European Yearbook of International Economic Law

EYIEL Monographs - Studies in European and International Economic Law

Volume 47

The European Yearbook of International Economic Law (EYIEL) is a Springer-publication in the field of International Economic Law (IEL), a field increasingly emancipating itself from Public International Law scholarship and evolving into a fully-fledged academic discipline in its own right. With the yearbook, editors and publisher make a significant contribution to the development of this "new" discipline and provide an international source of reference of the highest possible quality.

The EYIEL covers all areas of IEL, in particular WTO Law, External Trade Law of major trading countries, important Regional Economic Integration agreements, International Competition Law, International Investment Regulation, International Monetary Law, International Intellectual Property Protection and International Tax Law.

EYIEL publishes articles following a substantive review by the editors and external experts as appropriate.

The editors have published extensively in the field of IEL and European Law alike. They are supported by an international Advisory Board consisting of established scholars of the highest reputation.

EYIEL Monographs is a subseries of the European Yearbook of International Economic Law (EYIEL). It contains scholarly works in the fields of European and international economic law, in particular WTO law, international investment law, international monetary law, law of regional economic integration, external trade law of the EU and EU internal market law. The series does not include edited volumes. EYIEL Monographs are peer-reviewed by the series editors and external reviewers.

Nguyen Thi Lan Huong

Investment Protection and Environmental Governance

The EU-Vietnam IPA in Light of Emerging Economies

Springer

Nguyen Thi Lan Huong
Ho Chi Minh City University of Law
Ho Chi Minh City, Vietnam

ISSN 2364-8392 ISSN 2364-8406 (electronic)
European Yearbook of International Economic Law
ISSN 2524-6658 ISSN 2524-6666 (electronic)
EYIEL Monographs - Studies in European and International Economic Law
ISBN 978-3-032-05331-2 ISBN 978-3-032-05332-9 (eBook)
https://doi.org/10.1007/978-3-032-05332-9

This Springer imprint is published by the registered company Springer Nature Switzerland AG
The registered company address is: Gewerbestrasse 11, 6330 Cham, Switzerland

To my parents and my sons
—My love, my life, my light

Preface

This book explores specific innovations that affect Vietnam's ability to regulate environmental protection, a key objective of sustainable development as outlined in the EU–Vietnam Investment Protection Agreement. It aims to place this regulatory authority within the context of Vietnam's historical and contemporary economic development strategies. The goal is to identify challenges and suggest strategies for incorporating sustainable development objectives and environmental protection into negotiations of international investment agreements of Vietnam and other emerging economies facing similar challenges.

This book does not aim to evaluate all the levels of protection that an ideal investment treaty should include. Instead, it focuses on specific provisions that could help protect the regulatory actions the host state wishes to implement to achieve sustainable development and environmental protection goals, particularly in a developing economy like Vietnam. To date, most studies on investment protection standards have either examined them in isolation or in relation to environmental protection, usually from a general and impartial standpoint. While Vietnam or any other single state may share some commonalities with this general perspective, there can also be significant differences. These differences do not necessarily contradict the general view but highlight specific nuances. This divergence arises not only because any state seeking to negotiate an investment treaty will be particularly concerned about maximising benefits and minimising costs for itself but also due to the unique challenges each economy faces. These challenges may be linked to urgent environmental problems and the risk of "regulatory chill", where a state may be hesitant to adopt measures that protect human rights or the environment, especially compared to developed economies. As a result, countries like Vietnam must develop well-designed strategies that align with their policy preferences and address their specific circumstances.

This book, therefore, may serve as a resource for policymakers and international investment treaty negotiators from emerging economies, where foreign direct investment remains a key driver of economic development, yet environmental degradation has become an increasingly urgent concern. It is also intended to assist international organisations and negotiators from developed countries in better understanding the priorities and realities faced by their counterparts. After all, "each is a piece of the continent, a part of the main" (—John Donne). Sustainable development is a shared responsibility—one that can only be reached through the collective efforts of all stakeholders.

Ho Chi Minh City, Vietnam Nguyen Thi Lan Huong

Acknowledgements

This book is developed from my doctoral thesis completed at the Faculty of Law, Criminal Justice and Administration of the University of Lausanne between 2019 and 2024, under the supervision of Professor Andreas R. Ziegler. I am deeply grateful for his unwavering support, insightful guidance, and the trust and freedom he granted me to pursue my own research directions.

While this book is primarily based on my doctoral thesis, it has undergone extensive revision over the past year. Since I defended my thesis on December 3, 2024, several important developments have occurred in Vietnam's legal and policy landscape, which I have sought to integrate into this version. Since early 2025, Vietnam has entered a phase of substantial institutional restructuring. This process has taken place not only within central management agencies but also across local administrations, with large-scale mergers of provinces and cities. These changes in the administrative structure reflect the government's effort to strengthen its governance framework and to establish a solid foundation for the effective implementation of necessary policies in the current period. Within this evolving context, the issues discussed in this book have become even more relevant to Vietnam's pursuit of sustainable development.

I am deeply thankful to the distinguished members of my thesis committee—Professor Frédéric Erard, Professor Evelyne Schmid, Professor Catharine Titi, Professor Tran Viet Dung, and Professor Andreas R. Ziegler—for their invaluable comments and thoughtful critique, which significantly enriched the quality and depth of this research.

My sincere appreciation also goes to the editors of the European Yearbook of International Economic Law—first and foremost, to Marc Bungenberg, as well as to Christoph Herrmann, Markus Krajewski, and Andreas R. Ziegler—for kindly offering this book a home. I am equally grateful to Anja Trautmann, Pradeep Kuttysankaran, and Kala Palanisamy from Springer Nature for their generous assistance, guidance, and understanding throughout the editorial process.

My research stay in Switzerland was made possible by the European Union's Horizon 2020 Programme, and I am hugely grateful for their support. I also extend my sincere appreciation to the Swiss Institute of Comparative Law. The generous assistance from its staffs, along with privileged access to its resources, played an essential role in shaping and refining the arguments presented in this book.

The University of Lausanne holds a special place in my heart, as it was the setting for some of the most memorable times of my life. Its unique blend of high professionalism, openness, friendliness, and natural beauty truly sets UNIL apart as an ideal academic home.

I am equally grateful to my home institution, the Ho Chi Minh City University of Law, for granting me the academic leave necessary to pursue this research. I owe specially thanks to Professor Tran Viet Dung, former Dean of the International Law Faculty, for his guidance, constructive criticism, and invaluable encouragement during the final stages of this book's completion.

My sincere thanks also go to my dear colleagues in the International Trade Law Department for their invaluable support over the past years. I have had the privilege of collaborating with some of the most dynamic young academics working on trade policies, the energy transition, and international investment treaties. In particular, I would like to acknowledge Nguyen Hoang Thai Hy, who will soon begin his PhD at the University of Burgundy Europe this autumn. Our discussions during joint projects over the past three years have been instrumental in refining and developing some of the ideas presented in this book. I look forward to continuing our conversations in the years to come.

Above all, I am indebted to my family, whose steadfast encouragement and patience provided the bedrock for this endeavour, often at the expense of my presence. Finally, I extend my gratitude to all those who, though unnamed here, contributed in ways large and small to the completion of this book. Their presence and kindness have been a source of strength throughout this journey.

Lausanne, Autumn 2025

Nguyen Thi Lan Huong

Competing Interests The author has no competing interests to declare that are relevant to the content of this manuscript.

Contents

List of Abbreviations

ADB	Asian Development Bank
ASEAN	Association of Southeast Asian Nations
BAU	Business as Usual
BIT(s)	Bilateral Investment Treatie(s)
COP26	26th United Nations Climate Change Conference of the Parties
CPTPP	Comprehensive and Progressive Agreement for Trans-Pacific Partnership
CPV	Communist Party of Vietnam
CSR	Corporate Social Responsibility
DAGs	Domestic Advisory Groups
DONRE	(Vietnam) Department of Natural Resources and Environment
DOSTE	(Vietnam) Department of Science, Technology, and Environment
EIA	Environmental Impact Assessment
EVIPA	EU–Vietnam Investment Protection Agreement
FDI	Foreign Direct Investment
FET	Fair and Equitable Treatment
FTA(s)	Free Trade Agreement(s)
GATS	(WTO) General Agreement on Trade in Services
GATT	(WTO) General Agreement on Tariffs and Trade
GHG	Greenhouse Gas
ICS	Investment Court System
ICSID	International Center for Settlement of Investment Disputes
IET	International Environmental Treaty
IIA(s)	International Investment Agreement(s)
IIL	International Investment Law
IISD	International Institute for Sustainable Development
ILC	International Law Commission
IMF	International Monetary Fund
IPA(s)	Investment Protection Agreement(s)
IPPA(s)	Investment Promotion and Protection Agreement(s)
ISDS	Investor-State Dispute Settlement

MEA(s)	Multilateral Environmental Agreement(s)
MFN	Most Favoured Nation Treatment
MIT	(Vietnam) Ministry of Industry and Trade
MOC	(Vietnam) Ministry of Construction
MONRE	(Vietnam) Ministry of Natural Resource and Environment
MOST	(Vietnam) Ministry of Science and Technology
MOSTE	(Vietnam) Ministry of Science, Technology, and Environment
MPI	Ministry of Planning and Investment
MST	Minimum Standard of Treatment
NDCs	National Determined Contributions
NDPS	Non-disputing Party Submission
NEA	National Environmental Agency
NT	National Treatment
OECD	Organisation of Economic Cooperation Development
RCEP	Regional Comprehensive Economic Partnership
RTA(s)	Regional Trade Agreement(s)
SDGs	Sustainable Development Goals
TIP(s)	Trade with Investment Provisions
TSD Committee	Trade and Sustainable Development Committee
UNCITRAL	United Nations Commission on International Trade Law
UNCTAD	United Nations Conference on Trade and Development
UNDP	United Nations Development Programme
UNEP	United Nations Environment Programme
VNR	Voluntary National Review
VPA	Voluntary Partnership Agreement
WB	World Bank
WTO	World Trade Organization

Chapter 1
Introduction

Abstract This introductory outlines the context of this book. It explores the complex relationship between sustainable development, environmental protection, and the framework of international investment law. The chapter examines various established models and emerging proposals that aim to balance the interests of international investment with the goals of sustainable development. This chapter also outlines the scope of the book and describes the methodologies utilised, laying the groundwork for the subsequent analysis.

1.1 Background

The complex relationship between environmental protection and International Investment Law (IIL) has long been challenging to balance. Historically, environment as well as human right norms rarely appeared in the context of International Investment Agreements (IIAs), including Bilateral Investment Treaties (BITs) and multilateral investment agreements, as the aim of these treaties is to protect the investment and legitimate rights of the investor in the host state territory. Indeed, in traditional IIAs, the relevant doctrines in promoting the environment appear very faint and fragmentary, which is similar to the characteristics of IIL itself.

Tension between international investment and the environment has become hotter in this twenty-first century, leading by a series of financial crises, food security, and the environment.[1] In this context, sustainable development, with the emphasis on environmental protection, is capturing increasing attention in international trade and investment negotiations. These concerns may arise from the improvement of environmental protection standards and the progress in managing sustainable development, along with many environmental incidents related to investment activities. Adhering to environmental policy while being bound by investment protection obligations under trade and investment agreements can create a dilemma for host states.

[1] UNCTAD (2013).

N. T. Lan Huong, *Investment Protection and Environmental Governance*, European Yearbook of International Economic Law 47,
https://doi.org/10.1007/978-3-032-05332-9_1

Indeed, many investment disputes arise between host states and foreign investors because pursuing non-trade interests no longer ensures the legal protections that investors expect.[2]

In negotiating and implementing BITs and Free Trade Agreements (FTAs), countries face challenges arising from the conflict between foreign investors' rights to be protected and sustainable development goals. It has been observed that since the 2000s, investment policy-making has been experiencing a paradigm shift in which inclusive growth and sustainable development have emerged as key policy objectives.[3] Indeed, policy-making has faced multiple challenges in terms of how and to what extent to enhance the sustainability dimension in such a self-contained regime as IIAs might be most concerned. Along with this, how policy space can be reserved in a "hard" system of IIL, which has been traditionally framed by Germany from the end of the 1950s till the end of the twentieth century,[4] requires much effort at the international level. Lastly, fixing rising deficiencies in Investor - State Dispute Settlement (ISDS) is another challenge bringing the international investment regime to the centre of the debate.

Despite existing practices, the concept of sustainable development and its goals remain far from unified within the context of IIL and ISDS. However, modern treaties signed across various continents now commonly include language addressing concerns about sustainable development and tools to ensure that treaty obligations do not prevent parties from pursuing legitimate objectives. This often involves revisions to the preamble, general and specific environmental exceptions, provisions affirming the right to regulate, redefinitions of traditional investment protection standards such as Most Favored Nation Treatment (MFN), Fair and Equitable Treatment (FET), and providing conditions for expropriation and indirect expropriation. These regulations serve as pillars in protecting investments and are found in most modern investment agreements. These innovative clauses are hoping to narrow the scope of investment protection which has been built since the first generation BITs to balance it with the rights to regulate of the states in response to rising requirements.

---

[2] See a number of cases showing the complicated relationships between international investment and sustainable development, including environmental protection, socio-environmental impact assessment, and renewable energy, that happened in the 2010s, such as *Bear Creek Mining Corporation v. Republic of Peru* [2014] ICSID Case No. ARB/14/21, Award, 30 November 2017; *Eiser Infrastructure Limited and Energía Solar Luxembourg S.à r.l. v. Kingdom of Spain* [2013] ICSID Case No. ARB/13/36, Award, 04 May 2017; *Burlington Resources Inc. v. Republic of Ecuador* [2008] ICSID Case No. ARB/08/5, Award, 7 February 2017; *Perenco Ecuador Limited v. Republic of Ecuador* [2008] ICSID Case No. ARB/08/6, Award, 11 August 2015; *Urbaser S.A. and Consorcio de Aguas Bilbao Biskaia, Bilbao Biskaia Ur Partzuergoa v. Argentine Republic* [2007] ICSID Case No. ARB/07/26, Award, 8 December 2016; *Churchill Mining PLC and Planet Mining Pty Ltd v. Republic of Indonesia* [2012] ICSID Case No. ARB/12/14 and 12/40, Award, 6 December 2016; *Pac Rim Cayman LLC v. Republic of El Salvador* [2009] ICSID Case No. ARB/09/12, Award, 14 October 2016.

[3] UNCTAD (2013).

[4] Sacerdoti (2016), p. 28.

A notable example of this trend is the recently concluded trade and investment negotiations between the EU and Vietnam, finalised in 2019. This resulted in two separate agreements: (i) The EU-Vietnam Free Trade Agreement (EVFTA), covering trade facilitation in goods, services, government procurement, intellectual property rights, and other trade-related aspects; and (ii) the EU-Vietnam Investment Protection Agreement (EVIPA), which aims to protect investment activities in the EU and Vietnam. Alongside other successful negotiations with Canada and Singapore, these agreements with Vietnam introduce new formulations of traditional substantive standards and provisions supporting the host state's right to regulate.

While these developments may not be novel for the EU—similar elements are present in the model BITs of the US and Canada on the other side of the Atlantic and in studies by international organisations like the United Nations Conference on Trade and Development (UNCTAD) and the Organisation for Economic Cooperation and Development (OECD)—they signify a shift for Vietnam into a new trend of IIA formulation.[5] However, the potential impacts of these changes are difficult to predict, especially for a developing economy like Vietnam, which faces unique challenges in environmental management. This book investigates the extent to which the EVIPA can safeguard Vietnam's right to regulate, particularly in terms of environmental protection, and how it might contribute to the country's sustainable development goals.

1.2 Sustainable Development and Environmental Protection in International Investment Law

1.2.1 Literature Review

Studies on the interaction between IIL as a sub-system of international law and alternative value systems (such as those of environment and human health) have widely been conducted from different perspectives. In the context of international law that has so far been developed, it is critical to mention the following intensive works:

- *Foreign Investment and the Environment in International Law* by Jorge E. Viñuales

This study adopts policy-oriented and practical approaches to the relationship between IIL and environmental law. It identifies the major challenges states, foreign

[5] Some of these methods have appeared in the Comprehensive and Progressive Agreement for Trans-Pacific Partnership (CPTPP), which entered into force for Vietnam on January 14, 2019. However, while the CPTPP primarily focuses on promoting trade flow among its 11 member states, the concerns and scope of environmental protection and the preservation of national sovereignty related to these issues differ significantly from those in agreements with the EU.

investors, and their legal advisers face due to the potential friction between investment law and environmental law. It also provides a detailed analysis of the significant legal issues based on a comprehensive review of the jurisprudence from investment tribunals, human rights courts, and other adjudication mechanisms.

In this book, Viñuales maps the evolving relationship between environmental and investment law, conceptualising its dual nature as synergistic and conflicting. From this perspective, he argues that sustainable development primarily appears as a policy goal, with its operational contours defined by political declarations, recommendations, and soft-law instruments. The author provides a technical analysis of the relationship between environmental and investment law, focusing on various issues such as jurisdiction, applicable law, procedure, and damages that arise from incorporating environmental considerations into investment proceedings. Several general comments from the literature are noteworthy as they contribute to understanding the background of this relationship between these two branches of international law, which is central to this book. Notably, while environmental norms may exhibit some hierarchical effects through other channels, there is insufficient evidence to conclude that, in the current state of international law, any international environmental norms possess a peremptory nature. In contrast, most arguments supporting the *ius cogens* status of environmental norms are either purely theoretical or disproved by subsequent developments.[6]

In Part II of the book, the author adopts the perspective of an environmental lawyer to evaluate the consistency of foreign investment transactions—and their international legal protections—with the international legal framework for environmental protection. This section also examines legal techniques, both specific and general conflict norms, to manage normative conflicts between international investment law and international environmental law. When analysing general conflict norms, precisely the principle of *lex specialis derogat legi generali*, the author argues that while international investment law is a specialised field, this does not mean that investment disciplines should automatically be treated as *lex specialis* in cases of normative conflict. Nevertheless, in practice, investment tribunals may be inclined to do so.[7] The author concludes that investment tribunals might consider investment disciplines as *lex specialis* when resolving an investment dispute, partly due to their familiarity with investment disciplines and the need to qualify disputes as "arising out of" or "relating to" an investment to assert jurisdiction. This approach may emphasise the investment component over the environmental one, thereby favouring investment law.

Regarding the principle of *lex posterior derogat legi priori*, the author notes that when conflicts arise between provisions in treaties from different regimes, special attention should be given to the independence of the settlement means chosen. He suggests that aside from specialised tribunals' greater familiarity with the laws they regularly apply, investment tribunals are established based on an investment

[6] Viñuales (2012), p. 142.

[7] Ibid., p. 145.

instrument to decide specific investment disputes. This setup may introduce an implicit bias favouring investment law.

Part III of this book explores the impact of IIL on domestic environmental measures. The author analyses the consistency of domestic environmental measures with expropriation clauses, non-discrimination standards, and stability/due process commitments under international investment law. He also discusses three cross-cutting "defence arguments" based on environmental considerations: the police powers doctrine, the margin of appreciation doctrine, and emergency necessity clauses.

- *International Investment Law and the Environment* written by Saverio Di Benedetto[8]

In his study, Benedetto surveys the theoretical underpinnings of IIL to clarify the conceptual elements influencing the scrutinising of legal practices related to investments and the environment. He critically analyses theoretical approaches to IIL to determine whether integrating environmental concerns into investment rules is feasible or likely to be denied based on different theoretical perspectives.

Benedetto examines whether IIL functions as a cohesive unit or as a fragmented collection of elements, as well as the guiding purposes behind its interpretation. He concludes that the concept of fragmentation is particularly applicable to IIL, given that it consists of numerous autonomous legal instruments and the resolution of disputes is handled by independent tribunals. He investigates the debates surrounding investment disputes and non-commercial values, focusing on the applicable laws and interpretative methods used in international investment disputes. Benedetto also explores whether the choice of applicable law affects the consideration of non-commercial values. He discovers that the integration of values such as environmental and human health concerns into IIL is limited by the existing rules and practices governing investment treaty arbitration.

Benedetto emphasises key aspects of interpreting investment rules and suggests a fundamental approach for classifying interpretative arguments related to reconciling foreign investments with environmental protection. He evaluates how tribunals internally handle potential conflicts between investor rights and environmental protection, noting that the one-dimensional nature of IIL often leads to internal arguments that do not account for broader social values. This limitation arises because investment treaties prioritise legitimate investor rights over other values.

The book also explores systemic, external approaches that contrast with fragmented, internal methods. These approaches are supported by Article 31.3(c) of the Vienna Convention on the Law of Treaties (1969) (VCLT), which tribunals use to address conflicts between investor rights and environmental issues. In the final section, Benedetto analyses how various exceptions might allow for the integration of non-commercial issues into investment rules. He outlines potential scenarios for the

[8] Benedetto (2013).

evolution of investment regimes to better take into account environmental and human health concerns.

- *Integrating Sustainable Development in International Investment Law: Normative Incompatibility* written by Manjiao Chi[9]

In this book, the author addresses the challenge of integrating sustainable development into IIAs. He categorises provisions designed to promote sustainable development in modern IIAs into four main types: (i) the preamble, (ii) substantive sustainable development provisions, (iii) public interest provisions, and (iv) procedural sustainable development provisions. Chi observes that, aside from the preamble, which has limited effectiveness, the other types of provisions have a direct impact on promoting sustainable development.

In Part II, Chi evaluates four core sustainable development provisions in IIAs: substantive provisions, exceptive provisions, public interest provisions, and procedural provisions. In Part III, the author suggests improvements for IIA-making, including (i) achieving a better balance between protecting foreign investment and preserving state regulatory power, (ii) embedding the principles of good governance and the rule of law more deeply, and (iii) enhancing IIAs as norms within the global investment governance regime. Part III also proposes two ways to make IIAs more compatible with sustainable development: (i) reconceptualising IIAs from a governance perspective and (ii) bridging the compatibility gap between them. To achieve this, the author recommends exploring the issue from three perspectives: conceptual, normative, and governance.

- *Substantive Protection under Investment Treaties: A Legal and Economic Analysis* written by Jonathan Bonnitcha

In a book published in 2014,[10] Bonnitcha systematically analyses the advantages and drawbacks of the substantive protections provided by existing IIAs to foreign investors. The book aims to determine whether adjustments to the current regulatory framework are warranted to offer more or less protection. A central conclusion is that investment treaties' "economic" goals do not necessarily conflict with "non-economic" objectives, such as promoting human rights. This conclusion is based on the finding that the economic justifications for investment treaties are less robust than commonly assumed and that enhanced protections for foreign investors may not yield overall economic benefits.

Chapter 2 of Bonnitcha's book examines the justifications and criticisms of investment treaties in the existing literature. Two sections of interest address sovereignty (Sect. 2.3.4) and environmental norms (Sect. 2.3.6). Bonnitcha contributes valuable normative and causal assumptions that underpin existing arguments in the literature. An essential criticism highlighted is that investment treaties, particularly those with substantive standards such as expropriation provisions, constrain the

[9] Chi (2018).

[10] Bonnitcha (2014).

sovereignty of host states by requiring compensation even when pursuing legitimate policy objectives. In this context, sovereignty refers to a state's authority within its territory. However, Bonnitcha points out that an unqualified interpretation of sovereignty as a norm is not a coherent basis for critique. Instead, the more cohesive argument is that IIAs impede states' capacity to enact desirable policies within their territory, often referred to as the "right to regulate." He emphasises the need to clarify the extent to which investment treaties curtail states' exercise of their legitimate right to regulate.

The topic of environmental concerns and sustainable development has become a significant basis for critiquing IIAs. The arguments surrounding this issue closely resemble earlier discussions about state sovereignty. The obligations imposed by IIAs may discourage decision-makers in host countries from implementing new environmental regulations. This hesitation arises because such regulations can lead to compensation claims if they impact investors' interests or involve changes in laws that disrupt investors' legitimate expectations. However, in contrast to Manjiao Chi's view, Bonnitcha argues that there may not be a need to explicitly incorporate sustainable development as an additional primary norm within IIAs. Instead, if sustainable development is recognised as an integral aspect of existing primary norms, it would receive sufficient scrutiny. Treating sustainable development as a secondary norm might be more appropriate for later examination and consideration.[11]

This book underscores the importance of understanding the object and purpose of an investment treaty and how this understanding should influence the interpretative process, particularly in the VCLT context. Bonnitcha argues that treaty interpretation is inherently linked to underlying assumptions about the treaty's objectives and the implications of specific interpretations. This connection is especially significant for the substantive protections afforded by investment treaties.

Bonnitcha reviews the debate on the role of an investment treaty's purpose in interpreting its provisions and offers suggestions on how a treaty's purpose should be factored into the legal reasoning of tribunals. His study leads to several noteworthy conclusions. First, drawing from economic theory and evidence in Chap. 3, he asserts that "economic" arguments do not unconditionally justify heightened levels of investment treaty protection. In many instances, lower protection levels could yield more significant economic benefits. This challenges the traditional belief that stronger investment protection standards necessarily attract more Foreign Direct Investment (FDI) to host states.

Additionally, Bonnitcha argues there is no need to pit "economic" against "non-economic" objectives when drafting and interpreting Investment Promotion and Protection Agreements. Economic justifications for protecting investments are often weaker than assumed. He disagrees with the prevailing academic and policy debates on balancing investors' rights and states' regulatory autonomy, deeming such debates unnecessary. Bonnitcha suggests that lower levels of investment protection are generally preferable to higher levels. He argues that "existing arbitral

[11] Ibid., p. 39.

jurisprudence leans towards providing greater protection to foreign investment than can be justified."[12] He highlights the advantages of including exception clauses in future investment treaties, which can limit the circumstances in which a host state must pay compensation. However, he advises policymakers first to determine whether the core protection in question is warranted, as he finds no coherent justification for the levels of protection implied by current arbitral jurisprudence.

Bonnitcha also addresses whether Investment Promotion and Protection Agreements should grant tribunals jurisdiction to review policy measures taken by host states. He suggests achieving greater deference to domestic policy by excluding the possibility of substantive review under the FET standard. This would shift the focus of investment standards toward ensuring procedural fairness and protecting enforceable rights established under domestic law. However, he acknowledges the challenge of determining the appropriate level of respect for policy measures that may interfere with investors' rights, as these cases often involve competing objectives, making it sometimes more desirable to protect the substantive rights of foreign investors.

Bonnitcha critiques a significant minority of arbitral tribunals for providing protection without coherent justification. He accuses these tribunals of interpreting existing provisions "in a way that is profoundly misguided."[13] Thus, he underscores the necessity of precise drafting in future International Protection Agreements (IPAs) to reduce the interpretative discretion of arbitral tribunals. Contrary to much of the literature's discourse, he points out that in many situations, justifications for protecting foreign investment do not conflict with "public interest" objectives, eliminating the need for a delicate balance.

In his study, Bonnitcha examines the varying interpretations of the FET standard and indirect expropriation provisions in existing treaties by investment tribunals. He identifies eleven approaches to elements of the FET standard and five approaches to indirect expropriation in decisions from 2007 to 2014. Based on this analysis, Bonnitcha suggests three potential courses of action for host states: revising substantive protections in new treaties, amending protections in existing treaties, and negotiating interpretative statements for current investment treaties.

Another academic research focuses on the interaction between foreign investment, human rights, and the environment in international law, particularly in regions like South Asia.[14] However, this research takes a different approach by exploring how public international law can facilitate sustainable development, which is outside the context of this book. In general, the existing literature so far shows that academia appears to agree that some objectives are desirable in reforming IIL, including improvements in economic efficiency, the realisation of human rights, environmental conservation, greater foreign direct investment flows, and greater

---

[12] Ibid., p. 332.

[13] Ibid., p. 334.

[14] See for instance, Puvimanasinghe (2007). In this publication, Puvimanasinghe examined the role of different actors in international investment context including transnational corporations, host states, home states and non-state actors.

respect for the rule of law.[15] It also agreed that, except for Bonnitcha, IIAs contain competing interests that must be balanced in future concluded versions.

Above mentioned works set the fundamental foundation for this study, as the relationship between environmental protection and international investment has always been a challenging topic to deal with. This burgeoning literature shows that concerns on the relationship between international investment law and sustainable development remain. This has partly been rooted in the criticism that the traditional IIL system has been designed as an instrument to promote international investment, focusing on protecting the investors and investments rather than other legitimate values, and this leads to the assumption that current IIAs discourage states from taking legitimate regulatory measures to protect human rights and the environment. Part of the concern is that the traditional IIL, which usually considers itself as a self-contained regime, has limited the chance for external value to be examined and, therefore, led to unexpected results at the investment arbitration. To some extent, more development has been observed at both international and national levels in IIA-making, striking to respond to those critics. More proposals in combining sustainable dimensions into IIL are mostly related to reserving the state's policy space. This practice can be explored in a number of model BITs as well as completed negotiation BITs, though there may be variations in wording.[16] However, efforts to integrate these two areas continue to encounter new challenges stemming from the IIL regime, as highlighted by the mentioned studies. Ongoing discussions centre around the necessity and effectiveness of these proposals. If deemed necessary and practical, the key question becomes the extent to which they can support treaty parties' right to act for public purposes. An additional subquestion arises: is it reasonable to adapt a specialised legal system like IIL to protect non-investment values? In other words, are the protected rights of investors being increasingly constrained in favour of external values in this century?

1.2.2 Initiatives in Drafting Sustainable IIAs

As mentioned above, since the early of the twenty-first century, facing and predicting sustainable challenges in international investment, different players in the international community have prepared a number of model IIAs as well as proposals to (i) balance the relationship between international investment and sustainable development and to (ii) minimise practical weaknesses of the investor-state arbitration system.

[15] Bonnitcha (2014), p. 11.

[16] As mentioned by Tuerk and Rojid, fifteen out of the forty-seven investment treaties signed in 2011 incorporated sustainable development provisions recommended by UNCTAD's Investment Policy Framework for Sustainable Development. Tuerk and Rojid (2012).

1.2.2.1 IISD Model on International Investment Agreement for Sustainable Development

The first notable effort in this regard is the IISD Model International Agreement on Investment for Sustainable Development, published by the International Institute for Sustainable Development (IISD) published in 2005.[17] This work is recognised as the earliest comprehensive model designed with sustainable development as its core value.[18] The IISD Model IIA 2005 adopts a comprehensive perspective on sustainable development, explicitly incorporating the rights and obligations of foreign investors, host states, and home states. Unlike traditional ISDS, which primarily focuses on dispute settlement for investor rights, this model emphasises regime building for sustainable development. The IISD Model Agreement also outlines an agenda for future negotiations, presenting a comprehensive and consistent view of the connections between investment and sustainable development.[19] This model is believed to significantly advance BIT negotiations, treaty-making, and arbitration processes, promoting sustainable development principles within international investment frameworks.[20]

1.2.2.2 The UNCTAD Policy Framework for Sustainable Development

Another significant contribution to balancing international investment and sustainable development is the series of projects led by UNCTAD since 2012, beginning with the introduction of the first version of the Investment Policy Framework for Sustainable Development (UNCTAD Policy Framework). A revised version was released in 2015, which reviewed ongoing international efforts to reform investment governance[21] and provided specific guidelines for national investment policymaking. These guidelines emphasise enhancing the sustainable development impact of investment and promoting responsible investment. Specifically, the UNCTAD Policy Frameworks identify ambiguities in designing key investment protection terms and other weaknesses within the current IIA regime, proposing potential remedies in national policy agenda-setting and international treaty-making. The Framework suggests that the current IIL system is overly focused on protecting investors' rights and advocates for drafting agreements that better support sustainable development concerns. It offers core principles for investment policy-making and various options for revising investment standards to address these shortcomings.

In addition to these guidelines, which include concrete suggestions for drafting IIAs compatible with sustainable development, UNCTAD provides other policy

[17] Mann et al. (2005).

[18] Chi (2018), p. 27.

[19] Mann et al. (2005), p. vii.

[20] Mann (2008).

[21] UNCTAD (2015a).

tools to support the reform of the international investment regime. These include the Reform Package for the International Investment[22] and International Investment Agreements Reform Accelerator.[23]

1.2.2.3 OECD Studies

Various efforts have been made to address international investment and sustainable development, with notable initiatives undertaken by the Organisation for Economic Cooperation and Development (OECD) since 1998. Beginning in 2002, concerns related to the environment and sustainable development in the context of international investment became a frequent focus of OECD studies. One of the early studies evaluated the impact of FDI in the mining sector on sustainable development. It emphasised the roles of governments, multinational enterprises, donors, and international organisations in integrating investment and environmental policies.[24]

Several critical studies by Gordon and other researchers surveyed environmental concerns and sustainable development in investment treaty law, demonstrating significant efforts in this area.[25] Additionally, a study by Gaukrodger examined the balance between investor protection and the right to regulate in investment treaties.[26] This study outlined related issues in four areas: (i) the types of regulation potentially at issue in investment treaty claims; (ii) the types and levels of investor protection; (iii) the degree of impact of treaties on regulation; and (iv) the processes and institutions involved in balancing investor protection with regulatory rights. Gaukrodger emphasised the importance of evaluating the impact of specific rules rather than entire treaties and the value of comparative analysis across different regimes.

More recently, in 2021, the OECD released a study titled "The Future of Investment Treaties - Possible Directions," which provides a foundation for initial inter-governmental and public discussions. This study observes that trade and investment agreements may increasingly play a role in improving regulatory policies. It notes the emergence of sustainable development chapters in trade-investment treaties and highlights a growing interest in using State-to-State Dispute Settlement for investment disputes.[27] The study also points out that recent major treaties, such

---

[22] UNCTAD (2018).

[23] UNCTAD (2020).

[24] OECD (2002).

[25] Gordon (2008); Gordon and Pohl (2011); Gordon et al. (2014).

[26] Gaukrodger (2017).

[27] Gaukrodger (2021), pp. 15–16. The author has mentioned some treaties that adopt this approach, for instance, Brazil's Investment Facilitation Model, the United States - Mexico - Canada Agreement (2019) (USMCA), the EU - Japan Economic Partnership Agreement (EPA) (2018), the EU - China Comprehensive Agreement on Investment (CAI) (2020), the Canada - EU Comprehensive Economic and Trade Agreement (CETA) and the UK - Canada Trade Continuity Agreement (2020).

as the EU - Japan Economic Partnership Agreement (EPA) and the 2020 Regional Comprehensive Economic Partnership (RCEP), have given governments more significant roles in deciding on remedies.[28] However, the study implies that achieving sustainable development requires a strong regulatory framework where both domestic law and policy and trade-investment agreements are crucial for improving regulatory policies.[29]

In general, the OECD's approach differs from that of UNCTAD. The OECD argues that businesses, governments, and international treaties are vital in promoting sustainable development. Notably, the OECD has prepared "Guidelines for Multinational Enterprises",[30] which suggests general provisions on corporate social responsibility (CSR) concerning human rights, the environment, and corruption. These CSR norms are voluntary and rely on self-governance, acting as a "self-control mechanism" for foreign investors. The OECD Guidelines are considered a comprehensive code of conduct with voluntary standards covering the environment, competition, combating bribery, employment, science, and taxation.[31]

1.2.2.4 The Commonwealth Guide (2012)[32]

A noteworthy publication in this context is a practical handbook by the Commonwealth Secretariat, "Integrating Sustainable Development into International Investment Agreements: A Guide for Developing Country Negotiators," released in 2013. As indicated by its title, this guide is specifically aimed at helping developing countries negotiate BITs, economic partnership agreements, and investment provisions in preferential trading agreements. The guide aims to enhance understanding of the nature and effects of IIA obligations, thereby encouraging greater policy coherence from the perspectives of developing countries.[33] This guide follows a similar approach to the UNCTAD Policy Framework, identifying issues related to sustainable development within the current IIA framework and proposing various solutions to rebalance future IIAs to address these concerns. It underscores two core justifications for IIA reforms: (i) the evolving relationship between the environment and investment and (ii) the principle of sustainable development becoming the central goal of new policy initiatives.

The handbook surveys significant tools used in selected IIAs to provide a comprehensive overview of substantive and procedural provisions and their impacts on achieving sustainable development goals. It offers clear guidance for negotiators, particularly those from developing countries, distinguishing it from previous

---

[28] Ibid., p. 16.

[29] Ibid., p. 8.

[30] OECD (2011); Morgera (2006).

[31] Gehring and Kent (2013), p. 210.

[32] Vanduzer et al. (2013).

[33] Ibid., p. 4.

studies. Additionally, it addresses supplementary issues such as capacity-building and international cooperation, offering practical advice to support the negotiation process and implementing sustainable development principles in international investment agreements.

1.2.2.5 SADC Model BIT (2012)[34]

An effort from the Global South that merits attention is the SADC Model Bilateral Investment Treaty Template (SADC Model BIT), developed by the Southern African Development Community. Although the drafters do not explicitly state that their aim is to incorporate sustainable development, this orientation is evident throughout the model, from the preamble to the text.

The SADC Model BIT includes provisions typical of existing models, such as those related to expropriation (Article 6), regulatory measures (Article 20), and the obligations of states regarding environmental and labour standards (Article 22), which affirm the right to establish domestic environmental protection and development policies. It also features an article on exceptions (Article 25). Notably, the SADC Model BIT imposes duties on investors and investments to respect international human rights, environmental, and labour standards adopted by the host state (Article 15).

Regarding the right to regulate, Article 20.1 states:

> In accordance with customary international law and other general principles of international law, the Host State has the right to take regulatory or other measures to ensure that development in its territory is consistent with the goals and principles of sustainable development, and with other legitimate social and economic policy objectives.

Additionally, the model includes a provision titled "Right to Pursue Development Goals" (Article 21), which is especially connected to local conditions and the interests of identifiable ethnic or cultural groups. This template demonstrates the drafters' efforts to achieve a balanced and comprehensive approach, leading to a robust draft text for an investment treaty that integrates sustainable development principles effectively.

International efforts to reform the current IIA system to promote and facilitate sustainable development reflect a consensus that the existing system is not sufficiently aligned with Sustainable development goals.[35] The various proposals put forth demonstrate a comprehensive approach to IIA-making, rooted in the necessity of addressing sustainable development systemically within a broader context. These proposals aim to support countries in incorporating sustainable development features into their IIAs, although they differ in perspectives, primary approaches, and specific objectives. A common approach in these proposals is balancing investment rights with state regulatory powers. However, as mentioned by Bonnitcha, these

[34] SADC Model Bilateral Investment Treaty Template 2012.

[35] Chi (2018), p. 35.

resources are limited to providing a broad range of alternative levels of protection that might be adopted while articulating no ground for choosing between these options.[36] It, therefore, has been a lack of basis for addressing controversial objectives in order to support the policy-makers to decide which options are most suitable for their desirability of levels of protection. These practices illustrate a continuous trend in international investment law, a relatively young sub-system of international law, to evolve in response to social demands and changes, making it more compatible with sustainable development.

Despite these efforts, some argue that it is better to maintain the current regime of IIL as it stands. Critics suggest that changing the substance of IIL to focus more on sustainable development may reduce its flexibility and policy space.[37] Other commentators have expressed their scepticism regarding specific proposals to reform IIAs. Particularly, they have argued that a general exception clause is not necessary as a sufficient interpretation of substantive investor protection provisions will provide significant flexibility for the state in pursuing its legitimate rights.[38] In other words, they believe that current investment standards do not unduly limit host states' regulatory rights.

These differing opinions are part of the ongoing debate regarding new developments in IIL, though they are somewhat outside the scope of this study. Although sustainable development remains an indefinite concept within IIL, efforts to enhance this requirement have moved beyond merely inserting the term into the regime to addressing specific weaknesses. Consequently, these proposals are diverse and wide-ranging.

In summary, the proposals to enhance sustainability in IIL reflect a variety of approaches by governments and other stakeholders in response to rising concerns about international investment. This evolution is expected to make investment policymaking more complex, divergent, and uncertain.[39] Despite numerous studies from different perspectives contributing to the theoretical and practical understanding of sustainable development in IIL, scholars remain uncertain about how these new rules will impact the mainstream of IIAs.[40]

---

[36] Bonnitcha (2014), p. 337.

[37] The author proposes that Articles 31 and 33 of the Vienna rules of treaty interpretation can effectively reconcile the interests of investment protection and sustainable development, acting as a means to foster sustainable development. Berner (2016), p. 203.

[38] Newcombe (2012), p. 369.

[39] UNCTAD (2015b).

[40] Schefer (2020), p. 12.

1.3 Scope of the Study

The EVIPA includes standard provisions typically found in modern BITs, focusing on the preservation of sustainable values and the maintenance of state policy space. However, since the agreement was finalized in 2019, and similar to the other two agreements the EU made with Canada and Singapore, many questions remain, especially for Vietnam. As a developing economy with conditions that differ significantly from those of the EU and its developed partners, it is essential to understand the practical implications of these innovations for Vietnam. The country is currently undergoing international economic integration and facing rising environmental challenges, which have not yet been systematically examined in this context.

The following chapters of this book will not provide a complete and thorough discussion of the relationship between the two supporting yet often controversial areas of international law, as extensively studied by other scholars.[41] Nor will it attempt to evaluate the effectiveness of existing proposals aimed at reforming IIAs to align better with sustainable development. Instead, this research will assess how the EU - Vietnam Trade and Investment Agreement manages the balance between investment/trade and environmental protection. It will also consider what Vietnam needs to do to pursue its sustainable development goals based on legal arguments and precedent investment case law.

The book does not aim to provide a comprehensive examination of all sustainable development-friendly provisions within the EU - Vietnam Trade and Investment Agreements. Rather, it will focus on selected innovations that may directly impact Vietnam's rights to regulate its environment, one of the critical goals of sustainable development in the EVIPA. Additionally, this book seeks to contextualise the role of sustainable development within Vietnam's historical and present development strategies. It aims to identify areas that require further development and outline strategies for achieving these goals, with a particular emphasis on integrating sustainable development objectives into IIA negotiation strategies.

This research endeavours to delve into below main inquiries:

(i) Assessing the incorporation of environmental protection objectives within the EU - Vietnam Trade and Investment Agreements, scrutinising the extent to which environmental concerns are integrated into investment law in the context of current IIAs negotiations worldwide.
(ii) Investigating the regulatory impact on achieving the contracting parties' intentions on reserving the right to regulate and identifying constraints.
(iii) Anticipating and assessing the potential interpretations and applications of these changes in investment tribunals while elucidating the attendant challenges for Vietnam.

---

[41] For instance, see Benedetto (2013); Viñuales (2012); Chi (2018).

(iv) Analysing the stance on sustainable development within Vietnam's development strategy, focusing on strategies for enhancement through IIA negotiations and implementation.
(v) Assessing Vietnam's existing environmental protection and investment management frameworks. Identifying viable solutions for addressing urgent environmental challenges via FDI policies.

This book is not expected to evaluate all levels of protection included in an ideal investment treaty. Instead, only selected provisions that may contribute to the protection of regulatory actions that the host state may wish to adopt in order to pursue sustainable development and environmental protection targets, especially for a developing economy like Vietnam, will be examined. Until now, most studies evaluate investment protection standards, independently or in relationship with environmental protection, thus far, have been conducted from a general, impartial perspective. Vietnam, or any single state, may share similar points from the general perspective but, at the same time, may depart from it. This difference does not necessarily conflict with the general, impartial perspective but in a more particular way. This is not only because "any state seeking to negotiate an investment treaty will be particularly concerned to maximise the benefits and minimise the costs that accrue to that state itself",[42] but also because of the extent to which a specific economy faces particular rising problems is likely to vary with other states. Those problems may stem from urgent environmental requirements or in the mean that it is likely to be susceptible to "regulatory chill" in adopting measures to protect human rights or the environment compared to developed countries.[43] Therefore, a state may need to prepare well-designed strategies that reflect its own policy preferences.

Though considering the jurisdiction of investment tribunals, including the jurisdiction *ratione personae* and jurisdiction *ratione materiae,* as well as specific procedural requirements, may have affected the chance environmental-sensitive investment disputes will be examined or may have ensured a systemic approach to addressing sustainable development and environmental concerns in international investment context, the procedural issues in international investment arbitration is beyond the scope of this study.

Besides, the litigation practice shows that the applied approach may affect specific consideration and evaluation of an arbitral tribunal. It also proves that different ISDS tribunals have interpreted investment protection standards in several distinct ways.[44] Thus, it is suggested by the EU that a permanent tribunal system working under a strict set of rules agreed upon by the parties might help interpret the agreement in conformity with the mutual intention of the parties in comparison with traditional investment arbitration tribunals, especially in cases relating to the environment and sustainable development. In fact, under the EU viewpoint, ISDS is

---

[42] Bonnitcha (2014), p. 339.

[43] Regulatory chill is described as cases in which the states modify their behaviour to reduce the impact of IIAs provisions. Ibid., pp. 113–115.

[44] Ibid., p. 13.

an important part of investment protection which needs improvements.[45] According to the EU, in addition to fixing related vague investment protection rules, a clear set of dispute settlement procedures that ensures fair process and transparency should also be provided.[46] Therefore, since the negotiation of CETA, an Investment Court System (ICS) has been introduced with many crucial innovations from the traditional investor-state dispute system. The ICS is expected to fix widely acknowledged ISDS problems, which have attracted much discussion in the international community in recent years, as it highlights diverse ways to address those weaknesses. These include:[47]

- Preventing investors from bringing multiple or frivolous claims
- Improving transparency in the arbitration system
- Dealing with conflicts of interest and consistency of arbitral awards
- Introducing safeguards for the Parties.

Incorporating a tribunal system within the EVIPA holds notable potential for fostering sustainable development within its framework. Particularly significant is the endeavour to ensure the credibility of ISDS arbitrators by promoting stringent qualifications, particularly in matters of public policy.[48] As evidenced by numerous studies, including the ongoing examination in this book, ISDS arbitral awards demonstrate various interpretations concerning investment protection obligations. This variability partly stems from the fact that ISDS tribunals are typically appointed by disputing parties, raising concerns about their capacity to interpret international treaties. This highlights the necessity of bolstering consistency and coherence regarding norms within IIAs.

Consequently, establishing an international permanent investment court, comprised of judges serving fixed terms[49] and randomly selected to hear disputes,[50] holds promise for yielding substantial changes in decision-making compared to ad-hoc tribunals, especially when coupled with an appeal mechanism.[51] The absence of such a mechanism has contributed to inconsistent decisions among traditional

---

[45] Noting that the EU cannot use existing International Centre for Settlement of Investment Disputes (ICSID) and United Nations Commission on International Trade Law (UNCITRAL) dispute settlement mechanisms since the EU as such is a member of neither organisation, it is necessary for the EU to include a chapter on dispute settlement in each new EU investment treaty. European Parliament (2011).

[46] European Commission (2013), p. 6.

[47] Ibid., pp. 08–09.

[48] Schill (2017), p. 03.

[49] Article 8.27(5) of CETA, see also Article 8.28(3); Articles 3.9(5)-(7) and 3.10(5)-(7) of the EU - Singapore IPA; Articles 3.38(5),(8) and 3.39(5) of the EVIPA; Articles 11(5) and (9) and 12(5) of the EU - Mexico Agreement in Principle.

[50] Articles 8.27(7), (9), (17) and 8.27(5) of CETA; Articles 3.9(8) and 3.10(8) of the EU - Singapore IPA; Articles 3.38(7) and 3.39(9) of the EVIPA; Articles 11(8) and 12(9) of the EU - Mexico Agreement in Principle; See European Commission (2018).

[51] Article 8.28(2) of CETA; Article 3.19(1) of the EU - Singapore IPA; Article 3.54(1) of the EU - Vietnam IPA; Article 30(1) of the EU - Mexico Agreement in Principle.

investment tribunals.[52] Indeed, while such a mechanism may not be sufficient to safeguard contracting members' policy space,[53] a unified dispute resolution system comprising meticulously chosen judges and subject to close monitoring by both a mechanism and the parties offers a promising avenue for ensuring compliance with parties' intentions. This expectation is thoroughly justified, particularly if there is a mutual agreement among the parties that appointed judges must consider the protection of public interest or the right to regulate. In contrast to ad-hoc Tribunals, the expectation for an investment court system is firmly grounded. The EU's advocacy for a multilateral investment court underscores its recognition of the need for reform within the ISDS system to address concerns, including protecting the right to regulate.[54] The EU's emphasis on safeguarding governments' right to regulate through this mechanism[55] signifies its potential to significantly impact the preservation of parties' policy space through judicial activities.

While the potential of the ICS mechanism in reinforcing the right to regulate is promising, its establishment and implementation remain subject to various procedural hurdles and hinge largely on the concerted efforts of the involved parties.[56] Until this system is operationalised, any initial assessments made will offer limited insights. Hence, while acknowledging the significant influence of factors such as the procedure for appointing judges, litigation procedures, and the approach adopted by future tribunals on the interpretation of parties' right to regulate,[57] this book refrains from conducting an exhaustive examination of the ICS under the EVIPA.

Furthermore, assessments of trends and emerging approaches in IIA negotiations reveal diverse initiatives aimed at striking a balance between investment promotion and protection on one hand and the sovereign rights and broader societal interests of host states on the other. These include restrictions on investor access to dispute settlement, incorporating treaty language pertaining to states' regulatory rights, specifying limited investor obligations, clarifying essential investment protection standards, and introducing general exceptions.[58] While recognising these developments, this book does not aim to provide a comprehensive discussion on them.

[52] Brew (2019), pp. 213–214.

[53] Additional measures, such as providing explicit instructions to the tribunals regarding the parties' intentions for promoting sustainable development must be warranted. Furthermore, as observed in ISDS practice, the jurisprudence adopted by the ICS tribunal can significantly influence the practical outcome of a case. Hush (2018), p. 128.

[54] Indeed, for the EU, a multilateral investment court "is the only type of reform" that can effectively respond to the identified concerns with the current ISDS system, as shown in the EU's submission to the UNCITRAL Working Group III which presumably includes the concern on the protection of the right to regulate as well as the EU legal order. UNCITRAL Working Group III (2019).

[55] European Commission (2015).

[56] European Council (2016), p. 6.

[57] See the discussion on the contribution and the role of the ISDS arbitrators to the outcome of the arbitrations in Coleman et al. (2018), pp. 102–103; see also Waibel and Wu (2017).

[58] Coleman et al. (2018), p. 64.

Instead, it focuses solely on analysing the provisions within the EVFTA-EVIPA that support the state's policy space.

Notably, the mechanisms embedded within IIAs, including those within the EVFTA-EVIPA, aimed at fostering sustainable development objectives and safeguarding policy autonomy extend beyond the regulations scrutinised in this book. Research shows that right-to-regulate clauses and Corporate Social Responsibility (CSR) are increasingly included in IIAs.[59] For instance, Article 16 of the Benin-Canada BIT (2013) underscores the encouragement of enterprises to adhere to internationally recognised standards of corporate social responsibility, encompassing labour, environmental, human rights, community relations, and anti-corruption principles. Moreover, legislative measures concerning the right to regulate can intersect with provisions concerning free transfer treatment.

Besides, countries respond to the asymmetries and challenges posed by IIAs in diverse ways. Some opt to negotiate or renegotiate IIAs based on new models, exemplified by Brazil[60] and India. India, for instance, adopted an assertive stance, terminating existing BITs and initiating negotiations for new agreements, alongside issuing a Joint Interpretative Statement to clarify ambiguous provisions that often trigger repeated litigation.[61] Alternatively, certain nations opt for domestic legislative reforms to revamp their investment promotion and protection frameworks, as seen in Indonesia's drafting and adoption of domestic regulations facilitating the resolution of disputes between investors and the state.[62] Similarly, South Africa adopted the Protection of Investment Act, which allows for international arbitration of investment disputes but mandates the exhaustion of local remedies beforehand.[63]

While acknowledging these varied approaches globally, this book refrains from an exhaustive examination. Instead, it prioritises an analysis of relevant provisions within the EVIPA and, crucially, Vietnam's unique context to devise solutions aligned with the nation's distinctive circumstances and developmental aspirations. This book is grounded in Vietnam's current policy framework for FTA and BIT negotiations, which has evolved since the inception of the Đổi mới, or "opening-up," policy in 1986. This approach involves leveraging FTAs and BITs to drive institutional reform. Consequently, debates surrounding the impact of signing BITs on FDI attraction and the policy trend of reducing BIT networks, as observed in countries like India and South Africa, are deemed irrelevant to this book.

With these aims, the book is organised into four main parts:

- Part I provides the study's contextual background and theoretical framework, delving into the intricate relationship between environmental protection and investment protection.

[59] Levashova (2019), pp. 28–29.

[60] In 2015–2016, Brazil negotiated several new Cooperation and Facilitation Investment Agreements on the basis of its new model. Coleman et al. (2018), pp. 107–108.

[61] Ibid., pp. 48–49.

[62] Ibid.

[63] Ibid.

- Part II analyses Vietnam's legal and policy framework regarding investment management, sustainable development, and environmental protection within the broader context of its socio-economic policy. This part provides an analysis of the mechanisms and strategies employed by Vietnam's government to manage investment and environmental activities while highlighting the shortcomings and limitations inherent in its current policy landscape.
- Part III examines the potential effects of sustainable development provisions, focusing on regulations that protect the right to regulate within the EVIPA while taking into account Vietnam's unique situation.
- Part IV consolidates the main research findings from Parts II and III and elucidates institutional challenges while offering recommendations for Vietnam to prioritise sustainable development within its development strategy, particularly in the context of IIA negotiations.

This book contains ten chapters and an outlook chapter, as outlined below:

Chapter 1 presents an introductory overview of the context in which this study is unfolds. It examines the intricate relationship between sustainable development, environmental protection, and the principles of IIL. In doing so, it analyses a range of established frameworks and proposals aimed at reconciling international investment interests with the essential goals of sustainable development. This Chapter also outlines the scope of the book and details the methodologies employed in the research, thereby establishing a foundation for the subsequent analysis.

Chapter 2 focuses on the intricate interplay between sustainable development, the environment, and international investment within the realm of IIL over the past five decades. This chapter begins by tracing the evolution of IIL and elucidating its fundamental essence, which is providing investment protection commitments as embodied in BITs. Subsequently, the focus of this chapter shifts towards the multifaceted concerns of signatories of IIAs beyond investment protection. It particularly emphasises the pivotal role of sustainable development and the imperative of environmental protection as integral components of sustainable development within the context of IIAs. This background sets the stage for a comprehensive discussion on the imperative of preserving policy space within the framework of IIAs. Building upon this foundation, Chap. 2 explores novel proposals pertaining to the right to regulate within the context of IIAs negotiations. It also undertakes an in-depth review of treaties encompassing investment protection commitments, with particular emphasis on the Comprehensive and Progressive Agreement for Trans-Pacific Partnership (CPTPP), the United States - Mexico - Canada Agreement (USMCA), and the African Continental Free Trade Area (AfCFTA).

Chapter 3 provides an in-depth exploration of Vietnam's policy and legislative framework on investment. The chapter commences by conducting a retrospective examination of the economic development strategies and FDI attraction policies that Vietnam has employed, tracing their origins from the period when the country embarked on the path of economic liberalisation. Subsequently, it scrutinises the Vietnamese government's perspective on foreign investment, offering a comprehensive analysis of the policies devised to entice foreign direct investment. The practical implementation of these investment attraction policies is manifested through Vietnam's intricate system of investment legislation. Consequently, this chapter focuses on the evolution of Vietnam's investment legislation, tracking its journey as Vietnam integrated itself into the regional and global economic landscape. This review underscores the proactive nature of the Vietnamese government's endeavours and its unwavering commitment to cultivating an enabling environment for foreign investment. It is noteworthy that the Vietnamese government has displayed an increased capacity to formulate policies and effectively manage related issues over time. Ultimately, the analysis concludes that Vietnam's investment legal framework has been progressively evolving and aligning itself with the evolving requirements and norms of international investment practices. Particularly significant is the growing integration of environmental protection requirements into investment legislation, reflecting Vietnam's commitment to harmonising its legal framework with contemporary global standards in the realm of international investment.

Following a comprehensive examination of investment law and policy in Vietnam, *Chap. 4* shifts its focus towards a detailed assessment of environmental protection policies within the country, closely scrutinising the corresponding legal framework. Additionally, it introduces the complex network of state management agencies responsible for overseeing ongoing environment management activities. This analytical review underscores a noteworthy evolution in Vietnam's approach to environmental protection over time. The nation's growing acknowledgement of environmental concerns has been propelled by an increasing number of serious environmental incidents, extending beyond the primary objective of economic development.

However, this chapter also highlights systemic shortcomings in environmental policy management in Vietnam that impede effective environmental governance. Specifically, from a policy management perspective, although Vietnam has recognised environmental policies relatively early, they remain largely declarative and lack concrete implementation tools. Moreover, Vietnam's environmental management and investment management are presently separate activities that lack integration. In addition, within the realm of environmental management, numerous industries are involved, and as a result, the system of legal regulations and supervisory agencies responsible for overseeing this activity lacks coherence and systematic organisation. These inherent weaknesses in the domestic environmental management system, combined with the fragmentation of environmental laws and their separation from other national management branches, contribute to a lack of desired effectiveness in environmental governance in Vietnam.

Chapter 5 initiates by offering a contextual background for the negotiation and ultimate conclusion of the EVIPA. This contextual foundation is integral to cultivating a more comprehensive understanding of the specific commitments assessed in the following chapters. Subsequently, this chapter embarks on an analysis that centres around the theme of safeguarding regulatory autonomy for environmental protection within EVIPA. The analysis shows the convergence of concerns between the parties, accentuating their shared commitment to advancing sustainable development and environmental conservation. Additionally, this chapter extends its purview to encompass a broader discussion on the EU's extensive stance on sustainable development and human rights. These explorations collectively reveal the EU's consistent policy orientation, which promotes enduring values rooted in sustainability. Moreover, it explains the EU's strategic approach of employing commercial cooperation as a means to transcend the boundaries of purely commercial interests, enabling the fostering of shared non-commercial concerns with its partners, including Vietnam.

Chap. 6 presents an exhaustive examination of the provisions on indirect expropriation within the EVIPA. The primary objective of this Chapter is to assess the efficacy of the modifications introduced in EVIPA regarding one of the most frequently cited provisions in investor claims within the realm of international investment. The outcome of this analysis reveals that in contrast to contemporaneously negotiated or drafted agreements, for instance, Canada's 2021 Model Foreign Investment Promotion and Protection Agreement (FIPA), the provisions on indirect expropriation under the EVIPA do not exhibit significant innovations. This observation could be attributed to a deliberate policy choice made by the signatories. While Annex 4 of EVIPA may not universally receive acclaim for its meticulousness and comprehensiveness, it nonetheless furnishes a fundamental framework for arbitral tribunals to diligently adhere to the parties' original intentions when appraising specific measures. When evaluated with other enhancements featured in EVIPA, particularly those concerning regulatory measures, it consistently provides a discernible level of safeguard for the host state's policy measures. Notably, these disputes will fall under the purview of the ICS rather than any alternative arbitral tribunal, thus adding a layer of assurance for a standardised interpretation of these provisions. In a manner akin to the ISDS system's longstanding operation, the adjudicative processes developed by the ICS will progressively enhance the predictability of dispute resolution.

Similar to the assessments presented in Chap. 6, *Chap. 7* offers an analysis of the FET standard included in EVIPA. Commencing with an overview of FET provisions within the realm of IIL, this chapter subsequently delves into an examination of FET claims arising from policy measures directed at environmental protection, as observed in investment arbitration practice. Building upon this foundation, the chapter proceeds to conduct a thorough evaluation of the FET provisions under EVIPA.

The findings of this study underscore that EVIPA's FET clause possesses a degree of lucidity when compared to the verbiage commonly found in traditional FET clauses. Notably, this provision provides an exhaustive list of scenarios that constitute a breach of the FET standard, thus offering clearer assurances to the state in pursuit of its policy objectives, so long as the measures undertaken do not fall within the situations outlined in this clause. Furthermore, the chapter emphasises that the restriction placed on assessing legitimate expectations at the inception of the FET standard also limits the potential for this factor to be construed beyond the parties' original intentions. Crucially, these circumstances leading to a breach of the fundamental FET standard have already been codified as grounds within Vietnam's national legislation, reflecting a transparent legal framework. Consequently, the FET clause in EVIPA does not impose heightened obligations on Vietnam.

The nexus between the right to regulate and sustainable development underscores the need for their cohesive interpretation.[64] In practical terms, regulatory authority exercised by states to safeguard the environment also upholds the social pillars of sustainable development. *Chapter 8* of this book thus evaluates the potential impact of mentioning sustainable development in the Preamble and the provision on the right to regulate in broadening the protection afforded to state regulations, with a specific focus on Vietnam.

The findings of this chapter reveal that while the Preambles of both the EVFTA and EVIPA acknowledge concerns related to sustainable development, thereby guiding ICS tribunals to consider the broader objectives of the agreements beyond trade and investment promotion, they notably lack explicit mention of reserving the right to regulate. This omission stands in contrast to trade and investment agreements which the EU signed with two other partners, Canada and Singapore. Consequently, EVIPA falls short in providing a platform to safeguard the policy space for parties across the entire investment activities covered by the agreement.

Furthermore, while both the EVFTA and EVIPA incorporate substantive provisions affirming the right to regulate and expand public objectives, questions remain regarding how ICS tribunals will interpret and apply these provisions and the weight they will accord them. Assessing the effectiveness of these regulations in achieving a better balance between the host state's policy space and investment protection standards is inherently more complex compared to regulations concerning indirect expropriation and the FET standard. Therefore, obtaining more specific data on how ICS tribunals considered the first dispute involving these provisions is imperative for an accurate assessment.

Chapter 9 evaluates the role of the general exception provision in safeguarding the host state's right to regulate under the EVIPA. This chapter highlights that the exception clause of the EVIPA (Article 4.6) holds the potential for refining the interpretation and application of pertinent substantive obligations, including National Treatment (NT) and MFN treatment. This is logical, considering that, unlike provisions regarding indirect expropriation and FET, NT and MFN clauses in the EVIPA mirror their treatment in traditional IIAs.

One notable advantage of this regulation is its capacity to distribute the burden of proof between the aggrieved investor and the host state. However, the chapter also underscores that the effectiveness of the exception clause in preserving the host state's policy space hinges largely on the approach adopted by ICS tribunals. Therefore, ensuring the efficacy of this regulation necessitates ongoing discussions and clarifications between the contracting parties regarding the role of the exception clause and its interplay with relevant substantive obligations.

Chapter 10 comprehensively assesses the Vietnamese government's ability to pursue its policy objectives within the parameters outlined by the EVIPA. This

---

[64] Hush (2018), p. 128.

analysis is grounded in the common context shared by developing nations like Vietnam, which grapples with the delicate balance between investment attraction policies and the imperative of environmental protection. This equilibrium poses a significant challenge, especially in countries where FDI plays a crucial role in driving economic growth.

Vietnam's susceptibility to climate change and the environmental degradation resulting from rapid economic development policies underscores the urgency of addressing these issues within the country's development strategy. Nevertheless, existing constraints within Vietnam's environmental and investment management policies present substantial obstacles. This book proposes that the Vietnamese government leverage available tools, including international investment agreements, to redirect FDI flows towards supporting sustainable development goals.

While implementing such a strategy is complex, the potential of IIAs to foster a green economy for Vietnam and similarly positioned nations is considerable. Just as these agreements facilitate cross-border investment and mitigate risks for foreign investors, they can also contribute to improving the overall investment climate.[65] However, it is crucial to recognise that IIAs cannot substitute for robust domestic policies and regulatory frameworks.[66] Therefore, a proactive and resolute approach is imperative to address the challenging circumstances at hand effectively.

To date, the majority of research efforts have concentrated on analysing the evolution of the relationship and interaction between environmental law and investment law, as well as the inherent tension between these two paradigms or innovations aimed at preserving the right to regulate within IIAs, generally from a neutral standpoint. This book, therefore, does not intend to replicate these existing endeavours. Conversely, there have been relatively few studies that have examined the potential effects of new proposals concerning the host state's right to regulate, particularly from the perspective of a developing country like Vietnam, especially with regard to the regulations embedded in the trade and investment agreements between the EU and Vietnam.

1.4 Methods

The book mainly employs legal analytical methods to describe relevant IIAs, including text of EVIPA and other trade-investment agreements (CPTPP, CETA, Canada 2021 Model FIPA, USMCA,…) and practice reflected in ISDS awards. The methodology employed in this research navigates the evolving landscape presented by the EVIPA, recognising that its provisions have yet to be tested before the dispute resolution body within its framework, namely the ICS. Therefore, comments and proposals offered on related regulations of the EVIPA are grounded in

---

65 UNCTAD (2018), p. 16.

66 Ibid., p. 17.

an array of sources. Analysis of pertinent investment disputes, scholarly viewpoints, and doctrines in international law, particularly IIL, forms the backbone of this examination. Furthermore, a comparative study of specific provisions within the EVIPA with those of contemporaneous agreements aids in assessing the efficacy of these regulations in safeguarding the right to regulate. These approaches are contextualised within the broader context of IIAs and recent ISDS reform efforts.

Conducting empirical studies on policies and laws in the environmental and international investment management realm in Vietnam presents significant challenges. Information on the drafting and construction process of legal regulations or discussions within government agencies regarding international treaty participation is often not publicly disclosed. Similarly, details concerning investor-state disputes in which Vietnam is a defendant are classified as national secrets[67] and remain inaccessible to the public. Government officials responsible for negotiating and implementing investment treaties typically withhold information in this domain. Similarly, assessing the effectiveness of environmental policies and laws in Vietnam is another difficulty due to the lack of publicly available information. Official data or information regarding issues encountered during policy implementation or the enforcement of environmental laws is generally difficult to obtain. This lack of transparency hinders comprehensive evaluation and analysis, complicating efforts to gauge the country's impact and efficacy of environmental regulations. Therefore, assessments made in this book primarily rely on linguistic analysis of international treaties involving Vietnam, published policies, and legal documents, including reports from authoritative domestic and international entities. These encompass documents from the Communist Party, speeches of high-ranking officials, reports from government agencies, and information on official government websites. Additionally, insights from independent research conducted by domestic and international experts and reflections on the application of law in Vietnam through media reports are also considered.

ISDS Cases

Bear Creek Mining Corporation v. Republic of Peru [2014] ICSID Case No. ARB/14/21

Burlington Resources Inc. v. Republic of Ecuador [2008] ICSID Case No. ARB/08/5

Churchill Mining PLC and Planet Mining Pty Ltd v. Republic of Indonesia [2012] ICSID Case No. ARB/12/14 and 12/40

Eiser Infrastructure Limited and Energía Solar Luxembourg S.à r.l. v. Kingdom of Spain [2013] ICSID Case No. ARB/13/36

Pac Rim Cayman LLC v. Republic of El Salvador [2009] ICSID Case No. ARB/09/12

[67] Dung (2022), p. 267.

Perenco Ecuador Limited v. Republic of Ecuador [2008] ICSID Case No. ARB/08/6
Urbaser S.A. and Consorcio de Aguas Bilbao Biskaia, Bilbao Biskaia Ur Partzuergoa v. Argentine Republic [2007] ICSID Case No. ARB/07/26

Treaties

African Continental Free Trade Area (2018) (AfCFTA)
Brazil's Cooperation and Facilitation Investment Agreement (2015) (CFIA). Available via https://investmentpolicy.unctad.org/international-investment-agreements/treaty-files/4786/download
Benin - Canada BIT (2013)
Canada - EU Comprehensive Economic and Trade Agreement (2016) (CETA)
Canada's Model Foreign Investment Promotion and Protection Agreement (2021) (FIPA)
Comprehensive and Progressive Agreement for Trans-Pacific Partnership (2018) (CPTPP)
EU - Japan Economic Partnership Agreement (2018)
EU - Mexico Agreement in Principle (2018)
EU - China Comprehensive Agreement on Investment (2020)
EU - Singapore Investment Protection Agreement (2018) (EU - Singapore IPA)
EU - Vietnam Investment Protection Agreement (2019) (EVIPA)
Southern African Development Community (SADC) Model BIT (2012)
UK - Canada Trade Continuity Agreement (2020)
United States - Mexico - Canada Agreement (2019) (USMCA)

References

Bibliography

Benedetto SD (2013) International investment law and the environment. Edward Elgar Publishing
Berner K (2016) Reconciling investment protection and sustainable development-a plea for an interpretative U-Turn. In: Hindelang S, Krajewski M (eds) Shifting paradigms in international investment law: more balanced, less isolated, increasingly diversified. Oxford University Press
Bonnitcha J (2014) Substantive protection under investment treaties: a legal and economic analysis. Cambridge University Press
Brew R (2019) Exception clauses in international investment agreements as a tool for appropriately balancing the right to regulate with investment protection. Canterbury Law Rev 25:205
Chi M (2018) Integrating sustainable development in international investment law: normative incompatibility, system integration and governance implications. Routledge

Coleman J et al (2018) International investment agreements 2015–16: a review of trends and new approaches. In: Sachs LE, Johnson L (eds) 2015–2016 Yearbook on International Investment Law and Policy. Oxford University Press

Dung TV (2022) The impact of investment treaties on the rule of law in Viet Nam. In: Calamita NJ, Berman A (eds) Investment treaties and the rule of law promise: the internalisation of international commitments in Asia. Cambridge University Press

Gaukrodger D (2017) The balance between investor protection and the right to regulate in investment treaties: a scoping paper. OECD Working Papers on International Investment No 2017/02

Gaukrodger D (2021) The future of investment treaties - possible direction. OECD Working Papers on International Investment No 2021/03

Gehring MW, Kent A (2013) International investment agreements and the emerging green economy: rising to the challenge. In: Baetens F (ed) Investment law within international law – integrationist perspectives. Cambridge University Press

Gordon K (2008) International investment agreements: a survey of environmental, labour and anti-corruption issues. In: International investment law: understanding concepts and tracking innovations. OECD. Available via https://read.oecd-ilibrary.org/finance-and-investment/international-investment-law-understanding-concepts-and-tracking-innovations_9789264042032-en#page3

Gordon K, Pohl J (2011) Environmental concerns in international investment agreements: a survey. OECD Working Papers on International Investment No 2011/1

Gordon K, Pohl J, Bouchard M (2014) Investment treaty law, sustainable development and responsible business conduct: a fact finding survey. OECD Working Papers on International Investment No 2014/01

Hush E (2018) Where no man has gone before: the future of sustainable development in the comprehensive economic and trade agreement and new generation free trade agreements. Columbia J Environ Law 43(1):93. Available via https://journals.library.columbia.edu/index.php/cjel/article/view/3741

Levashova Y (2019) The right of states to regulate in international investment law: the search for balance between public interest and fair and equitable treatment. Wolters Kluwer

Mann H (2008) The IISD Model International Agreement on Investment for Sustainable Development: assessing progress at three years. OECD Global Forum on Investment VII. 28 March 2008. Available via http://www.oecd.org/investment/globalforum/40396943.pdf

Mann H, Moltke KV, Peterson LE, Cosbey A (2005) IISD Model International Agreement on Investment for Sustainable Development – negotiator's handbook, 2nd edn. International Institute for Sustainable Development. Available via https://www.iisd.org/system/files/publications/investment_model_int_handbook.pdf

Morgera E (2006) An environmental outlook on the OECD guidelines for multinational enterprises: comparative advantage, legitimacy, and outstanding questions in the lead up to the 2006 review. Georgetown Int Environ Law Rev 18(4)

Newcombe A (2012) General exceptions in international investment agreements. In: Segger MCC, Gehring M, Newcombe A (eds) Sustainable development in world investment law. Wolters Kluwer

OECD (2002) foreign direct investment and the environment - lessons from the mining sector. OECD Global Forum on International Investment

OECD (2011) Guidelines for Multinational Enterprises, Annex I to the Declaration on International Investment and Multinational Enterprises. Available via https://www.oecd-ilibrary.org/finance-and-investment/oecd-guidelines-for-multinational-enterprises-on-responsible-business-conduct_81f92357-en

Puvimanasinghe SF (2007) Foreign investment, human rights and the environment: a perspective from South Asia on the role of public international law for development. Martinus Nijhoff Publishers

Sacerdoti G (2016) Investment protection and sustainable development - key issues. In: Hindelang S, Krajewski M (eds) Shifting paradigms in international investment law: more balanced, less isolated, increasingly diversified. Oxford University Press

Schefer KN (2020) International investment law: text, cases and material, 3rd edn. Edward Elgar

Schill S (2017) Authority, legitimacy, and fragmentation in the (envisaged) dispute settlement disciplines in mega-regionals. ACIL Research Paper 2017-04. Available via https://papers.ssrn.com/sol3/papers.cfm?abstract_id=2932810

Tuerk E, Rojid F (2012) Towards a new generation of investment policies: UNCTAD's Investment Policy Framework for Sustainable Development. Investment Treaty News. Available via https://www.iisd.org/itn/en/2012/10/30/towards-a-new-generation-of-investment-policies-unctads-investment-policy-framework-for-sustainable-development/

UNCITRAL Working Group III (2019) Submission of the EU and its Member States, A/CN.9/WG.III/WP.159/Add.1. Available via https://undocs.org/en/A/CN.9/WG.III/WP.159/Add.1

UNCTAD (2013) Towards a New Generation of International Investment Policies: UNCTAD's Fresh Approach to Multilateral Investment Policy-making. Available via https://unctad.org/system/files/official-document/webdiaepcb2013d6_en.pdf

UNCTAD (2015a) Investment Policy Framework for Sustainable Development. Available via https://unctad.org/publication/investment-policy-framework-sustainable-development-2015-edition

UNCTAD (2015b) World Investment Report 2015: Reforming International Investment Governance. Available via https://unctad.org/system/files/official-document/wir2015_en.pdf

UNCTAD (2018) UNCTAD's Reform Package for the International Investment Regime. Available via https://investmentpolicy.unctad.org/uploaded-files/document/UNCTAD_Reform_Package_2018.pdf

UNCTAD (2020) International Investment Agreements – Reform Accelerator. Available via https://unctad.org/system/files/official-document/diaepcbinf2020d8_en.pdf

Vanduzer JA, Simons P, Maeda G (2013) Integrating sustainable development into international investment agreements: a guide for developing country negotiators. Commonwealth Secretariat. Available via https://www.thecommonwealth-ilibrary.org/index.php/comsec/catalog/book/168

Viñuales JE (2012) Foreign investment and the environment in international. Cambridge University Press

Waibel M, Wu Y (2017) Are arbitrators political? Evidence from international investment arbitration. University of Southern California 24. Available via https://www.yanhuiwu.com/documents/arbitrator.pdf

Documents

European Commission (2013) Investment Protection and Investor-to-State Dispute Settlement in EU Agreements - Fact Sheet. Available via http://www.sice.oas.org/TPD/USA_EU/Studies/tradoc_151916__Investment_e.pdf

European Commission (2015) Why the New EU Proposal for an Investment Court Systems in TTIP is beneficial to both Sates and Investors. Press Release MEMO/15/6060. Available via https://ec.europa.eu/commission/presscorner/detail/en/MEMO_15_6060

European Commission (2018) EU-Mexico Agreement: The Agreement in Principle. Available via https://policy.trade.ec.europa.eu/eu-trade-relationships-country-and-region/countries-and-regions/mexico/eu-mexico-agreement/agreement-principle_en

European Council (2016) Joint Interpretative Instrument on the Comprehensive Economic and Trade Agreement (CETA) between Canada and the European Union and its Member States, 13541/16 Brussels. Available via https://data.consilium.europa.eu/doc/document/ST-13541-2016-INIT/en/pdf

European Parliament (2011) Resolution on the Future European International Investment Policy, (2010/2203(INI)). Available via http://www.europarl.europa.eu/sides/getDoc.do?pubRef=-//EP//TEXT+TA+P7-TA-2011-0141+0+DOC+XML+V0//EN
European Union Council (2016) Joint Interpretative Instrument on the Comprehensive Economic and Trade Agreement (CETA) between Canada and the European Union and its Member States, 13541/16 Brussels. Available via https://data.consilium.europa.eu/doc/document/ST-13541-2016-INIT/en/pdf

Part I
Context and Theoretical Background

Chapter 2
Environmental Concerns and Sustainability in International Investment Law

Abstract This chapter focuses on the intricate relationship between sustainable development, the environment, and international investment within the framework of IIL over the past fifty years. It begins by tracing the evolution of IIL and clarifying its core purpose, which is to provide investment protection commitments as outlined in BITs. Next, the chapter shifts its focus to the diverse concerns of signatories of IIAs that extend beyond the mere protection of investments. It highlights the crucial role of sustainable development and emphasises the necessity of environmental protection as an essential component of development in the context of IIA negotiations. This background sets the stage for a comprehensive discussion on the importance of preserving policy space within IIAs. Building on this foundation, the chapter also explores new proposals regarding the right to regulate in the context of IIA negotiations. Additionally, it conducts an in-depth review of treaties that include investment protection commitments, with special attention given to the CPTPP, the USMCA, and the AfCFTA.

2.1 International Investment Law and Environmental Protection: A Complex Interplay

Historically, IIAs have been designed to provide a set of tools to protect foreign investors' properties inside the host state's border. Indeed, signing IIAs is a vital requirement for the home state to pave the way for capital export. Since their first appearance over sixty years ago, IIAs are usually drafted by developed economies[1] with a relatively short and straightforward format containing primarily substantive rights granted directly to the investors. The first modern BIT, the Germany - Pakistan BITs (1959), describes in its Preamble that the parties:

[1] VanDuzer (2016), pp. 172–173.

N. T. Lan Huong, *Investment Protection and Environmental Governance*, European Yearbook of International Economic Law 47,
https://doi.org/10.1007/978-3-032-05332-9_2

> Recognizing that an understanding reached between the two States is likely to promote investment, encourage private industrial and financial enterprise and to increase the prosperity of both the States.

In this wording, the aim to promote investment is mentioned as the core of the treaty, while there are no references to rights to regulate (regulatory autonomy, policy space, flexibility to introduce new regulations), sustainable development, or social investment aspects (e.g., human rights, labour, health, CSR, poverty reduction) as well as environmental aspects (e.g., plant or animal life, biodiversity, climate change).[2] The absence of those aspects in the Preamble makes no place for them in the treaty objectives and the treaty's substantive regulation. Specifically, besides a statement of the purpose of the BIT, an ideal format of traditional BITs includes:[3]

- a definition of investments protected by the BIT and the nationality of the protected investors;
- substantive rights granted to foreign investors: contingent standards (basically, the MFN and the NT standards; absolute standards (FET and Full Protection and Security); absolute general rights (the right to compensation for direct expropriation as well as for indirect expropriation); absolute specific rights (the right to repatriate dividends, profits, royalties, fees and the proceeds of divesting; …)
- procedural rights relating to the settlement of arising disputes, which usually suggests the availability of direct investment arbitration (ISDS).

As can be seen, traditional BITs or IIAs provide a one-way relationship in which the host state does not own any reciprocal rights compared to the investors. The above terms and substantive rights will further be interpreted in light of relevant international customary concepts when there is a lack of specific definitions or guidance for arbitral tribunals under the treaty.[4]

As mentioned above, BITs are drafted by developed economies to protect the investment of their citizens in a developing country's territory expecting FDI. Therefore, it is not necessary or a concern of the vague investor protection standards designed by themselves. Their primary focus is to set a high standard of protection for its investors and investments to protect them from the regulatory actions of the host state overseas, often in the developing world.[5] One may argue that BIT regulations are applied equally to both parties. However, it is rarely seen a claim, if any, submitted by an investor coming from a developing country at

[2] Chi supposes that the term "prosperity" carries similar meaning of "economic development" and this shows an implied positive investment-development relationship. However, this idea does not affect the fact that there is no clear linking between investment and sustainable development as well as environmental protection in this early form of BIT. Chi (2018), p. 17.

[3] Sacerdoti (2016), pp. 28–30.

[4] Ibid., p. 28.

[5] Collins (2012), p. 327.

investment arbitration because the direction of capital flow at this time mainly starts from developed countries to developing countries.[6]

For about 50 years since the 1950s, IIAs generally have conformed to this archetype and developed a surprisingly uniform structure, scope, and content. Stephan argues that the convergence of BITs stems from the shared interest of States in uniform rules, which promote fair investment conditions and efficient global capital allocation, benefiting both developed and developing countries.[7] There is also a comment that the one-way direction of the capital flow in this period encourages developed countries to focus on the strong protection of their investors, leading to the dominance of investor-protection provisions in BITs.[8] Such IIAs concluded in this period[9] is called as "one-sided international investment agreement". Scholars suppose that the IIA making process was driven and devised by capital-exporting countries. Therefore, IIAs' content could be viewed as a function of the hegemonic behaviour of those countries vi-à-vis their capital-importing counterparts.[10] For developing countries, these commitments are the price to pay to receive inward investment into the country. Therefore, it has been widely agreed that historically, the purposes of BITs were to attract investment by presenting competitive advantages to particular foreign investors.[11]

Over time, the diversion of capital flow from the North-South paradigm in the early days of foreign direct investment to the North-North, South-South relationship leads to a changing context. This shift in the capital flow at the regional and global levels has a connection with comprehensive regional and multilateral trade umbrellas.[12] The North-North paradigm aims to achieve deeper trade liberalisation and economic integration among developed countries, usually within a specific region, typically by forming agreements that include binding trade and investment rules. As for the South-South paradigm,[13] developing countries have negotiated more IIAs amongst themselves and, step by step, have become capital exporters.[14] With this switch in role and position, industrialised countries have realised that they are also bound by those obligations in their new role as host states. These investment standards have, indeed, limited their expected policy space in practice. Developed

[6] VanDuzer (2016), pp. 172–173; See also Vandevelde (2010), p. 8. A thorough discussion on negotiating position of two state parties in a BIT negotiation can be read in Mills (2014), pp. 441–443.

[7] Schill (2014), para. 26.

[8] VanDuzer (2016), pp. 172–173.

[9] Which is usually named as "Pax Americana"—a term used to describe the period in the second half of the 20th Century in which the US occupied a position of singular geopoliticaldominance. Collins (2012), p. 327.

[10] See further discussion in Schill (2014), para. 24; Benvenisti and Downs (2007), pp. 611–612.

[11] Mills (2014), p. 440.

[12] Read more about these trends in UNCTAD (2007), p. 4; VanDuzer (2016), pp. 173–174.

[13] UNCTAD (2005).

[14] Vanduzer et al. (2013), p. 2. However, the core provisions of BITs concluded between developing countries do not significantly differ from those concluded with developed countries. See further Chi (2018), p. 11; Schill (2014), para. 25.

economies can now be challenged at different dispute settlement forums under the signed IIAs or FTAs. In recent years, Austria, Belgium, France, Germany, Greece, Italy, Spain, Australia, Canada, and the United States have all been the targets of investor-state claims.[15] Among others, *Methanex v. USA*,[16] *Vattenfall v. Germany*,[17] *Eli Lilly v. Canada* and *Philip Moris v. Australia*[18] are disputes that have caught the international community's attention. Such problems arise from investment relationships between countries at the same level of development, which make them play as both capital importers and capital exporters in the South-South and North-North contexts where both partners have the same motivation to protect their right to pursue sustainable development goals, leading to a new trend in re-drafting IIA provisions to set the ground for the inclusion of sustainable development as well as provisions to reserve the rights to regulate of host states into BITs.

In addition, it has been noticed that the increasing participation of emerging economies such as China, India, and Malaysia into the world economy has contributed to accelerating this need. Indeed, developed economies like Canada, Australia, and the EU now have been negotiating treaties with developing economies, which are considered substantial sources of inward investment, forcing them to act more cautiously in IIA negotiations about reserving rights to regulate to achieve sustainable development. In practice, as shown in UNCTAD World Investment Reports, FDI flows to developed economies increased further in 2015 by 5% to 1 trillion USD, after significant growth in the previous year, while FDI outflows from developed countries remained weak.[19] In this context, the innovative feature of the BITs granting investors the right to directly challenge the host states' measures in breaching investment obligations at the international investment tribunal leads to a significant increase in investment claims. Notably, as of December 31, 2023, there are 1332 known treaty-based ISDS claims that had been filed, and at least 146 states have faced formal claims.[20] It has been highlighted that this "staggering" number is even more impressive if one notices that the first ISDS case was filed only approximately 30 years ago. Fewer than 50 cases had been filed before the year 2000,[21] meaning it takes only 23 years to reach that number of 1332 cases.

Together with the wave of investor-state disputes, sustainable development aspects such as human rights or environmental protection are subject to more claims

---

[15] VanDuzer (2016), pp. 174–175; Kläger (2016), p. 67; See also UNCTAD (2015a).

[16] *Methanex Corp. v. United States of America* [1999] UNCITRAL, 44 ILM 1345, Award, 3 August 2005.

[17] *Vattenfall AB, Vattenfall Europe AG, Vattenfall Europe Generation AG v. Federal Republic of Germany* [2009] ICSID Case No. ARB/09/6, Award, 11 March 2011.

[18] *Eli Lilly and Company v. The Government of Canada* [2017] UNCITRAL, ICSID Case No. UNCT/14/2, Award, 16 March 2017; *Philip Morris Asia Limited v. The Commonwealth of Australia*, UNCITRAL, PCA Case No. 2012-12, Award on Jurisdiction and Amssibility, 17 December 2015.

[19] UNCTAD (2015b), pp. x, xi.

[20] UNCTAD - Investment Policy Hub.

[21] Johnson et al. (2018), p. 5.

at investment arbitration,[22] along with (unpredictable) unjustified liabilities.[23] Indeed, ISDS practice shows that when determining investor protection standards, arbitrators need to take into account a wide range of factors on a case-by-case and fact-inquiring basis,[24] which leads to the risk of uncontrolled interpretation of investment tribunal as well as unpredictability for legislators and business. The traditional language of substantive investment standards is often vague and usually open to various interpretations.[25] Indeed, it is easy to find different interpretations of similar provisions by different investment tribunals. Many key terms in IIAs are drafted with vagueness, such as measure "tantamount to" or constitutes an "indirect expropriation," "compensational expropriation," the FET standard[26] which will be moreover entrusted ad-hoc tribunals to decide. The structure of ISDS mechanisms is another weakness of the IIA regimes, as pointed out by scholars because being composed of a variety of arbitrators chosen mostly by the parties themselves, not subject to an obligation to follow previous decisions, nor controlled by appeals mechanism capable of developing consistent case law, "the outcome is inevitably somehow unpredictable and inconsistent."[27] This lack of coherence and consistency regarding the interpretation of vital investment protection standards received much criticism.

At the same time, there are also critics that investment arbitrators often fail to take into account public interests or sustainable development goals pursued by the host states[28] or they tend to apply "unexpected" interpretations of investment standards or have allowed for "unwanted" challenges to state regulatory autonomy in pursuit of a public purpose.[29] This practice raises several questions for IIA negotiators as well as international organisations supporting international investment:

- Are current ISDS mechanisms providing too many rights for private entities to bring a claim against a host state that is a party to an IIA?
- Whether ISDS and IIAs' substantive obligations limit states' sovereignty in adjusting their policies and regulating the public interests, especially in the interests of the environment.

Along with those concerns, other weaknesses of investor-state arbitration have also been revealed through practice. Specifically, confidentiality, as one of the main features of arbitral proceedings, may lock all efforts to track investment disputes to

22 Osterwalder and Johnson (2011); Osterwalder et al. (2018).

23 These concerns are comprehensively presented in UNCTAD (2015c). See also Muchlinski (2016), p. 42.

24 Chi (2018), p. 60.

25 Hindelang and Krajewski (2016), pp. 10–11. See also Bonnitcha (2014), pp. 14, 355, Chapter 6.

26 In which the term "fair" and "equitable" has a similar problem.

27 Sacerdoti (2016), p. 35.

28 Chi (2018), pp. 60, 168; Kulick (2012), pp. 262–263; Brower and Schill (2009), p. 476; Kurt (2014), pp. 257–296.

29 Vanduzer et al. (2013), p. 102; Franck (2005), p. 1571.

assess the policy implications involved.[30] Another criticism related to the massive compensation paid by mainly developing countries as host states struggle with environmental management crises. All these problems have raised significant concerns to include an explicit guarantee to the policy space for regulating to achieve sustainable development, especially environmental protection, as in the practice of investor-state arbitration, states have come to realise that various IIA provisions can "unduly limit their regulatory power".[31] Therefore, in the past two decades, there has been a significant trend in IIAs focusing on sustainable development, particularly regarding the environmental aspect. This growing attention to environmental issues is reflected in various IIAs and trade agreements between countries across different continents. In light of these developments, at the international level, the expectation of enhancing the role of foreign investments in promoting sustainable development and its components has been recognised in different international forums. G20 Ministerial Meeting in July 2016, ministers of the world's largest economies agreed on Guiding Principles for Global Investment and Policymaking, which, among other purposes, is "promoting inclusive economic growth and sustainable development."[32] At the national level, countries have also paid more attention to sustainable development strategy and the right to governance on their territories.[33]

Since the mid-2000s, significant changes to IIL focusing more clearly on public interest considerations can be witnessed. Articles on the environment, labour rights, and opt-out clause for non-conforming can be found in the US 2004 Model BIT, provision on the general exception in the form of General Agreement on Tariff and Trade (GATT) Article XX under the World Trade Organisation (WTO) has been included in the Canadian 2004 Model BIT.[34] Those innovations have later appeared in BITs that those countries signed with their partners.

2.2 Sustainable Development and Environmental Protection in the Context of International Investment Law

2.2.1 Sustainable Development

As previously noted, traditional FTAs and BITs rarely address sustainable development or environmental protection. The primary purpose of these treaties is to create favourable conditions for investors from one country to invest in the territory of another. Consequently, expecting clauses promoting sustainable development or environmental protection in treaties specifically designed to provide investment

---

[30] Benedetto (2013), pp. 58–59.

[31] Chi (2018), p. 3; Kläger (2016), p. 67.

[32] G20 (2016).

[33] See, for example, the case of China in Chi (2015).

[34] See futher example in UNCTAD (2015b), pp. 102–103; Hindelang and Krajewski (2016), p. 4.

protection is unrealistic. The term "sustainable development" began to appear in treaties in the 1980s,[35] but its roots are most firmly embedded in international environmental law.[36] As has been observed, the concept of "sustainable development" is increasingly becoming part of the corpus of customary international law, necessitating an integrated approach to the various streams of international law.[37] The term can be found as an explicit objective in dozens of international treaties, notably, the Treaty on European Union (Article 21) or the Marrakesh Agreement establishing the WTO (Preamble), as well as in numerous soft-law instruments.[38] This term is also readily found in the preambles of BITs or preferential trade agreements with invesment provisions concluded by countries across the world today. Despite the ambiguity as to the normative content of sustainable development and its binding scope, in general terms, sustainable development has won international recognition as a broad legal principle, beyond being a policy principle.[39]

As can be seen, sustainable development functions as both a political and legal concept.[40].It first emerged as a political paradigm, articulating global norms that integrate economic growth, social equity, and environmental protection within policy-making frameworks.[41] At the same time, it has been incorporated into international law - appearing in treaty objectives, judicial reasoning, and doctrine - as a legal concept capable of guiding state obligations.[42] It is also a multi-level concept, carrying different meanings at different levels.[43] While a broad definition may initially facilitate consensus, building among diverse constituencies during international negotiations,[44] its inherent vagueness can later present challenges when applying this normative principle across different forums or contexts.

Despite its popularity, the meaning and scope of sustainable development have yet to be agreed upon and well-established. In its evolving process, the term is considered as a concept encapsulating the three-dimensional relationship of (i) economic development, (ii) social well-being and social development, and (iii) environmental protection.[45] At the international level, the law and policy relating to sustainable development deal predominantly with the environmental aspect, less with the other two components.[46] However, it is widely acknowledged that sustain-

---

[35] International Union for Conservation of Nature and Natural Resources, United Nations Environment Programme, World Wildlife Fund, World Conservation Strategy: Living Resource Conservation for Sustainable Development (1980).

[36] Puvimanasinghe (2007), p. 97.

[37] Sands et al. (2018), p. 219.

[38] Hindelang and Krajewski (2016), p. 7; Segger and Khalfan (2004), pp. 32–36.

[39] Sacerdoti (2016), pp. 25–26.

[40] Hindelang and Krajewski (2016), p. 7.

[41] Bantekas, Akestoridi (2023).

[42] Vinuales (2023), pp. 294–299.

[43] Viñuales (2012), p. 12; Dobson (1999), p. 23.

[44] Viñuales (2010), p. 246.

[45] Hindelang and Krajewski (2016), p. 7.

[46] Puvimanasinghe (2007), p. 159.

able development entails the delicate balance of various interests, as highlighted by the ICJ in the *Gabcikovo-Nagymaros* case.[47] In practice, stakeholders frequently find themselves tasked with the complex challenge of harmonising economic interests with environmental values.

Since the beginning of the twenty-first century, when trade liberalisation has been promoted with the support of the WTO, scholars have discussed and emphasised the importance of sustainable trade.[48] There is a high consensus among international institutions, states, and scholars on the significance of linking sustainable development with trade and investment development.[49] The term "sustainable development" is becoming more prominent in many new-generation trade agreements and IIAs.[50]

Indeed, the term sustainable development is usually found in the Preamble in FTAs. Although the Preamble does not create or limit obligations in the treaty directly,[51] it plays a vital role in guiding the interpretation of the overall treaty. This rule is guided by Article 31(1) of the VCLT, which requires that Treaties must be interpreted *"in good faith with the ordinary meaning to be given to the terms of the treaty in their context and in light of its object and purpose."* This provision is referred to by many arbitral tribunals as regards the interpretation of IIAs such as *Tokios Tokelės v. Ukraine*,[52] *Noble Ventures v. Romania*,[53] *Sempra v. Argentina*.[54]

In fact, the comprehensive agreement among 11 countries in the Trans-Pacific area – the Comprehensive and Progressive Agreement for Trans-Pacific Partnership (CPTPP) emphasises the priority to promote high levels of environmental protection and sustainable development in the Preamble of the Agreement as follows:

---

[47] In its judgment, the ICJ underscored that "the need to reconcile economic development with the protection of the environment is aptly expressed in the concept of sustainable development". I.C.J Judgment, Gabcikovo-Nagymaros Project (*Hungary v. Slovakia*), Rep. 7, Award, 25 September 1997, para. 140. This approach was later affirmed by the tribunal in *Belgium v. Netherlands (Iron Rhine Railway)* [2005] ICGJ 373, PCA 2005, Award, 24 May 2005, para. 59.

[48] See, for instance, WTO (2000); Robins and Roberts (2000); Sự (2004); Soubbotina (2004).

[49] Olson (2016); Anh (2020); Gehring and Kent (2013), p. 189.

[50] Recently concluded IIAs include sustainable development and its goals can be listed as the CPTPP, CETA, the EU Trade - Investment Agreements signed with its ASIA partners, including Vietnam and Singapore. Under ongoing BIT negotiations, such as China - EU BIT and China - US BIT, the parties have shown a consensus in promoting sustainable development and making BIT more compatible with sustainable development goals. Read more in Delegation of the European Union to the People's Republic of China (2013), pp. 09–14.

[51] Some scholars suppose that the Preamble's sole function is to set and limit the contextual space of the Agreement an therefore not to have actual binding authority. See Muchlinski (2016), p. 46; Vanduzer et al. (2013), p. 46.

[52] *Tokios Tokelės v. Ukraine* [2002] ICSID Case No. ARB/02/18, Award, 26 July 2007, para. 27.

[53] *Noble Ventures Inc. v. Romania* [2001] ICSID Case No. ARB/01/11, Award, 5 October 2005, paras. 50, 55.

[54] *Sempra Energy International v. Argentine Republic* [2002] ICSID Case No. ARB/02/16, Award, 28 September 2007, para. 381; Read more discussion on treaty interpretation in investment arbitration in Schreuer (2010).

> The Parties to this Agreement, resolving to:
>
> ...
>
> Promote high levels of environmental protection, including through effective enforcement of environmental laws, and further the aims of sustainable development, including through mutually supportive trade and environmental policies and practices;

In international investment, sustainable development often pertains to a state's rights to regulate. This right serves as a safeguard for various elements integral to sustainable development, encompassing environmental protection, health, safety, and the advancement of broader labour rights. Indeed, integrating sustainable development considerations into BITs gained prominence in the 2000s. One noteworthy instance is found in the BIT between Vietnam and Japan, enforced since December 2004. This agreement explicitly declares that the two nations will not compromise measures aimed at protecting health and the environment, underscoring their commitment to prioritising these concerns alongside investment promotion. Article 21 in this BIT further reinforces this stance.

Another noteworthy treaty is the US 2012 Model BIT. This model introduces provisions aligning investment encouragement with specific issues such as environmental protection, health, safety, and promoting broader labour rights. Notably, Article 12 on Investment and Environment within this model reflects a distinct governmental perspective pursuing non-commercial objectives.

1. The Parties recognise that their respective environmental laws and policies, and multilateral environmental agreements to which they are both party, play an important role in protecting the environment.
2. The Parties recognise that it is inappropriate to encourage investment by weakening or reducing the protection afforded in domestic environmental laws. Accordingly, each Party shall ensure that it does not waive or otherwise derogate from or offer to waive or otherwise derogate from its environmental laws in a manner that weakens or reduces the protections afforded in those laws, or fail to effectively enforce those laws through a sustained or recurring course of action or inaction, as an encouragement for the establishment, acquisition, expansion, or retention of an investment in its territory.
3. The Parties recognise that each Party retains the right to exercise discretion with respect to regulatory, compliance, investigatory, and prosecutorial matters, and to make decisions regarding the allocation of resources to enforcement with respect to other environmental matters determined to have higher priorities...

Moreover, this Article emphasises that *"Nothing in this Treaty shall be construed to prevent a Party from adopting, maintaining, or enforcing any measure otherwise consistent with this Treaty that it considers appropriate to ensure that investment activity in its territory is undertaken in a manner sensitive to environmental concerns."* (Article 12.5 US 2012 Model BIT). Although it is not genuinely considered as an exception as the provision is only applied to measure that is "otherwise consistent with" the treaty, this provision implies that measures of a party to *"ensure that investment activity in its territory is undertaken in a manner sensitive to environmental concerns" should not be found to be inconsistent with the treaty."*[55]

[55] VanDuzer (2016), p. 152.

However, because of its limited impact, this provision is not widely used except in recent United States' FTAs.[56]

The overarching observation from the practice above is the increasing prominence of concerns related to sustainable development and environmental protection in contemporary free trade and investment agreements. However, the critical number of contributions on the topic and the evolving definition of sustainable development make it difficult to determine the precise role played by the notion within the IIL framework.[57]

However, the concept of sustainable development is perceived as versatile, allowing it to be invoked to support the host state's environmental regulations while facilitating the influx of FDI capital.[58] Conversely, in areas such as renewable energy and resource utilisation, sustainable development can be wielded to argue for interpretations favouring investors, aligning with the overarching objective of IIAs to safeguard foreign investors and their investments.[59] Consequently, this concept can simultaneously bolster the positions of both the host state and the investor.

While the tangible impacts of provisions addressing these goals may currently be somewhat limited, the evolution within IIAs is anticipated to underscore the delicate balance between investors' economic interests and the imperative to safeguard society's non-economic benefits. This evolution is poised to reshape the rights and obligations of nations and investors in relevant cases.

2.2.2 *Environmental Protection in International Investment Law*

- **Since When and How?**

The interaction between the environment and other areas is very diverse. Indeed, environmental components can be discussed in the context of IIL, international human rights law, or international humanitarian law.[60] As mentioned by the OECD Report on International Investment conducted in 2011, starting from the mid-1990s, the number of newly concluded IIAs that include environmental concerns began to increase moderately.[61] The North American FTA (NAFTA), which came into force on January 1, 1994, is considered one of the first treaties that contain the specific language connecting IIL and international environmental law by mentioning relevant environmental treaties which would prevail over particular rules of the NAFTA

[56] The United States - Korea FTA (2012), Article 11.10, The United States - Australia FTA (2005), Article 11.11.

[57] Martini (2017), p. 562.

[58] Ibid.; see also Newcombe and Paradell (2009), p. 114.

[59] Martini (2017), p. 562.

[60] Viñuales (2012), p. 85.

[61] Gordon and Pohl (2011), p. 8.

in case of conflict (Article 104),[62] for example the Convention on International Trade in Endangered Species, the Montreal Protocol on Substances that Deplete the Ozone Layer, the Basel Convention on the Control of Transboundary Movements of Hazardous Wastes and Their Disposal,... Notably, NAFTA's Preamble prioritised environmental concerns by emphasising the need to act "*in a manner consistent with environmental protection and conservation*."

Along with the growing perception of the international community on sustainable development, many countries are more aware of environmental and social harms that can occur as a "consequence of unrestrained growth."[63] Environmental protection, therefore, has become more common in trade and investment agreements concluded worldwide. Similar wordings, though less precise than NAFTA Article 104, can be found in Article 72(c) of the CARIFORUM - European Union Economic Partnership Agreement 2008.[64] Model BITs prepared by developed countries,[65] concluded BITs and FTAs[66] have also showed this consideration.

- **Challenges in Enforcing the State's Environmental Protection Rights within the ISDS Context**

The case law suggests that investment disputes related to environmental regulatory measures arose from the 1990s onwards, but only since the 2000s has the number rapidly increased. According to a statistic conducted by Viñuales in his study, based on available data, one case was decided before 1990. Three others were decided during the 1990s, while twenty-four disputes were reported from 2000 to December 2011.[67] The number of investment claims kept growing in the 2010s with notable cases in connection with various environmental and sustainable development issues.[68]

In investment disputes, environmental considerations can appear in different ways, whether as (i) jurisdictional matters, (ii) applicable law, (iii) procedural matters, or (iv) damage evaluation.[69]

---

[62] Viñuales (2012), p. 137.

[63] Collins (2012), p. 327.

[64] Economic Partnership Agreement between the Cariforum States and the European Community and its Member States (2008), OJ 2008 L 289/I/3.

[65] For instance, the United States of America (2004 Model BIT of the USA Preamble, Articles 8, 12 and 32, and Annex B (expropriation)); Canada (Canada's 2004 Model BIT Articles 10 and 11); Belgium -Luxembourg (Belgium - Luxembourg's 2019 Model BIT Preamble, Article 5.3); Finland (Finland's 2004 Model BIT Article 5); the Netherlands (the Netherlands' 2004 Model BIT Preamble), and Sweden (Sweden's 2003 Model BIT Preamble).

[66] For instance, FTAs concluded by the United States and Australia, Chile, Morocco, Oman, Peru or Singapore (Article 18.8).

[67] Viñuales (2012), pp. 17–22.

[68] Osterwalder et al. (2018).

[69] The following summary is mainly based on the study of Viñuales and a survey conducted by the OECD in 2008 on 269 Investment and Free Trade Agreements. See Viñuales (2012) and Gordon (2008).

(i) Regarding jurisdiction, it can begin with a host state's violation of environmental norms, causing a breach of investment protection standards such as FET, full protection and security, and/or expropriation clauses.[70] Environmental claims can also appear in an international investment dispute as independent heads of claim when the investor claims that the host state's measures breach an environmental norm arising from a different instrument than the one covered by the arbitration clause.[71] Environmental claims can also appear as counterclaims of the host state, though the chance to bring such counterclaim depends on evaluation in both jurisdiction and applicable law.[72] Besides, as pointed out by Viñuales, investment tribunals may incorporate environmental considerations when determining the existence of a protected investment, either in connection with the definition of the rights or entitlements that can amount to a protected investment or, conversely, concerning the limits of protection of certain investments contrary to environmental law.[73]
(ii) Although human rights or environmental claims have often been deemed outside the scope of a tribunal's jurisdiction, human rights and environmental rules may still be relevant when considering an investment claim.[74] Regarding applicable law, environmental considerations can be included in the investment contract, domestic regulations, or applicable investment treaties.[75] These three sources constitute the legal framework potentially applicable to an investment.
(iii) In investment proceedings, environmental considerations can directly affect procedural issues via the role of non-disputing parties and additional challenges relating to evidentiary procedures.[76]
(iv) Last but not least, environmental considerations may affect the duty to compensate the host state. The investment dispute settlement practice shows a different approach regarding this issue. A few tribunals suppose that environmental justifications do not help the host states escape from that requirement.[77] In contrast, others hold that some deprivations of property based on environmen-

[70] *Peter A. Allard v. The Government of Barbados* [2010] PCA Case No. 2012-06, Award, 27 June 2016.

[71] *Biloune and Marine Drive Complex Ltd v. Ghana Investments Centre and the Government of Ghana* [1988] UNCITRAL, 95 ILR 183, Award, 27 October 1989. See futher in Viñuales (2012), pp. 90–91.

[72] Viñuales (2012), pp. 92–94; Bjorklund (2013), pp. 461, 466.

[73] Viñuales (2012), pp. 95–100.

[74] *Biloune and Marine Drive Complex Ltd v. Ghana Investments Centre and the Government of Ghana* [1988] UNCITRAL, 95 ILR 183, Award, 27 October 1989, paras. 202–203. See also Viñuales (2012), p. 100.

[75] Viñuales (2012), p. 100.

[76] Ibid., p. 113.

[77] *Compañia del Desarrollo de Santa Elena S.A. (CDSE) v. Republic of Costa Rica* [2000] ICSID Case No. ARB/96/1, Award, 17 February 2000; *Técnicas Medioambientales Tecmed, S.A. v. The United Mexican States* [2003] ICSID Case No. ARB(AF)/00/2, Award, 29 May 2003.

tal considerations[78] or a non-discriminatory ban on the sale and use of a substance harmful to water resources, enacted according to due process, are non-compensable.[79] A few tribunals recognised the right to establish high levels of environmental protection and emphasised the mutually supportive relationship between environmental protection and economic development.[80] A number of tribunals showed middle-ground positions.[81]

In general, environmental problems are usually dealt with under the IIL regime from an indirect point of view.[82] The causation lies at the root of the IIAs' nature: to protect the investors and the investments. Therefore, the regime rules do not provide for substantive obligations to protect non-economic interests. Meanwhile, the main principles of international investment law conceal potential conflicts with host states' measures.[83] Many host states' measures aimed at preserving the environment have been challenged as a violation of basic investment protection obligations such as expropriation[84] and FET standards with or without connection with minimum standards of treatment.[85] Therefore, it is no surprise that investment tribunals are

---

[78] *Saluka Investments B.V. v. The Czech Republic* [2001] PCA Case No. 2001-04, Award, 17 March 2006.

[79] *Methanex Corp. v. United States of America* [1999] UNCITRAL, 44 ILM 1345, Award, 3 August 2005. In this Award, Part IV, Chapter D, para. 7 stated: "*as a matter of general international law, a non-discriminatory regulation for a public purpose, which is enacted in accordance with due process and which affects, inter alios, a foreign investor or investment is not deemed expropriatory and compensable unless specific commitments had been given by the regulating government to the then putative foreign investor contemplating investment that the government would refrain from such regulation.*"

[80] However, the examination showed that the Canadian measure was discriminatory in intent and that there was no legitimate environmental reason for the export ban. See *S.D. Myers, Inc. v. Government of Canada* (*S.D. Myers v. Canada*) [1998] UNCITRAL, NAFTA, Award, 13 November 2000, paras. 195, 220.

[81] *Methanex Corp. v. United States of America* [1999] UNCITRAL, 44 ILM 1345, Award, 3 August 2005. *MTD Equity Sdn. Bhd. And MTD Chile S.A. v. Chile* [2001] ICSID Case No. ARB/01/7, Award, 25 May 2004. See further Viñuales (2012), p. 123.

[82] Benedetto (2013), p. 13.

[83] Ibid., p. 14.

[84] *S.D. Myers v. Canada* [1998] UNCITRAL, NAFTA, Award, 13 November 2000. *Abengoa, S.A. y COFIDES, S.A. v. United Mexican States* [2009] ICSID Case No. ARB(AF)/09/2, Award, 18 April 2013; *David Aven and others v. Costa Rica* [2014] ICSID Case No. UNCT/15/3, Award, 18 September 2018; *Pac Rim Cayman LLC v. Republic of El Salvador* [2009] ICSID Case No. ARB/09/12, Award, 14 October 2016; *Compañia del Desarrollo de Santa Elena S.A. (CDSE) v. Republic of Costa Rica* [2000] ICSID Case No. ARB/96/1, Award, 17 February 2000; *Copper Mesa Mining Corporation v. Republic of Ecuador* [2011] PCA No. 2012-2, Award, 25 August 2000; *Cosigo Resources, Ltd., Cosigo Resources Sucursal Colombia, Tobie Mining and Energy, Inc. v. Republic of Colombia* [2016] UNCITRAL (pending).

[85] *Vattenfall AB, Vattenfall Europe AG, Vattenfall Europe Generation AG v. Federal Republic of Germany* [2009] ICSID Case No. ARB/09/6, Award, 11 March 2011; *Occidental Petroleum Corporation and Occidental Exploration and Production Company v. Republic of Ecuador* [2006] ICSID Case No. ARB/06/11, Award, 05 October 2012; *The Renco Group, Inc. v. Republic of Peru* [2016] ICSID Case No. UNCT/13/1, awarded 09 November 2016; *Compañia del Desarrollo de*

reluctant to openly discuss potential conflicts between investment protection and public policy objectives, including environmental protection.[86]

2.3 The Autonomy of International Investment Law and the Application of Non-investment Obligations

2.3.1 International Investment Law as a Self-Contained Regime

In international law, IIL possesses all the characteristics to be considered a fragmented and self-contained system,[87] even though scholars have not directly labelled it as such. A self-contained regime is a system that revolves around its normative autonomy, distinct from the broader body of international law, due to the application of the lex specialis maxim to a specific set of rules and principles.[88] In the case of IIL, this fragmentation arises primarily from a lack of coordination with other fields of international law that address interests beyond those of investors.[89]

Regarding fragmentation, IIL, like other specialised systems within international law, is described as having its own principles and institutions.[90] This characteristic often results in an insularity from legislative and institutional activities in adjacent fields and from the general principles and practices of international law.[91] Fragmentation can lead to conflicting and incompatible rules, principles, rule systems, and institutional practices.[92] Given this context, examining IIL as a self-contained regime is essential, as self-contained regimes are closely linked to the broader theme of the fragmentation of international law.[93]

Santa Elena S.A. (CDSE) v. Republic of Costa Rica [2000] ICSID Case No. ARB/96/1, Award, 17 February 2000; *Metalclad Corporation v. The United Mexican States* [1997] ICSID Case No. ARB(AF)/97/1, Award, 25 August 2000; *Técnicas Medioambientales Tecmed, S.A. v. The United Mexican States* [2003] ICSID Case No. ARB(AF)/00/2, Award, 29 May 2003; *Clayton and Bilcon of Delaware Inc. v. Government of Canada* [2008] PCA Case No. 2009-04; *Infinito Gold v. Costa Rica* [2014] ICSID Case No. ARB/14/5 (pending).

[86] Viñuales (2012), p. 155.

[87] The fragmentation of international law has been discussed in detail a Report conducted by the International Law Commission (United Nations) in 2006. This report later has been referred to by many scholars including Viñuales (2012); Benedetto (2013). See ILC Report (2006).

[88] ILC Report (2006), pp. 65–102; see also Benedetto (2013), p. 24.

[89] Hindelang and Krajewski (2016), pp. 10–11.

[90] ILC Report (2006), para. 8.

[91] Ibid.

[92] See further discussion on the positive and negative sides of the fragmentation of international law in the ILC Report (2006), para. 14.

[93] Benedetto (2013), p. 24.

The International Law Commission Report on the Fragmentation of International Law (ILC Report) defines a self-contained regime as "a subcategory in a "strong form" of lex specialis within the law of state responsibility, in which it has set up its own "internal system."[94] The ILC Report references the 1925 advisory opinion of the Permanent Court of International Justice, which stated that it was unnecessary to refer to external sources to interpret certain expressions in a treaty: "*Everything, therefore, seems to indicate that, regarding this point, the Convention is self-contained and that the natural meaning of the words should be employed.*"[95] This notion underscores the importance of studying IIL as a self-contained regime within the broader discussion of the fragmentation of international law.

Following the evaluation, the ILC Report on Fragmentation of International Law comes to the conclusion that "self-contained regime" can be distinguished between two senses: in a narrow sense, it is used to denote a unique set of secondary rules under the law of state responsibility that claims primary to the general rules while in a broader sense, it is used to refer to interrelated systems or subsystem of rules that cover some particular problem differently from the way it would be covered under general law.[96] In this second sense, the characteristic of self-contained fuses with international law's contractual bias: in case the matter is included in a treaty, there will normally be no reason to recourse to other sources.[97]

This fragmented and self-contained characteristic of the IIL system supports the practice that external values, such as the environment, have little chance of being taken into account in the context of IIL. This practice has been examined in Benedetto's study, in which he comments that IIL provides little, if any, formal room for the consideration of other value systems while, at the same time, it increasingly interferes with alternative value systems.[98] More importantly, the self-contained logic is not only applied to IIL but has also been preferred at investment tribunals (*Metalclad v. Mexico*), especially in their application of the international rules on foreign investments to the integration of environmental concerns.[99] According to Benedetto, the patchwork nature of IIL makes it difficult to claim this field of international law to be understood as an autonomous legal system. However, it is also undeniable that the investment arbitral tribunals are influenced by a *self-contained approach* when examining cases involving environmental concerns.[100]

In practice, investment tribunals have generally lacked the intention to apply non-investment obligations and treaties, often citing a lack of jurisdiction over such claims (particularly in human rights cases) or ruling that a state's international obligations do not affect the nature of the challenged measure and, therefore, do not

[94] ILC Report (2006), para. 124.

[95] Permanent Court of International Justice (1925), p. 20. ILC Report (2006), para. 127.

[96] Ibid., para. 128.

[97] Ibid.

[98] Benedetto (2013), p. 16, Chapter 2.1 and Chapter 3.3.

[99] Ibid., see also Fauchald (2008).

[100] Benedetto (2013), pp. 31, 35.

influence the compensation to be paid in cases of expropriation. Although investment tribunals usually rely on classical canons of interpretation, this does not "inevitably affirm a self-contained vision of which virtually excludes any consideration of environment matters".[101] In other words, those tribunals have integrated external issues into investment rules by constructing internal arguments.

This approach is evident in dispute resolution practices where arbitral tribunals have developed open-ended interpretations of traditional investment concepts and standards. Specifically, arbitral tribunals rarely directly analyse environmental requirements in connection with investment standards, as there is no explicit basis for this relationship under IIAs. In cases of expropriation claims or claims of FET violations related to host state measures aimed at protecting the environment, tribunals typically assess whether the internal requirements related to those standards have been met. Suppose the host state is proven to have strictly followed these requirements. In that case, the tribunal can conclude that there is no violation of a specific IIA standard without considering the relevance to environmental protection. This practice aligns with the aforementioned characteristics and the conditions of IIAs. However, it also underscores the tenuous legal relationship between environmental and investment law, indicating a need for greater integration of environmental considerations into investment dispute resolutions.

In general, it has been observed that environmental protection is taken into account within the context of IIL through the interpretative activities of tribunals. Although clear expressions of a self-contained vision of IIL and arbitration are rare, and few legal authors explicitly apply self-contained logic to conceptualise IIL, arbitral tribunals seem influenced by this approach in developing their arguments.[102] Litigation practice shows that sustainable development and environmental protection are gradually being acknowledged by tribunals, although the common practice remains to interpret these issues within a self-contained logic, focusing on the meaning and application of investment rules themselves. Recently, there has been a trend towards including legal exceptions in model BITs, despite this not being widespread due to the fragmentation of IIL.[103] This development concerning legal exceptions will be analysed in the subsequent section of this book.

2.3.2 *Suggestions from the WTO's Experience*

The "humble" position of sustainable development and environmental protection within the IIL system, coupled with the growing awareness of these values' importance, clearly necessitates a new approach. This new approach can be inspired by the experience of a crucial institution in world trade, the WTO, in dealing with

---

101 Ibid., p. 84.

102 Ibid., pp. 28, 30, 31.

103 Ibid., p. 133.

non-trade issues. Prof. Jackson noted that WTO law was "the central illustration of legal jurisprudential developments influenced by phenomena of our contemporary world."[104] He emphasised that non-trade policies should not be disregarded in the WTO's trade policies.[105] Supporting this view, Laurence Boisson de Chazournes highlights that "complementarity is crucial to respond adequately to the challenges of a globalised and interdependent world." This complementarity can be understood in two ways: first, by externalising regulations on issues connected to trade previously considered outside the WTO's scope; second, by internalising regulatory approaches from other fora within the WTO.[106] This foundation has, in fact, been laid by WTO case law.[107]

This approach seems consistent with developments in the context of IIL. Similar to the WTO and its dispute settlement practices, there is a need to address IIL within the broader framework of the international legal system.[108] WTO case law demonstrates that trade-restrictive measures pursuing public policy objectives were initially perceived as barriers to trade but have since been integrated into the WTO trade agenda.[109] Likewise, state measures to pursue public purposes in international investment have faced compensation claims in investment arbitrations.[110] It is evident that the requirements imposed on the WTO legal system similarly apply to the IIL system. Sustainable development and environmental concerns should be viewed not as external but as integral to the IIA regime.

---

[104] Jackson (2006), p. 19. See Chazournes (2016), p. 379.

[105] Jackson (2006), p. 189. Environmental protection has, in fact, been a disjointed part in the WTO regime. The preamble of the Marrakesh Agreement establishing the WTO recognises that parties to the Agreement cooperate in the field of trade and economic endeavour with a view to "raising standards of living, ensuring full employment …while allowing for the optimal use of the world's resources in accordance with the objective of sustainable development, seeking both to protect and preserve the environment…". The only substantive regulation allow WTO member states to violate a specific obligation when follow legitimate objectives under GATT is Article XX on General Exceptions. However, reconciling free trade with environmental concerns has never been easy. Following disputes show this practice: *US - Gasoline* (WT/DS2/R/DSR, 1996; WT/DS2/AB/R/DSR, 1996), *US - Shrimp/Turtle* (WT/DS58/AB/R/DSR/1998), *Brazil - Measures Affecting Imports of Retreaded Tyres (Brazil - Retreaded Tyres)* (WT/DS332/AB/R, 2007), or *US - Tuna/Dolphin II* (WT/DS381/AB/R/DSR, 2012).

[106] Chazournes (2016), p. 379.

[107] WTO (1998) *The US – Import Prohibition of Certain Shrimp and Shrimp Products*, WT/DS58/AB/R, adopted on 6, November 1998. Chazournes (2016).

[108] Chazournes (2016), p. 380.

[109] Read more about the shift from the animosity towards so-called NTBs under GATT negotiation rounds to a more positive approach by referring to NTMs in the WTO period in Chazournes (2016).

[110] See, for instance, *S.D. Myers, Inc. v. Government of Canada* [1998] UNCITRAL, NAFTA, Award, 13 November 2000. *Abengoa, S.A. y COFIDES, S.A. v. United Mexican States* [2009] ICSID Case No. ARB(AF)/09/2, Award, 18 April 2013. *Copper Mesa Mining Corporation v. Republic of Ecuador* [2011] PCA No. 2012-2, Award, 25 August 2000. *Metalclad Corporation v. The United Mexican States* [1997] ICSID Case No. ARB(AF)/97/1, Award, 25 August 2000. *Clayton and Bilcon of Delaware Inc. v. Government of Canada* [2008] PCA Case No. 2009-04.

In the context of IIL, "externalisation" can be represented by applying a systemic approach to interpreting IIL. At the same time, "internalisation" involves the process of redrafting IIAs, which is becoming increasingly common in current IIA negotiations. These two strategies for redirecting IIAs towards a more environmentally sensitive system will be discussed in the following sections.

2.3.3 Promoting a Systemic Interpretation of International Investment Law

The systemic approach has usually been taken by the investment tribunal when dealing with the interactions and conflicts between the interests protected by IIAs and sustainable development requirements. This practice was based on Article 31.3(c) of the VCLT, which is prepared to deal with the plurality of rules and principles in the context of treaty interpretation.[111] Scholars consider Article 31.3(c) as a critical tenet in reducing the significance of lex specialis when autonomous regimes are involved in disputes.[112]

As mentioned before, conflict has frequently arisen between environmental issues and investment protection obligations in the context of ISDS since its appearance. The approach led by Article 31.3(c) of the VCLT has, therefore, received growing consideration in the last 15 years[113] in studies and different international legal regimes such as the WTO, the European Court of Human Rights or the International Court of Justice.[114] Article 31.3(c) is included within Part III Section 3 of the VCLT, which provides guidance for treaty interpretation. It provides that:

> There shall be taken into account, together with the context:
> … (c) any relevant rules of international law applicable in the relations between the parties.

In this case, the wording of Article 31.3(c) is not limited to general international law. Instead, it extends to "any relevant rules of international law applicable in the relations between the parties." "Any relevant rules" include both treaty rules and general international law.[115] While reference to general rules of international law in interpreting a treaty is a regular activity of the interpretation process, the principle of systemic integration goes a bit further than the meaning of general international law in the operation of particular treaties.[116] This principle, indeed, requires to

---

[111] ILC Report (2006), para. 208.

[112] Benedetto (2013), p. 135.

[113] Ibid., p. 134.

[114] For a study of case law relating to those forums, see ILC Report (2006), Chapter V(C).

[115] Ibid., paras. 470–472.

[116] Ibid., para. 415.

consider the normative environment "more widely."[117] At this point, this approach is relevant to the relationship between IIL and international environmental law.

In his study, Benedetto commented that for an autonomy treaty regime such as IIL, a systemic interpretation becomes more crucial as it may directly allow for the consideration of external values.[118] However, this method of interpretation is not commonly applied by investment tribunals to integrate external values into investment regimes.[119] In *Santa Elena v. Costarica,*[120] the first investment dispute dealing with environmental concerns, the tribunal refused to consider Costarica's obligations in other international environmental agreements.[121] This strict approach regarding IIL as a closed legal sub-system as well as several subsequent rulings giving due attention to environmental protection in this case have later been referred to by other tribunals.[122]

However, other arbitral tribunals tend to rely on the systemic approach in examining applicable law and interpretation issues, such as *SPP v. Egypt,*[123] and *Chemtura v. Canada.*[124] The *SPP v. Egypt* dispute has not directly dealt with environmental concerns but rather the protection of archaeological interests. In this case, the respondent has invoked its obligation to protect the site under the UNESCO Convention on World Cultural and Natural Heritage (the UNESCO Convention). The Tribunal has recognised the UNESCO Convention as a part of the applicable law in the case; therefore, it has to examine whether the international obligation to protect the pyramid site could "justify the measure taken by the respondence" and "exclude the Claimants' right to compensation."[125] The Tribunal later held that because the UNESCO Convention had not been effected for Egypt at the time of expropriation, it was not bound by the obligation to protect the site. Therefore, the Convention by itself "does not justify the measures taken by the Respondent to cancel the project, nor does it exclude the Claimants' right to compensation."[126] In case Egypt was obligated to protect the site, the continuation of the Claimant's activities interfering with antiquities in the area could be considered unlawful from

---

[117] Ibid., para. 416. In specific, it is acceptable to interpret a treaty by reference to another treaty. As hold by the Arbitral Tribunal in Franco-Belgian case from 1937. See UNRIAA Award (1937), p. 1713.

[118] Benedetto (2013), p. 136.

[119] Ibid., p. 137.

[120] *Compañia del Desarrollo de Santa Elena S.A. (CDSE) v. Republic of Costa Rica* [2000] ICSID Case No. ARB/96/1, Award, 17 February 2000.

[121] Benedetto (2013), p. 139.

[122] *Marion Unglaube and Reinhard Unglaube v. Republic of Costa Rica* [2009] ICSID Case No. ARB/08/1 and ARB/09/20, Award, 16 May 2012, paras. 214–18.

[123] *Southern Pacific Properties (Middle East) Limited v. Arab Republic of Egypt (SPP v. Egypt)* [1984] ICSID Case No. ARB/84/3, Award, 20 May 1992.

[124] *Chemtura Corporation (formerly Crompton Corporation) v. Government of Canada* [2002] PCA Case No. 2008-01, Award, 2 August 2010.

[125] *SPP v. Egypt* [1984] ICSID Case No. ARB/84/3, Award, 20 May 1992, para. 78.

[126] Ibid, para. 154.

the international point of view".[127] Although it has not been clearly stated, one can understand from this concern that if there is such an obligation to protect the site, Egypt would not pay compensation for its expropriation measure. This award and the applied approach have been supported by scholars as it has allowed for the examination of non-commercial issues into the investment legal dimension without jeopardising investor rights.[128]

In *Chemtura v. Canada*, the Tribunal relied on international conventions and focused on the public policy goals of the applied measures. The Tribunal has firstly confirmed that the States' rights to adopt and apply measures in order to protect the people's health and the environment are undeniable. It has examined whether the Canadian messures has been conducted in order to comply with international commitments of Canada (Aarhus Protocol to the LRTAP Convention)[129] which followed a systemic prespective. The Tribunal has come to a decision which support Canada's measures with the support of international conventions which it deemed sufficient to settle the point irrespective of the state of science.

In addition to the two significant cases mentioned above that apply systemic interpretation to investment standards to integrate non-investment concerns, other tribunals have also considered external factors related to environmental and health goals. These are often referenced through relevant environmental conventions, as seen in cases such as *Maffezini v. Spain*,[130] or *S.D. Myers v. Canada*.[131] In *Maffezini v. Spain*, the Tribunal had to assess whether a Spanish Environmental Impact Assessment (EIA) procedure caused damages to the claimant. The Tribunal supported the view that the EIA procedure was important "not only under Spanish and EEC law but also increasingly so under international law."[132] In *S.D. Myers. v. Canada*, the Tribunal referred to the Basel Convention and its policy objectives to determine that Canada's measures had legitimate goals.[133]

Scholars support systemic interpretation and Article 31.3(c) of the VCLT as they can effectively reconcile environmental values within the framework of international investment regimes[134] by supporting the consideration of environmental treaties in connection with IIA obligations in investment arbitrations. However, scholars also point out obstacles in applying this approach at investment tribunals:

---

[127] Ibid.

[128] Benedetto (2013), p. 143.

[129] *Chemtura Corporation (formerly Crompton Corporation) v. Government of Canada* [2002] PCA Case No. 2008-01, Award, 2 August 20100, para. 137.

[130] *Emilio Agustin Maffezini v. Spain* [2000] ICSID Case No. ARB/97/7, Award, 13 November 2000.

[131] *S.D. Myers, Inc. v. Government of Canada* [1998] UNCITRAL, NAFTA, Award, 13 November 2000, paras. 195, 220.

[132] *Maffezini v. Spain* [2000] ICSID Case No. ARB/97/7, Award, 13 November 2000, para. 67.

[133] *S.D. Myers v. Canada* [1998] UNCITRAL, NAFTA, Award, 13 November 2000, para 255. *Joseph Charles Lemire v. Ukraine* [2006] ICSID Case No. ARB/06/18, Award, 28 March 2011 has also been applied.

[134] Benedetto (2013), p. 152. See also Berner (2016).

(i) Arbitrators and scholars may have paid little attention to systemic interpretation and Article 31.3(c) of the VCLT. In some cases, such as *Marion Unglaube v. Costa Rica,*[135] *Chemtura v. Canada,*[136] and *Methanex v. USA,*[137] tribunals have avoided addressing the host states' arguments related to public purposes, which could have been supported by applying the VCLT rules.[138]

(ii) Many other tribunals have ignored the contextual arguments invoked by the host state, such as in *Metalclad v. Mexico,*[139] *Grand River Enterprises Six Nations Ltd v. USA,*[140] and *Compañía del Desarrollo de Santa Elena v. Costa Rica.*[141] Even when Article 31.3(c) is applied, it is often done cautiously.

(iii) Another difficulty lies in Article 31.3(c) itself, as "*any relevant rules of international law applicable*" must meet the requirement of being "*applicable in the relations between the parties*." Environmental treaties, typically concluded by states, are therefore not directly applicable to investors.[142]

These limitations suggest a need to directly integrate environmental and other non-investment values into IIL. The following section describes typical sustainable development and environmental protection provisions in IIAs.

2.3.4 Regulatory Authority and Regulatory Chill

2.3.4.1 Regulatory Authority

The concepts of regulatory authority, regulatory power, and the right to regulate have been increasingly discussed in the context of international investment law. Many contemporary IIAs reference this right, prompting scholars to seek a clearer understanding of what "the right to regulate" entails.[143] The right to regulate is

[135] *Marion Unglaube and Reinhard Unglaube v. Republic of Costa Rica* [2009] ICSID Case No. ARB/08/1 and ARB/09/20, Award, 16 May 2012.

[136] *Chemtura Corporation (formerly Crompton Corporation) v. Government of Canada* [2002] PCA Case No. 2008-01, Award, 2 August 2010.

[137] *Methanex Corp. v. United States of America* [1999] UNCITRAL, 44 ILM 1345, Award, 3 August 2005.

[138] See further discussion in Berner (2016), pp. 193–194.

[139] *Metalclad Corporation v. The United Mexican States* [1997] ICSID Case No. ARB(AF)/97/1, Award, 25 August 2000.

[140] *Grand River Enterprises Six Nations, Ltd., et al. v. United States of America* [2004] UNCITRAL, Award, 12 January 2011.

[141] *Compañia del Desarrollo de Santa Elena S.A. (CDSE) v. Republic of Costa Rica* [2000] ICSID Case No. ARB/96/1, Award, 17 February 2000.

[142] Benedetto (2013), pp. 153–154.

[143] See, for instance, Titi (2014); Giannakopoulos (2017), pp. 148–184; Nadakavukaren and Polanco Lazo (2023).

grounded in the international legal principle of state sovereignty,[144] which is a fundamental concept in international law[145] encompassing various elements.[146] State sovereignty includes both domestic and foreign aspects.[147] Specifically, the right to regulate reflects a state's sovereignty within its territory, granting it the authority to adopt legal regulations for the establishment of public order. Therefore, regulatory authority is often linked to a state's power to legislate and implement administrative actions in various areas of public interest. This right also plays a vital role in safeguarding the common interests of citizens, such as ensuring public safety and health.[148] Moreover, within the framework of international human rights law, some scholars argue that the adoption of legislation may not only be desirable but may also be required by international law in certain circumstances.[149]

2.3.4.2 Regulatory Chill

Investment treaty provisions may impede host states from fully exercising their regulatory authority, discouraging them from enacting or maintaining measures intended to safeguard human rights and environmental interests.[150] Within the framework of IIL, this concept is reflected in legal doctrines such as indirect expropriation, fair and equitable treatment, and national treatment.[151] The potential liability resulting from judicial decisions, legislative changes, and regulatory actions that adversely impact the economic interests of foreign investors may lead to a "regulatory chill."[152]

As pointed out by Bonnitcha, identifying the chilling effect of investment treaties is challenging because it requires "counterfactual evidence about the regulations that would have existed in the absence of the purported chilling."[153] Additionally, these effects may partly be attributed to other factors, such as the fear of losing future investments. In some cases, the reference to IIA obligations is merely a public excuse.[154] It has also been noted that very few empirical studies have examined the extent to which investment standards may cause regulatory chill.[155]

---

144 Levashova (2019), pp. 28–29.

145 Besson (2011).

146 Jackson (2008). p. 4.

147 Brownlie (2008); Crawford (2012).

148 Levashova (2019), p. 29.

149 Schmid (2015), pp. 573, 574.

150 Bonnitcha (2014), p. 114.

151 Trujillo (2018), p. 2739.

152 Johnson et al. (2015), p. 5.

153 Bonnitcha (2014), p. 115.

154 Tienhaara (2009), p. 263; Bonnitcha (2014), Ibid.

155 Bonnitcha (2014), p. 116.

Bonnitcha's research highlights two starting points in the existing discussion of the chilling effect.[156] The first is doctrinal inquiry, which assumes that investment provisions may (or may not) have significant chilling effects on host states' decisions. Another criticism is based on the argument that the uncertainty in the interpretation of IIA provisions, or the cost of potential investment litigation, tends to discourage decision-makers from adopting measures that would have little or no chance of constituting a violation of IIAs.

Existing discussions indicate two distinct types of regulatory chill stemming from the standards within IIAs:[157]

- Chilling of measures that "clearly give rise to liability": This type typically occurs under two specific conditions: first, when decision-makers are acutely aware of the particular IIA commitments that may pertain to the proposed measures. Second, when they are cognizant that the host state is likely to be obligated to provide compensation.
- Chilling of measures that "may not give rise to liability": For this type, the additional empirical condition that must be met is the uncertainty surrounding whether the intended measure or a series of measures can be deemed a violation of the IIA's provisions.

These observations suggest that regulatory chill is influenced by clear liability risks and the uncertainty of potential violations, leading to a reluctance to adopt necessary regulations.

The chilling effect can manifest at any stage of decision-making within host states, affecting the adoption, maintenance, and enforcement of individual measures or a series of measures. This effect can arise from two sources: an investor's warning of a potential treaty violation, referred to as "threat chill,"[158] or decision-makers' awareness of investment treaty obligations, known as "internalisation chill."[159] Scholars have also pointed out that while pertinent evidence can be found in the factual records of arbitration proceedings concerning "threat chill", relatively few previous studies have delved into the phenomenon of "internalisation" chill.[160]

Considerable discussion has emerged around this phenomenon, particularly in light of practical cases. The first observation suggests differing levels of awareness between national and subnational governments. Decision-makers at subnational levels with significant autonomy from the national government are often less aware of IIA regulations and less sensitive to the risk of IIA liability than national governments.[161]

[156] Ibid., pp. 116–117.

[157] Ibid.

[158] Tienhaara (2009), p. 262.

[159] Bonnitcha (2014), p. 118.

[160] Ibid., p. 119.

[161] Ibid., p. 119. The case of *Abitibi-Bowater v Canada* illustrates this hypothesis. See *Anbitibi Bowater Inc., v. Government of Canada* [2009] ICSID Case No. UNCT/10/1, Award, 15 December 2010.

The second observation is that decision-makers in developing countries are likely more affected by the threat of investment treaty provisions than those in developed countries. This could be due to limited state budgets for litigation or restricted access to high-quality legal expertise.[162] Indeed, there have been instances where developing country governments reversed their decisions after investors threatened to submit claims to investment arbitrators over issues like mining permits.[163] In contrast, governments in developed countries upheld their decisions in similar situations.[164] However, it is recognised that these limited practices are insufficient for a generalisation that developing countries are more concerned about litigation under IIAs than developed countries. The final decisions of governments often result from complex considerations that are not easily clarified for arbitrators and scholars. Nonetheless, this practice provides evidence of the potential threat of regulatory chill, particularly for governments in developing countries.

Bonnitcha's empirical test of regulatory chill, examining cases such as *Metalclad v. Mexico*, *Tecmed v. Mexico,* and *Santa Elena v. Costa Rica*, supports the assumption that states are less likely to maintain measures that might lead to liability.[165] Furthermore, investors' objections or threats of claims tend to have a more substantial chilling effect than when decision-makers consider the risks themselves.

However, exploring the nexus between uncertainty regarding potential liability and the chilling effect yields limited empirical evidence. Bonnitcha, in examining three cases related to tobacco plain packaging, initially arising in Australia and subsequently considered by the governments of New Zealand and the United Kingdom, demonstrates the intricate impact of investment treaty protection on domestic decision-making processes.[166] Despite this prevailing uncertainty, Bonnitcha contends that IIAs offering greater clarity and protection in applying policy measures are likely to mitigate the chilling effect.[167] This conclusion partly supports the ongoing trend in IIA negotiations, which seeks to establish more defined IIA standards and more explicit provisions concerning the legitimacy of the policy rights of host states.

Bonnitcha's analysis of previous cases involving environmental measures challenged by investors offers several noteworthy conclusions.[168] Firstly, in most cases, the central focus has been on whether the contested measure constituted "an unjustified interference with the investors' interests" rather than examining whether the environmental objective was a pretext. This observation highlights the conventional approach adopted by arbitral tribunals, which prioritise protecting foreign invest-

[162] Bonnitcha (2014), pp. 119–120. Tienhaara (2011), p. 612.

[163] See Indonesia case in Gross (2003), p. 894; and *Vannessa Ventures v. Costa Rica* ([2004] ICSID Case No. ARB(AF)/04/6, Award, 16 January 2013) in Tienhaara (2009), p. 239.

[164] *Glamis Gold Ltd. v. United States of America* [2003] UNCITRAL, NAFTA, Award, 8 June 2009.

[165] Bonnitcha (2014), pp. 120–121.

[166] Ibid., pp. 125–126.

[167] Ibid., p. 127.

[168] Ibid., p. 131.

ments as the primary objective of IIAs. This approach results in limited consideration for external issues such as environmental protection and human rights within investment arbitration. Secondly, the diverse array of environment-inspired measures that have been subject to arbitration claims indicates that these types of measures were not adequately anticipated during the negotiation of investment treaties. Bonnitcha suggests that states should make more general assessments for prospective judgments if they wish to preserve their regulatory authority in future IIAs. Thirdly, in most instances, measures aimed at environmental support are implemented in good faith. If chilling effects impact such measures, it could lead to a constrained scope for protecting human rights and the environment in the context of international investment.

2.4 Balancing Investor Protection and Regulatory Rights in IIA Negotiations: The Need for Substantive Regulations

2.4.1 Current Development in IIA Negotiations

Significant and noteworthy observations indicate a substantial shift in national attitudes towards the status and role of BITs. In the contemporary landscape, FTAs with investment chapters have gained greater popularity than traditional BITs.[169] Consequently, the framework for delineating investment protections has become notably more diverse and expansive than classic BITs. Additionally, concerns regarding non-investment issues, particularly sustainable development, have garnered increasing prominence and have been explicitly articulated in the Preambles of these agreements. This shift has led to an extension of the objectives and purposes of traditional IIAs. In this context, the objective of investment agreements no longer exclusively revolves around investment protection but aims to strike the necessary balance between investment protection requirements and the state's regulatory freedom.

Furthermore, nations have taken a proactive stance by including supplementary explanations for their investment protection commitments to ensure that the interpretation of these obligations accurately reflects the contracting parties' intentions. This reflects the considerable caution exercised by countries when providing investment protection obligations to foreign investors. These developments are anticipated to enhance the predictability of the application and interpretation of investment treaties, thereby legitimising the reference to constitutional adjudicative techniques like "proportionality" in this system.[170]

[169] Calamita (2013), pp. 164–184.

[170] Ibid.

2.4.2 Innovations in Reserving Regulatory Space to Support IIA Negotiations

It is evident that the systemic approach alone is insufficient to address the challenges arising from the self-contained nature of IIL. Traditionally, principles of sustainable development and states' inherent regulatory authority have not been explicitly included in conventional IIAs. Recognising this gap, international organisations and states have acknowledged the need to internalise sustainable development objectives into IIL and enhance the state's right to regulate globally and nationally.

Since the early twenty-first century, various studies by international organisations, notably the OECD, UNCTAD, and the Commonwealth, have aimed to assist countries in crafting IIAs that align effectively with their specific development strategies. A significant international initiative in this regard is the UNCITRAL Reform Negotiations, launched in 2017 under UNCITRAL Working Group III.[171]

Although the focus of discussions under UNCITRAL Working Group III is primarily on procedural standards, particularly ISDS reform, these discussions significantly impact the role of the right to regulate within IIL. The issues deliberated within this framework are deeply intertwined with or have repercussions on the state's right to regulate. For example, participating parties have explored concerns about investment arbitrators' potential lack of awareness regarding public interest matters compared to judges and the necessity to clearly define "public interest."[172] Particularly noteworthy is identifying the right to regulate as a cross-cutting issue, especially pertinent to developing countries. This led to a proposal in July 2021 to enhance its emphasis within the work plan of Working Group III.[173] Other discussions have focused on further understanding this right and setting expectations for ongoing deliberations throughout the negotiation process.[174]

Leading economies like the EU and Canada have been pioneers in integrating sustainable development standards and enhancing the state's regulatory rights in BITs and FTAs through negotiations with their partners. As a result, an increasing number of contemporary trade and investment treaties now include provisions to promote sustainable development and reinforce the state's regulatory authority through various mechanisms. However, there is no prompt and universally accepted solution to address the multidimensional problems of the current IIL system, given the conflicting interests and diverse objectives among actors.[175] This reform process

[171] UNCITRAL Reports. Working Group III.

[172] UNCITRAL (2018), para. 84. See other discussions relating to the right to regulate in different Phase of the UNCITRAL Working Group III as observed by Titi in Titi (2022), pp. 86–88.

[173] UNCITRAL (2021a) para. 256.

[174] UNCITRAL (2021b).

[175] Sacerdoti (2016), p. 35.

is predicted to take time and effort due to the massive number of existing BITs and the diversity of views on the advisable changes.[176]

In a 2011 survey conducted by the OECD of 1623 IIAs, the proportion of newly concluded IIAs containing environmental language began to increase moderately from 2002, peaking in 2008, with 89% of freshly concluded treaties referencing environmental concerns.[177] Structural challenges of traditional IIAs stem from fragmentation, incoherence, and the broad nature of obligations established in IIAs. Current suggestions focus on revising substantive obligations and integrating sustainable development objectives into IIAs and the ISDS. This results in a rather complex set of alternative formulations that are open to discussion.[178]

Depending on the parties' targets, different options can be considered:[179]

(i) Revision in treaty design by adding sustainable development aims into the preamble. Although the preamble usually does not impose legal obligations, it may assist in interpreting the agreement.
(ii) Resolving controversial interpretations by clarifying existing substantive provisions such as FET, expropriation, MFN, NT, and narrowing the scope and definition of "investment." The expropriation clause and FET, which have traditionally controlled state regulatory autonomy,[180] remain crucial focus areas.
(iii) Inclusion of new sustainable development-oriented provisions:
    - General exceptions
    - Provisions on the right to regulate
    - Investor responsibilities: includes a general obligation to obey host state laws with a simultaneous denial of rights under the treaty if an investment is made in violation of host country law.
    - State obligations and institutional structures: providing for no-lowering of standards clauses, specialised home state obligations, and establishing institutional structures for cooperation between the state contracting parties to the IIA.
    - Special and differential treatment provisions: designed to address the concerns of least developed countries.
    - Sustainability assessments

Among these suggestions, a general exception clause and a provision on the right to regulate are particularly notable. According to the OECD survey,[181] reserving policy space for environmental regulation across the entire treaty is the most common category of language found in IIAs, and this likely remains true today.

---

[176] Ibid.

[177] Gordon and Pohl (2011), p. 10.

[178] Muchlinski (2016), p. 46.

[179] Ibid., pp. 45–63.

[180] Hindelang and Krajewski (2016), p. 11.

[181] Gordon and Pohl (2011), p. 8.

While the effectiveness of these initiatives in promoting sustainable objectives or expanding the state's regulatory space has yet to be universally accepted by scholars, scepticism and opposition persist. For example, Sornarajah criticises the right to regulate, arguing that balanced investment treaties incorporating this provision are impractical and that states should terminate their investment treaties instead.[182] Another scholar, Titi, contends that the requirement on the non-lowering of environmental and other public welfare standards imposes an obligation on the host state not to relax its standards but does not grant the host state a "right."[183]

Despite ongoing debates, these initiatives continue to be a part of national and international discussions and are incorporated into models for investment treaties. However, since investment tribunals in specific disputes have not yet considered them, the precise contribution of each initiative and their collective impact on individual countries' choices in the IIAs they conclude remains unclear.

2.4.3 Sustainability-Support Regulations in Selected New-Generation FTAs

The number of trade-investment negotiations in which states show more concern for protecting sustainable values and legitimate objectives has rapidly increased recently. This trend can be found in different negotiations from different continents, and it significantly changes the design of traditional trade-investment treaties, which show more balance between investment protection and nations' rights. The CPTPP and a series of FTAs recently signed by the EU with its partners, such as Canada, Singapore, and Vietnam, are typical representations of this trend.

- The Comprehensive and Progressive Agreement for Trans-Pacific Partnership

The CPTPP, a comprehensive trade agreement among 11 countries in the Trans-Pacific region, represents one of the largest trading areas globally, accounting for nearly 13.5% of global GDP.[184] The agreement was renegotiated starting in 2017 following the withdrawal of the United States.[185] and entered into force for Vietnam on January 14, 2019. It is expected to have positive effects on the country's economy. The CPTPP is envisioned to be more comprehensive than the Regional Comprehensive Economic Partnership (RCEP). With China's application to join the CPTPP, it has the potential to serve as the cornerstone for Asia-Pacific supply chains.[186]

---

[182] Sornarajah (2015), chs. 06-07.

[183] Titi (2014), pp. 105–107.

[184] Global Affairs Canada (2018).

[185] Government of Canada (2018).

[186] Meltzer and Coulibaly (2022), p. 45.

The CPTPP emphasises the priorities of promoting high levels of environmental protection and sustainable development in its Preamble. More importantly, the Preamble underscores the right of the contracting parties to regulate by stating:

> Recognise their inherent right to regulate and resolve to preserve the flexibility of the Parties to set legislative and regulatory priorities, preserve public welfare, and protect legitimate public objectives, such as public health, safety, the environment, the conservation of living or non-living exhaustible natural resources…

Additionally, the Preamble emphasises the pursuit of high levels of environmental protection through various directions. Furthermore, Chapter 20 on Environment of the CPTPP prioritizes environmental protection goals alongside members' trade interests. Notably, Article 20.3 on General Commitments states that:

> … 2. The Parties recognise the sovereign right of each Party to establish its own levels of domestic environmental protection and its own environmental priorities, and to establish, adopt or modify its environmental laws and policies accordingly.
>
> 3. Each Party shall strive to ensure that its environmental laws and policies provide for, and encourage, high levels of environmental protection and to continue to improve its respective levels of environmental protection.
>
> 4. No Party shall fail to effectively enforce its environmental laws through a sustained or recurring course of action or inaction in a manner affecting trade or investment between the Parties, after the date of entry into force of this Agreement for that Party.
>
> 5. The Parties recognise that each Party retains the right to exercise discretion and to make decisions regarding: (a) investigatory, prosecutorial, regulatory and compliance matters; and (b) the allocation of environmental enforcement resources with respect to other environmental laws determined to have higher priorities…
>
> 6. Without prejudice to paragraph 2, the Parties recognise that it is inappropriate to encourage trade or investment by weakening or reducing the protection afforded in their respective environmental laws. Accordingly, a Party shall not waive or otherwise derogate from, or offer to waive or otherwise derogate from, its environmental laws in a manner that weakens or reduces the protection afforded in those laws in order to encourage trade or investment between the Parties.
>
> …

This regulation explicitly guarantees the right of the contracting parties to regulate, allowing them to issue policy measures aimed at environmental protection. Article 20.3 plays a central role in conserving the regulatory rights of CPTPP Members, as it is the only regulation that mentions the sovereignty rights of Member governments to establish their levels of domestic environmental protection and set their environmental priorities throughout the agreement. Significantly, Article 20.3 prohibits the parties from diminishing or diluting the protections offered by their individual environmental laws to promote trade or investment.

Regarding investment protection commitments, Chapter 9 of the CPTPP on Investment contains typical regulations with traditional designs of investment protection, including Expropriation and Compensation (Article 9.8) and Minimum Standard of Treatment (Article 9.6). Annex 9-B of the CPTPP is particularly notable, as it clarifies actions that constitute expropriation, specifying that these are measures that "*interfere with a tangible or intangible property right or property interest in an investment*" (Annex 9-B(1) CPTPP). This annex also provides specific legal grounds to determine indirect expropriation (Annex 9-B(3)a CPTPP). This clarification is a new development compared to traditional BITs and is expected to support investment tribunals in examining host state measures. Additionally, the annex excludes the possibility of legitimate measures being considered indirect expropriations as long as those actions are conducted in a non-discriminatory manner, except in rare circumstances (Annex 9-B(3)b CPTPP). This revision significantly improves the preservation of policy space for member countries.

Furthermore, Article 9.16 on Investment and Environmental, Health, and Other Regulatory Objectives provides a legal basis for CPTPP member countries to adopt, maintain, and enforce measures to ensure investment activity is undertaken with appropriate caution:

> Nothing in this Chapter shall be construed to prevent a Party from adopting, maintaining or enforcing any measure otherwise consistent with this Chapter that it considers appropriate to ensure that investment activity in its territory is undertaken in a manner sensitive to environmental, health or other regulatory objectives.

While this provision has faced criticism for its circular language, stipulating that regulatory measures must still align with the provisions of the Investment Chapter, it affirms the right to regulate in harmony with other terms of the investment chapter.[187] The inclusion of this substantive provision supporting the right to regulate is seen as a positive step in safeguarding countries' policy space during IIA negotiations.

Additionally, Article 9.3 of the CPTPP guides investment tribunals in the event of any inconsistency between the Investment Chapter and another chapter of the CPTPP, stating that the other chapter shall prevail to the extent of the inconsistency. This means that if there is a conflict between investment protection regulations and Chapter 20 on Environment, Article 20.3 will take priority. This regulation effectively addresses the relationship between the Investment Chapter and other agreement chapters.

Chapter 29, Article 29.1 of the CPTPP on General Exceptions also mentions that Article XX of GATT 1994 can be invoked in case of a violation of National Treatment. This general exception clause, also found in the EU's Trade-Investment Agreements, will be discussed in detail in Chapter 9 of this book.

The CPTPP generally represents a new approach in multilateral trade-investment negotiations, where sustainable development and regulatory rights are carefully considered. Although the preamble may be too general to create any practical effect in interpreting Members' rights and obligations in specific circumstances, Article 20.3, Paragraphs 2 and 5, can help justify governments' environmental decisions or measures as long as those measures are not enforced in a manner affecting trade or investment between the Parties (Paragraph 4, Article 20.3).

- The United States - Mexico - Canada Agreement

The United States - Mexico - Canada Agreement (USMCA) was negotiated to replace NAFTA among the three North American countries: the United States,

[187] Zamir and Barker (2017), pp. 215–216. See also Kawharu (2015), pp. 07, 09.

Canada, and Mexico. It came into effect on July 1, 2020. Like recent FTAs signed by the EU with its partners, the USMCA is often regarded as one of the most comprehensive and high-standard trade agreements ever negotiated among these three member countries. It is expected to drive economic prosperity, promote fairer and more balanced trade, and ensure North America remains the world's most competitive region.

In terms of sustainability, this agreement has been heralded for incorporating the strongest, most advanced, and most comprehensive environmental obligations in any United States trade agreement.[188] Notably, it strongly emphasises sustainable development through mutually supportive trade and environmental policies and practices, as articulated in the Preamble. Furthermore, environmental protection goals are typically addressed in a dedicated Environmental Chapter (Chapter 24), treated as an independent component similar to the CPTPP, rather than being intertwined with trade-related aspects, as seen in the EU's FTAs. While emphasising the importance of a healthy environment and sustainable development in the joint development policies of member countries, the agreement also recognises that it is inappropriate to use environmental laws or measures in a manner that would constitute a disguised restriction on trade or investment between the Parties (Para. 5, Article 24.2 USMCA).

Much like other contemporary FTAs, USMCA member countries affirm their sovereign right to establish their own levels of domestic environmental protection and environmental priorities and to establish, adopt, or modify their environmental laws and policies accordingly (Article 24.3 USMCA). A noteworthy feature of the USMCA's environmental provisions is their incorporation into the agreement's text, making them fully enforceable. Similar to the CPTPP and the EU's trade-investment agreements, this agreement mandates parties to fulfil their obligations under Multilateral Environmental Agreements (MEAs) (Article 24.8 USMCA). What sets these commitments apart is that USMCA parties have strengthened them by making the environmental provisions subject to enforceable USMCA dispute settlement. This commitment bolsters the enforcement of obligations included in MEAs, especially in addressing climate change, which often lack enforcement mechanisms.[189]

Furthermore, this chapter outlines the Parties' commitment to facilitate and promote trade and investment in environmental goods and services, as stipulated in Article 24.24. It also recognises the importance of cooperation among the Parties in the research and development of clean energy and the encouragement of innovative investments in the clean energy sector. Moreover, the Agreement specifies various cooperative efforts dedicated to managing environmental issues. For instance, Annex 12-D details the expected cooperation to harmonise energy performance standards and test procedures among the Parties. Similar to the EU's trade-investment agreements, the USMCA establishes an Environment Committee

---

[188] See the USMCA Factsheet; Office of the United States Trade Representative.

[189] It should be noticed that the list of MEAs does not encompass the United Nations Framework Convention on Climate Change or the Paris Agreement.

composed of senior government representatives responsible for implementing this Chapter (Article 24.26). This Committee oversees the implementation of environmental commitments, ensuring regular monitoring of the obligations. This mechanism operates similarly to the Trade and Sustainable Development Committee (TSD Committee) under the EU's trade-investment agreements, promoting strict adherence to and continuous monitoring of environmental commitments.

Regarding investment protections, the USMCA includes Chapter 14 on Investment, which provides substantive protections and mechanisms for settling disputes arising from violations of these investment protections. This chapter features two protection schemes: The first applies to general investments, offering fundamental substantive protections such as NT, MFN, and direct expropriation. The second scheme applies to covered sectors, including oil and gas production, telecommunications, transportation, specific infrastructure, and power generation, under written agreements between investors and the government. In these cases, investors benefit from the general investment protections and additional provisions, including minimum standard of treatment (MST), transfers, performance requirements, senior management and boards of directors, and indirect expropriation.

A more detailed examination of these substantive investment protections reveals adjustments and clarifications compared to NAFTA, which were the basis of many ISDS claims. For instance, the MST under the USMCA references customary international law but includes new clarifications. It specifies that the concepts of "fair and equitable treatment" and "full protection and security" do not necessitate treatment beyond the minimum standard of treatment of aliens under customary international law (Annex 14-A). Additionally, the USMCA clarifies that implementing a new regulation does not constitute a breach of MST simply because it is inconsistent with an investor's expectations (Para. 4, Article 14.6 USMCA). Concerning indirect expropriation, the agreement includes provisions clarifying that nondiscriminatory regulatory actions designed to protect legitimate public welfare objectives would not amount to indirect expropriation, except in "rare circumstances," aligning with the language found in more recent United States IIAs (Annex 14-B).

Furthermore, the agreement delineates specific limitations on the types of disputes investors may bring before ISDS tribunals. This chapter exclusively applies to the United States and Mexico, with no jurisdiction over Canada. Existing investments in Canada and investments made by Canadian investors will continue to be safeguarded under the existing NAFTA regime for three years following the implementation of the USMCA. After this transitional period, the ISDS mechanism under NAFTA will be gradually phased out. Since Mexico and Canada are both members of the CPTPP, their investors will enjoy the investment protections and dispute settlement mechanisms stipulated in this agreement.[190] For Mexico, ISDS will still be applicable, but such claims will be limited to situations involving breaches of NT, MFN treatment, and direct expropriation. Claims prevalent during the NAFTA era,

[190] The USMCA Factsheet; Office of the United States Trade Representative.

such as those alleging violations of the MST or citing indirect expropriation, will no longer be covered.

Another method employed to curtail the authority of ISDS in the USMCA is the requirement for investors to "exhaust local remedies" by initially filing their complaints in the courts or administrative tribunals of the host state and waiting for 30 months before initiating arbitration (Article 14.D.5 USMCA).[191] The agreement also includes a provision aimed at preserving the regulatory autonomy of the parties, stating: *"Nothing in this Chapter shall be interpreted to prevent a Party from adopting, maintaining, or enforcing any measure otherwise consistent with this Chapter that it considers appropriate to ensure that investment activity in its territory is undertaken in a manner sensitive to environmental, health, safety, or other regulatory objectives.* (Article 14.6 USMCA).

In summary, the USMCA upholds many core investment provisions from NAFTA but introduces new qualifications and provisions that align with more recent United States investment agreements.[192] These amendments, combined with restrictions on the extent to which foreign investors can submit claims against host states through the ISDS mechanism, are designed to manage the proliferation of claims under NAFTA.

- The African Continental Free Trade Area

This book also explores the African Continental Free Trade Area (AfCFTA), a recent free trade agreement with objectives that closely align with those of the previously discussed agreements. However, unlike the other agreements, AfCFTA was primarily negotiated among developing countries in Africa, a continent facing unique challenges in trade development. The negotiations for AfCFTA began in January 2012 and took effect on January 1, 2021, following a multi-phase negotiation process. Phase I focused on tariff concessions related to trade in goods, service schedules, dispute settlement, and the finalisation of various trade-related annexes. Additional phases, which include competition, intellectual property, investment, and e-commerce, are still ongoing.

AfCFTA shares a common goal with the EU, aiming to establish a single market for goods and services while facilitating the movement of people, ultimately promoting deeper economic integration across the African continent. As of 2024, 54 of the 55 countries have signed the agreement, with 44 ratifying it, creating a market comprising over 1.3 billion people. However, it is worth noting that despite acknowledging environmental sustainability in "Africa's Agenda 2063: The Africa We Want," AfCFTA does not feature robust provisions for sustainable development.

Parallel to the other FTAs discussed, the preamble of AfCFTA asserts the parties' right to regulate within their territories and the flexibility to pursue legitimate policy goals across various areas, including public health, safety, the environment, public

---

[191] It's important to note that this requirement does not apply to covered government contracts in sectors such as oil and gas, power generation, telecommunication, transportation, and infrastructure.

[192] Congressional Research Service (2020).

morals, and the promotion and protection of cultural diversity. AfCFTA includes a general exception clause (Article 26) that safeguards the regulatory rights of State parties, particularly in the pursuit of legitimate objectives within their sovereign jurisdiction. Among these objectives, environmental protection is encompassed, along with measures necessary to protect human, animal, or plant life or health; measures preserving national treasures of artistic, historic, or archaeological value; and measures related to the conservation of exhaustible natural resources. This general exception clause resembles Article XX of the GATT 1994 under the WTO. It permits adopting and applying measures that may breach obligations within the agreement, provided they do not manifest as arbitrary or unjustifiable discrimination between parties or constitute a disguised restriction on international trade. However, the lack of jurisprudence in AfCFTA raises concerns about how the adjudicatory body will interpret the general exception clause and which environmental measures will be justified under its scope. This uncertainty stems from the realisation that not all environmental measures will be justifiable within the bounds of the general exceptions clause.[193]

Similarly, the Preamble of the Protocol on Trade in Services, a component of AfCFTA with implications for future foreign investors operating in these markets, underscores the priority of national policy objectives and the preservation of the right to introduce new regulations within their territories to achieve legitimate national policy objectives and sustainable development. The preamble also reflects state parties' standpoints in adhering to the Protocol on Trade in Services provisions, emphasising that they should not compromise environmental protection and sustainable development. This policy is subsequently translated into a substantive provision (Article 8 Right to Regulate). Several provisions within the Protocol on Trade in Services allocate particular importance to sustainable development by referencing sustainable development goals.

In terms of the agreement's scale, the number of clauses addressing sustainable development and environmental protection in AfCFTA is relatively limited compared to other contemporaneously signed FTAs previously discussed, including CPTPP, EVFTA, and, notably, USMCA. Nevertheless, this limitation is expected to be mitigated by implementing supplementary measures to advance environmental protections. These proposals can operate on regional or cooperative levels, such as creating a level playing field to prevent countries with lower environmental regulations from gaining a competitive advantage. They can also focus on reducing trade barriers for green products and services, both regionally and nationally. Furthermore, they may encompass reducing or eliminating market access barriers related to environmental goods and services and facilitating the adoption of environmentally friendly measures.[194]

Despite the relatively modest regulations supporting sustainable development within the AfCFTA, it is essential to recognise that this agreement, when viewed in

[193] See further Ven and Signe (2021), pp. 07–08.

[194] Ibid.

the context of global trade and investment agreement negotiations, aligns with the overall pace of international development. This is promising for the continent, as it indicates that AfCFTA is keeping up with broader global trends. Given the current developmental stage of the member countries in this FTA, it may be challenging to prioritise sustainable development and environmental protection over immediate economic benefits. The economic dimension still tends to take precedence in these nations. To advance non-trade standards, African countries may need to reach a certain level of economic development. Developed countries, such as the EU, have a vital role in promoting and elevating non-trade standards on the continent, and this role needs to continue expanding.

In international and regional trade and investment negotiations, the agreements reviewed in this section provide insights into several notable trends concerning specific efforts to address environmental issues and promote sustainable development. First, countries have considered solving these challenges, especially responding to climate change, as an urgent target in addition to the goal of facilitating trade. The second observation is that developed countries tend to use trade benefits offered within the framework of regional economic integration to urge their partners to share environmental concerns. This is more or less effective, as in the case of the EU's Trade and Investment Agreements and the USMCA. The third observation is that, within the framework of these new-generation FTAs, various instruments have been designed to ensure that environmental commitments are closely monitored and enforced. However, the most common approach is cooperation, regardless of regional or inter-regional scope. This may stem from the non-economic nature of promoting sustainable development and environmental protection. Although calling for cooperation is not quite an effective tool, as in the case of international environmental agreements signed from the twentieth century onwards (United Nations Framework Convention on Climate Change 1992, Kyoto Protocol, and the Paris Agreement on Climate Change), these are still good premises in the meantime preparing for stronger approach for taking affirmative actions to mitigate and adapt to climate change.

2.5 Interim Conclusion

As we enter the twenty-first century, humanity grapples with formidable environmental, ecological, public health, safety, security, and morality challenges. The protection of public interests and the environment has taken on a central role in the development strategies of nations. Consequently, recently concluded agreements exhibit greater detail and reflect the signatory parties' specific needs, economic structures, and policy objectives. This evolution has brought a significant challenge for investment treaty drafters in the modern era. They now face the complex task of redesigning IIAs with dual objectives: safeguarding the interests of investors and their investments and advancing sustainable goals. Developments in this arena have thus far encompassed different investment standards, the introduction of sustainable development objectives in the Preamble, and the inclusion of exceptions and substantive provisions that protect the regulatory rights of states. These suggestions for integrating sustainable development into IIAs appear fragmented, like the IIL regime. Consequently, combined with increased government interventions in investment projects, these changes have reduced the predictability of investment policies for investors and have the potential to influence international investment flows, albeit not straightforwardly.[195] Further examination of these modifications within diverse interaction contexts is necessary, especially in light of the evolving investment court system, as the specifics of its operation have yet to be fully determined.

Compared to traditional investment treaties, recent IIAs and preferential trade agreements place a greater emphasis on sustainable development and preserving the host state's legitimate rights. This underscores the prioritisation of sustainability and environmental protection in this century, taking precedence over various other factors in national policies and trade and investment forums worldwide. Negotiating new-generation preferential and investment protection agreements demonstrates substantial efforts to promote sustainable development and revise trade and investment provisions. However, due to the limitations of discussion within investor-state arbitration, scholars remain cautious about evaluating or predicting the practical effects of these proposals.[196] Others criticise that the new treaty language only marginally increases policy flexibility for states while omitting direct mention of climate change.[197]

International investment law has consistently represented one of the most intricate domains of international law.[198] This complexity arises from the divergent objectives of the stakeholders involved. Home states are inclined toward explicit standards that prioritise the interests of their private investors, ensuring that foreign investors receive at least equal treatment to domestic businesses. Motivated by the fear of asset nationalisation by the host states, private investors seek to secure their investments. Host states, in turn, have a vested interest in establishing transparent treaty guidelines to circumvent litigation initiated by private investors.[199]

Reconciling these diverse or competing interests within a single international treaty is challenging. Nevertheless, various factors have propelled foreign investment law to evolve in response to these realities. As evidenced in the earlier analysis, the multidimensional nature of FDI flows and the shift in capital movements have made developed countries more discerning and cautious. Additionally, experiences of being challenged at investment tribunals have made developed countries careful in their approach to the language and scope of investment protection provisions. It is worth noting that developing countries have encountered analogous situations as they grapple with concerns about potential ISDS claims resulting from measures aimed at pursuing their policy objectives. Furthermore, over the past

[195] Vanduzer et al. (2013), p. 26.

[196] Read more in Chi (2018), pp. 163–164.

[197] Thrasher (2021).

[198] Subedi (2006), p. 121.

[199] Edsall (2006), p. 935.

decade, sustainable development has increasingly become a widely pursued value in both developed and developing nations. The confluence of these factors underscores the growing recognition of states' rights to regulate in the current generation of IIAs. While it may be too early to assess the effectiveness of these developments in safeguarding and advancing public welfare regulations and their impact on the functioning of global FDI flows, this evolution represents a significant milestone in the development of IIAs over the past six decades.

ISDS Cases

Abengoa, S.A. y COFIDES, S.A. v. United Mexican States [2009] ICSID Case No. ARB(AF)/09/2

Anbitibi Bowater Inc., v. Government of Canada [2009] ICSID Case No.UNCT/10/1

Bear Creek Mining Corporation v. Republic of Peru [2014] ICSID Case No. ARB/14/21

Belgium v. Netherlands (Iron Rhine Railway) [2005] ICGJ 373, PCA 2005

Biloune and Marine Drive Complex Ltd v. Ghana Investments Centre and the Government of Ghana [1988] UNCITRAL, 95 ILR 183

Burlington Resources Inc. v. Republic of Ecuador [2008] ICSID Case No. ARB/08/5

Chemtura Corporation (formerly Crompton Corporation) v. Government of Canada [2002] PCA Case No. 2008-01

Churchill Mining PLC and Planet Mining Pty Ltd v. Republic of Indonesia [2012] ICSID Case No. ARB/12/14 and 12/40

Clayton and Bilcon of Delaware Inc. v. Government of Canada [2008] PCA Case No. 2009-04

Compañia del Desarrollo de Santa Elena S.A. (CDSE) v. Republic of Costa Rica [2000] ICSID Case No. ARB/96/1

Copper Mesa Mining Corporation v. Republic of Ecuador [2011] PCA No. 2012-2

Cosigo Resources, Ltd., Cosigo Resources Sucursal Colombia, Tobie Mining and Energy, Inc. v. Republic of Colombia [2016] UNCITRAL (pending)

David Aven and others v. Costa Rica [2014] ICSID Case No. UNCT/15/3

Eiser Infrastructure Limited and Energía Solar Luxembourg S.à r.l. v. Kingdom of Spain [2013] ICSID Case No. ARB/13/36

Eli Lilly and Company v. The Government of Canada [2017] UNCITRAL, ICSID Case No. UNCT/14/2

Emilio Agustin Maffezini v. Spain [2000] ICSID Case No. ARB/97/7

Glamis Gold Ltd. v. United States of America [2003] UNCITRAL, NAFTA

Grand River Enterprises Six Nations, Ltd., et al. v. United States of America [2004] UNCITRAL

Infinito Gold v. Costa Rica [2014] ICSID Case No. ARB/14/5

Joseph Charles Lemire v. Ukraine [2006] ICSID Case No. ARB/06/18

Marion Unglaube and Reinhard Unglaube v. Republic of Costa Rica [2009] ICSID Case No. ARB/08/1 and ARB/09/20

Metalclad Corporation v. The United Mexican States [1997] ICSID Case No. ARB(AF)/97/1
Methanex Corp. v. United States of America [1999] UNCITRAL, 44 ILM 1345
MTD Equity Sdn. Bhd. And MTD Chile S.A. v. Chile [2001] ICSID Case No. ARB/01/7
Noble Ventures Inc. v. Romania [2001] ICSID Case No. ARB/01/11
Occidental Petroleum Corporation and Occidental Exploration and Production Company v. Republic of Ecuador [2006] ICSID Case No. ARB/06/11
Pac Rim Cayman LLC v. Republic of El Salvador [2009] ICSID Case No. ARB/09/12
Perenco Ecuador Limited v. Republic of Ecuador [2008] ICSID Case No. ARB/08/6
Peter A. Allard v. The Government of Barbados [2010] PCA Case No. 2012-06
Philip Morris Asia Limited v. The Commonwealth of Australia [2012] UNCITRAL, PCA Case No. 2012-12
S.D. Myers, Inc. v. Government of Canada [1998] UNCITRAL, NAFTA
Saluka Investments B.V. v. The Czech Republic [2001] PCA Case No. 2001-04
Sempra Energy International v. Argentine Republic [2002] ICSID Case No. ARB/02/16
Southern Pacific Properties (Middle East) Limited v. Arab Republic of Egypt [1984] ICSID Case No. ARB/84/3
The Renco Group, Inc. v. Republic of Peru [2016] ICSID Case No. UNCT/13/1
Técnicas Medioambientales Tecmed, S.A. v. The United Mexican States [2003] ICSID Case No. ARB(AF)/00/2
Tokios Tokelės v. Ukraine [2002] ICSID Case No. ARB/02/18
Urbaser S.A. and Consorcio de Aguas Bilbao Biskaia, Bilbao Biskaia Ur Partzuergoa v. Argentine Republic [2007] ICSID Case No. ARB/07/26
Vannessa Ventures v. Costa Rica [2004] ICSID Case No. ARB(AF)/04/6
Vattenfall AB, Vattenfall Europe AG, Vattenfall Europe Generation AG v. Federal Republic of Germany [2009] ICSID Case No. ARB/09/6

Treaties

African Continental Free Trade Area (2018) (AfCFTA)
Belgium - Luxembourg Model BIT (2019)
Canada Model BIT (2004)
CARIFORUM - European Union Economic Partnership Agreement 2008
Comprehensive and Progressive Agreement for Trans-Pacific Partnership (2018) (CPTPP)
European Economic Area Agreement (1992)
Finland Model BIT (2004)
Germany - Pakistan BIT (1959)
Kyoto Protocol to the UNFCCC (1997)
North American FTA (1992) (NAFTA)
Netherlands Model BIT (2004)

Paris Agreement on Climate Change (2016)
Southern African Development Community (SADC) Model BIT (2012)
Sweden Model BIT (2003)
Treaty on European Union (1992) (The Maastricht Treaty)
UNESCO Convention on World Cultural and Natural Heritage (1972) (UNESCO Convention)
United Nations Framework Convention on Climate Change (1992)
United States - Korea Free Trade Agreement (2007) (US - Korea FTA)
United States - Australia Free Trade Agreement (2004) (US - Australia FTA)
United States - Mexico - Canada Agreement (2019) (USMCA)
US Model BIT (2004)
US Model BIT (2012)
Vienna Convention on the Law of Treaty (1969) (VCLT)
WTO General Agreement on Tariffs and Trade (1994) (GATT)
WTO Marrakesh Agreement (1994)

References

Other Cases

Belgium v. Netherlands (Iron Rhine Railway) [2005] ICGJ 373, PCA 2005, Award, 24 May 2005. Available via https://legal.un.org/riaa/cases/vol_XXVII/35-125.pdf
I.C.J Judgment, Gabcikovo-Nagymaros Project (*Hungary v. Slovakia*). Rep. 7, Award, 25 September 1997. Available via http://www.worldcourts.com/icj/eng/decisions/1997.09.25_gabchkovo.htm
Permanent Court of International Justice (1925) Exchange of Greek and Turkish Populations (Lausanne Convention VI, January 30th, 1923, Article 2). Advisory opinion No. 10. 1925 P.C.I.J. (ser. B) No. 10 (Feb. 21). Available via https://www.worldcourts.com/pcij/eng/decisions/1925.02.21_greek_turkish.htm
UNRIAA Award (1937) Différend concernant l'accord Tardieu-Jaspar (Belgium/France). Vol. III. 01 March 1937. Available via https://legal.un.org/riaa/cases/vol_III/1701-1716.pdf
WTO (1996) *US - Standards for Reformulated and Conventional Gasoline (US - Gasoline)*, WT/DS2/R/DSR, WT/DS2/AB/R/DSR, 20 May 1996
WTO (1998) *US - Import Prohibition of Certain Shrimp and Shrimp Products*, WT/DS58/AB/R, adopted on 6 November 1998
WTO (2007) *Brazil - Measures Affecting Imports of Retreaded Tyres (Brazil - Retreaded Tyres)*, WT/DS332/AB/R, 17 December 2007
WTO (2012) *United States - Measures Concerning the Importation, Marketing and Sale of Tuna and Tuna Products* (*US - Tuna/Dolphin II*), WT/DS381/AB/R/DSR, 13 June 2012

Bibliography

Anh Le Nguyen Dieu (2020) Phát triển Thương mại Theo hướng Bền vững ở Việt Nam trong Bối cảnh Hội nhập Quốc tế [Developing Sustainable Trade in Viet Nam in the Context of International Integration]. Dphil in Economic Management Thesis, Institute of Postgraduate Training. Thuong mai University

Bantekas I, & Akestoridi K, (2023) Sustainable Development Goals, Between Politics and Soft Law: The Emergence of "Political Normativity" in International Law, 37 *Emory International Law Review 449*, https://scholarlycommons.law.emory.edu/cgi/viewcontent.cgi?params=/context/eilr/article/1314/&path_info=Bantekas_ELSC_8.14.23.pdf.

Benedetto SD (2013) International investment law and the environment. Edward Elgar Publishing

Benvenisti E, Downs GW (2007) The Empire's new clothes: political economy and the fragmentation of international law. Stanford Law Rev 60:595

Berner K (2016) Reconciling investment protection and sustainable development - a plea for an interpretative U-Turn. In: Hindelang S, Krajewski M (eds) Shifting paradigms in international investment law: more balanced, less isolated, increasingly diversified. Oxford University Press

Besson S (2011) Sovereignty, international law and democracy. Eur J Int Law 22(2):373–387

Bjorklund AK (2013) The role of counterclaims in rebalancing investment law. Lewis Clark Law Rev 17:461

Bonnitcha J (2014) Substantive protection under investment treaties: a legal and economic analysis. Cambridge University Press

Brower CN, Schill SW(2009) Is arbitration a threat or a boon to the legitimacy of international investment law? Chic J Int Law 9(2):471. Available via https://chicagounbound.uchicago.edu/cjil/vol9/iss2/5

Brownlie I (2008) Principles of public international law, 7th edn. Oxford University Press

Calamita NJ (2013) International human rights and the interpretation of international investment treaties: constitutional considerations. In: Baetens F (ed) Investment law within international law-integrationist perspectives. Cambridge University Press

Chazournes LB (2016) WTO and non-trade issues: inside/outside WTO. J Int Econ Law 19:379

Chi M (2015) The "Greenization" of Chinese BITs: an empirical study of the environmental provisions in Chinese BITs and its implications for China's future BIT-Making. J Int Econ Law 18

Chi M (2018) Integrating sustainable development in international investment law: normative incompatibility, system integration and governance implications. Routledge

Collins D (2012) Sustainable international investment law after the Pax Americana: the BOOT on the other foot. J World Invest Trade 13(3)

Congressional Research Service (2020) USMCA: Investment Provisions. Available via https://crsreports.congress.gov/product/pdf/IF/IF11167

Crawford J (2012) Brownlie's principles of public international law, 8th edn. Oxford University Press

Dobson A (ed) (1999) Fairness and futurity: essays on environmental sustainability and social justice. Oxford University Press

Edsall RD (2006) Indirect expropriation under NAFTA and DR-CAFTA: potential inconsistencies in the treatment of state public welfare regulations. Boston Univ Law Rev 86(4):931. Available via https://www.bu.edu/law/journals-archive/bulr/documents/edsall.pdf

Schmid E (2015) The identification and role of international legislation duties in a contested area: must Switzerland legislate in relation to business and human rights. Swiss Rev Int Eur Law 25:563–589

Fauchald OK (2008) The legal resoning of ICSID tribunals – an empirical analysis. Eur J Int Law 19(2):301

Franck SD (2005) The legitimacy crisis in international treaty arbitration: privatizing public internationl law through inconsistent decisions. Fordham Law Rev 73:1521

G20 (2016) Guiding Principles for Global Investment Policy Making (2016). Available via https://investmentpolicy.unctad.org/uploaded-files/document/Annex%20III%20G20%20Guiding%20Principles%20for%20Global%20Investment%20Policymaking.pdf

Gehring MW, Kent A (2013) International investment agreements and the emerging green economy: rising to the challenge. In: Baetens F (ed) Investment law within international law – integrationist perspectives. Cambridge University Press

Giannakopoulos C (2017) The right to regulate in international investment law and the law of state responsibility: a Hohfeldian approach. In: Pazartzis P, Merkouris P (2019) Permutations of responsibility in international law. Brill Nijhoff

Gordon K (2008) International investment agreements: a survey of environmental, labour and anti-corruption issues. In: International investment law: understanding concepts and tracking innovations. OECD. Available via https://read.oecd-ilibrary.org/finance-and-investment/international-investment-law-understanding-concepts-and-tracking-innovations_9789264042032-en#page3

Gordon K, Pohl J (2011) Environmental concerns in international investment agreements: a survey. OECD Working Papers on International Investment No 2011/1

Gross SG (2003) Inordinate Chill: BITs, Non-NAFTA MITs, and host state regulatory freedom – an Indonesian case study. Mich J Int Law 24:894

Hindelang S, Krajewski M (2016) Towards a more comprehensive approach in international investment law. In: Hindelang S, Krajewski M (eds) Shifting paradigms in international investment law: more balanced, less isolated, increasingly diversified. Oxford University Press

ILC Report (2006) Fragmentation of International law: Difficulties Arising from the Diversification and Expansion of International Law. The Study Group of the International Law Commission. International Law Commission. A/CN.4/L.682. 13 April 2006. Available via https://legal.un.org/ilc/documentation/english/a_cn4_l682.pdf

Jackson JH (2006) Sovereignty, the WTO, and the changing fundamentals of international law. Cambridge University Press

Jackson JH (2008) Sovereignty: outdated concept or new approaches. In: Shan W, Simons P, Singh D (eds) Redefining sovereignty in international economic law. Hart Publishing

Johnson L, Sachs L, Sachs J (2015) Investor - State Dispute Settlement, Public Interest and U.S. Domestic Law. Columbia Center on Sustainable Investment. Policy Paper

Johnson L, Sachs L, Güven B, Coleman J (2018) Cost and Benefits of Investment Treaties - Practical Consideration for States. Columbia Centre on Sustainable Investment. Policy paper. Available via https://ccsi.columbia.edu/sites/default/files/content/pics/Cost-and-Benefits-of-Investment-Treaties-Practical-Considerations-for-States-ENG-mr.pdf

Kawharu A (2015) TPPA: Chapter 9 on Investment. Expert Paper No.2 WordPress.com: TPP Legal. Available via https://tpplegal.files.wordpress.com/2015/12/ep2-amokura-kawharu.pdf

Kläger R (2016) Revising treatment standards - fair and equitable treatment in light of sustainable development. In: Hindelang S, Krajewski M (eds) Shifting paradigms in international investment law: more balanced, less isolated, increasingly diversified. Oxford University Press

Kulick A (2012) Global public interest in international investment law. Cambridge University Press

Kurt J (2014) Building legitimacy through interpretation in investor-state arbitration: on consistency, coherence, and the identification of applicable law. In: Douglas Z, Pauwelyn J, Viñuales JE (eds) The foundation of international investment law: briging theory into practice. Oxford University Press

Levashova Y (2019) The right of states to regulate in international investment law: the search for balance between public interest and fair and equitable treatment. Wolters Kluwer

Martini C (2017) Balancing investors' rights with environmental protection in international investment arbitration: an assessment of recent trends in investment treaty drafting. Int Lawyer 50(3)

Meltzer J, Coulibaly B (eds) (2022) USMCA Forward. Brookings Institution. Available via https://www.brookings.edu/wp-content/uploads/2022/02/usmca_2022_Report.pdf

Mills A (2014) The balancing and unbalancing of interests in international investment law and arbitration. In: Douglas Z, Pauwelyn J, Viñuales JE (eds) The foundation of international investment law: briging theory into practice. Oxford University Press

Muchlinski P (2016) Negotiating new generation international investment agreements: new sustainable development oriented initiatives. In: Hindelang S, Krajewski M (eds) Shifting paradigms in international investment law: more balanced, less isolated, increasingly diversified. Oxford University Press

Nadakavukaren K, Polanco Lazo R (2023) Legal Opinion on Right to Regulate on Investment Treaties - Canada, European Union, Japan, Netherlands, and United States of America. E-Avis ISDC 2023. Available via www.isdc.ch

Newcombe A, Paradell L (2009) Law and practice of investment treaties: standards of treatment. Kluwer Law International

Office of the United States Trade Representative. Benefits for the Environment in the United States - Mexico - Canada Agreement. Available via https://ustr.gov/trade-agreements/free-trade-agreements/united-states-mexico-canada-agreement/benefits-environment-united-states-mexico-canada-agreement

Olson S (2016) The case for sustainable trade. Hindrich Foundation. Available via https://www.hinrichfoundation.com/research/article/sustainable/the-case-for-sustainable-trade/

Osterwalder NB, Johnson L (eds) (2011) International Investment Law and Sustainable Development: Key Cases from 2000-2010. IISD

Osterwalder NB, Brauch MD, Schacherer S (2018) International Investment Law and Sustainable Development: Key Cases from 2010s. IISD

Puvimanasinghe SF (2007) Foreign investment, human rights and the environment: a perspective from South Asia on the role of public international law for development. Martinus Nijhoff Publishers

Robins N, Roberts S (eds) (2000) The reality of sustainable trade. International Institute for Environment and Development. Available via https://www.iied.org/sites/default/files/pdfs/migrate/8861IIED.pdf

Sacerdoti G (2016) Investment protection and sustainable development - key issues. In: Hindelang S, Krajewski M (eds) Shifting paradigms in international investment law: more balanced, less isolated, increasingly diversified. Oxford University Press

Sands P et al (2018) Principles of international environmental law, 4th edn. Cambridge University Press

Schill SW (2014) Ordering paradigms in international investment law: bilateralism - multilateralism – multilateralization. In: Douglass Z, Pauwelyn J, Viñuales JE (eds) The foundations of international investment law: bringing theory into practice. Oxford University Press

Schmid E (2015) The identification and role of international legislative duties in a contested area: must Switzerland legislate in relation to "business and human rights"? Schweizerische Zeitschrift für internationales und europäisches Recht (SZIER)/Swiss Rev Int Eur Law 25:563–589

Schreuer C (2010) Diversity and harmonization of treaty interpretation in investment arbitration. In: Merkouris P, Elias O, Fitzmaurice M (eds) Treaty Interpretation and the Vienna Convention on the Law of Treaties: 30 Years on. Brill

Segger MCC, Khalfan A (2004) Sustainable development law: principles, practices, and prospects. Oxford University Press

Sornarajah M (2015) Resistance and change in the international law on foreign investment. Cambridge University Press

Soubbotina TP (2004) Beyond economic growth: an introduction to sustainable development. World Bank. Available via https://documents.worldbank.org/en/publication/documents-reports/documentdetail/454041468780615049/beyond-economic-growth-an-introduction-to-sustainable-development

Sự Hà Văn (2004) Những Giải pháp chủ yếu nhằm Phát triển Thương mại theo Tiếp cận Phát triển bền vững trong Bối cảnh Hội nhập Kinh tế Quốc tế của Việt Nam [Main Sollutions for Trade development following Sustainable development Approach in the Context of Vietnam's International Economic Integration]. Scientific project. Ministry of Trade. Vietnam

Subedi SP (2006) The challenge of reconciling the competing principles within the law of foreign investment with special reference to the recent trend in the interpretation of the term "expropriation". Int Lawyer 40(1)

Thrasher R (2021) Room to move: building flexibility into investment treaties to meet climate-change commitments. Columbia FDI Perspective No. 296. Columbia Centre on Sustainable Development

Tienhaara K (2009) The expropriation of environmental governance: protecting foreign investors at the expense of public policy. Cambridge University Press

Tienhaara K, (2011) Regulatory Chill and the Threat of Arbitration: A view from Political Science, *Brown C, Miles K. Evolution in Investmeent Treaty Law and Arbitration. Cambridge University Press*, https://doi.org/10.1017/CBO9781139043809.034.

Titi A (2014) The right to regulate in international investment law. Hart Nomos

Titi C (2022) The right to regulate in international investment law (revisited). Courses of the Summer school on Public International Law 2022. Available via https://papers.ssrn.com/sol3/papers.cfm?abstract_id=4058447

Trujillo E (2018) Balancing sustainability, the right to regulate, and the need for investor protection: lessons from the trade regime. Boston Coll Law Rev 59:2735

UNCITRAL (2018) Report of Working Group III: Investor-State Dispute Settlement Reform on the Work of its Thirty-fifth Session. New York. Available via https://documents-dds-ny.un.org/doc/UNDOC/GEN/V18/029/59/PDF/V1802959.pdf?OpenElement

UNCITRAL (2021a) Report of the United Nations Commission on International Trade Law Fifty-fourth Session, 28 June – 16 July 2021. A/76/17. Available via https://uncitral.un.org/sites/uncitral.un.org/files/report_54th.pdf

UNCITRAL (2021b) Report of Working Group III (Investor-State Dispute Settlement Reform) on the work of its resumed Fortieth Session. Vienna, 4 - 5 May 2021. A/CN.9/1054. Available via https://documents.un.org/doc/undoc/gen/v21/038/72/pdf/v2103872.pdf?token=SrAMfPMMvzMk3nGVKZ&fe=true

UNCITRAL Reports. Working Group III: Investor-State Dispute Settlement Reform. Accessed via https://uncitral.un.org/en/working_groups/3/investor-state

UNCITRAL Working Group III (2019) Submission of the EU and its Member States, A/CN.9/WG.III/WP.159/Add.1. Available via https://undocs.org/en/A/CN.9/WG.III/WP.159/Add.1

UNCTAD (2005) South-South Cooperation in International Investment Arrangements. Available via https://unctad.org/system/files/official-document/iteiit20053_en.pdf

UNCTAD (2007) Investor-State Dispute Settlement and Impact on Investment Rulemaking. Available via https://unctad.org/system/files/official-document/iteiia20073_en.pdf

UNCTAD (2013) Towards a New Generation of International Investment Policies: UNCTAD's Fresh Approach to Multilateral Investment Policy-making. Available via https://unctad.org/system/files/official-document/webdiaepcb2013d6_en.pdf

UNCTAD (2015a) Investor-States Dispute Settlement: Review of Developments in 2015, IIA Issues note. UNCTAD (2015) Investor-States Dispute Settlement: Review of Developments in 2015. IIA Issues. Available via https://investmentpolicy.unctad.org/publications/144/investor-state-dispute-settlement-review-of-developments-in-2015

UNCTAD (2015b) World Investment Report 2015: Reforming International Investment Governance. Available via https://unctad.org/system/files/official-document/wir2015_en.pdf

UNCTAD (2015c) Investment Policy Framework for Sustainable Development. Available via https://unctad.org/publication/investment-policy-framework-sustainable-development-2015-edition

UNCTAD (2018) UNCTAD's Reform Package for the International Investment Regime. Available via https://investmentpolicy.unctad.org/uploaded-files/document/UNCTAD_Reform_Package_2018.pdf

UNCTAD (2020) International Investment Agreements – Reform Accelerator. Available via https://unctad.org/system/files/official-document/diaepcbinf2020d8_en.pdf

UNCTAD - Investment Policy Hub. Investment Dispute Settlement Navigator. Available via http://investmentpolicyhub.unctad.org/ISDS

USMCA Factsheet. Available via https://ustr.gov/sites/default/files/files/Press/fs/USMCA/USMCA_Environment.pdf

Vandevelde KJ (2010) Bilateral investment treaties-history, policy, and interpretation. Oxford University Press
VanDuzer JA (2016) Sustainable development provisions in international trade treaties. In: Hindelang S, Krajewski M (eds) Shifting paradigms in international investment law: more balanced, less isolated, increasingly diversified. Oxford University Press
VanDuzer JA, Simons P, Maeda G (2013) Integrating sustainable development into international investment agreements: a guide for developing country negotiators. Commonwealth Secretariat. Available via https://www.thecommonwealth-ilibrary.org/index.php/comsec/catalog/book/168
Ven CVD, Signe L (2021) Greening the AfCFTA: it is not too late, Africa Growth Initiative at Brookings. Available via https://www.brookings.edu/wp-content/uploads/2021/09/21.09.15-Greening-the-AfCFTA.pdf
Viñuales JE (2010) Foreign investment and the environment in international law: an ambiguous relationship. Br Yearb Int Law 80. Available via https://papers.ssrn.com/sol3/papers.cfm?abstract_id=1652763
Viñuales JE (2012) Foreign investment and the environment in international law. Cambridge Univesity Press
Viñuales J, (2023) Sustainable Development, *Rajamani L (ed.) The Oxford Handbook of International Environmenatl Law (2nd ed.),* https://doi.org/10.1093/law/9780198849155.003.0017.
WTO (2000) Trade, development and the environment. Kluwer Law International
Zamir N, Barker P (2017) The Trans-Pacific Partnership Agreement and States' Right to Regulate under International Investment Law. Denver J Int Law Policy 45(2)

Documents

Delegation of the European Union to the People's Republic of China (2013) EU-China 2020 Stratergic Agenda for Cooperation. Available via https://www.eeas.europa.eu/sites/default/files/20131123.pdf
Economic Partnership Agreement between the Cariforum States and the European Community and its Member States (2008) OJ 2008 L 289/I/3. Available via https://www.consilium.europa.eu/en/documents-publications/treaties-agreements/agreement/?id=2008034
EU Council (2016) Joint Interpretative Instrument on the Comprehensive Economic and Trade Agreement (CETA) between Canada and the European Union and its Member States, 13541/16 Brussels. Available via https://data.consilium.europa.eu/doc/document/ST-13541-2016-INIT/en/pdf
European Commission (2013) Investment Protection and Investor-to-State Dispute Settlement in EU Agreements - Fact Sheet. Available via http://www.sice.oas.org/TPD/USA_EU/Studies/tradoc_151916__Investment_e.pdf
European Commission (2015) Why the New EU Proposal for an Investment Court Systems in TTIP is beneficial to both Sates and Investors, Press Release MEMO/15/6060. Available via https://ec.europa.eu/commission/presscorner/detail/en/MEMO_15_6060
European Parliament (2011) Resolution on the Future European International Investment Policy (2010/2203(INI)). Available via http://www.europarl.europa.eu/sides/getDoc.do?pubRef=-//EP//TEXT+TA+P7-TA-2011-0141+0+DOC+XML+V0//EN
Global Affairs Canada (2018) Economic Impact of Canada's Participation in the Comprehensive and Progressive Agreement for Trans-Pacific Partnership. Available via https://www.international.gc.ca/trade-commerce/trade-agreements-accords-commerciaux/agr-acc/CPTPP-ptpgp/impact-repercussions.aspx?lang=eng
Government of Canada (2018) CPTPP Timeline Negotiation. Available via https://www.international.gc.ca/trade-commerce/trade-agreements-accords-commerciaux/agr-acc/cptpp-ptpgp/timeline_negotiations-chronologie_negociations.aspx?lang=eng

Part II
FDI and Environmental Governance in Vietnam

Chapter 3
Vietnam's Evolving Framework for FDI Policy and Legislation

Abstract This chapter provides a detailed exploration of Vietnam's policy and legislative framework regarding investment. It begins with a retrospective examination of the economic development strategies and FDI attraction policies that Vietnam has implemented since the country started its economic liberalisation. Following this overview, the chapter analyses the Vietnamese government's perspective on foreign investment, offering a comprehensive discussion of the policies created to attract FDI. The practical application of these investment attraction policies is reflected in Vietnam's complex system of investment legislation. The chapter also traces the evolution of Vietnam's investment legislation, highlighting its progress as it integrated into the regional and global economic landscape. This review emphasises the proactive approach of the Vietnamese government and its steadfast commitment to creating an enabling environment for foreign investment. It is noteworthy that the Vietnamese government has demonstrated an enhanced ability to formulate effective policies and manage associated issues over time. Ultimately, the analysis concludes that Vietnam's investment legal framework has continuously evolved to align with international investment practices' changing requirements and norms. The growing incorporation of environmental protection measures into investment legislation is particularly significant as it reflects Vietnam's dedication to harmonising its legal framework with contemporary global standards in international investment.

3.1 Economic Reform in Vietnam: Shifting Policies Toward Trade Liberalisation

Since gaining independence in 1975, Vietnam has focused on establishing socialism. In about ten years, the agricultural economy, which had been heavily damaged by a 30-year war, implemented a centrally planned economic development model while the country was subject to economic sanctions following the war. Under this

N. T. Lan Huong, *Investment Protection and Environmental Governance*, European Yearbook of International Economic Law 47,
https://doi.org/10.1007/978-3-032-05332-9_3

model, all land, natural resources, and productive activities were state-controlled.[1] The state oversaw most economic activities, including distributing agricultural products and consumer goods.[2] State-owned enterprises predominantly operated vital industries and foreign trade activities, while non-state enterprises were restricted in size, number of employees, and capital investment.[3]

Despite the challenges posed by a closed economy and post-war trade embargoes, which led to severe economic and social imbalances, Vietnam remained committed to its integration goals. In 1976, the country became an official member of the International Monetary Fund (IMF) and the World Bank (WB) and joined the Asian Development Bank (ADB) the same year. Vietnam also became a member of the United Nations in 1977. Additionally, on June 29, 1978, Vietnam joined the Council for Mutual Economic Assistance, and on November 31, 1978, it signed the Treaty of Friendship and Comprehensive Cooperation with the Soviet Union. Despite these integration efforts, as noted by Litvack, by the mid-1990s, over half of Vietnam's population lacked the resources to obtain essential food, making poverty reduction a high priority for the country.[4]

Two significant events in the early 1980s notably influenced a shift in the government's perspective: the collapse of the Soviet Union and the economic reforms in China that began in 1976. As Thayer noted, the collapse of the Soviet Union compelled Vietnam to transition from a "one-one relationship" to a "multi-directional foreign policy."[5] In addition, China's economic achievements urged the Vietnamese government to expedite its socio-economic reform plans.

In 1986, at the Sixth National Congress of the Communist Party of Vietnam (CPV), the "Đổi mới" (renovation) policy was unified, marking a significant turning point for the country's socio-economic development.[6] The essence of the 1986 renovation theory was the transition from a centrally planned economy to a socialist-oriented market economy,[7] later officially enshrined in the 1992 Constitution (Articles 15–29 and Article 57). This developmental orientation was consistently emphasised in subsequent CPV meetings. The Seventh (1991), Eighth (1996), Ninth (2001), and Tenth National Party Congress (2006) all underscored the solution of actively integrating into the international economy to promote rapid, effective, and sustainable economic development.[8]

---

[1] World Bank (1999), para. 3.

[2] Ibid.

[3] Ibid.

[4] Litvack (1999), p. 47.

[5] Thayer and Amer (2000), pp. 1–24.

[6] Communist Party of Vietnam (1986).

[7] This objective may be gained by (i) liberalizing domestic prices, (ii) increasing the number of trading entities, (iii) developing trade policy instruments and (iv) removing exchange rate distortions. Auffret (2003), p. 2.

[8] Communist Party of Vietnam (1991); Communist Party of Vietnam (2001); Communist Party of Vietnam (2006).

During the Seventh National Party Congress (1991), the CPV proposed "The Outline for Constructing the Nation in the Transition Period to Socialism" and "The Strategy for Stability and Socio-economic Development until 2000 (1991–2000)." The CPV also introduced an independent foreign policy aimed at diversification and multilateralisation, with the directive: "Vietnam seeks to be friends with all countries, striving for peace, independence, and development."[9]

Another objective of the reforms was to promote export-oriented industries by adjusting the protectionist regime while simultaneously safeguarding the manufacturing sector developed during the centrally planned era.[10] The political report at the Sixth CPV Congress highlighted the need to increase export volumes rapidly, meet import demands, and address the inefficiencies in trade that were damaging both domestic and foreign markets.

Numerous reforms have been implemented across various economic sectors, including macroeconomic management, agriculture, price control, finance, and state enterprises since 1986. The most fundamental changes aimed to enhance the efficiency of the enterprise sector, boost agricultural production, leverage foreign trade and investment, and reform government operations.[11] These changes initially set the basis for Vietnam's economic development in these years.

In the shift towards a market-oriented economy, private firms and foreign investments were permitted, except in critical industrial sectors such as chemicals, coal, communication, electricity, fertilisers, steel, and transport, where the government maintained direct control over certain light consumer goods. Control over state-owned enterprises was reduced, promoting privatisation and the growth of private firms. Recognising the crucial role of FDI in industrialisation, the Law on Foreign Investment was adopted and enacted in January 1988.

After disrupting trade with the Soviet Union and Eastern European countries in the early 1990s, Vietnam redirected its export focus to the Asian market. In 1991, Vietnam signed a trade agreement with China. By November 1992, Japan had resumed Official Development Assistance (ODA) to Vietnam. In 1993, Vietnam re-engaged with the international financial system, including the IMF, WB, and ADB. During this period, Vietnam made significant efforts to integrate into the regional and global economy.

A landmark event occurred in 1995 when Vietnam and the United States normalised their diplomatic relations. That same year, Vietnam joined the Association of Southeast Asian Nations (ASEAN). Membership in this regional organisation connected Vietnam to multiple regional players, providing it with greater bargaining power with superpowers like the United States and China.[12]

ASEAN cooperation efforts have promoted intra-regional links to build a robust ASEAN Economic Community. A key instrument of economic cooperation in the

[9] Communist Party of Vietnam (1991).

[10] See Auffret (2003), p. 2.

[11] Abonyi (2005); Dodsworth et al. (1996).

[12] Chauhan (2013).

region is the ASEAN Free Trade Agreement (AFTA), based on the Common Effective Preferential Tariff Scheme (CEPT). The CEPT, implemented in 2001, provided a schedule for tariff reductions among ASEAN members. Subsequently, Vietnam extended most-favored-nation and national treatment to ASEAN member countries.[13] Subsequently, Vietnam extended MFN and NT to ASEAN member countries. Moreover, ASEAN has signed a series of FTAs with significant economies such as Japan, China, India, and South Korea, which have helped expand the regional market. Vietnam's decision to join ASEAN at this time was strategically sound, aiming to secure a peaceful regional and international environment conducive to economic development and to ensure favourable external conditions for its economic renovation.[14] ASEAN membership also improved Vietnam's standing with other countries, particularly China and the United States (see Table 3.1). These strategic objectives motivated Vietnam to join ASEAN despite foreseeable economic disadvantages.[15]

Following the "Đổi mới" reforms, Vietnam experienced significant economic growth, with its GDP expanding at an average annual rate of 6.6% over the subsequent decade. Inflation, which had been at triple-digit levels, fell to 12.7% in 1995 and 4.5% in 1996. This economic success was mainly due to proactive measures by the Vietnamese government to ensure regional stability, particularly in addressing disputes in the East Sea.[16] However, the East Asian economic crisis interrupted this growth trajectory, causing FDI in Vietnam to plummet from a record 2 billion USD in 1997 (around 10% of GDP) to below 800 million USD in 1998. FDI continued to decline in 1999, reaching approximately 600–700 million USD.[17] Despite the crisis, significantly reducing the country's export value, Vietnam remained committed to enhancing trade cooperation with regional neighbours and pursuing agreements with broader markets, including Europe[18] and North America.

Vietnam became a founding member of the Asia-Europe Cooperation Forum in March 1996. In November 1998, it joined the Asia-Pacific Economic Cooperation (APEC) Forum. In 1999, Vietnam signed a framework agreement with China to promote friendship and comprehensive cooperation between the two countries. On July 13, 2001, Vietnam made a significant stride in integrating into the global economy by signing a Bilateral Trade Agreement (BTA) with the United States. This agreement, resulting from sustained efforts within the country, was drafted following WTO regulations and covered various trade and investment-related fields, including trade in goods, intellectual property rights, trade in services, development of investment relations, business facilitation, and transparency-related provisions.

[13] By 2003, 92% of all tariff lines used by Vietnam was cut down under the CEPT scheme.

[14] Thayer (2001), p. 7.

[15] Ibid., p. 11.

[16] Chauhan (2013).

[17] World Bank (1999), para. 46.

[18] Trade between Vietnam and European countries increased rapidly during the latter half of the 1990s after the establishment of diplomatic relations between the two partners.

Table 3.1 Vietnam's timeframe of integration[a]

1986	Đổi mới (Renovation) Policy
1987	
1988	
1989	
1990	Australia – Vietnam Agreement on Trade & Economic Cooperation
1991	China – Vietnam Trade Agreement
1992	Singapore – Vietnam Trade Agreement
	Vietnam – China Agreement on Economic Cooperation Vietnam – China Agreement on Encouragement & Reciprocal Protection of Investments
1993	
1994	Canada – Vietnam Agreement on Economic Cooperation
	New Zealand – Vietnam Agreement on Economic Cooperation
1995	(WTO Accession Process Started)
	ASEAN membership
	ASEAN Framework Agreement on Services (AFAS)
	EC – Vietnam Framework Cooperation Agreement
1996	ASEAN Free Trade Area (AFTA)
1997	
1998	ASIA – PACIFIC Economic Cooperation forum (APEC)
1999	
2000	US – Vietnam Agreement on Trade Relations
2001	(CEPT/AFTA tariff reduction implementation)
2002	ASEAN – China Framework Agreement on Comprehensive Economic Cooperation
2003	ASEAN – India Framework Agreement on Comprehensive Economic Cooperation (AIFTA)
2004	
2005	ASEAN – Korea Framework Agreement on Comprehensive Economic Cooperation (AKFTA)
	ASEAN Member Countries & Russia Agreement on Economic & Development
2006	
2007	WTO membership
2008	Vietnam – Japan Economic Partnership Agreement (VJEPA) (Came into force in 2009)
	ASEAN – Japan Comprehensive Economic Partnership Agreement (AJCEP)
2009	ASEAN Comprehensive Investment Agreement (ACIA)
	ASEAN Trade in Goods Agreement (ATIGA)
	Agreement Establishing ASEAN – Australia – New Zealand FTA (Came into effect from 2010)
2010	
2011	Vietnam – Chile Free Trade Agreement (VCFTA)
2012	
2013	
2014	

(continued)

Table 3.1 (continued)

2015	Vietnam – Korea Free Trade Agreement (VKFTA)
	Vietnam – The EURASIAN Economic Union & Its member States Free Trade Agreement (Vietnam – EAEU FTA)
2016	
2017	ASEAN – Hongkong Free Trade Agreement (AHKFTA)
2018	The Comprehensive and Progressive Agreement for Trans – Pacific Partnership (CPTPP)
2019	EVFTA – EVIPA
2020	Regional Comprehensive Economic Partnership (RCEP)
	UK – Vietnam Free Trade Agreement (UKVFTA)
2021	
2022	
2023	Vietnam – Israel Free Trade Agreement (VIFTA)

[a] In this table, agreements signed by Vietnam with smaller economies, such as Cuba, are not included. Additionally, agreements currently under negotiation, such as the Vietnam–EFTA Free Trade Agreement, are not mentioned

The BTA effectively opened the United States market to Vietnamese exports such as agricultural products, textiles, and footwear. Vietnam committed to adhering to WTO-level standards in intellectual property rights within 18 months. Vietnam agreed to progressively open critical services such as telecommunications, finance, banking, distribution, construction, and tourism for 2 to 10 years in the service sector for the first time since implementing market-opening policies. The successful signing of the BTA with the United States is vital to Vietnam's accession to the WTO.

In 2001, Vietnam announced a strategic partnership with Russia, followed by a collaboration with Japan in 2002. According to a World Bank report, within 15 years of the Đổi Mới reforms initiated in 1986, Vietnam transformed from a marginal food importer to one of the world's largest rice exporters. By 1998, rice export volumes had surged to 3.8 million tons, with significant improvements in quality.[19] Additionally, exports of other agricultural products such as coffee and rubber more than doubled between 1992 and 1997.[20] A subsequent World Bank report highlighted that between 2003 and 2008, Vietnam's economy doubled from 40 billion to 90 billion USD, and its exports more than tripled from 20 billion to 63 billion USD. A key milestone during this period was Vietnam's official admission as the 150th member of the WTO on January 11, 2007.[21] This achievement marked the culmination of twelve years of continuous efforts in institutional reform and market opening to WTO members. It represented a significant milestone in Vietnam's first wave of economic integration.[22] Vietnam's accession to the WTO involved negotiating approximately 20 bilateral agreements with various members, including the

[19] World Bank (1999), para 24.

[20] Ibid.

[21] For WTO accession process of Vietnam, refer Thanh (2005).

[22] Anh (2020), p. 68.

United States, the EU, China, Japan, India, Korea, and Australia,[23] to establish the terms of its entry. As a WTO member, Vietnam continued implementing trade policy reforms for greater transparency and liberalisation. These reforms were reflected in multilateral commitments related to laws and institutions and commitments to opening up the goods and services markets. Trade liberalisation efforts included the establishment of a predictable and transparent regime for international trade, significant tariff reductions, the elimination of export subsidies, and the phased opening of the services market.[24]

In addition to its trade relationships with WTO members and cooperation within ASEAN, the Vietnamese government has been highly proactive in negotiating trade and investment agreements. These efforts have led to the second wave of integration, characterised by Vietnam joining new-generation FTAs with comprehensive scopes. These FTAs address traditional trade issues, as covered by WTO agreements, as well as competition, public procurement, human rights, the social dimension, and sustainable development provisions.

Since 2010, Vietnam has participated in the negotiation of the Trans-Pacific Strategic Economic Partnership Agreement (TPP), which was later renamed the Comprehensive and Progressive Agreement for Trans-Pacific Partnership (CPTPP or TPP-11) following the withdrawal of the United States. This agreement includes 11 Asia–Pacific economies: Australia, Brunei, Canada, Chile, Japan, Malaysia, Mexico, New Zealand, Peru, Singapore, and Vietnam. The CPTPP aims to provide freer trade and investment access within the region. The agreement entered into force on December 30, 2018, for the first six ratifying countries (Australia, Canada, Mexico, Japan, Singapore, and New Zealand). Vietnam ratified the agreement, making it the seventh member, with the CPTPP taking effect on January 14, 2019. The CPTPP is considered a thorough FTA that supports digital trade and includes high-standard provisions for investors, supply chains, goods, rules of origin, certification, services, labour, and environmental protections. It also covers many institutional aspects and is expected to positively impact member countries' economies while presenting significant challenges, particularly for less developed countries like Vietnam.

Another notable agreement is the FTA between the Eurasian Economic Union (EAEU), its member states, and Vietnam. This agreement was signed on May 29, 2015, and entered into force on October 6, 2016. Under this agreement, Vietnam agreed to immediately eliminate 59% of duties on goods from EAEU members and gradually reduce the rates on 29% of imported goods to zero for 5 to 10 years, depending on the product involved.

Around the same time, in 2015, Vietnam and the European Member States concluded negotiations on the EU - Vietnam Free Trade Agreement.[25] This agreement was split into two separate agreements at the EU's request due to new issues related

[23] Abbott et al. (2006), p. 11.

[24] World Bank (2011), pp. 16–17.

[25] The negotiation was started since October 2010.

to the EU's competence to ratify FTAs: the EVFTA and the Investment Protection Agreement (EVIPA), which includes provisions for investment protection and investor-state dispute settlement mechanisms. Both agreements were officially signed in Hanoi on June 30, 2019. The EVFTA entered into force on August 1, 2020, while the EVIPA is expected to be ratified by the EU Parliament and Member States' parliaments within the next two years. As of February 2022, twelve EU Member States had ratified the EVIPA.[26]

The CPTPP and the EVFTA are among the most comprehensive FTAs Vietnam has entered into force since joining the WTO. Concurrently, Vietnam actively participated in the negotiations of several other agreements, including the RCEP.[27] The RCEP includes ASEAN member countries and six additional states with which ASEAN has existing FTAs: China, South Korea, Japan, India, Australia, and New Zealand. These agreements extend Vietnam's commitments beyond WTO obligations, covering areas such as trade in services, investment, intellectual property rights, competition, state-owned enterprises, labour rights, and sustainable development.

These integration initiatives have transformed Vietnam into an open economy with a high degree of liberalisation. As a result, Vietnam's business environment and economic institutions have become more aligned with global practices and fundamental market economy standards. By 2019, Vietnam had established trade and investment relationships with approximately 230 countries and territories across five continents. These FTAs have significantly boosted Vietnam's export value, created employment opportunities, increased incomes, and attracted more significant foreign direct investment. They have also provided a conducive environment for refining economic institutions and enhancing the nation's competitive capabilities.

While scholars have raised concerns about managing overlapping obligations within the framework of numerous concluded treaties, signing international trade and investment agreements remains a crucial component of Vietnam's long-term strategy to enhance institutional capacity. Legal reforms have played a pivotal role in Vietnam's transformation to meet bilateral and multilateral commitments. This journey began with introducing customs tariff reductions in 1988, eliminating the state monopoly over international trade in 1989, and establishing export processing zones in 1990. Notably, the legal reform process gained significant momentum following the US Vietnam BTA.[28]

In March 2002, Decision No. 35/2002/QĐ-TTg concerning the Government Action Program for implementing the US - Vietnam BTA was issued. Accessing the WTO further motivated the country to pursue comprehensive legal and institutional reforms. Since then, key legislation such as the Law on Enterprise, Commercial Law, Law on Foreign Investment, Law on Bankruptcy, Law on Tax, Law on Banking, and the Civil Code have been revised.

---

[26] See European Commission (2020).

[27] Entry into force on 1 January 2022.

[28] Abbott et al. (2006), p. 7.

Specifically, on December 3, 2004, the National Assembly enacted the Competition Law (Law No. 27/2004/QH11). In 2005, Vietnam introduced the Law on Investment, replacing the 1996 Law on Foreign Investment and the 1994 Law on Promotion of Domestic Investment. This new investment law established equal investment rules for domestic and foreign investors: "This law applies to investors and organisations and individuals engaged in business investment activities in the Vietnamese territory." These significant amendments created a trade policy and legal system consistent with international practices, facilitating Vietnam's smooth operation within WTO market principles.[29]

In 2013, the National Assembly ratified the 2013 Constitution and enacted several laws to institutionalise its provisions. Following these constitutional changes, Vietnam revised trade and commercial management laws to enhance its legal framework. Notably, on November 26, 2014, the National Assembly approved amendments to the 2005 Law on Investment and the 2005 Law on Enterprise by introducing Law No. 67/2014/QH13 on Investment. This law governs business investment activities within Vietnam and offshore business investments from Vietnam.

Subsequently, on June 12, 2017, the National Assembly ratified Law No. 05/2017/QH14 on Foreign Trade Management. This law oversees foreign trade operations, promotes foreign trade activities, and addresses dispute resolution concerning the application of foreign trade management measures. It applies to state management agencies, traders engaged in foreign trade activities, and other relevant domestic and foreign organisations and individuals.

Over more than 30 years of reform, Vietnam has amended its Constitution three times and issued or amended over 150 laws and regulations, along with more than 70 ordinances. These legislative efforts have laid the foundation for establishing and promoting a socialist-oriented market economy. Consequently, they have positively impacted ongoing reforms, gradually enhancing market economy institutions and improving the country's long-term economic competitiveness. The result is a business environment that is increasingly fair, transparent, predictable, and aligned with international standards and practices.[30]

In its pursuit of economic growth, the Vietnamese government has prioritised investment and business environment improvements alongside legal reforms. Recognising the importance of administrative reform, initiatives were launched as early as 1990 to lay the groundwork for economic transformation. The 8th Plenum of the Central Party Committee emphasised this objective, leading to the approval of the Master Programme on Public Administration Reform for 2001–2010 through Decision No. 136/2001/QĐ-TTg signed by the Prime Minister on September 17, 2001.[31] The reform agenda aimed to evolve Vietnam's centrally planned public administration system into a "*democratic, clean, strong, professionalised, modernised, effective and efficient public administration system which operates in line*

[29] Anh (2020), p. 70.

[30] Ibid.

[31] Acuña-Alfaro (2009), p. 5.

with the principle of the State socialist ruled-of-law under the leadership of the Party; public cadres and civil servants will have appropriate capacities and ethical qualities able to respond to the requirements of the cause of national building and development." While progress has been noted in enhancing public administration and restructuring administrative apparatus, the pace has been gradual. It has yet to fully meet Vietnam's socio-economic development and global integration needs.[32]

A significant challenge remains the capacity limitations among current civil servants.[33] Looking forward, the next phase of public administration reform in Vietnam is envisioned to modernise the public sector by enhancing its policy implementation responsibilities and promoting active engagement of non-state actors in evaluating public administration performance.[34] Since 2018, the government has initiated preparations for e-government implementation. On August 28, 2018, Prime Minister Nguyen Xuan Phuc signed Decision 1072/QĐ-TTg to establish the National Committee on E-Government. This committee is tasked with researching and proposing guidelines, strategies, and mechanisms to foster a legal framework conducive to e-government development.[35] Concurrently, the Vietnamese government and individual ministries have endeavoured to reduce and streamline administrative procedures, facilitating business operations and other sectors within Vietnam.[36] The combined efforts of economic and legal reforms, alongside Vietnam's international integration process, have significantly bolstered the country's economic prowess. Vietnam has transitioned from a war-torn centrally planned economy to a middle-income nation, with per capita income nearly quintupling to 4163.5 USD (in 2022).[37]

In Asia, Vietnam presents a compelling proposition for investors, underscored by its low cost of doing business, robust economic expansion, and deregulated economic environment.[38] Strategic advantages such as competitive production costs, a prime location in Southeast Asia, strong economic fundamentals, and a burgeoning domestic consumer market further enhance its appeal.[39] Achieving a rank of 68 out of 190 countries in the World Bank's Ease of Doing Business index in 2018[40] highlights the efficacy of Vietnam's efforts in fostering trade and improving the investment climate.

According to the General Statistics Office of Vietnam, the country's GDP grew 7.5% in 2018 and 7.4% in 2019. However, the GDP contracted to approximately

---

[32] Ibid.

[33] The authors point out that a number of severe shortcomings such as poor human resource management and development, inadequate remuneration, low motivation, poor work ethics and performances, as well as a lack of transparency and systemic corruption that hampers the effectiveness of the government. Ibid., pp. 199, 210.

[34] Ibid, p. 40.

[35] Prime Minister of Vietnam (2018) Decision No. 1072/2018/QĐ-TTg, Article 2.

[36] EuroCham (2019), p. 20.

[37] World Bank (2022a).

[38] EuroCham (2019), p. 19.

[39] Ibid.

[40] World Bank (2018).

2.6-2.9% in 2020 and 2021 due to the Covid-19 pandemic impact, rebounding significantly to 8% in 2022.[41] With an average GDP growth rate of 6.1% from 2013 to 2022, Vietnam has surpassed the Asia–Pacific-average of 4.4%, solidifying its position as one of the world's fastest-growing economies.[42]

Moreover, recent data published by the World Bank indicates that from 2011 to 2022,[43] the net inflow of FDI into Vietnam has exhibited consistent growth, rising from 7.43 billion USD in 2011 to 17.9 billion USD in 2022. This growth trajectory experienced temporary declines in 2020 (15.8 billion USD) and 2021 (15.66 billion USD) due to the adverse effects of the COVID-19 pandemic. These fluctuations are partly attributed to the global economic landscape, which has witnessed significant shifts in recent years, including the United States–China Trade war and instability in Europe stemming from the Russia–Ukraine conflict, thereby positioning Asia as an emerging hub for global development.

Since 2022, FDI inflows into Vietnam are expected to resume their upward. This resurgence can be attributed to Vietnam's robust political stability and effective policies aimed to attract FDI. Vietnam has established itself as a reliable destination for foreign investors. Notably, Vietnam has benefited from the relocation of production facilities from China to other Asian countries due to the repercussions of the United States–China Trade War since 2018. Nevertheless, like many other economies, the country has encountered significant challenges stemming from the adoption of protectionist tariff measures introduced during the second term of United States President Donald J. Trump.

As outlined in the Vietnam 2035 Report, the reform agenda in Vietnam is founded on three vital pillars: achieving a balance between economic prosperity and environmental sustainability, promoting equity and social inclusion, and enhancing the capacity and accountability of the state. However, Vietnam's ongoing economic development faces various challenges, including issues related to the management of state-owned enterprises, the efficiency of public investments, and transparency deficiencies. Nonetheless, international commitments, particularly those tied to new-generation agreements such as the EVFTA and the CPTPP, are expected to play a central role in instigating a fresh wave of economic and governance reforms in Vietnam. This builds upon the successes achieved by the country upon its accession to the WTO.

---

[41] Focus Economic.

[42] Lee (2024).

[43] World Bank (2022b).

3.2 The Evolution of Vietnam's Policy and Legal Framework for Foreign Direct Investment

3.2.1 Vietnam's Policy on Foreign Direct Investment

As previously mentioned, since 1986, the Vietnamese government has consistently adhered to a policy of integrating into the regional and global economy. This enduring commitment, complemented by the objective of attracting foreign investments, has remained unwavering. Indeed, the signing and ratifying IIAs have emerged as strategic instruments in Vietnam's pursuit of its integration strategy.[44] In the early 1990s, the act of signing IIAs served a dual purpose, not only as a means to attract foreign investments but also as a diplomatic tool to foster the normalisation of relations with Western countries following more than two decades of United States-imposed embargoes.[45]

Like numerous other developing nations, the Vietnamese government highly values FDI capital. It anticipates that foreign investment endeavours will facilitate the mobilisation of capital, infusion of technology, introduction of advanced management practices, and expansion of export markets to propel industrialisation and modernisation. This approach has been enshrined in various documents of the Communist Party, which emphasise the significant role of FDI resources. These documents acknowledge FDI as indispensable to Vietnam's development and have formulated specific investment attraction policies. The 13th Party Congress underscored the significance of FDI capital, particularly emphasising that "the foreign-invested economy constitutes an essential component of the overall economy, exerting a significant influence in mobilising investment capital, infusing technological advancements, implementing modern management methodologies, and broadening export markets."

Recognising the critical role of FDI capital in economic development, the Vietnamese government has diligently enacted a series of policies to attract foreign investments. These comprehensive policies encompass various measures, such as import tax exemptions and reductions, corporate income tax incentives, and preferential land lease arrangements. Furthermore, there has been a concerted effort to streamline investment procedures, specifically focusing on creating a business-friendly environment that eliminates obstacles hindering the establishment and operation of investment projects.

The process of international economic integration has also involved the liberalisation of the market mechanisms, offering foreign investors lucrative business opportunities within Vietnam. Indeed, Vietnam's commitments under the General Agreement on Trade in Services (GATS) and other FTAs it has entered have opened doors for foreign investors in various service sectors, including insurance, banking,

[44] Dung and Huong (2021), p. 43.

[45] Mutrap (2008).

education, logistics, tourism, telecommunications, and so forth. Throughout this progression, the legal framework governing investment activities has undergone significant enhancements to ensure the efficient organisation of such endeavours. Critical components of this framework include legislation related to investment activities, enterprise law, corporate income tax law, and import-export tax laws, which have been progressively introduced and amended over time.

In addition to cultivating and progressively enhancing its domestic preferential investment environment, Vietnam has actively engaged in negotiated and signed international investment treaties with various partners, starting from its BIT with Italy in 1990. According to data sourced from UNCTAD, as of 2023, Vietnam has emerged as a signatory to 67 BITs and Multilateral Investment Treaties (MITs), comprising 39 BITs and 28 treaties incorporating investment provisions.[46] Broadly speaking, Vietnam's framework of international commitments related to investment protection spans multiple levels, encompassing Multilateral Agreement on Investment (MAI), FTAs, and BITs.

Within the realm of MAI, Vietnam, as a member of the ASEAN, signed the ASEAN Comprehensive Investment Agreement (ACIA) on February 26, 2009, which subsequently came into effect on March 29, 2012. Additionally, the country has engaged in "ASEAN-Plus" FTAs with major trading partners, culminating in signing investment agreements between ASEAN and these significant trade counterparts.[47] Noteworthy among the group of FTAs featuring investment protection provisions that Vietnam is a part of are the 2009 ASEAN-New Zealand and Australia FTA (AANZFTA) and the CPTPP. Lastly, within the ambit of BITs, Vietnam has established agreements with a diverse range of nations. These encompass development partners such as Australia, Denmark, Sweden, Finland, the United Kingdom, various European countries (including France, the Netherlands, Germany, and others, which will soon be replaced by the EVIPA, as well as burgeoning economies in the Asian region, including but not limited to Japan, South Korea, Indonesia, Thailand, Malaysia, Laos, and so forth.[48]

Over more than three decades devoted to promoting economic integration and encouraging foreign investment, Vietnam's IIA system has made remarkable progress. It currently ranks as the third-most robust in Asia, trailing only behind China and Korea.[49] However, it is essential to note that the landscape of Vietnam's IIA policy has undergone significant transformations compared to the 1990s. This transformation is closely linked to Vietnam's evolution from a primarily capital-importing nation to one where an increasing number of Vietnamese enterprises are expanding their operations abroad. In 2022 alone, Vietnam's total newly granted and adjusted investment capital in foreign markets reached nearly 534 million USD. Among

[46] See UNCTAD Investment Policy Hub. Vietnam's International Investment Treaties.

[47] See ASEAN - Japan EPA (2008); ASEAN - Hong Kong, China SAR Investment Agreement (2017); ASEAN - Korea Investment Agreement (2009).

[48] See UNCTAD Investment Policy Hub. Vietnam's International Investment Treaties.

[49] Dung and Huong (2021), p. 46.

these investments, state-owned enterprises accounted for 70.8 million USD, constituting approximately 13% of the total registered capital invested overseas by Vietnamese enterprises during that year.

As of December 20, 2022, Vietnam has amassed a portfolio of 1611 valid overseas investment projects, representing a cumulative Vietnamese investment capital exceeding 21.75 billion USD. Among these projects, 141 are associated with state-owned enterprises, collectively contributing nearly 11.67 billion USD to the nation's overall foreign investment capital, representing a substantial 53.7% share. Notably, Vietnam's foreign investments have found their focal points in sectors such as mining industries (comprising 32% of investments) and agriculture, forestry, and fisheries (contributing 15.8% of investments). Geographically, the countries receiving the largest share of Vietnam's foreign investments include Laos (accounting for 24.6%), Cambodia (13.5%), and Venezuela (8.4%).[50]

In light of these developments, it has become imperative for Vietnam's BITs/IIAs to adopt a more balanced approach in the current integration phase. Beyond their traditional role of providing investment guarantees, contemporary BITs/IIAs must also be structured to ensure the safeguarding of investments and the protection of Vietnamese investors operating within the territories of their partners. Interviews with officials from the Ministry of Planning and Investment (MPI) revealed that MPI, as the state agency responsible for negotiating investment treaties, aimed to enhance investment protection standards during negotiations with Mozambique (2007), Venezuela (2008), Slovakia (2009), Kazakhstan (2009), and the Eurasian Economic Union (2015).[51] As a result, these treaties offer extensive safeguards for foreign investors and their investments, as evidenced by the broad definition of investment and the inclusion of provisions ensuring full compensation for expropriation, FET, robust security protection for investors' assets, and unhindered transfer of investment capital.[52]

In terms of the substantive protection commitments within the IIAs that Vietnam actively participates in, it is evident that, in addition to stipulating definitions for "investment" and "investor," analysis reveals that virtually all publicly accessible BITs involving Vietnam contain robust commitments aimed at ensuring the protection of foreign investments. These commitments encompass a range of critical provisions, such as MFN and NT, FET, full protection and security, provisions for repatriation of capital and compensation for losses, explicit commitments against expropriation and the commitment to adhere to the ISDS mechanism. These extensive networks of commitments serve as a firm legal foundation for foreign investment activities within Vietnam and furnish the necessary legal framework for resolving investment disputes in which one of the parties involved is the Vietnamese state.

[50] Foreign Investment Department, Ministry of Planning and Investment (2022).

[51] Dung (2022), pp. 273–274.

[52] Ibid.

Furthermore, upon conducting an in-depth review, it becomes apparent that the submission of investment disputes to the ICSID for conciliation or arbitration proceedings has been a prevalent choice under Vietnam's IIAs, often exercised by investors and the host state.[53] Nevertheless, it is crucial to note that Vietnam has yet to become a party to the 1965 Convention on the Settlement of Investment Disputes between States and Nationals of Other States, commonly known as the ICSID Convention. Consequently, although the ICSID mechanism is acknowledged in the relevant BITs, its practical utilisation for dispute resolution remains unfeasible in Vietnam. Consequently, despite the availability of ISDS provisions, any investor seeking final binding arbitration will need to resort to alternative arbitration mechanisms.

Most of Vietnam's BITs offer investors the option of arbitration under the UNCITRAL Rules,[54] and in certain cases, arbitration under the ICSID Additional Facility is explicitly designated.[55] Furthermore, Vietnam's BITs frequently provide various dispute resolution avenues should an amicable settlement prove unattainable. These options include resolving disputes before national courts or the contracting parties, as well as recourse to an ad-hoc arbitral tribunal, constituted explicitly by the two contracting parties or, in certain instances, the use of pre-established arbitral tribunals agreed upon by both contracting parties.[56]

Concerning the landscape of ISDS cases involving Vietnam, data compiled by the UNCTAD reveals a noteworthy trajectory. This analysis spans from the inception of the first ISDS case against the Vietnamese government, initiated by an investor holding Dutch nationality back in 2004, precisely the case of *Trinh and Binh Chau v. Vietnam* (I).[57] As of present, Vietnam has encountered a total of 13 ISDS cases. Within this set of 13 cases, 06 cases remain pending, 01 case discontinued, 3 cases decided in favour of the Vietnamese government, while one case has resulted in a finding that a state measure did indeed violate the relevant BIT.[58] In these ISDS disputes, foreign investors have invoked various grounds for their claims against Vietnam. These claims are primarily rooted in a range of substantive principles enshrined in the IIAs, including NT, MFN, FET, full protection and security and commitment not to expropriate. This pattern of claims aligns with the broader global landscape of investment disputes.

---

[53] For instance, Article 9.19(4) CPTPP; Article 14.3(1) Vietnam - Japan BIT (2003); Article 4 Chapter 4 on Development of Investment Relations Vietnam - U.S BTA (2000).

[54] Article 14.3 Vietnam - Japan BIT (2003); Article 8.2 Vietnam - France BIT (1992); Article 9.19(4) CPTPP; Article 4 Chapter 4 on Development of Investment Relations Vietnam - U.S BTA (2003).

[55] Article 9.19(4) CPTPP; Article 4 Chapter 4 on Development of Investment Relations, Vietnam - U.S BTA (2003).

[56] Malintoppi and Tan (2016), p. 434.

[57] *Trinh Vinh Binh and Binh Chau Joint Stock Company v. Socialist Republic of Viet Nam* (I) [2004] SCC, Award, 1 March 2007.

[58] *Trinh Vinh Binh and Binh Chau Joint Stock Company v. Socialist Republic of Viet Nam* (II) [2014] PCA Case No. 2015-23. For other cases, see Table 3.2 below.

ISDS cases involving Vietnam reveal that these disputes stem from both sides: the Government, particularly state agencies, and foreign investments.[59] For the Government and state agencies overseeing foreign investment activities in Vietnam, conflicts typically arise due to the following factors:

(i) Investment agreements or contracts are sometimes drafted with a degree of laxity, occasionally making excessive commitments and investment assurances during the investment promotion phase.
(ii) Changes in the legal framework and inconsistent law enforcement contribute to disputes.
(iii) State agencies demonstrate a lack of goodwill in addressing investor concerns, and there is a lack of standardised procedures for resolution.
(iv) Certain local authorities do not sufficiently screen investors for their capacity and past investment practices abroad, leading to the approval of numerous unscrupulous or dishonest investors. This includes investors with a history of legal violations in other countries who subsequently engage in misconduct during the investment process and then resort to legal action against the government.

In some cases, foreign investors lack a clear understanding of Vietnam's legal landscape. Some investors utilise ISDS litigation to apply pressure on Vietnamese state agencies. Notably, the presence of ISDS cases involving Vietnam highlights the complex nature of investor-state relations and emphasises the significance of these IIAs in regulating and safeguarding foreign investments. This practice in Vietnam reflects broader trends in international investment activities, illustrating the critical role played by ISDS mechanisms in addressing disputes and upholding the principles of investment protection that underpin these agreements on a global scale.[60]

As shown in Table 3.2, the number of ISDS cases involving Viet Nam has markedly increased since 2017. In response to this trend, the Vietnamese government has demonstrated growing proactivity in pursuing ISDS reform initiatives on both international and domestic fronts. This proactive stance reflects Vietnam's commitment to addressing the challenges posed by ISDS disputes and fortifying its position in the evolving landscape of international investment governance.

Internationally, Vietnam's engagement has been increasingly robust. Since 2018, after years of participating as an observer, Vietnam officially assumed the status of a member of the United Nations Commission on International Trade Law (UNCITRAL). Within UNCITRAL, Vietnam has taken on a more active role, participating in negotiations within specific working groups, notably Working Groups II, III and V,[61] and also in BIT negotiations. An emblematic example of this proactive approach is Vietnam's acceptance of the EU's proposal on ICS within the framework of the EVIPA. Additionally, Vietnam has been receptive to new

59 Tuyet (2020), p. 12.

60 UNCTAD (2019).

61 Ha (2022).

Table 3.2 Viet Nam ISDS cases as respondent state[a]

No.	Year of initiation	Case name	IIA breaches alleged	Outcome of original proceedings	Home state of investor
1.	2023	*Power China and others v. Viet Nam (II)*	N.A	Pending	China
2.	2022	*Immobilien Partner and others v. Viet Nam*	N.A	Pending	Germany Portugal
3.	2022	*Itaco and Dangelas v. Viet Nam*	N.A	Pending	United States of America
4.	2022	*Power China and China Railway v. Viet Nam (I)*	N.A	Pending	China
5.	2019	*Dangelas and others v. Viet Nam*	– National treatment – Fair and equitable treatment/Minimum standard of treatment, including denial of justice claims – Full protection and security, or similar – Arbitrary, unreasonable and/or discriminatory measures – Indirect expropriation	Pending	United States of America
6.	2018	*Shin Dong Baig v. Viet Nam*	N.A	Pending	Korea, Republic of
7.	2017	*Conoco Phillips and Perenco v. Viet Nam*	N.A	Pending	United Kingdom
8.	2014	*Crockrell v. Viet Nam*	N.A	Discontinued	United States of America
9.	2014	*Trinh and Binh Chau v. Vietnam (II)*	– Direct expropriation – Fair and equitable treatment/Minimum standard of treatment, including denial of justice claims	Breaches found: – Direct expropriation – Fair and equitable treatment/Minimum standard of treatment, including denial of justice claims	Netherlands

(continued)

Table 3.2 (continued)

No.	Year of initiation	Case name	IIA breaches alleged	Outcome of original proceedings	Home state of investor
10.	2013	*Recofi v. Viet Nam*	N.A	Jurisdiction declined All claims dismissed at the merits stage	France
11.	2011	*Dialasie v. Viet Nam*	– Indirect expropriation – Fair and equitable treatment/Minimum standard of treatment, including denial of justice claims – Full protection and security, or similar		France
12.	2010	*McKenzie v. Viet Nam*	– Indirect expropriation – Fair and equitable treatment/Minimum standard of treatment, including denial of justice claims – Others	Jurisdiction declined	United States of America
13.	2004	*Trinh and Binh Chau v. Vietnam (I)*	Direct expropriation	Not applicable - settled or discontinued before decision on liability	Netherlands

[a] Compiled from UNCTAD Investment Policy Hub. Vietnam's ISDS Cases

developments in the formulation of substantive investment protection obligations, reflecting its commitment to keeping pace with international standards.

At the domestic level, the Vietnamese government has exhibited an increased dedication to implementing solutions designed to assist the state in resolving international investment disputes. Commencing in 2014, the Vietnamese government initiated research and issued regulations pertaining to the coordination among ministries, government branches, and local authorities in handling international investment disputes, as detailed in Decision 04/2014/QĐ-TTg.[62] More recently, this regulatory framework was updated through the issuance of Decision 14/2020/QĐ-TTg, which came into effect on June 1, 2020.[63] These actions underscore the

[62] Prime Minister of Vietnam (2014) Decision No. 04/QĐ-TTg.

[63] Prime Minister of Vietnam (2020) Decision No. 14/QĐ-TTg.

government's recognition of the significance of preventing ISDS disputes from arising and highlight its commitment to establishing the necessary mechanisms to support the government in future ISDS cases.

One of the most challenging issues facing the government is the lack of sufficient knowledge among government officials regarding investment obligations in general and Vietnam's commitments under IIAs in particular. Insufficient awareness of the state's obligations under IIAs, such as FET, NT, and MFN, coupled with a failure to consider these requirements in investment management decision-making, can easily result in decisions that risk violating IIAs. In response to this challenge, the Vietnamese government has recently intensified efforts to enhance officials' understanding of Vietnam's commitments under IIAs. Notably, in 2022, a Handbook on Obligations in International Investment Treaties was compiled with financial support from the Australian Government and distributed to officials in various provinces and cities across the country. This handbook, drafted by international and domestic experts, provides a concise and practical explanation of Vietnam's investment treaty obligations and how they apply to government decision-making processes.

The objective of compiling this handbook is to disseminate knowledge about investment protection obligations to officials across all branches of government (executive, legislative, and judiciary), at all levels (central, local, regional), and across various regulatory areas (administrative, environmental, taxation, labour, etc), as well as across all sectors of the economy (natural resources, services, manufacturing, etc). This initiative by the Vietnamese government is commendable as it aims to raise awareness among government officials in their day-to-day activities and functions,[64] about Vietnam's obligations under international investment treaties. However, measuring the effectiveness of these activities remains challenging. Continuous efforts to foster knowledge about IIAs among individuals involved in investment management activities are necessary and should be organised regularly.

Regarding the current status of foreign investment activities in Vietnam, data provided by the Foreign Investment Agency indicates that as of March 2022, there are 36.881 valid investment projects in Vietnam originating from 143 countries and territories. The total registered capital for these projects amounts to an impressive 444.1 billion USD.[65] Regarding capital structure, data from March 2023 highlights that foreign investors have allocated their investments across 17 of the 21 national economic sectors. Among these sectors, the processing and manufacturing industry emerges as the front-runner, boasting a total investment capital of nearly 4 billion USD. This accounts for a substantial 73% of the overall registered investment capital, although it reflects a decrease of 25% compared to the same period. The real

[64] Viet Nam's Ministry for Planning and Industry (2021).

[65] Foreign Investment Agency (2023).

estate business sector occupies the second position with a total investment capital of nearly 766 million USD, constituting almost 14.1% of the total registered investment capital.[66] However, it experienced a notable decline of 71.6% during the same period. Meanwhile, the wholesale and retail sectors, along with warehousing and transportation, have attracted increased investment capital during this time, ranking third and fourth with total registered capital of nearly 276 million USD (a twofold increase over the same period) and almost 151 million USD (a growth of 37 million USD), respectively. The remaining investments are distributed across various other industries.[67]

The government's open and incentive-driven policy towards foreign investors has resulted in significant profit gains from attracting FDI capital in recent years. However, on a broader scale, the use of FDI capital in Vietnam remains less than fully effective. Notably, the proportion of foreign investment in critical sectors such as agriculture, fish and seafood processing, renewable energy, and software production remains relatively low. Additionally, attracting foreign investment to economically challenged and underdeveloped regions proves to be more challenging than in other areas. These limitations can be attributed to factors such as geographical location, infrastructure deficiencies, limitations in skilled human resources, and complications in inter-regional transportation and logistics. Moreover, sector-specific policies lack synchronisation and consistency, and the regulatory environment for state-owned enterprises does not always provide foreign investors with a truly conducive operational landscape.[68] Hence, it remains imperative to continue researching and adjusting policies to attract foreign investment to ensure they receive attention and contribute effectively to Vietnam's economic development goals.

3.2.2 Vietnam's Investment Legislation

Vietnam's legislative framework for investment has evolved over the past 37 years, underscoring its commitment to the aforementioned policies. This framework began to take shape during the "Đổi mới" period and has since been refined. It facilitates investment activities and reflects Vietnam's shifting approach to attracting investments. This section delineates the evolution and maturation of Vietnam's legislative investment framework from the inception of the "Đổi mới" period to the contemporary era. Additionally, it examines legislative instruments encompassing environmental protection and delineates the obligations incumbent upon foreign investors within the purview of investment law. This multifaceted analysis serves to elucidate

[66] Ibid.

[67] Ibid.

[68] See, for instance, the constraints in the policy implementation for advancing offshore wind power development in Vietnam in Huong and Phong (2023).

the dynamic transformations witnessed in Vietnam's investment attraction policies throughout its historical trajectory.

- **Law on Foreign Investment 1987 and Two Amendments**

In the early stages of economic reforms, Vietnam faced a shortage of investment capital for social development and infrastructure. Vietnam's inflation rate during this period reached over 453.50% in 1986.[69] To tackle these challenges and mobilise domestic and foreign capital, Vietnam introduced numerous incentive policies. Foreign investment, in particular, played a crucial role. Consequently, the first significant legislative step following the announcement of the "Đổi mới" policy was the enactment of the Law on Foreign Investment (LFI) in Vietnam in 1987. This law laid the foundation for encouraging foreign investment in Vietnam during the initial phase of economic reform.[70] Although significant, the LFI 1987 was not Vietnam's first legal framework for attracting foreign investments. Prior to this, Vietnam issued the Investment Charter in 1977, facilitating the signing of various investment agreements. However, no investment licenses were directly granted under the 1977 Investment Charter.[71]

It is essential to highlight that in 1987, Vietnam operated under the 1980 Constitution, which recognised only two economic sectors within a centrally planned economy: the state-owned and collective economies. In this context, introducing the LFI 1987 in Vietnam, which primarily targeted FDI, can be viewed as a pioneering and innovative approach.[72]

The promulgation of the LFI 1987 shows synchronous innovative thinking in economic development policies associated with attracting foreign investment. This law, comprised of 42 articles, primarily delineated legal modalities of investments within Vietnam's territory (Chapter 2). It significantly encouraged foreign entities and individuals to establish 100% foreign-owned enterprises in Vietnam, which is in stark contrast to the more gradual approaches adopted by other Asian countries like Thailand and Indonesia. For instance, durings this same period, Thailand only encouraged foreign private sector funds by allowing share investment as a form of capital expansion.[73] Moreover, the law introduced a pioneering provision allowing capital contributions through land use rights tailored to Vietnam's specific circumstances.[74]

In terms of investment protection, the LFI 1987 encompassed comprehensive principles and measures. It assured ownership rights, facilitated investment

---

[69] Hung and Cong (2024).

[70] Quang (2021), p. 44.

[71] Prof. Nguyen Mai, former Deputy Chairman of the State Committee for Cooperation and Investment (SCCI) in Nguyen Duc (2017).

[72] Ibid.

[73] Thailand's policy on economic development prior to 1987 was characterized by a limited dependence on FDI due to the substantial loans obtained from foreign countries. See Government of Thailand.

[74] Hoang (2014).

activities in Vietnam (Article 2.1), committed to non-expropriation (Article 21), provided fair and equitable treatment to foreign investors (Article 20), allowed the repatriation of capital and profits, and enabled foreign employees to remit their income (Article 22). Additionally, the law incorporated mechanisms for dispute resolution, accommodating disputes arising from business cooperation contracts, joint venture contracts, or disputes among joint venture enterprises, enterprises with 100% foreign capital, and Vietnamese economic organisations. These mechanisms included negotiation, conciliation, and arbitration.

The State Committee for Cooperation and Investment (SCCI) was instituted alongside establishing legislative instruments to facilitate investment activities in March 1989. Conceived in compliance with Article 36 of the LFI 1987 and further substantiated by Decree 139 issued by the Council of Ministers, the SCCI functioned as the central agency overseeing foreign investment initiatives during this period. Operating as an inter-ministerial authorisation committee vested with substantial authority, it expeditiously approved investment projects. Subsequently, provincial foreign economic relations committees were instituted to monitor the law's implementation and anticipate the inflow of foreign capital. On November 1, 1995, the government issued Decree No. 75/CP, delineating the functions, duties, powers, and organisational structure of the Ministry of Planning and Investment following the merger of the State Committee on Planning and the SCCI.

The imperatives of rectifying inconsistencies within vital legal sources governing investment activities, coupled with the need to enhance the legal framework to align with the economic, social, and financial objectives of investment activities as derived from the practical application of the LFI 1987, necessitated two significant amendments to the law on foreign direct investment in 1990 and 1992. Notable modifications encompassed extending the operating term for foreign-invested enterprises from a maximum of 20 years, as stipulated in Article 15 of the LFI 1987, to a maximum of 50 years, as specified in Article 15 of the LFI 1992 (amendment). Furthermore, the LFI 1992 (amendment) codified regulations concerning export processing zones (Article 19 (a) LFI 1992 (amendment)) and was designed to foster confidence among foreign investors contemplating investments in such zones. Moreover, Article 19(b) was introduced in the revised LFI of 1992, governing the build-operate-transfer investment model, thereby establishing a legal framework conducive to expanding innovative investment approaches that would attract a diverse array of investors across various sectors, especially in the infrastructure domain - an imperative for Vietnam's economic development at that juncture. Another noteworthy addition in the LFI 1992 (amendment), in contrast to the LFI 1987, was the state's commitment to taking appropriate measures to redress the rights of investors in cases where changes in Vietnamese regulations undermined the interests of parties involved in business cooperation contracts and licensed foreign-invested enterprises (Article 21). This overt alignment with a principle widely applied in international investment activities underscored Vietnam's reverence for customary international law and its commitment to fostering an enabling legal foundation to safeguard the legitimate rights of foreign investors.

Concurrently, sub-legislative documents delineating the implementation of the LFI in Vietnam underwent corresponding amendments to align with the evolving legal landscape. Many domestic regulations governing investment activities were promulgated in tandem with these amendments. For instance, the Company Law (Law No. 47-LCT/HĐNN8 (December 21, 1990)) and the Law on Private Enterprises (Law No. 48-LCT/HĐNN8 (December 21, 1990)) were among the notable legal instruments adopted in 1990.

Significantly, in 1992, the Socialist Republic of Vietnam made amendments to its constitution, explicitly stating: "*The State encourages foreign organisations and individuals to invest capital and technology in Vietnam in accordance with Vietnamese law, international law, and practice; ensures legal ownership of capital, assets, and other rights of foreign organisations and individuals. Enterprises with foreign investment shall not be subject to nationalisation*" (Article 25 of the 1992 Constitution of Vietnam). This constitutional provision unequivocally affirms the government's policy of promoting foreign investment in Vietnam, underscoring its commitment to adhere to Vietnamese and international legal standards for safeguarding the rights and interests of foreign investors.[75] Due to these legal developments, the period characterised by the implementation of the LFI 1987, with its subsequent amendments, saw the emergence of the first wave of investments in Vietnam, encompassing 459 investment projects with a total capital of 5.28 billion USD.

- Law on Foreign Investment 1996 and Law on Foreign Investment 2000 (Amendment)

The Laws on Foreign Investment in 1996 and subsequent amendments in 2000 were vital in the evolution of Vietnam's foreign investment framework. In the context of a centrally planned economy governed by the 1980 Constitution, which recognised only two economic sectors, state-owned and collective, enacting the LFI 1987 marked a significant departure from traditional economic policies. However, after a decade of implementation, it became clear that improvements were necessary. These included vague and non-specific provisions, overlapping regulations, complex administrative procedures, and a lack of clarity in policy and planning.[76] Consequently, investors faced challenges in navigating the intricate system, and state agencies encountered difficulties in performing their duties effectively.

Recognising the critical role of FDI in Vietnam's economic development, the 9th National Assembly, in its 10th session on November 12, 1996, promulgated the Law on Foreign Investment in 1996 (LFI 1996) to replace the LFI 1987 and its 1990 and 1992 amendments. The LFI 1996 introduced a comprehensive set of 68 articles that provided more detailed regulations than its predecessor. It affirmed Vietnam's commitment to attracting foreign investment while protecting investors' rights and simplifying investment procedures. The law also prioritised projects contributing to

[75] Dung and Huong (2021), p. 42.

[76] Hoang (2014).

technological transfer, advanced technological capacity, exports, and economic growth (Article 3 LFI 1996).

This legislation also outlines the government's responsibility to periodically align its economic development plans with the release of lists that include encouraged and particularly encouraged projects, along with those either restricted from foreign investment or subject to conditional FDI.

This strategic approach aims to facilitate foreign investors in selecting projects while providing management agencies with clear guidance for project evaluation and approval. This framework fosters a transparent environment that empowers investors to assess project viability and effectiveness. Furthermore, to direct FDI capital towards BOT projects and investments in remote and underserved regions, LFI 1996 incorporates various special incentives, as outlined in Articles 39 and 46.

Regarding foreign investment management, the LFI 1996 elucidates the coordination mechanisms among ministries, branches, and local authorities by adopting a "one-door" system utilising the State Investment Management Agency as the designated focal point, as mandated by law. This "focal point" agency is pivotal in overseeing the harmonisation of efforts among ministries, branches, and localities throughout the entire foreign direct investment process. This comprehensive coordination encompasses strategy formulation, planning, policy development, issue resolution, monitoring and ensuring compliance with investment license provisions and legal requirements. Its overarching objective is to safeguard the interests of the Vietnamese government and the Vietnamese State. The focal agency collaborates directly with ministries, branches, and local People's Committees to accomplish this. While these entities are entrusted with executing state management functions related to FDI within the boundaries of their mandates, extending from project initiation through implementation to post-production phases, it is vital to clarify that the State Investment Management Agency neither acts as the managing entity for foreign-invested enterprises nor supplants the roles of ministries, branches, and local authorities. Instead, ministries, branches, and People's Committees at the provincial and central levels remain fully accountable for the comprehensive state management of foreign direct investment. They handle various aspects throughout the investment lifecycle, encompassing project implementation and post-production activities.

Regarding investment licensing procedures, the LFI 1996 introduces provisions designed to enhance the principle of democratic centralism, bolster the self-responsibility of the state administrative mechanism, and elevate management efficiency. This is achieved by decentralising investment licensing authority to Provincial People's Committees (PPC), extending the issuance of Investment Licenses for projects located in Industrial Zones and Export-Processing Zones (Article 55). Additionally, the LFI 1996 establishes a more robust legal framework to simplify investment procedures and reinforce investment activities's legality. It incorporates explicit regulations outlining deadlines for issuing investment licenses and related licenses, focusing on streamlining processes and reducing bureaucratic delays.

Furthermore, to augment the accountability of state management agencies, the LFI 1996 grants foreign investors the right to lodge complaints and initiate legal action in cases of protracted procedures causing disruption by state agencies, organisations, or civil servants (Article 64). Moreover, the law prescribes sanctions against those who violate foreign investment regulations, encompassing foreign investors, foreign-invested enterprises, parties involved in business cooperation contracts, organisations, individuals, and state officials (Article 63).

The LFI 1996 also incorporates a noteworthy amendment of regulations governing the principle of unanimity within the Board of Directors of joint venture enterprises, specifically regarding decisions on operational direction, business plans, and key personnel appointments, a provision initially outlined in Article 13 of the LFI 1987. In this context, the LFI 1996 introduces revisions and additions to critical aspects such as the appointment and dismissal of the General Director, First Deputy General Director, Chief Accountant, amendments to the enterprise charter, approval of annual financial income and expenditure statements, project settlements, and borrowing of investment capital. In these scenarios, decision-making follows the principle of consensus among attending Board of Directors members during meetings. Furthermore, the LFI 1996 establishes a mechanism that permits joint venture parties to stipulate in the Enterprise Charter that specific issues necessitating unanimous decisions may instead be subject to majority rule (Article 14).

Additionally, the LFI 1996 formalises the regulations concerning Industrial Parks and Export Processing Zones, extending equivalent incentives for profit tax and import and export duties to both foreign investors and Vietnamese investors engaged in developing industrial park infrastructure and investing in Industrial Zones. These incentives align with the provisions of the Foreign Investment Law and the Industrial Parks Regulations (as exemplified in Decree 192-CP dated December 28, 1994 adopting Industrial Parks Regulations). The primary aim of these adjustments is to address inequalities in the treatment of domestic enterprises and foreign investors conducting business in export processing zones, which disparate laws had previously governed. Specifically, domestic enterprises were subject to the Law on Enterprises, while foreign investors were governed by the Law on Foreign Investment. These adjustments are designed to encourage domestic capital to invest in industrial parks and simultaneously enhance the efficiency of industrial park management and law enforcement.

In addition to the well-recognised build-operate-transfer method established in the LFI 1992 (amendment), the 1996 LFI introduces various other investment methods, such as build-transfer-operate contracts and build-transfer contracts. These provisions aim to diversify investment approaches and expand avenues to attract foreign investment, particularly for infrastructure development projects (Article 19 of the LFI 1996).

Following the enactment of the LFI 1996, although foreign investment played a vital role in contributing positively to the nation's economic development, subsequent years witnessed a continuous decline in the pace of foreign investment inflow into Vietnam. This decline could be attributed to several factors, including challenges arising from the evolving investment landscape and overlapping and inconsistent regulatory frameworks, notably in areas concerning high-income tax, value-added tax, land, foreign exchange, and labour policies. Additionally, external factors such as the regional economic crisis had a detrimental impact on foreign investment.

In response to this challenging environment, in 2000, the National Assembly passed a significant amendment to the 1996 LFI, known as the LFI 2000 (amendment). This amendment swiftly addressed issues and mitigated risks associated with foreign-invested enterprises, particularly concerning foreign currency balance and account management (Articles 33 and 35). Furthermore, it provided solutions to challenges related to land use rights mortgages and compensation for site clearance (as specified in Article 46). Additionally, the LFI 2000 (amendment) extended greater autonomy in foreign-invested enterprises' management and organisational structure, thereby reducing unnecessary state intervention in their operations. Notably, this amendment introduced a range of tax incentives for foreign investment projects, enhancing Vietnam's investment environment's attractiveness and competitiveness as elaborated in Articles 40, 43, 44, and 47 of the LFI 2000 (amendment).

- **Law on Investment 2005**

In 2005, to enhance the domestic legal and institutional framework in preparation for Vietnam's accession to the WTO and meet the non-discrimination principle requirement within this global trade system, the National Assembly approved the Law on Investment 2005 (LOI 2005).[77] This crucial legislation came into effect on July 1, 2006, supplanting the LFI 1996 and the Law on Domestic Investment Promotion. Shortly after that, on September 22, 2006, Decree 108/2006/NĐ-CP was issued to provide detailed guidance on several articles of the LOI 2005, commonly referred to as Decree 108.

The LOI 2005, in conjunction with its implementing regulations, was meticulously designed to further refine the investment and business environment. It aimed to establish legal consistency within the investment framework, fostering a level playing field without discrimination among investors. Additionally, the law sought to streamline investment procedures, fostering an environment conducive to attracting and efficiently utilising investment capital. Moreover, the law was tailored to meet the demands of Vietnam's integration into the global economy while fortifying state oversight of investment activities. Notably, the LOI 2005 significantly deviated from its predecessor, as it focused solely on matters related to investment activities. Organisational and operational aspects of enterprises were transferred to the Law on Enterprises, while tax incentives were incorporated into tax-related legislation. Furthermore, specialised fields such as securities, insurance, banking, and finance were addressed by specific sectoral laws.

Concerning the state's role in investment management, the LOI 2005 delineated the powers and responsibilities of each relevant state authority. Particular emphasis was placed on the role and duties of PPC in overseeing investment activities. These

[77] National Assembly of Vietnam (2005) Law on Investment No. 59/2005/QH11.

Committees, operating as local administrative units, assumed a comprehensive role in managing local socio-economic development, including issuing investment certificates and supervising investment activities within their respective provinces.

One noteworthy feature introduced by the LOI 2005 is the policy of decentralisation, whereby the authority to issue Investment Certificates and oversee investment activities was devolved to the PPC and the Management Board of Industrial Parks, Export Processing Zones, High-Tech Parks, and Economic Zones (hereafter referred to as the Management Board). This decentralisation was a strategic move aligned with administrative reform in economic management. By granting these agencies the direct oversight of investment resources such as land, labour, environment, and planning, and enabling them to closely monitor the conditions and progress of local projects, the policy sought to curtail the number of projects requiring approval from the Prime Minister. Empowering the PPC and the Management Board served a dual purpose: it streamlined governance structures by reducing the burden on central governing agencies, thereby allowing ministries and state management bodies to concentrate on policy formulation, forecasting, and the critical tasks of monitoring and supervising investment activities.

The LOI 2005 also introduced a more precise delineation of the rights and responsibilities of investors compared to its predecessors. Under this law, investors were granted various rights, including the autonomy to engage in business investments, access to investment resources, utilisation of credit capital, land, and multiple assets. They also possessed rights relating to labour management, account management, foreign currency transactions, and the facilitation of import, export, advertising, processing, and reprocessing activities. This comprehensive specification of investor rights aimed to provide greater clarity and security in the investment process, fostering a more conducive environment for economic activities.

It is worth noting that the LOI 2005 introduced a significant development in Vietnam's legislative landscape by establishing a more comprehensive framework for ISDS dispute resolution mechanisms within its domestic context. This progress is embodied in Article 12 of this law. For the first time, the LOI 2005 explicitly outlines the procedures for resolving disputes that may arise between foreign investors and Vietnamese state management agencies concerning investment activities conducted within Vietnamese territory. The law mandates that these disputes are to be resolved through arbitration or by Vietnamese courts unless alternative provisions are stipulated in a contract signed between a representative of a competent state agency and a foreign investor or within the framework of an international treaty to which Vietnam is a signatory. This represents a noteworthy advancement in Vietnam's legislative approach, mainly because before the enactment of this law, the 1996 LFI did not directly address this form of dispute resolution. Specifically, Article 24 of the 1996 LFI merely indicated that disputes arising from build-operate-transfer contracts, build-transfer-operate contracts, and build-transfer contracts would be resolved in accordance with the method agreed upon by the parties as specified in the contract. Article 12 of the LOI 2005 should be read in conjunction with the legal framework about Public-Private Partnerships (PPPs) during that period, subsequently detailed in Decree No. 78/2007/N-CP,[78] which was later replaced by Decree No. 108/2009/NĐ-CP.[79] This decree regulated the resolution of investment disputes involving state agencies in the context of PPP-related contracts.[80]

- **Law on Investment 2014**

In 2014, the Law on Investment No. 67/2014/QH13, which became effective on July 1, 2015 (LOI 2014), was ratified by the National Assembly of Vietnam on November 26, 2014. Alongside the LOI 2014, its corresponding implementing regulation, Decree 118/2015/NĐ-CP, was concurrently enacted, along with Decree 136/2015/NĐ-CP, which offers guidance on implementing specific Law on Public Investment provisions.

A significant departure from previous legislation, the LOI 2014 makes a significant statement in Article 5.1 by affirming that "Investors are entitled to make investments in the business lines that are not banned in this Law." This law takes a more specific approach to delineating industries prohibited from investment, as seen in Article 6, rather than employing a general regulation akin to Article 30 in the LOI 2005. Furthermore, 2014 LOI dedicates an entire chapter to investment assurance (Chapter 2).

The LOI 2014 carries forward commitments related to critical investment protections found in IILs. These protections encompass transparency requirements, equal treatment of both foreign and domestic investors, safeguards against expropriation, and adherence to investment treaties to which Vietnam is a party (Article 5 LOI 2014). Notably, the law underscores that, in cases of conflict, the legal weight of the treaty to which Vietnam is a signatory supersedes that of the LOI 2014 (Article 4.3 LOI 2014). The LOI 2014 recognises that foreign investors are subject to sector-specific laws and regulations contingent upon the industry in which they intend to invest. These sector-specific laws encompass credit institutions, petroleum, publishing, and others (Article 4.1 LOI 2014).

The law broadens incentives for foreign investors by modifying regulations about issuing Investment Registration Certificates for foreign-invested projects. It also narrows the scope of application for the requirement to procure investment registration certificates for foreign investors, significantly reducing the issuance period for Investment Registration Certificates for projects that necessitate investment policy decisions from 45 days to 15 days (Article 37, 40 LOI 2014).

The LOI 2014 reaffirms the dispute resolution mechanisms between investors and the state, as initially outlined in the LOI 2005, which include arbitration and recourse to Vietnamese courts as articulated in Article 14 of the LOI 2014. To further elucidate, the regulatory framework for Public-Private Partnerships (PPP) is comprehensively detailed in Decree No. 63. This decree governs the provisions

[78] Government of Vietnam (2007) Decree No. 78/2007/NĐ-CP, Article 2.

[79] Government of Vietnam (2009) Decree No. 108/2009/NĐ-CP, Article 44.

[80] See further Dung and Huong (2021), p. 270.

related to dispute resolution in accordance with the corresponding provisions articulated in the LOI 2014.[81]

In summary, the LOI 2014 lays a clear legal framework that safeguards the constitutional principle of citizens' right to invest and participate in business ventures in areas not prohibited by law. Furthermore, it removes ambiguous and unjustifiable barriers to professions and business investments. The most notable reforms introduced by the LOI 2014 focus on administrative procedures, leading to more streamlined documentation, simplified processes, and shorter timelines for issuing Investment Registration Certificates to foreign investors.

- **Law on Investment 2020 and its Environmental Responsibility Provisions for Investors**

In addition to international agreements, the Law on Investment 2020 (LOI 2020),[82] which came into effect on January 1, 2021, alongside its accompanying legal documents,[83] which regulates the procedures for evaluating important national projects and monitors investment activities, serves as the primary regulatory framework governing investment activities in Vietnam.

Concurrently with adopting the new LOI 2020, the Vietnam Law on Enterprises (Law No. 59/2020/QH14, enacted on June 17, 2020) was also implemented, replacing the previous Vietnam Law on Enterprises 2014. The Law on Enterprises 2020 applies to all business activities conducted in Vietnam. Furthermore, by this law, specialised laws take precedence in the event of any discrepancies between the provisions of LOI 2020 and the relevant specialised laws (Article 4.3 LOI 2020).

Within the LOI 2020, Article 4 has been amended to explicitly delineate the scope of regulation and the principles governing the application of the Investment Law in conjunction with other laws that govern business activities in Vietnam. Additionally, the LOI 2020 has modified and supplemented ten sets of regulations found in the LOI 2014 to ensure alignment with laws about land and taxes. It has also introduced amendments to six other laws, including the Environmental Protection Law, Housing Law, Real Estate Business Law, Urban Planning Law, Corporate Income Tax Law, and Cinema Law, to harmonise them with the provisions outlined in the LOI 2020.

In regard to investment guarantee commitments, the LOI 2020 dedicates an entire chapter, Chapter 2, to elucidate the state's commitments to ensuring the security and protection of business investment activities conducted within Vietnam's borders. This chapter encompasses crucial aspects such as asset ownership guarantees (Article 10), assurances for unimpeded business investment activities (Article 11), and safeguards for the transfer of foreign investors' assets abroad (Article 12). Of particular significance is Article 13, which outlines guarantees provided when

[81] Government of Vietnam (2018) Decree No. 63/2018/NĐ-CP, Article 67.

[82] National Assembly of Vietnam (2020) Law on Investment No. 61/2020/QH14.

[83] Government of Vietnam (2021) Decree No. 31/2021/NĐ-CP and Decree 29/2021/NĐ-CP (26 March 2021).

legal changes occur. Article 13 serves as a safeguard, assuring investors they will retain certain advantages even when new laws are enacted. Specifically, if a new law introduces more favorable investment incentives, investors can continue to benefit from these advantages for the remaining duration of their project's incentive period (Article 13.1 LOI 2020). Conversely, suppose a new law diminishes the investment incentives that were previously enjoyed by investors. In that case, they are entitled to maintain those existing incentives for the remaining duration of their project's incentive period (Article 13.2 LOI 2020). However, it's important to note that Article 13.3 introduces a reservation clause, which specifies that the provisions of Article 13.2 may not apply if changes in legal documents are necessitated by reasons such as national defense, national security, social order and safety, social ethics, community health, and environmental protection. It's worth highlighting that this provision on the right to regulate of Vietnam applies exclusively to the investment guarantee commitments outlined in Article 13.2 and does not extend as a general principle governing investment guarantee obligations.

Regarding investment incentives and supporting policies, the LOI 2020 has introduced amendments and additions to investment incentives and supportive measures. These changes are designed to ensure a discerning and high-quality approach to investment attraction, aligning with the directives outlined in Resolution No. 50/NQ-Central Committee of the Politburo.[84] Simultaneously, the LOI 2020 aims to maintain consistency and coherence in implementing investment incentives and support policies, per the provisions set forth in the Investment Law, tax legislation, and related laws.

Specifically, the LOI 2020 incorporates provisions to encourage various activities, including research and development initiatives, the production and trade of products resulting from scientific research outcomes, innovation endeavours, the manufacturing of goods, or the provision of services that contribute to or engage with value chains and industry clusters, as well as the promotion of environmental, industrial development.

Furthermore, the LOI 2020 establishes regulations delineating the principles and conditions for applying investment incentive policies, focusing on ensuring the quality and effectiveness of their implementation. For instance, these principles entail granting incentives for a finite duration, contingent upon the outcomes of project execution. Investors are mandated to adhere to preferential conditions throughout the incentive period by the stipulations of the law. Additionally, the LOI 2020 augments the framework by conferring authority upon the Prime Minister to institute special incentives. This latitude empowers the government to create mechanisms and policies that are exceptionally attractive and timely, intending to swiftly draw in FDI flows that are currently in rapid motion. This special incentive

[84] Central Committee of the Politburo of Vietnam (2019) Resolution No. 50/NQ-TW (20 August 2019). This Resolution has been supported by Resolution No. 58/NQ-CP issued by the Government (27 April 2020) which introduces the Government's Action Program aimed at Implementing Resolution No. 50-NQ/TW.

provision allows for applying incentives at a level up to 50% higher than the highest level stipulated following the prevailing laws.

Regarding environmental protection concerns, the LOI 2020 stands out as the most comprehensive legislative document to date in Vietnam, as it contains a substantial number of provisions and requisites on environmental protection. Notably, the LOI 2020 prioritises to projects with a distinct focus on environmental considerations. For instance, entities engaged in the manufacturing and providing of technologies, equipment, products, and services that align with the requirements outlined in the Law on Environmental Protection[85] are eligible for investment incentives under this law (Article15.2(đ) LOI 2020).

Moreover, Article 30.1 of the LOI 2020 stipulates that investment projects with significant or potentially severe environmental ramifications, such as nuclear power plants or projects necessitating the conversion of land designated as special-use forests, headwater protection forests, or border protection forests spanning at least 50 hectares, among others, require investment guideline approval from the National Assembly. Regardless of whether investment projects fall under the authority of the National Assembly, the Prime Minister, or PPC, they must include a preliminary assessment of their environmental impact, if applicable, following the regulations outlined in environmental protection laws (Article 33.1(d) LOI 2020).

Under this law, state agencies must consider preliminary assessments of the socio-economic efficiency and environmental impact, if any, as part of the procedures for evaluating requests for investment guideline approval (Article 33.3(c) LOI 2020).

Furthermore, the LOI 2020 underscores the imperative of adherence to its provisions and those outlined in other pertinent national laws, such as those governing planning, land use, environmental protection, construction, and labour. (Article 42.3 LOI 2020). Investors are required to secure written approvals for investment guidelines, if applicable, and investment registration certificates, if applicable, during the execution of their investment projects

Besides, the Vietnamese government maintains a consistent policy in managing investment projects with potential environmental impacts. Investment projects that employ outdated technologies, pose environmental risks or consume excessive resources are ineligible for extensions (Article 44.4(a)). Additionally, the law grants state agencies the authority to suspend or terminate an investment project either partially or entirely in different situations listed under Articles 47 and 48. Legal situations permitting investment authority to suspense investment projects due to environmental concerns comprise: (Article 47.2 LOI 2020)

- to protect sites/monuments, relics, antiques or national treasures following the Law on Cultural Heritage;
- to rectify a violation of the law on environmental protection at the request of the environmental authority;
- under a judgment or decision of a court or an arbitral award;

[85] National Assembly of Vietnam (2020) Law on Environment Protection No. 72/2020/QH14.

Legal situation allowing investment authority to terminate investment projects due to environmental concerns comprise (Article 48.2 the LOI 2020):

- the investor fails to overcome the difficulties that lead to project suspension in the cases mentioned in Paragraphs 2 and 3 Article 47 of this Law;
- the investor is no longer permitted to keep using the investment location and fails to complete the procedures for change of investment location within 06 months from the date on which the investor is no longer permitted to use the investment location;
- the State expropriated land reserved for the investment project for the reason that the land is not used or the land use is delayed in accordance with regulations of law on land;
- the investment project is terminated according to a judgment or decision of a court or an arbitral award;

In summary, the LOI 2020 exhibits a more lenient approach toward foreign investment, underscoring the government's continued commitment to attracting foreign investment to stimulate and advance the domestic economy. However, in contrast to the LOI 2014, the LOI 2020 introduces numerous specific environmental requirements for investment projects, aiming to curtail and prevent potentially risky investment practices that could lead to environmental pollution. Indeed, when compared to the LFI 1987, in which the environmental protection obligations of foreign investors were addressed rather inadequately in Article 34, specifying that foreign-invested enterprises must take necessary measures to protect the environment during their operations, the LOI 2020 represents a substantial advancement. This law seamlessly integrates environmental protection requirements into various stages of the licensing process, project implementation, and investment project management on Vietnamese territory. These regulations underscore the Vietnamese government's considerable emphasis on environmental protection measures within this latest iteration of the investment law. They also reflect the government's acute awareness of the significance of reserving national rights to oversee investment activities carrying potential environmental risks and to ensure the effective operation and management of these investments.

Despite advancements in raising awareness about integrating and safeguarding the right to regulate environmental protection within the national investment legal framework, deficiencies persist in the implementation of these regulations. In Vietnam, the system of legal documents undergoes frequent adjustments and new enactments, as exemplified by the laws and regulations governing investment activities outlined earlier. However, this does not guarantee the effectiveness of state management endeavours. More specifically, the execution of legal regulations in Vietnam encounters numerous challenges during the implementation phase. Legal provisions may be subject to inconsistent interpretation and enforcement by central and local authorities, potentially violating of investment protection principles such as FET and non-discrimination.

3.3 Investment Laws and Policies in Vietnam: Proactive and Continuous Improvements

It is worth noting that the Vietnamese legal system and economy demonstrate a significant degree of openness. Regarding the legal system, the observations presented in this chapter illustrate that numerous international values and standards related to trade and investment are incorporated and enshrined within the national legislative framework. This ongoing process reinforces Vietnam's commitment to openness and its aspiration to align domestic standards more closely with the common standards and requirements of the international community.

With regard to economic openness, Vietnam's national import-export indicators have shown consistent growth over the years, and the foreign investment sector has also witnessed significant increases in its targets. Foreign investors are permitted to engage in various forms of investment as outlined in Article 21 of the LOI 2020. Moreover, the list of industries and sectors available for investment has expanded significantly, and domestic businesses are actively encouraged to invest overseas. This economic openness not only enables the country to capitalise on its competitive advantages and harness potential resources but also fosters the development of new industries.

However, it is essential to note that these indicators do not fully capture the quality of economic openness, particularly concerning the absorption of advanced science and technology and the effectiveness of management within the foreign-invested sector. Additionally, excessive economic openness can expose the country to economic and environmental risks, as it becomes directly influenced by external factors such as fluctuations in the global economy. Therefore, state management in the economic and environmental domains necessitates vigilant and timely supervision.

Overall, in the realm of investment law, Vietnam has been proactive in issuing and amending several legal documents related to investment in order to meet evolving requirements as it integrates into the global economy. The Investment Law, as the highest-ranking legal document within the investment legal framework, has undergone numerous revisions and promulgations in the Vietnamese context. This reflects the government's proactive approach in creating conducive conditions for attracting FDI capital. The government's commitment is evident through the allocation of resources and the prioritisation of improving the investment legal framework to meet the demands of compelling foreign investment attraction and utilisation. Thanks to these persistent integration policies, continuous legal system improvements, and enhancements to the administrative-judicial system, Vietnam has successfully attracted FDI capital.

Regarding ISDS dispute resolution methods, Vietnam's proactive engagement in ISDS reform at both international and domestic levels highlights the government's clear awareness of the necessity to mitigate the risk of ISDS disputes and its commitment to creating an environment conducive to responsible and sustainable foreign investment. This commitment illustrates Vietnam's evolving role in the global investment landscape and its aspiration to align with contemporary standards and practices in international investment governance.

Within the ISDS mechanisms established by the IIAs that Vietnam has entered into, it is important to note that these agreements largely reflect Vietnam's status as a developing country seeking foreign investments to support its developmental objectives. Consequently, most IIAs acknowledge the authority to settle investment disputes through international arbitration institutions, including the recently concluded EVIPA. However, these agreements exhibit a certain degree of heterogeneity in the mechanisms they recognise. This diversity in ISDS mechanisms carries inherent risks. Firstly, it elevates the risk of encountering disputes subject to various distinct mechanisms, thereby increasing the complexities and costs of managing and pursuing these disputes. Each arbitration mechanism or centre follows distinct procedural requirements, necessitating unique strategies for each case. Furthermore, the expertise and perspectives of arbitral tribunals operating under different mechanisms can significantly differ, which may influence the state's defence strategy in a specific dispute. For each ISDS mechanism, the state must formulate a tailored litigation strategy, incurring costs across multiple dimensions. This practice underscores the need for Vietnam to consider a more unified and streamlined approach to ISDS mechanisms in its future IIAs, enhancing both efficiency and cost-effectiveness in dispute resolution. Such efforts would align Vietnam with international best practices and contribute to the efficient and effective resolution of investment disputes while minimising the complexities and associated expenses for the state as a defendant in these cases.

The prevailing trend in the legislative documents adopted by the Vietnamese government is twofold. On one hand, it continues to offer advantages and incentives for investors, thereby fostering a conducive environment for investment. On the other hand, it reinforces the responsibilities of investors, particularly concerning activities that may adversely impact the environment. Furthermore, the processes related to licensing and the management of investment activities concerning environmental aspects have become more stringent and rigorously enforced. Nevertheless, there remains a need to develop specific criteria to assess the effectiveness of foreign investments across various dimensions, including the economy, society, environment, defence, and security. In fact, this requirement was initially outlined in Resolution 50/NQ-TW issued on August 20, 2019.[86] Unfortunately, these criteria have not yet been realised through appropriate mechanisms. These criteria would serve to elucidate the performance of investment activities, the extent to which domestic and highly specialised labour forces are engaged, the degree of scientific and technological integration into production activities, the environmental impact of investment projects, the evaluation of the added value brought by foreign-invested projects, and the potential for collaboration with domestic enterprises, among other aspects. Implementing such a mechanism to screen and categorise sources of FDI would enable precise measurement of FDI attraction and utilisation outcomes. Furthermore, it could significantly enhance the efficiency of managing and deploying these capital inflows. Such an approach forms the basis for strategic

[86] Central Committee of the Politburo of Vietnam (2019) Resolution No. 50/NQ-TW.

planning to harness FDI in priority sectors aligned with Vietnam's economic development objectives for each stage, both in the current and forthcoming periods.

3.4 Interim Conclusion

Since the implementation of the Đổi mới policies, particularly the revisions made to the investment laws to align with WTO standards from 2005 to the present, Vietnam's iterations of investment laws have been meticulously designed to ensure equitable application to both domestic and foreign investors. This concerted effort has significantly improved the investment environment in Vietnam, promoting fairness and transparency for all market participants. Notably, Vietnam's legal framework governing investment and environmental considerations has seen considerable advancements through various amendments and new regulations.

Over time, Vietnam's domestic investment legislation has shown steady and progressive improvement, partly due to the influence of international agreements. Vietnam's current investment law framework fundamentally acknowledges and aligns with the state's commitments to safeguarding investments. Furthermore, the methods for resolving ISDS disputes, as recognised under national law, have gradually evolved, drawing closer to international best practices.

Vietnam's economic development, international economic integration, and attraction of foreign investment highlight its unique and distinctive characteristics. In the past four decades, the rapid and remarkable economic growth and a significant level of integration can be attributed primarily to the government's strong political will and the CPV's leadership. In the initial stages of economic integration, the country's laws and policies may have been limited. Nevertheless, they evolved and matured during the implementation process, particularly under the pressure of international commitments, both bilateral and multilateral. This evolution is especially evident in Vietnam's adherence to its international commitments, notably following its accession to the WTO. Vietnam's proactive and enthusiastic approach to fulfilling these commitments and meeting the demands of its trading partners has established the country as a dependable partner on the global stage. Although Vietnam's dynamism and economic potential have made it an attractive destination for foreign investment, it is imperative to recognise that the nation's political will and determination to build a reputation as a trustworthy partner have significantly contributed to its sucess in economic development.

ISDS Cases

Trinh Vinh Binh and Binh Chau Joint Stock Company v. Socialist Republic of Viet Nam (I) [2004] SCC, awarded 1 March 2007.

Trinh Vinh Binh and Binh Chau Joint Stock Company v. Socialist Republic of Viet Nam (II) [2014] PCA Case No. 2015-23

Treaties

Agreement between the United States of America and the Socialist Republic of Vietnam on Trade Relations (Vietnam – U.S BTA) (2003). Available via https://ustr.gov/sites/default/files/US-VietNam-BilateralTradeAgreement.pdf.

ASEAN - Hong Kong, China SAR Investment Agreement (2017)

ASEAN - Japan EPA (2008)

ASEAN - Korea Investment Agreement (2009)

Comprehensive and Progressive Agreement for Trans-Pacific Partnership (2018) (CPTPP)

Vietnam - France BIT (1992)

Vietnam - Japan BIT (2003)

References

Bibliography

Abbott P, Bentzen J, Tarp F (2006) Vietnam's accession to the WTO: lessons from past trade agreements. MPRA Discussion Paper No. PRG2.06.02. Available via https://mpra.ub.uni--muenchen.de/61679/

Abonyi G (2005) Policy reform in Vietnam and The Asian Development Bank's State-Owned Enterprise Reform and Corporate Governance Program Loan. ERD Working Paper No.70. Asian Development Bank

Acuña-Alfaro J (ed) (2009) Reforming public administration in Vietnam: current situation and recommendations. The National Political Publishing House

Anh LND (2020) Phát triển thương mại theo hướng bền vững ở Việt Nam trong bối cảnh hội nhập quốc tế [Developing sustainable trade in Viet Nam in the context of international integration]. Dphil in Economic Management Thesis. Institute of Postgraduate Training. Thuongmai University

Auffret P (2003) Trade reform in Vietnam – opportunities with emerging challenges. WPS3076 The World Bank Policy Research Working Paper 2

Chauhan S (2013) Vietnam's role in ASEAN. Observer Research Foundation. Available via https://www.eastasiaforum.org/2013/10/23/vietnams-role-in-asean/

Dodsworth JR et al (1996) Vietnam transition to a market economy. International Monetary Fund. Available via https://www.elibrary.imf.org/view/IMF084/07830-9781557755384/07830-9781557755384/front.xml?redirect=true

Dung TV (2022) The impact of investment treaties on the rule of law in Viet Nam. In: Calamita NJ, Berman A (eds) Investment treaties and the rule of law promise: the internalisation of international commitments in Asia. Cambridge University Press

Dung TV, Huong NTL (eds) (2021) Các Cơ chế Trọng tài Đầu tư Quốc tế: Quy tắc, Thủ tục và Thực tiễn [Investor-state arbitration: rules, procedures and practices]. Ho Chi Minh City National University Publishing

Focus Economic. Vietnam GDP (2014–2024). Available via https://www.focus-economics.com/country-indicator/vietnam/gdp/#:~:text=The%20Vietnamese%20economy%20recorded%20average,information%2C%20visit%20our%20dedicated%20page

Foreign Investment Agency (2023) Tình hình đầu tư nước ngoài tại Việt Nam 3 tháng đầu năm 2023 [Foreign investment in Vietnam in the first 3 months of 2023]. Available via https://fia.mpi.gov.vn/Detail/CatID/457641e2-2605-4632-bbd8-39ee65454a06/NewsID/d702c50b-26db-4f64-9beb-c34327550dfd

Foreign Investment Department, Ministry of Planning and Investment (2022) Tình hình đầu tư của Việt Nam ra nước ngoài năm 2022 [Vietnam's Investments Abroad in 2022]. Available via https://fia.mpi.gov.vn/Detail/CatID/90c0e0c8-58ee-4737-bf70-5f08acea5ca8/NewsID/6ccbd876-c6ed-4a5e-a4ea-1fbc82d82c05/MenuID/5ef9e864-dd1c-48a5-b6b0-6bed77ece7dc

Ha TTP (2022) Statement at the Sixth Committee of the 77th Session of the General Assembly, Agenda item 75: Report of the United Nations Commission on International Trade Law on the Work of its 55th Session. New York. Available via https://www.un.org/en/ga/sixth/77/pdfs/statements/uncitral/15mtg_vietnam.pdf

Hoang DN (2014) Quá trình Hình thành và Phát triển của Luật Đầu tư Nước ngoài tại Việt Nam [The Formation and Development Process of the Foreign Investment Law in Vietnam]. Foreign Investment Agency, Ministry of Planning and Investment. Available via https://fia.mpi.gov.vn/Detail/CatID/80a3a429-cc68-4621-94a8-9ebecf86aae6/NewsID/1b85b856-4f4f-4a34-a162-c1851888298b

Hung LD, Cong PT (2024) Phối hợp chính sách tài khóa và tiền tệ nhằm ổn định lạm phát tại Việt Nam [Combining fiscal and monetary policy to stabilize inflation in Vietnam, State bank of Vietnam]. Banking Review. Available via https://tapchinganhang.gov.vn/phoi-hop-chinh-sach-tai-khoa-va-tien-te-nham-on-dinh-lam-phat-tai-viet-nam-6647.html

Huong NTL, Phong PB (2023) Pro-sustainable development via EVFTA – the case of climate change response and promoting offshore wind power in Viet Nam. International Workshop on Trade and Marine Environment Protection: Status and Perspective of International, Regional and National Laws. The Foreign Trade University. Ha Noi, Viet Nam

Lee S (2024) Vietnam's renewables surge, but serious pollution concerns persist. Asia Pacific Foundation of Canada. Available via https://www.asiapacific.ca/publication/vietnams-renewables-surge-serious-pollution-concerns-persist

Litvack JI (1999) The dilemmas of change: revitalizing social services in a period of transition. In: Litvack JI, Rondinelli DA (eds) Market reform in Vietnam: building institutions for development. Quorum Books

Malintoppi L, Tan C (eds) (2016) Investment protection in Southeast Asia: a country-by-country guide on arbitration laws and bilateral investment treaties. Brill Nijhoff

Mutrap (2008) Đánh giá Tác động Tổng thể khi Việt Nam Trở thành Thành viên WTO đến Thay đổi Xuất nhập khẩu và thể chế [Assessing the overall impact of Vietnam becoming a Member of the WTO on import-export and institutional changes]. Vietnam Ministry of Industry and Trade and European Commission. ASIE/2003/005711

Nguyen Duc (2017) 30 năm FDI: Dự luật lịch sử và những chuyên cơ chở tỷ phú [30 Years of FDI: Historic bill and Jets carrying billionaires]. Đầu tư Online. Available via https://baodautu.vn/30-nam-fdi-du-luat-lich-su-va-nhung-chuyen-co-cho-ty-phu-d74458.html

Quang CH (2021) Investor-state dispute settlement mechanism in the context of reform to Vietnam's investment and judicial framework. Hongduc Publishing

Thanh VT (2005) Vietnam's trade liberalisation and international economic integration: evolution, problems, and challenges. ASEAN Econ Bull 22(1):75. Available via https://www.jstor.org/stable/25773845

Thayer (2001) Vietnam and ASEAN. Conference on Vietnam: Prospects for Economic and Social Progress

Thayer CA, Amer R (eds) (2000) Vietnamese foreign policy in transition. Institute of Southeast Asian Studies, Singapore

Tuyet DA (2020) Research Report 2019-2020: improving the effectiveness of ISDS dispute resolution in Vietnam. Ministry of Justice of Vietnam, UK Government and UNDP Vietnam. Available via https://moj.gov.vn/tttp/tintuc/Pages/nghien-cuu-trao-doi.aspx?ItemID=62

UNCTAD (2019) Fact Sheet On Investor-State Dispute Settlement Cases in 2018. Available via https://unctad.org/en/PublicationsLibrary/diaepcbinf2019d4_en.pdf

UNCTAD Investment Policy Hub. Vietnam's ISDS Cases. Available via https://investmentpolicy.unctad.org/investment-dispute-settlement/country/229/viet-nam

UNCTAD Investment Policy Hub. Vietnam's International Investment Treaties. Available via https://investmentpolicy.unctad.org/international-investment-agreements/countries/229/viet-nam?type=bits

Viet Nam's Ministry for Planning and Industry (2021) Vietnam handbook on obligations in international investment treaties. Privately introduced in Training Workshop on Feb 24 - 25th, 2022 in Ho Chi Minh City. The information regarding this Workshop is available via https://asean.org/viet-nam-finalises-handbook-for-implementing-international-investment-commitments/

World Bank (1999) Vietnam Development Report 2000: Attacking Povert. Available via https://documents1.worldbank.org/curated/en/929551468780565502/pdf/Viet-Nam-Development-report-2000-attacking-poverty-country-economic-memorandum.pdf

World Bank (2011) Vietnam Development Report 2012: Market Economy for a Middle-income Vietnam. 6 December 2011. Available via https://documents.worldbank.org/en/publication/documents-reports/documentdetail/495721468327934602/vietnam-development-report-2012-market-economy-for-a-middle-income-vietnam

World Bank (2018) Doing business 2018: reforming to create jobs. Available via https://www.doingbusiness.org/content/dam/doingBusiness/media/Annual-Reports/English/DB2018-Full-Report.pdf

World Bank (2022a) GDP per Capita - Vietnam. Available via https://data.worldbank.org/indicator/NY.GDP.PCAP.CD?locations=VN

World Bank (2022b) Foreign Direct Investment: net inflows. Available via https://data.worldbank.org/indicator/BX.KLT.DINV.CD.WD?end=2022&locations=VN&start=1970&view=chart

Documents

Central Committee of the Politburo of Vietnam (2019) Resolution No. 50/NQ-TW (20 August 2019) Regarding the Strategic Direction for Refining Institutional Frameworks and Policies, Enhancing the Quality, and Boosting the Effectiveness of Foreign Investment Cooperation until 2030

Communist Party of Vietnam (1986) Document of the Sixth National Congress of the Communist Party of Vietnam. The National Political Publishing House. Hanoi

Communist Party of Vietnam (1991) Document of the Seventh Meeting. The National Political Publishing House. Hanoi

Communist Party of Vietnam (2001) Document of the Ninth Meeting. The National Political Publishing House. Hanoi

Communist Party of Vietnam (2006) Document of the Tenth Meeting. The National Political Publishing House. Hanoi

EuroCham (2019) White Book 2019: Trade and Investment Issues and Recommendations. Available via https://www.scribd.com/document/408504041/WhiteBook-2019-pdf

European Commission (2020) EU-Viet Nam Trade Agreement and Investment Protection Agreement. Available via https://policy.trade.ec.europa.eu/eu-trade-relationships-country-and-region/countries-and-regions/vietnam/eu-vietnam-agreement_en

Government of Thailand. The Sixth National Economic and Social Development Plan (1987-1991). Available via https://data.thailand.opendevelopmentmekong.net/dataset/6-2530-2538

Government of Vietnam (2007) Decree No. 78/2007/NĐ-CP (11 May 2007) on Investment in the Form of Build-Operate-Transfer Contracts, Build-Transfer-Operate Contracts, Build-Transfer Contracts

Government of Vietnam (2009) Decree No. 108/2009/NĐ-CP (27 November 2009) on Investment in the Form of Build-Operate-Transfer Contracts, Build-Transfer-Operate Contracts, Build-Transfer Contracts
Government of Vietnam (2018) Decree No. 63/2018/NĐ-CP (4 May 2018) on Investment in the Form of Public - Private Partnerships
Government of Vietnam (2020) Resolution No. 58/NQ-CP (27 April 2020) Government's Action Program Aimed at Implementing Resolution No. 50-NQ/TW
Government of Vietnam (2021) Decree No. 29/2021/NĐ-CP (26 March 2021) on Prescribing Procedures for Appraisal of Projects of National Significance, and Supervision and Assessment of Investment
Government of Vietnam (2021) Decree No. 31/2021/NĐ-CP (26 March 2021) on Providing Detailed Guidance on the Implementation of the Law on Investment
National Assembly of Vietnam (2005) Law No. 59/2005/QH11 (29/11/2005) on Investment
National Assembly of Vietnam (2020) Law No. 61/2020/QH14 (17 June 2020) on Investment
National Assembly of Vietnam (2020) Law No. 72/2020/QH14 (17 November 2020) on Environment Protection
Prime Minister of Vietnam (2014) Decision No. 04/QĐ-TTg (14 January 2014) on Adopting the Regulation on Coordination in Resolving International Investment Disputes
Prime Minister of Vietnam (2018) Decision No. 1072/QĐ-TTg (28 August 2018) on Approving the strategy for development of the lawyer profession through 2020
Prime Minister of Vietnam (2020) Decision No. 14/QĐ-TTg (4 April 2020) on Adopting Regulations on Coordination for Resolution of International Investment Disputes

Chapter 4
Vietnam's Environmental Protection Regime: Gaps Behind the Growth

Abstract Given the extensive existing literature on environmental governance in Vietnam, this chapter does not intend to provide a comprehensive analysis. Instead, it seeks to illuminate Vietnam's current environmental landscape following nearly four decades of economic liberalisation, drawing connections between this reality and the ongoing process of economic development to outline the environmental challenges confronting the nation. Additionally, the chapter examines the evolution of policies and legal frameworks in Vietnam aimed at addressing environmental management issues and responding to climate change. Furthermore, it highlights the shortcomings and weaknesses within the relevant environmental policy and legal structures, laying the groundwork for recommendations to ensure that foreign investment contributes to sustainable development, as explored in the latter part of this book.

4.1 Current Environmental Challenges in Vietnam

It is widely recognised that Vietnam has attained a notable degree of success in economic development and integration due to well-conceived socio-economic development policies. However, the rapid economic growth accompanied by industrialisation and swift urbanisation has exerted significant pressure on the country's environmental sustainability and citizens' health. As of 2020, Vietnam had 862 cities and municipal areas with a combined population of approximately 97.58 million.[1] Notably, urban drainage systems can fulfil only 60% of the total drainage needs, with many of these systems lacking synchronisation with centralised wastewater treatment facilities, resulting in suboptimal treatment effectiveness. Approximately 15% of urban domestic wastewater is subjected to collection and treatment processes.[2]

[1] Ministry of Natural Resource and Environment (MONRE) (2021), p. 8.

[2] Ibid, p. 9.

N. T. Lan Huong, *Investment Protection and Environmental Governance*, European Yearbook of International Economic Law 47,
https://doi.org/10.1007/978-3-032-05332-9_4

The rapid urbanisation driven by the expanding construction sector, alongside a rise in personal vehicle ownership due to tariff reductions under signed FTAs, has resulted in severe air pollution in major cities such as Hanoi and Ho Chi Minh City. These urban centres are responsible for two-thirds of the overall energy demand and carbon emissions, stemming from diverse sources, including transportation, industrial operations, construction, and building activities.

The demand for energy development is placing significant pressure on Vietnam's environment. Like many emerging economies, the country's industrialisation process necessitates considerable energy consumption. This results in increased fuel and energy consumption, heightened waste generation, and environmental strain.[3] Despite having favourable natural conditions to exploit variety of energy sources such as fossil fuels, hydropower, wind power, and solar power, Vietnam has primarily met its energy needs by developing hydropower and coal-fired power, largely due to limited financial resources.[4] Renewable energy sources have only recently gained attention in the past decade.[5]

However, reliance on coal-based energy policies has notably adverse effects on Vietnam's environment, particularly regarding the deteriorating air quality surrounding coal power projects. Coal power plants emit significant amounts of dust and gases, including SO2, NOx, and NO2, as well as considerable volumes of ash and slag, leading to severe air pollution, particularly in northern cities where numerous coal power projects are located.[6] For instance, cities like Hanoi experience increased incidences of respiratory diseases, blood circulation issues, and cardiovascular diseases due to the proximity of coal-fired power plants.[7]

Moreover, the exploitation of hydroelectric resources has led to the establishment of various small hydroelectric projects, frequently without sufficient regard for their economic, social, and environmental consequences. These projects have resulted in deforestation, decreased biodiversity, and disrupted water ecosystems downstream of hydroelectric dams, heightening the risk of drought, desertification, erosion, landslides, and saltwater intrusion.[8]

Despite having low greenhouse gas emissions during the first decade of economic opening, Vietnam's total greenhouse gas emissions doubled and even tripled from 2014 to 2016, increasing from 103.8 million to 316.7 million tons of CO2.[9] Notably, emissions from the energy sector surged significantly, being approximately 08 times higher than in 1994, driven by a rapid rise in energy demand.[10] A document

[3] Ibid, p. 10.

[4] Ibid, p. 17.

[5] Vy et al. (2020), p. 670.

[6] Ibid.

[7] Schirmbeck (2017), p. 3.

[8] MONRE (2021), p. 17.

[9] Ibid, p. 30.

[10] Ibid.

published by the World Bank in 2019[11] highlighted that water quality in Vietnam is deteriorating, and pollution levels have been increasing recently. Contamination affects both surface and groundwater, with minimal treatment of municipal and industrial wastewater. Most sewage, industrial discharge, and solid waste end up in watercourses. In the area of industrial wastewater management, data from the Ministry of Natural Resource and Environment reveals the presence of 369 industrial zones primarily located in the Southeast Delta and the Red River Delta.[12] Most industrial zones had been established by the end of 2015, with approximately 74.9% having constructed centralised wastewater treatment facilities, while the percentage for industrial clusters until 2014 remained at 3–5%.[13] Given the substantial volume of waste generated, only 60% of wastewater undergoes treatment, with the remainder being either self-disposed or directly discharged into the environment.[14]

Wastewater from the operations of industrial establishments and industrial zones creates significant pressure on the surface water environment in Vietnam.[15] Until recently, many industrial zones and individual large factories discharged untreated wastewater into nearby rivers and lakes, causing water pollution in several river sections. Due to the high costs of constructing and operating wastewater treatment systems, the number of enterprises establishing these systems in industrial parks and complexes is limited. Although the enterprises possess pollution treatment equipment, it is not consistently operational, resulting in wastewater quality that fails to meet Vietnamese standard (QCVN).[16] Indeed, the water quality in the basins of major rivers where industrial zones are situated has seriously declined, failing to comply with national technical regulations (QCVN 08: 2008/BTNMT).[17] The Report on the National Environment 2016–2020 indicates that approximately 60% of active industrial clusters have not submitted environmental impact assessment reports.[18] This highlights a lack of specific environmental protection measures within these industrial clusters.

Additionally, the adoption of modern technology in Vietnam's production facilities remains relatively low compared to other countries in the region. Consequently, the production process often requires more raw materials and energy, leading to increased waste generation that is frequently inadequately managed, leading to significant environmental pollution. To date, large-scale enterprises are spread across various regions of the country and operate in sectors that potentially have substantial impacts on the environment, including mineral exploitation, electricity

[11] World Bank (2019).

[12] Ibid, p. 11.

[13] MONRE (2015), pp. 09–11.

[14] Ibid, p. 10. Accordingly, Viet Nam's industrial zones discharge around 240.000 cubic meters of untreated industrial sewage into the environment every day.

[15] MONRE (2010), pp. 66–67. See also MONRE (2015), p. 9.

[16] See figures in MONRE (2018), p. 29.

[17] MONRE (2010), pp. 71–75.

[18] MONRE (2021), p. 12.

generation, oil and gas exploration and processing, mechanics, chemicals, metallurgy, shipbuilding, construction material production, and food processing.[19] In fact, a considerable number of these industrial establishments do not ultilise advanced or modern technology and show little interest in investing in environmental treatment facilities, thereby causing severe environmental pollution in many localities.[20]

The FDI sector is instrumental in driving Vietnam's export growth. However, it is disheartening to note that activities demanding high levels of expertise, such as research and development (R&D) within FDI enterprises in Vietnam, remain limited.[21] Instead, a significant portion of FDI is funneled into industries that heavily consume energy and resources, primarily sectors like metallurgy, ship repair, textiles, footwear, and mining.[22] This trend has resulted in both pollution and environmental degradation. Furthermore, these foreign investment enterprises have predominantly employed medium-level technologies rather than the cutting-edge innovations the country had hoped to attract.[23]

Studies suggest that while trade liberalisation helps to promote economic growth in Vietnam,[24] this process has led to some adverse environmental consequences.[25] In the past years, for different reasons, natural resources, especially water and biodiversity resources in Vietnam, have been seriously degenerated. Available data shows that forest destruction and deforestation continue at an alarming rate. Indeed, the country has lost 67% of the area of mangrove forests compared to 1943.[26] Notably, as mentioned in a statistic in 2012, 56% of the total area of mangrove forests across the country is newly planted has single species, and is of poor quality in terms of size, height and species diversity; which means the primary mangrove forests are almost gone.[27] Between 70% and 80% of the nation's marine waste is generated by factories, coastal and urban industrial zones, and residential areas that discharge unprocessed wastewater and solid waste into rivers and canals in coastal areas or directly into the sea.[28] In 15 years (2000–2015), about 15–20% of the coral reefs were lost.[29] By 2015, about 100 species of marine organisms in Vietnam are

[19] MONRE (2017).

[20] MONRE (2015), pp. 13, 15.

[21] Dordi et al. (2008), p. 9.

[22] Chu (2020), p. 2; Mani and Hja (2006), p. 24.

[23] According to a survey in 2001, 42.9% of foreign investment enterprises operating in the mining and quarrying industry used modern technology and 50% of them used medium technology. See Hong et al. (2009), p. 31.

[24] The country has enjoyed one of the fastest GDP per capita growth rates in the world, averaging 6.4% a year in the 2000s and transform to a low-to-middle-income country by 2010. In 2010, nominal GDP per capita of Vietnam reached USD 1168 compared with USD 416 in 2001. See World Bank (2023).

[25] Mani and Hja (2006), p. 25.

[26] MONRE (2015).

[27] Korea Environment Institute (2017), p. 174.

[28] Ibid, p. 170.

[29] Ibid, p. 173.

threatened. They are included in the Red Book of Vietnam and the International Union for Conservation of Nature Red List, which require protection measures.[30] In certain localities, land and minerals resources have suffered from exhaustive or highly wasteful exploitation.[31] Environmental pollution and emissions have worsened, both in urban and rural areas.[32] As can be seen, the pollution of water, air, and soil, as well as the degradation of land in Vietnam, are contributed by both anthropogenic activities and natural factors. After more than 30 years of reform, the country is facing a big challenge in mitigating pollution and natural resource degradation, requiring urgent actions.

Vietnam faces a dual challenge as it copes with the pollution stemming from industrialisation and the repercussions of climate change and natural disasters.[33] With its extensive coastline stretching over 3200 km and numerous low-lying cities and river delta regions, Vietnam is highly susceptible to sea-level rise. Without effective adaptation measures, modelling projections suggest that coastal flooding could impact 06 to 12 million people by 2070–2100, depending on global emissions trends.[34]

The country's two primary economic hubs on major river deltas are particularly vulnerable to climate change. Hai Phong, a key trading port in the north, and the capital city, Hanoi, home to 8 to 9 million residents,[35] are forecasted to face significant impacts by the end of the century.[36] In the southern region, the situation is exacerbated by factors such as ongoing sand mining and the erosion of coastlines and riverbanks due to sea level rise. Ho Chi Minh City, Vietnam's most significant and fastest-growing urban centre, is situated in the Mekong Delta, where most of the country's industrial development and agricultural production, including rice, fish/shrimp farming, and fruit cultivation, are located. The increasing intrusion of saltwater into the delta's waterways, declining water levels, and land subsidence pose a grave threat to livelihoods in the region. These changes may even render rice farming unsustainable in the long term.[37]

The Vietnam Climate and Development Report highlights the severe vulnerability of the Mekong Delta to climate change, noting that nearly half of the delta area could be submerged if sea levels rise by 75–100 centimetres compared to 1980–1999 levels.[38] A meter of sea-level rise would inundate 79% of Ca Mau province and 76%

---

[30] MONRE (2015).

[31] Vietnam (2012), p. 16.

[32] Korea Environment Institute (2017), p. 23.

[33] Vietnam is one of the world's most affected countries by climate change. See United Nations (2018), p. 18; See also Kreft et al. (2015).

[34] World Bank (2022), p. 6.

[35] MONRE (2021), p. 8.

[36] Schirmbeck (2017), p. 2.

[37] Ibid.

[38] World Bank (2022), p. 27.

of Kien Giang province.[39] The Vietnamese government recognises climate change as a major impediment to the country's growth. Without effective adaptation measures, a temperature increase of 1.0 °C and 1.5 °C could result in GDP losses of about 1.8% and 4.5%, respectively, with economic losses estimated at around 4.3 billion USD over the next decade.[40] In the worst-case scenario, with rising sea levels and temperatures, it is projected that 3.1 million Vietnamese people will need to migrate internally by 2050.[41] These threats have positioned Vietnam at 127th out of 182 countries in the Notre Dame Global Adaptation Initiative rankings and as the 13th most vulnerable country in the Germanwatch Global Climate Risk Index for 2000–2019, highlighting its extreme vulnerability to climate-related risks.[42] Addressing this situation places significant pressure on the Vietnamese government in the present and upcoming years.

4.2 Legislation, Policy Instruments, and Institutions in Environmental Management in Vietnam

Since 1975, following the country's reunification and the aftermath of the war, environmental protection has not been a priority in Vietnam's centrally planned economy. The introduction of the Đổi mới Policy marked a significant turning point, creating conditions that fostered economic development. From this point onward, international integration became a crucial policy for the Communist Party of Vietnam (CPV) and the government, serving as a cornerstone of the country's national renewal process since 1986. This transformation acted as a powerful catalyst, moving Vietnam from a nation primarily engaged in economic and trade relations with socialist countries to an active participant deeply integrated into the regional and global economy.

Historically, Vietnam had an agrarian economy, and its environmental conditions were relatively less damaged before the industrialisation process began, except for pollution from the post-war period. In 1985, the Council of Ministers promulgated Resolution No. 246, titled "The Survey and Rational Use of Natural Resources and Environmental Protection." However, this resolution did not encompass specific policies related to environmental protection.

Vietnam's policy on sustainable development was officially articulated and underscored in the Socio-Economic Development Strategy for 1991–2000, which was adopted at the Seventh National Congress of the CPV. This pivotal strategy emphasised the correlation between economic growth and other critical dimensions, including social progress, equity, cultural development, and environmental

[39] Ibid.

[40] Vietnam's NDCs (2022), p. 17.

[41] Ibid.

[42] World Bank (2022), p. 6.

protection. The CPV Politburo's Directive No. 36-CT/TW, issued on June 25, 1998, further reinforced this commitment by highlighting that environmental protection is an integral and fundamental component of socio-economic development guidelines, policies, and plans across all levels and government agencies. It was deemed crucial in ensuring sustainable development and successfully realising of the national industrialisation and modernisation process.

Vietnam's sustainable development policy has continued to evolve and has been reaffirmed in all subsequent documents adopted by CPV Congresses, becoming the guiding principle and official state policy. Building on this orientation, Vietnam's environmental legislation began to take shape mainly in the 1990s. This legislative momentum started with the issuance of the "National Action Plan on the Environment and Sustainable Development for 1991–2000" in 1991 by the Council of Ministers. This plan a significant shift in Vietnam's approach to environmental protection by recognising the importance of preserving the environment and directing policy approaches for sustainable development. It was the beginning of incorporating environmental protection into Vietnam's legal framework. The significance of environmental preservation was further enshrined in the 1992 Constitution, articulated in Article 17 and Article 29. The most recent 2013 Constitution reaffirmed the importance of environmental protection, with relevant provisions found in Articles 43, 53, and 63.

The "National Plan on Environment and Sustainable Development for 1991–2000" established an institutional framework for environmental protection and management in Vietnam. At the national level, this framework comprised the Ministry of Science, Technology, and Environment (MOSTE). Recognising the multifaceted sources of environmental pollution, other government organisations, such as the Ministry of Construction, the Ministry of Transportation, the Ministry of Agriculture and Rural Development, and the Ministry of Health, were also tasked with environmental protection duties.

MOSTE, established in 1992, held the highest authority for environmental protection. It was divided into two branches: the Directorate for Standards and Quality and the National Environmental Agency (NEA). As the executive department under MOSTE, the NEA was responsible for implementing environmental policy, formulating regulations and standards, developing comprehensive strategies, assessing Environmental Impact Assessment reports, and issuing and revoking environmental licenses. The NEA played a crucial role in ensuring compliance with environmental legislation across various ministries and the Department of Science, Technology, and Environment (DOSTE), conducting pollution control inspections, resolving environmental disputes, and sanctioning non-compliance.

In 2002, the Ministry of Science and Technology (MOST) and the Ministry of Natural Resources and Environment (MONRE) were established as separate entities. As a result, MONRE took over responsibility for environmental issues, along with the Vietnam Environmental Protection Agency, which was previously known as NEA, while continuing its functions

At the provincial level, Department of Natural Resources and Environment (DONRE) was entrusted with environmental protection tasks delegated by the MONRE. However, regarding political, administrative, and financial control, DONRE operated under the jurisdiction of the PPC.[43] Similarly, at the district level, Environmental Bureaus, under the district People's Committees, functioned as local departments of DONRE.

The Ministry of Construction (MOC) manages pollution associated with construction activities by formulating policies, requirements, and guidelines for housing, public infrastructure, drainage and sanitation, waste management, slum improvement, and urban planning. Provincial units of MOC are responsible for the local implementation of these policies. The Ministry of Industry is the designated authority for developing industrial strategies and providing technical assistance for pollution reduction related to industrial activities.

Environmental management in Vietnam is primarily overseen by MONRE, with various specialised management ministries also playing significant roles. This decentralised model of management has resulted in dispersed responsibilities and overlapping jurisdictions among multiple ministries. With its inherent overlaps, this management model is also mirrored at the provincial and district levels.[44] Despite suggestions for organisational and structural changes,[45] the enactment of the new Law on Environmental Protection in 2020 did not bring significant developments to the environmental protection structure in Vietnam. The following section will elucidate the evolution of the environmental legal system over time and highlight the key policy instruments currently used for environmental management in the country.

4.2.1 Environmental Legislation in Vietnam: A Continuing Evolution

Following discussions within the Council of Ministers in 1991, the Law on Environmental Protection (LEP 1993) was promulgated and officially came into effect in 1994.[46] It was with the enactment of LEP 1993 that environmental protection became a prominent political concern in Vietnam. This law explicitly articulated its purpose as safeguarding public health and promoting the country's sustainable development. It established the foundational principles of environmental protection in Vietnam, emphasising that "environmental protection must be in harmony with economic development and ensure social progress for national sustainable development…" (Article 4.1 LEP 1993). This law reaffirmed Vietnam's commitment to environmental protection, highlighting the state's policy of

[43] Nam and Thi (2023), p. 8.

[44] Tin (2019), p. 72.

[45] Ibid.

[46] National Assembly of Vietnam (1993) Law on Environmental Protection No. 29-L/CTN.

diversifying capital investment sources for environmental protection and allocating separate funds for environmental activities in the annual state budgets (Article 5.5 LEP 1993). Furthermore, it emphasised the importance of expanding and enhancing "the effectiveness of international cooperation, fully realising international commitments to environmental protection, and encouraging organisations and individuals to participate in international cooperation for environmental protection" (Article 5.8 LEP 1993).

The LEP 1993 also outlined the rights and responsibilities of the MOSTE, along with other ministries and DOSTE, in managing environmental protection activities. The implementation of this law was supported by several additional documents, including Decree 175/CP (October 18, 1994), which provided guidelines for enforcing the Law on Environmental Protection. Decree No. 26/CP (April 26, 1996) outlined regulations on administrative fines for violations of the Law on Environmental Protection. Moreover, Circular No. 490/1998/TT-BKHCNMT, issued by MOSTE in April 1998, offered guidelines for the environmental impact assessment of investment projects.

In 1995, MOSTE published Vietnam's environmental standards, known as "TCVN-1995," following the requirements of LEP 1993 and Decree No. 175/CP. Subsequently, a multitude of TCVN standards were developed. In general, all projects executed within Vietnam's territory must adhere to the Vietnam environmental standards issued by MOSTE. For projects implemented in localities with their environmental standards, the use of local standards is permissible as long as they are more stringent than those issued by MOSTE.[47]

The LEP 1993 and Decree No. 175/CP brought about a significant transformation in environmental policy in Vietnam, making the Environmental Impact Assessment (EIA) procedure compulsory for both the approval of new investment projects and the continued operation of existing industries. Under the provisions of LEP (Articles 17 and 18) and Decree No. 175/CP (Article 9), both new and existing projects are mandated to submit an EIA report for assessment and approval by the authorities. The EIA report evaluates the environmental conditions of the site where the project is to be located and assesses the potential environmental impact resulting from the project's activities. Furthermore, it must propose adequate measures to control emissions, thereby mitigating any adverse environmental effects of the project (Article 10 Decree No. 175/CP).

Based on the submitted EIA report, the authorities evaluate whether the proposed measures meet environmental standards. Projects that fail to comply with TCVN standards may be given a timeframe to make adjustments. If they continue to fall short of the requirements, they can face penalties or even suspension of factory operations. According to Decree No. 175/CP, various types of projects are reviewed and approved by different government agencies, contingent on the scope and scale

[47] Prime Minister of Vietnam (1998) Circular No. 490/1998/TT-BKHCNMT, Article IV.1 and Article IV.

of the project. The project's significance determines whether it requires approval from national or provincial authorities.

Once the project receives approval, the authorities will begin the process of issuing land use and construction permits. After the construction is completed, an environmental agency will visit the site to verify whether the pollution control technologies detailed in the approved EIA report have been implemented. If all requirements are fulfilled, the project will be allowed to commence operations. The next step is to apply for a "Certificate of Implementing Pollution Control Measures," as required by Article 6 of Circular No. 276-TT/MTg issued by MOSTE on March 6, 1997. Both the approved EIA and the Certificate of Implementing Pollution Control Measures are necessary to obtain an environmental license. The duration of this license can range from three to five years, depending on the factory's scale and the type of industry involved.

In conjunction with the environmental license, the EIA has been a crucial policy tool for environmental protection in Vietnam since the introduction of the 1993 Law on Environmental Protection (LEP 1993). Following the Asian economic crisis, Circular No. 490/1998/TT-BKHCNMT was enacted, providing "Guidelines on Preparing and Appraising Environmental Impact Assessment Reports for Investment Projects." This circular made significant changes, allowing projects located in industrial zones that had their own EIA approvals (referred to as Project Type II) to bypass the full EIA process (Article I.2.1).

On the other hand, domestic investment projects, joint ventures, projects in cooperation with foreign countries, projects with 100% foreign capital investment, and other forms of investment (collectively referred to as investment projects) implemented within Vietnam's territory and possessing the potential to cause large-scale environmental pollution, environmental incidents that are challenging to manage, or pose difficulties in establishing environmental standards, were required to prepare and submit a comprehensive EIA report (Article I.1 and I.2.1). For Project Type II investments, a simpler procedure was introduced, allowing these projects to submit a "Registration for Securing Environmental Standards" to the Department of Science, Technology, and Environment (DOSTE). This policy change aimed to encourage investment in industrial zones (Article II.1.2).

The inclusion of EIA requirements mandated by the LEP 1993 and Decree No. 175/CP, which apply to all economic endeavours regardless of their scope, has been perceived as unduly burdensome and indicative of a policy design flaw. Circular No. 490/1998/TT-BKHCNMT was introduced as part of measures to streamline the EIA process; however, its implementation yielded limited results. The issuance of Circular No. 490/1998/TT-BKHCNMT underscored deficiencies in the execution of the EIA framework, thereby accentuating its shortcomings as an ineffective instrument for environmental governance in Vietnam.

- **National Strategy for Environmental Protection to 2010 (NSEP 2010)**

Despite the implementation of the LEP 1993, Vietnam's environmental policy during this period proved ineffective in controlling pollution. Decision 64/2003/QĐ-TTg identified 439 factories and production facilities as significant sources of pollution and mandated various remedies. These remedies included suspending operations, relocating facilities, altering production processes, and establishing wastewater treatment systems to mitigate further environmental damage (refer to Annex I and II of Decision 64/2003/QĐ-TTg). In response, the MOSTE drafted the National Strategy for Environmental Protection, which was submitted to the government in 2002. This strategy received approval from the Prime Minister through Decision 256/2003/QĐ-TTg, dated December 2, 2003. It is titled "Approval of the National Environmental Protection Strategy up to 2010, with orientation up to 2020" (NSEP to 2010).

The Strategy confirmed the viewpoint of Vietnam's government regarding environmental protection as follows: (Article 1.1 Decision 256)

> The Strategy for Environmental Protection is an inseparable part of the Socio-Economic Development Strategy and is an important basis for national sustainable development. Economic development must be closely and harmoniously combined with social development and environmental protection. Investment in environmental protection is an investment in sustainable development.

The text outlines five main aims and objectives, which are as follows: (i) preventing and controlling pollution; (ii) addressing severe environmental pollution and degradation in affected sites, areas, and regions; (iii) protecting and sustainably utilising natural resources; (iv) safeguarding and enhancing the environment in critical areas; and (v) conserving nature and biodiversity. The strategy emphasises the importance of strengthening environmental protection through effective state management, capable institutions, and robust legislation (as stated in Article 1.1 of Decision 256). Additionally, it establishes four key targets (as mentioned in Article 1.3.1 of Decision 256):

- Limiting pollution increases: This target requires that 100% of newly constructed production facilities implement clean technologies or be equipped with pollution reduction and waste treatment systems that comply with environmental standards. Additionally, 50% of production and business establishments should obtain certifications demonstrating adherence to environmental standards or ISO 14001 certifications. It is also aimed that 40% of urban areas and 70% of industrial parks and export processing zones will have centralised wastewater treatment systems that meet environmental standards.
- Improving environmental quality: Focus on enhancing the overall quality of the environment.
- Ensuring a high level of ecological balance.
- Meeting environmental requirements for international economic integration while minimising the negative impacts of globalisation.

The NSEP to 2010 outlined 36 national priority programs, plans, subjects, and projects related to environmental protection, each assigned to various relevant ministries based on sectors. Notable examples include a hazardous waste treatment program, which was allocated to the Ministry of Natural Resources and Environment, and a program focused on renovating heavily polluted and degraded canals, rivers, and lakes in urban areas, which fell under the responsibility of the Ministry of Construction.

Other programs addressed various aspects such as improving state management capacity, enhancing the legal system, developing wastewater treatment systems in industrial zones, and promoting environmentally friendly technological innovations. These initiatives were managed by various relevant ministries, including the Ministry of Industry and the Ministry of Science and Technology. While these programs encompassed a broad spectrum of environmental issues, many of them were simply reiterations of existing policies already governed by laws and related documents, and they lacked specific mechanisms for implementation.

- **From 2005 to 2013**

In 2005, the National Sustainable Development Council was established by the Prime Minister's Decision No. 1032/QĐ-TTg on September 29, 2005.[48] The council's role is to advise the Prime Minister on implementing sustainable development initiatives in accordance with the Strategic Orientation for Sustainable Development. It is chaired by a Deputy Prime Minister and consists of 30 members from various government bodies, ministries, agencies, social and professional organisations, businesses, and the media.

Between 2005 and 2010, significant efforts were made to accelerate the development and refinement of the legal system concerning environmental protection. The National Assembly adopted the Law on Environmental Protection in 2005 (LEP 2005)[49] to replace the LEP 1993, introducing several new regulations. Under this new law, state management for environmental protection was decentralised.[50] Each ministry was given the authority to develop its own environmental regulations and oversee the environmental protection efforts of its subordinate entities, while the PPCs were granted greater autonomy in approving environment-related permits. This decentralisation has resulted in fragmented environmental management.[51]

Several new laws were also enacted during this period, including the Law on Biodiversity (2008), which laid the foundation for legal frameworks concerning biodiversity conservation in Vietnam. The Law on Efficient Use of Energy (2010) and the Law on Environmental Protection Tax (2010) were also introduced during this period.

In 2008, the Vedan Corporation faced significant scrutiny after discharging wastewater into the Thi Vai River, which resulted in several changes to environmental protection regulations in Vietnam. An investigation uncovered ten violations by Vedan, including exceeding wastewater discharge standards, failing to implement

[48] This Council has later been renamed as 'National Council on Sustainable Development and Competitiveness Enhancement'.

[49] The implementation of this Law is guided by Government of Vietnam (2006) Decree 80/2006/NĐ-CP on Guidelines for the Implementation of a number of articles of the Law on Environmental Protection, admended by Decree 21/2008/NĐ-CP (28 February 2008).

[50] Nam and Thi (2023), p. 10.

[51] Ibid.

environmental monitoring fully, neglecting to register a commitment to protect the environment, and not complying with hazardous waste management regulations, among others. Despite these violations, Vedan was only required to pay an administrative fine of 267.5 million VND, according to Decree 81/2006/NĐ-CP (August 9, 2006), which outlined administrative sanctions for environmental violations. This outcome sparked debate among scholars and the public, as many believed the relatively lenient fine could incentivise companies to accept penalties instead of investing in wastewater treatment systems from the outset.[52]

In response to these concerns, Decree 81 was replaced by Decree 117/2009/NĐ-CP (December 31, 2009). Subsequent decrees, such as Decree 179/2013/NĐ-CP (November 14, 2013) and Decree 155/2016/NĐ-CP (November 18, 2016), addressed environmental protection violations and established administrative fines of up to 2 billion VND.[53] These updates aimed to impose stricter penalties for environmental violations to deter non-compliance and enhance the effectiveness of environmental protection regulations.

During this period, Vietnam established and progressively refined its legal framework for managing water resources and protecting the water environment. Key components of this framework include the Law on Water Resources of 2012[54] and the associated guiding documents. These legal provisions regulate the management, protection, exploitation, and use of water resources, as well as efforts to mitigate harmful effects related to water within Vietnam's territory.

- **From 2014 to 2020**

During this period, several significant developments took place in Vietnam's environmental protection efforts. One of the most important events was the adoption of the Law on Environmental Protection 2014 (LEP 1993), which replaced the LEP 2005. This new legislation introduced a variety of regulations aimed at addressing current environmental challenges, including climate change response, promotion of green growth, and the development of environmental planning. While the prevention of pollution and environmental degradation remained key objectives, the LEP 2014 implemented comprehensive policies and measures that covered all aspects of environmental protection activities. It also defined the rights, obligations, and responsibilities of environmental protection agencies, organisations, households, and individuals (as stated in Article 4.1 of the LEP 2014). The law emphasised that environmental protection is a collective responsibility and obligation for all members of society.

Additionally, this period saw the issuance of various legal regulations related to environmental management, such as the Law on Planning (2017),[55] Law on Fisheries

---

[52] Tin (2019), p. 70.

[53] Ibid.

[54] National Assembly of Vietnam (2012) Law No. 17/2012/QH13, replacing the Law No. 08/1998/QH10 on Water Resources 1998.

[55] National Assembly of Vietnam (2017) Law No. 21/2017/QH14.

(2017),[56] Land Law (2013),[57] Law on Natural Disaster Prevention and Control (2013),[58] Law on Cultivation (2018),[59] Law on Husbandry (2018),[60] Law on Biodiversity (2018),[61] Forestry Law (2017);[62] Law on Natural Resources and Environment of Sea and Islands (2015),[63] Law on Hydrometeorology (2015),[64] Law on Water Resources (2012).[65]

Besides, the Government and the Prime Minister have issued several resolutions, master plans, plans and programs related to climate change, including Resolution No. 76/NQ-CP on Natural Disaster Prevention and Control (2018); Resolution No. 120/NQ-CP of the Government on climate resilient and sustainable development of the Mekong Delta (2017); Decree No. 119/2016/NĐ-CP of the Government on several policies on management, protection and sustainable development of coastal forests to respond to climate change (2016).

During this period, the system of national technical standards and regulations on surface water quality, domestic wastewater and wastewater for manufacturing industries continues to be reviewed and revised.[66] A significant shift occurred in the regulation of wastewater discharge into water sources, emphasizing the protection of sources that are under substantial pressure from wastewater activities.[67] Economic instruments, including taxes, environmental fees, sanctions, and compensation, were more robustly applied. Tax policies related to the water environment were developed in alignment with sustainability goals, leading to effective fee collection. This strategy has increased awareness among businesses regarding the responsible use of water resources and has encouraged initiatives to conserve water and reduce wastewater discharge, thereby alleviating environmental pollution.[68]

In Vietnam, violations of environmental laws and related regulations can result in four types of legal responsibilities: administrative responsibility, civil liability, disciplinary responsibility, and criminal responsibility. Among these, administrative sanctions are the most commonly applied form of punishment, and there are comprehensive guidelines in place to enforce these sanctions. However, the

[56] National Assembly of Vietnam (2017) Law No.18/2017/QH14.

[57] National Assembly of Vietnam (2013) Law No. 45/2013/QH13 .

[58] National Assembly of Vietnam (2013) Law No. 33/2013/QH13.

[59] National Assembly of Vietnam (2018) Law No. 31/2018/QH14.

[60] National Assembly of Vietnam (2018) Law No. 32/2018/QH14.

[61] Office of the National Assembly of Vietnam (2018). Integrated document No. 32/VBHN-VPQH.

[62] National Assembly of Vietnam (2018) Law No.18/2017/QH14

[63] National Assembly of Vietnam (2015) Law No. 82/2015/QH13.

[64] National Assembly of Vietnam (2015) Law No. 90/2015/QH13.

[65] National Assembly of Vietnam (2012) Law No. 17/2012/QH13.

[66] See National Technical Regulations related to Water Environment in MONRE (2010), p. 88.

[67] Ibid., p. 99.

[68] The environmental protection fee for waste water has been regulated and implemented since 2003. Up to now, the regulations on environmental protection fees on waste water have been adjusted twice in Government of Vietnam (2013) Decree No. 25/2013/NĐ-CP and Government of Vietnam (2016) Decree No. 154/2016/NĐ-CP.

implementation of these sanctions remains limited for various reasons.[69] The Prime Minister has demonstrated a commitment to enforcing regulations by continuing to approve programs aimed at ensuring fair prosecution for violations of waste regulations, particularly during the period from 2016 to 2020.[70]

4.2.2 Policy Tools and Institutions for Environmental Protection in Vietnam

Various economic instruments have been actively encouraged and implemented in Vietnam to control pollution and promote environmental protection. These instruments are crucial in incentivising businesses and industries to adopt environmentally responsible practices. These instruments include:

- Vietnam Environment Protection Fund (VEPF): Decision 82/2002/QĐ-TTg established the VEPF, which is financed through domestic and foreign sources. The fund provides loans at preferential interest rates to support environmental protection investment projects that borrow from financial institutions. It also provides financial support for national and inter-regional programs, projects, and activities to prevent, combat, and mitigate environmental pollution, degradation, and incidents.
- Sanctions and Compensation for Damages: Decision 64/2003/QĐ-TTg introduced a plan for organisations contributing to severe environmental pollution. Owners of such organisations who implemented this plan were entitled to various incentives, including tax exemptions or reductions related to corporate income tax, import tax benefits for clean and environmentally friendly machinery and equipment, preferential policies, as well as reductions or exemptions for land use levies, land rentals, and land use taxes. These incentives were offered to encourage polluting organisations to take corrective actions, such as suspending operations, changing technologies, or installing wastewater treatment systems.
- Environmental Protection Fees: Several Decrees and decisions were adopted to impose environmental protection fees for activities such as wastewater discharge and mining. These fees are financial mechanisms that provide revenue for environmental protection initiatives.
- Revolving Fund for Pollution Reduction Program: Regional authorities, such as Ho Chi Minh City, introduced economic instruments like the revolving fund for pollution reduction programs. This initiative grants low-interest loans to industries investing in pollution control measures and technologies.

While economic instruments have been employed, supplementary tools like pollution control subsidies, product charges, tradable permits, development impact fees,

[69] See further Tin (2019), pp. 70–71; Chu (2020), p. 6.

[70] Prime Minister of Vietnam (2018) Decision No. 807/QĐ-TTg.

and resource depletion charges were not extensively adopted in Vietnam during this period. Exploring these alternative mechanisms is imperative to bolster the efficacy of environmental protection and sustainability efforts.

4.2.3 Laws and Policies for Mitigating Climate Change Effects

In 2012 and 2013, Vietnam adopted several significant strategies and decisions to promote sustainable development, environmental protection, and addressing climate change. These initiatives reflect the country's commitment to environmental conservation and resilience to climate change. Below is a summary of the key strategies and decisions:

- Law on Environmental Protection Tax: The Law on Environmental Protection Tax, adopted by the National Assembly in 2010 and effective from January 1, 2012, marked a crucial step in legalising economic instruments for environmental protection in Vietnam. This law imposes taxes on activities that harm the environment, serving as a financial mechanism to encourage cleaner and more sustainable practices.
- Vietnam Strategy for Sustainable Development (2011–2020): Decision No. 432/QĐ-TTg, dated April 12, 2012, approved by the Prime Minister outlines the country's vision for sustainable development from 2011 to 2020, emphasising the importance of balancing economic growth with environmental protection and social development. It sets objectives and directions for various sectors to achieve sustainable development.
- Strategy for Environmental Protection to 2020, Vision to 2030: Decision No. 1216/QĐ-TTg, dated September 5, 2012, approved by the Prime Minister, sets out a comprehensive strategy for environmental protection. This strategy establishes environmental protection goals and objectives, addressing pollution control, natural resource management, and biodiversity conservation. The vision extends to 2030, emphasising the long-term commitment to environmental sustainability.
- National Committee on Climate Change: Decision No. 43/QĐ-TTg, dated January 9, 2012, marked the establishment of the National Committee on Climate Change. This Committee is designed to enhance institutional capacity in dealing with the adverse effects of climate change. It signifies Vietnams recognition of the importance of addressing climate change at the national level.
- Resolution 24-NQ/TW (2013): Adopted by the 11th Central Committee of the Communist Party of Vietnam (CPV), Resolution 24-NQ/TW is titled "Actively Respond to Climate Change, Improve Natural Resource Management, and Protect the Environment." This resolution underscores the need for active responses to climate change and highlights the importance of enhancing natural resource management and environmental protection. It outlines specific objec-

tives to tackle climate change and improve environmental conservation in Vietnam.

– Other Environmental and Biodiversity Strategies: In addition to the climate change-related strategies, several other strategies were adopted in 2013, including the Strategy on Forestry Development (2006–2020),[71] Strategy on management of special forests systems, marine protected areas, reservation zones of domestic water area of Vietnam to 2020, with the vision to 2030,[72] and the National Strategy on bio-diversity up to 2020, with a vision to 2030.[73] These strategies focus on various aspects of environmental conservation, sustainable forestry, biodiversity protection, and the management of natural resources.

These initiatives collectively demonstrate Vietnam's commitment to fostering sustainable development, protecting the environment, addressing climate change and biodiversity conservation. The legal and strategic framework provides a comprehensive approach to balancing economic growth with environmental and social well-being.

- **National Strategy for Environmental Protection to 2020**

In 2013, after a decade of implementing the National Strategy for Environmental Protection (NSEP) up to 2010, there was a notable reduction in the number of production establishments causing severe pollution, with the list decreasing to 326 such establishments, representing a decrease from the previous period. Of these, approximately 3% had received investments from foreign investors.[74]

The Prime Minister approved the second National Strategy for Environmental Protection, covering the next ten years (NSEP up to 2020), in Decision 1216/QĐ-TTg.[75] This strategy was followed by Decision 166/QĐ-TTg (January 21, 2014), which outlined the plan for implementing the national environmental protection strategy up to 2020, with a vision to 2030. The NSEP up to 2020 reaffirmed the Vietnamese government's commitment to integrating environmental protection into its socioeconomic and sustainable development strategies, recognising the changing context of pollution management in Vietnam.

The NSEP up to 2020 emphasises the necessity of clearly defining responsibilities across various ministries and management levels to enhance environmental management and pollution control. It advocates for stronger enforcement of administrative measures that embody the "polluter pays" principle, ensuring accountability for polluters. The strategy also highlights the importance of integrating environmental protection into socioeconomic development plans and projects to achieve sustainable development. Additionally, it calls for improvements in the EIA

[71] Prime Minister of Vietnam (2007) Decision No. 18/QĐ-TTg.

[72] Prime Minister of Vietnam (2014) Decision No. 218/QĐ-TTg.

[73] Prime Minister of Vietnam (2013) Decision No. 1250/QĐ-TTg.

[74] Prime Minister of Vietnam (2013) Decision No. 1788/QĐ-TTg. This Decision does not include facilities that were mandated to cease operations or prohibited from operating.

[75] Prime Minister of Vietnam (2012) Decision 1216/QĐ-TTg.

process to prevent outdated, polluting technologies in new developments. There is also a push for targeted actions within industrial zones that do not meet environmental standards, potentially leading to the closure of non-compliant facilities and a prohibition on new investments. Furthermore, strict regulations on investment licensing are deemed essential for enforcing compliance with environmental protection laws, along with an increased focus on controlling pollution from the mining sector through the promotion of economic instruments and clean energy sources. These measures and strategies demonstrate Vietnam's ongoing commitment to addressing environmental issues and ensuring a sustainable and eco-friendly development path. The focus on integration with economic activities, effective management, and pollution control highlights the government's proactive approach to environmental protection.

The NSEP up to 2020 highlights several critical areas for enhancing environmental protection, emphasising the strengthening of legal frameworks and institutions to bolster law enforcement capabilities. NSEP to 2020 has suggested establishing a dispute settlement mechanism and compensation for environmental issues. It advocates for the consolidation of management systems across state agencies, focusing on improving the capacity of law enforcement while streamlining responsibilities at national, provincial, district, and commune levels to eliminate overlaps and fragmentation. Additionally, the strategy recognises the importance of international cooperation in environmental initiatives, particularly in the context of securing bilateral and multilateral trade agreements, alongside commitments to the WTO on environmental services to attract foreign investment. The MONRE continues to lead coordination efforts, while the Ministry of Planning and Investment and the Ministry of Finance manage financial coordination, supported by various other ministries and People's Committees responsible for implementing specific objectives and measures within the strategy (Part IV Decision 1216/QĐ-TTg).

Vietnam's legal framework for environmental protection has seen significant improvements compared to the previous period. These enhancements include the development of specific guiding documents in various environmental fields, such as pollution control, waste management, river basin management, sea and island environment management, biodiversity conservation, and promoting environmental protection through public participation. Additionally, the system of environmental technical regulations has undergone review and revision, indicating an effort to keep standards up to date with current environmental challenges.

The period 2020 to present marks a strong explosion of policies issued to respond to climate change. Indeed, Viet Nam has issued and implemented many guidelines, policies, strategies, programs and plans in its efforts to respond to climate change and implement international commitments, specifically the new Law on Environmental Protection (2020), which has been approved by the National Assembly focusing on climate change adaptation. Circular No. 01/2022/TT-BTNMT detailing the implementation of the Law on Environmental Protection in response to climate change has also been issued.

Overall, in terms of policy, in 2022, Vietnam took significant strides in climate action with the approval of two vital initiatives by Prime Minister Decisions. Firstly,

Decision No. 896/QĐ-TTg (July 26, 2022) of the Prime Minister approved the Vietnam National Strategy on Climate Change to 2050, aimed at proactively adapting to and mitigating climate change impacts while striving for net-zero greenhouse gas (GHG) emissions by 2050. This strategy underscores Vietnam's commitment to international climate protection efforts and prioritises the development of climate resilience techniques to bolster economic competitiveness. Central to the strategy are two ambitious objectives: reducing GHG emissions and enhancing climate resilience. By 2030, Vietnam targets a 43.5% reduction in total GHG emissions compared to business-as-usual projections. Simultaneously, Decision 942 endorsed Vietnam's Action Plan on Methane Emissions Reduction by 2030.[76] This plan outlines measures to curtail methane emissions by 30% from various sources such as crop production, animal husbandry, waste management, and industrial activities like petroleum exploitation and coal mining. Besides, the Government and the Prime Minister have also issued many resolutions, master plans, plans and programs related to climate change, notably:

- National Adaptation Plan (2020);
- Master Plan for the Mekong Delta in 2021–2030, Vision to 2050 (2022);
- National Monitoring and Evaluation System of Climate Change Adaptation Activities (2022).

In summary, Vietnam's regulations governing environmental protection are present in the Law on Environmental Protection and various other legal documents, which have significantly expanded over time. This comprehensive system of legal documents underscores Vietnam's commitment to addressing environmental challenges and promoting responsible environmental stewardship through legal regulations, enforcement mechanisms, and punitive measures when necessary.

Furthermore, Vietnam's recently established national planning system reflects decisive actions signalling the country's dedication to addressing climate change and reducing its negative repercussions at the domestic level. Through establishing precise objectives and implementing tangible strategies, the Vietnamese government exhibits a proactive stance in mitigating climate impacts and promoting sustainability.

4.3 Engaging in Global Environmental and Climate Treaties

Over the past three decades, Vietnam has proactively engaged with the global community, becoming a signatory to approximately 20 international conventions and agreements focused on sustainable development and environmental protection. The country has demonstrated a strong commitment to fulfilling its obligations within these international accords. Among these agreements, the 1982 Convention on the

[76] Prime Minister of Vietnam (2022) Decision No. 942/QĐ-TTg.

Law of the Sea, the 1985 Vienna Convention for the Protection of the Ozone Layer and the Montreal Protocol on Substances that Deplete the Ozone Layer, the 1989 Basel Convention on the Control of Trans-boundary Movements of Hazardous Wastes and Their Disposal (Basel Convention), the 1973 Convention on International Trade in Endangered Species of Wild Fauna and Flora (CITES 1973), the 1971 Convention on Wetlands of International Importance, especially as Waterfowl Habitat (RAMSAR Convention 1971), the 1973 International Convention for the Prevention of Pollution from Ships (1973 MARPOL Convention), the 1992 Convention on Biological Diversity; the 1972 Convention concerning the Protection of the World Cultural and Natural Heritage; the United Nations Convention to Combat Desertification; the Stockholm Convention on Persistent Organic Pollutants are most notable. Additionally, as a nation highly vulnerable to climate change, Vietnam has ratified the 1992 United Nations Framework Convention on Climate Change, the Kyoto Protocol, and the Paris Agreement. These commitments reflect the country's dedication to addressing pressing global environmental issues.

Vietnam has actively developed sustainable cooperative relationships with both its traditional partners and other countries, as well as international organisations. This strategy has enabled the country to access international resources for environmental protection initiatives. Vietnam has fostered cooperation across various regions, including Asia-Europe, Asia-Pacific, ASEAN, and ASEAN+3. It has also contributed to environmental cooperation mechanisms among East Asia countries and those in the Mekong sub-region.[77]

As part of ASEAN's framework for environmental cooperation, Vietnam has been an active participant in the ASEAN Ministerial Meetings on the Environment, the ASEAN Senior Officials on Environment, and various working groups of the ASEAN Special Organization on Environment. These groups focus on areas such as multilateral environmental treaties and conventions, marine environment issues, coastal region management, nature conservation and biodiversity, sustainable urban development, integrated water resource management, and the ASEAN Haze Technical Task Force.

Beyond participating in international conventions, Vietnam has taken proactive steps to foster both multilateral and bilateral cooperation in environmental protection. The country has implemented several major programs and projects in collaboration with key partners, including Japan, Korea, Switzerland, Denmark, and Sweden, along with support from international organisations such as the United Nations Development Programme (UNDP), the United Nations Environment Programme (UNEP), the WB, the Global Environment Facility, and the ADB. From 2011 to 2015, Vietnam attracted more than 30 international environmental projects with a total budget exceeding 750 million USD.[78] This international cooperation has significantly enhanced Vietnam's scientific and technological capabilities, incorporated modern methodologies and best practices from other nations, and

[77] MONRE (2015), p. 232.

[78] Ibid, p. 214.

strengthened the country's policy and legal framework regarding natural resources and environmental concerns.[79]

Regarding environmental legislation, Vietnam has demonstrated its commitment to translating international principles into domestic law as a signatory to numerous international environmental treaties and conventions. Key principles of environmental protection, particularly the principle of sustainable development, have been integrated into Vietnam's national legal framework. The principle of sustainable development, found in Principle 11 of the Stockholm Declaration and Principle 12 of the Rio de Janeiro Declaration, has been reflected in Vietnam's internal legal documents. For example, Article 63 of the 2013 Vietnam Constitution enshrines this principle. Additionally, the Law on Environmental Protection 2014 emphasises sustainable development in Article 4.2. This law underscores the importance of balancing environmental protection with economic growth, social security, the well-being of children, gender equality, biodiversity conservation, climate change response, and the right to live in a clean environment.

Vietnam's commitment to the principle of sustainable development goes beyond legal documents. It has been effectively integrated into various national development policies and strategies, including the 2011–2020 Social and Economic Development Strategy and the 2016–2020 Social and Economic Development Plan. Furthermore, this principle is evident in laws and action plans implemented at various levels, including those established by ministries, agencies, and provinces.

As a United Nations member, Vietnam actively participates in the global sustainable development agenda. In July 2018, Vietnam launched its Voluntary National Review. It has also formulated a national system of statistical indicators for monitoring and evaluating sustainable development. International development partners have strongly supported Vietnam's implementation of sustainable development goals, which have been integrated into its development cooperation strategies.[80] In specific, sustainable development goals were nationalised in the National Action Plan to implement the 2030 Agenda for Sustainable development goals in May 2017.[81] Following this National Action Plan, many orienting documents, policies and measures have been promulgated and implemented in order to achieve 17 sustainable development goals (SDGs) identified by the United Nations, especially in:

- Ensuring availability and sustainable management of water and sanitation for all (Goal 6)[82]

---

[79] Ibid.

[80] Baum (2020), p. 17.

[81] Prime Minister of Vietnam (2017) Decision No. 622/QĐ-TTg. See seventeen global SDGs have been nationalized into 115 Viet Nam SDG targets in the 'National Action Plan for Implementation of the 2030 Agenda for Sustainable Development' in United Nations (2018).

[82] Law No. 17/2012/QH13 on Water Resources, National Assembly of Vietnam (2012) and National Strategy on Water Resources until 2020, approved by Decision No.81/QĐ-TTG of the Prime Minister, are two important policies to implement SDG 6. In addition, the National Target Program on New Rural Development 2016–2020, approved by Decision No. 1600/QĐ-TTg of the Prime

- Ensuring access to affordable, reliable, sustainable energy for all (Goal 7)[83]
- Promoting sustained, inclusive and sustainable economic growth, full and productive employment and decent work for all (Goal 8)[84]
- Developing sustainable and resilient cities and rural areas; ensuring safe and resilient working and living areas; maintaining relevant regional allocation of population and labour (Goal 11)[85]
- Taking urgent action to combat climate change and natural disasters (Goal 13)[86]
- Strengthening the means of implementation and revitalising the global partnership for sustainable development (Goal 17)[87]

Besides, Vietnam recognises the importance of a green growth policy and has incorporated it into the National Green Growth Strategy for the 2021–2030 period, with a vision for 2050. This policy is viewed as a crucial approach to achieving sustainable development and reducing greenhouse gas emissions, ultimately working

---

Minister, is especially focussed on meeting the needs of the poor, ethnic minorities and those living in remote areas.

[83] The main requirements of SDG 7 are delineated in the Law No. 28/2004/QH11 on Electricity, National Assembly of Vietnam (2004), amended by Law No. 24/2012/QH13, National Assembly of Vietnam (2012); Law No. 50/2010/QH12 on Economical and Efficient Use of Energy, National Assembly of Vietnam (2010) and National Strategy for Energy Development until 2020 with a Vision to 2045, approved by Decision No. 215/QĐ-TTg of the Prime Minister.

[84] National Assembly of Vietnam (2019) Law No. 45/2019/QH14 on Labour Code; National Assembly of Vietnam (2017) Law No. 04/2017/QH14 on Support for Small and Medium-sized Enterprises; National Assembly of Vietnam (2021) Resolution No. 31/2021/QH15 on the Overall Plan for Economic Restructuring during 2013–2020 associated with the transformation of the growth model towards improved quality, efficiency and competitiveness capacity during 2013–2020; Prime Minister of Vietnam (2021) Decision No 1658/2QĐ-TTg on National Green Growth Strategy 2021–2030, Vision to 2050; Government of Vietnam (2020) Resolution No. 124/2020/NQ-CP on the Government's Action Program to implement Resolution No. 23-NQ/TW of the Politburo on National Industry Development Policies until 2030, Vision to 2045.

[85] Prime Minister of Vietnam (2021) Decision No. 2161/QĐ-TTg on the National Strategy on Housing Development for 2021–2030, Vision to 2045; National Assembly of Vietnam (2023) Law No. 27/2023/QH15 on Housing; National Assembly of Vietnam (2009) Law No. 30/2009/QH12 on Urban Planning; and the Prime Minister of Vietnam (2016) Decision No.1600/QĐ-TTg on the National Target Program on New Rural Development 2016–2020 are important policies that aim to reach SDG 11.

[86] National Assembly of Vietnam (2013) Law No. 33/2013/QH13 on Preventing and Controling Natural Disaster; Prime Minister of Vietnam (2021) Decision No. 397/QĐ-TTg on National Strategy for Natural Disaster Prevention, Response and Mitigation until 2030, Visiton to 2050; Prime Minister of Vietnam (2022) Decision No.896/QĐ-TTg National Strategy on Climate Change until 2050; Prime Minister of Vietnam (2021) Decision No 1658/QĐ-TTg National Green Growth Strategy 2021–2030, Vision to 2050; and related action plans.

[87] National Assembly of Vietnam (2020) Law on Investment No.61/2020/QH14; Prime Minister of Vietnam (2016) Decision No. 40/QĐ-TTg on Overall Strategy for International Integration to 2020 with a Vision to 2030; and Prime Minister of Vietnam (2022) Decision No. 493/QĐ-TTg on Export-Import Strategy until 2030. See the list of adopted documents and policies in different areas in Korea Environment Institute (2017); United Nations (2018).

towards a carbon-neutral economy in the long run.[88] Acknowledging the interplay between these concepts, Vietnam actively participates in international environmental treaties on climate change. The country continues to negotiate comprehensive commitments on sustainable development, including climate change initiatives, in agreements such as the EVFTA and other new-generation FTAs. Vietnam has made significant efforts to integrate international principles, particularly the principle of sustainable development, into its domestic legal and policy framework. These efforts reflect the country's commitment to addressing global environmental and developmental challenges while striving for a harmonious balance between economic growth, social development, and environmental protection.

During the 26th United Nations Climate Change Conference of the Parties (COP26) hosted in Glasgow on October 31 to November 13, 2021 COP26, Vietnam's Prime Minister Pham Minh Chinh made significant commitments. These include achieving a net-zero carbon emission target by 2050, halting deforestation by 2030, and phasing out coal-fueled power generation by 2040.[89] These commitments are seen as a goodwill gesture by the government to attract foreign direct investment into Vietnam in the wake of the COVID-19 pandemic. The emphasis is on exploring and advancing clean energy sources.

To fulfill its commitments outlined at COP26, the Vietnamese government aims to reduce total greenhouse gas (GHG) emissions by approximately 9% compared to the Business as Usual (BAU) scenario by 2030, which translates to 83.9 million tonnes of CO2 equivalent.[90] With international assistance through bilateral and multilateral cooperation and the adoption of new mechanisms under the Paris Agreement, this target could increase by up to 27% relative to the BAU scenario, amounting to 250.8 million tonnes of CO2 equivalent. Moreover, the emission reduction targets in Vietnam's NDCs 2022 show even greater ambition. The targets for emission reductions across various sectors, including energy, agriculture, land use, land-use change and forestry, waste, and industrial processes, by 2030—compared to the BAU scenario in the NDCs 2022—exceed those set in the NDCs 2020. Specifically, the unconditional contribution has increased from 9% to 15.8%, while the conditional contribution has risen from 27% to 43.5%.[91] In general, a comprehensive array of measures has been delineated to attain these ambitious objectives. Efforts to advance the implementation of the NDCs primarily concentrate on developing and enacting of institutional and legislative frameworks pertaining to climate change.[92]

---

[88] Prime Minister of Vietnam (2021) Decision No 1658/QĐ-TTg on National Green Growth Strategy 2021–2030, Vision to 2050.

[89] Shira (2021).

[90] UNFCCC (2020), p. 8.

[91] Vietnam's NDCs (2022), p. 2.

[92] Ibid, p. 26.

4.4 Challenges in Environmental Management and Responding to Climate Change in Vietnam

After over 30 years of renovation, environmental protection in Vietnam has developed progressively alongside the country's economic growth. Funding for environmental initiatives has significantly increased. In fact, state budget expenditures for environmental protection have grown over the years, representing 1% of the total budget and amounting to approximately 6 trillion VND in 2010, which is triple the amount in 2004. Additionally, funding sourced from Official Development Assistance between 2000 and 2009 totaled around 3.2 billion USD, with loans making up about 2.4 billion USD and grants accounting for approximately 0.79 billion USD.[93]

Vietnam has actively participated in key international environmental conventions, and the legal framework for environmental protection has been gradually developed. Since 1994, the LEP has been adopted and admended multiple times, with the fourth version reflecting the government's increasing concern for this issue. The legal documents related to environmental protection and management systems have been strengthened. However, the pressures from socio-economic development, along with the impacts of climate change and natural disasters, have created significant environmental challenges. These issues have affected public health and the economy and have increased conflicts related to environmental concerns within society.

As of 2024, the legal framework for environmental protection in Vietnam is relatively comprehensive and well-defined, addressing nearly all environmental concerns. The consolidation of state management organisations focused on environmental issues has continued, which includes improvements in organisational structure and human resources. However, despite the early recognition of environmental issues during the country's economic development, Vietnam's environmental protection policies have not been systematically or cohesively designed or implemented.[94] Several regulations and decisions related to the environment that emerged in the 10 to 20 years following the Đổi mới reforms were primarily reactive, addressing immediate issues rather than being part of a comprehensive long-term strategy. Additionally, the enforcement of environmental laws, regulations, decrees, and directives in Vietnam has been weak in practice, leading to several underlying problems as pointed out below:

- ***Weakness in the organisational system***

[93] Vietnam (2012).

[94] For instance, although the majority of industrial zones were established in 1994, it was not until 2002 that the MOSTE issued 'Regulation on the Protection of the Environment in Industrial Zones'. This Regulation comprehensively encompassed all relevant environmental protection provisions applicable to industrial zones as delineated in the Law on Environmental Protection, Decree No. 175/CP, and Circular No. 490/1998/TT-BKHCNMT. Consequently, this document had a minimal impact on the management of environmental protection within industrial zones.

There is an overlap in functions, duties and responsibilities in the current management system from national to local levels.[95] At the national level, cooperation among different ministries, such as The Ministry of Planning and Investment, The Ministry of Finance, The Ministry of Agriculture and Rural Development, The Ministry of Labour, Invalids and Social Affairs with MONRE, in implementing environmental policies in their sectors is neither consistent nor efficient.[96] There is a noticeable lack of communication and, in some cases, competition among these ministries.[97] Despite the establishment of interministerial coordination committees for various strategies, a cohesive policy framework has yet to be developed.[98]

Additionally, the fragmentation of environmental management across different ministries without clear roles and mechanisms for addressing critical environmental and development connections results in ineffective management.[99] The complex web of overlapping responsibilities among various sectors, combined with suboptimal collaboration among government agencies, has frequently led to delays in decision-making regarding emerging environmental issues. This fundamental weakness has significant implications, undermining the effective enforcement of policies related to sustainable development and diminishing the authority of the MOSTE/MONRE in enforcing environmental regulations. Improving governance remains the greatest challenge in environmental management in Vietnam, partly due to the low awareness and capacity among planners regarding how to collaborate effectively.[100]

At the local level, environmental protection management has not received the necessary attention. Generally, there is a lack of understanding of environmental integration in certain provinces, districts, and municipalities.[101] Studies have found that provincial and district leaders perceive their performance to be judged principally on economic growth and conflict avoidance. However, the environmental objective seems to conflict with both criteria.[102] Additionally, the absence of a central government decree or policy, as well as clear guidelines, targets, and indicators, presents another challenge. This situation leads to inefficient or ineffective investigations into high-risk or unproven demonstration projects.

- ***The top-down approach in adopting environmental policies and incoherence and incomplete policies and legislative system***

[95] MONRE (2015), p. xxxii; Chu (2020), p. 5.

[96] Tin (2019), p. 75; Chu (2020), p. 3; Bass et al. (2009), pp. 15–16.

[97] Schirmbeck (2017), p. 5.

[98] Ibid.

[99] This challenge in cooperating among different ministries has been empirically investigated in Bass et al. (2009), p. 16; Tin (2019), p. 75; MONRE (2015), pp. 193–194.

[100] Bass et al. (2009), pp. 38, 48.

[101] Ibid, p. 43.

[102] Ibid, p. 44.

Vietnam's single-party governance often leads to strategies being primarily conceived and approved at a national level. As a result, the valuable input, existing capacities, and effective local initiatives of subnational entities and key stakeholders aren't always fully utilized.[103] Furthermore, although mechanisms for public contribution on draft legislation have been in place on government information portals since the 2000s to meet transparency requirements associated with WTO accession, the broader public is rarely consulted during the drafting process or informed about newly enacted policies.[104] Consequently, policies in Vietnam, both in general and specifically in environmental management, are typically proclaimed and enforced without establishing meaningful engagement with the actual capacities and incentives of subnational actors and key stakeholders, resulting in implementation challenges or lack of attention to these policies.

Regarding the substance of published environmental policies, it has been observed that strategies and documents having the same goals in some cases do not refer to each other.[105] Scholars have also pointed out that almost none of the policies are harmonised with other political sectors, although creating such links would be crucial for the implementation of those strategies.[106] In specific, the Vietnam National Green Growth Strategy has almost not referred to the overall socio-economic development plans of the country despite the orientation to link social development with green development can be found in many documents adopted by the Communist Party of Vietnam, which sets the framework of political action in Vietnam, as well as in different versions of the National Strategy on Environmental Protection.

This incoherence indicates a lack of collaboration among relevant political actors. More importantly, it raises concerns that some political decision-makers intentionally endorse ambitious policies designed to attract "donor money" for their mere existence on paper, but these policies will only be implemented to a very limited extent.[107] This disjointed approach to policy-making has led to inadequate implementation control. Subnational levels and key stakeholders often lack the capacity, motivation, and sufficient guidance needed to carry out the adopted strategies. An example of this issue is highlighted in a study by Sonja Schirmbeck. When the Action Plan for implementing the Vietnam National Green Growth Strategy was adopted, all provinces were instructed to develop their own provincial action plans. However, most provinces merely copied the templates provided by the national government rather than tailoring them to the specific needs of their respective regions.[108]

---

[103] Schirmbeck (2017), p. 6.

[104] Ibid.

[105] For instance, Vietnam's Greenhouse Gas (GHG) emissions reduction targets of the Climate Change Strategy, see Prime Minister of Vietnam (2021) Decision No 1658/QĐ-TTg on National Green Growth Strategy 2021–2030, Vision to 2050; and the intended NDC are inconsistent. See further incoherence between relevant policies and documents in Schirmbeck (2017), p. 5.

[106] Ibid, p. 6.

[107] Ibid.

[108] Ibid, p. 7.

Vietnam has made some progress in developing legal documents to support environmental protection by regularly reviewing, amending, and strengthening them. However, this system of documents is fragmented, overlapping, ambiguous, incomplete, and lacks uniformity. For instance, environmental standards and technical regulations, particularly those not related to waste, remain insufficient. This gap results in inadequate criteria for a comprehensive assessment of environmental impacts caused by projects. Additionally, there are no specific legal documents systematically regulating the management and control of marine waste. The management of marine biodiversity is often complicated by overlapping regulations and even contradictions in some cases.[109]

- ***A serious lack of environmental experts***

A significant challenge in managing environmental pollution in Vietnam is the shortage of qualified human resources in management agencies, particularly those with expertise in environmental issues. There is a lack of both quantity and quality in personnel, especially in critical areas such as environmental impact assessment, biosafety, biodiversity conservation, and environmental economics.[110] Research indicates that limited institutional and financial resources result in an average of only eight environmental inspectors per province. This number is far from adequate to cover the extensive responsibilities involved in environmental protection, mineral resource extraction, water resource management, and land administration.[111]

- ***Weaknesses in inspecting and monitoring production activities***

The weak execution and monitoring of implementing environmental protection laws and regulations is considered a big issue, especially at the local level.[112] The inability to effectively supervise environmental compliance has led to policy ineffectiveness.[113] In Vietnam, the inspecting and monitoring activities are not well organised by the authorisations in the implementation phase of the projects, which leads to the chance that the investors will ignore the implementation of the approved pollution control measures. The Formosa case serves as a notable example of this problem.

> In 2016, a steel plant built in Vietnam by a Taiwanese company named Hung Nghiep Formosa Ha Tinh, Ltd. (FHS) was discovered to dump industrial wastes into the sea through underwater drainage pipes and seriously damaged the marine environment causing at least 70 tons of dead fish, affecting 450 hectares (1,112 acres) of coral reefs and making fisherman in the area to be jobless.
>
> This FHS plant was set up in 2012 in the Vung Ang Economic Zone, Ha Tinh Province, thereby taking advantage of associated infrastructure, local tax policies, and preferences in

[109] See further in United Nations (2018), p. 72.

[110] MONRE (2015), pp. 193–194.

[111] Nam and Thi (2023), p. 18.

[112] Korea Envestment Institute (2017), p. 23.

[113] Nam and Thi (2023), p. 19.

tariffs with countries belonging to the ASEAN Free Trade Area.[114] This is a joint factory that produces iron and steel from the initial raw materials of iron ore and coal into steel products. The project includes 6 blast furnaces with a capacity of 4,350 m3, the capacity is estimated at 15 million tons of finished cast iron with a total investment of 28.5 billion USD.[115] FHS is recognised as the largest FDI enterprise in Vietnam, contributing over 50% of the total budget revenue in Ha Tinh.[116] It should be noticed that Ha Tinh is a relatively impoverished province, accounting for only 1.1% of the national gross domestic product.[117]

When the environmental incident happens, followed by the protest of civic groups and local communities, the information released by the authorities and the FHS shows the conflict regarding the hidden sewage pipeline system constructed by FHS. Indeed, in Ha Tinh, on April 22, Mr Ho Anh Tuan, Head of the Provincial Economic Zone, said that the 1.5 km long waste pipeline system was approved by the Ministry of Natural Resources and Environment to be installed to discharge treated wastewater. This system was included in the environmental impact assessment (EIA) report, which was approved by the authorities.

Mr Hoang Duat Thuyen, Director in charge of the safety of Formosa Group, also said that "the Waste discharge permits were issued by the Ministry of Natural Resources and Environment in accordance with standard 52/2013. From March 2015, the system started to be tested and received a license from the Ministry of Natural Resources and Environment in December 2015".[118]

However, Mr Hoang Duong Tung (Deputy Director of Vietnam Environment Administration, MONRE) affirmed: "Up to now, Formosa has not been licensed to discharge waste into the sea directly. Currently, the relevant agencies of the Ministry are still conducting necessary inspection and appraisal procedures."[119]

Following the incident, an interdisciplinary agency comprising representatives from seven ministries, including the Ministry of Natural Resources and Environment; Ministry of Agriculture Rural Development; Ministry of Public Security; Ministry of Health; Ministry of Industry and Trade; Ministry of Science and Technology; alongside approximately 100 experts from Israel, Japan, and Germany, conducted a comprehensive joint investigation.[120]

However, the cause of the pollution was officially announced following a three-month investigation.'[121] Accordingly, it was determined that Formosa had discharged untreated wastewater into the sea through an underground pipe system. The discharged wastewater contained Phenol, Cyanide, and Iron Hydroxide toxins in concentrations exceeding permissible levels.[122]

---

[114] Fan et al. (2020).

[115] Đức Hùng and Bạch Dương (2016).

[116] As mentioned by Director of Department of Industry and Trade Hoang Van Quang, see Văn Đức (2020).

[117] Dat (2024), p. 198.

[118] Ibid.

[119] Danh Toại, M. Hà (2016).

[120] VnExpress (2016); Binh Minh (2016); Ministry of Science and Technology (2016).

[121] (2016).

[122] Minh Hà, Đông Sơn (2016).

> Notably, in a report prepared by the Ministry of Natural Resource and Environment, one among 53 administrative violations of FHS which were identified in 2016 was that the investor installed a wet cooler system applying for coke rather than the dry system which was presented in the EIA.[123]

> On June 29 and 30, at the headquarters of the Ministry of Natural Resources and Environment, Mr Tran Nguyen Thanh, Chairman of the Board of Directors of Formosa, admitted that the company's waste discharge activities caused environmental incidents that caused mass deaths of seafood in four provinces in central Vietnam. Formosa commits to compensating to fix the marine environment and compensating people for economic losses in the amount of 11,500 billion VND (equivalent to 500 million USD).

This incident has highlighted numerous weaknesses in Vietnam's environmental management, as outlined below:

(i) Investment Licensing Procedure

FHS was licensed to operate in 2008, with capital from Formosa Plastics Group, a Taiwanese conglomerate known for its controversial practices. The company has faced allegations of wrongdoing globally, including fraud in Texas in 1998 and environmental violations in Taiwan, Cambodia, and the United States.[124] The decision to license such a company for an investment project, despite economic experts deeming the project economically inefficient, raises significant concerns. Furthermore, FHS received considerable incentives in Vietnam, such as a 10% corporate income tax rate during the project period (compared to 22% for domestic enterprises), 04 years of income tax exemption followed by a 50% reduction for the next nine years, 15 years of land rent exemption, exemption from import tax on machinery and equipment, and exemption from natural resources tax for sand pumping and levelling activities. Economists, including Pham Chi Lan and Bui Trinh, have heavily criticised these incentives, arguing that they contradict economic analysis.[125] The decision to grant such incentives to a company with a questionable history and limited economic and technological benefits raises questions about the competency of Vietnamese agencies in reviewing FDI investment projects. It also suggests that the Vietnamese government may be excessively favoring FDI projects, potentially at the expense of environmental and economic considerations.

Another notable issue related to the investment licensing procedure for the FHS concerns the investor's technological accountability. Prior to the adoption of the LEP 2005, the Law on Foreign Direct Investment in Vietnam required investor to include a detailed explanation of the technology to be used in their projects within their application. However, the LEP 2005 only mandates that the investor be "responsible for the technology", simplifying the application process. During the investment licensing stage, FHS was only required to submit a pre-feasibility report,

---

[123] Đức Hùng (2017).

[124] Centre for International Environmental Law (2021), p. 16.

[125] Bich Ngoc (2014a, b).

which did not provide sufficient detail on whether dry or wet cup stamping technology would be employed. Subsequently, according to its specialised management function, the Ministry of Industry and Trade was responsible for approving the facility design.

This situation leads to several preliminary conclusions:

- Simplifying procedures, reducing document requirements, and shortening the review time for issuing investment certificates for FDI projects result in management agencies lacking the necessary information on technology to assess environmental safety at the investment licensing stage. This situation increases the risk of importing pollution from developed countries, as warned by Castleman,[126] or transferring air pollution from regions with strict environmental regulations to less developed, low-income countries that have more lenient regulatory enforcement.[127] This concern is evident in the case of FHS, where the technology used for the project was inadequately evaluated during the investment licensing stage. Additionally, it is impossible to change production or waste treatment technology once the factory has been constructed.[128]
- The investment licensing procedures are overly simplistic and fail to clearly define the responsibilities of the relevant agencies, as well as the coordination required between them. As a result, no agency takes full responsibility, leading to inadequate oversight of the investment licensing process. This situation also allows outdated technologies to infiltrate the domestic production environment. In the case of FHS, Ms. Tran Thi Tuyet Nhung, the Deputy Director of the Department of Technology Assessment, Appraisal and Assessment at the Ministry of Science and Technology, stated that the responsibility for technology appraisal rests with the Ministry of Industry and Trade.[129] However, when the People's Committee of Ha Tinh province, the local authority responsible for issuing investment certificates, sent an official request along with the pre-feasibility study project report, the Ministry of Science and Technology simply responded that the technology in question was commonly used by steel mills worldwide and was not considered new.[130] Additionally, Do Hoai Nam, the Director of the Department of Technology Assessment, Appraisal and Assessment, could not confirm whether the Ministry of Industry and Trade invited the Ministry of Science and Technology to participate in the technology assessment and appraisal of the FHS project during the appraisal process.[131]

[126] Castleman (1979), p. 569.

[127] Ben-David et al. (2021), p. 415; Dat (2024), p. 206.

[128] Director of the Department of Technology Evaluation - Appraisal and Assessment Do Hoai Nam answered an interview with the press at the regular press conference of the Ministry of Science and Technology held on July 5, 2016. See Thu Hằng (2016).

[129] Ibid.

[130] Ibid.

[131] Ibid.

This situation reveals a notable weakness in the organisation and division of responsibilities among the relevant agencies involved in investment licensing procedures in Vietnam during this time. It also highlights that environmental protection in economic development has not received adequate attention, despite the emphasis placed on this goal in various policy documents of the Communist Party of Vietnam and the regulations set by the Government.

(ii) Project Management During Operation

The FHS incident highlights significant weaknesses in the management of investment projects during their operational phase. Despite being examined and licensed by MONRE in 2015, FHS's wastewater treatment system failed to comply with environmental protection rules. This suggests that inspections and licensing may have been conducted merely to fulfil procedural requirements rather than to ensure actual wastewater treatment capacity. Additionally, while an EIA report was submitted, it appeared to be a formality for obtaining land use and construction permits rather than a genuine environmental safeguard. The underground wastewater pipeline to the sea, included in the EIA, only became a concern after untreated wastewater was discharged directly into the sea, leading to widespread fish deaths and severe impacts on local livelihoods. This situation underscores the limitations in the inspection and supervision capabilities of Vietnam's environmental management agencies during the operation of investment projects.

(iii) State Capacity to Manage Environmental Incidents

The third limitation lies in the capacity of Vietnamese state agencies to manage and address environmental incidents. The nearly three-month-long investigation into the marine environmental incident caused by FHS revealed significant deficiencies in the state agencies' handling skills and response experience. International experts had to be invited to assist in determining the cause of the fish deaths, highlighting the institutional weaknesses of Vietnam's environmental management agencies. The government's handling of the incident faced substantial criticism from both domestic and international observers, reflecting a broader issue of inadequate institutional capacity. These points illustrate the critical need for strengthening Vietnam's environmental management framework, particularly in terms of investment licensing, project oversight, and incident response capabilities.

The 2016–2020 Report on National Environment published by the Ministry of Natural Resources and Environment shows that the Central Coastal Environmental Incident caused by FHS is ranked first in the list of prominent environmental pollution cases.[132] This case highlights the shortcomings in the capacity of state authorities to manage environmental issues related to investment projects. Inspection activities aimed at assessing compliance with environmental policies—whether regular, random, or based on specific complaints—are poorly coordinated. Specifically, oversight of projects with potential environmental pollution risks, such

[132] MONRE (2021), p. 147.

as thermal power plants, mineral extraction, and chemical ventures, receives inadequate attention.

There is an argument that the Vietnamese government has both the capability and obligation to address this issue decisively as a regulatory body rather than simply accepting a compensation of 500 million USD from FHS. However, implementing more punitive measures, such as requiring the factory to close until all environmental standard violations are corrected or temporarily revoking its operating license, could worsen the situation. Such actions might be viewed as indirect expropriation and could not be executed without providing adequate compensation to investors, as specified in the bilateral investment promotion agreement between Taiwan and Vietnam, signed in 1993 (Articles 4 and 8). In this case, the Vietnamese government opted for a flexible approach to addressing foreign investors' violations of environmental protection regulations. While concerns about investor protection commitment under the BIT likely played a role, the primary motivation appears to be maintaining the country's reputation as an FDI-friendly country. Moreover, significant violations partly stem from deficiencies in managing and supervising investment projects with high environmental impact risks.

This incident, along with numerous recent environmental pollution cases in Vietnam, highlights a trend in which many localities prioritise attracting investment over environmental protection. Additionally, there has been a lack of thorough screening of investors before granting licenses. In the case of FHS, despite readily available information about the investor's track record, this essential aspect may not have been adequately considered during the licensing process.

Overall, while Vietnam possesses a comprehensive policy and legal framework for environmental protection, its effectiveness is undermined by various limitations in policy formulation, management, and enforcement. As a result, doubts persist regarding the Vietnamese government's ability to effectively address climate change under current circumstances.

Scholars have suggested that to pursue sustainable development and environmental management, the government should "Actively implement multilateralisation, diversify foreign relations and intensively integrate into the world, especially participating in free trade agreements with the developed economic regions of the world."[133] Vietnam has applied this strategy in its development process, as evidenced by the numerous international treaties it has concluded, primarily focused on encouraging trade and investment. However, as a developing country partner, it rarely shows its initiative in negotiating non-trade/investment issues such as labour, human rights or environment. The inclusion of these regulations in recent bilateral and multilateral new-generation trade-investment agreements, such as the CPTPP and EVFTA/EVIPA, has largely been driven by the suggestions and encouragement of its developed partners.

Similar to most other developing economies, Vietnam has not established its own Model BIT, especially one aligned with sustainable development requirements. In

[133] Tien et al. (2020), p. 77.

the context of trade and investment agreements, the country has not developed a specific strategy for negotiating matters related to sustainable development and environmental protection. This practice is evident in its bilateral and multilateral negotiations. A mere expectation that trade and investment agreements can prioritise investment in developing road, transport, medical, educational and urban infrastructures to enhance economic capacity and competitiveness while also limiting environmental waste[134] has proven impractical over the past 38 years. Among the 17 SDGs, goals 3, 6, 7, 8, 9, 11, 16, and 17 are particularly relevant to this book. These goals emphasise the importance of promoting sustainable economic growth, leveraging technology to ensure the well-being of both human and biological life, and enhancing the means of implementation while revitalising global partnerships for sustainable development. Pursuing these goals requires sufficient strategies in negotiating and effectively implementing international treaties with proper roadmaps to maximise national benefits, particularly in fostering motivation for changes in national policies. Nevertheless, the specific impacts of participation in these agreements and the strategies for negotiating trade and investment agreements in support of sustainable development in Vietnam remain unclear.

For instance, let's take a closer look at the efforts of the Vietnamese government to fulfill its commitments made at COP26 in 2021. Over the past two years since these important announcements, a National Steering Committee has been established, led by Prime Minister Pham Minh Chinh, to oversee Vietnam's commitments from the 26th Conference of the Parties to the United Nations Framework Convention on Climate Change.[135] This committee consists of key ministers from essential sectors, including the Ministry of Natural Resources and Environment (headed by Mr Tran Hong Ha), the Chairman of the Government Office (Mr Tran Van Son), the Ministry of Foreign Affairs (Mr Bui Thanh Son), the Ministry of Justice (Mr Le Thanh Long), the Ministry of Information and Communications (Mr Nguyen Manh Hung), and the Ministry of Construction (Mr Nguyen Thanh Nghi). Additionally, leaders from other ministries, agencies, and central authorities also participate in this committee.

In conjunction with these committee sessions, various projects, strategies, and action plans have been devised and implemented to translate the outcomes of the COP26 Conference into action.[136] However, these initiatives, despite being comprehensive, lack specific criteria and processes for effective implementation

---

[134] Ibid.

[135] Ministry of Industry and Trade (2022).

[136] For instance, endeavours like finalizing the National Electricity Development Plan spanning from 2021 to 2030, with a future perspective extending to 2045, have been initiated. Moreover, projects including the formulation of a Project delineating tasks and strategies to implement the COP26 Conference outcomes, the crafting of a National Strategy on climate change up to 2050, and the initiation of an Action program focusing on transitioning to green energy and reducing carbon and methane emissions in the transportation sector are underway. Additionally, action plans such as the National Action Plan on Green Growth spanning from 2021 to 2030 and the Action Plan aimed at curbing methane emissions until 2030 have been devised. Various ministries and sectors are actively developing sector-specific Action Plans in alignment with Vietnam's commit-

and evaluation. Additionally, there is limited engagement from relevant stakeholders in policy discussions. While the predominant top-down approach may work in some contexts, it falls short in addressing complex issues like climate change and sustainable development, which require broad mobilisation of resources and close collaboration between government and society.

The Vietnamese government currently possesses a strong policy framework to tackle environmental challenges, garnering praise from scholars,[137] notably in comparison to other emerging economies. Participation in new trade agreements, particularly those addressing non-trade issues like environmental protection, is expected to elevate environmental standards in Vietnam.[138] Furthermore, pressure from markets with stringent environmental regulations is anticipated to incentivise the country to enhance its domestic environmental standards. The government also acknowledges that effective implementation of environmental policies is essential to ensure access to new markets.[139] This understanding drives the country's commitment to pursue sustainable development objectives more effectively.

4.5 Interim Conclusion

This chapter examines how Vietnam's economic development and international economic integration have significantly influenced the evolution of its environmental policy and legal system. Over time, these systems have been gradually improved and expanded, primarily due to the proactive efforts of the government and the CPV to meet the requirements of international partners. Ensuring the implementation of international commitments remains a priority for the Vietnamese government, reflecting its desire to demonstrate goodwill to its global partners.

Vietnam's policies on natural resource and environmental management have been established at various levels. These range from international declarations, such as the Vietnam Climate Change Strategy and the Vietnam National Green Growth Strategy signed by the Prime Minister, to the resolutions of the Communist Party, the Environmental Protection Law, and detailed decrees on wastewater treatment, solid waste management, and species protection adopted by the National Assembly.[140] This strategic orientation towards sustainable development highlights the country's commitment to environmental protection as a critical component of its development process. These policies, which date back to the early 1990s, have seen

ments at COP26, with the overarching goal of attaining net zero emissions equilibrium. Thanh Huong (2023).

[137] Schirmbeck (2017), p. 5.

[138] Ibid, p. 8.

[139] Opening Speech of Dr. Tran Hong Ha, Vice Minister of MONRE, at a Conference on 'Implementing the Environmental Commitments of the Trans-Pacific Partnership' held on 8 April 8 2016 in Hanoi.

[140] Schirmbeck (2017), p. 5.

significant improvements over time. However, progress in achieving environmental protection has been limited due to various factors, including ineffective management structures and institutional capacity challenges at all levels. Despite the comprehensive promulgation of regulations, institutional limitations have rendered environmental management in Vietnam largely ineffective.

Vietnam has historically treated economic development and environmental management as separate objectives. Environmental policies have often been less effectively integrated into economic policies. Although there is a growing awareness of the importance of environmental protection in economic development, as evidenced in early official documents, environmental protection is still viewed as an independent mission rather than a correlative component of sustainable development. Additionally, Vietnam's environmental policy and regulations lack systematicity, often being issued in response to problems that arise or to fulfil international commitments. Indeed, separate institutions and policies have been designed to achieve individual objectives at different stages of Vietnam's economic development.[141] Consequently, although various environmental management policies and laws have been promulgated over time, the regulatory system fundamentally lacks cohesion, leading to implementation difficulties.

Vietnam's accession to the WTO and participation in various regional FTAs and BITs have opened significant avenues for attracting foreign investment. However, amidst the economic gains, the imperative of securing domestic environmental standards has become more pronounced. Notably, sectors attracting foreign investment often involve heavy or primary industries that demand substantial capital, such as mineral extraction and steel production, in expansive and remote areas. This scenario increases the likelihood of governmental intervention to preserve the environment. Additionally, developing countries like Vietnam face a heightened risk of discord with investors in environmental protection matters due to evolving and rapidly changing environmental regulations. Vietnam's current national development policies across various sectors often lack clarity and cohesive alignment, resulting in difficulties reconciling investor protection with comprehensive environmental protection measures. Nonetheless, it is essential to emphasise that, despite the limitations in policy formulation and environmental management, consistent political will can gradually address these shortcomings.

The challenges of integrating environmental management and economic development are significant and complex, and few countries have found perfect solutions.[142] While there have been some promising plans to better link environmental and developmental needs, many policy, coordination, and capacity constraints persist in Vietnam.[143] It is crucial to prepare for a new approach to institutional change that incorporates sustainable development and environmental protection into

[141] Bass et al. (2009), p. 9.

[142] Ibid.

[143] Ibid., p. 10.

various policies, with investment encouragement being a potential option. This approach will be explored further in Part IV of this book.

References

Bibliography

Bass S et al (2009) Integrating environment and development in Vietnam: achievements, challenges and next step. Paper resulting from the Viet Nam Environmental Mainstreaming 'Lessons Learned Review'. IIED. The Viet Nam/UNDP Poverty Environment Programme 2010

Baum A (2020) Vietnam's development success story and the unfinished SDG agenda. IMF Working Paper. Asia Pacific Department. Available via https://www.imf.org/en/Publications/WP/Issues/2020/02/14/Vietnam-s-Development-Success-Story-and-the-Unfinished-SDG-Agenda-48966

Ben-David I et al (2021) Exporting pollution: where do multinational firms emit CO2? Econ Policy 36(107)

Bich Ngoc (2014a) Formosa nhận bồi thường và ưu đãi kịch trần [Formosa receives extraordinary compensation and incentives]. Dat Viet Press. Available via https://fica.dantri.com.vn/thoi-su/dau-tu/formosa-nhan-boi-thuong-va-uu-dai-kich-tran-16953.html

Bich Ngoc (2014b) Biệt đãi Formosa: Việt Nam muốn được gì? [Special treatment for Formosa: What does Vietnam want?]. Dat Viet Press. Available via https://vietstock.vn/2014/07/biet-dai-formosa-viet-nam-muon-duoc-gi-768-355193.htm

Binh Minh (2016) Vụ cá chết: Bộ Công an vào cuộc [Fish death case: Ministry of Public Security intervenes]. Government News. Available via https://baochinhphu.vn/news-102202153.htm

Castleman BI (1979) The export of hazardous factories to developing nations. Int J Health Serv

Centre for International Environmental Law (2021) Formosa Plastics Group: A Serial Offender of Environmental and Human Rights - A Case Study. Available via https://www.ciel.org/reports/formosa-plastics-group-a-serial-offender-of-environmental-and-human-rights/

Chu XD (2020) Laws of environmental protection in Vietnam - situation and solutions. J Phys: Conf Ser 1515 052082. Available via https://iopscience.iop.org/article/10.1088/1742-6596/1515/5/052082/pdf

Danh Toai, M. Ha (2016) Formosa xả thải ra biển [Formosa discharges untreated wastewater into the sea] Thanh nien Press. Available via https://thanhnien.vn/thoi-su/formosa-xa-thai-ra-bien-695002.html

Dat HT (2024) Reassessing environmental protection in international investment agreements: the case of Vietnam. Review of European, Comparative & International Environmental Law, Wiley Periodicals LLC

Dordi C et al (2008) Đánh giá Tác động Tổng thể khi Việt Nam trở thành Thành viên của WTO đến Thay đổi Xuất nhập khẩu và Thể chế [Final Report on 'Evaluating the Effects of Joining the WTO to the Export-Import and Institution of Vietnam']. Vietnam Ministry of Industrial and Trade and the European Committee. ASIE/2003/005711

Đức Hùng (2017) Thủ tướng thị sát hệ thống xử lý nước thải của Formosa' [The Prime Minister inspected Formosa's Wastewater Treatment System] Vnexpress. Available via https://vnexpress.net/thu-tuong-thi-sat-he-thong-xu-ly-nuoc-thai-cua-formosa-3617565.html

Đức Hùng, Bạch Dương (2016) Formosa thải ra môi trường những gì' [What does Formosa release to the environment?]. Vnexpress. Available via https://vnexpress.net/formosa-thai-ra-moi-truong-nhung-gi-3393475.html

Fan MF, Chiu CM, Mabon L (2020) Environmental justice and the politics of pollution: the case of the Formosa Ha Tinh Steel Pollution Incident in Vietnam. Sage Journal. Available via https://doi.org/10.1177/2514848620973164

Hong VXN et al (2009) Sustainable development impacts of investment incentives - A case study of the mining industry in Vietnam. Central Institute for Economic Management

Korea Environment Institute (2017) Environmental sustainability in Asia: progress, challenges and opportunities in the implementation of the Sustainable Development Goals-Series 1 – Vietnam. Available via https://www.greenpolicyplatform.org/research/environmental-sustainability-asia-vietnam

Kreft S et al (2015) Global Climate Risk Index 2015 - who suffers most from extreme weather events? Weather-related loss events in 2013 and 1994 to 2013. German Watch Briefing Paper. Available via https://germanwatch.org/de/download/10333.pdf

Mani M, Hja S (2006) Trade liberalisation and the environment in Vietnam. World Bank Policy Research Working Paper 3879

Minh Hà, Đông Sơn (2016) Công bố nguyên nhân sự cố môi trường làm hải sản chết bất thường tại 4 tỉnh ven biển miền Trung [Revealing the Root Cause of the Environmental Incident Leading to Unusual Deaths of Seafood in Four Central Coastal Provinces] People's Army Newspaper. Available via https://www.qdnd.vn/xa-hoi/cac-van-de/cong-bo-nguyen-nhan-su-co-moi-truong-lam-hai-san-chet-bat-thuong-tai-4-tinh-ven-bien-mien-trung-482056

Ministry of Industry and Trade of Vietnam (2022) Nỗ lực thực hiện các cam kết của Việt Nam tại Hội nghị COP26 [Efforts to implement Vietnam's commitments at the COP26 Conference]. Available via https://moit.gov.vn/bao-ve-moi-truong/no-luc-thuc-hien-cac-cam-ket-cua-viet-nam-tai-hoi-nghi-cop26.html

Ministry of Natural Resource and Environment (MONRE) (2010) Báo cáo Môi trường Quốc gia 2010: Tổng quan Môi trường Việt Nam [Report on National Environment 2010: Overview of Vietnam Environment]. Available via https://congnghemoitruong.com.vn/bao-cao-hien-trang-moi-truong-quoc-gia_2010/

Ministry of Natural Resource and Environment (MONRE) (2017) Báo cáo Hiện trạng Môi trường Quốc gia 2017: Quản lý Chất thải [Report on National Environment 2017: Waste Management]. Available via https://climatelearning.undp.org.vn/wp-content/uploads/2021/09/bao-cao-moi-truong-2017-danen-compressed-1.pdf

Ministry of Natural Resource and Environment (MONRE) (2018) Báo cáo Hiện trạng Môi trường Quốc gia 2018: Môi trường nước các lưu vực sông [Report on National Environment 2018: Water Environment of River basins]. Available via http://dwrm.gov.vn/uploads/download/files/bao-cao-htmt-quoc-gia-2018-moi-truong-nuoc-cac-lvs_signed.pdf

Ministry of Natural Resource and Environment (MONRE) (2021) Báo cáo hiện trạng Môi trường Quốc gia 2016-2020 [Report on National Environment 2016-2020]. Dan Tri Publishing. Available via https://www.monre.gov.vn/Portal/Documents/2021/11/20211108_Bao%20cao%20HTMT%202016-2020_F.pdf

Nam DT, Thi TD (2023) Vietnam's environmental policy: a 30-year critical review. ZCEAP Working Paper 04-23. Available via https://iceds.anu.edu.au/files/GC%20Working%20Paper-Thang-cover-combined.pdf

Schirmbeck S (2017) Vietnam's environmental policies at a crossroads - Salinated Rice Fields, Hunted-Out National Parks, and Eroding Beaches - and What We Can Do About It. Friedrich Ebert Stiftung, p 3. Available via https://asia.fes.de/news/vietnams-environmental-policies-at-a-crossroads

Shira D (2021) COP26: Vietnam's commitment to reducing emissions. Vietnam Briefing. Available via https://www.vietnam-briefing.com/news/cop26-climate-change-vietnams-commitment-reducing-emissions.html/

Thanh Huong (2023) Nhìn lại 2 năm Việt Nam hiện thực cam kết COP 26' [Reflecting on Vietnam's Implementation of COP26 Commitments Over the Past Two Years] Natural Resources and Environment Press. Available via https://baotainguyenmoitruong.vn/nhin-lai-2-nam-viet-nam-hien-thuc-cam-ket-cop-26-366323.html>

Thu Hằng (2016) Bộ Khoa học – Công nghệ "né" trách nhiệm vụ Formosa [The Ministry of Science and Technology "avoided" responsibility for the Formosa case] Thanh Nien News. Available via https://thanhnien.vn/bo-kh-cn-ne-trach-nhiem-vu-formosa-185574781.htm
Tien NH et al (2020) Sustainable development and environmental management in Vietnam. Int J Res Finance Manag 3(1):72–79
Tin VT (2019) Assessing Vietnam's environmental laws and direction for improvement. Vietnamese J Leg Sci 1(1):64–76
UNFCCC (2020) Vietnam's updated NDCs' submitted to the UNFCCC. Available at https://unfccc.int/sites/default/files/NDC/2022-06/Viet%20Nam_NDC_2020_Eng.pdf
United Nation (2018) Viet Nam's Voluntary National Review on the Implementation of the Sustainable Development Goals. Available via https://vietnam.un.org/en/4122-viet-nams-voluntary-national-review-implementation-sustainable-development-goals
Văn Đức (2020) Động lực tăng trưởng từ dự án FDI lớn nhất Việt Nam [Growth motivation from Vietnam's largest FDI project]. Ha Tinh News. Available via https://baohatinh.vn/dong-luc-tang-truong-tu-du-an-fdi-lon-nhat-viet-nam-post199422.html
Vietnam (2012) Implementation of Sustainable Development in Vietnam. Vietnam's National Report at the United Nations Conference on Sustainable Development (Rio+20). Available at https://sdgs.un.org/publications/vietnam-implementation-sustainable-development-national-report-un-conference
Vietnam's NDCs (2022) Vietnam's Nationally Determined Contributions. Available via https://unfccc.int/sites/default/files/NDC/2022-11/Viet%20Nam_NDC_2022_Eng.pdf
VnExpress (2016) 84 Ngày truy tìm nguyên nhân cá chết [84 Days of Investigating the Mystery behind fish death] Available via https://vnexpress.net/interactive/2016/84-ngay-ca-chet
Vy NNT, Hy NHT, Hien NXM (2020) Remarks for European Renewable Energy Investors in Vietnam under EU-Vietnam Investment Protection Agreements. Int Bus Law J 2020(5–6):667–688
World Bank (2019) Vietnam: toward a safe, clean, and resilient water system. Washington. Available via https://www.worldbank.org/en/country/vietnam/publication/vietnam-toward-a-safe-clean-and-resilient-water-system
World Bank (2022) Vietnam - Country Climate and Development Report. Available via https://openknowledge.worldbank.org/server/api/core/bitstreams/a27f1b05-910d-59ab-ba2c-84206bf107c2/content
World Bank (2023) GDP per capita – Vietnam. Available via https://data.worldbank.org/indicator/NY.GDP.PCAP.CD?locations=VN

Documents

Government of Vietnam (1994) Decree No. 175-CP (18 October 1994) on Guidelines for the Implementation of the Law on Environmental Protection
Government of Vietnam (2006) Decree No. 80/2006/NĐ-CP (9 August 2006) on Guidelines for the Implementation of a number of articles of the Law on Environmental Protection; amended by Decree No. 21/2008/NĐ-CP (28 February 2008)
Government of Vietnam (2013) Decree No. 25/2013/NĐ-CP (29 March 2013) on Environmental Protection Fees for Waste water
Government of Vietnam (2016) Decree No. 154/2016/NĐ-CP (16 November 2016) on Environmental Protection Fees for Waste water
Government of Vietnam (2020) Resolution No. 124/2020/NQ-CP on the Government's Action Program to implement Resolution No. 23-NQ/TW dated 22 March 2018 of the Politburo on National Industry Development Policies until 2030, Vision to 2045
Ministry of Science, Technology, and Environment (MOSTE) (2002) Decision No. 62/2002/QĐ-BKHCNMT (9 August 2002) on the Adoption of Regulation on the Protection of the Environment in Industrial Zones

Ministry of Science and Technology (2016). Công bố nguyên nhân gây ra hiện tượng cá chết hàng loạt ở 4 tỉnh miền Trung [Official Announcement on the Causes of Mass Fish Deaths in Four Central Provinces], *Government Press Conference*, https://mst.gov.vn/cong-bo-nguyen-nhan-gay-ra-hien-tuong-ca-chet-hang-loat-o-4-tinh-mien-trung-197132121.htm

National Assembly of Vietnam (1993) Law No. 29-L/CTN (27 December 1993) on Environmental Protection

National Assembly of Vietnam (1998) Law No. 08/1998/QH10 (20 May 1998) on Water Resources

National Assembly of Vietnam (2004) Law No. 28/2004/QH11 (3 December 2004) on Electricity, amended by Law No. 24/2012/QH13 (20 November 2012) on Electricity

National Assembly of Vietnam (2009) Law No. 30/2009/QH12 (17 June 2009) on Urban Planning

National Assembly of Vietnam (2010) Law No. 50/2010/QH12 (17 June 2010) on Economical and Efficient Use of Energy

National Assembly of Vietnam (2012) Law No. 17/2012/QH13 (21 June 2012) on Water Resources

National Assembly of Vietnam (2013) Law No. 45/2013/QH13 (29 November 2013) on Land

National Assembly of Vietnam (2015) Law No. 82/2015/QH13 (25 June 2015) on Natural Resources and Environment of Sea and Islands

National Assembly of Vietnam (2018) Law No. 31/2018/QH14 (19 November 2018) on Cultivation

National Assembly of Vietnam (2019) Law No. 45/2019/QH14 (20 November 2019) on Labour Code

National Assembly of Vietnam (2020) Law No. 61/2020/QH14 (17 June 2020) on Investment

National Assembly of Vietnam (2021) Resolution No. 31/2021/QH15 (12 November 2021) Plan for Economic Restructuring in 2021-2025

National Assembly of Vietnam (2023) Law No. 27/2023/QH15 (27 November 2023) on Housing

National Assembly of Vietnam (2013) Law No. 33/2013/QH13 (19 June 2013) on Natural Disaster Prevention and Control

National Assembly of Vietnam (2015) Law No. 90/2015/QH13 (23 November 2015) on Hydro-meteorology

National Assembly of Vietnam (2017) Law No. 04/2017/QH14 (12 June 2017) on Support for Small and Medium-sized Enterprises

National Assembly of Vietnam (2017) Law No. 16/2017/QH14 (15 November 2017) on Forestry

National Assembly of Vietnam (2017) Law No. 18/2017/QH14 (21 November 2017) on Fisheries

National Assembly of Vietnam (2017) Law No. 21/2017/QH14 (24 November 2017) on Planning

National Assembly of Vietnam (2018) Law No. 32/2018/QH14 (19 November 2018) on Animal Husbandry

Office of the National Assembly of Vietnam (2018) Integrated document No. 32/VBHN-VPQH (10 December 2018) Law on Biodiversity

Prime Minister of Vietnam (1998) Circular No. 490/1998/TT-BKHCNMT (29 April 1998) Guiding on Preparing and Appraisal of Environmental Impact Assessment Report for Investment Projects

Prime Minister of Vietnam (2006) Decision No.81/QĐ-TTg (14 April 2006) National Strategy on Water Resources until 2020

Prime Minister of Vietnam (2007) Decision No. 18/QĐ-TTg (5 February 2007) Approving Vietnam's Forestry Development Strategy in the 2006-2020 Period

Prime Minister of Vietnam (2012) Decision 1216/QĐ-TTg (5 September 2012) Approving the National Environmental Protection Strategy to 2020, Vision to 2030

Prime Minister of Vietnam (2013) Decision No. 1250/QĐ-TTg (31 July 2013) on Viet Nam's NBS to 2020, Vision to 2030

Prime Minister of Vietnam (2014) Decision No. 218/QĐ-TTg (7 February 2014) Approving the Strategy for management of systems of special-use forests, marine reserves and internal water reserves of Vietnam through 2020, Vision to 2030

Prime Minister of Vietnam (2016) Decision No.1600/QĐ-TTg (16 August 2016) on the National Target Program on New Rural Development 2016-2020

Prime Minister of Vietnam (2017) Decision No. 622/QĐ-TTg (10 May 2017) Approving the National Action Plan for Implementing the Agenda 2030 for Sustainable Development

Prime Minister of Vietnam (2018) Decision No. 807/QĐ-TTg (3 July 2018) Approving the Program on Thoroughly Handling Facilities Causing Serious Environmental Pollution in 2016 – 2020

Prime Minister of Vietnam (2021) Decision No. 397/QĐ-TTg (17 March 2021) Approving the National Strategy for Natural Disaster Prevention, Response and Mitigation until 2030, Vision to 2050

Prime Minister of Vietnam (2022) Decision No. 493/QĐ-TTg (19 April 2022) on the Export-Import Strategy until 2030

Prime Minister of Vietnam (2024) Decision No. 215/QĐ-TTg (1 March 2024) Approving National Strategy for Energy Development until 2020 with a Vision to 2045

Prime Minister of Vietnam (2013) Decision No. 1788/QĐ-TTg (1 October 2013) Approving the Plan to Handling Production Establishments Causing Serious Environmental Pollution by 2020

Prime Minister of Vietnam (2016) Decision No. 40/QĐ-TTg (7 January 2016) on the Overall Strategy for International Integration to 2020, Vision to 2030

Prime Minister of Vietnam (2021) Decision No. 1658/QĐ-TTg (1 October 2021) Approving the National Green Growth Strategy 2021–2030, Vision to 2050

Prime Minister of Vietnam (2021) Decision No. 2161/QĐ-TTg (22 December 2021) on the National Strategy on Housing Development for 2021–2030, Vision to 2045

Prime Minister of Vietnam (2022) Decision No. 896/QĐ-TTg (26 July 2022) on the National Strategy on Climate Change until 2050

Prime Minister of Vietnam (2022) Decision No. 942/QĐ-TTg (5 August 2022) on Approving the Action Plan on Methane Emissions Reduction by 2030

Vietnam's Politburo (2018) Resolution No. 23-NQ/TW (22 March 2018) on National Industry Development Policies until 2030, Vision to 2045

Part III
Environmental Regulatory Space under the EVIPA

Chapter 5
Preserving Environmental Regulatory Space in the EVIPA

Abstract This Chapter begins by providing a contextual background for the negotiation and eventual conclusion of the EVIPA. This context is essential for a deeper understanding of the specific commitments discussed in the subsequent chapters. The Chapter then analyses the crucial theme of preserving regulatory autonomy for environmental protection within the framework of EVIPA. This analysis highlights the shared concerns of both parties, emphasising their commitment to promoting sustainable development and environmental conservation.

Furthermore, the Chapter discusses the EU's broader position on sustainable development and human rights. These explorations collectively reveal the EU's consistent policy orientation, which promotes enduring values rooted in sustainability. Additionally, it explains the EU's strategic approach of using commercial cooperation to go beyond mere economic interests, facilitating the advancement of shared non-commercial concerns with its partners, including Vietnam.

Unlike traditional BITs, many contemporary investment protection agreements are now incorporated into broader trade frameworks. The EVIPA follows this trend, forming part of the broader negotiations within the EVFTA. Under the EVFTA, alongside the primary objective of boosting trade, there is increased emphasis on non-commercial aspects like environmental protection and investment promotion. Therefore, when examining the pertinent investment protection provisions within the EVIPA, it is essential to consider this overarching context. This chapter thus focuses on discussing the general legal framework established by the EVFTA concerning the advancement of sustainable development while also addressing the shared concerns that the parties seek to address within the current trade and investment relationship.

N. T. Lan Huong, *Investment Protection and Environmental Governance*, European Yearbook of International Economic Law 47,
https://doi.org/10.1007/978-3-032-05332-9_5

5.1 The EU - Vietnam Trade and Investment Agreements: Sustainable Development Concerns and the Right to Regulate

Among its partners, the EU is one of the most important trade and investment partners of Vietnam. In fact, as announced by the European Commission, the EU is one of the largest foreign investors in Vietnam. EU investors committed 1.8 billion USD in FDI, reaching a total investment stock of 21.6 billion USD to Vietnam in 2017 and rising to 24 billion USD by the end of 2018, spread over more than 2000 projects.[1] The top three sectors of investment by the EU are Industrial Processing and Manufacturing (8.4 billion USD), the production and transmission of electricity (5 billion USD) and real estate (2.6 billion USD).[2] According to a statistic conducted by Vietnam Customs, in 2024, the United States, China and the EU are the three most significant markets of Vietnam exports.[3] Furthermore, two-way trade between the EU and Vietnam expanded to 56.3 billion USD in 2018, according to the general statistics office of Vietnam. Main imports from the EU to Vietnam are high-tech products, including electrical machinery and equipment, aircraft, vehicles, and pharmaceutical products. Vietnam's main exports to the EU are footwear, textiles and clothing, coffee, rice, seafood, and furniture.[4]

As previously mentioned, the EU and Vietnam established a diplomatic relationship at the beginning of the 1990s. Since that year, the country has been one of the main partners of the EU in Southeast Asia. From that time, the two partner have strengthened their partnership step by step by signing the EU–Vietnam Framework Cooperation Agreement (FCA) in 1995, the EU-Vietnam Framework Agreement on Comprehensive Partnership and Cooperation (PCA) in 2012. This PCA contains nearly all common concerns of both sides: trade, environment, energy, science and technology, good governance, human rights, as well as tourism, culture, migration and the fight against corruption and organised crime. This agreement also provides a chance to enhance the coherence and synergy between the EU and the Member State policies. A high level of discussions on trade and politics and related development issues such as human rights have been organised.[5]

In 2012, the two partners started negotiating a thorough free trade and investment agreement called EVFTA, which later took three years of negotiation to realise the trade and investment principles established in the PCA. The concluding agreement has been separated into the EU–Vietnam FTA (EVFTA) and the Investment Protection Agreement (IPA or EVIPA). The EVFTA is expected to eliminate approximately 99% of all tariffs, reduce regulatory barriers and overlapping red tape, ensure the

[1] EuroCham (2020), p. 17.

[2] Ibid.

[3] Vietnam Customs (2024).

[4] EuroCham (2020), p. 18.

[5] Delegation of the European Union to Vietnam (2019), p. 6.

protection of geographical indications and open up services and public procurement markets once in force.[6]

In addition, the IPA is prepared to replace the bilateral investment agreement currently in place between 21 EU Member States and Vietnam. This IPA suggests modern rules on investment protection enforceable through a new Investment Court System. However, many obstacles still need to be overcome to gain those potential benefits, as EVFTA (and another new-generation FTA - the CPTPP) are high-quality agreements with higher commitments than traditional FTAs.

Since the deadlock of WTO's Doha Round, which began in 2001, international trade has been covered by a new wave of regional agreements. Indeed, since 1999, the number of regional trade agreements (RTAs) has kept dramatically growing. As of 2019, there are 294 physical RTAs in force, while the number sorted by notification is 472.[7]

Although some scholars suppose that the tendency to enter into regional negotiation among the developed economies[8] continues to stall the WTO,[9] others argue that the objectives cannot be concluded in the DOHA negotiation have let countries reach their aims via regional negotiations.[10] The trade war between the United States and China from 2018, which has escalated into a number of disputes at the WTO with other territories like Canada, EU, Mexico, Norway, Russia, and Turkey, has also partly contributed to accelerating the negotiating process of regional and inter-regional agreements.[11]

In this protectionism trend, Asia-Pacific economies have significantly contributed to the overall increase of the world economy.[12] The Asia-Pacific area continues to be noticed as a potentially attractive market consisting of both developed nations like Japan, Singapore, and Australia, to emerging markets like China and frontier

---

[6] Ibid, p. 26.

[7] WTO Secretariat (2019). Signing RTAs to address bilateral and regional concerns remains the dominant trend in the global trade landscape as of 2024. Specifically, in 2024, there are 369 RTAs currently in force, with a total of 608 cumulative notifications of RTAs in effect. See WTO Secretariat (2024).

[8] The mentioned economies are the United States and the EU. Indeed, in October 2015, the United States concluded negotiations with Japan and 10 other economies on a vast new Pacific rim pact: the Trans-Pacific Partnership (TPP). It is after the United States' President decided to withdraw TPP, the Agreement was change the name to The Comprehensive and Progressive Agreement for Trans-Pacific Partnership (CPTPP) with 11 members not including the United States. Since 2013, the United States was also in a negotiation with the European Union on the Transatlantic Trade and Investment Partnership (TTIP). The negotiations were stopped until at the end of 2016. About the EU, since the middle of the 2000s, the Union has entered into trade negotiations with different countries and regions around the world such as the United States, Canada, Japan, China, ASEAN, Singapore, Vietnam, India, Australia, New Zealand, Mexico, Chile, Mercosur,… See European Commission (2017a).

[9] As warned by WTO former Director-General, Mr. Supachai Panitchpakdi in 2002. See Panitchpakdi (2002). See also Wolfe (2015); Baldwin (2011), p. 31.

[10] Rodriguez Mendoza (2014); Abbott (2012); Ha and Sicurelli (2017), p. 369.

[11] This is at least true for the case of Vietnam. See Hutt (2019).

[12] Economic and Social Commission for Asia and the Pacific (2018), p. 87.

markets like India, Vietnam, Cambodia,... Although the effects of the United States–China trade war and other trade tensions are unlikely to weaken, partly due to the blockage of the appointment of new judges under the WTO dispute settlement system from the United States, according to the United Nations, the Asia–Pacific increased the region's shares of global merchandise trade further to 38.3%.[13] The Region remained the main destination for FDI, attracting 39% of global FDI inflows in 2017, a rise of 09 percentage compared to 2016.[14] Therefore, big economies like the United States and the EU are predicted to continue developing trade cooperation with the region.

In this area, ASEAN countries are considered to be central to the efforts to "build a more robust regional security order in the wider Asia-Pacific."[15] Indeed, the joint communication between the European Parliament and the Council has mentioned that "investing in the EU–ASEAN relationship will bring significant returns for EU interests, both economically and politically."[16] This context is ideal for negotiating recently promoted bilateral agreements between the EU and a few ASEAN partners. In fact, negotiations with a group of seven ASEAN member states were conducted in July 2007. However, in 2009, the 7th Joint Committee agreed to take a pause in the negotiation given that it would be sufficient if the EU pursued FTA negotiation in a bilateral format with ASEAN countries. Negotiations with Singapore and Malaysia were launched in 2010, with Vietnam in June 2012, and with Thailand in March 2013. Negotiations with the Philippines and Indonesia were launched in 2016.[17] The result of these negotiations is a series of preferential trade agreements signed from 2010 until now. In specific, the European Union has signed bilateral FTAs with South Korea in 2010 (EU–Korea FTA);[18] with Japan (the EU Japan Economic Partnership Agreement)[19] and Singapore (EU–Singapore FTA and IPA) during 2017–2018.[20] In 2013, the EU also launched negotiations with China for an investment protection agreement. In the past seven years, the EU has also followed negotiations with other ASEAN countries, including Thailand, the Philippines, Indonesia and Myanmar.[21] Besides, the Union has recently opened negotiations with two other countries in the Pacific area, including Australia and New Zealand, from May 2018.[22]

---

[13] Ibid.

[14] Ibid, pp. 50, 90.

[15] European Commission (2015a).

[16] Ibid.

[17] European Commission (2017a).

[18] The Agreement entered into force on 13 December 2015. See European Commission. Negotiations and Agreements.

[19] The Agreement has entered into force on 1 February 2019.

[20] The EUSFTA entered into force on 21 November 2019.

[21] Ibid.

[22] Ibid.

In the last few months of 2018, the EU has promoted the process of negotiating and signing free trade agreements with Asian countries, including Vietnam, Japan, and Singapore. Regarding the FTA with Vietnam, as mentioned in Chapter 1, the EU–Vietnam FTA officially launched negotiations on June 26, 2012, in Brussels, Belgium. This is an important FTA prioritised by both the Vietnamese government and the EU. The agreement went through 14 rounds of negotiation. On August 4, 2015, in Brussels, the EU and Vietnam agreed in principle on the trade and investment agreement, although provisions on investment protection and dispute settlement are still being negotiated.[23] As the purposes of cooperation are boosting development in economics, trade and investment in connection with sustainable development, the agreements deal with issues related to trade in goods, services, intellectual property, rules of origin, public procurement, labour, environment, technical barriers, sanitary and phytosanitary measures, state enterprises, competition, trade facilitation, and investment.[24]

- **The Investment Court System and the EU's Competence to Sign and Conclude FTA**

After the above-mentioned development, the adoption and ratification process of the EU Vietnam Trade and Investment Agreement has been slow due to the internal EU discussion regarding the EU's competence to sign and conclude the FTA with its trading partners. The debate arose when the European Council and the governments of all Member States asserted that the EU could not conclude the agreement by itself because certain parts of the agreement fall within a competence shared between the EU and the Member States or even within the exclusive competence of the Member States.[25] Specifically, besides other issues, the Council and the Member States mentioned in their request for explanation that "Chapter 9 of the envisaged agreement relates only to investment protection and not to the admission of investments. It follows that, even as far as that chapter relates to foreign direct investment, it cannot be approved by the EU alone. As investment protection is not specifically linked to international trade, it does not fall within the common commercial policy."[26] Regarding this issue, the European Court of Justice gave the opinion as below:[27]

> The Free Trade Agreement between the European Union and the Republic of Singapore falls within the exclusive competence of the European Union, with the exception of the following provisions, which fall within a competence shared between the European Union and the Member States:

[23] European Commission (2015c).

[24] European Commission (2018b).

[25] Court of Justice of the European Union (2017).

[26] Ibid, para. 27. The "envisaged agreement" mentioned here is the free trade agreements which are under negotiation between EU and a few ASEAN countries including Singapore and Vietnam.

[27] Ibid, para. 305.

- the provisions of Section A (Investment Protection) of Chapter 9 (Investment) of that agreement, in so far as they relate to non-direct investment between the European Union and the Republic of Singapore;
- the provisions of Section B (Investor-State Dispute Settlement) of Chapter 9; and
- the provisions of Chapters 1 (Objectives and General Definitions), 14 (Transparency), 15 (Dispute Settlement between the Parties), 16 (Mediation Mechanism) and 17 (Institutional, General and Final Provisions) of that agreement, in so far as those provisions relate to the provisions of Chapter 9 and to the extent that the latter fall within a competence shared between the European Union and the Member States.

Therefore, the three aforementioned related issues will come under the shared jurisdiction of the EU and its member states. This decision has important implications for the conclusion of the FTA between the EU and Singapore and other FTAs of the EU in the future. As mentioned by Michel Trochu, on the one hand, all so-called "new generation" trade agreements to be concluded in the future by the EU will have to be validated not only by the Council and the Parliament but also by all the national parliaments of the EU Member States. This procedure may seriously slow down and thus weaken the Union's trade policy.[28]

For the above opinion, as explained in the Draft Recommendation provided by the EU Committee on International Trade, later discussions between the EU institutions on the new architecture of future FTAs led to the decision that the free trade agreements between the EU and Member States with Vietnam and with Singapore were split into free trade agreements and investment protection agreements.[29] Consequently, in September 2018, the EU–Vietnam Trade and Investment Agreement was divided into an FTA and an IPA to streamline the approval process, similar to the arrangement made for the EU–Singapore FTA. According to this Draft Recommendation, the existing 21 BITs in force between Vietnam and the EU Member States will be replaced by the EVIPA once it enters into force.[30] This EVIPA will help extend access of EU investors to the Vietnam service market beyond current WTO obligations.

It should be noted that the EVIPA contains investment protection commitments (Chapter 2) and investment dispute resolution (Chapter 3), including the establishment of the ICS, the independent arbitral tribunal model was proposed and discussed in recent negotiations of FTAs between the EU and other partners, including the Transatlantic Trade Investment Partnership (TTIP),[31] the FTA with Canada (CETA),[32] with Mexico,[33] with Singapore, and Vietnam. It is a new and improved ICS not based on *ad hoc* tribunals as traditional investor-state dispute settlement mechanisms.[34] Specifically, the ICS will be a permanent public tribunal with

[28] Trochu (2018), p. 38.

[29] Zahradil (2018).

[30] Ibid.

[31] European Commission (2015d). The negotiations on TTIP were launched in 2013 and ended without conclusion in 2016. See also European Council (2019).

[32] European Commission (2016a).

[33] European Commission (2018c).

[34] European Commission (2017b).

professional and independent judges appointed by the EU and its partners. The tribunal's procedure will be held transparently, limiting cases when an investor can challenge a state. Another crucial improvement in the suggested dispute settlement mechanism is that it includes an appeal tribunal,[35] which may provide a chance to re-examine the tribunal awards for legal correctness and reverse where an error arises.

The improvements mentioned above highlight the EU's pioneering efforts to address the weaknesses in the current international investment dispute settlement system.[36] However, since this reform is also a new aspect for the EU Member States, the ICS is excluded from the provisional application of CETA. This means that this part will only be implemented once all EU Member States conclude their national ratification procedures.[37] A similar situation occurred with the trade and investment agreements between the EU and its other partners, Vietnam and Singapore. In October 2018, the European Commission announced that it had submitted proposals for the signature and conclusion of both the EVFTA and the EVIPA to the European Council.[38] These agreements must be signed and then presented to the European Parliament. After receiving the Parliament's consent, the Council will conclude the EVFTA, allowing it to enter into force. The EVIPA, on the other hand, will require ratification by all EU Member States and must follow each nation's national procedures.

As the European Parliament's 2019 agenda unfolds, it is marked by several key events, including the European elections scheduled for May 23–26,2019;Brexit;and discussions surrounding the EU's long-term budget; the signing and ratification procedure may not be prioritised by the EU, at least in the first six months of 2019.[39] As mentioned by the Chairman of the European Parliament's Committee on International Trade - Bernd Lange in a discussion held in April 2019 with Vietnamese National Assembly Chairwoman Nguyen Thi Kim Ngan: the signing and the approving procedure is expected to be promoted in June or July after the European Parliament completes its elections and begins its new term.[40]

The two Agreements were signed by the EU and Vietnam on June 30, 2019, in Hanoi, marking the culmination of nearly a decade of negotiations. Meanwhile, EVFTA is considered the most significant new-generation FTA in the country's history regarding direct benefits for Vietnam.[41] On February 12, 2020, the European

[35] EU Council (2016), p. 6.

[36] Efforts to reform the ISDS system have also been carried out by many other agencies for many years. On March 15, 2019, the ICSID issued a Working paper (WP#2) follow its rule amendment process launched in October 2016. Besides, the UNCITRAL has entrusted a working group (WG III) with a broad mandate to work on the possible reform of ISDS from 2017 until now. See more in United Nations Commission on International Trade Law. Working Group III.

[37] European Commission (2017b).

[38] European Commission (2018a).

[39] European Parliament (2018). See also Oortwijn (2019).

[40] Vietnamnet News (2019).

[41] EuroCham (2020), p. 19.

Parliament voted in favour of both agreements. By the end of March 2020, the European Council had adopted a decision on the ratification of the EVFTA.[42]

On June 8, 2020, Vietnam's National Assembly XIV, at its second phase of the ninth session, approved the ratification of the EVFTA and EVIPA, as well as the International Labour Organisation Convention 105 on the abolition of forced labour.[43] As of March 2021, Hungary and the Czech Republic were the only two EU member states to have completed the ratification of the EVIPA.[44] It is anticipated that other EU member states will finalise their ratifications within the next two years.[45]

5.2 The EU - Vietnam Trade and Investment Agreements: Exploring Shared Concerns

As one of the world's three largest economies, alongside China and the United States, the EU places substantial emphasis on promoting sustainable values, both within the Union and beyond, through trade agreements with its global partners. The endeavour to foster sustainable economic development, hand in hand with environmental protection, holds a vital position among the EU's myriad political and economic objectives. This policy finds consistent reflection in numerous EU documents, decisions, and statements, with legislative proposals being a prominent example, such as those adopted by the European Commission on July 14, 2021, as part of the European Green Deal initiative.[46] Complementing the European Green Deal, the European Digital Strategy has also been introduced to harness digital transformation as a vital driver of sustainable development. In alignment with the objectives outlined in the European Green Deal and the European Digital Strategy, the new EU Trade Policy was unveiled in February 2021, with sustainability taking on an explicit and central role in the EU's trade agenda. This policy underscores the imperative of deploying all available tools to champion social equity and environmental sustainability. Notably, trade agreements have emerged as a crucial instrument for advancing sustainability. Consequently, it is paramount to effectively implement relevant trade agreements and uphold the rights and obligations enshrined within them.[47]

This policy is not a new proposal in response to new internal and external challenges to the EU's trade regime in this era. Still, it was shaped approximately 15

---

[42] EU Council (2020).

[43] Vietnamplus (2020).

[44] Hungary ratified the EVIPA on December 24, 2019, followed by the Czech Republic on February 13, 2020.

[45] EuroCham (2020), p. 19.

[46] European Commission. The European Green Deal.

[47] See the communication from the European Commission (2021a).

years ago, dating back to the establishment of the European Community. More specifically, a key objective of the EU's foreign trade policy, as articulated in the Treaty of Lisbon (Lisbon Treaty),[48] Article 206: "The Union contributes, in the common interest, to the harmonious development of world trade, the progressive abolition of restrictions on international trade and FDI, and to reduce all barriers including tariff barriers". It's essential to note, however, that as underscored in official documents,[49] the EU does not limit its goals to simply reducing restrictions on trade and investment but to increasingly combine political values and other standards in its external relations. This Treaty at Article 207:1 also places the Common Commercial Policy under that part of the Union's external action to which Article 21:2 Treaty of European Union apply:[50]

> 2. The Union shall define and pursue common policies and actions, and shall work for a high degree of cooperation in all fields of international relations, in order to:

(a) safeguard its values, fundamental interests, security, independence and integrity;
(b) consolidate and support democracy, the rule of law, human rights and the principles of international law;
(c) preserve peace, prevent conflicts and strengthen international security, in accordance with the purposes and principles of the United Nations Charter, with the principles of the Helsinki Final Act and with the aims of the Charter of Paris, including those relating to external borders;
(d) foster the sustainable economic, social and environmental development of developing countries, with the primary aim of eradicating poverty;
(e) encourage the integration of all countries into the world economy, including through the progressive abolition of restrictions on international trade;
(f) help develop international measures to preserve and improve the quality of the environment and the sustainable management of global natural resources, in order to ensure sustainable development;
(g) assist populations, countries and regions confronting natural or man-made disasters; and
(h) promote an international system based on stronger multilateral cooperation and good global governance.

Non-trade issues pertaining to sustainable development, environmental protection, and human rights, as outlined in Article 21.2 of the Treaty on European Union, have consistently manifested in the EU's new-generation FTAs. This inclusion serves the purpose of ensuring that the regulations established in significant markets align with European standards. Moreover, the EU's trade agreements mandate adherence to international environmental norms, the effective enforcement of environmental legislation, sustainable trade in natural resources, the combatting of illegal trade in endangered species, the promotion of climate change mitigation through trade, and the cultivation of practices such as corporate social responsibility.[51]

---

[48] The Lisbon Treaty amending the Treaty on European Union and the Treaty establishing the European Community (OJC 306, 17.12.2007); signed on 13 December 2007 in Lisbon, enter into force on 1 December 2009 after ratification by 27 countries of the Union.

[49] See, for instance EU Parliamentary Assembly (2017).

[50] Gstohl and Hanf (2014).

[51] To gain a more comprehensive understanding of the significance of this concern within the European Union's system of agreements, it is pertinent to reference a document adopted by the United Nations General Assembly on September 25, 2015, titled 'Transforming Our World: the

The advantages of engaging in trade with the European Union are evident. It offers not only commercial benefits but also added value in terms of upholding global standards. Importantly, the integration of non-trade concerns into international trade agreements has become a shared priority for countries worldwide, irrespective of their developmental status. Consequently, the EU's objective for addressing the multifaceted challenges of this era has been closely shared by its partners.

The EVFTA–EVIPA negotiation is an ideal illustration of the EU's vision and strategy among its agreements with other potential partner countries such as South Korea, India, the ASEAN countries, members of MERCOSUR, Russia, the Gulf Cooperation Council and China.[52] As mentioned above, in 2009, after the failure to form the EU–ASEAN Free Trade Area due to slow progress and different concerns among ASEAN countries, the EU expressed its intention to promote FTA with Vietnam as soon as possible.[53] This determination significantly impacts the success of later negotiations between the two partners.[54] The EU–Vietnam Trade and Investment Agreement is a step toward reaching one of the Union's aims: to "secure greater market access for European business and deepen regulatory cooperation with major trade partners."[55]

Indeed, Vietnam is the second largest trading partner of the European Union, behind Singapore, within the ASEAN, with trade amounting to 47.6 billion Euros per year for goods and 3.6 billion Euros for services. Suppose the Union's stock of investments in Vietnam remains modest at 8.3 billion Euros in 2016. In that case, more European companies are establishing themselves in this country to set up a platform serving the Mekong region. The main EU imports from Vietnam concern telecommunications equipment, clothing and food products. The main products the Union exported to Vietnam are machinery and transport equipment, chemicals and agricultural products.

From the EU viewpoint, a growing middle-income economy like Vietnam is an attractive market for the EU's goods, services and investment. At the time of the negotiation, the average tariff rate of Vietnam applied for EU's goods was 9.3%, and this tariff rate was even higher on many strong products from the EU (tariff on pharmaceutical products has been at 10% and on automotive products at 90%).[56] Therefore, tariff reduction under an FTA will certainly bring significant benefits to

---

2030 Agenda for Sustainable Development'. This document identifies a diverse array of sustainable development concerns encompassing economic, social, and environmental dimensions, all of which are corroborated in various chapters of EU agreements. These concerns have been explicitly integrated into many agreements signed by the EU with its global partners. See United Nations General Assembly (2015).

[52] European Commission (2006), p. 9.

[53] As commented by Mr. Sean Doyle, EU Ambassador, Head of the EU delegation to Vietnam in 2011. See Nguyễn Nhuần (2011).

[54] Vietnam Chamber of Commerce and Industry (2011), p. 9.

[55] European Commission (2010b).

[56] Vietnam Chamber of Commerce and Industry (2011), p. 17.

EU exporters. The experts also believe that as a developing economy focusing on exports, there is a high demand for producing services, including infrastructure and financial services, in Vietnam. At the same time, the country has not prioritised market access for any partners yet.[57] Vietnam is also one of the most attractive destinations in Asia for FDI. Thus, a preferential trade agreement with Vietnam will certainly bring substantial benefits to the EU.

Moreover, the EU - Vietnam Trade and Investment Agreements will create a balance position for EU's goods, services and investors with other competitors in the country market as Vietnam has entered into many free trade agreements (CPTPP, RCEP, Vietnam–US BTA, …) which provide preferential treatment for its trading partners. Therefore, the EU–Vietnam agreements will provide opportunities for agricultural, industrial, and services exporters from the EU, which have been curtailed by existing trade barriers.[58] This agreement has been mentioned as "the most ambitious and comprehensive trade agreement which the EU has concluded to date with a developing country", and it will serve as a "benchmark for future negotiations with developing countries" and also give a reference case for future negotiations of EU with other ASEAN countries.[59]

The successful conclusion of the EVFTA - EVIPA is also meaningful for the EU, offering substantial opportunities for collaboration across various domains. Although the concerns are quite broad, within the EU framework, specific objectives for engagement with Vietnam have also been clearly articulated, as outlined in a document presented to the Senate on November 14, 2018.[60]

These objectives encompass:

(i) Establishing an ambitious and comprehensive framework for trade cooperation between the two parties,
(ii) Crafting an investment protection agreement to generate fresh opportunities and legal certainty, thereby promoting trade and investment growth between the two parties.

The EU's selection of the adjectives "ambitious" and "comprehensive" in its approach underscores its intent to pursue commercial development goals in tandem with other non-commercial objectives, all of which are geared towards realising sustainable development for both Vietnam and the EU.

With due regard to the enhancing awareness of linking sustainable development with trade,[61] the EU has been including this issue in trade negotiations with its partners since the conclusion of the EUKorea Free Trade Agreement in 2010.[62] This is the first time that sustainable development was included in a preferential trade

[57] Ibid.

[58] European Commission (2017c), p. 4.

[59] Ibid.

[60] Committee on European Affairs (2018).

[61] Jutten (2023), p. 2.

[62] Cuyvers (2014), pp. 01–02.

agreement of the EU.[63] Since then, the EU has quickly brought this concern into its trade negotiations, namely the EU agreements with Central America, Colombia, Peru, Georgia, Moldova, and Ukraine. It is also worth mentioning that European countries expressed concerns about this issue very early. Indeed, the "principle of sustainable development" was considered as first appeared in the Preamble of the 1992 European Economic Area (EEA).[64] Discussing and including a separate "Trade and Sustainable Development" chapter has been encouraged in all trade and investment negotiations with its partners. This concern, therefore, can be found in all recently concluded agreements in which the EU is a partner, specifically, CETA (Chapter 22, Chapter 24); TTIP;[65] EU–Japan Economic Partnership Agreement (Chapter 16); EU–Singapore Trade and Investment Agreement (Chapter 12), and the EVFTA (Chapter 13). In general, sustainable development has been mentioned as one of the core values that the EU has prepared to spread out[66] via different trade cooperation with its partners. Regarding the scope of "sustainable development" under the EU's FTAs, including CETA, EU Singapore FTA, and EVFTA, despite a slight change in design,[67] all three agreements determine sustainable development in connection with labour and environmental management.

During the EU–Vietnam negotiations, one of the significant issue discussed was the inclusion of human rights in the trade agreement. As the negotiation with Vietnam was the first since the publication of the Strategic Framework on Human Rights and Democracy in 2012,[68] the EU addopted an ambiguous approach to the human rights implications of its bilateral trade with Vietnam.[69] However, due to many reasons, which are mostly from the internal EU, from the preparation stage of the trade negotiation with Vietnam, the Commission preferred separate institutional venues to negotiate trade and human rights.[70] The Commission also decided not to endorse the Parliament's request to conduct a specific human rights assessment in the case of Vietnam.[71] The two partners later agreed to cooperate in promoting human rights in a joint document - The Framework Agreement on Comprehensive Partnership and Cooperation between the EU and its Member States and The Socialist Republic of Vietnam in October 2012. This document also aims to establish

[63] Jutten (2023), p. 2.

[64] Agreement on the European Economic Area 1992. See Sands et al. (2018), p. 218.

[65] Although the negotiation has been interrupted, the EU indeed proposed provisions on sustainable development with the United States under Part 3 relating to Trade rules by protecting the environment. See European Commission (2016b).

[66] European Commission (2014).

[67] In CETA, labour and environment protections are separately regulated from chapter on sustainable development while in EVFTA and EU - Singapore FTA both issues are included in chapter on sustainable development.

[68] The Framework states that the 'EU will promote human rights in all areas of its external action without exception'. European Union Council (2012).

[69] Sicurelli (2015), p. 232.

[70] Ibid.

[71] Ibid, p. 241.

the premises for both sides to negotiate an FTA. Therefore, the EVFTA has not included human rights in Chapter 13 on Trade and Sustainable Development. Instead, the Agreement only addressed labour and environmental issues related to trade and investment.

In the EVFTA, a two-pronged approach was designed to target the interconnection between trade and investment, labour and environmental policies.[72] By applying this approach, both parties, on the one hand, will promote mutual supportiveness and, on the other hand, limit the adverse effects arising from increased trade and investment at the expense of labour and environmental protection.[73] In specific, the two partners have agreed to include an article on "Multilateral Labour Standards and Agreements" (Article 13.4) in which "each party reaffirms its commitments, in accordance with its obligations under the International Labour Organisation (ILO) and the ILO Declaration on Fundamental Principles and Rights at Work and its Follow-up… to respect, promote and effectively implement the principles concerning the fundamental rights at work."

Besides, the final text of EVFTA also includes an agreement to ratify and effectively implement MEAs, including, among others, the Paris Agreement, the United Nations Framework Convention on Climate Change (UNFCCC), the United Nations Convention on Biological Diversity, the United Nations Convention on International Trade in Endangered Species (CITES) and the Kyoto protocol on climate change as well as to cooperate in other environmental protection issues (Article 13.6). The chapter also includes specific actions to help advance the conservation and sustainable management of natural resources from both sides (Article 13.7). A Committee on Trade and Sustainable Development is established to review the implementation of the related commitments (Article 13.5). The chapter also supports good administrative practices in regulating and applying measures aimed at protecting the environment and labour conditions that may affect trade and investment by requesting that those measures be developed, introduced and implemented transparently. (Article 13.12)

On September 17, 2018, a group of 32 European parliamentarians sent an open letter to the High Representative of the Union for Foreign Affairs and Security Policy Mrs. Federica Mogherini and EU Trade Commissioner Cecilia Malmström,[74] a primary player in the Vietnam - EU trade negotiation calling on the EU to establish several human right criteria that Vietnam must meet before the EVFTA is submitted to the National Assembly for approval, particularly in the areas of freedom of speech and association establishment, religious freedom and workers' rights. In the first few months of 2019, human rights organisations have also convinced the European Parliament and the European Council to postpone the ratification of the proposed EU - Vietnam FTA as the country does not improve human rights, especially the adoption of Vietnam's new cybersecurity law (Law No. 24/2018/, June 12, 2018)

[72] Tröster et al. (2019), p. 9.

[73] Ibid.

[74] Nessel and Verhaeghe (2020), p. 5.

and other limitation in freedom of speech. The country has also not shown intention to ratify ILO conventions.[75] In fact, the discussion in the EU Parliament shows that despite undisputed economic benefits for both sides, some European Council Members still have concerns about social and labour rights and cyber security legislation.[76] As the ratification of ILO Conventions will be decisive in considering the EU,[77] goodwill from the Vietnamese government is also critical to the future of the agreement. However, given that this trade relationship benefits both partners, the signing and ratification process is not so obscure.

Indeed, during negotiation rounds, although agreed to include the above commitments in the EVFTA, Vietnamese negotiators raised strong resistance against the suggestion of freedom of association for workers. This right is not recognised in the Vietnamese Constitution and thus becomes a significant obstacle in bilateral negotiation.[78] However, as the CPTPP, which Vietnam signed in November 2018, has also included this commitment, it is predicted that the Vietnamese government will consider making a concession with the EU on this issue. In a recent discussion between the Vietnamese National Assembly Chairwoman Nguyen Thi Kim Ngan with Chairman of the European Parliament's Committee on International Trade - Bernd Lange, during her working visit to the European Parliament,[79] Mrs Ngan mentioned that: "Vietnam has been improving legal regulations in line with international law and commitments that Vietnam has signed and involved. Vietnam's Labour Code has been built in the spirit of protecting the interests of labourers, adding that the revision of the Code has been started, and the National Assembly is scheduled to discuss the revision at its May meeting." She admitted that: "there are differences in the views of Vietnam and the EU on some labour issues, but Vietnam will carefully consider the recommendations made by the EU."

As can be seen, the EU' comprehensive strategy[80] to achieve sustainability goals has led to encouraging results. The Chapter on Trade and Sustainable Development in the EVFTA reflects the EU's vision of linking trade and investment with sustainable development. However, given that both political interests and civil society actors in Vietnam are rather weak,[81] benefits of this chapter depend on the active participation of EU institutions and support for cooperation between the two parties.

For Vietnam, the EU has been one of the most essential partners since the two regions established their cooperation. Compared with previous trade negotiations

[75] Human Rights Watch (2019).

[76] EuroCham (2019), p. 22.

[77] The European Parliament Resolution on trade and economic relations with ASEAN mentioned that "a Partnership and Cooperation Agreement (PCA), containing enforceable human rights clauses, is a prerequisite for the Union to conclude an FTA with any country". See European Parliament (2008).

[78] Sicurelli (2015), p. 34.

[79] Vietnamnet News (2019).

[80] See EU policy on promoting sustainable development in European Commission. Sustainable development.

[81] Tröster et al. (2019), p. 4.

(WTO accession, AFTA and other FTA under the ASEAN+ framework) in which the country took a passive role, Vietnam has a certain equilibrium position in the negotiation with the EU. Since the launch of bilateral FTA negotiations in March 2010,[82] Vietnam seems to be cautious about being involved in further negotiations between the two partners.[83] An FTA with a significant partner like the EU may considerably influence Vietnam's economy. Notwithstanding, at that time, Vietnam was focusing on a strategy to implement a series of FTA already in force[84] while concentrating its resources on participating in the Trans-Pacific Partnership Agreement negotiations with another major trading partner the United States. For those reasons, starting another "wide and deep" FTA while not preparing a comprehensive "FTA participation strategy" seems too risky for the country. However, after numerous discussions, considerations and assessments, negotiations between the two parties were officially launched in 2012.

The impact assessment of the EU–Vietnam Trade and Investment Agreements on the Vietnamese economy at this time cannot be comprehensive. However, some studies make predictions based mainly on econometric methods. In a report conducted by a group of economists in 2011,[85] the preferential trade agreement with the EU is predicted to impact the Vietnamese economy in all possible scenarios positively.[86] In another research, the EVFTA is predicted to offer many opportunities and pose challenges to Vietnam's economy.[87] First, the commitment to improving the business environment, including greater transparency in public procurement markets, will encourage more investment from the EU.[88] Second, using quantitative analysis, the authors suppose that the reduced tax rates under EVFTA can lead to trade diversion effects, especially in electronics and machinery industries, because imports from the EU can replace imports from China in Vietnam's market. It may also lead to trade creation in automotive.[89] Using quantitative analysis, the authors suppose that the tariff reduction also brings an advantage for Vietnam's products over its rivals in the EU market.[90]

---

[82] European Commission (2010a).

[83] Vietnamnet (2011).

[84] Vietnam is actively pursuing FTA policy. Until 2018, the country is following 16 FTAs including those under negotiation, eight involve ASEAN, four are bilateral (FTA with Japan, Chile, Korea, Israel), the rest are Mega-RTAs. See Kikuchi et al. (2018), p. 6.

[85] Philip et al. (2011).

[86] Ibid., pp. 06–07. This report predicts that the fiscal revenue would increase substantially as the revenue from the growth of imports exceed the losses due to the reduction of tariffs (529 billion Dong yearly from the first year of liberalisation in the rapid dismantling scenario and from 0 in the first year to 6305 billion Dong after 15 years in the progressive dismantling one). Besides, the impact on the GDP will be largely positive: around +2.7% yearly in case of rapid dismantling, while in the case of progressive dismantling there will be a gradual increase since the second year of implementation up to +3.7% after fifteen years.

[87] Duong et al. (2015), pp. 18–19.

[88] European Commission (2017), p. 4.

[89] Duong et al. (2015), pp. 15–16.

[90] Ibid.

Vietnam is an export-driven economy, and establishing an FTA that eliminates 99% of tariffs on both sides is expected to significantly boost Vietnam's exports to a large market, such as the EU, which has a population of approximately 745 million.[91] Although the EU provides developing countries with relatively open access to its market through the General System of Preferences, the tariffs on competitive export products from Vietnam remain high - 11.7% on textiles, 10.8% on seafood, and 12.4% on footwear, with some products facing tariffs as high as 57%.[92]

According to Mr. Nguyen Anh Duong, a domestic expert involved with the EU-MUTRAP project, EVFTA will significantly reduce tariff barriers for Vietnam's agricultural and fishery products, as well as implement progressive tax mechanisms for these goods. Additionally, the tax incentives for processed products are expected to promote the export of Vietnam's goods to the EU market.[93] Thus, a strong FTA with the EU could enhance access for Vietnamese exports and improve the competitiveness of Vietnam's products within this market. However, studies also suggest that the benefits of the FTA will only be attainable if Vietnamese businesses enhance the quality of their products to comply with the EU's technical standards concerning epidemiology, hygiene, and animal and plant quarantines.[94] The main challenges stem from non-tariff barriers, as the European market maintains high standards. Scholars believe that this FTA presents a valuable opportunity for Vietnam to engage in discussions with the EU regarding the reduction of non-tariff barriers,[95] which include trade defence instruments such as anti-dumping measures; rule of origin; as well as sanitary and phytosanitary and technical barriers to trade measures. Experts also noted that Vietnam may have a positive position in requesting the EU to recognise it as a market economy in this trade deal.[96]

Obviously, to gain the tariff preferences of the EU, Vietnam has to, in turn, provide market access to EU goods and services, and this has received the most criticism from experts. The study of Binh Duong and his colleagues also mentions the challenges in the development gap between both sides and the competition pressure placed on Vietnamese enterprises as the country conducts its tariff reduction obligation and market access obligation in services.[97] The risk of opening the service sector (banking, postal, insurance, and maritime transport) will be even more significant

[91] Worldometer (2024).

[92] Vietnam Chamber of Commerce and Industry (2011), p. 23.

[93] Minh Long (2017).

[94] Duong et al. (2015), p. 16.

[95] Philip et al. (2011), p. 12.

[96] Vietnam Chamber of Commerce and Industry (2011), p. 28. As mentioned by the experts, the ability to succeed in this issue under EVFTA negotiation is much higher than the discussion within the framework of the Vietnam - EU working group on the recognition of market economy status to Vietnam.

[97] It should be noticed that other economical experts give optimistic comment on this challenge. Ibid., p. 30.

as Vietnamese service providers are usually less competitive in terms of capital size, experience, diversity, and quality[98] compared with well-experienced EU firms.

Despite these challenges, Former Prime Minister of Trade of Vietnam - Mr Truong Dinh Tuyen, who is in charge of the WTO accession procedure of Vietnam, has supposed that: "the most important thing that Vietnam needs to focus on is to stimulate the institutional improvements in Vietnam, especially in the government's procurement programs, law enforcement mechanism and sanctions."[99] In doing so, the country may have a chance to take full advantage of other commitments in competition, environment, and labour to support the country's business environment in a safer and more stable way.[100]

Recently, the environment has become a hot topic in Vietnam as the country is facing corollary issues of its industrial-development-priority policy, including serious environmental incidents caused by foreign investors and fast-rising heat extremes due to the effects of climate change. A Report of "Vietnam 2035: Toward Prosperity, Creativity, Equity, and Democracy" implies that evidence is increasing that climate change is already occurring in Vietnam and will intensify over the coming decades.[101] This document also points out that "climate change poses a major threat to development in Vietnam, where more than 50% of the workforce and income depends on climate-sensitive natural resources."[102]

As announced in the Socio-Economic Development Strategy 2011–2020, the aim of the Vietnamese government is to make the country a modern, industrialised nation. To achieve this target, the strategy has focused on structural reforms, environmental sustainability, social equity, and emerging issues of macroeconomic stability. This requires changes to the banking system, market institutions and State-owned Enterprises.[103] All these points are, indeed, significantly matched with the overall effects of the preferential trade relationship with the EU. It has been mentioned that new-generation FTAs like EVFTA are expected to create positive pressure on the Vietnamese government to adjust its economic, social, and environmental policies.[104] The legal frame that the EVFTA has set is expected to support Vietnam taking another step forward to be a reliable part of the global supply chain.

Mr Tran Hong Ha, Vice Minister of MONRE, at a conference held in 2016 on "Implementing the Environmental Commitments of the Trans-Pacific Partnership", emphasised that "after the conclusion of those agreements, Vietnam would have to effectively implement its environmental policies because, otherwise, it might

[98] Ibid.

[99] Ngoc Ha (2014).

[100] Vietnam Chamber of Commerce and Industry (2011), p. 32.

[101] World Bank, Ministry of Planning and Investment of Vietnam (2016), p. 57.

[102] Ibid, p. 245.

[103] EuroCham (2019), p. 24.

[104] Schirmbeck argued in her research that FTAs, which were heavily criticized by left-wing actors in the "Global North" and beyond, positively affected Vietnam's environmental policies. See Schirmbeck (2017), p. 8.

jeopardise access to new markets".[105] This opinion is not simply an encouragement but an urgent requirement as Vietnam's international trade strategy at this moment still based on export-orientation. In order to bring its products into a strict import-control market like the EU, standards, manufacturing process, product quality, and labour standards need to be enhanced to achieve its export expectations. In fact, the National Assembly of Vietnam approved a revised Labour Code in 2019,[106] which allows independent trade unions to operate with permission from state authorities. The new Labour Code also reflects Vietnam's clear commitments to collective bargaining, combating forced labour, and combating workplace discrimination. Although much work remains to be done as various Decrees and Circulars implementing the current Labour Code need to be revised to comply with the new Labour Code, these revisions show a step towards Vietnam aligning with international labour standards by implementing core Conventions of the ILO as a requirement proposed in the EVFTA negotiation framework.[107]

One year before the conclusion of the EVFTA, the Vietnam–EU Voluntary Partnership Agreement (VPA) on implementing Forest Law Enforcement, Governance and Trade was also signed in October 2018 after nearly nine years of negotiation. This binding agreement, which entered into force in June 2019, aims to address illegal logging, improve forest governance and promote trade in legal timber products. It also includes commitments to improve transparency, accountability, legislative clarity and other aspects of governance. Vietnam's VPA commitments have been reflected in its new Forestry Law, which entered into force in January 2019.

These examples show that international treaties are necessary incentives for reforming and upgrading governance capacity in Vietnam's socioeconomic development. With such an open-minded, outward-looking policy, the EVFTA is believed to create a strong motivation for the Vietnamese national reform process and to raise suspicions of sustainable development among the Vietnamese government and non-governmental actors. These are likely the expectations of the Vietnamese government as they engage in this extensive and comprehensive trade and investment partnership with the EU.

5.3 The EU–Vietnam Trade and Investment Agreements: Addressing Shared Concerns

The preceding section addressed the EU and Vietnam's concerns within their trade and investment cooperation relationship. It highlighted the goal of promoting trade while also pursuing various non-commercial objectives. A comprehensive agreement characterised by the near-total removal of bilateral tariffs and customs duties,

[105] Vice Minister of MONRE Tran Hong Ha (2016).

[106] National Assembly of Vietnam (2019) Labour Code No. 45/2019/QH14.

[107] Ebbighausen (2020).

coupled with a substantial reduction in non-tariff barriers across service and investment sectors, encompassing government procurement, intellectual property rights, competition, and regulatory coherence, creates a rigorous set of obligations for both parties. Therefore, it becomes imperative to define the scope of regulatory autonomy for each party to guide the development and implementation of future policies.

This section offers an overview of how both parties balance environmental protection with trade and investment under the concept of "sustainable development" within the EU–Vietnam Trade and Investment Agreements. The focus will be on examining the agreement's provisions related to sustainable development, particularly those about the state's regulatory power.

- **The Integration of "Sustainable Development" in the EVFTA**

In the EVFTA, "sustainable development" has been repeatedly mentioned throughout the Agreement, starting from the Preamble as below:[108]

> Determined to strengthen their economic, trade and investment relationship in accordance with the objective of sustainable development, in its economic, social and environmental dimensions, and to promote trade and investment under this Agreement in a manner mindful of high levels of environmental and labour protection and relevant internationally recognised standards and agreements;

The term "sustainable" has later been affirmed in Chapter 7 on non-tariff barriers to trade and investment in renewable energy generation. In this Chapter, the two parties declare the objectives of promoting, developing and increasing energy generation of energy from renewable and sustainable sources, mainly through facilitating trade and investment in line with global efforts to reduce greenhouse gas emissions. (Article 7.1). The scope of this chapter covers measures that affect trade and investment between the Parties in relation to the generation of energy from renewable and sustainable sources (Article 7.3).

In addition, Chapter 12 on intellectual property has also encouraged a more sustainable and inclusive economy for both sides (Article 12.1). More precisely, Vietnam and the EU have expressed a strong and unified viewpoint on a chapter on Trade and Sustainable Development to promote sustainable development by fostering the contribution of trade and investment-related aspects of labour and environmental issues (Article 13.1.1). Article 13.1(1) underscores the primary objective of the chapter on Trade and Sustainable Development, which is to promote sustainable development, focusing on "fostering the contribution of trade and investment-related aspects to labour and environmental issues." Within this chapter, the parties commit to pursuing sustainable development by simultaneously emphasising three key elements: economic development, social development, and environmental protection (Article 13.1(3)).

The critical regulations highlighted in this chapter are those outlined in Article 13.2 (Right to Regulate and Levels of Protection) and 13.3 (Upholding Levels of Protection) of the agreement. These provisions serve as crucial safeguards for

[108] The term "principles of sustainable development" is also repeated in the Preamble of EVIPA.

parties to pursue their sustainable development objectives, strategies, policies, and priorities (Article 13.2.1(a)), as well as the right to establish their levels of domestic protection in environmental areas as it deems appropriate (Article 13.2.1(b)). Moreover, Article 13.2.1 emphasises the right to adopt or modify laws and policies in line with MEAs to which a Party is a signatory (Article 13.2.1(c)). It encourages enacting high-level domestic environmental laws and policies (Article 13.2.2 EVFTA).

Furthermore, Article 13.3 imposes an affirmative obligation on the parties to ensure that trade and investment activities do not undermine the levels of protection provided in domestic environmental or labour laws (Article 13.3.1 EVFTA). This provision mirrors language commonly found in Model BITs drafted by Finland, the Netherlands, and the United States.[109] Since Articles 13.2 and 13.3 explicitly preserve the parties' right to regulate, these regulations serve as the primary basis for interpreting obligations under the Agreement. As long as these rights are exercised reasonably, they guarantee the parties' policy space. Additionally, Paragraph 4 of Article 13.5 underscores the parties' right to adopt or maintain measures to implement MEAs to which they are signatories, provided such measures are not applied in a discriminatory manner or as disguised trade restrictions.

This chapter encourages both parties to ensure compliance and effective implementation of multilateral environmental treaties to which they sign within their domestic laws and practices (Article 13.5(2)). Additionally, as deemed appropriate, the Parties are urged to engage in consultation and cooperation regarding trade-related environmental issues of mutual interest (Article 13.5(1)). These regulations reflect the shared commitment of both parties toward the advancement of sustainable development in general and environmental matters in particular. Notably, this includes a dedicated response to climate change, as outlined in Article 13.6 of the EVFTA. In more specific terms, Article 13.6 of the EVFTA delineates the obligations of the Parties, encompassing cooperative efforts in effectively implementing the UNFCCC, the Kyoto Protocol, and the Paris Agreement (Article 13.6(1)). It also involves consultation, information-sharing, experiences in carbon pricing, the promotion of domestic and international carbon markets, and the advancement of energy efficiency, low-emission technology, and renewable energy (Article 13.6(2)).

Moreover, numerous commitments related to sustainable development, particularly environmental protection, are enumerated in the agreement. These include pledges on the conservation and sustainable use of biological diversity (Article 13.7 EVFTA), sustainable forest management and trade in forest products (Article 13.8 EVFTA), and cooperation on the sustainable management of marine resources and aquaculture products (Article 13.9 EVFTA). Additionally, commitments to enhance the contribution of trade and investment to sustainable development goals are outlined in Article 13.10 EVFTA, encompassing endeavours to facilitate trade and investment in goods and services essential for climate change mitigation (Article 13.10.2(c)) and promote corporate social responsibility (Article 13.10.2(e)).

[109] Martini (2017), p. 560.

In Chapter 13, regarding labour rights, the EVFTA recognise the commitment to implement all ratified ILO conventions. (Article 13.4.2); to respect and effectively implement the principles of the ILO concerning fundamental rights at work, such as the freedom of association or the elimination of forced labour and child labour (Article 13.4). Regarding environmental protection, the Agreement emphasises the commitment to effectively implement international environmental agreements (Article 13.1, 13.5) as well as the right to protect the environment at the appropriate level of each party (Article 13.2). As mentioned in an evaluation of the EU, most of the EU's FTA partners are still unfamiliar and, as a consequence, face challenges in implementing those chapters.[110] Indeed, a few EU stakeholders suppose that current implementation mechanisms regarding these commitments do not provide sufficiently visible responses to concerns put to the attention of governments or addressing long-standing implementation issues as well as lack of cooperation.[111] For instance, Chapter 13 on Trade and Sustainable Development of EVFTA contains regulations on encouraging members to make compliance with the ILO conventions and other international environmental agreements. The effect of this kind of commitment mainly depends on the voluntary of the parties and requires significant effort from coordination mechanisms.

Chapter 13 of the EVFTA contains a crucial agreement outlined in Article 13.13, which stipulates that "The Parties shall, jointly or individually, review, monitor, and assess the impact of the implementation of this Agreement on sustainable development through their respective policies, practices, participative processes, and institutions."[112] This mechanism enables the evaluation of the EVFTA's implementation and its contribution to sustainable development through the processes and institutions of the involved parties.

While some argue that monitoring and enforcing sustainable development is challenging,[113] it is worth noting that sustainable development does not necessarily require specific, predetermined outcomes and doesn't need to be enforced in the same manner as trade or investment obligations, as highlighted by Hush.[114] As long as the Parties are clear about the collaborative objective of promoting sustainable development, they have the flexibility to proactively determine the level of sustainable development they aim to achieve. The mechanism outlined in Article 13.13 provides a means to monitor the agreement's implementation. It allows the parties to gather sufficient data to make necessary adjustments to ensure the agreement continually evolves to address their shared concerns. Although questions remain regarding the effectiveness of this mechanism, its inclusion is a possitive development that holds the potential to foster meaningful progress.

[110] European Commission (2016b).

[111] Ibid, pp. 04–05.

[112] The EU - Japan Economic Partnership Agreement, Trade and Sustainable Development Chapter contain a similar provision in Article 16.11.

[113] Ederington (2010), pp. 84, 91.

[114] Hush (2018), p. 153.

Notably, the EU–Singapore FTA includes a provision aimed at reducing subsidies for fossil fuels to mitigate greenhouse gas emissions (Article 12.3 EU–Singapore FTA). However, a similar provision was not included in the EVFTA.[115] This disparity may be attributed to Vietnam's significant reliance on fossil fuels, with many state-funded projects still heavily invested in this sector. Additionally, when negotiating and concluding the EVFTA, Vietnam's energy development policies did not demonstrate a strong orientation toward transitioning to low-carbon fuels, as has been observed in more recent years.

To support the cooperation between the two partners, Chapter 16 on cooperation and capacity building sets the ground for the cooperation between the EU and Vietnam within the scope of existing legal and institutional frameworks and according to the rules and procedures governing the relations between the Parties to foster sustainable development in all its dimensions, including sustainable growth and the reduction of poverty. (Articles 16.1 and 16.2 EVFTA). This cooperation may cover different areas such as regional cooperation and integration; trade facilitation; trade policy and regulations; trade-related aspects of agriculture, fishery and forestry; sustainable development, etc… by means of exchange of information, experience and best practices as well as by means of policy cooperation. Where appropriate, seminars, workshops, training, studies, technical assistance and capacity building. (Article 16.2 EVIPA). These means of cooperation are expected to provide Vietnam with the necessary technical assistance and support in capacity building, especially in areas that need to be developed as sustainable development.

In terms of management, the EVFTA establishes a Committee on Trade and Sustainable Development (Article 17.2 EVFTA) to supervise and facilitate the implementation and application of the Agreement as well as to supervise and coordinate the work of all specialised committees, working groups and other bodies established under this Agreement, recommend to those bodies any necessary action, and evaluate and adopt decisions, where provided for in this Agreement, regarding any subject matter referred to it by those bodies. This is also the chanel to exchange information and to support the cooperation between the two partners.

In addition, in promoting cooperation to facilitate the development of renewable energy, the EVFTA has included a separate Chapter regulating the restriction on the use of non-tariff barriers in renewable energy generation, which shows the priority interests of the Parties in this field. Most notably, Article 7.1, Paragraph 1, Article 7.3 and Article 7.4, sections (a) and (b) emphasise that Parties shall refrain from adopting measures providing for local content requirements and measures requiring to form a partnership with local companies. These provisions prevent a party from applying policies to encourage and develop domestic enterprises in the renewable energy sector. In other words, this field requires fair treatment between foreign and domestic investors.

[115] Vietnam has recently secured an agreement to receive 15 billion USD in public funding from the Just Energy Transition Partnership, which includes active participation from the European Union. This funding is aimed at supporting Vietnam's efforts to decarbonize its energy systems. See European Commission (2022).

However, it is essential to note that, in accordance with Article 13.16(1) of the EVFTA, disputes on matters covered under Chapter 13 can only seek recourse through friendly procedures established under Article 13.16 (Government Consultations) and Article 13.17 (Panel of Experts). Chapter 15 (Dispute Settlement) and its Annex 15-C (Mediation Mechanism) do not apply to Chapter 13 on Trade and Sustainable Development. However, the current enforcement mechanisms show that Vietnam is more rigorously bound by the EVFTA's environmental and labor commitments than countries without similar agreements with the EU.[116]

Evidently, the EVFTA does not introduce new provisions or solutions but rather reaffirms the commitments already established in environmental treaties related to climate change to which the Parties are signatories. Nonetheless, the agreement provides a comprehensive framework for consultation and information-sharing obligations between the Parties. Indeed, the EU - Vietnam Trade and Sustainable Development (TSD) Committee, established under the EVFTA, serves as a platform for exchanging information and experiences related to the ratification of multilateral environmental agreements or their amendments (Para. 3, Article 13.5 EVFTA). This committee's meetings, as outlined in Article 13.5, also provide a forum to address issues that may arise during the implementation of the provisions in Chapter 13 (Article 13.16 EVFTA). This includes obligations related to cooperation in implementing the UNFCCC, the Kyoto Protocol, and the Paris Agreement, as mentioned in Article 13.6 of the EVFTA. This mechanism is expected to pressure the Vietnamese government to develop comprehensive plans for climate change response.

According to Decision 1201/QĐ-TTg,[117] which approves the implementation plan for the EVFTA, the focal agency involved in Vietnam's TSD consists of representatives from several ministries. These include the Ministry of Industry and Trade, Ministry of Labour, Invalids and Social Affairs, Ministry of Natural Resources and Environment, and Ministry of Agriculture and Rural Development.

In fact, during the first EU - Vietnam TSD Committee Meeting, Vietnam updated the EU on its NDCs and policies regarding energy efficiency. This includes the Law on Economical and Efficient Use of Energy 2010 and Politburo's Resolution 55-NQ/TW on the Orientation of Vietnam's National Energy Development Strategy to 2030, with a vision to 2045.[118] TSD Committee meetings, therefore, can serve as a tool for closely monitoring the implementation of obligations related to sustainable development and environmental protection outlined in the EVFTA, thereby exerting political pressure on Vietnam.

The EVFTA not only incorporates national-level mechanisms but also encourages active participation from the public and various sectors of society in promoting sustainable development. This is achieved through the establishment of Domestic Advisory Groups (DAGs), which include individuals and non-state organisations

[116] Huong et al. (2025), p. 7.

[117] Prime Minister of Vietnam (2020).

[118] The Joint Report of this meeting is available at: TSD Committee (2021).

involved in these efforts (Article 13.15(4)). Notably, most FTAs negotiated between the EU and its partners, starting with the EU - Korea FTA in 2010, have led to the formation of DAGs in both the EU and its partner countries. These groups aim to facilitate consultation and the effective implementation of the chapters on Trade and Sustainable Development included in these FTAs.[119] Essentially, the comprehensive commitments outlined in the EVFTA reflect the parties' strong willingness to promote extensive collaboration for advancing sustainable development alongside economic growth and investment. The inclusion of various mechanisms in the EVFTA aligns with the global trend among nations striving to actively mobilise investment aligned with sustainable development goals.[120] While some provisions may not receive full recognition due to their limited scope and the lack of specific implementation or enforcement mechanisms, they are expected to provide insights on how countries can strategically designate sectors, activities, standards, and approaches to effectively stimulate desired investment flows between treaty parties.[121] In the broader context of FTA negotiations worldwide, the EVFTA stands out as an agreement that integrates non-trade concerns into the promotion of cooperation and trade development.

- **Investment Protection Commitments and the Right to Regulate under EVIPA**

To understand EVIPA's regulations and their context, it is worth observing the EU's point of view regarding investment protection and ISDS. Historically, despite being a large common market, the EU did not have a unified policy for investment protection. This lack of uniformity was largely due to the significant regulatory costs associated with harmonising the diverse systems existing in the Member States, as noted by Tudor.[122] The Lisbon Treaty grants the EU exclusive competence over the common commercial policy, which includes foreign direct investment since 2009 (Article 3.1(e) Treaty on the Functioning of the European Union (TFEU)). Only the Union can create and implement legally binding acts in this area. Member States can legislate independently only if authorised by the Union (Article 2.1 TFEU). Chapter 4 of Title IV of Part Three TFEU laid the foundation for crucial aspects such as common rules for capital movement between Member States and third countries, which also cover investments. These rules may be influenced by the Member States' international agreements on foreign investment. Indeed, a report indicates that EU member states have entered into approximately 1200 investment protection agreements.[123] Therefore, to protect the interests of Union investors and their investments in third countries, as well as Member States hosting foreign investors, it is necessary to maintain existing bilateral investment agreements while

[119] For further information regarding the DAGs, see European Commission (2021b). In line with Decision No. 1972/QĐ-BCT (17 August 2021) of the Ministry of Industry and Trade, a Domestic Advisory Group has been established in Vietnam.

[120] See more discussions about this trend in Coleman et al. (2021), pp. 118–121.

[121] Ibid, p. 121.

[122] Tudor (2008), p. 39.

[123] Hallak (2022), p. I.

gradually preparing and negotiating Union investment agreements with high investment protection standards.[124]

In addition to the above-mentioned concerns, against a backdrop of widespread concerns surrounding the ISDS arbitration system and the huge amount of compensation payments that EU Member States are required to pay due to the introduction of new regulations,[125] combined with an increasing emphasis on the pursuit of legitimate policies, significant shifts in the perspectives of both EU Member States and the EU have emerged. These concerns have become prominent discussion topics within the Union, particularly during the CETA and TTIP negotiations. CETA is the first investment agreement negotiated by the EU since its assumption of exclusive competence in matters of FDI under the Lisbon Treaty in 2009. In the EU, the main result of public consultation on investment protection and investor-to-state dispute settlement in the TTIP Agreement shows the opposition to ISDS.[126] This opposition led to the call for reopening the negotiations over the ISDS aspects of CETA from the governments of France and Germany.[127]

In response to these pressing concerns, which encompass the promotion of sustainable development and the protection of member states' regulatory rights, the EU has actively advocated for establishing IPAs with its trading partners across all continents. These IPAs are integrated into FTAs or treated as separate agreements alongside the signed FTAs, serving as crucial steps towards addressing these current challenges.

The EU's new approach to investment protection in the current era is reflected in numerous published documents and directives. According to the EU, investment protection provisions, including ISDS, need to be enhanced. The focus is on "finding a better balance between the right of states to regulate and the need to protect investors" and reforming the investment arbitration system itself.[128] This balance can be achieved through a two-pronged approach: (i) clarifying and improving investment protection rules (right to regulate, indirect-expropriation, FET) and (ii) improving the operation of the dispute settlement system.[129] Thus, the EU has two key objectives in its investment policy reform. First, investment protection rules must be clearly defined to avoid any interpretative ambiguity, particularly regarding

[124] European Parliament and Council (2012) Regulation No. 1219/2012 of 12 Dec 2012 establishing transitional arrangements for bilateral investment agreements between Member States and third countries.

[125] Research findings reveal that from 2000 to 2021, there were 1146 disputes initiated worldwide. Of these, 267 cases involved current EU Member States as respondents. The highest award within this group, as of 2021, reached 4.379 billion US Dollar. See Hallak (2022), pp. 02–03.

[126] European Commission (2015b).

[127] Nyer (2015), p. 698.

[128] Indeed, the EU emphasises that "when the state is protecting the public interest in a non-discriminatory way, the right of the state to regulate should prevail over the economic impact of those measures on the investor." See European Commission (2013), p. 2.

[129] Ibid.

the state's right to regulate for public policy objectives.[130] Second, it is essential to establish a framework for arbitrators in investor-to-state procedures that applies specific rules contained in an investment agreement.[131]

This policy is consistently emphasised in official EU documents and in agreements negotiated with its partners. Specifically, within the EU, the directives for modernising the Energy Charter Treaty (ECT) emphasise that while prioritising investment protection, the ECT should explicitly uphold the "right to regulate" in critical areas such as health, safety, the environment, public morals, and consumer rights.[132] The repeated emphasis on this issue in various published communications indicates that safeguarding policy autonomy during FTA and IIA negotiations has become a central aspect of the EU's investment policy.[133]

Regarding the EU's concern on the right to regulate, the Court of Justice of the European Union (CJEU) has adopted a notable document, Opinion 1/17 (April 30, 2019), which explains its view on the compatibility of the dispute settlement mechanism in the CETA with EU law. This Opinion addresses concerns raised by the Kingdom of Belgium regarding the compatibility of the proposed ISDS mechanism with various aspects. These include its alignment with the autonomy of the EU legal system, adherence to the principle of equal treatment and effectiveness, and compatibility with the right of access to an impartial tribunal. Among these observations, it is noticeable mention the doubt that "in order to give rulings on disputes brought before it against the Union, the CETA Tribunal might, in the course of its examination of the relevant facts, which may include the primary law based on which the contested measure was adopted, weigh the interest constituted by the freedom to conduct business, relied on by the investor bringing the claim, against public interests, set out in the EU and FEU Treaties and the Charter, relied on by the Union in support of its defence." (Opinion 1/17, Para. 137). That tribunal would accordingly be called upon, without having to undertake an interpretation as such of those Treaties or of the Charter, to make findings as to the effect of those texts and to decide based on that weighing of interests, inter alia, whether that EU measure is "fair and equitable", within the meaning of Article 8.10 of the CETA, whether it constitutes indirect expropriation, within the meaning of Article 8.12 of that agreement. The specific concern is whether such situations, which are likely to occur often, would adversely affect the Court's exclusive jurisdiction over the definitive interpretation of EU law and, accordingly, the autonomy of the EU legal order.

To address these concerns, the CJEU underscores that the ISDS Tribunal established under the CETA will not possess jurisdiction, as explicitly stated in the initial clause of Article 8.31.2 of the agreement, to assess the legality of a measure, which is implied to breach the terms of the agreement under the domestic legislation of a member state. As articulated in Article 8.31.1 of CETA, this provision significantly

[130] Ibid, p. 6.

[131] Ibid.

[132] The EU Council (2019).

[133] Coleman et al. (2018), p. 77.

confines the authority of the CETA Tribunal, as it lacks the jurisdiction to interpret and apply EU laws beyond the provisions outlined in CETA. Consequently, domestic law is excluded from consideration as applicable law in disputes under this provision. The CJEU proceeded to affirm that "EU legislation is enacted through the democratic process delineated in the EU and FEU Treaties, and is deemed, in accordance with the principles of conferral of powers, subsidiarity, and proportionality outlined in Article 5 TEU, to be both suitable and necessary for achieving a legitimate objective of the Union." (Para. 151) Subsequently, the CJEU examined the provisions of CETA and highlighted the following key observations: Article 28.3.2 of CETA on general exceptions permits a Party to adopt or enforce measures necessary to safeguard public objectives, provided that such measures are not applied in a manner that would result in arbitrary or unjustifiable discrimination among the Parties where similar conditions exist, or constitute a disguised restriction on trade between the Parties. (Para. 152) Drawing from this provision, the CJEU reasoned that the CETA Tribunal lacks jurisdiction to declare incompatible with CETA the level of protection of a public interest established by EU measures in such circumstances and, consequently, to mandate the Union to pay damages (Para. 153).

Besides, Point 1(d) and Point 2 of the Joint Interpretative Instrument between the EU and Canada emphasise that the agreement "will … not lower [the standards and regulations of each Party] related to food safety, product safety, consumer protection, health, environment or labour protection', that 'imported goods, service suppliers and investors must continue to respect domestic requirements, including rules and regulations", and that the CETA 'preserves the ability of the European Union and its Member States and Canada to adopt and apply their laws and regulations that regulate economic activity in the public interest' has also been quoted. (Para. 155). Based on all the above-mentioned statements, the CJEU concluded that the discretionary powers of the CETA Tribunal and Appellate Tribunal do not extend to permitting them to call into question the level of protection of public interest determined by the Union following a democratic process (Para. 156).

The relevant provisions of CETA highlighted by the CJEU raise several critical issues. For instance, Article 8.31.3 of CETA departs from the practice observed in some investment treaties, which explicitly designate the applicable law for disputes. This provision also diverges from the majority of investment treaties that allow arbitration rules to incorporate the host state's domestic law as part of the law to be applied by a tribunal, akin to Article 42(1) of the ICSID Convention.[134] It seems inconceivable to assess the legality of a measure without considering domestic law. Moreover, the argument based on Article 28.3.2 of CETA regarding General Exceptions, suggesting that the tribunal lacks jurisdiction over measures aimed at protecting the public interest, is deemed insufficient because the exception does not preclude the jurisdiction of an investment tribunal or court to determine whether the measure or series of measures falls within its scope.[135]

---

[134] Titi (2021), p. 514.

[135] Ibid.

Although numerous concerns have been raised, it is believed that such provisions are deliberate and may significantly influence the formulation of future provisions on investment dispute settlement, extending well beyond the confines of the EU.[136] Although this book does not extend into a detailed examination of Opinion 1/17, which has already been scrutinised, its mention is relevant to this study. Opinion 1/17 is viewed as a "jurisprudential precedent shaping future law," as its conditions bind not only the EU but also, indirectly, third states.[137]

In terms of trade and investment relations with its partners, the above-mentioned policy is emphasised by the EU to be applied to investment protection provisions included in the EU agreements, in which the clarification of two key provisions, including indirect expropriation and FET, will be focused.[138] The recent signing of IPAs with Canada,[139] Vietnam, and Singapore exemplifies the EU's approach. These agreements are notable for their comprehensive and detailed provisions, which include the establishment of an "investment court system" whose structure and procedures are collaboratively determined by the involved parties. These developments indicate that the EU intends to use IPAs as a policy instrument, seeking greater control over them to promote the values it aims to disseminate.

5.4 Interim Conclusion

The FTAs established with Vietnam and other partners represent the most comprehensive and impactful negotiations ever undertaken by the EU.[140] A comprehensive agreement with almost full elimination of bilateral tariffs and custom taxes, in addition to a substantial reduction of NTBs in the area of services and investment with the range of covers areas from government procurement, intellectual property rights, competition, to regulatory coherence will create strict bound obligations for both sides. Thus, determining the regulatory space for parties is crucial for designing and applying future related policies.

As former Trade Minister of Vietnam - Mr Truong Dinh Tuyen - remarked, the EU–Vietnam economic relationship is mutually supportive.[141] From the EU's perspective, the Agreement facilitates easier access for its products, services, and investors to the Vietnamese domestic market. It is accompanied by heightened protection afforded by high-level investment standards and a revamped investment dispute resolution mechanism. For Vietnam, building on the positive experiences from its WTO accession process, the EU–Vietnam FTA, along with the CPTPP,

---

[136] Ibid.

[137] Ibid.

[138] European Commission (2013), p. 7.

[139] For Canada, investment protection provisions has been included in the Canada – EU FTA (CETA).

[140] de Mestral (2015), p. 641.

[141] Ngoc Ha (2014).

demonstrates a robust commitment across various domains, transcending traditional trade norms to include labour rights, human rights, and environmental protection. Consequently, the concept of "deep integration" is met with a more receptive attitude within Vietnam's internal community and government.

EVFTA, in general, and EVIPA, in specific, act as regulatory frameworks that provide the foundation for domestic reforms in Vietnam, enabling the country to advance further into the global supply chain. In addition to promoting trade and investment, these agreements are anticipated to encourage transparency and adherence to internationally recognised standards in environmental protection, labour rights, and human rights. The EVFTA is expected to be a conduit for European expertise to readily reach Vietnam. This will encompass cutting-edge, innovative, and environmentally friendly solutions and technologies, fostering mutual learning in high-quality services, advanced management practices, and the training of local employees. A more significant EU business presence in Vietnam instills corporate responsibility, promotes environmental protection, elevates quality standards and food safety, fortifies intellectual property rights protection, and enhances the recognition of local products under Geographical Indications.[142] These elevated standards are vital for propelling Vietnam through a successful reform process. For these reasons, the conclusion of the Agreement is heralded as a "win-win" trade project, with high expectations from both partners.

While the objective of trade development holds significant importance for both parties, the contemporary landscape underscores a heightened emphasis on non-trade matters, particularly environmental protection. In this context, the EVFTA - EVIPA deliberately addresses the integration of these concerns into the agreement's content through multiple avenues. These concerns extend beyond general statements of purpose found in the Preamble and are more specifically delineated in the substantive provisions of the agreement. The EVIPA is considered a tool to bolster investment promotion while safeguarding the signatories' rights to regulate. Nevertheless, as the practical application of these regulations remains somewhat constrained, the following chapters will progressively assess their efficacy in harmonising associated objectives, especially in light of Vietnam's present circumstances.

Jurisprudence

Court of Justice of the European Union (2017), Opinion 2/15 of the Court, 16 May 2017. Available via https://curia.europa.eu/juris/document/document.jsf?text=&docid=190727&pageIndex=0&doclang=EN&mode=req&dir=&occ=first&part=1&cid=2831024.

[142] EuroCham (2018), p. 51.

Treaties

Canada - EU Comprehensive and Economic Trade Agreement (2016) (CETA)
Comprehensive and Progressive Agreement for Trans-Pacific Partnership (2018) (CPTPP)
Energy Charter Treaty (1994) (ECT)
European Economic Area Agreement (1992) (EEA)
EU - Japan Economic Partnership Agreement (2019)
EU - Korea FTA (2010)
EU - Singapore Free Trade Agreement (2019) (EU - Singapore FTA)
EU - Singapore Investment Protection Agreement (2018) (EU - Singapore IPA)
Lisbon Treaty (2007)
EU - Vietnam FTA (2019) (EVFTA)
EU - Vietnam Framework Cooperation Agreement (1995)
EU - Vietnam Framework Cooperation Agreement on Comprehensive Partnership and Cooperation (2012)
EU - Vietnam IPA (2019) (EVIPA)
Convention on the Settlement of Investment Disputes between States and Nationals of other States (1965) (ICSID Convention)
ILO Declaration on Fundamental Principles and Rights at Work (1998, amended 2022)
Kyoto Protocol on Climate change (1997)
Paris Agreement (2015)
Treaty on the Functioning of the European Union (1957) (TFEU)
Transatlantic Trade and Investment Partnership (TTIP)
United Nations Framework Convention on Climate Change (1992) (UNFCCC)
United Nations Convention on Biological Diversity (1992)
United Nations Convention on International Trade in Endangered Species (1973) (CITES)

References

Bibliography

Abbott R (2012) The future of the multilateral trading system and the WTO. In: Melendez-Ortiz R, Bellmann C, Rodriguez Mendoza M (eds) The future and the WTO: confronting the challenges. International Centre for Trade and Sustainable Development

Baldwin R (2011) 21st century regionalism: filling the gap between 21st century trade and 20th century trade rules. WTO Staff Working Paper No. ERSD-2011-08. Available via https://www.wto.org/english/res_e/reser_e/ersd201108_e.pdf

Coleman J, Sachs L, Johnson L, Gupta K (2018) International Investment Agreements 2015-16: a review of trends and new approaches. In: Sachs LE, Johnson L (eds) Yearbook on International Investment Law and Policy 2015-2016. Oxford University Press, Oxford

Coleman J, Johnson LJ, Merrill E, Sachs LE (2021) Investment treaties and models in 2019: (mis) aligned with the SDGs? In: Sachs LE, Johnson LJ, Coleman J (eds) Yearbook on International Investment Law & Policy 2019. Oxford University Press, Oxford

Cuyvers L (2014) The sustainable development clauses in free trade agreements of the EU with Asian countries: perspectives for ASEAN? J Contemp Eur Study 22(4). Available via https://www.tandfonline.com/doi/abs/10.1080/14782804.2014.923752

de Mestral A (2015) When does the exception become the rule? Conserving regulatory space under CETA. J Int Econ Law 18:641–654. https://doi.org/10.1093/jiel/jgv033

Delegation of the European Union to Vietnam (2019) Guide to the EU - Vietnam Trade and Investment Agreements. Available via https://www.eeas.europa.eu/sites/default/files/eu_fta_guide_final.pdf

Duong NB, Anh TT, Trang NT (2015) Future Vietnam - EU Free Trade Agreement: an analysis of trade creation and trade diversion effects. External Econ Rev 72

Ebbighausen R (2020) EU - Vietnam trade deal puts spotlight on workers' rights. Deutsche Welle. https://www.dw.com/en/eu-vietnam-trade-deal-puts-spotlight-on-workers-rights/a-52040200

Economic and Social Commission for Asia and the Pacific (2018) Asia-Pacific Trade and Investment Report 2018: Recent Trends and Developments. Available via https://www.unescap.org/publications/APTIR2018

Ederington J (2010) Should trade agreements include environmental policy? Rev Environ Econ Policy 4(1):84–102

EuroCham (2018) EVFTA Report 2018. Available via https://www.eurochamvn.org/sites/default/files/uploads/180724_tax%20update/The%20EVFTA%202018%20Report.pdf

EuroCham (2019) Whitebook 2019: Trade and Investment Issues and Recommendations. Available via https://www.scribd.com/document/408504041/WhiteBook-2019-pdf

EuroCham (2020) Whitebook 2020: Trade & Investment issues and Recommendations. Available via https://camnangxnk-logistics.net/wp-content/uploads/2020/08/Whitebook-EuroCham-2020.pdf

Gstohl S, Hanf D (2014) The EU's Post-Lisbon Free Trade Agreements: commercial interests in a changing constitutional context. Eur Law J 20(6):733–748

Ha HH, Sicurelli D (2017) The EU's preferential trade agreements with Singapore and Vietnam: market vs. normative imperatives. Contemp Polit 23(4):369–387. https://doi.org/10.1080/13569775.2017.1289303

Hallak I (2022) Investor–state protection disputes involving EU Member States. European Parliamentary Research Service. PE738.216. Available via https://www.europarl.europa.eu/RegData/etudes/IDAN/2022/738216/EPRS_IDA(2022)738216_EN.pdf

Human Rights Watch (2019) EU: postpone vote on Vietnam Free Trade Agreement. Available via https://www.hrw.org/news/2019/01/10/eu-postpone-vote-vietnam-free-trade-agreement

Huong NTL, Hy NHT, Giang TTT (2025) EU Green Deal: Green Regionalism or Trade Protectionism? A Discussion on the Conditions for Free Trade to Promote Deforestation Prevention in Selected ASEAN Countries. Available via https://ssrn.com/abstract=5181329

Hush E (2018) Where no man has gone before: the future of sustainable development in the comprehensive economic and trade agreement and new generation free trade agreements. Columbia J Environ Law 43(1):93–128. Available via https://journals.library.columbia.edu/index.php/cjel/article/view/3741

Hutt D (2019) Europe, Vietnam reach towards major trade deal. Asia Times. https://www.asiatimes.com/2019/02/article/europe-vietnam-reach-towards-major-trade-deal/

Jutten M (2023) Trade and sustainable development in EU free trade agreements. European Parliamentary Research Service. Available via https://www.europarl.europa.eu/RegData/etudes/BRIE/2023/754613/EPRS_BRI(2023)754613_EN.pdf

Kikuchi T, Yanagida K, Huong V (2018) The effects of mega-regional trade agreements on Vietnam. J Asian Econ 4. https://doi.org/10.1016/j.asieco.2017.12.005

Martini C (2017) 'Balancing Investors' rights with environmental protection in international investment arbitration: an assessment of recent trends in investment treaty drafting. Int Lawyer 50(3):529–584

Minh Long (2017) Việt Nam cần động lực mới cho cải cách để hưởng lợi từ EVFTA. Công Thương Newspapers. Available via https://congthuong.vn/viet-nam-can-dong-luc-moi-cho-cai-cach-de-huong-loi-tu-evfta-96568.html

Nessel C, Verhaeghe E (2020) Unfolding the European Commission's storytelling on ethical trade relations with Vietnam. CEVIPOL Working Papers 2(2):2–32. Available via https://www.cairn-int.info/revue-cevipol-working-papers-2020-2-page-2.htm

Ngoc Ha (2014) EVFTA: challenges for Vietnam lie in non-tariff barriers. VietNamNet News. Available via https://english.vietnamnet.vn/fms/business/96985/evfta%2D%2Dchallenges-for-vietnam-lie-in-non-tariff-barriers.html

Nguyễn Nhuần (2011) Liên minh châu Âu và Việt Nam Hướng tới một năm Hợp tác Thành công 2011 [The European Union and Vietnam Look forward to a Successful year of Cooperation in 2011]. Thanh Tra Press, 11 Jan 2011. Available via https://thanhtra.com.vn/chinh-tri/doi-noi/Lien-minh-chau-Au-va-Viet-nam-huong-toi-mot-nam-hop-tac-thanh-cong-2011-24771.html

Nyer D (2015) The Investment chapter of the EU - Canada Comprehensive Economic and Trade Agreement. J Int Arbitr 32(6):697

Oortwijn J (2019) EU - Vietnam Free Trade Agreement delayed to 2020. Available via https://www.bike-eu.com/laws-regulations/nieuws/2019/01/eu-vietnam-free-trade-agreement-delayed-to-2020-10135214?vakmedianet-approve-cookies=1&_ga=2.25321979.716361221.1555518938-1720667938.1555518938

Panitchpakdi S (2002) The Doha Development Agenda: Challenges Ahead. European Parliament. Brussels. Available via https://www.wto.org/english/news_e/spsp_e/spsp07_e.htm

Philip JM et al (2011) The Free Trade Agreement between Vietnam and the European Union: quantitative and qualitative impact analysis. EU-Vietnam MUTRAP III

Rodriguez Mendoza M (2014) Mega-regionals and the Doha negotiations: implications for developing countries. Bridges Africa 3(10)

Sands P et al (2018) Principles of international environmental law, 4th edn. Cambridge University Press, Cambridge

Schirmbeck S (2017) Vietnam's Environmental Policies at a Crossroads - Salinated Rice Fields, Hunted-Out National Parks, and Eroding Beaches - and What We Can Do About It. Friedrich Ebert Stiftung. Available via https://asia.fes.de/news/vietnams-environmental-policies-at-a-crossroads

Sicurelli D (2015) The EU as a promoter of human rights in bilateral trade agreements: the case of the negotiations with Vietnam. J Contemp Eur Res 11(2):230–245. Available via https://doi.org/10.30950/jcer.v11i2.655

Titi C (2021) Opinion 1/17 and the future of investment dispute settlement: implications for the design of a Multilateral Investment Court. In: Sachs L, Johnson L, Coleman J (eds) Yearbook on International Investment Law & Policy 2019. Oxford University Press, Oxford

Trochu M (2018) The evolution of investor-states dispute settlement methods in free trade agreements between the EU and some states in East and South-East Asia. In: Viet DT, Lan HNT (eds) Giải quyết tranh chấp đầu tư quốc tế: Một số vấn đề pháp lý và thực tiễn trong bối cảnh hội nhập [Investor-State Dispute Settlement: Legal Issues and Practice in the Context of Integration]. Ho Chi Minh City National University Publishing, Ho Chi Minh City

Tröster B, Grumiller J, Grohs H, Raza W, Staritz C, Arnim RV (2019) Combining trade and sustainability? The Free Trade Agreement between the EU and Vietnam. Policy Note, Research Report 29/201, Austrian Foundation for Development Research (ÖFSE). Available via https://www.econstor.eu/handle/10419/192973

Tudor I (2008) The fair and equitable treatment standard in the international law of foreign investment. Oxford University Press, Oxford

United Nations Commission on International Trade Law. UNCITRAL Working Group III: Investor-State Dispute Settlement Reform. Available via https://uncitral.un.org/en/working_groups/3/investor-state

United Nations General Assembly (2015) Resolution: Transforming Our World: The 2030 Agenda for Sustainable Development. Available via https://sustainabledevelopment.un.org/post2015/transformingourworld/publication

Vice Minister of MONRE Tran Hong Ha (2016) Opening Remark at Conference on Implementing the Environmental Commitments of the Trans Pacific Partnership. 8 April 2016. Hanoi

Vietnam Chamber of Commerce and Industry (2011) Kiến Nghị Chính Sách: Hiệp định Thương mại Tự do Việt Nam - Liên Minh Châu Âu [Policy Recommendation: Vietnam - European Union Free Trade Agreement]. International Trade Policy Advisory Committee. Available via https://trungtamwto.vn/file/16536/Khuyen%20nghi%20Chinh%20sach%20Vietnam%20-%20EU%20FTA.pdf

Vietnam Customs (2024) Tình hình xuất khẩu, nhập khẩu hàng hóa của Việt Nam tháng 3 và 3 tháng năm 2024 [Vietnam's Export and Import of goods in March and 3 months of 2024]. Available via https://www.customs.gov.vn/index.jsp?pageId=442&tkId=7503

Vietnamnet (2011) FTA Talks between Vietnam, EU Almost Stalled. Available via https://english.vietnamnet.vn/en/business/8403/fta-talks-between-vietnam%2D%2Deu-almost-stalled.html

Vietnamnet News (2019) NA Chairwoman meets Chairman of EP's International Trade Committee. Available via https://en.vietnamplus.vn/na-chairwoman-meets-chairman-of-eps-international-trade-committee-post149440.vnp

Vietnamplus (2020) Legislature to vote on resolutions ratifying EVFTA, EVIPA. Available via https://en.vietnamplus.vn/legislature-to-vote-on-resolutions-ratifying-evfta-evipa/174515.vnp

Wolfe R (2015) First diagnose, then treat: what ails the Doha Round? World Trade Review. Cambridge University Press

World Bank, Ministry of Planning and Investment of Vietnam (2016) Vietnam 2035: Toward Prosperity, Creativity, Equity, and Democracy. Available via https://openknowledge.worldbank.org/handle/10986/23724

Worldometer (2024) Europe population. http://www.worldometers.info/world-population/europe-population/

WTO Secretariat (2019) RTAs currently in force 1948-2019 WTO Regional Trade Agreements Database. Available via http://rtais.wto.org/UI/PublicMaintainRTAHome.aspx

WTO Secretariat (2024) RTAs currently in force 1948-2024 WTO Regional Trade Agreements Database. Available via http://rtais.wto.org/UI/charts.aspx

Zahradil J (2018) Draft Recommendation on the Proposal for a Council decision on the Conclusion of the Investment Protection Agreement between the European Union and its Member Sates, of the one part, and the Socialist Republic of Viet Nam. European Union, Committee on International Trade. 16 November 2018. Available via https://www.europarl.europa.eu/doceo/document/INTA-PR-629564_EN.pdf?redirect

Documents

Committee on European Affairs (2018) Accord de libre-échange entre l'Union européenne et la République socialiste du Viêt Nam: proposition de décision du Conseil relative à la signature, au nom de l'Union européenne, de l'accord de libre-échange entre l'Union européenne et la République socialiste du Viêt Nam [Free Trade Agreement between the European Union and the Socialist Republic of Vietnam: Proposal for a Council Decision on the signing, on behalf of the European Union, of the Free Trade Agreement between the European Union and the Socialist Republic of Vietnam]. Examination under Article 88-4 of the Constitution, COM(2018) 692 final. 17 October 2018. Available via https://www.senat.fr/ue/pac/EUR000004780.html

EU Council (2012) EU Strategic Framework and Action Plan on Human Rights and Democracy. 11855/12. 25 June 2012. Luxemburg. Available via https://www.consilium.europa.eu/uedocs/cms_data/docs/pressdata/en/foraff/131181.pdf
EU Council (2016) Joint Interpretative Instrument on the Comprehensive Economic and Trade Agreement (CETA) between Canada and the European Union and its Member States. 14 January 2017. Available via https://eur-lex.europa.eu/legal-content/EN/TXT/PDF/?uri=CELEX:22017X0114(01)
EU Council (2019) Negotiating Directive for the Modernisation of the Energy Charter Treaty. Annex of the Council Decision 10745/19. 2 July 2019. Brussels. Available via https://data.consilium.europa.eu/doc/document/ST-10745-2019-ADD-1/en/pdf
EU Council (2020) Council Decision 2019/753 on The Conclusion of the Free Trade Agreement between the European Union and the Socialist Republic of Viet Nam. 30 March 2020. Available via https://eur-lex.europa.eu/eli/dec/2020/753/oj/eng
EU Parliamentary Assembly (2017) "New generation" Trade Agreements and their Implications for Social Rights, Public Health and Sustainable Development. Resolution 2152. 27 January 2017. Available via http://assembly.coe.int/nw/xml/XRef/Xref-XML2HTML-EN.asp?fileid=23489
European Commission (2006) Global Europe: Competing in the world – A contribution to the EU's growth and jobs strategy. Communication from the Commission to the Council, the European Parliament, the European Economic and Social Committee and the Committee of the Regions. COM(2006) 567 final. Brussels. 4 July 2006
European Commission (2010a) Press Release - EU and Vietnam To Launch Free Trade Negotiation. March 2010. Available via http://europa.eu/rapid/press-release_IP-10-219_en.htm
European Commission (2010b) European Council Conclusions. September 2010. Available via http://europa.eu/rapid/press-release_DOC-10-3_en.htm
European Commission (2013) Investment Protection and Investor-to-State Dispute Settlement in EU Agreements - Fact Sheet. Available via http://www.sice.oas.org/TPD/USA_EU/Studies/tradoc_151916__Investment_e.pdf
European Commission (2014) Trade for All: Towards a More Responsible Trade and Investment Policy. Available via https://op.europa.eu/en/publication-detail/-/publication/d90eda7c-7299-11e5-9317-01aa75ed71a1
European Commission (2015a) The EU and ASEAN: A Partnership with a Strategic Purpose. Joint Communication to the European Parliament and the Council. May 2015. Available via http://eeas.europa.eu/archives/delegations/cambodia/documents/press_corner/2015/eu_asean_partnership_en.pdf
European Commission (2015b) Report on Online Public Consultation on Investment Protection and Investor-to-State Dispute Settlement (ISDS) in the Transatlantic Trade and Investment Partnership. January 2015. Available via https://ec.europa.eu/commission/presscorner/api/files/document/print/hr/memo_15_3202/MEMO_15_3202_EN.pdf
European Commission (2015c) Memo: EU and Vietnam reach Agreement on Trade Deal. August 2015. Available via https://ec.europa.eu/commission/presscorner/detail/mt/IP_15_5467
European Commission (2015d) Why the new EU proposal for an Investment Court System in TTIP is beneficial to both States and investors. Press Release MEMO/15/6060. November 2015) Available via https://ec.europa.eu/commission/presscorner/detail/en/MEMO_15_6060
European Commission (2016a) CETA: EU and Canada Agree on New Approach on Investment in Trade Agreement. February 2016. Available via https://ec.europa.eu/commission/presscorner/detail/en/IP_16_399
European Commission (2016b) Text of The Transatlantic Trade Investment Partnership. July 2016. Available via http://trade.ec.europa.eu/doclib/press/index.cfm?id=1230
European Commission (2017a) Overview of FTA and other Trade Negotiations. September 2017. Available via https://www.consilium.europa.eu/media/31365/ongoing-trade-negotiations.pdf
European Commission (2017b) CETA - a Trade Deal That Sets a New Standard for Global Trade. Press Release. 15 February 2017. Available via https://ec.europa.eu/commission/presscorner/detail/en/memo_17_271

European Commission (2017c) The Economic Impact of the EU-Vietnam Free Trade Agreement. 1 January-31 December 2017. Available via https://mglobale.promositalia.camcom.it/kdocs/1986231/impatto_economico_dellaccordo_ue_vietnam.pdf
European Commission (2018a) Commission Presents EU-Vietnam Trade and Investment Agreements for Signature and Conclusion. 17 October 2018. Available via https://ec.europa.eu/commission/presscorner/detail/en/ip_18_6127
European Commission (2018b) EU-Vietnam Trade Agreement - Memo. 17 October 2018. Available via https://policy.trade.ec.europa.eu/news/eu-vietnam-trade-agreement-memo-2018-10-17_en
European Commission (2018c) EU and Mexico Reach New Agreement on Trade. April 2018. Available via https://ec.europa.eu/commission/presscorner/detail/en/IP_18_782
European Commission (2021a) Trade Policy Review - An Open, Sustainable and Assertive Trade Policy. Communication from the Commission to the European Parliament, the Council, the European Economic and Social Committee and the Committee of the Regions. February 2021. Available via https://ec.europa.eu/commission/presscorner/detail/en/ip_21_644
European Commission (2021b) Participation of civil society organisation in the implementation of trade agreements - TSD Committees and civil society meetings. December 2021. Available via https://trade.ec.europa.eu/doclib/press/index.cfm?id=1870
European Commission (2022) Political Declaration on establishing the Just Energy Transition Partnership with Viet Nam. December 2022 Available via https://ec.europa.eu/commission/presscorner/detail/en/statement_22_7724
European Commission. Negotiations and Agreements. Available via http://ec.europa.eu/trade/policy/countries-and-regions/negotiations-and-agreements/#_being-negotiated
European Commission. Sustainable development. Available via http://ec.europa.eu/trade/policy/policy-making/sustainable-development/
European Commission. The European Green Deal: Striving to be the First Climate-neutral Continent. Available via https://climate.ec.europa.eu/eu-action/european-green-deal_en
European Council (2019) Making Trade Policy. Available via http://ec.europa.eu/trade/policy/in-focus/ttip/
European Parliament (2008) Trade and Economic Relations with the Countries of South East Asia (ASEAN) P6_TA(2008)0195. 8 May 2008. Brussels. Available via http://www.europarl.europa.eu/sides/getDoc.do?type=TA&reference=P6-TA-2008-0195&language=EN
European Parliament (2018) Coming up in 2019: European Elections, EU Budget, Brexit. Available via http://www.europarl.europa.eu/news/en/headlines/eu-affairs/20181122STO19861/coming-up-in-2019-european-elections-eu-budget-brexit
European Parliament and Council (2012) Regulation No. 1219/2012 (12 December 2012) Establishing Transitional arrangements for Bilateral Investment agreements between Member States and third countries
National Assembly of Vietnam (2019) Labour Code No. 45/2019/QH14 (1 January 2021)
Prime Minister of Vietnam (2020) Decision 1201/QĐ-TTg (6 August 2020) Approving the EVFTA Agreement Implementation Plan
TSD Committee (2021) 1st Meeting – November 2021 – Joint Report. In: CIRCABC. Available at https://circabc.europa.eu/ui/group/09242a36-a438-40fd-a7af-fe32e36cbd0e/library/84ff4c1b-dde0-4c40-ac8d-52ffeaeb3bf0/details
Vietnam Ministry of Industry and Trade (2021) Decision No. 1972/QĐ-BCT (17 August 2021) Establishing Domestic Advisory Group – Vietnam. Available via https://trungtamwto.vn/file/21031/2021.08.17-qd-1972%2D%2Dbct-thanh-lap-dag.pdf

Chapter 6
Indirect Expropriation Under the EVIPA

Abstract This Chapter provides a comprehensive examination of the provisions regarding indirect expropriation within the EVIPA. The primary aim of this chapter is to evaluate the effectiveness of the changes introduced in EVIPA, particularly concerning one of the most commonly referenced provisions in investor claims in international investment arbitration. The analysis shows that, compared to contemporaneously negotiated or drafted agreements, such as Canada 2021 Model FIPA, the provisions on indirect expropriation in EVIPA do not demonstrate significant innovations. This observation may be attributed to a deliberate policy choice made by the signatories. While Annex 4 of the EVIPA may not be universally praised for its detail and comprehensiveness, it does provide a basic framework for arbitral tribunals to follow the parties' original intentions when evaluating specific measures. Importantly, these disputes will be under the jurisdiction of the ICS rather than any alternative arbitral tribunal, adding an extra layer of assurance for a standardised interpretation of these provisions. The adjudicative procedures developed by the ICS will gradually enhance the predictability of dispute resolution.

6.1 Expropriation and Indirect Expropriation in International Investment Law and Environmental Protection

6.1.1 Expropriation and Indirect Expropriation in International Investment Law

Expropriation under IIL has its roots in customary international law, which means the host state takes the investors' assets without their consent.[1] There are two types of taking in international investment practice: direct expropriation and indirect

[1] Subedi (2008), p. 120.

N. T. Lan Huong, *Investment Protection and Environmental Governance*, European Yearbook of International Economic Law 47,
https://doi.org/10.1007/978-3-032-05332-9_6

expropriation. Direct expropriation refers to a situation in which a state formally transfers or extinguishes an investor's title to the property.[2] This act deprives investors of the right "to manage, use or control" their investment. Direct expropriation can be identified through the host state's clear, intentional actions aimed at foreign investors' assets or investments. In this context, it is necessary to mention the concept of "nationalisation" because "direct expropriation" and "nationalisation" are often mentioned together or interchangeably. However, these two concepts have certain differences in scope and magnitude.

While nationalisation is inherently a form of direct expropriation, it typically refers to large-scale takings of private property across all economic sectors or within specific industries.[3] This measure is often carried out as part of broader economic and social reforms. Nationalisation is also frequently driven by political motives to end foreign domination of the domestic economy and industry and expand state-controlled sectors.[4] Historically, nationalisation was widespread in Latin America, Asia, Africa, and Eastern Europe after World War II, as many newly independent states nationalised foreign investments to lay the foundation for a new economic and social order.[5] Nationalisation often targets significant industries or national resources such as oil, insurance, banking, and mining.[6] While less common today, nationalisation still occurs, exemplified by Venezuela's nationalisations within the oil industry based on a law enacted by its National Assembly in 2009.[7]

In contrast, direct expropriations generally refer to property-specific or enterprise-specific takings where the property rights remain with the state or are transferred by the state to other economic operators.[8] Direct expropriation, therefore, has a narrower target and scope than nationalisation. Instead of expropriating ownership rights across all industries or businesses within the same sector nationwide, direct expropriation targets specific entities within particular industries as determined by the state.[9]

The commonality between nationalisations and direct expropriations is that both involve the transfer of title or outright physical seizure. These acts are easy to identify because they are based on an open, deliberate, and unequivocal intent, typically reflected in a formal law, decree, or physical act.[10] The concept of direct expropriation, therefore, is straightforward to define and generally not controversial in international investment activities. The second type of expropriation, indirect expropriation, is more likely to occur and presents additional challenges due to its

[2] Bonnitcha (2014), pp. 229–230.

[3] UNCTAD (2012), p. 05.

[4] Plimmer and McCluskey (2019), p. 171.

[5] Henkin (1989), p. 216.

[6] Qian (2020), p. 16.

[7] Isakoff (2013), p. 192.

[8] UNCTAD (2012), pp. 05–06.

[9] Dung (2014), p. 29.

[10] UNCTAD (2012), pp. 06–07.

complicated characteristics. Indirect expropriation refers to a situation in which the host country interferes in the use of the property or with the enjoyment of the benefits without taking it, and the legal title to the property is not affected.[11] In the mentioned cases, those measures have a similar effect to expropriation.

The discussion on what constitutes an indirect expropriation and the liability in case of indirect expropriation has received much debate over the last fifteen years.[12] In particular, the liability to compensate in case of direct expropriation is widely recognised, while such a requirement in case of indirect expropriation appears in a greater multiplicity in litigation practice.[13] As pointed out by commentators, although not all measures that affect the investments constitute indirect expropriation, traditional IIAs do not provide sufficient guidance for the arbitral tribunal on delineating the boundary between non-compensable measures and indirect expropriation.[14] This practice was affirmed by the Saluka tribunal, which commented that "international law has yet to identify in a comprehensive and definitive fashion precisely what regulations are considered 'permissible' and 'commonly accepted' as falling within the police or regulatory power of States and, thus, non-compensable. In other words, it has yet to draw a bright and easily distinguishable line between non-compensable regulations on the one hand and, on the other, measures that have the effect of depriving foreign investors of their investment and are thus unlawful and compensable in international law.[15]

The decisions of different tribunals in regard to such matters, therefore, are manifold. In the case of environmental measures alleged to be indirect expropriation, the doctrine of police power has frequently been invoked by the host states, mostly in connection with non-compensable measures.[16] Despite the lack of a uniform definition identifying a clear scope of state police powers, such powers are generally accepted as a matter of customary international law/general international law[17] both

[11] Dolzer (1986), p. 56; Bonnitcha (2014), p. 230; OECD (2004), p. 2; UNCTAD (2007), p. 56.

[12] Subedi (2008), p. 120; Hoffmann (2018), p. 151.

[13] Viñuales (2012), p. 299.

[14] Bonnitcha (2014), p. 230; Dolzer (1986), p. 56; UNCTAD (2007), p. 56.

[15] *Saluka Investments BV v. Czech Republic*, UNCITRAL, Partial Award, 17 March 2006, paras. 263–264.

[16] See *S.D. Myers, Inc. v.. Canada* [1998] UNCITRAL, NAFTA, Award, 13 November 2000; *Methanex Corporation v. United States of America* [1999] UNCITRAL, 44 ILM 1345, Award, 3 August 2005; *Glamis Gold Ltd. v. United States of America* [2003] UNCITRAL, NAFTA, Award, 16 May 2009; *Chemtura Corporation v. Government of Canada* [2002] PCA Case No. 2008-01, Award, 2 August 2010; *Suez, Sociedad General de Aguas de Barcelona S.A., and InterAguas Servicios Integrales del Agua S.A. v. The Argentine Republic* [2003] ICSID Case No. ARB/03/17; *Quiborax S.A. and Non Metallic Minerals S.A. v. Bolivia*, ICSID Case No. ARB/06/2, Award, 16 September 2015. See further Viñuales (2012), p. 369; Titi (2018), p. 336.

[17] Viñuales (2012), p. 367.

in litigation practice[18] and in legal discussions.[19] It has also been considered as one of the most important defence arguments in investment-environment disputes.[20]

However, case law shows that the majority of decisions are based on the "sole effect doctrine" when tribunals evaluate potential indirect expropriation. This doctrine requires the inquiry to focus on the impact of the measure applied to the interests of the investor when determining if a measure constitutes an indirect expropriation. The sole effect doctrine focuses on the economic damage of the investor, while the police power doctrine's concern is the legitimate intentions and purposes of the applied measure. Therefore, these tribunals may evaluate the effect an administrative action or decision has on the investor's rights (i.e., the economic value of the use, enjoyment, or disposition of assets or rights) instead of considering the intention of the host country.[21] In this context, the reasonable, legitimate expectation of the investor has also been considered by some tribunals in the context of regulatory expropriation claims, although this concept has primarily been associated with the FET standard in investment case law. Some tribunals also examine whether such actions or measures are proportional to the *public interest* or *public welfare* presumably protected thereby and to the protection legally granted to the investments.[22] The requirement for a public interest motivation of an expropriation measure, both direct and indirect, is rooted in customary international law[23] and can be widely found in IIAs, although the terminology varies slightly. For example, IIAs may mention: "public benefit" (Germany–Pakistan BIT (2009)), "public interest" (China–Peru FTA (2009)), "public order and social interest" (Canada–Colombia FTA (2008)), "public necessity" (Peru–Singapore FTA (2008)) or "public purpose related to internal needs" (Angola–United Kingdom BIT (2000)).[24] This requirement is also reflected in most domestic legal systems. Despite this divergence in formulations of the concept, not many IIAs provide a clear scope to determine the "public purpose" of the host state's measure, which means arbitrators must ascertain the public purpose on a case-by-case basis.[25]

In relating to the liability of compensation, although IIL "makes no distinction when it comes to paying compensation," whether direct or indirect expropriation,[26]

---

[18] *Methanex Corporation v. United States of America* [1999] UNCITRAL, 44 ILM 1345, Award, 3 August 2005; *Saluka Investments BV v. The Czech Republic* [2001] PCA Case No. 2001-04, Award, 17 March 2006; *Chemtura Corporation v. Government of Canada* [2002] PCA Case No. 2008-01, Award, 2 August 2010.

[19] For instance, see Chi (2018), p. 46. See also Viñuales (2014), p. 329.

[20] The other two arguments are the margin of appreciation doctrine and emergency and necessity clauses. See further in Viñuales (2012), p. 366.

[21] *Técnicas Medioambientales Tecmed, S.A. v. The United Mexican States* [2003] ICSID Case No. ARB(AF)/00/2, Award, 29 May 2003, para. 116.

[22] Ibid., para. 122.

[23] Reinisch (2018), p. 178. See also Hobér (2007), p. 38; UNCTAD (2012), p. 27.

[24] UNCTAD (2012), p. 29.

[25] Chi (2018), pp. 48–49.

[26] Subedi (2008), p. 125.

the tribunal's decisions show a different practice. Indeed, while it is widely recognised that providing compensation in case of a direct expropriation is necessary, in case of indirect expropriation, such requirements may vary depending on the specific circumstances of the case.[27] This practice of the "case-by-case" approach is widely accepted, especially in IIL, because of the "diversity of situations" that may arise in practice.[28] However, such diversity has not been expected from a rule-making perspective because it would create unpredictable possibilities for host states and, therefore, creates, theoretically, a legal risk to them, especially when it comes to measures that had been adopted and applied in order to pursue sustainable development goals.

6.1.2 Indirect Expropriation and Environmental Protection in Investment Arbitration Practice

In ISDS practice, indirect expropriation and FET frequently emerge as central issues brought before investment arbitral tribunals, particularly in cases related to the host state's environmental protection measures. Measures that lead to disputes have usually arisen in the following situations:

(i) The rejection or termination of the project or the revocation of license for foreign investors to engage in investment activities, typically involving the operation of hazardous waste treatment systems or hazardous waste landfills (as in *Metaclad v. Mexico*;[29] *Tecmed v. Mexico*;[30] *Biwater v. Tanzania*;[31] *Crystallex v.*

---

[27] In *SPP v. Egypt* when counting the amount of compensation, the tribunal have considered the environmental aim of the government's measure and decided that the amount of compensation claimed should be reduced (para 191). In *Metalclad v. Mexico*, however, the environmental dimension of the case was not been taken into account because the tribunal considered that the host state's evaluation of environmental risks posed by the investor's activities had no basis (para 106). In *Tecmed v. Mexico*, the tribunal did examined environmental context of the adopted measure in assesing whether such measure amounted to a compensable expropriation. See further analysis in Viñuales (2012), pp. 299–301.

[28] *Chemtura Corporation v. Government of Canada* [2002] PCA Case No. 2008-01, Awarded, 2 August 2010, para. 249.

[29] *Metalclad Corporation v. United Mexican States* [1997] ICSID Case No. ARB(AF)/97/1, Award, 30 August 2000.

[30] *Técnicas Medioambientales Tecmed, S.A. v. The United Mexican States* [2003] ICSID Case No. ARB(AF)/00/2, Award, 29 May 2003.

[31] *Biwater Gauff (Tanzania) Ltd. v. United Republic of Tanzania* [2005] ICSID Case No. ARB/05/22, Award, 24 July 2008.

Venezuela;[32] *Abengoa v. Mexico*[33] or related to nuclear power projects (as in *Vattenfall v. Germany (I))*.[34]

(ii) Introduce stricter regulations to enhance the preservation of biodiversity (as in *Marion Unglaube v. Costa Rica)*,[35] or to protect the area of traditional cultural concern (as in *Glamis Gold v. USA)*.[36]

(iii) Prohibition of the utilisation, sale, or disposal of harmful substances with adverse environmental effects (as in *SD Myers v. Canada*,[37] *Chemtura v. Canada*,[38] *Methanex v. The United States)*.[39]

(iv) Amend tax legislation to enforce environmental policies (as in *Yuri Bogdanov and Yulia Bogdanova v. Moldova)*.[40]

As previously mentioned, traditional IIAs frequently emphasise investment protection obligations while often neglecting environmental conservation objectives or the host state's legitimate policy interests. Consequently, when evaluating a host state's policy measures, investment tribunals typically centre their analysis on the wording of pertinent investment protection standards to assess potential violations. However, it is crucial to acknowledge that investment protection obligations, particularly those on expropriation and indirect expropriation in IIAs, present intricate and nebulous concepts. Defining these concepts precisely and constraining their scope through traditional interpretations is no straightforward task. Moreover, investment arbitration tribunals do not adopt a uniform approach when interpreting these obligations. The litigation practice demonstrates a lack of substantial consensus in distinguishing between acts of indirect expropriation and measures designed to pursue legitimate policy objectives. This inconsistency can be attributed, in part, to the various doctrines applied in the evolution of international investment law, which dictate what considerations should be weighed when determining whether a host state's regulatory measure constitutes an indirect expropriation.

---

[32] *Crystallex International Corporation v. Bolivarian Republic of Venezuela* [2011] ICSID Case No. ARB(AF)/11/2, Award, 4 April 2016.

[33] *Abengoa S.A. y COFIDES S.A. v. United Mexican States*, [2009] ICSID Case No. ARB(AF)/09/2, Award, 18 April 2013.

[34] *Vattenfall AB, Vattenfall Europe AG, Vattenfall Europe Generation AG v. Federal Republic of Germany* [2009] ICSID Case No. ARB/09/6 (no award).

[35] *Marion Unglaube and Reinhard Unglaube v. Republic of Costa Rica* [2009] ICSID Case No. ARB/08/1 and ARB/09/20, Case No. ARB/08/1 and ARB/09/20, Award, 16 May 2012.

[36] *Glamis Gold Ltd. v. United States of America* [2003] UNCITRAL, NAFTA, Award, 8 June 2009, para. 103–104. This is a new concept suggested by KEA Environmental, Inc. to protect the interests of a local tribe under a cultural studies retained by the United States Bureau of Land Management.

[37] *S.D. Myers, Inc. v. Canada* [1998] UNCITRAL, NAFTA, Final Award, 30 December 2002.

[38] *Chemtura Corporation v. Government of Canada* [2002] PCA Case No. 2008-01, Award, 2 August 2010.

[39] *Methanex Corporation v. United States of America* [1999] UNCITRAL, 44 ILM 1345, Award, 3 August 2005.

[40] *Yulia Bogdanova v. Republic of Moldova* [2012] SCC Case No. 091/2012, Award, 16 April 2013.

Up to the present, the primary doctrines employed to assess breaches of the indirect expropriation clause include the sole effect doctrine, the police power doctrine, and the proportionality doctrine. Tribunals and researchers advocate for the "sole effect" doctrine, which posits that the primary, though not exclusive, criterion for determining whether expropriation has occurred hinges on the impact of a regulatory measure on an investor's assets. Several prominent arbitral tribunals have supported this doctrine, including *Patrick Mitchell v. Congo,*[41] *Metalclad v. Mexico,*[42] *Tecmed v. Mexico,*[43] *Santa Elena v. Costa Rica,*[44] and *Siemens v. Argentina.*[45] The central focus of this doctrine lies in elucidating the economic repercussions of the host state's regulatory measures on the investments of foreign investors. The underpinning principle of the sole effect doctrine is that any significant deprivation of value, irrespective of the measure's intended purpose, must be classified as indirect expropriation and necessitate appropriate compensation.

In contrast, the "police powers" doctrine asserts that when assessing the applied measure, the tribunal must consider the broader context and objectives of that measure. Notable Tribunals that have applied this doctrine include *Saluka v. Czech Republic*[46] and *Methanex v. United States.*[47] According to the police powers doctrine, lawful regulatory measures aimed at safeguarding public health or environmental protection, executed without discrimination, should not be construed as indirect expropriation, and therefore, compensation is not warranted unless the measure's impact significantly outweighs its intended purpose. However, within the framework of the police powers doctrine, different "formulas" have emerged in dispute resolution practice. Some tribunals maintain that regulatory measures aimed at protecting legitimate public interests are the principal determinant, absolving the measure from any obligation to compensate foreign investors automatically.[48] Others perceive the objective of the applied measure as one factor among several to be evaluated alongside considerations such as the measure's impact. Nevertheless, the common thread among these approaches is that arbitral tribunals meticulously examine the context in which measures are applied, encompassing the objectives pursued by the host country while also considering other pertinent factors, including proportionality, impact, and the original intent of the host country.

---

[41] *Patrick Mitchell v. Congo* [1999] ICSID Arbitral Tribunal Case No. 99/7, 9 February 2004.

[42] *Metalclad Corporation v. United Mexican States* [1997] ICSID Case No. ARB(AF)/97/1, Award, 30 August 2000.

[43] *Técnicas Medioambientales Tecmed, S.A. v. The United Mexican States* [2003] ICSID Case No. ARB(AF)/00/2, Award, 29 May 2003.

[44] *Compañia del Desarrollo de Santa Elena S.A. (CDSE) v. Republic of Costa Rica* [2000] ICSID Case No. ARB/96/1, Award, 17 February 2000.

[45] *Siemens A.G. v. Republic of Argentina* [2002] ICSID Case No. ARB/02/8, Award, 6 February 2007.

[46] *Saluka Investments BV v. The Czech Republic* [2001] PCA Case No. 2001-04, Award, 17 March 2006.

[47] *Methanex Corporation v. United States of America* [1999] UNCITRAL, 44 ILM 1345, Award, 3 August 2005.

[48] OECD (2004).

The aforementioned doctrines aim to establish a more consistent approach for determining conduct constituting indirect expropriation, thereby enhancing predictability within the investment arbitration system. Nevertheless, each of these doctrines imposes certain limitations on the factors that the tribunal takes into account, consequently introducing a degree of imbalance into investor-state dispute resolution. This, in turn, undermines the overall predictability of the system.

In fact, a comprehensive and equitable approach is required to assess indirect expropriation effectively rather than simply concentrating on the economic impact of a measure or the legitimate policy objectives pursued by the host country. It's essential to recognise that the mere implementation of a measure in the interest of public welfare does not automatically absolve it from being considered a form of indirect expropriation. States also have policy objectives that warrant protection for the greater benefit of society. Hence, researchers and legal practitioners have increasingly focused on achieving a balanced approach that harmonises investors' rights to protection with a state's prerogative to pursue legitimate public policies.[49] This approach, often referred to as the "doctrine of proportionality," has gained prominence and gradually found its way into generations of international investment agreements since the early 2000s.[50]

The doctrine of proportionality mandates that arbitral tribunals, when evaluating measures potentially constituting indirect expropriation, strike a balance between assessing of the measure's economic impact and its specific characteristics, including its purpose, context, and the government's intent in its implementation. In recent times, several investment arbitration awards have adopted this balanced perspective. These tribunals have, in various ways, held that administrative measures enacted for public purposes generally should not be regarded as indirect expropriation. However, they have also cautioned that the mere existence of a public purpose for a measure is insufficient to entirely exempt it from scrutiny under the police powers doctrine.[51]

Scholars have highlighted that, even when employing proportionality analysis, the standard of review applied by tribunals in evaluating the host state's measures can be the vital factor influencing liability and, consequently, the allocation of risk between host states and investors.[52] The "standard of review" in this context refers to the level of scrutiny or deference that a court or tribunal grants to the primary

[49] See, for instance, Kriebaum (2007); Olynyk (2012).

[50] See, for instance, recently signed FTA between the United States and its partners like Chile (Annex 10-D(4) the United State - Chile FTA; Morroco (Annex 10-B(4) The United States - Morocco FTA); Australia (Annex 11-B(4) Australia - US FTA. Different version of the Canadian Model BITs have also included similar provision. In specific, see Annex B.13(1) Canadian Model BITs 2004 and Article 9 Canadian Model BITs 2021.

[51] See *Azurix Corp. v. Argentina* [2001] ICSID Case No. ARB/01/12, Award, 14 July 2006; *S.D. Myers, Inc. v. Canada* [1998] UNCITRAL, NAFTA, Award, 13 November 2000; *LG&E Energy Corp., LG&E Capital Corp. and LG&E International Inc v. Argentine Republic* [2002] ICSID Case No. ARB/02/1, Decision on Liability, 3 October 2006.

[52] Oesch (2003); Henckels (2012), p. 238.

decision-maker when assessing factual and legal matters.[53] The degree of deference that investment tribunals show toward the autonomy of the host state is crucial in determining the state's accountability for the applied measure. Despite its significance, investment tribunals have not yet established a consistent standard of review for cases involving the exercise of public power.[54] Furthermore, commentators have raised various concerns regarding the application of this standard of review and the entity conducting these reviews, namely the investment tribunal.[55] Lastly, the crucial point remains that the relationship between proportionality analysis and the standard of review, particularly concerning the discrete stages of proportionality analysis, has not been fully elucidated in the context of ISDS.[56]

In each expropriation claim, the specific measures taken by the host state under a particular BIT can vary significantly. However, regardless of whether the arbitral tribunal applies the sole effect doctrine, the police powers doctrine, or the proportionality doctrine, the practice of resolving investment disputes consistently underscores the need for a case-by-case evaluation. Determining whether a measure constitutes a breach of indirect expropriation necessitates a nuanced analysis, drawing on principles derived from investment treaties, customary international law, and precedents established in previous arbitral awards.[57]

Broadly speaking, when addressing expropriation claims, arbitral tribunals continue to take the environmental protection objectives of the applied measures into account. This is particularly evident in cases where tribunals endorse the police powers approach and, more recently, the proportionality approach. Nevertheless, from the host states' perspective, there remains a pressing demand for stronger assurances regarding the state's right to regulate, especially in light of the increasing

---

[53] Henckels (2012), p. 238.

[54] Ibid., p. 239.

[55] As noted by Caroline Henckels, these concerns may include (i) a strict proportionality analysis might vest excessive discretion in arbitrators, as the assessment of the value of a host state's regulatory objective allows substantial room for deeming the regulatory objective illegitimate relative to the investment's cost; and (ii) necessity analysis may involve empirical judgments that tribunals are not ideally positioned to make, given their limited expertise compared to national authorities. See Ibid., p. 238.

[56] Ibid, p. 241.

[57] In international investment arbitration, arbitral tribunals frequently turn to the assessments rendered by preceding investment tribunals in relevant situations. However, it's crucial to underscore that Investment tribunals consistently emphasise a fundamental principle: each arbitral award is independent and holds binding authority solely over the parties involved in the dispute. Moreover, every tribunal retains its competence and may arrive at a distinct conclusion on any given matter. This principle was articulated in the *AES Summit Generation Limited and AES-Tisza Erömü Kft. v. Republic of Hungary* [2007] ICSID Case No. ARB/07/22, Decision on Jurisdiction, 26 April 2005, para. 30. Nevertheless, striving to reach conclusions that align with the decisions of previous tribunals, even though not legally binding, serves several critical purposes. It fosters consistency and stability within the investment arbitration system, thereby enhancing predictability. This consistency ensures that outcomes are not arbitrary and are grounded in precedent, promoting fairness in the resolution of disputes in this intricate and evolving area of international law. See further in Olynyk (2012), p. 258.

frequency with which investor claims are arising in the context of environmental measures enacted by the host state. Furthermore, as environmental concerns continue to grow in complexity and unpredictability, governments will increasingly rely on their right to regulate to address these challenges. This trend is expected to intensify shortly, underscoring the need for a delicate balance between protecting the interests of foreign investors and ensuring the host states ability to enact and enforce environmental regulations effectively.

As of September 2023, nearly half of the known treaty-based ISDS cases resolved by various investment arbitration forums have involved claims of indirect expropriation.[58] This significant figure highlights a noticeable trend: claims of indirect expropriation are becoming increasingly common compared to other substantive standards within the framework of IIAs. The rise in indirect expropriation claims, combined with the lack of a clear and universally accepted definition of this concept, has created a compelling case for revising the indirect expropriation clause in modern IIAs. This revision process has resulted in several options for drafting a new and more robust expropriation clause.

Rather than designing the expropriation provision as a "simple clause" that encompasses both direct and indirect expropriation (as seen in NAFTA Article 1110), many "modern" IIAs have transitioned towards a "comprehensive clause." This comprehensive approach includes the indirect expropriation clause and incorporates additional provisions to provide clarity and guidance for its interpretation and application. A notable example of this approach is found in Article 6 and Annex B on Expropriation within the US 2012 Model BIT. Similar comprehensive provisions can be identified in various international agreements, such as the 2004 Canadian Model BIT (Annex B 13(1)), the China Canada–BIT (Annex B.10), the CPTPP (Annex 9-B), the CETA, the Central America–Dominican Republic–United States FTA (CAFTA - DR) (Annex 10 - C), the ACIA (Article 15 and Annex 2), and the EVIPA. These changes reflect a global shift towards a more nuanced and comprehensive approach to addressing expropriation matters.

The next section provides a detailed evaluation of specific developments in drafting indirect expropriation provisions under the EVIPA.

[58] As of December 31, 2024, 570 out of 1401 cases have involved claims of breach of indirect expropriation. This information is sourced from the UNCTAD database, which provides valuable insights into ISDS cases. UNCTAD Investment Policy Hub.

6.2 Expropriation and Indirect-Expropriation Provisions Under the EVIPA

6.2.1 Article 2.7 EVIPA on Expropriation

The commitment not to conduct expropriation and/or indirect expropriation has been mentioned in Article 2.7 below:

ARTICLE 2.7 Expropriation

1. A Party shall not nationalise or expropriate the covered investments of investors of the other Party either directly, or indirectly through measures having an effect equivalent to nationalisation or expropriation (hereinafter referred to as "expropriation"), except:

(a) for a public purpose;
(b) under due process of law;
(c) on a non-discriminatory basis; and
(d) against payment of prompt, adequate and effective compensation.

2. The compensation referred to in paragraph 1 shall amount to the fair market value of the covered investment at the time immediately before the expropriation or the impending expropriation became public knowledge, whichever is earlier, plus interest at a reasonable rate established on a commercial basis, from the date of expropriation until the date of payment. Such compensation shall be effectively realisable, freely transferable in accordance with Article 2.8 (Transfer) and made without delay.
3. Notwithstanding paragraphs 1 and 2, in the case that Viet Nam is the expropriating Party, any measure of direct expropriation relating to land shall be:

(a) for a purpose in accordance with the applicable domestic laws and regulations[1]; and
(b) upon payment of compensation equivalent to the market value, while recognising the applicable domestic laws and regulations.

(Footnote 1: The applicable domestic laws and regulations is Viet Nam's Land Law No. 45/2013/QH13 and Decree No. 44/2014/NĐ-CP Regulating Land Prices, as at the date of entry into force of this Agreement.)

4. The issuance of compulsory licences in relation to intellectual property rights does not constitute an expropriation within the meaning of paragraph 1, to the extent that such issuance is consistent with the Agreement on Trade-Related Aspects of Intellectual Property Rights contained in Annex 1C of the WTO Agreement (hereinafter referred to as "TRIPS Agreement").
5. An investor affected by an expropriation shall have a right, under the law of the expropriating Party, to prompt review of its claim and of the valuation of its investment, by a judicial or other independent authority of that Party.
6. This Article shall be interpreted in accordance with Annex 4 (Understanding on Expropriation).

Article 2.7 EVIPA is an ideal clause of expropriation which provides traditional limitations regarding the action of nationalisation or expropriation of the host state. This provision has a similar language to Article 6 of the US 2012 Model BIT and other BITs signed by the United States following this Model BIT, for instance, Article 10.7(1) of the Dominican Republic–Central American FTA (DR-CAFTA). Investment Chapter of CPTPP (Chapter 9), especially provisions on expropriation, has the same language and structure as the US 2012 Model BIT as the United States is the CPTPP's "former architect". On its face, this provision only prohibits the practice of direct and indirect expropriation while does not mention other "measures tantamount to expropriation" as provided in Article 1110(1) NAFTA. In its arbitration practice, this language of Article 1110(1) NAFTA has given rise to so much ambiguity.[59] The omission of the vague term "measure tantamount to expropriation" significantly limits the scope of future direct and indirect measures to be challenged in front of the EVIPA Tribunal.

Paragraph 1 Article 2.7 EVIPA mentions four traditional elements that may classify an action as "legal" expropriation, which have been mentioned since the first generation of IIAs and have become part of customary international law:

(a) *for a public purpose;*
(b) *under due process of law;*
(c) *on a non-discriminatory basis; and*
(d) *against payment of prompt, adequate and effective compensation.*

This language indicates that even if a legal expropriation is imposed, it will not exempt the host state from the obligation to provide sufficient compensation.

Investment tribunals and scholars have consistently agreed that expropriation may happen in ways other than by formal decree. Therefore, it has been accepted that expropriation "must be analysed in consequential rather than formal terms".[60] In other words, the effect of the government's measure will be at the centre of the tribunal's analysis but not other characteristics. For this reason, a similar clause in EVIPA can be seen in such a way.

In Vietnamese national legislation, expropriation has generally been clearly regulated, and the act of expropriation has to be accompanied by appropriate compensation equivalent to *fair market value*.[61] As earlier introduced, expropriation happens when investors' rights to property have been limited by the host state's official measures. In the context of international law, property encompasses both tangible and intangible assets, including but not limited to movable and immovable objects, real estate, shares, intellectual property, and contractual rights.[62]

Notably, this article contains a provision applied for the government of Vietnam regarding direct expropriation relating to land (Paragraph 3), which requires the measure to be applied "for a purpose in accordance with the applicable domestic laws and regulations" and upon payment of compensation equivalent to the market value. Paragraph 3 of Article 2.7 EVIPA demonstrates Vietnam's strong commitment to direct expropriation measures concerning land. In such cases, the measure must align with the pertinent domestic legal framework while also ensuring that fair and adequate compensation, equivalent to the market value, is provided. The requirement for compensation to be recognised in accordance with domestic laws

[59] Edsall (2006), p. 937.

[60] Reisman and Sloane (2004), p. 121.

[61] National Assembly of Vietnam (2020) Law on Investment No. 61/2020/QH14; National Assembly of Vietnam (2013) Land Law, No. 45/2013/QH13; National Assembly Office (2019) Law on Compulsory Purchase and Requisition of Property, Integrated document, No. 37/VBHN-VPQH.

[62] OECD (2004), p. 4.

underscores the need to address this specific issue within Vietnamese legislation. While similar provisions can be found in numerous IIAs signed by Vietnam, particularly since 2008,[63] the acceptance of such a stringent commitment demonstrates Vietnam's positive intentions. This trade and investment agreement with the European Union further showcases Vietnam's proactive stance in deeper regional and international integration, solidifying its reputation as a reliable destination for FDI inflows.

This article also includes a specific exception for Vietnam regarding the issuance of compulsory licenses for intellectual property rights (IPRs). Intellectual property is generally recognised as a common exception to expropriation.[64] This is evident in many IIAs, such as the Canada 2004 Model BIT (Article 13.5), US 2012 Model BIT (Article 6.5), and Article 10.12(6) 2009 India–Korea CEPA. EVIPA follows this trend. Specifically, Article 2.7 Paragraph 4 EVIPA serves as an omission of compulsory licenses from the scope of expropriation action in the agreement, showing specific concerns of both parties. This exception ensures that IPR holders cannot challenge the compulsory licenses issued by host states as forms of indirect expropriation of their rights. Similar exception can be found in China - Canada BIT (Article 10.2) and other previous IIAs to which Vietnam is a party, especially IIAs concluded by ASEAN with its partners.[65] While this exception excludes the issuance of compulsory licenses related to intellectual property rights from being classified as indirect expropriation, it primarily addresses issues related to human rights rather than environmental protection. Therefore, a further evaluation of this exception will not be included within the scope of this book.

In general, Paragraph 1 Article 2.7 EVIPA is a typical expropriation clause found in many existing investment treaties with the commitment of not taking a measure tantamount to nationalisation or expropriation except when all conditions are complied with. This regulation follows previous IIAs approach in determining a legal expropriation by four elements, including the aim of the applied measures is (i) for a public purpose, (ii) under due process of law, (iii) on a non-discriminatory basis, and (iv) adequate and effective compensation. Thus, this regulation retains the format of the expropriation clause in previous IIAs, which introduced two types of

[63] See, for instance, Vietnam - Kazakhstan BIT (Art 6.3); Vietnam - Greece BIT Art 5.2; Vietnam - Oman BIT (Art 6.2); Vietnam - Macedonia BIT (Art 6.3); Vietnam - Slovakia BIT (Art 6.3); ASEAN - China Investment Agreement (Art 8.4); ASEAN - Korea Investment Agreement (Art 12.4); ASEAN Comprehensive Investment Agreement - ACIA (Art 14); ASEAN - Australia - New Zealand FTA (ANZ FTA) Chapter 11 (Art 9.6); ASEAN - Hong Kong Investment Agreement (Art 10.4); Vietnam - Korea FTA (Art 9.7(5)); Vietnam - Eurasian Economic Union (Vietnam - EAEU FTA) (Art 8.35(5)); CPTPP (Art 9.8), Annex 9-C. See also EU-Vietnam Investment Protection Agreement - EVIPA (Art 2.7); Regional Comprehensive Economic Partnership (RCEP) (Art 10.13(5)).

[64] Faccio (2012), p. 98.

[65] For instance, ASEAN - China Investment Agreement (Art 8.6); ASEAN - Korea Investment Agreement (Art 12.5); ACIA (Art 14.5); ASEAN - ANZ FTA (Chapter 11 Art 9.5); Vietnam - EAEU FTA (Art 8.35); Vietnam - Korea FTA (Art 9.7(6)); ASEAN - Hong Kong Investment Agreement (Art 10.5); CPTPP (Art 9.8(5)). See further Ha (2021), p. 120.

direct and indirect expropriation measures. However, paragraph 6 of Article 2.7 EVIPA adds further guidance on the interpretation of expropriation that this Article shall be interpreted in accordance with Annex 4. The approach based on adding clarification in the annex while keeping the original language of the traditional definition helps maintain the continuity with past treaty practice.[66]

6.2.2 *Annex 4 EVIPA on Expropriation*

6.2.2.1 Paragraph 1 Annex 4 EVIPA

Annex 4 EVIPA provides a definition of expropriation and indirect expropriation in detail:

> 1. Expropriation as referred to in paragraph 1 of Article 2.7 (Expropriation) may be either direct or indirect as follows:
>
> (a) direct expropriation occurs if an investment is nationalised or otherwise directly expropriated through formal transfer of title or outright seizure; and
>
> (b) indirect expropriation occurs if a measure or series of measures by a Party has an effect equivalent to direct expropriation, in that it substantially deprives the investor of the fundamental attributes of property in its investment including the right to use, enjoy and dispose of its investment, without formal transfer of title or outright seizure.

In this definition, direct and indirect expropriation measures are specified separately. The definition of expropriation itself is uncontroversial in the context of investment dispute resolution. Indirect expropriation refers to a measure or series of measures implemented by a state that "substantially deprives the investor of the fundamental attributes of property… without the formal transfer of title or outright seizure."

In fact, the broad determination of measures tantamount to expropriation or creeping expropriation in dispute resolution poses a significant threat to the state's right to regulate and creates a reluctance to exercise its regulatory authority. Therefore, clear guidelines with specific characteristics that constitute indirect expropriation are necessary to safeguard the state's regulatory rights. According to existing jurisprudence, when examining cases of expropriation or indirect expropriation, the degree of economic impact is the primary and most critical factor to assess. In most international investment rulings, expropriation occurs when a regulation or measure significantly impairs an investor's economic rights—such as ownership, use, enjoyment, or management of their business—effectively rendering those rights useless.[67] Second, the context and purpose of the measure in question will be accounted for. In this analysis, two main questions should be addressed: Is the measure adopted and applied to protect legitimate public policy objectives? and (ii) Is there a proportional relationship between the state's legitimate purpose and

[66] Ortino (2016), p. 354.

[67] OECD (2004), p. 11.

the impact on the economic value of foreign investments? Finally, the interference of the measure with the expectations based on the investment must be taken into account.

As can be seen, Paragraph 1 Annex 4 EVIPA closely reflects this jurisprudence in drafting the expropriation clause. In this wording, indirect expropriation occurs when the applied measure has "an effect equivalent to direct expropriation" based on the assessment of whether it "substantially deprives the investor of the fundamental attributes of property in its investment". Jurisprudence defines indirect expropriation as happening when the value of an investment has been significantly reduced. Regarding the term "substantially," although most tribunals establish the standard slightly below "complete deprivation," certain investment tribunals seem to have embraced a stance that necessitates a greater degree of deprivation.[68] Specifically, "substantially" means that the decrease in value must have been significant and more or less total for a measure to amount to indirect expropriation.[69]

Scholars believe that codifying the notion of "substantial deprivation" in the test for indirect expropriation may not have provided much clarity, as tribunals have been reluctant to offer clear guidance on the degree of interference required to establish substantial deprivation, citing the fact-specific nature of the evaluation.[70] Furthermore, the term "substantial deprivation" does not resolve the "denominator" issue, as tribunals must first determine the investment's boundaries to determine if the host state has caused significant deprivation.[71]

Regarding the phrase "fundamental attributes of property", the jurisprudence shows that the object of property deprivation in evaluating the act of expropriation pertains to the control, use, benefit, enjoyment, and value of the investment.[72] The ambiguity in using this phrase lies in the fact that the jurisprudence does not clarify whether each factor alone is adequate to establish expropriation or if they are cumulative prerequisites. In contrast, each individual factor has a distinct meaning and applying one over another could yield different outcomes based on the case's

---

68 Ortino (2016), p. 356.

69 *Venezuela Holdings BV, Mobil Cerro Negro Holding LTD et al. v. Venezuela* [2007] ICSID Case No. ARB/07/27, Award, 9 October 2014, para. 286. See also *Técnicas Medioambientales Tecmed, S.A. v. The United Mexican States* [2003] ICSID Case No. ARB(AF)/00/2, Award, 29 May 2003, para. 115 and *Cargill v. Mexico* [2005] ICSID Case No. ARB(AF)/05/2, Award, 18 September 2009, para. 360.

70 Ortino (2016), p. 356.

71 Ibid.

72 *Metalclad Corporation v. United Mexican States* [1997] ICSID Case No. ARB(AF)/97/1, Award, 25 August 2000, para. 103; *Técnicas Medioambientales Tecmed, S.A. v. The United Mexican States* [2003] ICSID Case No. ARB(AF)/00/2, Award, 29 May 2003, para. 115; *Chemtura Corporation v. Government of Canada* [2002] PCA Case No. 2008-01, Award, 2 August 2010, para. 247; *Glamis Gold Ltd. v. United States of America* [2003] UNCITRAL, NAFTA, Award, 8 June 2009, paras. 357–358; *Venezuela Holdings BV, Mobil Cerro Negro Holding LTD et al. v.Venezuela* [2007] ICSID Case No. ARB/07/27, Award, 9 October 2014, para. 286. These factors are usually examined by investment tribunal with different combinations. See further Ortino (2016).

circumstances.[73] Furthermore, it remains unclear whether the three examples listed in Annex 4(1)(b) referring to the loss of fundamental property attributes are exhaustive or if there are other fundamental property attributes beyond those explicitly mentioned.[74]

The other two paragraphs of Annex 4 are designed to provide guidance for the Tribunal to examine a potential indirect expropriation:

> 2. The determination of whether a measure or series of measures by a Party, in a specific factual situation, constitutes an indirect expropriation requires a case-by-case, fact-based inquiry that considers, inter alia:
>
> (a) the economic impact of the measure or series of measures, although the fact that a measure or series of measures by a Party has an adverse effect on the economic value of an investment, standing alone, does not establish that such an (indirect) expropriation has occurred;
> (b) the duration of the measure or series of measures or of its effects; and
> (c) the character of the measure or series of measures, in particular its object, context and intent.

The language, as can be seen in Paragraph 2 Annex 4 EVIPA is similar to those suggested by the 2004 and 2012 US Models BIT (in specific, US 2012 Model BIT, Annex B, Article 4(a)) as well as 2004 Canadian Model BIT (Canada 2004 Model BIT, Annex B.13(1)) although with slight differences.[75] The Annex B, paragraph 4(a) US 2012 Model BIT mentions three considerations:

> (i) the economic impact of the government action, although the fact that an action or series of actions by a Party has an adverse effect on the economic value of an investment, standing alone, does not establish that an indirect expropriation has occurred;
> (ii) the extent to which the government action interferes with distinct, reasonable investment-backed expectations; and
> (iii) the character of the government action.

In fact, in the US 2012 Model BIT, the requirements on evaluating the duration of the measure in EVIPA have been replaced by the interferences of the government action on reasonable investment-backed expectations. These provisions have been included in later concluded BITs of the United States and Canada, such as the United States Uruguay BIT (2005), Annex B; and the Canada Peru BIT (2006), Annex B.13(1).

6.2.2.2 Paragraph 2 Annex 4 EVIPA

Paragraph 2 of Annex 4 EVIPA emphasises the importance of evaluating measures or series of measures on a case-by-case, fact-based inquiry. This evaluation should consider three non-exhaustive factors within a balancing framework: (i) the economic impact of the measures, (ii) the duration of the measure applied, and (iii) the

---

[73] Ibid.

[74] Ibid, p. 357.

[75] It has been mentioned that these three criteria have origin from the US Supreme Court jurisprudence on "regulatory taking". See further Bonnitcha (2014), p. 268.

characteristics of the measure applied. These assessments to clarify an indirect expropriation measure indeed have been pointed out by scholars[76] and the OECD since 2004.[77]

The determination of a potential indirect expropriation will depend on the assessment/analysis of the tribunal in a specific case. It underscores the necessity of examining measures or series of measures individually, using a fact-based approach that considers the economic impact, duration, and nature of the measures involved. This case-by-case approach has long been recognised as essential in assessing diverse and complex regulatory actions. Under this analysis, a number of elements, including the economic impact, duration, and nature, should be taken into account. The severity of the economic impact caused by the state's measures—particularly on the legal status of the property and the owner's practical ability to use and enjoy it—has traditionally been the primary factor in determining indirect expropriation.[78]

Paragraph 2(a) of Annex 4 of the EVIPA offers a clearer explanation of the term "economic impact" described in Paragraph 1(b) of the same Annex. For a measure or series of measures enacted by a Party to qualify as an indirect expropriation, the impact must be "substantial," along with other characteristics. This clarification regarding the substantial impact of a measure in determining indirect expropriation has been supported by case law and is a common practice among investment tribunals. For instance, the Tribunal in *Philip Morris v. Uruguay* supposed that "in order to be considered an indirect expropriation, the government's measures interference with the investor's rights must have a major adverse impact on the claimant's investments".[79] This means that the regulatory measure must cause a significant reduction in the value, usage, or enjoyment of the claimant's investment for it to be considered a "substantial deprivation."

Based on this practice, in the case of EVIPA, it can be anticipated that merely having an adverse impact on an investment does not automatically equate to an

[76] This characterisation approach has been analised in Bonnitcha (2014). Section 5.6.2.1.

[77] OECD (2004), p. 10.

[78] Several international tribunals have determined that a regulation could be considered expropriation if it substantially impairs the investor's economic rights, i.e. ownership, use, enjoyment or management of the business, by rendering them useless. See OECD (2004), pp. 10–11.

[79] *Philip Morris Brands Sàrl, Philip Morris Products S.A. and Abal Hermanos S.A. v. Oriental Republic of Uruguay* [2010] ICSID Case No. ARB/10/7, Award, 8 July 2016, para. 192. Other Tribunals follow this practice include: *Pope & Talbot Inc. v. The Government of Canada* [1999] Ad-hoc Tribunal, UNCITRAL, Interim Award, 26 June 2000, para. 96; *PSEG v. Turkey* [2002] ICSID Case No. ARB/02/5, Award, 19 January 2007, paras. 278–280; *CMS Gas Transmission Company v. The Republic of Argentina* [2001] ICSID Case No. ARB/01/, Award, 12 May 2005, para. 262; *LG&E Energy Corp., LG&E Capital Corp. and LG&E International Inc v. Argentine Republic* [2002] ICSID Case No. ARB/02/1, Decision on Liability, 3 October 2006, para. 194; *BG Group Plc. V. Argentina* [2003] UNCITRAL, Award, 24 December 2007, paras. 258–266; *Enron Creditors Recovery Corporation and Ponderosa Assets, L.P. v. Argentine Republic* [2001] ICSID Case No. ARB/01/3, Award, 22 May 2007, para. 245; *AWG Group Ltd. v. The Argentine Republic* [2003] UNCITRAL, Decision on Liability, Award, 30 July 2010, para. 134; *Corn Products International, Inc. v. United Mexican States* [2003] ICSID Case No. ARB(AF)/04/1, Decision on Responsibility, Award, 15 January 2008, para. 91.

indirect expropriation. This interpretation gives host states considerable latitude to exercise their regulatory authority without the fear of being accused by foreign investors of expropriation, unless the strict threshold of substantial deprivation is met. Therefore, the term "substantially" carries significant implications that require attention from all parties involved, including the state, investors, and the ICS tribunals. This proposition is perceived unfavourably by investors as it may result in rejecting their expropriation claims, while states may view it as an opportunity to continue implementing regulatory measures. However, challenges may arise for states in proving their case, as economic impact analysis needs to be conducted with care. This analysis must consider factors such as costs for the investor, welfare gains, and socio-economic benefits, which investment tribunals and scholars have often found difficult to define accurately.[80]

Paragraph 2(b) of Annex 4 adds an element of the duration of the applied measure or its effects to the test of indirect expropriation. This provision highlights the importance of the severity of the measure applied on the investors' property to constitute a taking. With regard to the duration of the regulation, dispute resolution practices indicate there is no specific reference point for this issue. A tribunal has suggested that "in some contexts and circumstances, it would be appropriate to view a deprivation as amounting to an expropriation even if it were partial and temporary".[81] Meanwhile, in *Hauer v. Land Rheinland-Pfalz*, the European Court of Justice concluded that a three-year prohibition of the European Commission did not violate the German winegrower's property right. In other words, despite the measure being only partial and temporary, it may be deemed as expropriation. Thus, the duration of the regulation remains at the discretion of the arbitral tribunal and is assessed on a case-by-case basis, making it a significant consideration for the host state.

Paragraph 2(c) of Annex 4 of the EVIPA is drafted more clearly than the US 2012 Model BIT, as it requires all relevant factors of the applied measure—including the object, context, and intent—to be taken into account. By requesting the tribunal to consider the context in which the measure is applied, the drafters of the EVIPA have adopted a "police power" approach. This approach, which has been utilised in numerous disputes,[82] ensures that the host state's right to regulate is carefully evaluated in the assessment. It implies that the parties intend to give greater weight to the objective of the measure when determining whether expropriation has occurred.

However, studies indicate that a case-by-case inquiry can lead to varying potential decisions for future investment tribunals. Therefore, paragraph 2 is insufficient in addressing the nature of such an inquiry and its relationship with the effect-based

[80] Gazzini (2010), p. 47.

[81] *S.D. Myers, Inc. v. Canada* [1998] UNCITRAL, NAFTA, Award, 13 November 2000, para. 232.

[82] *S.D. Myers, Inc. v. Canada* [1998] UNCITRAL, NAFTA, Award, 13 November 2000; *Técnicas Medioambientales Tecmed, S.A. v. The United Mexican States* [2003] ICSID Case No. ARB(AF)/00/2, Award, 29 May 2003; Judgement by the European Court of Human Rights, case of *Sporrong and Lönnroth v. Sweden* No.7151/75, 7152/75 of 23 September 1982.

test proposed in paragraph 1.[83] Scholars have noted that this case-by-case approach has been developed within litigation practice. Indeed, this analysis, which considers the effect of the measures applied as well as their characteristics, has been demonstrated in the case of *Feldman v. Mexico*.[84] This approach suggests that when examining indirect expropriation, the Tribunal should balance its assessment between the economic impact of the measure with the character of the measure in which its object, context and intent are highlighted. As observed, this approach differs slightly from the methods used in previous cases interpreting traditional expropriation clauses, such as *Metalclad v. Mexico* and *Tecmed v. Mexico.* In those instances, the tribunals defined indirect expropriation primarily by the severe loss of economic value of the investment, which would then be subject to a proportionality review.[85]

In both *Metalclad v. Mexico* and *Tecmed v. Mexico*, the Tribunals focused on the impact of the economic value of the investment.[86] In contrast, in the annexe approach, the economic impact of the measure is required but not playing that much important compared with the two mentioned cases in order to establish an indirect expropriation. This direction is secured by a clarification included in Paragraph 2(a) Annex 4: *"The fact that a measure or series of measures by a Party has an adverse effect on the economic value of an investment, standing alone, does not establish that such an expropriation has occurred"*. In this case, substantial deprivation is still required, probably but in a more balanced way with other characters of the measure (in particular, its object, context and intent) in the specific context in the host state.

In general, the three requirements outlined in Paragraph 2 of Annex 4 ensure that the ICS tribunals do not apply the sole effect doctrine to determine indirect expropriation. Under this test, economic impact is only one component, and economic impact alone is insufficient to conclude that indirect expropriation has occurred. This provision raises two fundamental questions: (i) Is the list in Paragraph 2 comprehensive, or does it allow for additional factors? and (ii) Is consideration of these three factors mandatory, discretionary, or contingent upon the specific circumstances of the case? These questions will shape the tribunals' assessments and influence the final outcome.

To address the first question, if it is determined that this list is exhaustive, assessing whether indirect expropriation has occurred will primarily depend on these three factors. In this case, examining only these three criteria would be sufficient to establish the existence of indirect expropriation. Consequently, excluding other factors not included in this list, such as a violation of the government's prior binding

[83] See further Ortino (2016), pp. 360–361.

[84] *Marvin Roy Feldman Karpa v. United Mexican States* [1999] ICSID Case No. ARB(AF)/99/1, Award, 16 December 2002, paras. 102, 106. See Bonnitcha (2014), p. 168. In fact, the examination of legitimate welfare objective and non-discrimination requirement have been conducted by the tribunal in this case.

[85] See further discussion in a study that seek to compare different approaches in drafting and interpreting indirect-expropriation clause in Bonnitcha (2014), pp. 229–272.

[86] The tribunal in Tecmed applied a higher threshold of economic impact in compared with Metalclad. See further Bonnitcha (2014), p. 320.

written commitment to the investor or interference with distinct and reasonable investment-backed expectations, would reduce the likelihood of considering a state measure as constituting indirect expropriation.

Concerning the second question, among the three factors outlined in Paragraph 2 of Annex 4 EVIPA, the economic impact is intrinsically linked to the adverse nature of indirect expropriation, as indicated in jurisprudence. It is considered a mandatory element that must be proven as a basis for a claim. However, the status of the remaining two factors in Paragraphs 2(b) and 2(c) is less clear. If the fulfillment of these two requirements is seen as discretionary or contingent upon specific factual circumstances, then, in addition to demonstrating a substantial economic impact, meeting just one of the two criteria, either the duration of the measure in Paragraph 2(b) or the characteristics of the measure in Paragraph 2(c), would suffice to establish the existence of indirect expropriation.

Research supports this interpretation, arguing that the formulation of the expropriation provision does not explicitly state that all three factors are mandatory.[87] Additionally, the term "inter alia" in the English version, which means "among other things," has been translated as "for example" in the Vietnamese version of EVIPA. Understanding "inter alia" as "for example," and considering the wording and structure in the Vietnamese version, suggests that these three elements may serve as examples for the Tribunal to consider in their analysis. However, this book argues that the structure of Paragraph 2 of Annex 4 EVIPA should be understood as presenting an open list. Therefore, the factors listed in Paragraphs 2(a), 2(b), and 2(c) should all be initially taken into account alongside other relevant considerations. This provision should be interpreted through a structural analysis of Paragraph 2, particularly the term "inter alia" or "among other things." This interpretation clarifies that to determine whether a measure or series of measures by a Party constitutes indirect expropriation, the Tribunal must consider various factors, including the three specified in the paragraphs.

Dispute resolution practices regarding provisions with similar wording, while limited, suggest that Tribunals follow the guidance set forth in the relevant BIT provision. In the case of *Railroad Development Corporation v. Guatemala*[88] under the Central America Free Trade Agreement (CAFTA), which included an indirect expropriation provision similar to that found in EVIPA, the Tribunal took into account all the elements listed in CAFTA Chapter 10, Annex-C, paragraph 4(a). These elements included the character of the government's action, the measure's purpose, investment-backed expectations, and the economic impact of the government's action.

Although the practices observed in individual disputes may not offer a definitive prediction of how future Tribunals will interpret Paragraph 2 of Annex 4 of the EVIPA, they can serve as potential examples of such an approach. Moreover, the

---

[87] Ha (2021), p. 154.

[88] *Railroad Development Corporation v. Republic of Guatemala* [2007] ICSID Case No. ARB/07/23.

legal understanding of indirect expropriation has evolved significantly over the years, providing investment tribunals with a solid foundation for conducting these analyses, as discussed in the first section of this chapter. This body of practice challenges the idea that it is sufficient to demonstrate an additional factor, such as the duration of the measure or frustration of the investor's reasonable expectations, combined with severe economic impact, to conclude that indirect expropriation has occurred.

Paragraph 2 of Annex 4 EVIPA with three evaluation requirements, however, does not include the fourth requirement that has been mentioned in Paragraph 2(c) Annex 8-A CETA on indirect expropriation measure, which is "the extent to which the measure or series of measures interferes with distinct, reasonable investment-backed expectations". This provision in CETA allows for the potential relevance of the subjective expectations of the claimant when assessing whether an expropriation has occurred.[89] Reasonable expectation means that investors have to take into account normal regulatory changes or adjustments, and the host state will not be liable for any damages arising from these changes. The burden of proving that reasonable expectations were not met falls on the investor. The lack of consideration for reasonable investment-backed expectations highlights the case-by-case nature of the inquiry,[90] suggesting that the list of relevant factors is not exhaustive and that additional factors could be examined, as discussed earlier.

In fact, the absence of the requirement to assess the impact of the disputed measure on investment-backed expectations aligns with the established practice of the EU legal system.[91] While the absence of formal recognition regarding the impact of the disputed measure on legitimate expectations does not necessarily eliminate the possibility of it being considered in future ICS, the fact that this requirement is not prioritised in the EU's perspective indicates that it may not carry significant weight in this test.

Paragraph 2 of Annex 4 of the EVIPA rectifies the deficiency of the sole effect doctrine, which only addresses the critical question of whether the measure results in a substantial deprivation of the investment while failing to consider other essential attributes of the relevant measure. By specifying the characteristics that must be evaluated, namely the degree of deprivation, object, purpose, and context of the

[89] Henckels (2016), pp. 40–41.

[90] Ortino (2016), p. 360.

[91] Indeed, in the case of *Atlanta AG and Others v. EC*, the Court of Justice of the European Union ruled that: "The principle of protection of legitimate expectations is one of the fundamental principles of the Community legal order. Nevertheless, traders cannot have a legitimate expectation that an existing situation which is capable of being altered by the Community institutions in the exercise of their discretionary power will be maintained. This is particularly true in an area such as the common organisation of the markets the objectives of which require constant adjustments in order to meet changes in economic circumstances." See Judgment of the Court of First instance, case of *Atlanta AG and Others v. EC*, C-104/97 P 1999 ECR I-6983, para. 55. For further details on the EU's approach to legitimate expectations in the context of indirect expropriations, see Luca (2014).

measure itself, this paragraph establishes a framework for states to enact legislation in the public interest while balancing the interests of the investors.

6.2.2.3 Paragraph 3 Annex 4 EVIPA

As discussed above, under Paragraph 2 Annex 4 EVIPA, once a host state's measure or a series of measures undergo rigorous tests for complicated characteristics, including severe economic impact, the duration, as well as the object, context and intent to be considered as an indirect expropriation measure; will that states be liable to pay compensation to a foreign investor? The agreement provides the answer to this question in the last paragraph:

> 3. Non-discriminatory measures or series of measures by a Party that are designed to protect legitimate public policy objectives do not constitute indirect expropriation, except in the rare circumstances where the impact of such measure or series of measures is so severe in light of its purpose that it appears manifestly excessive.

Similar to Paragraph 2, this Paragraph 3 Annex 4 EVIPA is not a new invention of EVIPA draters (see Table 6.1). In fact, among different ways to balance the host states' right to regulate to pursue sustainable development goals with investors' rights, the inclusion of exceptions in expropriation provisions has become very popular in modern IIAs.[92] This model of provision on expropriation with such exception has been widely spread in recently concluded BITs beyond North America. For instance, several BITs signed by India with its partners Jordan (2006), Iceland (2007), Trinidad and Tobago (2007), Senegal (2008), Syria (2008), Mozambique (2009), Latvia (2010), Lithuania (2011) or FTA signed by Australia with Chile (2008) and with Malaysia (2012). Regarding multilateral treaties, in a recently conducted research, the 2012 Japan–Korea–China Trilateral Investment Treaty contains a similar protocol on indirect expropriation, while other recent BITs, such as Agreement Establishing the ASEAN–Australia–New Zealand FTA (ASEAN–ANZ FTA) (2009), Chapter 11 and Annex, do include the carve-out paragraph (Annex on Expropriation and Compensation, Article 4).[93] This broad-spread trend in including such exceptions in indirect expropriation clauses from America to Western and Eastern countries indicates a particular preference for this suggestion worldwide.

[92] For instance, see 2004/2012 US Model BIT at Annex B.4(b), Canadian Model FIPA 2004, Annex B.13(1) Art (c). This explanatory clause has later been appeared in agreements signed by the US (Dominican Republic - Central America FTA - CAFTA - DR FTA (2004), Chile - United States FTA (2003), Morocco - United States FTA (2004), Rwanda - United States BIT (2008)) and Canada (Canada Czechnia, Latvia and Romania BIT - Annex A (2009); Canada - Jordan BIT (2009), Canada - Peru BIT (2006), Canada - Slovak Republic BIT (2010), CETA Chapter X Annex X.11.

[93] Bonnitcha (2014), p. 267.

Table 6.1 Criteria to be taken into account in determining indirect expropriation claims in selected treaties[a]

No.		EVIPA (Article 2.7, Annex 4)	CETA (Article 8.12, Annex 8-A)	Canada 2021 Model FIPA (Article 9)	US 2012 Model BIT (Article 6, Annex B)	ASEAN Comprehensive Investment Agreement (Article 14, Annex 2)	CPTPP (Article 9.8, Annex 9-B)
1.	The interference with a tangible or intangible property right or property interest in a covered investment	×	×	✓	✓	✓	✓
2.	Measure has an effect equivalent to direct expropriation	✓	✓	✓	✓	✓	✓
3.	Case-by-case, fact-based inquiry	✓	✓	✓	✓	✓	✓
4.	Economic impact of the measure	✓	✓	✓	✓	✓	✓
5.	The breach of government's prior binding written commitment to the investor	×	×	×	×	✓	×
6.	Duration of the measure	✓	✓	✓	×	×	×
7.	Character of the measure	✓	✓	✓	✓	✓ (objective and the proportionate)	✓
8.	Interference with distinct, reasonable investment-backed expectations	×	✓	✓	✓	×	✓

(continued)

Table 6.1 (continued)

No.		EVIPA (Article 2.7, Annex 4)	CETA (Article 8.12, Annex 8-A)	Canada 2021 Model FIPA (Article 9)	US 2012 Model BIT (Article 6, Annex B)	ASEAN Comprehensive Investment Agreement (Article 14, Annex 2)	CPTPP (Article 9.8, Annex 9-B)
9.	Exception for public welfare measures, except in the 'rare circumstances'	✓	✓	✓ (not include the term "except in rare circumstances)	✓	✓ (not include the term "except in rare circumstances)	✓

[a] This table, inspired by Caroline Henckels' work, has been compiled by the author. See Henckels (2016)

In general, this regulation first helps distinguish between indirect expropriation and a regulatory act not subject to compensation.[94] This offer stems from the litigation practice that prompts the need to develop the theory of regulatory takings. Second, such language sets a limit for the arbitral tribunal in evaluating regulatory measures. Accordingly, not all regulatory measures that negatively affect the investments (which resulted in indirect expropriation) are excluded from the obligation of compensation, but only those pursuing legitimate public welfare objectives.[95] This paragraph 3, therefore, confirms the right to regulate principle, which has been mentioned earlier in Article 2.2 Chapter 2 EVIPA.

The wording of Paragraph 3 Annex 4 EVIPA is similar to relevant provisions included in CETA and CPTPP as it identifies the mentioned "rare circumstances" while the US 2012 Model BIT, Annex B, Article 4(b) has not included such clarification, although this provision does provide such carve-out. This provision constitutes an exception for the host state in case it applies legitimate regulation. Under such language, it depends on the tribunal to clarify whether the disputed measure(s) meet those three requirements:

(i) be applied *non-discrimination*
(ii) be conducted to protect *public welfare objectives*
(iii) whether "rare circumstances" happen in the case and are capable of refuting this presumption[96]

If these three elements are satisfied, a regulatory measure would not constitute indirect expropriation. This provision is expected to strengthen the state's position within the IIA framework by discouraging investors from submitting unfounded

[94] UNCTAD (2013), p. 86.
[95] Benedetto (2013), p. 128.
[96] Berner (2016), pp. 193, 194.

claims and providing guidance to arbitral tribunals in distinguishing between legitimate regulatory actions without compensation and indirect expropriation.[97]

However, this "public purpose" exception does not fully exempt governments from liability for expropriation.[98] Instead, it creates a presumption in favor of legitimate regulation. While this provision establishes a presumption that government actions for public purposes are not expropriatory, tribunals must still assess whether "rare circumstances" could undermine this presumption.[99] In the absence of such a presumption, tribunals would require a more detailed legal justification for why a public purpose should exempt regulatory actions from compensation.

As stated in paragraph 6 Article 2.7, Annex 4 is an integral part of the treaty; thus, when examining a measure or series of measures, the arbitrators need to not only put in their consideration the effects and characteristics that have been mentioned in Paragraph 2 Annex 4, but also to clarify whether the measures constitute non-discrimination and whether such measures are applied to pursuit legitimate public policies provided in Paragraph 3 Annex 4. It means that, in this case, in spite of the fact that a measure or a series of measures may amount to/constitute indirect expropriation under the examination set in Paragraph 2 Annex 4, those measures still have a chance to escape if the mentioned conditions in Paragraph 3 are all met. Determining these three conditions requires a thorough inquiry on a case-by-case basis, considering the context, and the process with all specific circumstances taken into consideration.[100]

The first requirement that the applied measure has to meet under Paragraph 3 Annex 4 EVIPA is that it must not target or unfairly affect one investor compared to others to be considered proportionate and not violate equal protection. Hence, when adopting any regulatory measure, the host state has to make sure whether it disproportionately restricts property or places a "special burden" on particular investors[101] as this discrimination may lead to compensation.

Second, the language of Paragraph 3 Annex 4 EVIPA ensures that the measure's purpose would be taken into account in evaluating a potential indirect expropriation measure. Thus, the legitimate objectives here have their chance to weigh against a finding of liability.[102] In a specific situation, when a measure is specified to exceed the threshold of effect for indirect expropriation, this new approach directs the tribunals to consider, among other factors, its non-discriminatory characteristic and its legitimate objectives. This wording is obviously clearer than expropriation clauses included in traditional IIAs. However, there is still little doubt over whether this new approach is more favourable to the investor or the host state.[103] This guidance

[97] Korzun (2017), p. 408.

[98] Berner (2016), pp. 192–193.

[99] Ibid.

[100] Chi (2018), p. 58.

[101] Brower and Schill (2009), p. 486.

[102] Bonnitcha (2014), p. 323.

[103] Ibid, pp. 320–321.

contained a substantive carve-out for a public policy measure or series of measures that have been adopted and applied non-discriminatorily from the scope of liability for indirect expropriation. Obviously, the liability could have its chance to be triggered in "rare circumstances", but this requires further analysis with regard to the severe impact of the measure. The assessment of whether the applied measure leads to a severe impact that is beyond the protected objective is left to the judgment of the tribunal.

Paragraph 3 Annex 4 EVIPA confirmed that legitimate public policy, along with its effect, is a criterion that must be considered in dispute resolution. In this context, the term "legitimate" is synonymous with "reasonable" and prompts the tribunal to address the question of proportionality. The proportionality requirement will be defined by evaluating whether the applied measures cause discrimination and misuse. For this reason, a measure that is disguised by the goal of protecting public interests, causing a manifestly excessive impact on investors' assets, can still result in an indirect expropriation. Although not yet strongly conceptualised, this proportionality test has been applied by several tribunals[104] with the aim of balancing the regulatory rights of the host state with the investors' rights.

As can be seen, the application of Paragraph 3 requires the ICS tribunal to apply an applicable test to establish if a particular conduct by the host state meets the presumption in this provision. In this applicable test, the tribunal have to be faced with several options, including good faith, reasonableness, necessity and even cost/benefit balancing.[105]

Although the aim of Paragraph 3 is to establish a safeguard for the host states' right to regulate, some studies are still sceptical about the scope and operation of this mechanism. In particular, the language used in paragraph 3 may require an evaluation to determine if the measure in question is appropriately connected to a valid public policy objective pursued by the host State.[106] The reasonableness test has to focus on establishing a satisfactory causal relationship between the desired legitimate objective and the conduct that is deemed reasonable.[107] This Paragraph 3 Annex 4 EVIPA, however, does not explain legitimate public policy objectives like other new-generation IIA.[108] However, as the understanding of public welfare objectives in existing jurisprudence as well as in IIA negotiating practice has been not so

104 Brower and Schill (2009), p. 484.

105 See further Ortino (2016), p. 362.

106 Ibid.

107 Ibid.

108 For instance, Annex on Expropriation and Compensation, Art 4 ASEAN - ANZ FTA mentions "Non-discriminatory regulatory actions by a Party that are designed and applied to achieve legitimate public welfare objectives, such as the protection of public health, safety, and the environment do not constitute expropriation of the type refred to in Paragraph 2(b)". Many Canadian and US IIAs, and the COMESA investment agreement have also clarified this terms as: "Except in rare circumstances, non-discriminatory regulatory actions by a Party that are designed and applied to protect legitimate public welfare objectives, such as public health, safety, and the environment, do not constitute indirect expropriations." [Annex B, Art 4(b) of the US - Uruguay BIT. See also Annex 10-D, Chapter 10, Art 4(b) of the US - Chile FTA].

controversial when it comes to the scope of these terms, the author, therefore, supposes that future tribunals will face no difficulty in interpreting this language of Paragraph 3 Annex 4 EVIPA.

Third, EVIPA provides guidance to future ICS tribunals that the term "rare circumstance" refers to a situation where "the impact of a measure or series of measures is so severe" considering its purpose, to the extent that it is *manifestly* excessive. As suggested by Henckels, this language implies that a tribunal is expected to consider the relative significance of the measure's objective in relation to its impact on the investment, which involves making a judgment based on values.[109] Moreover, the word "manifest" in this paragraph shows that a very high threshold will be applied.[110] Such strong language reflecting policy objectives while also guarding against extreme regulation has not yet become widely prevalent in most IIAs, as shown in a survey analysing 38 IIAs recently signed between 2018 2020.[111]

Except for the abovementioned guidance, EVIPA provides no more clarification on the term "rare circumstances". Based on the vague nature of this term, it is believed to create a comparatively broad exception to the presumption in favour of "nondiscriminatory regulatory actions.[112] Therefore, it is expected to result in a reduction of predictability and certainty for both host states and private parties. However, this book supposes that the context of this annexe ensures that a restrictive approach will be applied.[113] In addition, the choice of wording "so severe" and "manifestly excessive" indicates that the applicable threshold must be high. Even so, there might be a worry that it hardly concretises how tribunals should apply the test in practice.[114] In addition, determining the point at which a measure becomes "severe" or "*manifestly* excessive" is challenging. This language has clearly placed the final decision in the tribunal's hands. However, this book argues that maintaining this discretion is essential because the balance test necessitates an interactive assessment of the criteria outlined in Paragraph 3 Annex 4 EVIPA. The determination of what is deemed "excessive" relies on a proportional evaluation of the measure(s) in relation to its intended purpose. The tribunal's extensive experience in evaluating such matters over time suggests that providing excessive guidance could hinder their ability to assess cases effectively. There are also proposals[115] to establish specific regulatory criteria, such as clearly defined objectives, to differentiate non-discriminatory regulatory actions pursued for legitimate purposes from indirect expropriations which appears in Article 20(8) Common Market for Eastern and Southern Africa Investment Agreement (2007) or Annex 2(4) ACIA (2009).

[109] Henckels (2016), p. 43.

[110] Baltag et al. (2023), p. 385.

[111] Ibid, p. 409.

[112] Edsall (2006), p. 958; Schwebel (2011), p. 158.

[113] Kawharu (2015), p. 12.

[114] Henckels (2016), p. 43.

[115] Ibid.

However, this direct approach may not currently hold much relevance in the EU context.

The challenges posed by Paragraph 3 Annex 4 EVIPA have been effectively eliminated in Canada 2021 Model FIPA by expanding the definition of indirect expropriation while completely excluding legitimate policy measures from the scope of indirect expropriation action by excluding the term "except in rare circumstances" from Article 9.3 on indirect expropriation.[116] Specifically:

> 3. An indirect expropriation under paragraph 1 may occur when a measure or a series of measures of a Party has an effect equivalent to direct expropriation without formal transfer of title or outright seizure. A non-discriminatory measure of a Party that is adopted and maintained in good faith to protect legitimate public welfare objectives, such as health, safety and the environment, does not constitute indirect expropriation, even if it has an effect equivalent to direct expropriation. The determination of whether a measure or a series of measures of a Party has an effect equivalent to direct expropriation requires a case-by-case, fact-based inquiry that shall consider:

(a) the economic impact of the measure or the series of measures, although the sole fact that a measure or a series of measures of a Party has an adverse effect on the economic value of a covered investment does not establish that an indirect expropriation has occurred;
(b) the duration of the measure or series of measures of a Party;
(c) the extent to which the measure or the series of measures interferes with distinct, reasonable investment-backed expectations; and
(d) the character of the measure or the series of measures.

While still maintaining the "traditional" criteria for assessing the violation of indirect expropriation, Canada 2021 Model FIPA has taken further steps to safeguard the state's rights to regulate. This provision ensures that all legislative measures meeting the conditions of non-discrimination, good faith adoption and application, and aiming to protect public welfare objectives are unequivocally not considered indirect expropriation. Notably, unlike the Canada 2004 Model BIT, the Canada 2021 Model FIPA incorporates this regulation in the main text instead of mentioning it in the Annex. Furthermore, Canada 2021 Model FIPA does not introduce any other possibilities for policy measures to be classified as indirect expropriation by excluding the term "except in rare circumstances." The concept of indirect expropriation drawn by this regulation, therefore, is more precise than that of EVIPA. Alongside the provisions of Article 3 on the Right to Regulation and Article 4 on Non-derogation, this regulation (Article 9.3 Canada 2021 Model FIPA) demonstrates the Canadian government's strong stance in protecting the authority to regulate policy objectives within its jurisdiction. In comparison, the EVIPA and its Annex 4 are evidently less effective in this regard.

The wording of EVIPA's annex also differs slightly from the US 2012 Model BIT, as it mentions regulatory actions that are "designed..." but not "designed and

[116] A study indicates that the inclusion or omission of the phrase "except in rare circumstances" in this regulation does not alter its content or meaning. Essentially, both formulations have an equivalent impact. See further Ha (2021), p. 160.

applied," as included in the US 2012 Model BIT.[117] However, this difference does not impact the content of this regulation. In a dispute arising under the US 2012 Model BIT context, the tribunal need to evaluate "the procedures by which a measure was adopted only so far as "this is incidental to the determination of whether a measure was "designed and applied to protect a legitimate public welfare objective."[118] This means that in this case, the evaluation of due process is only necessary to evaluate a measure's legitimate objectives. It seems that the EVIPA's annex does not fully articulate at this point. It is unclear why Paragraph 3 of Annex 4 EVIPA has been designed as published while other IIAs signed between the EU and its other partners, including Canada and Singapore, have the same wording with the US 2012 Model BIT in relating to the term "designed and applied".[119] It is unclear whether this difference is intentional or not, but this slight difference in drafting this provision may not lead to severely different interpretations as both agreements share the same approach with a similar structure of consideration/inquiry. In addition, an "as such" discriminatory measure, once it has been proven, is essentially considered to constitute a violation. However, the wording of this provision may create a situation that a particular regulation which fully meets all mentioned requirements but causes discrimination when applied will not be excluded. In other words, such regulation is still faced with compensation.

Some scholars view the provision in the EVIPA, along with similar provisions in concurrently negotiated IIAs, with scepticism, suggesting that it serves more as a clarification of indirect expropriation rather than an exception.[120] This scepticism arises from the broad language used, reminiscent of statements regarding the police power doctrine. Ha argues that based on this wording, even measures that significantly impact foreign investments remain non-compensable. According to the author, this interpretation contradicts the typical legal consequences associated with treaty expropriation provisions and undermines their intended purpose.[121] This perspective may be warranted when considering the provision in isolation and within the context of some Investment tribunals' view that the primary objective of IIAs is to promote and protect foreign investment. Yet, the landscape of IIAs negotiations has evolved significantly. In addition to clarifying investment protection standards, many innovations now address economic development goals and other policy

---

[117] The US 2012 Model BIT Annex B, Paragraph 4(b) "*Except in rare circumstances, non-discriminatory regulatory actions by a Party that are designed and applied to protect legitimate public welfare objectives, such as public health, safety, and the environment, do not constitute indirect expropriations.*"

[118] Bonnitcha (2014), p. 329.

[119] In specific, Paragraph 3 Annex 8-A CETA provides: "For greater certainty, except in the rare circumstance when the impact of a measure or series of measures is so severe in light of its purpose that it appears manifestly excessive, non-discriminatory measures of a Party that are designed and applied to protect legitimate public welfare objectives, such as health, safety and the environment, do not constitute indirect expropriations." Paragraph 2 Annex 1 EU - Singapore IPA have exactlly the same format with those included in CETA.

[120] Ha (2021), p. 160.

[121] Ibid.

objectives in a more balanced manner. These include provisions securing countries' right to regulate, as will be explored in Chapter 8. Moreover, an essential effort to safeguard parties' control over their agreements lies in establishing the ICS tribunals composed of highly qualified judges with powers akin to those of members of permanent international jurisdictions, such as the International Court of Justice and the WTO Appellate Body.[122] With such a diverse array of tools, although the definitive effectiveness of these regulations remains unproven in practice, the cumulative impact of these innovations is worth anticipating.

Some authors, like Muchlinski, have commented that such exclusion of public policy measures from the scope of indirect expropriation may not offer the clarity as the regulation appears to give at first sight because, in such cases, the investors may still question whether their economic loss is the outcome of a legitimate measure or in fact of an indirect expropriation.[123] However, as has been clarified above in this study in regard to the structure of the indirect expropriation inquiry required by the EVIPA Annex, this provision does not, of course, preclude the inquiry into the measure being taken but rather instructs the tribunal on different stages of the inquiry as closely as possible to the intention of the parties.

This annex approach has been believed to provide a better balance between a measure's effects and its characteristics and, therefore, was more desirable compared with traditional approaches.[124] The clarification of investment treaty language would avoid potential conflicts, if there are, between investment and sustainable development. Furthermore, this new approach is better designed to address hold-up problems, help entail net economic benefits and is more likely to encourage stability and certainty in the domestic legal systems.[125] However, these characters are additional values which are not much rellevant to this study.

In general, such clarification, as suggested in Paragraph 3 Annex 4 EVIPA, and the similar clauses included in the above-mentioned treaties, is expected to reduce uncertainty in determining a state's legal liability in case of public policy measures and, therefore, would reduce regulatory chill.[126] Scholars commented that such clear insurance would contribute to reducing the likelihood of a measure or a series of measures to be considered as indirect expropriation because not all substantial deprivation that breaches the investor's reasonable expectations constitutes indirect expropriation under this language.[127] Such a clear approach also contributes to

[122] While the appointment procedure for judges in the jurisdictional system of investments may raise suspicions about meeting international requirements for judicial independence, this feature supports the parties' initiative to ensure investment tribunals adhere closely to the language of IIAs when interpreting them. The aforementioned commentary was provided by the Deutscher Richterbund (a German association of judges and judges) on February 4, 2016, as cited by Trochu (2018), p. 45.

[123] Muchlinski (2016), p. 52.

[124] Bonnitcha (2014), p. 324.

[125] Ibid, pp. 321–322.

[126] Ibid, p. 319.

[127] Ibid, pp. 327–328.

reducing regulatory chill in host state governance processes relating to human right protection and environmental conservation.

The less attractive side of this annexe approach, is that such carve-out from indirect-expropriation claim implies, at least in principle, that it would be less effective at attracting FDI as it can decrease the substantive protection granted by IIAs.[128] However, if this limitation exists, it may only be theoretical. This is because if it were true, one may question why this approach has become so popular in negotiating of IIAs across various continents. Indeed, the common trend in IIA negotiation trying to strike the right balance between competing objectives shows different options: (i) omitting ISDS in investment treaties, (ii) withdrawing from current treaties; the left solution, which is not that serious in the acting of this concern is re-drafting substantive regulations in traditional IIAs. In this general context, such clauses included in EVIPA have been more common in BITs as well as in new-generation trade-investment FTAs. Therefore, it is less likely that this provision may lead to unattracting potential FDI. Not to mention that few studies have provided quantitative evidence of the relevance between the signing of IIAs/BITs and the FDI-attracting effect, especially in the case of Brazil.[129]

The annexe approach in drafting expropriation provisions has not been well appreciated as to the reason that this approach requires an ad-hoc inquiry including a number of factors, and the outcome of such inquiry may not be easy for decision-makers to predict in advance, and such uncertainty is likely to lead to greater regulatory chill.[130] Besides, some scholars point out that an approach based on preserving continuity with past treaty practice carries potential risks in maintaining the traditional level of uncertainty with regard to the concept of indirect expropriation and preserving the treaty's emphasis on affording a high level of protection to foreign investment at the expense of the host state's regulatory autonomy.[131] It has been also believed that the language of the Annex with 3 paragraphs simply refers more or less expressly to a variety of legal approaches while not clarifying their contour and relationship.[132] Furthermore, the contours of each approach remain, in some important respects, unclear.[133]

However, this book supposes that these potential risks will be effectively managed by the general framework for indirect expropriation determinations included in the relevant Annex. In addition, although the mentioned criteria will be considered on a case-by-case basis, the guiding value of these provisions for interpreting relevant provisions cannot be denied. Indeed, under EVIPA, the assessment of a breach of the indirect expropriation clause involves a two-tier test. Firstly, there is an examination of whether the measure in question constitutes indirect expropriation, which

[128] Bonnitcha (2014), pp. 327–328; Gehring and Kent (2013), p. 287; Diepeveen et al. (2014), p. 147.

[129] See Johnson et al. (2018), pp. 6–7.

[130] Bonnitcha (2014), pp. 328–329.

[131] Ortino (2016), p. 355.

[132] Ibid, p. 363.

[133] Ibid, p. 364.

is determined through a case-by-case, fact-based inquiry. Secondly, if it is established that the measure in dispute amounts to indirect expropriation, the question arises as to whether the measure falls within the exception outlined in Paragraph 3, which would prevent it from being classified as indirect expropriation and thus not subject to compensation. In the second test, non-discriminatory measures adopted by a state for the purpose of public welfare do not amount to indirect expropriation provided the regulatory measure is proportionate, which means that the measure is suitable for the regulatory goal, is necessary and balances the effects with the benefits that it seeks to achieve. The introduction of the concept of proportionality implies an acknowledgement that legitimate non-discriminatory regulatory measures implemented for public welfare, such as those related to public health, may amount to expropriation if their impact on foreign investment is disproportionate to their benefits.[134] In contrast, host states are not required to provide compensation for proportional regulatory measures. It should be noted that all these tests, including proportionality, have earlier appeared in legal literature.[135] Due to this, it is reasonable to assume that the future EVIPA tribunals have prior experience conducting these inquiries.

6.3 Experiences from ISDS Practice

Dispute settlement practice to date does not provide an adequate approach or specific view of arbitration tribunals regarding such clarification and exception of the indirect expropriation clause. This fact may limit the clarification of investment tribunal's approaches to some extent on these developments. Until 2014, there was only one case that examined investment treaties containing an annex on indirect expropriation clause—Central American FTA (CAFTA), which is *Railroad Development Corporation (RDC) v. Guatemala.*

For convenience of reference, it will be useful to reproduce here the relevant provisions of CAFTA (Chapter 10, Annex-C on Expropriation):

> 4. The second situation addressed by Article 10.7.1 is indirect expropriation, where an action or series of actions by a Party has an effect equivalent to direct expropriation without formal transfer of title or outright seizure.
>
> (a) The determination of whether an action or series of actions by a Party, in a specific fact situation, constitutes an indirect expropriation, requires a case-by- case, fact-based inquiry that considers, among other factors:
>
> (i) the economic impact of the government action, although the fact that an action or series of actions by a Party has an adverse effect on the economic value of an investment, standing alone, does not establish that an indirect expropriation has occurred;

[134] Ranjan (2019), p. 113.

[135] For instance, when determining if a balance existed in the case at hand, the Tecmed tribunal examined the investor's legitimate expectations, the significance of the regulatory objective pursued by the host state, and the impact and weight of the restriction. See Brower and Schill (2009), p. 486. See also Subedi (2006), p. 130.

(ii) the extent to which the government action interferes with distinct, reasonable investment-backed expectations; and

(iii) the character of the government action.

(b) Except in rare circumstances, nondiscriminatory regulatory actions by a Party that are designed and applied to protect legitimate public welfare objectives, such as public health, safety, and the environment, do not constitute indirect expropriations.

The wording of Annex 10-C CAFTA on Expropriation is slightly different from EVIPA, but it shares similar requirements in the "case-by-case, fact-based inquiry" in which the examination of the economic impact of the measure (with the emphasis on "the fact that an action or series of actions by a Party has an adverse effect on the economic value of an investment, standing alone, does not establish that an indirect expropriation has occurred") and the character of the measure are noticeable. Instead of requiring the consideration of the duration of the measure like EVIPA, CAFTA requires the tribunal to evaluate "the extent to which the government action interferes with distinct, reasonable investment-backed expectations"

The dispute arose between a private-owned railway investment and management company—Railroad Development Corporation (RDC), which was awarded a 50-year right to rebuild and operate the Guatemalan rail system (Usufruct)[136] and the Republic of Guatemala for indirectly expropriating its investment by adopting Lesivo Declaration declaring the signed contract void to protect the cultural and historical patrimony[137] which created a devastating effect for the claimant's investment.[138]

When examining the claim of indirect expropriation, the tribunal has sequentially reviewed factors mentioned in CAFTA Chapter 10, Annex-C, Paragraph 4(a) relating to the claim of indirect expropriation, including the character of the government's action, the purpose of the measure, investment-backed expectations and the economic impact of the government's action. In this process, regarding the character of the measure, the tribunal confirmed the validity of Contract 143/158. It turned to evaluate whether the Lesivo Declaration expropriated the Claimant's investment and to which extent it affected his investment.[139] The effect of the Lesivo Declaration was later confirmed by the drop in the volume of freight carried by the railroad after the publication of the Lesivo Declaration as compared with the previous year and the refusal of FVG credit by suppliers.[140] In the tribunal's analysis, the purpose of the Lesivo Declaration was decided not to deprive the Claimant of its Usufruct rights.[141] Regarding investment-backed expectations, the tribunal admitted the

[136] *Railroad Development Corporation v. Republic of Guatemala* [2007] ICSID Case No. ARB/07/23, Award, 29 June 2012, para. 30.

[137] Ibid, paras. 35 and 42.

[138] Ibid, para. 43.

[139] Ibid, para. 84.

[140] Ibid, para. 150.

[141] Ibid, para. 110.

expectation of the Claimant regarding a legally valid contract created and contributed by the actions of the Respondent as well as its agency—FEGUA.[142]

In this case, the tribunal did not have the opportunity to engage in the balancing process because the economic impact of the measure was initially determined not to amount to indirect expropriation.[143] Consequently, from a theoretical standpoint, there was no significant legal contribution to clarify how this annex approach might preserve the host state's right to regulate. However, the tribunal demonstrated respect for the guidance provided by the treaty, particularly the Annex, when assessing the impact of the disputed measure. It emphasised that "the fact that an action... has an adverse effect on the economic value of an investment, standing alone, does not establish that an indirect expropriation has occurred." This attitude has a positive impact on clarifying the language used in investment treaties concerning investment protection standards.

6.4 Exercising Regulatory Rights Under Indirect Expropriation Provisions in EVIPA: Considerations for Vietnam

EVIPA's regulations on expropriation incorporate various criteria commonly used in investment dispute settlement practice, especially the reasonableness, proportionality test, and the police power doctrine. Indeed, the emphasis on considering the disputed measures' character, object, and intent reflect the reasonableness and proportionality test. Additionally, the requirement that measures be designed and applied to protect legitimate public welfare objectives in order to be released from the obligation to adequate compensation corresponds to the spirit of the police power doctrine.[144]

Based on the language found in Annex 4 of the EVIPA, the procedure for determining whether a legislative measure qualifies as an indirect expropriation can be elaborated as follows: In this examination, three familiar factors concerning the economic impact of regulatory measures, the duration of the measure, and the character of the measures are sequentially analysed. This regulation emphasises the need to balance these factors, particularly between the measure's economic impact and the other two factors. Doing so ensures that the economic impact does not play a decisive role in determining indirect expropriation, in contrast to the sole effect

[142] Ibid, para. 123.

[143] Ibid, para. 152. This approach is similar with the tribunal's view in *Fireman's Fund in which* an initial threshold of effect was take priority over further evaluation process. See further Bonnitcha (2014), p. 269.

[144] Titi assumed that this phrasing would reject the sole effect doctrine and instead adopt a moderated version of the police powers doctrine. Titi (2018), p. 339.

doctrine approach. Additionally, based on Paragraph 3, legislative measures that aim to safeguard public policy objectives can be accepted to a certain extent, provided they neither create a severe impact nor exceed their intended purpose in a manifestly excessive manner.

At present, there may still be uncertainty surrounding the protection of the host state's right to regulate within the framework of this regulation, particularly when evaluating its practical application. In particular, one may suppose that it remains unclear how these criteria will be collectively assessed, as each one emphasises a different aspect of the measure. It is also uncertain whether these factors will be weighed equally in the test for determining a violation of expropriation or if one factor may be deemed more significant than the others. Without providing any additional direction, the drafters of EVIPA appear to entrust discretionary power to the ICS tribunals.[145] Given that the included criteria are well-known elements in investment dispute resolution practice, both parties may have presumed that the tribunal would not encounter any challenges in evaluating them. Along with the exception provided in Paragraph 3 Annex 4 and guidance included in the Preamble, Article 2.2 on the regulatory measure, the host state will be well protected in applying legitimate policy measure

In general, Annex 4 of the EVIPA takes a similar approach to expropriation as the CETA and the US 2012 Model BIT or the CPTPP. As outlined in Paragraph 2 of Annex 4, the EVIPA grants tribunals significant discretion to determine whether a measure by a Party constitutes an indirect expropriation when it "requires a case-by-case, fact-based inquiry." Moreover, the tribunal is obligated to consider other important factors while examining the factual background of the case, such as the economic impact, duration, effects, and character of the measure, including its object, context, and intent. This approach imposes a more balanced interpretation and application of the expropriation clause than in previous BITs, where past disputes have resulted in numerous dissenting opinions regarding tribunals' decisions. The EVIPA has undoubtedly incorporated classic cases concerning expropriation claims under NAFTA because of the substantially similar wording. However, the environmental purpose holds greater significance in the preamble of EVIPA, as it is considered one of the primary objectives for maintaining economic integration. This is in contrast to NAFTA, which had relatively lower concerns regarding environmental protection. The EVIPA's granting of specific yet limited power to tribunals in determining the conduct of indirect expropriation is a cautious approach toward Vietnam and the EU.

Some scholars argue that the EU drafters have not been clear in determining whether the primary function of an investment agreement is to protect foreign investors or subject host countries to certain principles of good public governance, evidenced by the ambiguous language in which the annex is currently drafted.[146] This opinion is partially accurate as the objective of investment agreements has evolved

[145] Henckels (2016), p. 30.

[146] Ortino (2016), pp. 364–365.

to encompass multiple goals. Instead of solely focusing on investment protection, modern IIAs are designed to safeguard both the host state's sovereignty in domestic policymaking and serve as a means to promote sustainable development. Therefore, it is reasonable to anticipate that the EVIPA is expected to accomplish a broader range of objectives beyond safeguarding the interests of foreign investors. However, balancing different policy goals, especially for complex concepts such as expropriation clauses, is not an easy task. Obviously, balancing different policy goals in relation to complex concepts such as expropriation is not an easy task, and the drafters' choice is to try to incorporate experiences from past tribunals' practice into this expropriation clause model. Of course, given that there is limited practice on disputes based on the expropriation clause attached to the annexe, it is difficult to assert that this provision will provide absolute clarity to the host state's practice of the right to regulate. Nonetheless, this model provides at least some reassurance, based on past disputes, that the country's right to regulate has a better chance of being protected with codified guidelines. The remaining aspects are left in the hands of ICS tribunals might be familiar with how the traditional expropriation clause works, which means that applying the necessary applicable tests will not cause much confusion. In fact, while the number of disputes concerning expropriation clauses under the EVIPA or CETA models is limited when examining comparable provisions in other international investment agreements, it has been observed that the tribunal adhered to the guidance provided by the wording while also attempting to align with the intentions of the parties.

In comparison to recent investment agreements signed by Vietnam, particularly the CPTPP (Annex 9-B s 3(b)), Vietnam–Korea FTA (Annex 9-B Para. c(ii)) and investment agreements within the ASEAN framework, such as ACIA (Annex 2 Para. 4), as well as ASEAN agreements signed with partners like ASEAN–ANZ FTA (Annex on Expropriation and Compensation Paragraph 4), ASEAN–Hong Kong Investment Agreement (Annex 2 Para. 4), the EVIPA basically includes similar provision regarding exclusions pertaining to public welfare measures. However, it is worth noting that the indirect expropriation provision in EVIPA does not incorporate certain factors found in other modern IIAs, which are (see Table 6.1):

- The breach of the government's prior binding written commitment to the investor[147]
- The interference with distinct, reasonable investment-backed expectations[148]

This raises the question of whether there are any variations in the inquiry applied by the tribunal when evaluating violations of indirect expropriation among the different models mentioned above. As mentioned earlier, since the list included in Paragraph 2 of Annex 4 has an open-ended nature, the absence of these factors does not imply that EVIPA's tribunal did not take them into account during its examination. On the

[147] ASEAN - ANZ FTA Annex on Expropriation and Compensation; ACIA annex 2; ASEAN - Hong Kong Investment Agreement Annex 2; RCEP Article 10.13 Annex 10B.

[148] CPTPP Annex 9-B; Vietnam - Korea FTA Annex 9-B.

contrary, tribunals established under the CPTPP or ACIA may also consider all pertinent factors, including those not explicitly included in the indirect expropriation clause. In other words, these alternative rules may not significantly impact the tribunals in the aforementioned forums when assessing potential cases of indirect expropriation. However, the absence of formal regulations grants the tribunals more discretion in determining which factors should be included in the analysis as relevant features of potential expropriation. In this instance, granting greater discretion to the tribunal may not necessarily be advantageous for the parties involved, as it significantly diminishes the predictability of the dispute resolution process.

Table 6.1 reveals that, while there are some variances in the approaches taken, the corresponding provisions in the EVIPA largely align with the prevailing international consensus on how such clauses should be formulated. These provisions are designed to circumscribe the latitude of interpretation granted to investment tribunals. While the EVIPA's model for such an indirect expropriation provision may not be groundbreaking, it represents a prudent and well-established choice for the parties involved in the EVIPA at this stage.

The subsequent section provides an analysis of the domestic regulatory framework concerning environmental protection in Vietnam and the country's investment laws governing expropriation and indirect expropriation measures. As previously outlined, the Law on Environmental Protection 2020 and the LOI 2020 serve as the primary legislative instruments governing the conduct of foreign investors that may have adverse effects on the environment. Additionally, numerous subsidiary regulations have been issued to provide further elaboration and specific guidelines beyond the scope of these two foundational laws.

Concerning direct expropriation, the LOI 2020 provides explicit protection by recognising and safeguarding the ownership of assets, capital, income, and other lawful rights and interests of investors (Article 5.4 LOI 2020). This commitment is reinforced in Article 10 of the law, which guarantees asset ownership. Under this provision, investors' lawful assets cannot be nationalised or administratively confiscated. In cases where the state requisitions or purchases assets for reasons such as national defence, security, national interests, emergencies, or natural disaster management, investors are entitled to reimbursement or compensation in compliance with the Law on Compulsory Purchase and Requisition of Property No. 15/2008/QH12 (3 June 2008).

The requisition or purchase of assets is allowed only under conditions of absolute necessity (such as for national defence or security reasons or in national interest); ensuring property owners' legal rights and interests without discrimination (Article 4 Law on Compulsory Purchase and Requisition of Property). Similarly, properties subject to compulsory requisition include houses and land-attached assets, machines, equipment, transportation means, communication, and other technical assets. Compensation for requisitioned or purchased property is determined based on prevailing local market prices. It must be paid in a single instalment to the property owner within a timeframe ranging from 30 to 45 days from the effective date of the asset requisition or purchase decision (Article 18.1(a) and Article 19.1).

The amended Enterprise Law 2020[149] also includes the same commitment as Article 5 of the LOI 2020. Article 5 Enterprise Law 2020 highlights three key points: Firstly, the state acknowledges the sustained existence and growth of enterprises defined by this Law and ensures legal equality among all enterprises, irrespective of their business type or economic sector, while also recognising the legality of profitable business operations. Secondly, the state recognises and safeguards the rights pertaining to asset ownership, capital, income, and other lawful rights and interests of both enterprises and their owners. Thirdly, it stipulates that lawful assets and capital of enterprises and their owners are protected against nationalisation or administrative confiscation, with the state being permitted to purchase or requisition enterprise assets only when strictly necessary. In such cases, enterprises must be compensated in accordance with asset purchase and requisition laws, ensuring their interests and avoiding discrimination based on business types.

Regulations governing direct expropriation measures serve as the fundamental framework for safeguarding investors' property rights. However, determining the circumstances leading to indirect expropriation is notably more complex than in the case of direct expropriation. Concerning indirect expropriation measures, the challenge for the host state resides in how it exercises its authority to manage investment activities while also fulfilling environmental protection mandates within the domestic context.

As discussed in the previous section, analysis of investment disputes related to environmental protection management measures reveals that claims of indirect expropriation violations typically stem from the state's implementation of administrative measures. These may include prohibitions on using, selling, or disposing of hazardous substances, introducing more stringent environmental protection regulations, or deciding to reject, terminate, or revoke licenses for foreign investors. Consequently, the risk of facing claims related to indirect expropriation violations primarily arises from regulatory actions that lack a legal foundation, insufficient scientific basis, or actions that fail to meet transparency and nondiscrimination requirements during implementation.

While Vietnam's investment law acknowledges the state's right to apply measures for environmental protection, as detailed in Article 47 and Article 48 of the LOI 2020, as discussed in Chapter 3, it is essential to exercise caution in implementing these measures. Article 47.2 outlines five cases in which the state is permitted to suspend or partially suspend the operation of an investment project:[150]

a) *To protect sites/monuments, relics, antiques or national treasures in accordance with the Law on Cultural Heritage;*

[149] A new Law on Enterprises - Law No. 59/2020/QH14 (17 June 2020) has been passed by the National Assembly to replace the Enterprise Law 2014 since 1 January 2021.

[150] The conditions and procedures for decommissioning investment projects are outlined in Article 56 of Decree 31/2021/NĐ-CP (came into effect on 26 March 2021) which provides detailed regulations and instructions for the implementation of certain articles of the Investment Law.

b) *To rectify a violation of the law on environmental protection at the request of the environment authority;*
c) *To take measures to ensure occupational safety at the request of the labour authority;*
d) *Pursuant to a judgment or decision of a court or an arbitral award;*
e) *The investor fails to adhere to the written approval for investment guidelines or the investment registration certificate and recommits administrative violations after incurring penalties.*

Article 47 of the LOI 2020 grants the state management agency for investment the authority to suspend or partially suspend the operation of an investment project in various circumstances, including those related to environmental protection (Para. (b)), safeguarding cultural heritage, or investor non-compliance with written approval for investment guidelines or the investment registration certificate, particularly if they repeat administrative violations following penalties.

In essence, Vietnam has laid sufficient groundwork by promulgating its domestic legislation concerning expropriation and the measures that may constitute indirect expropriation. However, it is crucial for regulatory agencies to be mindful of the criteria that tribunals will consider when assessing specific measures employed to manage the particular investment—environmental issues discussed in this chapter. The formulation of the indirect expropriation clause within the EVIPA suggests that future tribunals will likely continue to draw from established interpretations of this provision as developed through ISDS practice. In situations where the Vietnamese government must implement a measure that results in effects akin to an indirect expropriation, it must carefully consider the factors outlined in Annex 4 to ensure that the measure qualifies as an exception under specific circumstances.

6.5 Interim Conclusion

In general, the inclusion of an annex on indirect expropriation serves the EU's intention in investment protection negotiations with its partners by offering guidance on the interpretation of this concept while codifying existing practices.[151] However, it's important to note that this approach may not be universally appreciated, primarily because uncertainties remain regarding both the "quantum" and the "object" of necessary deprivation outlined in Paragraph 1 of Annex 4. Furthermore, some provisions in the annex are still somewhat vague, providing ICS tribunals with a degree of discretion. This approach reflects the parties' desire to strike a balance between protecting the state's right to regulate and investors' rights, while also avoiding regulatory abuse. It's worth noting that more specific norms can restrict the decision-making criteria of adjudicators, limiting their discretion to make evaluative

[151] See this proposal of the EU Council (2012).

judgments, as observed by Henckels.[152] Furthermore, it is important to recognise that expropriation is inherently one of the most complex provisions within IIAs. As a result, creating precise regulations in this area can be a daunting task. Given this inherent complexity, opting for a moderate level of guidance in the regulations while affording tribunals the necessary flexibility to conduct thorough evaluations in each unique case might be a well-considered policy choice on the part of the drafters.

On the other hand, adopting an approach that grants more rights to the state, as seen in the provisions of the Morocco - Nigeria BIT (2016),[153] is not suitable in the context of EVIPA, given that both parties are potential capital exporters in future trade relations and seek to protect their investors to a certain extent. Research also indicates that a BIT that is more favourable to the host state may limit the protection of its investors in the other party's territory. Consequently, this section concludes that adhering to the current model for recognising expropriation clauses, especially indirect expropriation, is a policy choice that benefits both parties.

However, the dual objective and the complex nature of the expropriation provision make the annex-based approach in EVIPA less effective. Therefore, this model of indirect expropriation has not been well-supported by scholars, especially in guiding tribunals to reach more comprehensive evaluations of specific measures. Consequently, the language used in the Canada 2021 Model FIPA is preferable in terms of legal precision.

Although it may not be praised for its strictness and completeness in language, the analysis in this chapter shows that the provisions on indirect expropriation in EVIPA contribute to increased predictability, particularly in interpreting specific relevant provisions, while offering better protection of the right to regulate for states compared to similar provisions in traditional IIAs. In the event of a dispute, the fairly clear instructions provided in Annex 4 can assist the tribunal in adhering more closely to the parties' intentions concerning the interpretation of the expropriation clause and relevant reservations on the state's right to regulate. As a result, there is still a foundation to believe that this provision bolsters more policy space for both parties, serving the interests of host states in their decision-making processes.

ISDS Cases

Abengoa S.A. y COFIDES S.A. v. United Mexican States, [2009] ICSID Case No. ARB(AF)/09/2

AES Summit Generation Limited and AES-Tisza Erömü Kft. v. Republic of Hungary [2007] ICSID Case No. ARB/07/22

[152] Henckels (2016), p. 27.

[153] The Morocco - Nigeria BIT has empowered the host State to enact regulations related to legitimate welfare concerns, effectively striking a balance between investor protection and a set of obligations governing investment conduct. See further Ejims (2019), p. 84.

AWG Group Ltd. v. The Argentine Republic [2003] UNCITRAL

Azurix Corp. v. Argentina [2001] ICSID Case No. ARB/01/12

BG Group Plc. v. Argentina [2003] UNCITRAL

Biwater Gauff (Tanzania) Ltd. v. United Republic of Tanzania [2005] ICSID Case No. ARB/05/22

Cargill v. Mexico [2005] ICSID Case No. ARB(AF)/05/2

Chemtura Corporation v. Government of Canada [2002] PCA Case No. 2008-01

CMS Gas Transmission Company v. The Republic of Argentina [2001] ICSID Case No. ARB/01/8 Award, 12 May 2005

Compañia del Desarrollo de Santa Elena S.A. (CDSE) v. Republic of Costa Rica [2000] ICSID Case No. ARB/96/1

Corn Products International, Inc. v. United Mexican States [2003] ICSID Case No. ARB(AF)/04/1

Crystallex International Corporation v Bolivarian Republic of Venezuela [2011] ICSID Case No. ARB(AF)/11/2

Enron Creditors Recovery Corporation and Ponderosa Assets, L.P. v. Argentine Republic [2001] ICSID Case No. ARB/01/3

LG&E Energy Corp., LG&E Capital Corp. and LG&E International Inc v. Argentine Republic [2002] ICSID Case No. ARB/02/1

Marion Unglaube and Reinhard Unglaube v. Republic of Costa Rica [2009] ICSID Case No. ARB/08/1 and ARB/09/20, Case No. ARB/08/1 and ARB/09/20

Marvin Roy Feldman Karpa v. United Mexican States [1999] ICSID Case No. ARB(AF)/99/1

Methanex Corporation v. United States of America [1999] UNCITRAL, 44 ILM 1345

Patrick Mitchell v. Congo [1999] ICSID Arbitral Tribunal Case No. 99

Philip Morris Brands Sàrl, Philip Morris Products S.A. and Abal Hermanos S.A. v. Oriental Republic of Uruguay [2010] ICSID Case No. ARB/10/7

Pope & Talbot Inc. v. The Government of Canada [1999] UNCITRAL

PSEG v. Turkey [2002] ICSID Case No. ARB/02/5

Quiborax S.A. and Non Metallic Minerals S.A. v. Bolivia, ICSID Case No. ARB/06/2

Railroad Development Corporation v. Republic of Guatemala [2007] ICSID Case No. ARB/07/23

S.D. Myers, Inc. v. Canada [1998] UNCITRAL, NAFTA

Saluka Investments BV v. The Czech Republic [2001] PCA Case No. 2001-04

Siemens A.G. v. Republic of Argentina [2002] ICSID Case No. ARB/02/8

Suez, Sociedad General de Aguas de Barcelona S.A., and InterAguas Servicios Integrales del Agua S.A. v. The Argentine Republic [2003] ICSID Case No. ARB/03/17

Técnicas Medioambientales Tecmed, S.A. v. The United Mexican States [2003] ICSID Case No. ARB(AF)/00/2

Vattenfall AB, Vattenfall Europe AG, Vattenfall Europe Generation AG v. Federal Republic of Germany [2009] ICSID Case No. ARB/09/6

Venezuela Holdings BV, Mobil Cerro Negro Holding LTD et al. v. Venezuela [2007] ICSID Case No. ARB/07/27
Yulia Bogdanova v. Republic of Moldova [2012] SCC Case No. 091/2012

Other Cases

Atlanta AG and Others v. European Community [1999] Judgment of the Court of First instance, 11 December 1996, C-104/97 P 1999 ECR I-6983
Sporrong and Lönnroth v. Sweden [1982] Judgement by the European Court of Human Rights, of 23 September 1982, case No.7151/75, 7152/75

Treaties

Angola - United Kingdom BIT (2000)
ASEAN - Australia - New Zealand FTA (ASEAN - ANZ FTA)
ASEAN - China Investment Agreement (2009)
ASEAN - Hong Kong Investment Agreement (2017)
ASEAN - Korea Investment Agreement (2009)
ASEAN Comprehensive Investment Agreement (2009) (ACIA)
Australia - The United States FTA (2004)
Australia - Chile FTA (2008)
Australia - Malaysia (2012)
Canada - Colombia FTA (2008)
Canada - Jordan BIT (2009)
Canada - Peru BIT (2006)
Canada - Slovak Republic BIT (2010)
Canada Model BIT (2004)
Canada Foreign Investment Promotion and Protection Agreement (2021) (FIPA)
Canada - Czechnia, Latvia and Romania BIT (2009)
Canada - EU Comprehensive Economic and Trade Agreement (2016) (CETA)
Comprehensive and Progressive Agreement for Trans-Pacific Partnership (CPTPP)
Chile - United States FTA (2003)
China - Canada BIT (2012)
China - Peru FTA (2009)
Common Market for Eastern and Southern Africa Investment Agreement (2007)
Dominican Republic - Central America FTA (2004) (CAFTA-DR)
EU - Singapore Investment Protection Agreement (2018)
EU - Vietnam Investment Protection Agreement (2019) (EVIPA)
Germany - Pakistan BIT (2009)
India - Iceland BIT (2007)
India - Jordan BIT (2006)

India - Korea Comprehensive Economic Partnership Agreement (2009) (CEPA)
India - Latvia BIT (2010)
India - Lithuania BIT (2011)
India - Mozambique BIT (2009)
India - Senegal BIT (2008)
India - Syria BIT (2008)
India - Trinidad and Tobago BIT (2007)
Japan - Korea - China Trilateral Investment (2012)
Morocco - Nigeria BIT (2016)
North America Free Trade Agreement (1994) (NAFTA)
Peru - Singapore FTA (2008)
Regional Comprehensive Economic Partnership (2020) (RCEP)
United State - Chile FTA (2003)
United States - Morocco FTA (2004)
United States - Rwanda BIT (2008)
United States - Uruguay BIT (2005)
US Model BIT (2004/2012)
Vietnam - Eurasian Economic Union (2015) (VN-EAEU FTA)
Vietnam - Greece BIT (2008)
Vietnam - Kazakhstan BIT (2009)
Vietnam - Korea FTA (2015)
Vietnam - Macedonia BIT (2014)
Vietnam - Oman BIT (2011)
Vietnam - Slovakia BIT (2009)

References

Bibliography

Baltag C, Joshi R, Duggal K (2023) Recent trends in investment arbitration on the right to regulate, environment, health and corporate social responsibility: too much or too little? ICSID Rev 38(2):381–421

Benedetto SD (2013) International investment law and the environment. Edward Elgar Publishing, Cheltenham

Berner K (2016) Reconciling investment protection and sustainable development-a plea for an interpretative U-turn. In: Hindelang S, Krajewski M (eds) Shifting paradigms in international investment law: more balanced, less isolated, increasingly diversified

Bonnitcha J (2014) Substantive protection under investment treaties: a legal and economic analysis. Cambridge University Press

Brower CN, Schill SW (2009) Is arbitration a threat or a boon to the legitimacy of international investment law? Chic J Int Law 9(2):471–488. Available via https://chicagounbound.uchicago.edu/cjil/vol9/iss2/5

Chi M (2018) Integrating sustainable development in international investment law: normative incompatibility, system integration and governance implications. Routledge

Diepeveen R et al (2014) Bridging the gap between international investment law and the environment. Utrecht J Int Eur Law 30(78):145–160

Dolzer R (1986) Indirect expropriation of Alien property. ICSID Rev - Foreign Invest Law J

Dung TV (ed) (2014) Tước quyền Sở hữu Tài sản của Nhà đầu tư nước ngoài và Bồi thường trong Pháp luật Đầu tư Quốc tế - Những vấn đề Pháp lý và Kinh nghiệm cho Việt Nam [Depriving foreign investors' property rights and compensation under international investment law - legal issues and experiences for Vietnam]. Research Project, Ho Chi Minh University of Law

Edsall RD (2006) Indirect expropriation under NAFTA and DR-CAFTA: potential inconsistencies in the treatment of state public welfare regulations. Boston Univ Law Rev 86(4):931–962. Available via https://www.bu.edu/law/journals-archive/bulr/documents/edsall.pdf

Ejims O (2019) The 2016 Morocco - Nigeria Bilateral Investment Treaty: more practical reality in providing a balanced investment treaty? ICSID Rev 34(1)

Faccio S (2012) Indirect expropriation in international investment law between states regulatory powers and investors protection. Doctoral Dissertation. University of Verona

Gazzini T (2010) Drawing the line between non-compensable regulatory powers and indirect expropriation of foreign investment - an economic analysis of law perspective. Manchester J Int Econ Law 7(3):36–51

Gehring MW, Kent A (2013) Sustainable development and IIAs, from objective to practice. In: De Mestral A, Levesque C (eds) Improving international investment agreements. Routledge

Ha LTN (2021) Vietnam's international investment agreements: various substantive compatibility thresholds for legislative measures. Doctoral Dissertation. La Trobe University

Henckels C (2012) Indirect expropriation and the right to regulate: revisiting proportionality analysis and the standard of review in investor-state arbitration. J Int Econ Law 15(1):223–255. https://doi.org/10.1093/jiel/jgs012

Henckels C (2016) Protecting regulatory autonomy through greater precision in investment treaties: the TPP, CETA and TTIP. J Int Econ Law 19(1):27–50. https://doi.org/10.1093/jiel/jgw001

Henkin L (1989) International law: politics, values and functions general - course on public international law. Available via https://referenceworks.brill.com/display/entries/HACO/A9780792310488-01.xml

Hobér K (2007) Investment arbitration in Eastern Europe: in search of a definition of expropriation. JurisNet, LLC

Hoffmann AK (2018) Indirect expropriation. In: Reinisch A (ed) Standards of investment protection. Oxford University Press, Oxford

Isakoff PD (2013) Defining the scope of indirect expropriation for international investments. Global Bus Law Rev 3(2):189–209. Available via https://engagedscholarship.csuohio.edu/cgi/viewcontent.cgi?referer=&httpsredir=1&article=1033&context=gblr

Johnson L, Sachs L, Güven B, Coleman J (2018) Cost and benefits of investment treaties - practical consideration for states. Columbia Centre on Sustainable Investment, Policy paper. Available via https://ccsi.columbia.edu/sites/default/files/content/pics/Cost-and-Benefits-of-Investment-Treaties-Practical-Considerations-for-States-ENG-mr.pdf

Kawharu A (2015) TPPA: Chapter 9 on investment. Expert Paper No. 2, WordPress.com: TPP Legal. Available via https://tpplegal.files.wordpress.com/2015/12/ep2-amokura-kawharu.pdf

Korzun V (2017) The right to regulate in investor - state arbitration: slicing and dicing regulatory carve-outs Vand. J Transnatl Law 50(2):355–414

Kriebaum U (2007) Regulatory takings: balancing the interests of the investor and the state. J World Invest Trade 8(5):717–744. https://doi.org/10.1163/221190007X00152

Luca AD (2014) Indirect expropriations and regulatory takings: what role for the "legitimate expectations" of foreign investors? In: Sacerdoti G, Acconci P, Valenti M, De Luca A (eds) General interests of host states in international investment law. Cambridge University Press, Cambridge

Muchlinski P (2016) Negotiating new generation international investment agreements: new sustainable development oriented initiatives. In: Hindelang S, Krajewski M (eds) Shifting para-

digms in international investment law: more balanced, less isolated, increasingly diversified. Oxford University Press, Oxford
OECD (2004) "Indirect Expropriation" and the "Right to Regulate" in International Investment Law. OECD Working Papers on International Investment 2004/04. Available via https://www.oecd.org/en/publications/indirect-expropriation-and-the-right-to-regulate-in-international-investment-law_780155872321.html
Oesch M (2003) Standards of review in WTO dispute resolution. J Int Econ Law 6(3):633–659
Olynyk S (2012) A balanced approach to distinguishing between legitimate regulation and indirect expropriation in investor-state arbitration. Int Trade Bus Law Rev 15
Ortino F (2016) Defining indirect expropriation: the transatlantic trade and investment partnership and the (elusive) search for 'greater certainty'. Leg Issues Econ Integr 43(4)
Plimmer F, McCluskey W (2019) The Routledge handbook of contemporary issues in expropriation. Routledge
Qian X (2020) Water services disputes in international arbitration. Kluwer Law International
Ranjan P (2019) Police power, indirect expropriation in international investment law, and Article 31(3)(c) of the VCLT: a critique of *Phipip Morris v. Uruguay*. Asian J Int Law 9(1):98–124
Reinisch A (2018) Legality of expropriations. In: Reinisch A (ed) Standards of investment protection. Oxford University Press, Oxford
Reisman WM, Sloane R (2004) Indirect expropriation and its valuation in the BIT generation. Br Yearb Int Law 75:115–150. Available via https://scholarship.law.bu.edu/cgi/viewcontent.cgi?article=1555&context=faculty_scholarship
Schwebel SM (2011) The United States 2004 Model Bilateral Investment Treaty: an exercise in the regressive development of international law. In: Justice in international law: Further selected writings. Cambridge University Press, Cambridge
Subedi SP (2006) The challenge of reconciling the competing principles within the law of foreign investment with special reference to the recent trend in the interpretation of the term "Expropriation". Int Lawyer 40(1)
Subedi SP (2008) International investment law - reconciling policy and principle. Hart Publishing
Titi C (2018) Police powers doctrine and international investment law. In: Gattini A, Tanzi A, Fontanelli F (eds) General principles of law and international investment arbitration. Brill Nijhoff
Trochu M (2018) The evolution of Investor-states Dispute settlement methods in Free Trade Agreements between the EU and some states in East and South-East Asia. In: Dung TV, Huong NTL (eds) Giải quyết tranh chấp đầu tư quốc tế: Một số vấn đề pháp lý và thực tiễn trong bối cảnh hội nhập [Investor-State Dispute Settlement: legal issues and practice in the context of integration]. Ho Chi Minh City National University Publishing, Ho Chi Minh City
UNCTAD (2007) Investor-State Dispute Settlement and Impact on Investment Rulemaking. Available via: https://unctad.org/system/files/official-document/iteiia20073_en.pdf
UNCTAD (2012) Expropriation – UNCTAD Series on Issues in International Investment Agreements II. United Nations, New York and Geneva. Available via: https://unctad.org/system/files/official-document/unctaddiaeia2011d7_en.pdf
UNCTAD (2013) Series on International Investment Agreements II: Expropriation
UNCTAD Investment Policy Hub. Available via: https://investmentpolicy.unctad.org/investment-dispute-settlement/advanced-search
Viñuales JE (2012) Foreign investment and the environment in international law. Cambridge University Press
Viñuales JE (2014) Sovereignty in foreign investment law. In: Douglas Z, Pauwelyn J, Viñuales JE (eds) The foundations of international investment law: bringing theory into practice. Oxford University Press

Documents

EU Council (2012) Meeting Document from the European Commission to the Trade Policy Committee on EU Canada Comprehensive and Economic Trade Agreement - landing zones. DS 1744/12. Available via https://www.bilaterals.org/IMG/pdf/-29.pdf

Government of Vietnam (2021) Decree 31/2021/NĐ-CP Provides detailed regulations and instructions for the implementation of certain articles of the Investment Law (26 March 2021)

National Assembly of Vietnam (2013) Law No. 45/2013/QH13 on Land (29 November 2013)

National Assembly of Vietnam (2020) Law No. 59/2020/QH14 on Enterprises (17 June 2020)

National Assembly of Vietnam (2020) Law No. 61/2020/QH14 on Investment (17 June 2020)

National Assembly Office (2019) Law No. 37/VBHN-VPQH on Compulsory Purchase and Requisition of Property, Integrated document (16 December 2019)

Chapter 7
Fair and Equitable Treatment Standard Under the EVIPA

Abstract This chapter analyses the FET standard included in the EVIPA. It begins with an overview of FET provisions within the context of IIL, followed by an examination of FET claims related to policy measures aimed at environmental protection, as seen in investment arbitration practice. Building on this foundation, the chapter then evaluates the FET provisions under EVIPA. The findings of this study highlight that the FET clause in EVIPA is more clearly defined compared to the language typically found in traditional FET clauses. This clarity offers greater assurance to the state in pursuing its policy objectives, as long as the measures undertaken do not fall within the outlined scenarios. Additionally, the chapter emphasises that the restriction on assessing legitimate expectations at the inception of the FET standard limits the potential for this factor to be interpreted beyond the original intentions of the parties. Importantly, the circumstances leading to a breach of the fundamental FET standard have already been codified in Vietnam's national legislation, indicating a transparent legal framework.

7.1 Fair and Equitable Treatment Standard in International Investment Law and Environmental Protection

7.1.1 Fair and Equitable Treatment Standard in International Investment Law

Much like other substantial protection offered by typical IIAs, the FET clause is constructed to oblige states to ensure a specific level of treatment for foreign investors.[1] Alongside the expropriation clause, FET is among the core standards in IIAs, serving to protect foreign investors and their investments from the actions of host states that lack good faith. In fact, research indicates that only a minority of treaties

[1] Bonnitcha (2014), p. 59.

N. T. Lan Huong, *Investment Protection and Environmental Governance*, European Yearbook of International Economic Law 47,
https://doi.org/10.1007/978-3-032-05332-9_7

did not incorporate the FET clause.[2] This standard signifies the commitment of the host state to establish a legal framework or legal stability for investments within the country's investment climate.

Inherent to its nature as a standard, FET in IIL lacks a precise and universally accepted definition.[3] As Schill observed, the concept of fair and equitable treatment lacks a standardised core definition, thereby rendering its straightforward application challenging.[4] It is established that this treatment standard exists independently of national legal systems and encompasses more than merely preventing bad faith actions by host states.[5] In general, the FET standard is diversely included with different formulations in IIL. It can be referred to as a free-standing standard or juxtaposed to other standards like full protection and security (Article 2.2 Germany 2008 Model BIT). It can also be combined with a reference to general international law (Article 4.1 France Mexico BIT 1998) or to the minimum standard of customary international law (US 2012 Model BIT). It can be described as the host state's treatment having to be "fair and equitable", "just and equitable", or "according to international law".

Based on its autonomous or conditional nature, FET can be divided into two types.[6] A Conditional FET is a clause which is linked to international or national law standards while an autonomous FET simply imposes the obligation to grant FET to foreign investors without the requirement of external qualification onto the FET.[7] Conditional FET clauses can be divided into several subgroups depending on the external standards to which they are linked, such as general international law, customary international law, domestic law and regulations.[8] This type of FET can usually be found in BITs concluded by the United States and the United Kingdom while autonomous FET standards are widely used by European countries.[9]

The typical language of an FET clause reads as follows: "Investments of investors of each Contracting Party shall at all times be accorded fair and equitable treatment and full protection and security in the territory of the other Contracting Party."[10] An FET clause adding guidance that refers to international law can be read as NAFTA Article 1105:

> Each Party shall accord to investments of investors of another Party treatment in accordance with international law, including fair and equitable treatment and full protection and security.

---

[2] In a study conducted in 2008, the author finds out that only 19 out of 365 BITs do not include fair and equitable treatment clause. See Tudor (2008), p. 23.

[3] Ibid, p. 15.

[4] Schill (2009), p. 263.

[5] Ibid.

[6] Chi (2018), p. 51.

[7] Dolzer (2007), p. 961. Chi (2018), pp. 51, 52.

[8] Chi (2018), Ibid.

[9] Ibid.

[10] Article 2(2), Bulgaria - United Kingdom BIT (1995).

A mere declaration as above highlights several significant issues stemming from the ambiguous nature of the FET standard, which grants substantial interpretive authority to international investment tribunals.[11] The diverse use of language in FET clauses makes it increasingly challenging to anticipate how these provisions will be interpreted in practice. In fact, some investment arbitrators have voiced concerns that the broad interpretation of the FET standard has led tribunals to impose obligations on parties that do not directly arise from the language used by the parties themselves to define their commitments.[12]

Even more concerning is the perception that the FET clause could encroach further into the host state's traditional *domaine réservé* than any other treaty rule.[13] Notably, scholars have observed that despite using common terminology, such as references to an investor's "legitimate expectations," tribunals attribute significantly different legal content to various elements of the FET provision.[14] As mentioned earlier, this is because notions of "fairness" and "equity" allow for a significant degree of subjective judgment.[15] The ambiguity of the FET clause has compelled tribunals to develop a set of essential criteria to determine acts that constitute a violation of the FET clause. However, during this development, the tribunals faced criticism for interpreting FET provisions too broadly compared to the general wording of such clauses or their negotiating intentions.[16]

It is evident that not every adverse action by a state constitutes a treaty violation, but rather, only "acts showing a wilful neglect of duty, an insufficiency of action falling far below international standards, or even subjective bad faith",[17] which also forms the international minimum standard, qualify as a breach of the FET standard. Therefore, the central assessment for an FET violation is whether the state has acted in good or bad faith.[18] Indeed, the Saluka tribunal asserted that any government conduct affecting an investment must be "reasonably justifiable by public policies" to comply with the FET standard.[19] This perspective has been agreed upon by

---

[11] Schefer (2020), p. 327.

[12] *Suez, Sociedad General de Aguas de Barcelona SA, and InterAguas Servicios Integrales del Agua SA v. The Argentine Republic* [2003] ICSID Case No. ARB/03/17 and *AWG Group Ltd. v. The Argentine Republic* [2003] UNCITRAL, Decision on Liability, 30 July 2010, Separate Opinion of Arbitrator Pedro Nikken, para. 27.

[13] Dolzer (2007), p. 964.

[14] Bonnitcha (2014), p. 145.

[15] UNCTAD (2012b), p. 43; Berner (2016), p. 186.

[16] Subedi (2008), pp. 168-171; Muchlinski (2016), p. 48.

[17] *Alex Genin, Eastern Credit Limited, Inc. and A.S. Baltoil v. The Republic of Estonia* (*Genin v. Estonia*) [1999] ICSID Case No.ARB/99/2, Award, 25 June 2001, para. 367.

[18] Swedish National Board of Trade (2015), p. 14.

[19] *Saluka Investments BV v. The Czech Republic* (*Saluka v. Czech Republic*) [2001] UNCITRAL, Partial Award, 17 March 2006, para. 307.

academic scholars. Scholars often refer to this substantive aspect of the FET under labels such as "unreasonableness",[20] proportionality,[21] or arbitrariness.[22]

Over time, primarily through dispute resolution practice, the content of the FET clause has been progressively clarified.[23] In particular, when assessing FET standard violations, investment arbitral tribunals commonly evaluate the following seven non-exclusive elements associated with the rule of law:[24]

(a) *requirement of legality*
(b) *transparency*
(c) *non-discrimination*
(d) *procedural due process and the denial of justice, stability and predictability of the legal framework*
(e) *reasonableness and proportionality*
(f) *consistency in decision-making and*
(g) *the protection of investors' legitimate expectations*

It should be noted that common terms are not always mentioned consistently among tribunal decisions. Furthermore, these factors are often interconnected and may even represent competing interests, and assessing them requires consideration of other elements. Therefore, tribunals must carefully establish an adequate standard of review, burdens of proof, and appropriate levels of deference.[25] Among these elements, investors' legitimate expectations have been identified as a key component of the FET standard, especially in the context of long-term investment projects.[26]

The term "legitimate expectation," much like the concept of indirect expropriation, is subject to various criteria for evaluation by investment arbitration tribunals. Generally, legitimate expectations pertain to situations in which a host state's actions breach the consistency principle by deviating from prior promises or assurances upon which the investor had relied.[27] However, dispute resolution practice has demonstrated that this requirement can be interpreted too broadly, potentially severely limiting a nation's right to regulate. For instance, in the Tecmed case, the tribunal suggested that: "the foreign investor expects the host state to act in a consistent manner, free from ambiguity and totally transparently in its relations with the foreign investor, so that it may know beforehand any and all rules and regulations that will govern its investments, as well as the goals of the relevant policies and

[20] Vandevelde (2010a), p. 202.

[21] Kläger (2011), p. 236.

[22] Bonnitcha (2014), p. 211.

[23] Kläger (2016), p. 67.

[24] See a full analysis of these seven FET elements in Jacob, Schill (2017), p. 18.

[25] See further Kingsbury, Schill (2010), p. 96.

[26] Chi (2018), pp. 52–53.

[27] Vandevelde (2010b), p. 68.

administrative practices or directives, to be able to plan its investment and comply with such regulations."[28]

In the ISDS context, the term "legitimate expectation" has been explored through three distinct approaches, as observed by Andrew Newcombe and Lluis Paradell.[29] The first interpretation involves expectations arising from the foreign investor's reliance on specific host state conduct, which may include oral or written representations or commitments made by the host state concerning the investment. The second interpretation, frequently referenced by tribunals, pertains to stable and predictable legal and administrative frameworks that meet certain minimum standards. These standards encompass factors such as consistency and transparency in decision-making. Finally, the third and broadest level of legitimate expectations refers to the expectation that the conduct of the host state subsequent to the investment will be fair and equitable.

Overall, scholars have identified a set of requirements for the protection of legitimate expectations under the FET standards by examining decisions from investment arbitrators. For instance, Viñuales suggested that in order to be considered legitimate expectations, a measure or series of measures should meet the following characteristics:[30]

(i) They must result from State conduct.
(ii) They must be sufficiently clear.
(iii) They must arise prior to the moment when the investment is made.
(iv) They must be legitimate and reasonable in the light of the overall circumstances surrounding the investment.
(v) The investor must specifically rely on such expectations in making its investment.

From the law and economic perspective, Bonnitcha's research on investment tribunals' decisions reveals that decisions embody four different views of the basis for expectations protected by the FET standard. Each of these views can be characterised as a distinct, coherent interpretation of the legitimate expectations element of the FET standard:[31]

(i) The legal rights approach: expectations must be based on specific rights that the investor has acquired under domestic law.
(ii) The representations approach: expectations may be based on specific unilateral representations of government officials.
(iii) The stability approach: expectations may rest on the regulatory framework in force in the host state when the investor invests.

[28] *Tecnica Mediambientales Tecmed S.A. v. United Mexican* States (*Tecmed v. Mexico*) [1999] ICSID Case No. 1 ARB (AF)/00/2, Award, 29 May 2003, para. 154.

[29] Newcombe and Paradel (2009), pp. 279–280.

[30] Viñuales (2012), p. 353.

[31] Bonnitcha (2014), p. 194.

(iv) The business plan approach: expectations may be based on the investor's business plans.

Although not completely consistent, both jurisprudence and legal economics approaches suggest that investors' legitimate expectations often need to be (i) sufficiently clear to determine; (ii) based on state conduct (either under domestic law or the behaviour of government officials); (iii) arising before the investment. In addition, fair expectations also need to be (iv) reasonable within a specific context, considering parameters such as business risk or the industry's regular patterns.

The most important point that can be observed from arbitral litigation is that legitimate expectations constitute a separate and distinct component of FET.[32] This means that a violation of this requirement alone is sufficient to constitute a breach of the FET standard.[33] A tribunal in Saluka has referred to it as the "dominant element" of the FET standard.[34] Some tribunals support the view that a violation of legitimate expectations can be regarded as one of several contributing factors to a FET breach.[35]

Overall, as observed by the tribunal in *Waste Management v. Mexico:* [36] "evidently the standards [FET] is to some extent a flexible one which must be adapted to the circumstances of each case." Due to the diversity in its formulation and the imprecision in its content, examining a violation of the FET standard needs to be decided on a state-specific and case-by-case basis.[37] However, among the criteria listed above, the second requirement that expectations must exist and be enforceable by law is considered the critical requirement.[38] Meanwhile, in the context of investment law and environmental protection, scholars have identified the requirement regarding the legitimacy and reasonableness of expectations as the key component of the FET standard.[39]

With this connotation, FET, as a general substantive clause, typically serves as a gateway for integrating external principles into the investment process, such as

---

[32] Swedish National Board of Trade (2015), p. 23.

[33] See for instance, *Glamis Gold Ltd. v. United States of America* (*Glamis Gold v. USA*) [2003] UNCITRAL, NAFTA case, Award, 8 June 2009, para. 627; *International Thunderbird Gaming Corporation v. United Mexican States (Thunderbird v. Mexico)* [2002] UNCITRAL, Award, 26 January 2006, para. 147.

[34] *Saluka v. Czech Republic* [2001]UNCITRAL, Partial Award, 17 March 2006, para. 302.

[35] See *Waste Management v. United Mexican States (II)* [2000] ICSID Additional Facility, ICSID Case No ARB(AF)/00/3, Award, 30 April 2004, para. 98; *Mesa Power Group, LLC v. Canada* [2011] UNCITRAL, PCA Case No 2012-17, Award, 24 March 2016, para. 502. See further Banerjee and Weber (2021), p. 544.

[36] *Waste Management v. United Mexican States (II)* [2000] ICSID Additional Facility, ICSID Case No ARB(AF)/00/3, Award, 30 April 2004, para. 99.

[37] Chi (2018), p. 52.

[38] See *LG&E Energy Corp., LG&E Capital Corp. and LG&E International Inc v. Argentine Republic* [2002] ICSID Case No. ARB/02/1, Decision on Liability 3 October 2006, para. 130.

[39] Viñuale (2012), p. 353; Drukteiniene and Paleviciene (2020), p. 1201.

equity.[40] Recent scholarship has further suggested that there are conceptual parallels between sustainable development and fair and equitable treatment, which support the incorporation of arguments derived from social and environmental objectives within the current fairness discourse on fair and equitable treatment. Both concepts share a similar requirement for the legitimacy of state measures that align with sustainable development objectives. Despite these conceptual parallels, there is an absence of an environmental or social perspective in the current discussion on FET or in international investment arbitration in general.[41]

In fact, some arbitral tribunals support the view that the correct approach to legitimate expectations is to evaluate both the investor and the host state. Specifically, in *Saluka Investments BV v. Czech Republic*, the tribunal stated that "in order to determine whether the frustration of the foreign investor's expectations was justified and reasonable, the host state's legitimate right to subsequently regulate domestic matters in the public interest must be taken into consideration as well."[42]

Another tribunal in *EDF (Services) Limited v. Rumani* supported this view by stating that: "Legitimate expectations cannot be solely the subjective expectations of the investor. They must be examined as the expectations when the investment is made, as they may be deduced from all the circumstances of the case, due regard being paid to the host State's power to regulate its economic life in the public interest."[43]

The tribunal in another case, *Spyridon Roussalis v. Romania*,[44] took the same approach when evaluating a public health support measure of the government of Romania. The tribunal rejected the claim by stating that the disputed measure, carried out by the Romanian Food Safety Authority, was part of fulfilling the state's obligations to enforce food safety regulations. Consequently, these regulations were seen as having a clear and legitimate public purpose. This rationale led to the conclusion that the claimant could not reasonably have expected the state to abstain from enacting regulations in the public interest.[45] In this instance, the investor's expropriation was deemed legitimate due to the state's legitimate purpose and aim behind its measure.[46]

---

[40] See Kläger (2011), p. 203; Grierson-Weiler and Laird (2008), p. 259.

[41] See further in Kläger (2011), pp. 203–205.

[42] *Saluka v. Czech Republic* [2001] UNCITRAL, Partial Award, 17 March 2006, paras. 304–336. It should be noted that this case is not related to state management measures but rather concerns Czechia's regulations of its banking sector, which is examined within a commercial context.

[43] *EDF (Services) Limited v. Rumani* [2005] ICSID Case No. ARB/05/13, Award, 08 October 2009, para. 219.

[44] *Spyridon Roussalis v. Romania* [2006] ICSID Case No. ARB/06/1, Award, 7 December 2011.

[45] Ibid, para. 691.

[46] This interpretive model was dicussed by Benedetto as "double scope" legitimacy. Benedetto (2013), p. 108.

The *Marion Unglaube v. Costa Rica* case[47] shares similarities with the Saluka and Spyridon cases yet introduces novel aspects as the tribunal acknowledges the host state's right to regulate, particularly in situations involving "the action or decision taken for the State's responsibility towards safeguarding public health, safety, morals, or welfare."[48]

In another dispute, the Glamis case, when assessing the violation of the FET standard, the tribunal opted for a narrower interpretation of legitimate expectations, considering the absence of a quasi-contractual relationship between the State and the investor. The tribunal did not delve into the environmental rationale behind the State's measure. However, a pivotal statement by the tribunal suggests that the impact on environmental consequences can be considered an "autonomous argument which may support the absence of legitimate expectations,"[49] thus contributing to limiting the scope of the FET standard in this case.[50]

As observed, the prevailing perspective on legitimate expectations in litigation practice indicates that protecting legitimate expectations does not undermine the host states' regulatory authority. In other words, host states possess the right to implement measures to pursue public policies as long as these policies are implemented bona fide by conduct[51] Enacting, modifying or cancelling a law is essentially the privilege right of a state in the territory over which that state has sovereignty except in case an agreement exists, in the form of a stabilisation clause or otherwise. The enactment, alteration, or revocation of a law is fundamentally a privilege of a state within its sovereign territory unless there is an agreement in place, such as a stabilisation clause or another similar provision.[52]

Conversely, policy objectives are not exempt from violating the FET standard. All measures or actions have to be conducted in good faith. These actions should not blatantly contravene the principles of consistency, transparency, impartiality, and non-discrimination. Specifically, any differential treatment of a foreign investor should avoid unreasonable distinctions and requirements. Such treatment must be substantiated by demonstrating a rational link to policies that are not influenced by a preference for other investments over foreign-owned ones.[53]

[47] *Marion Unglaube and Reinhard Unglaube v. Republic of Costa Rica* (*Marion Unglaube v. Costa Rica*) [2009] ICSID Case No. ARB/08/1 and ARB/09/20, Award, 16 May 2012.

[48] Ibid, para. 246.

[49] *Glamis Gold Ltd. v. United States of America* [2003] UNCITRAL, NAFTA case, Award, 8 June 2009, para. 766.

[50] Benedetto (2013), p. 113.

[51] *Saluka v. Czech Republic* [2001] UNCITRAL, PCA Case No. 2001-04, Partial Award, 17 March 2006, para. 307.

[52] See also *Parkerings-Compagniet v. Lithuania* [2005] ICSID CaseNoARB/05/8, Award, 11 September 2007, para. 332.

[53] These are expected behaviors that demonstrate the goodwill of the host state in the treatment of investors as prominently highlighted by the tribunal in the *Saluka v. Czech Republic*, Partial Award, 17 March 2006, para. 307.

Over time, when assessing violations of the FET standard concerning policy measures implemented by host states, issues related to public welfare have gained equal importance alongside investors' expectations.[54] For instance, in the *Genin v. Estonia* case,[55] it was determined that Estonia's measure was undertaken for legitimate regulatory reasons and was deemed consistent with the FET standard.[56] This approach considers FET treatment in connection with the principles of reasonableness and proportionality to elucidate the level of interference at which a host state's conduct can be deemed acceptable when the measure is applied to pursue legitimate interests.[57] This approach bears a resemblance to the proportionality test often employed in evaluating indirect expropriation claims, as discussed in the preceding chapter, and is also frequently used when addressing conflicts between equal sovereign entities.[58] Scholars generally endorse this approach.[59] However, even in cases where a legitimate purpose is evident, it is essential that the applied measure adheres to due process, ensuring it is not administered in an arbitrary or discriminatory manner, as underscored by the tribunal in the case of *Marion Unglaube v. Costa Rica.*[60]

7.1.2 Fair and Equitable Treatment Standard and Environmental Protection in ISDS Practice

Statistics demonstrate that, alongside indirect expropriation, FET is the clause most commonly invoked when countries implement measures to achieve policy objectives, particularly in environmental protection.[61] This holds regardless of the formulation of the FET in those BITs.

These measures may encompass:

(i) Rejection or termination of projects or the revocation of licenses for foreign investors engaged in investment activities, often involving the operation of

---

[54] See for instance, *Saluka v. Czech Republic* [2001] UNCITRAL, PCA Case No. 2001-04, Partial Award, 17 March 2006, para. 306.

[55] *Genin v. Estonia* [1999] ICSID Case No. ARB/99/2, Award, 25 June 2001.

[56] See also, *Impregilo S.p.A. v. Argentine Republic* [2007] ICSID Case No. ARB/07/17, Award, 21 June 2011, para. 291; or *Marvin Roy Feldman Karpa v. United Mexican States* [1999] ICSID Cases No.ARB(AF)/99/1, Award, 16 December 2002, para. 112, or *Eiser Infrastructure Limited and Energia Solar Luxembourg S.à.r.l v. Kingdom of Spain* [2013] ICSID Case No. ARB/13/36, Award, 4 May 2017, para. 362.

[57] Kingsbury and Schill (2010), p. 97.

[58] Ibid, p. 36.

[59] Benedetto (2013), p. 115; Vandevelde (2010b), p. 55.

[60] The tribunal explained that "even if such measures are taken for an important public purpose, governments are required to use due diligence in the protection of foreigners and will not be excused from liability if their action has been arbitrary or discriminatory." *Marion Unglaube v. Costa Rica* [2009] ICSID Case No. ARB/08/1 and ARB/09/20, Award, 16 May 2012, para. 117.

[61] Osterwalder, Brauch, Schacherer (2018), p. 2.

hazardous waste treatment facilities or landfills,[62] or cases related to nuclear power projects such as *Vattenfall v. Germany*.[63] Individually, the rejection of investors' projects following a negative environmental assessment process may lead to a FET claim, as seen in cases *Clayton/Bilcon v. Canada*.[64]

(ii) Implementation of stricter regulations to enhance biodiversity preservation, as observed in the *Unglaube v. Costa Rica* case[65] or the protection of areas of traditional cultural significance, as in the *Glamis Gold v. USA* case.[66]

(iii) Prohibition of the utilisation, sale, or disposal of harmful substances with adverse environmental effects, as seen in cases such as *SD Myers v. Canada*,[67] *Chemtura v. Canada*,[68] and *Methanex v. The United States*.[69]

(iv) Amendment of tax legislation to enforce environmental policies, as illustrated in the *Yuri Bogdanov and Yulia Bogdanova v. Moldova* case.[70]

In disputes that arise, most measures implemented are geared towards preserving biodiversity or mitigating investment activities' adverse environmental impacts. However, as previously discussed, when evaluating claims made under relevant IIAs, tribunals still have to assess certain components of the FET standard while recognising the host state's authority to implement policy measures. These factors include good faith, due process, and non-discrimination, under international and domestic law, to determine the nature of the applied measure. To conduct these assessments, it is essential to understand the meanings of these terms within international law, considering their ordinary meanings, the evolution of international

[62] Examples include cases such as *Metalclad Corporation v. United Mexican States* (*Metalclad v. Mexico*) [1997] ICSID Case No. ARB(AF)/97/1, Award, 25 August 2000; *Técnicas Medioambientales Tecmed, S.A. v. The United Mexican States* (*Tecmed v. Mexico*) [1999] ICSID Case No. ARB(AF)/00/2, Award, 29 May 2003; *Biwater Gauff (Tanzania) Ltd. v. United Republic of Tanzania* [2005] ICSID Case No. ARB/05/22, Award, 24 July 2008; *Crystallex International Corporation v. Bolivarian Republic of Venezuela* [2011] ICSID Case No. ARB(AF)/11/2, Award, 4 April 2016; *Abengoa S.A. y COFIDES S.A. v. United Mexican States* [2009] ICSID Case No. ARB(AF)/09/2, Award, 18 April 2013.

[63] *Vattenfall AB, Vattenfall Europe AG, Vattenfall Europe Generation AG v. Federal Republic of Germany* [2009] ICSID Case No. ARB/09/6, Award, 11 March 2011.

[64] *Clayton and Bilcon of Delaware Inc. v. Government of Canada* (*Bilcon v. Canada*) [2008] UNCITRAL, NAFTA, PCA Case No. 2009-04, Award on damage, 10 January 2019.

[65] *Marion Unglaube v. Costa Rica* [2009] ICSID Case No. ARB/08/1 and ARB/09/20, Case No. ARB/08/1 and ARB/09/20, Award, 16 May 2012.

[66] *Glamis Gold v. USA* [2003] UNCITRAL, NAFTA, Award, 8 June 2009.

[67] *S.D. Myers, Inc. v. Canada* [1998] UNCITRAL, NAFTA, Award, 20 December 2002.

[68] *Chemtura Corporation v. Government of Canada* [2002] PCA Case No. 2008-01, Award, 2 August 2010.

[69] *Methanex Corporation v. United States of America* [1999] UNCITRAL, 44 ILM 1345, Award, 3 August 2005.

[70] *Yulia Bogdanova v. Republic of Moldova* [2012] SCC Case No. 091/2012, Award, 16 April 2013.

law, and the specific context in which they are used.[71] The disputes outlined below illustrate this practice:

In the *MTD v. Chile* case, when evaluating a claim under the FET clause with no reference to customary international law in the BIT, the tribunal employed an interpretation approach in accordance with the norms established by Article 31(1) of the VCLT. This approach requires that a treaty be "interpreted in good faith in accordance with the ordinary meaning to be given to the terms of the treaty in their context and in the light of its object and purpose."[72] By following this method, they first (i) determined the ordinary meaning of fair and equitable treatment,[73] and then (ii) examined the object and purpose of the BIT as outlined in its Preamble.[74]

Applying this approach, they concluded that "in terms of the BIT, fair and equitable treatment should be understood as being treated in an even-handed and just manner, supportive of fostering the promotion of foreign investment." Its terms are framed as a pro-active statement—"to promote," "to create," "to stimulate"—rather than prescriptions for passive behaviour by the State or avoidance of prejudicial conduct toward investors (Para. 113). Based on this clarification, the tribunal then applied these requirements to the actions of the host state (Para. 115), which displayed inconsistency in decision-making regarding project approval and subsequent project blockage and actions taken in bad faith (Para. 116). In combination with the unreasonable application and discriminatory measures (Para. 190–196), the tribunal found that Chile had violated the FET standard under the Malaysia—Chile BIT. Although consideration is given to the environmental management procedure relevant to the project at issue (Para. 195), no significant consideration is given by the tribunal to the relevant policy objective.

In a prior dispute, the *Metalclad v. Mexico* case, when evaluating a claim under the FET clause referencing MST under NAFTA Article 1105, the tribunal took into consideration (i) NAFTA's objective, which aims "to promote and increase cross-border investment opportunities and ensure the successful implementation of investment initiatives" (NAFTA Article 1102(1)) (Para. 75); (ii) whether there was a "promise" made by the representations of the federal government (Para. 86–89). Additionally, the Tribunal considered (iii) the transparency of all relevant domestic legal requirements relating to the investment procedure, which should "leave no room for doubt or uncertainty." (Para. 76). Ultimately, the tribunal found that Metalclad's investment was not accorded fair and equitable treatment in accordance with international law and that Mexico had violated NAFTA Article 1105(1).

Numerous studies have addressed the determination and comparison of whether different drafting models of the FET clause result in a higher or lower threshold for

---

[71] *Marion Unglaube v. Costa Rica* [2009] ICSID Case No. ARB/08/1 and ARB/09/20, Case No. ARB/08/1 and ARB/09/20, Award, 16 May 2012, para. 244. See also *Tecmed v. Mexico* [2003] ICSID Case No. ARB(AF)/00/2, Award, 29 May 2003, para. 113.

[72] *MTD Equity Sdn and MTD Chile SA. v. Republic of Chile* (*MTD v. Chile*) [2001] ICSID Case No. ARB/01/7, Award, 25 May 2004, para. 112.

[73] Ibid, paras. 109–113.

[74] Ibid, para. 113.

breaching the FET standard.[75] According to Ying Zhu's research, several models have emerged: First, the "autonomous-low" model interprets the FET standard as an autonomous treaty standard, establishing a low threshold for violations. Cases adopting this model include *Tecmed S.A. v. Mexico* and *MTD v. Chile*.[76] Second, the "autonomous-high" model has been employed when examining the FET standard as an autonomous treaty standard. Tribunals in *Biwater v. Canada* and *Marion Unglaube v. Costa Rica* established a high threshold for determining a breach of FET by reference to cases equating FET to MST. Third, the "MST-Neer" Model is linked to the FET standard under NAFTA Article 1105, where some tribunals have equated the FET standard to the MST standard in the Neer case. This model requires a high threshold for the host state's conduct to constitute a breach, as seen in *Glamis Gold v. USA*. Fourth, the "MST-Evolved Neer" Model has been applied in cases such as *Chemtura v. Canada, Gold Reserve v. Venezuela, and Bilcon v. Canada*. This model suggests that the MST has evolved from the Neer standard. While it maintains a high threshold for the host state's conduct to reach the level of a NAFTA Article 1105 breach under the FET standard, it does not necessarily require that the challenged conduct reaches the level of shocking or outrageous behaviour.[77]

Generally, regardless of the specific model in which the FET clause is drafted and interpreted, investment tribunals tend to assess applied measures based on similar criteria. These criteria include:

- Examination of the Preamble to identify BIT's context and purpose;
- Examination of the nature of the applied measure;
- Examination of compliance with due process and transparency;
- Examination of impact on legitimate expectations.

The last two criteria are the most critical aspect of the evaluation. In addition to these factors, specific sub-elements are considered, which can contribute to a breach of the FET clause. These sub-elements include the stability of the legal framework for environmental protection, which can influence the legitimate expectations of investors and the due process requirements.[78] Regarding the consideration of international environmental obligations in FET assessments, there are three main approaches observed in ISDS practice:[79]

(i) When the investment treaty has included a conflict clause (e.g., Article 104 of NAFTA), this clause is very useful in helping the tribunals assess the situation, as seen in the S.D. Myers case.

[75] See, for instance, Zhu (2018), p. 319; or Ha (2021), p. 88.

[76] Cases adopting such model includes, for instance, *Tecmed v. Mexico* [2003] ICSID Case No. ARB(AF)/00/2, Award, 29 May 2003 and *MTD v. Chile* [2001] ICSID Case No. ARB/01/7, Award, 25 May 2004.

[77] *Bilcon v. Canada* [2008] PCA Case No. 2009-04, Award, 17 March 2024, para. 444.

[78] Zhu (2018), pp. 335–336.

[79] Ibid, p. 353.

(ii) In case there's no conflict clause or this clause is inapplicable, while both parties are bound by the international environmental treaty (IET) in question, tribunals have varying opinions on whether to consider the IET when interpreting the investment treaty. In this case, the S.D. Myers tribunal did consider a relevant environmental treaty in interpreting NAFTA, while the Glamis Gold tribunal did not.
(iii) In case there's no conflict clause or this clause is inapplicable, while only the host state is obligated under the IET, tribunals differ in how they apply the IET. For instance, the Chemtura tribunal considered the host state's IET obligations as evidence of good faith, but the S.D. Myers and Marion Unglaube tribunals did not.

Although the environmental protection objective of the measure is considered, it mainly contributes to determining the legitimate objective of the applied measures. In some cases, a country's commitments under the FET are also examined by tribunals. However, these situations illustrate the complexity of reconciling foreign investor protection with a host state's environmental commitments within the context of investment treaties. Different tribunals take varying approaches. The core of the tribunal's analysis still primarily revolves around evaluating the characteristics of the FET standard. In these assessments, a violation of the FET standard is typically concluded after inquiries are made, including:[80]

- Existence of an environmental objective.
- Reasonableness of the applied measure to achieve such an objective.
- Non-discriminatory application of the measure.
- Due process in conducting the measure.
- Absence of specific commitments made by the host state to the foreign investor.

In general, while recent cases have witnessed tribunals adopting a more balanced approach in considering the host state's public interest concerns alongside investors' rights under the FET standard, ISDS practice also indicates that the FET clause has remained the most frequently relied upon and successful basis for claims made by investors under IIAs. This observation is widely acknowledged among scholars. For instance, Dolzer and Schreuer note that "the concept is the most frequently invoked standard in investment disputes, with the majority of successful claims pursued in international arbitration being based on a violation of the FET standard."[81] More recently, Muchlinski has commented that "this general standard is expanding to become the prevailing standard of protection enjoyed by investors."[82] In addition, in ISDS practice, FET claims are commonly raised on their own or in conjunction with expropriation claims.[83]

[80] Ibid, p. 332.

[81] Dolzer and Schreuer (2012), p. 119.

[82] Muchlinski (2016), p. 48. See also UNCTAD (2012a), p. 1.

[83] Read more in Chi (2018), p. 52; Tudor (2008), p. 15; Martini (2017), p. 538.

Research also reveals that the FET standard can place significant constraints on a state's sovereignty due to the broad interpretation of this standard. It can potentially subject State administrative actions to extensive review, which might be at odds with the state's right to regulate for its development.[84] Therefore, in an attempt to safeguard the right to regulate of the host state in investment agreements, different stakeholders have proposed new FET clauses; the EVIPA is not an exception. The subsequent section will provide a detailed evaluation of this FET clause under EVIPA.

7.2 Fair and Equitable Treatment Standard Under the EVIPA

In this section, an analysis of the FET clause within EVIPA will be undertaken, paragraph by paragraph. Additionally, this section will involve a comparative examination of EVIPA's provisions with those of contemporary agreements. This comparative approach is intended to glean valuable insights for evaluating the extent of influence exerted by the FET clause on the host state's right to regulate. For that reason, the FET clause in the EVIPA has been quoted here:

> *ARTICLE 2.5 Treatment of Investment*
>
> *1. Each Party shall accord fair and equitable treatment and full protection and security to investors of the other Party and covered investments in accordance with paragraphs 2 to 7 and Annex 3 (Understanding on the Treatment of Investments).*
>
> *2. A Party breaches the obligation of fair and equitable treatment referred to in paragraph 1 where a measure or series of measures constitutes:*
>
> *(a) a denial of justice in criminal, civil or administrative proceedings;*
>
> *(b) a fundamental breach of due process in judicial and administrative proceedings;*
>
> *(c) manifest arbitrariness;*
>
> *(d) targeted discrimination on manifestly wrongful grounds, such as gender, race or religious belief;*
>
> *(e) abusive treatment such as coercion, abuse of power or similar bad faith conduct; or*
>
> *(f) a breach of any further elements of the fair and equitable treatment obligation adopted by the Parties in accordance with paragraph 3.*
>
> *3. Treatment not listed in paragraph 2 may constitute a breach of fair and equitable treatment where the Parties have so agreed in accordance with the procedures provided for in Article 4.3 (Amendments).*
>
> *4. When applying paragraphs 1 to 3, a dispute settlement body under Chapter 3 (Dispute Settlement) may take into account whether a Party made a specific representation to an investor of the other Party to induce a covered investment that created a legitimate expectation, and upon which the investor relied in deciding to make or maintain that investment, but that the Party subsequently frustrated.*
>
> *5. For greater certainty, the term "full protection and security" referred to in paragraph 1 refers to a Party's obligations to act as may be reasonably necessary to protect physical security of the investors and the covered investments.*

[84] Muchlinski (2016), p. 48; Kläger (2011), p. 206.

6. Where a Party has entered into a written agreement with investors of the other Party or covered investments that satisfies all of the following conditions, that Party shall not breach that agreement through the exercise of governmental authority. The conditions are:

(a) the written agreement is concluded and takes effect after the date of entry into force of this Agreement;

(b) the investor relies on the written agreement in deciding to make or maintain the covered investment other than the written agreement itself and the breach causes actual damages to that investment;

(c) the written agreement creates an exchange of rights and obligations in connection to the said investment, binding on both parties; and

(d) the written agreement does not contain a clause on the settlement of disputes between the parties to that agreement by international arbitration.

7. A breach of another provision of this Agreement, or of a separate international agreement, does not establish that there has been a breach of this Article.

- In *Paragraph 1*, there is a combination of two treatment standards: fair and equitable treatment and full protection and security. The practice of combining these two standards within a single provision is not uncommon in treaty drafting.[85] This approach resembles the FET clause found in the US 2012 Model BIT Article 5.1. However, unlike Article 5.1 of the US 2012 Model BIT and the entire Article 5, Paragraph 1 of Article 2.5 in EVIPA does not establish a linkage between the FET standard and the customary international minimum standard of treatment of aliens.[86]
- Following the previous statement, *Paragraph 2* of this provision offers a dual assessment, encompassing procedural and substantive review of government conduct. Specifically, it outlines scenarios where a host state measure or behavior could potentially breach the FET standard. This list of situations serves to enhance clarity, which has been lacking in traditional FET clause models. In essence, this paragraph provides a set of administrative law-based standards for evaluating whether a measure constitutes a FET violation. This regulation fundamentally resembles the sample clause presented by the UNCTAD in the Policy Framework for Sustainable Development.[87] However, unlike UNCTAD's sample clause, EVIPA's FET clause does not explicitly mention "legitimate expectations." The connection to legitimate expectations only arises in the tribunal's considerations in Paragraph 4 of Article 2.5, which will be examined further in the subsequent discussions.

- For Paragraph 2(a), "denial of justice", a long-recognised element of the minimum standard of treatment[88] is noted, similar to IIAs of the same generation, such as CETA. Many scholars have discussed broad and narrow perspectives on

---

[85] Tudor (2008), p. 28.

[86] Article 5.1 US Model BIT "Each Party shall accord to covered investments treatment in accordance with customary international law, including fair and equitable treatment and full protection and security."

[87] UNCTAD (2015), p. 97.

[88] Newcombe and Paradel (2009), p. 238.

this element.[89] However, a complete and working definition of this element is suggested by Andrew Newcombe, Lluis Paradel as quoted below:[90]

- A denial of justice relates to serious inadequacies in the state's judicial or administrative system with respect to the judicial protection of foreigners and their rights.

Thus, denial of justice is mainly related to procedural defects in judicial and administrative proceedings. Specific acts related to denial of justice were listed by the tribunal in *Robert Azinian, Kenneth Davitian & Ellen Bacca v. Mexico* as follows:[91] firstly, there is a refusal to entertain a suit by the relevant court; secondly, subjecting the suit to undue delay, thirdly, administering justice in a seriously inadequate way, and fourthly, there is clear and malicious misapplication of the law.

ISDS practice shows that the threshold for finding a denial of justice has consistently been found relatively high.[92] Besides, over time, arbitral tribunals have drawn some essential guidelines in determining a denial of justice of a domestic court, as quoted below:

* Merely an incorrect ruling by a national court is insufficient grounds to establish that an investor was denied justice.[93]
* To determine whether a denial of justice has taken place, a standard test should be applied in which the domestic court decision must be deemed "clearly improper and discreditable," and it must also give rise to "justified concerns regarding the judicial propriety of the case."[94]
* To qualify as a denial of justice under international law, there must be either "clear evidence of an egregious failure of the judicial system," a demonstration of "systemic injustice", or proof that "the contested decision was unmistakably improper and discreditable."[95]

However, these discrete instructions may not be enough to effectively limit the space for the future tribunal to consider a breach of denial of justice, especially when the scope of this obligation has not yet been defined.[96] For instance, Keller pointed out that Article 8.10.2(a) CETA. which included the same provision, does

---

[89] On this discussion, see, for instance, Newcombe and Paradel (2009), p. 239.

[90] Ibid.

[91] *Robert Azinian, Kenneth Davitian, & Ellen Baca v. The United Mexican States* [1997] ICSID Case No. ARB(AF)/97/2, Award, 1 November 1999, paras. 102–103.

[92] *Jan Oostergetel and Theodora Laurentius v. Slovak Republic* (*Oostergetel v. Slovalia*) [2006] UNCITRAL, Award, 23 April 2012, para. 291. See Keller (ed) (2023), pp. 184, 188.

[93] *Oostergetel v. Slovalia*, Ibid., para. 273

[94] *Mondev International Ltd v. United States of America* (*Mondev v. USA*) [1999] ICSID Case No. ARB(AF)/99/2, Award, 11 October 2002, para. 127.

[95] *Philip Morris Brands Sàrl, Philip Morris Products S.A. and Abal Hermanos S.A. v. Oriental Republic of Uruguay* [2010] ICSID Case No. ARB/10/7, Award, 8 July 2016, para. 500.

[96] Valenti (2014), p. 54.

not limit the review of the actions of domestic courts on other grounds. Furthermore, the role of a well-established principle in customary international law, which is the rule of exhaustion of local remedies as a procedural requirement for initiating international law claims, appears to be absent in this regulation of denial of justice.[97]

- Regarding the due process requirement outlined in Paragraph 2(b), it is important to note that this requirement refers to customary international law standards and is widely recognised as a component of the FET standard. Furthermore, it is an integral element of the concept of "denial of justice." As Andrew Newcombe and Lluis Paradell have observed, if the judicial system fails to rectify a breach of due process, it can result in a denial of justice.[98]

As explicitly mentioned in this paragraph, the due process requirements are typically applied to both judicial and administrative proceedings. This regulation obligates the host state to ensure fairness in its interactions with investors and to afford affected investors the opportunity for advance notice and the ability to present their perspectives before certain decisions are made.[99] However, using the term "fundamental" in this context signifies that determining a factual breach related to due process necessitates an evaluation based on the specific circumstances. The ordinary interpretation of this language intuitively suggests that a significant threshold must be met for a host state to be found in violation of the due process standard.

In the case of Article 8.10 of CETA, the concept of a "fundamental breach of due process" is formulated somewhat differently than in Article 2.5 of EVIPA. CETA goes a step further by explicitly defining the content of a fundamental breach of due process, including a fundamental breach of transparency. Notably, Article 2.5 of EVIPA does not mention the transparency factor. Still, this omission does not definitively preclude the possibility of bringing transparency-related claims before investment tribunals or addressing their jurisdiction under EVIPA. Historically, transparency has been integral to early FET claims, rooted in customary international law and substantiated by arbitral practice. However, some scepticism may persist until EVIPA comes into effect, as interpretations of the transparency requirement may vary and necessitate further clarification.[100]

- Regarding the concept of "manifest arbitrariness" mentioned in Paragraph 2(c), jurisprudential observations suggest that the scope of FET encompasses protection against arbitrary treatment, whether explicitly stated in the FET clause or not.[101] This understanding has been affirmed by numerous tribunals, as demonstrated in cases such as *Frontier Petroleum Services v. Czech Republic* and *CMS*

[97] See further the discussion on the requirement of the exhaustion of local remedies and the relationship with a claim for a denial of justice in Keller (2023), p. 185.

[98] "If a breach of due process is not corrected by the judicial system, a denial of justice will result." Newcombe and Paradel (2009), p. 244.

[99] Henckels (2016), p. 39.

[100] Ibid., p. 40.

[101] Swedish National Board of Trade (2015), p. 20.

v. Argentina.[102] Specifically, in the case of *CMS v. Argentina*, the tribunal explicitly states that "any measure that might involve arbitrariness or discrimination is in itself contrary to fair and equitable treatment."[103] Nevertheless, defining what constitutes arbitrariness is a complex task for "manifest arbitrariness" into the scope of the FET obligation has led to controversial decisions, as evident in the *Bilcon v. Canada* case.[104]

In essence, the primary obligation to prevent arbitrary actions that undermine the vested rights of foreign investors is grounded in principles aimed at averting the abuse of rights and promoting good faith.[105] The provision itself contains language that necessitates a fact-based assessment. Therefore, it becomes crucial to determine the approach that a tribunal will employ when conducting this evaluation. In this regard, the factors constituting arbitrariness, as identified by Professor Schreuer, a recognised legal expert in the field, in the case of *EDF v. Romania,* have generally been accepted and endorsed:[106]

a. a measure that inflicts damage on the investor without serving any apparent legitimate purpose;
b. a measure that is not based on legal standards but on discretion, prejudice or personal preference;
c. a measure taken for reasons that are different from those put forward by the decision maker;
d. a measure taken in willful disregard of due process and proper procedure.

As previously noted, investment tribunals, particularly those under NAFTA, have considered actions deemed "manifestly arbitrary" as a breach of the FET standard.[107] The provision in Paragraph 2(c) of Article 2.5 EVIPA mirrors this established practice.

- Regarding the requirement relating to targeted discrimination on manifestly wrongful grounds, such as gender, race, or religious belief under Paragraph 2(d), fair and equitable treatment has long been associated with the principle of non-discrimination; however, it typically prohibits only unreasonable discrimination.[108]

[102] *Frontier Petroleum Services v. Czech Republic* [2007] UNCITRAL Award, 12 November 2010, para. 285; *CMS Gas Transmission Company v. The Republic of Argentina* (*CMS v. Argentina*) [2001] ICSID Case No. ARB/01/, Award, 12 May 2005. See also, *Glamis Gold Ltd. V. United States of America* [2003] UNCITRAL, NAFTA, Award, 8 June 2009, paras. 625, 803-805 and *International Thunderbird Gaming Corporation v. United Mexican* States (*Thunderbird v. Mexico*) [2002] UNCITRAL, NAFTA, Award, 26 January 2006, para. 197; or *Saluka v. Czech Republic* [2001] UNCITRAL, PCA Case No. 2001-04, Award, 17 March 2006, paras. 284, 305–309, 337.

[103] *CMS v. Argentina* [2001] ICSID Case No. ARB/01/8, Award, 12 May 2005, para. 290.

[104] *Bilcon v. Canada* [2008] UNCITRAL, NAFTA, PCA Case No. 2009-04, Award on Jurisdiction and Liability, 17 March 2015, paras. 442–443, 591.

[105] Newcombe and Paradel (2009), p. 246.

[106] Legal Opinion of Prof. Schreuer accepted and applied by the Tribunal in *EDF (Services) Limited v. Rumani* [2005] ICSID Case No. ARB/05/13, Award, 08 October 2009, para. 303.

[107] Levashova (2019), p. 258; Kriebaum (2016), p. 19.

[108] Vandevelde (2010b), p. 63.

Research has categorised four distinct types of discrimination claims that may arise within the context of IIAs.[109] The first type pertains to discrimination prohibited by international human rights law, particularly involving individual characteristics such as gender, race, or religious beliefs, as noted in Paragraph 2(d). The second type arises when a state engages in discriminatory practices based on nationality in its legislative measures. The third type of discrimination occurs when the host state fails to apply national law to investors in a non-discriminatory manner. The final type of discrimination emerges when the state makes arbitrary or unreasonable distinctions between similarly situated investors or investments.

Paragraph 2(d) is crucial in delineating the scope of responsibility for discriminatory actions. It specifies that only acts of "targeted" and "manifest" discrimination give rise to potential claims. While not explicitly stated, jurisprudence suggests that, for a claim to be valid, the discrimination must have resulted in a decrease or impairment of the investment's value.[110]

The provided guidance assists future ICS tribunals in identifying specific violations of the nondiscrimination requirement; however, the terminology lacks qualitative precision, leaving the ultimate determination to future tribunals.

- In Paragraph 2(e), the factors of the abusive treatment of investors, such as coercion, duress and harassment, have been mentioned. Arising from state authority, abusive treatment of investors is not uncommon. Instances of coercion and harassment have been examined in several ISDS cases.[111] Paragraph 2(e) is designed to shield investors from such mistreatment. Muchlinski suggests that the FET provision recognition model strives to offer a clear set of criteria for evaluating specific host state conduct. It "has the advantage of demanding a more focused factual inquiry but retains the disadvantages of the first-generation provision by leaving major questions of factual judgment to the tribunal."[112]

The criteria delineated in Paragraph 2, from (a) to (e), constitute a comprehensive list derived from jurisprudence. This exhaustiveness serves a dual purpose: it guides ICS tribunals in interpreting the FET clause consistently and grounded in sufficient reasoning while also effectively delimiting the scope of the FET clause compared to traditional BITs. This regulatory approach yields markedly different consequences than the US 2012 Model BIT, which provides an illustrative list. In the US 2012 Model BIT, any measure falling outside the listed cases cannot constitute a breach of the relevant FET standard.

[109] Newcombe and Paradel (2009), p. 252.

[110] Swedish National Board of Trade (2015), p. 20.

[111] *Pope & Talbot Inc. v. The Government of Canada* (*Pope & Talbot v. Canada*) [1999] UNCITRAL, Award, 26 June 2000; *Tecmed v. Mexico* [2003] ICSID Case No. ARB(AF)/00/2, Award, 29 May 2003; *Total S.A. v. The Argentine Republic* [2004] ICSID Case No. ARB/04/1, Award, 27 December 2010; and *Desert Line Projects LLC v. The Republic of Yemen* [2005] ICSID Case No. ARB/05/17, Award, 8 February 2008. See further Swedish National Board of Trade (2015), p. 21.

[112] Muchlinski (2016), p. 50.

- In addition to the five acts listed in Paragraph 2 that constitute a violation of the FET standard, Paragraph 2(f) and *Paragraph 3* of Article 2.5 EVIPA introduce the possibility that specific acts or measures may also be deemed violations of this obligation if the parties agree so. On the one hand, this provision ensures that investors' interests can still be protected when a country's measure does not fit into any specifically regulated situations. On the other hand, this regulatory approach demonstrates the parties' desire to maintain full control over the application of the FET standard between them, even in new and unforeseen situations that may emerge in the future. This power contributes to enhancing the parties' regulatory power, which is similar to the case of Article 8.10 CETA. This highlights the parties' utmost commitment to preserving their proactive rights in constraining the FET standard. Aside from the listed situations, only measures agreed upon by both parties can be considered a breach of the FET clause. Consequently, a state can confidently pursue environmental policies it deems necessary as long as these measures don't fall into the categories specified in the agreement.
- *Paragraph 4* serves as a caution to future ICS tribunals tasked with evaluating state conduct within the scope of the FET standard. It emphasises the need to determine whether the host state made specific representations to the investor, creating a legitimate expectation on which the investor relied when deciding to initiate or maintain their investment. A breach of the FET clause is established if this legitimate expectation is confirmed, along with the factors outlined in paragraphs 1 to 3 of Article 2.5 in EVIPA. This provision is rooted in the observed practices of ISDS, particularly regarding the decision-making processes of tribunals concerning legitimate expectations. Most ISDS tribunals adhere to the principle that a state's specific representations can create legitimate expectations for investors.[113] According to Levashova's research, a particular representation is characterised by several factors: first, it is provided by a competent authority with decision-making authority over the investment; second, it is aimed at expressly and specifically inducing investment, often formalised in written agreements, licenses, or other assurances; and third, it is directed at a specific investor rather than a broad group of potential investors.[114]

Notably, the absence of legitimate expectation in the criteria for determining FET violations in Paragraph 2 of Article 2.5 in EVIPA reveals the drafters' active effort to narrow the broad interpretation of the standard. By placing legitimate expectations in a separate provision from the closed list presented in Paragraph 2, the consequence is that an investor who has been disappointed by a specific policy cannot claim a breach of the FET standard if their situation does not fall within the cases specified in Paragraph 2. In this context, the language of Paragraph 4, which refers to "When applying Paragraphs 1 to 3," implies that legitimate expectation no longer

[113] Levashova's work outlines the steps taken by ISDS tribunals to determine the specificity of a state's representation. See Levashova (2019), p. 246.

[114] Ibid., pp. 246–247.

stands as a standalone factor but must be considered alongside the situations enumerated in Paragraphs 2(a) to 2(e). This regulation significantly restricts the scope of legitimate expectation claims, enhancing the protection of a state's policy space when compared to the FET clause in traditional IIAs.

As highlighted in Paragraph 4, the legitimate expectation is only considered in specific situations involving particular representations. With these limitations, the scope of "legitimate expectation" is notably narrow compared to interpretations of this term in ISDS practice, especially compared to broader approaches observed in cases like Tecmed. This limitation may lead to concerns that restricting regulatory actions could undermine the protection of legitimate expectations. However, as Levashova points out, this provision reinforces the parties' priorities, ensuring that a state retains the right to exercise its regulatory powers. It confirms the parties' intentions to safeguard a state's ability to regulate in line with their policies.[115]

Just like in the cases of CETA and the EU—Singapore IPA, another aspect of legitimate expectations concerning the stability of the overall regulatory framework is restricted by an independent regulation linked to the host state's right to regulate in the EVIPA, specifically outlined in Paragraph 2 of Article 2.5. This regulation will be examined more closely in the forthcoming chapter.

- *Paragraph 5* serves to clarify that the scope of "full protection and security" mentioned in Paragraph 1 only obligates the host state to ensure the physical safety of investors and their covered investments. Notably, this wording excludes "legal protection" from the purview of the "full protection and security" requirement. This distinction has led to divergent interpretations in jurisprudence, with some tribunals considering "legal protection" as part of "full protection and security,"[116] while others reject this view.[117] This provision has important implications for future ICS tribunals, as it precludes the host state's liability for legitimate changes in domestic policies and laws over time. This limitation, therefore, holds significant importance in preserving a country's policy space. This regulation applies insofar as the host state has not made a specific commitment regarding "legal protection" or "stabilisation clauses" in individual agreements with investors, as such commitments would override this provision.[118]

The language used in Paragraph 5 of Article 2.5 in EVIPA offers valuable guidance for future ICS tribunals. However, in terms of effectiveness in restricting the scope of this obligation, Article 6.1(b) of the Moroccan 2019 Model BIT employs stronger language:

---

[115] Ibid, p. 270.

[116] See for instance, *Plama Consortium Limited v. Republic of Bulgaria* [2003] ICSID Case No. ARB/03/24, Award, 27 August 2008, para. 180. See, further Reinisch, Schreuer (2020), pp. 570–573.

[117] See further Swedish National Board of Trade (2015), p. 17.

[118] Ibid.

(b) the full protection and security set out in paragraph 1 refers only to the Party's obligations with respect to the physical security of investors and their investments in its territory and not to any other obligations.

This provision's structure is more explicit than Paragraph 5 in Article 2.5 of EVIPA, as it clearly conveys the drafter's intention to prevent the extension of the Full Protection and Security standard to include an obligation to provide legal security.

- In the EVIPA, the FET standard is designed to provide a stronger legal foundation for pursuing public policies. However, violating an agreement with an investor is still considered a breach of Article 2.5 if the specific conditions outlined in *Paragraph 6* are all met. Paragraph 6 underscores that state actions must not violate a written agreement made after EVIPA enters into force, where the host state and investor have exchanged rights and obligations. In addition, that agreement doesn't include a provision for resolving disputes through international arbitration. In such cases, the state is still obligated to adhere to its FET commitments. This regulation imposes a good faith obligation on the state to honour the agreement with the investor, preventing potential abuse of power by the state in exercising its authority.
- The provision outlined in *Paragraph 7* of Article 2.5 in EVIPA indicates that the FET standard in EVIPA has not been crafted in conjunction with other provisions within or beyond EVIPA. This differs from FET clauses in certain traditional BITs that incorporate the FET clause alongside either an NT or an MFN reference as seen in agreements like the France—El Salvador BIT (1978) (Article 3) or the Romania—Czech Republic BIT (1993) (Article 3).

In general, the FET clause in EVIPA represents one of several more precise drafting options observed in new-generation IIAs by UNCTAD in 2018. It aims to clarify the FET standard by presenting an exhaustive list of specific FET obligations.[119] Within EVIPA, the FET standard is combined with several other standards of treatment, following a traditional approach to drafting FET clauses. This approach aligns with two different methods for drafting FET standards: either as a freestanding obligation or as a standard mandated by "international law."[120] In the case of EVIPA, the FET standard is incorporated alongside the standard of Full Protection and Security, akin to Article 10.1 of the ECT and Article 8.10 of CETA. Further clarification is provided in Paragraph 2, offering specific guidance on scenarios that may breach these standards without invoking general international law. Such FET provisions are rooted in contemporary principles of judicial review, focusing on modern notions of good governance, which extends beyond condemning only the worst administrative practices and denial of justice, as discussed by scholars.[121]

---

[119] Other three options are: (i) adding reference to minimum standard of treatment of aliens under customary international law, (ii) clarifying through an open-ended list of FET obligations; and (iii) omiting FET clause. See further in UNCTAD (2018), pp. 36–38.

[120] Dolzer, Schreuer (2012), p. 121.

[121] Muchlinski (2016), p. 49.

Significantly, the FET clause model in EVIPA, as well as in CETA, does not explicitly mention customary international law. This decision serves to reduce the ambiguity often associated with traditional FET clauses that reference the minimum standard of treatment under customary international law because, as scholars have noted, the precise nature and implications of this linkage are not always clear.[122] This approach reflects the extensive negotiations between the EU and Canada within the framework of their Trade—Investment Agreement. The EU resisted Canada's suggestion to link FET to the MST, as seen in Canada's practice, due to concerns about reducing the level of investment protection offered by the FET standard. The current language in the FET clause of CETA and EVIPA is consistent with the EU's preference to clearly outline the criteria for FET application, effectively codifying jurisprudential outcomes that are generally accepted.[123]

The question that arises is how this FET clause's level of protection will be determined. This issue was raised in a document released by the European Parliament in 2006, which proposed that the scope of the FET clause in any IIAs entered into by the EU should align with the protection afforded by customary international law.[124] Nevertheless, the exact level of protection under customary international law remains undetermined. Nonetheless, the merit of this provision lies in its detailed enumeration of actions that constitute FET violations, which serves to restrict the interpretation space of future ICS tribunals.

Overall, Article 2.5 of EVIPA serves as an autonomous treaty standard clause that is sufficient for assessing a breach of the FET standard. However, if necessary, tribunals may consider other sources in interpreting the FET standard as suggested in Article 31 of the VCLT. This approach has been employed by tribunals in cases such as *Enron v. Argentina*;[125] *National Grid v. Argentina*;[126] *MTD v. Chile*;[127] *Plama v. Bulgaria*;[128] *Tecmed v. Mexico*.[129] Furthermore, it's critical to recognise that the interpretation of the FET standard is not solely contingent on the provision's wording but also on the broader treaty context. In Lauder, for instance, the tribunal conducted an extensive analysis of the articles interacting with the provision under

---

[122] This observation can be found in Coleman et al. (2019), p. 110. Additionally, the authors of this work also highlighted the drawbacks that FET clause models lacking clarity on the connection between the FET clause and customary international law may encounter.

[123] See the EU Council (2012).

[124] European Parliament (2011), para. 19.

[125] *Enron Creditors Recovery Corporation and Ponderosa Assets, L.P. v. Argentine Republic* [2001] ICSID Case No. ARB/01/3, Award, 22 May 2007, para. 258.

[126] *National Grid P.L.C. v. Argentine Republic*, UNCITRAL Arbitration, Award, 3 November 2008, para. 167.

[127] *MTD v. Chile* [2001] ICSID Case No. ARB/01/7, Award, 25 May 2004, paras. 110–112.

[128] *Plama Consortium Limited v. Republic of Bulgaria* [2003] ICSID Case No. ARB/03/24, Award, 27 August 2008, para. 163.

[129] *Tecmed v. Mexico* [2003] ICSID Case No. ARB(AF)/00/2, Award, 29 May 2003, para. 155.

examination to ascertain its precise meaning. In this case, the provision pertained to the prohibition of "arbitrary or discriminatory" treatment by the host State.[130]

Compared with EVIPA, CETA has included a binding Joint Interpretative Instrument (Instrument)[131] adopted alongside the agreement, clarifying the contracting states' intentions on CETA provisions. As this instrument is binding, future CETA tribunals must consider it when interpreting CETA's provisions. Although the content of this Instrument lacks detailed elaboration, it effectively highlights various perspectives of the parties, which were already addressed in the existing provisions of CETA. For instance, in Section 6 on Investment Protection, both Parties affirm that CETA encompasses contemporary rules on investment while still safeguarding governments' rights to regulate in the public interest (Section 6 Para. (a)). Furthermore, it clarifies that governments have the authority to modify their laws, even if such changes may negatively impact an investment or an investor's profit expectations (Section 6 Para. (b)), which is one element falling under the FET standard. Notably, concerning the FET standard, it emphasises the commitment of the EU and Canada to regularly review the scope of the obligation, ensuring it aligns with their intentions and is not interpreted in a broader manner than intended (Section 6 Para. (d)). The subsequent paragraph introduces a mechanism to prevent and address any misinterpretations of CETA by CETA's tribunals through binding notes of interpretation (Section 6 Para. (e)). All these instruments collectively underscore the importance placed by the contracting parties on tribunals' interpretations of relevant terms in accordance with their intentions.

Additionally, CETA incorporates a "built-in treaty mechanism," empowering states to retain control over the interpretation of investment provisions. (Article 8.10(3) CETA.[132] The utilisation of these reminder tools plays a significant role in guiding future tribunals to understand the intentions of both parties involved. Unfortunately, these mechanisms are not included within the scope of EVFTA and EVIPA.

Existing scholarship has put foward valuable suggestions to enhance the clarity and understanding of the FET clause under EVIPA. These suggestions encompass:

- Elaborating on "manifest arbitrariness": A more detailed explanation of the "manifest arbitrariness" factor is recommended. The terms "manifest" and "arbitrary" may lack precision in practice and could benefit from further legislative definition to enhance predictability. The proposed solution, which involves giving tribunals instructive interpretations through clear definitions of "manifestly

[130] *Ronald S Lauder v. Czech Republic* [1999] UNCITRAL Arbitration, para. 219-220; Tudor (2008), pp. 36–37.

[131] EU Council (2016).

[132] Article 8.10.3 CETA: *"The Parties shall regularly, or upon request of a Party, review the content of the obligation to provide fair and equitable treatment. The Committee on Services and Investment, established under Article 26.2.1(b) (Specialised committees), may develop recommendations in this regard and submit them to the CETA Joint Committee for decision."* See detailed discussion on the significance of various tools employed by states to monitor the implementation of core investment protection standards in Levashova (2019), p. 68.

arbitrary," is a convincing approach. This could involve attaching a threshold for manifest arbitrariness to elements like bad faith or irrationality, thereby achieving a clearer and more standardised understanding.[133]
- Defining elements of legitimate expectation: The FET clause should clearly identify the elements related to legitimate expectations. For instance, it could specify the form that a representation must take (written or verbal) and the character of such representations. It should also address whether an expectation can ever be inferred from laws or regulations.[134]
- Clarity on fundamental breach of due process: There should be further clarification regarding the content of a fundamental breach of due process. This could entail specifying whether the content of administrative proceedings encompasses all forms of administrative decision-making. Enhanced clarity in this regard would contribute to a more precise interpretation of the due process requirement, reducing ambiguity for investors and host states.[135]

7.3 Experiences from ISDS Practice

The *Windstream Energy LLC v. Government of Canada* case,[136] which concerns Article 1105 of NAFTA Chapter 11 on the MST, represents an FET clause formulated in the traditional manner. It essentially considers "fair and equitable treatment" and "full protection and security" as components of the MST without providing specific explanations. This dispute is examined in this book due to its notable implications for the application of public policy measures aimed at environmental protection.

The dispute arose from an offshore wind electricity generation project known as the WWIS Project in Ontario, Canada. This project was initiated following the enactment of the Green Energy and Green Economy Act of 2009 and the establishment of a Feed-in-Tariff (FIT) Program for renewable energy projects, including onshore and offshore wind power.

Windstream Energy LLC, a United States company and the claimant, submitted an application to the Ontario FIT Program through its Canadian subsidiary, Windstream Wolfe Island Shoals. They sought a contract for the development of an offshore wind energy facility. The claimant argued that after being awarded a FIT Contract, the Government of Ontario delayed the approval of necessary permits and authorisations, eventually leading to a moratorium on offshore wind development

[133] Henckels (2016), p. 37.

[134] Ibid., p. 38.

[135] Ibid., p. 40.

[136] *Windstream Energy LLC v. Government of Canada* (*Windstream v. Canada*) [2013] PCA Case No. 2013-22, Award, 27 September 2016.

on February 11, 2011. This moratorium frustrated their efforts to develop the Project.

Windstream contended that the conduct of the Government, including the Ontario Power Authority, is attributable to the Respondent, and they claimed that the measures taken by Ontario authorities were inconsistent with the Respondent's obligations under Chapter 11 of NAFTA, specifically Articles 1110, 1105, 1102, 1103, and, if the Ontario Power Authority is deemed a state enterprise, Article 1503(2).

The Claimant challenged the Respondent's assertion that the threshold for proving a breach of Article 1105(1) was "extremely high." They cited previous cases, such as *Bilcon v. Canada* and *Mondev v. USA*, where tribunals rejected arguments that the challenged conduct must reach the level of shocking or outrageous behaviour. These cases supported the idea that what is considered unfair or inequitable does not necessarily equate to behaviour that is outrageous or egregious.[137]

In this case, the tribunal posited that fair and equitable treatment should adhere to customary international law standards and that "The concepts of 'fair and equitable treatment' and 'full protection and security' do not require treatment in addition to or beyond that which is required by the customary international law minimum standard of treatment of aliens."[138] While these assessments are not groundbreaking in further clarifying the content of the FET standard, the tribunal's evaluation of the Canadian Government's moratorium is particularly noteworthy. Specifically, the tribunal concluded that the moratorium itself did not breach the fair and equitable treatment standard. Instead, it was the Ontario government's actions following the moratorium that were considered problematic. In particular, the government's failure to address the scientific uncertainty of the project, which had been relied upon to enact the moratorium initially, was found to be in violation of fair and equitable treatment. The tribunal determined that "the Government on the whole did relatively little to address the scientific uncertainty surrounding offshore wind that it had relied upon as the main publicly cited reason for the moratorium."[139]

Furthermore, after the imposition of the moratorium, the Government of Ontario failed to take sufficient action to address Windstream's legal and contractual uncertainty. Despite the regulatory framework still allowing for offshore wind development, detailed regulations specific to offshore wind were never established. The negotiations with Windstream were conducted by the Ontario Power Authority, despite the Government's decision to impose a moratorium. However, the Government did not provide any direction to the Ontario Power Authority for these negotiations, even though it had the authority to do so under the Green Energy and Green Economy Act of 2009. Consequently, the negotiations failed, resulting in a situation where the Project became financially unfeasible by May 2012.[140]

---

137 Ibid, paras. 295–296.

138 This explaination is provided by NAFTA Free Trade Commission (2001). See *Windstream v. Canada* [2013], Award, 27 September 2016, para. 356.

139 *Windstream v. Canada* [2013] PCA Case No. 2013-22, Award, 27 September 2016, para. 378.

140 Ibid., para. 379.

The tribunal underscored that the Government did not take any decisive steps to clarify the situation throughout this period. They failed to promptly complete the necessary scientific research or establish the appropriate regulatory framework for offshore wind. Nor did they reactivate Windstream's FIT Contract. Alternatively, the Government did not amend the relevant regulations to exclude offshore wind as a renewable energy source and terminate Windstream's FIT Contract in accordance with applicable law.

The tribunal also concluded that "the failure of the Government of Ontario to take the necessary measures, including, when necessary, directing the Ontario Power Authority, within a reasonable period after the imposition of the moratorium to bring clarity to the regulatory uncertainty surrounding the status and development of the Project created by the moratorium constitutes a breach of Article 1105(1) of NAFTA."[141] Thus, the applied measure, which is the moratorium itself, does not constitute a violation of the FET. Instead, the failure to resolve the scientific uncertainty of the project on which it is based, and the government's inaction that left the investor to resolve the difficulties after the moratorium was issued without making a timely decision, rendered the project unable to continue implementation, constituting a violation of FET.

This case demonstrates that while FET regulations may or may not be specific, the tribunal's evaluations are always based on implementing general principles. Specific provisions must inevitably be interpreted and applied to the case's particular facts. As with the Mondev tribunal's observation, "a judgment of what is fair and equitable cannot be reached in the abstract; it must depend on the facts of the particular case."[142]

Another observation that can be drawn from ISDS practice is that disputes related to FET claims often involve procedural requirements, which host states frequently encounter. In addition to the abovementioned disputes, cases like *Bilcon v. Canada*[143] or *Pop & Talbot*[144] illustrate this practice. In *Bilcon v. Canada*, the process conducted by state agencies was judged by the tribunal as arbitrary and lacking in transparency. The Bilcon case also demonstrates the tribunal's extensive assessment of host state regulatory measures. Meanwhile, in *Pope and Talbot v. Canada*, the tribunal considered that a domestic agency failed to produce a legal basis under domestic law for the administrative proceedings it initiated against a foreign investor in a situation where the relations with the investor were more like combat than cooperative regulation. From the perspective of domestic administrative law, that is hardly extraordinary: improper motives and bad faith, e.g., the pursuit of vindictiveness or extraneous political objectives, are typical indicators of illegal public decision-making.[145]

---

141 Ibid., para. 380.

142 *Mondev v. USA* [1999] ICSID Case No. ARB(AF)/99/2, Award, 11 October 2002, para. 118.

143 *Bilcon v. Canada* [2008] PCA Case No. 2009-04.

144 *Pope & Talbot v. Canada* [1999] UNCITRAL, Award, 26 June 2000.

145 Jacob and Schill (2017), p. 20.

From this practice, it is evident that implementing government policy measures, in general, needs to be done carefully. The management of specific investment projects, especially the implementation of administrative procedures at various stages during the life of an investment, under the requirements of FET standards, must be carried out in good faith and promptly. Relevant regulations, therefore, need to ensure a solid legal basis, providing sufficient guidance for the government's close management. These requirements are set out in accordance with the principle of proportionality or reasonableness,[146] which mandates a balanced approach between the foreign investors' interests and the host states' right to regulate, an increasingly prevalent aspect of FET.[147]

7.4 Fair and Equitable Treatment Standard Under the EVIPA: A Potential Contributor to the Right to Regulate and Considerations for Vietnam

Article 2.5 EVIPA offers a precise definition of the FET standard and the full protection and security obligation. This level of detail signifies the parties' intention to ensure a more transparent application of this standard compared to traditional FET clauses. Nevertheless, the core principle derived from case law on the traditional FET standard remains consistent, emphasising that a state's conduct must be sufficiently grave to constitute a breach of the FET standard.[148]

Overall, the criteria outlined in Paragraph 2 of Article 2.5 EVIPA for assessing violations of the FET standard essentially mirror the evaluation practices that have evolved within investment tribunals. Scholars have summarised these practices, which include consistency, non-discrimination, transparency, and due process considerations.[149] Nevertheless, elements that allow the investment tribunal to have a broader evaluation, space such as "reasonableness" or "proportionality", play an essential role in the tribunals' evaluation to clarify the relationship between the objective and the measure in question under the FET standard, were not explicitly included in Article 2.5 of EVIPA.[150] It is speculated that, from the perspective of the EU, including these elements is unlikely to significantly improve the balance between the host state's regulatory authority and the investor's rights under the FET

---

[146] As pointed out by scholars by examining the case law, there is an extensive overlap between proportionality and reasonableness requirement under the context of FET evaluation. See Ortino (2017), p. 87; Levashova (2019), p. 253.

[147] See further Jacob and Schill (2017), p. 39.

[148] Levashova (2019), p. 269.

[149] See detail analysis regarding these five principles in interpreting FET treatment in Vandevelde (2010b), p. 104.

[150] Coleman et al. (2019).

standard.[151] Another indication is that these elements have been integrated into the specific criteria outlined in Paragraph 2 of Article 2.5 of EVIPA. In essence, a measure that falls within the scope of one of the scenarios violating the FET standard as delineated in the regulations above inherently breaches the principles of "reasonableness" and "proportionality." Consequently, such a measure violates the FET standard regardless of whether it satisfies the "reasonableness" and "proportionality" criteria or not.

Investigating FET clauses within contemporary trade and investment agreements sheds light on the extent of protection afforded to the right to regulate under EVIPA in comparison to other treaties of a similar generation (see Table 7.1). Another significant treaty that should be mentioned in this context is the CPTPP. In the CPTPP, Article 9.6 on Minimum Standard of Treatment is to be construed in alignment with Annex 9-A (Customary International Law). Specifically, Article 9.6 CPTPP stipulates that each party shall accord treatment to covered investments in accordance with applicable customary international law principles, including FET and full protection and security. However, this obligation is constrained to the level equivalent to the requirements set out in the customary international law minimum standard and does not establish additional substantive rights. This approach in the CPTPP regarding the FET standard is reminiscent of NAFTA's prior adoption.[152]

In fact, the reference to the customary international law's minimum standard of treatment, which obliges the fair treatment of foreign entities, is based on historically recognised state practices in contemporary international law. This approach provides flexibility to the parties but places a challenging burden on investors to prove a breach of the FET standard. Nonetheless, there is dissension among scholars and tribunals concerning the contents of the minimum standard of treatment due to its customary nature.[153] This lack of precision can lead to confusion and hesitation among states, particularly when addressing urgent environmental issues. As a result, this FET clause still lacks the necessary clarity to empower the host state to confidently pursue its environmental policies.

To furnish tribunals with direction regarding the customary international law as perceived by contracting parties, the CPTPP specifies that "*fair and equitable treatment includes the obligation not to deny justice in criminal, civil, or administrative adjudicatory proceedings in accordance with the principle of due process embodied in the principal legal systems of the world*" (Article 9.6.2(a)). By utilising the term "includes", it has been proposed that the parties to this agreement keep the door open for the potential inclusion of additional obligations pertaining to the treatment of aliens within the customary international law concept of FET.[154] More significantly, this provision of CPTPP includes an important exclusion related to investor expectations. It explicitly states that "the mere fact that a Party takes or fails to take

[151] See further discussion on the absence of these element in Levashova (2019), pp. 271–272.

[152] Henckels (2016), p. 37.

[153] Coleman et al. (2019), p. 110.

[154] Ibid., p. 113.

Table 7.1 Criteria to be taken into account in determining FET standard breach in selected treaties[a]

No.		EVIPA (Article 2.5)	CETA (Article 8.10)	Canada 2021 Model FIPA (Article 8)	US 2012 Model BIT (Article 5)	ASEAN Comprehensive Investment Agreement (Article 11)	CPTPP (Article 9.6 and Annex 9-A)
1.	Title of the provision	Treatment of Investment	Treatment of investors and of covered investments	Minimum Standard of Treatment	Minimum Standard of Treatment	Treatment of Investment	Minimum Standard of Treatment
2.	Link to customary international law minimum standard of treatment	×	×	✓	✓	×	✓
3.	Provide exhaustive list of FET violation	✓	✓	✓	× (illustrative list)	× (illustrative list)	× (illustrative list)
	• Denial of justice	✓	✓ (with a reference to including a fundamental breach of transparency)	✓	✓	✓	✓
	• Breach of due process	✓	✓	✓	✓	✓	✓
	• Arbitrariness	✓	✓	✓	×	×	×
	• Discrimination on manifestly wrongful grounds	✓	✓	✓	×	×	×
	• Abusive treatment	✓	✓	✓	×	×	×

4.	Further element agreed by the Parties	✓	✓	×	×	×	×
5.	Legitimate expectation	✓ But Rather limited	✓ But Rather limited	×	×	×	× (fails to take an action that may be inconsistent with an investor's expectations does not constitute a breach of FET standard)
6.	Declaration of no connection with other provisions/international agreement	✓	✓	✓	✓	✓	✓
7.	Declaration of breaches domestic law does not establish a breach of FET standard	×	✓	×	×	×	×

[a]This table, inspired by Caroline Henckels' work, has been compiled by the author. See Henckels (2016)

an action that may be inconsistent with an investor's expectations does not constitute a breach of this Article, even if there is a loss or damage to the covered investment as a result." This language not only limits the role of investor expectations in assessing a breach of the FET clause but also provides clear guidance to Tribunals about the parties' intention to set limits on the interpretation of the FET standard. Accordingly, this regulation raises the possibility that a measure inconsistent with an investor's expectations does not constitute a breach of this Article, even if the measure results in loss or damage to the covered investment as a result.

In general, while this provision in the CPTPP has raised the threshold for violating the FET standard, its primary limitation is that it does not clarify the level of protection required by customary international law principles. Additionally, it does not provide precise guidance through an enumerated list of FET violations. Consequently, as pointed out in several studies, the interpretation of this provision is left to the tribunals.[155] In this regard, the approach of EVIPA and CETA would address the inadequacies of the CPTPP's customary international law-based approach regarding the predictability and accuracy of the FET norm.

When comparing Article 2.5 of the EVIPA with another innovative FET clause found in the Canada 2021 Model FIPA, it becomes evident that the FIPA takes a more traditional approach. In the Canada 2021 Model FIPA, minimum standards of treatment are directly addressed in Article 8, rather than being encompassed under the heading of "fair and equitable treatment," as is the case in the EVIPA. Even though the term "fair and equitable treatment" is not explicitly mentioned in Article 8 of the Canada 2021 Model FIPA, the content of FET is fully acknowledged within it. In specific:

> Canada 2021 Model FIPA, Article 8: Minimum Standard of Treatment
>
> "1. Each Party shall accord in its territory to a covered investment of the other Party and to an investor with respect to their covered investment treatment in accordance with the customary international law minimum standard of treatment of aliens. A Party breaches this obligation only if a measure constitutes:
>
> (a) denial of justice in criminal, civil or administrative proceedings;
>
> (b) fundamental breach of due process in judicial and administrative proceedings;
>
> (c) manifest arbitrariness;
>
> (d) targeted discrimination on manifestly wrongful grounds such as gender, race or religious beliefs;
>
> (e) abusive treatment of investors, such as physical coercion, duress and harassment; or
>
> (f) a failure to provide full protection and security.

1. A determination that there has been a breach of another provision of this Agreement, or of a separate international agreement, does not establish that there has been a breach of this Article.
2. The fact that a measure breaches domestic law does not establish a breach of this Article."

As observed, this regulation confirms that the level of treatment required by Article 8 is the customary international law minimum standard of treatment and provides an exhaustive list of FET violations. This list closely resembles Article 2.5 of the EVIPA. However, Article 8 of the Canada 2021 Model FIPA directly recognises a

[155] For instance, see Henckels (2016).

"failure to provide full protection and security" as a violation of the minimum standard of treatment. In contrast, in the EVIPA, the obligation to provide "full protection and security" is specified separately in Paragraph 5, apart from the regulations on the FET treatment. This distinction arises from the structural differences in framing the two clauses. In EVIPA, treatment obligations to investors, including FET and full protection of treatment, are regulated together. In contrast, the Canada 2021 Model FIPA addresses the minimum standard of treatment, where FET and full protection of treatment are two separate components within the scope of this treatment. Notably, the closed list of actions that may violate the standard provided in both provisions is quite similar. However, the FIPA's list does not include the consideration of legitimate expectations, as suggested in EVIPA.

In general, the FET clause model in the Canada 2021 Model FIPA combines two options recognised by UNCTAD in 2018, as it both acknowledges the minimum standard of treatment and offers an exhaustive list. Linking FET to the minimum standard of treatment can elevate the threshold for State liability and enable states to adapt their policies in line with evolving objectives, depending on a particular tribunal's interpretation of the minimum standard of treatment under customary international law.[156] However, such regulations do not always guarantee complete control over the decision-making power of the tribunals, as some NAFTA Arbitral tribunals have emphasised the "evolutionary nature" of customary international law to broaden the scope of the FET standard.[157] This practice suggests that the Canada 2021 Model FIPA drafters have taken a dual approach by limiting the actions deemed to violate FET, essentially constraining the space within which tribunals can interpret this FET clause. Consequently, the tribunals have two points of reference when considering this standard, with the provided list being more instructive due to its specificity.

Moreover, since this list is exhaustive and each criterion is listed independently, ISDS practice indicates that a single violation of any of these factors is sufficient to establish a breach of the minimum standard of treatment. Besides, this regulation also provides important guidance on what constitutes a measure that is manifestly arbitrary in footnote 1, clarifying that a measure is manifestly arbitrary when it is evident that the measure is not rationally connected to a legitimate policy objective, such as when it is based on prejudice or bias rather than on reason or fact.

It should be noted that, in the Canada 2021 Model FIPA, the scope of the full protection and security standard is limited to footnote number (2) rather than being included in the main text. In essence, this FET clause model, according to Canada's perspective, encompasses two contents: fair and equitable treatment and full protection and security. This provision addresses the uncertainties associated with traditional MST by offering an exhaustive list to guide future tribunals in determining specific breaches.

---

[156] UNCTAD (2018), p. 36.

[157] See *Merrill and Ring Forestry v. Government of Canada* [2006] ICSID Case No. UNCT/07/1, Award, 31 March 2010, paras. 192–213. See further Nyer (2015), p. 702.

While the use of undefined terms such as "a fundamental breach of due process" or "manifest arbitrariness" has received criticism from scholars due to the discretion they may grant to arbitrators,[158] this study supports the notion that this regulation widens the policy space for the host state. According to Article 2.5 EVIPA, a Party is only implied to breach the FET obligation when a measure or series of measures constitute "a fundamental breach" or "manifest arbitrariness" when adopting regulations within its territory. By employing these terms, the burden of proof on investors claiming a breach of the FET standard against the host state under EVIPA becomes more demanding. The tribunal's analysis, therefore, must ensure that only severe measures can lead to a finding of a breach of the FET standard. This high threshold for determining a breach of the FET standard aligns with past practice, such as *Glamis Gold v. USA* under NAFTA, in which the tribunal explained that "To violate the customary international law minimum standard of treatment codified in Article 1105 of the NAFTA, an act must be sufficiently egregious and shocking—a gross denial of justice, manifest arbitrariness, blatant unfairness, a complete lack of due process, evident discrimination, or a manifest lack of reasons—so as to fall below accepted international standards and constitute a breach of Article 1105(1)."[159] Therefore, Article 2.5 EVIPA is expected to set a high threshold for proving a breach of the FET standard.

In general, the restrictive wording of the FET clause in EVIPA seems to respond to the ambiguities in the scope of this provision. This regulatory approach narrows the scope of the FET standard compared to the traditional version of FET clauses. The next aspect to consider is whether this FET provision offers greater investor protection than what is provided by national law. If the answer to these questions is "no," the requirements under Article 2.5 EVIPA do not create higher obligations for Vietnam. Therefore, this section proceeds by assessing Vietnam's relevant domestic regulations, with a primary focus on transparency in the legal system, which is closely related to procedural fairness and due process. These requirements are intertwined with the element of transparency in the legal system.[160]

(i) Denial of Justice

While the concept of the "right to seek justice" is not explicitly articulated in Vietnam's constitution and specific legal regulations,[161] the broader goal of protecting justice has been acknowledged in the Constitution of Vietnam of 2013. Furthermore, elements related to the right to seek justice, such as the principle of equality before the law (Article 16) and the right to a fair, public, and expeditious

---

[158] Henckels has made some suggestions to improve these regulations. Refer Henckels (2016).

[159] *Glamis Gold v. USA* [2003] UNCITRAL, NAFTA, Award, 8 June 2009, para. 22. Two other earlier cases applied the same interpretation are *Waste Management v. United Mexican States (II)* [2000] ICSID Additional Facility, ICSID Case No. ARB(AF)/00/3, Award, 30 April 2004, para. 98; *Thunderbird v. Mexico* [2002] UNCITRAL, NAFTA, Award, 26 January 2006, para. 194. See further Nyer (2015), p. 702.

[160] Valenti (2014), p. 52.

[161] Hai (2019), p. 73.

trial by the court (Article 31), are also enshrined in the Constitution of Vietnam of 2013.

Vietnam's legal framework has included specialised laws that facilitate access to justice for vulnerable groups. For instance, the Law on People with Disabilities in 2010 and the Law on Legal Aid in 2017 are designed to support cases involving marginalised or disadvantaged individuals. However, the right to seek justice is most explicitly regulated in Vietnamese procedural law, which encompasses laws like the Vietnamese Criminal Procedure Code;[162] the Vietnamese Law on Administrative Procedure;[163] and the Vietnamese Civil Procedure Code 2015.[164] Notably, the Vietnamese Civil Procedure Code 2015, Article 4.1, stipulates that agencies, organisations, and individuals possess the right to "petition the court to protect justice, protect human rights, civil rights, and the interests of the State, their rights, and the legitimate interests of others." Similarly, Article 13.2 dictates that "The court is duty-bound to protect justice, protect human rights, civil rights, social regimes, the interests of the State, and the legitimate rights and interests of organisations and individuals." Moreover, the Vietnamese Law on State Compensation Liability in 2017[165] specifies that state agencies conducting criminal, civil or administrative proceedings must provide compensation in instances where an unlawful act by an official in the line of duty results in damage.

Generally, Vietnamese law acknowledges the fundamental rights associated with the right to seek justice. Investors are thus assured of this right within Vietnam's territory. In summary, the requirement in Paragraph 2(a) Article 2.5 EVIPA is largely aligned with domestic law and does not impose additional obligations on Vietnam. However, as vital as establishing a comprehensive domestic legislative framework is the effective enforcement of legal regulations by relevant entities. Without efficient enforcement, the rights stipulated hold little practical significance, especially when enforcement entities lack sufficient resources, professional capabilities, and ethical standards.

The Justice Index,[166] a collaborative effort by the Vietnam Lawyers Association, the Centre for Community Support and Development Studies under the Vietnam Union of Science and Technology Associations, and the UNDP in 2015, highlighted critical issues within Vietnam's dispute resolution landscape. These concerns encompassed unclear procedures for dispute settlement, protracted processing times, and inefficiencies in dispute resolution. State agencies' assistance in resolving disputes and complaints was notably less effective than support provided by

[162] National Assembly of Vietnam (2015), Criminal Procedure Code, No. 101/2015/QH13, 27 November 2015.

[163] National Assembly of Vietnam (2015), Law on Administrative Procedures, No. 93/2015/QH13, 25 November 2015.

[164] National Assembly of Vietnam (2015), Civil Procedure Code, No. 92/2015/QH13, 25 November 2015 with amendments in 2019.

[165] National Assembly of Vietnam (2017) Law on State Compensation Liability, No. 10/2017/QH14, 20 June 2017.

[166] VLA and UNDP Vietnam (2016), pp. 54–55.

lawyers and legal aid providers. Furthermore, limitations in accessing the court stemmed from concerns about the cost, procedural complexity, and confidence in the integrity of judges and court staff. Moreover, disparities in access to justice persisted among diverse social groups, with those who were economically disadvantaged, possessed lower educational attainment, or were not part of the social elite encountering difficulties accessing information and local justice institutions due to their limited personal and social capital.

Addressing these systemic weaknesses presents a substantial challenge, and improvements remain elusive in the short-term. Thus, the Justice Index of Vietnam for 2015 retains its relevance as it continues to reflect the persisting issues within the country's administrative and judicial management system. The index's portrayal of ineffectiveness underscores that the central and enduring challenge within Vietnam's legal system lies in the enforcement of laws. Neglecting to address this issue may engender the possibility of breaches of the denial of justice requirement under FET clause of the EVIPA.

(ii) Due process

While not explicitly enshrined, the 2013 Constitution of Vietnam indirectly embodies the essence of due process,[167] which is closely akin to the global concepts of the "right to due process" and the "right to a fair trial." Drawing from the foundational principles outlined in the 2015 Civil Procedure Code, it is evident that Vietnamese law recognises fundamental procedural fairness rights in civil proceedings. These include:[168]

- The right to petition the court to safeguard legitimate rights and interests (the right to access the court) (Article 4); the right to be trialed by an independent, impartial, and unbiased court (Article 12).
- The right to a prompt, equitable, and public trial (Article 15). Additionally, the court's principle of a prompt, fair, and public trial is acknowledged in Article 103 of the 2013 Constitution and Article 11 of the Law on the Organisation of the People's Courts in 2014.
- The right to ensure litigation: The principle of ensuring litigation within trials is officially recognised in Article 103 of the 2013 Constitution, Article 13 of the Law on the Organisation of the People's Courts in 2014, and Article 24 of the Civil Procedure Code in 2015.

The assurance of rights related to due process under Vietnamese law closely parallels the provisions in Paragraph 2(b) of Article 2.5 of the EVIPA. Therefore, investors' due process rights are fundamentally protected. Nevertheless, as research has indicated,[169] the approach of Vietnamese legislators is not inherently "rights-based," which results in the indirect derivation of due process rights from the principles of

[167] Dat (2020), p. 3.

[168] See rights of due process in Civil procedures in Vietnam in Quan and Thao (2020), pp. 51–62.

[169] Ibid.; Dung (2019), p. 98.

civil procedure law. Indeed, the 2015 Vietnamese Civil Code notably lacks explicit principles articulating litigants' rights while primarily concentrating on regulations concerning the responsibilities and status of the entity conducting the proceedings.[170]

As for the litigation practices within the court, as shown by studies, a multitude of legal proceedings have encountered issues with proper execution.[171] Numerous cases involving the temporary suspension of case resolutions often lack a legal basis, infringing upon trial preparation deadlines. Furthermore, the collection of documents and evidence within court proceedings tends to be incomplete and insufficient, and the evaluation of evidence frequently lacks objectivity and comprehensiveness. As a result, improper application of the law frequently leads to erroneous decisions in dispute settlements. A report summarising the court's activities in 2022 revealed that the rate of judgments and decisions annulled or amended due to subjective reasons of the Court was approximately 0.9%.[172] While this figure may not appear substantial in isolation, it becomes more significant when viewed within the context of the total number of cases the court handles each year. In 2022 alone, the Court accepted a staggering 567.521 cases and resolved 504.681 cases.[173] However, it is important to note that this rate is a relative indicator, as it does not encompass other, albeit less severe, cases of procedural errors. These errors may include violations of trial preparation deadlines, incorrect legal determinations, or flawed liability assessments, even if they do not result in annulled or amended judgments.

This practice in Vietnam shows that the requirements for due process in international law may not perfectly align with the framework established in Vietnamese legislation and dispute settlement practice. These disparities in approach and the constraints in applying due process could be a notable concern for Vietnam upon the entry into force of the EVIPA.

(iii) Arbitrary

In Vietnam, efforts to control arbitrary conduct primarily revolve around legal measures aimed at enhancing the efficiency of both the judicial and administrative systems. These measures include the provisions mentioned earlier concerning due process requirements, along with regulations pertaining to the responsibilities of state judicial and administrative agencies, and state judicial officers such as judges and prosecutors. For instance, Article 266.2(b) of the 2015 Civil Procedure Code stipulates that: "*The court must base its decisions on the results of the litigation and the evidence examined during court hearings to analyse, evaluate, and comment on the circumstances of the case, the legal grounds, etc., to accept or reject the requests or proposals of the parties...*"

---

[170] Quan and Thao (2020), p. 61.

[171] Dung (2019), p. 98.

[172] Supreme People's Court of the Socialist Republic of Viet Nam (2022).

[173] Ibid.

However, the practical implementation of these regulations has proven to be relatively ineffective. This observation is supported by the findings of a specific study, which indicates that in numerous instances, the court issues awards without providing detailed explanations, merely invoking the applicable law.[174] As a result, the litigation process may appear to be a mere formality if the court's decision fails to reflect the outcomes of the parties' arguments. In addition, it is not uncommon for judgments or decisions to exhibit an incomplete consideration of the arguments presented by the parties, and in some instances, they may even lack a coherent rationale based on the court's decision-making process.[175]

Furthermore, in the context of investment and environmental management activities, as presented in Chaps. 3 and 4, licensing and management activities are gradually improving in the legislative system towards greater transparency and decentralisation of responsibilities. However, similar to the limitations mentioned above, this requirement can be violated, especially in cases where the capacity and moral qualities of state officials are not guaranteed. Therefore, administrative and judicial decisions must be carefully considered before being issued.

(iv) Discrimination

In Vietnam, regulations against discrimination are enshrined in various laws, with the Constitution of 2013 being the most prominent. Article 16 of the 2013 Constitution underscores the principle of equality and non-discrimination. The State is committed to ensuring equal rights and opportunities for all genders (Article 26.1) and explicitly prohibits gender-based discrimination (Article 26.3). Furthermore, Article 35 of the 2013 Constitution prohibits discrimination, forced labour, and the exploitation of workers below the minimum working age.

In response to the need to fulfil commitments arising from recently signed FTAs like the CPTPP and EVFTA, which are linked to the ILO Conventions, adjustments have been made to the Vietnam Labour Code. These changes incorporate requirements to prohibit sex-based discrimination, bringing the country's legislation closer to the principles outlined in ILO Conventions 111 and 100.

In addition to being guaranteed in the 2013 Constitution, the principle of non-discrimination is further elaborated in specialised legal documents, such as the 2015 Criminal Code (Amended in 2017) (Article 3.1(b)), 2015 Criminal Procedure Code (Article 9), 2015 Civil Code (Article 8), 2015 Civil Procedure Code (Article 8).[176]

In commercial business relationships, this regulation is included in Vietnam's Enterprise Law 2020 (Law No. 59/2020/QH14) (Article 5.3), especially in activities involving the nationalisation of assets and capital of enterprises. The Vietnam Commercial Law 2005 provides fundamental principles in commercial activities, with Article 10 emphasising that "traders of all economic sectors are equal before the law in commercial activities."

[174] Quan and Thao (2020), p. 62.

[175] Ibid., p. 62.

[176] Nghi (2012), p. 6.

This demonstrates Vietnam's comprehensive approach to combating discrimination and promoting equal treatment under the law. Therefore, the provisions concerning non-discrimination, particularly the obligation of equal treatment in commercial activities, are firmly established within the framework of national legislation. While not documented with the same level of detail, the fundamental rationale for this requirement has been articulated. Consequently, through the effective implementation of these regulations, the essential prerequisites related to the FET clause are firmly established, thereby minimising potential challenges for Vietnam.

(v) Abusive Treatment of Investors, such as Coercion, Duress and Harassment

Under Vietnamese law, coercion and harassment are not classified as criminal offences; however, administrative sanctions are in place to address such behaviours.[177] In cases where public officials engage in illegal conduct during state administrative activities, criminal proceedings, civil proceedings, or administrative proceedings, resulting in actual damage, the 2017 Law on State Compensation Liability (Articles 8, 9, 10) allows for compensation claims against the state. Essentially, the provisions in Paragraph 2(e) Article 2.5 EVIPA do not impose more stringent requirements than those already present in Vietnamese law.

However, in environmental protection, actions taken by the executive branch in implementing regulations and decisions made by the judicial power often result in an increased number of specific and targeted cases compared to legislative measures.[178] Therefore, it is essential to exercise prudence when implementing administrative and judicial decisions regarding investment and environmental management to prevent the potential establishment of grounds for FET standard violations.

7.5 Interim Conclusion

Numerous design models have been proposed by international institutions such as the Commonwealth and UNCTAD for drafting the FET clause. Nevertheless, the selection of the final model ultimately rests with the parties, contingent on their objectives and expectations within their relationship. In the case of EVIPA, the analysis in this chapter demonstrates that the FET provisions included in the EVIPA offer a solid foundation for future tribunal assessments of claims related to FET standard violations. The choice of the Parties to include an exhaustive list can be considered as an innovative approach that moves beyond the longstanding debate about whether the FET standard is purely derived from customary international law or functions as an independent treaty standard. This progress allows the host state to regulate more effectively, leading to enhanced predictability and minimising

[177] Art 7.5(đ) Decree 144/2021/NĐ-CP (31 December 2021) on Administrative penalties for violations against regulations on social safety, security, order; social evils, fire prevention and firefighting; rescue; domestic violence prevention and control.

[178] Martini (2017), p. 544.

situations that trigger legitimate expectations of investors. The improvements aim to significantly limit the role of investor's legitimate expectations in the relationship with FET standards in IPAs signed by the EU, thereby arguably helping preserve the state's policy space to regulate in the public interest.[179]

While there may be some clarity issues in the wording, the choices made by the Parties are anticipated to establish a high threshold for determining a breach of the FET standard. This provision, therefore, provides the contracting state with increased regulatory authority over environmental matters, alongside the investor's ability to file claims against the state. This grants the state greater flexibility in implementing reasonable environmental measures, but it must exercise due diligence. Striking the right balance is crucial, as an overly broad scope may lead to underutilisation by the state while jeopardising the investor's rights, resulting in an imbalance of interests between the two parties.

The analysis in this chapter yields the following conclusions:

(i) The FET clause has been clarified and significantly limited to aid tribunals in better interpreting the parties' intentions. This is especially evident in the provision of an exhaustive list and the restriction on applying of legitimate expectations within the initial scope of the FET standard. The exhaustive list of FET standard violations in Article 2.5 EVIPA closely aligns with dispute resolution practices concerning fair and equitable treatment. This familiarity is expected to facilitate tribunals in conducting the necessary examinations. Thus, this provision ensures the exercise of public authority in management, administrative, and judicial activities without resulting in manifestly arbitrary or discriminatory treatment of investors. It provides a basic standard of treatment to investors, maintaining the essence of investment protection while limiting the scope of these standards, ultimately safeguarding the state's right to implement policy measures. From this perspective, such FET clauses help mitigate the risk of regulatory interference compared to those with illustrative lists.

(ii) Requirements related to the FET standard, such as regulations ensuring the right to seek justice, the right to a fair trial, protection against discrimination, and protection against arbitrary treatment, are essentially recognised in Vietnamese law. Therefore, the provisions outlined in the FET clause do not impose greater obligations on Vietnam. Nonetheless, a critical concern lies in the law enforcement by state agencies to guarantee compliance with the principles of the rule of law. Generally, promoting transparency is widely recognised as an effective strategy to reduce the likelihood of arbitrary and discriminatory government decision-making, thus minimising the potential for disputes.[180] This observation is also supported by insights from dispute resolution practice[181] as stated by the tribunal in *Urbaser v. Argentina* that the state's

[179] Levashova (2019), p. 265.

[180] Grierson-Weiler and Laird (2008), p. 285.

[181] See, for instance, *Waste Management v. United Mexican States* [2000] ICSID Case No. ARB(AF)/00/3, Award, 30 April 2004, para. 98.

conduct must align with the specific requirements under the FET standard.[182] Therefore, this issue is of paramount importance and requires enhancement to minimise the risk of breaching the FET clause. Conversely, ensuring adherence to the requirements delineated by the FET standard also offers advantages to the host state by promoting good governance.[183] This aspect is undeniably a vital factor contributing to a nation's broader development objectives.

References

ISDS Cases

Abengoa S.A. y COFIDES S.A. v. United Mexican States [2009] ICSID Case No. ARB(AF)/09/2
Alex Genin, Eastern Credit Limited, Inc. and A.S. Baltoil v The Republic of Estonia [1999] ICSID Case No. ARB/99/2
AWG Group Ltd. v. The Argentine Republic [2003] UNCITRAL
Biwater Gauff (Tanzania) Ltd. v United Republic of Tanzania [2005] ICSID Case No. ARB/05/22
Chemtura Corporation v Government of Canada [2002] PCA Case No. 2008-01
Clayton and Bilcon of Delaware Inc. v. Government of Canada [2008] UNCITRAL, NAFTA, PCA Case No. 2009-04
CMS Gas Transmission Company v. The Republic of Argentina [2001] ICSID Case No. ARB/01/8
Crystallex International Corporation v. Bolivarian Republic of Venezuela [2011] ICSID Case No. ARB(AF)/11/2
Desert Line Projects LLC v. The Republic of Yemen [2005] ICSID Case No. ARB/05/17
EDF (Services) Limited v. Rumani [2005] ICSID Case No. ARB/05/13
Eiser Infrastructure Limited and Energia Solar Luxembourg S.à.r.l v. Kingdom of Spain [2013] ICSID Case No. ARB/13/36
Enron Creditors Recovery Corporation and Ponderosa Assets, L.P. v. Argentine Republic [2001] ICSID Case No. ARB/01/3
Frontier Petroleum Services v. Czech Republic [2007] UNCITRAL
Glamis Gold Ltd. v. United States of America [2003] UNCITRAL, NAFTA
Impregilo S.p.A. v. Argentine Republic [2007] ICSID Case No. ARB/07/17
International Thunderbird Gaming Corporation v. United Mexican States [2002] UNCITRAL, NAFTA
Jan Oostergetel and Theodora Laurentius v. Slovak Republic [2006] UNCITRAL

[182] *Urbaser S.A. and Consorcio de Aguas Bilbao Bizkaia, Bilbao Biskaia Ur Partzuergoa v. The Argentine Republic* [2007] ICSID Case No. ARB/07/26, Award, 8 December 2016, para. 622.
[183] UNCTAD (2018), p. 35.

LG&E Energy Corp., LG&E Capital Corp. and LG&E International Inc v. Argentine Republic [2002] ICSID Case No. ARB/02/1
Marion Unglaube and Reinhard Unglaube v Republic of Costa Rica [2009] ICSID Case No. ARB/08/1 and ARB/09/20
Marvin Roy Feldman Karpa v. United Mexican States [1999] ICSID Case No. ARB(AF)/99/1
Merrill and Ring Forestry v. Government of Canada [2006] ICSID Case No. UNCT/07/1
Mesa Power Group, LLC v. Canada [2011] PCA Case No. 2012-17
Metalclad Corporation v. United Mexican States [1997] ICSID Case No. ARB(AF)/97/1
Methanex Corporation v. United States of America [1999] UNCITRAL, 44 ILM 1345
Mondev International Ltd v. United States of America [1999] ICSID Case No. ARB(AF)/99/2
MTD Equity Sdn and MTD Chile SA. v. Republic of Chile [2001] ICSID Case No. ARB/01/7
National Grid P.L.C. v. Argentine Republic [2006] UNCITRAL
Parkerings-Compagniet v. Lithuania [2005] ICSID Case No. ARB/05/8
Philip Morris Brands Sàrl, Philip Morris Products S.A. and Abal Hermanos S.A. v. Oriental Republic of Uruguay [2010] ICSID Case No. ARB/10/7
Plama Consortium Limited v. Republic of Bulgaria [2003] ICSID Case No. ARB/03/24
Pope & Talbot Inc. v. The Government of Canada [1999] UNCITRAL
Robert Azinian, Kenneth Davitian, & Ellen Baca v. The United Mexican States [1997] ICSID Case No. ARB(AF)/97/2
Ronald S Lauder v. Czech Republic [1999] UNCITRAL
S.D. Myers, Inc. v. Canada [1998] UNCITRAL, NAFTA
Saluka Investments BV v. The Czech Republic [2001] UNCITRAL, PCA Case No. 2001-04
Spyridon Roussalis v. Romania [2006] ICSID Case No. ARB/06/1
Suez, Sociedad General de Aguas de Barcelona SA, and InterAguas Servicios Integrales del Agua SA v. The Argentine Republic [2003] ICSID Case No. ARB/03/17
Técnicas Medioambientales Tecmed, S.A. v. The United Mexican States [1999] ICSID Case No. ARB(AF)/00/2
Total S.A. v. The Argentine Republic [2004] ICSID Case No. ARB/04/1
Urbaser S.A. and Consorcio de Aguas Bilbao Bizkaia, Bilbao Biskaia Ur Partzuergoa v. Argentine Republic [2007] ICSID Case No. ARB/07/26
Vattenfall AB, Vattenfall Europe AG, Vattenfall Europe Generation AG v. Federal Republic of Germany [2009] ICSID Case No. ARB/09/6
Waste Management v. United Mexican States (II) [2000] ICSID Additional Facility, ICSID Case No. ARB(AF)/00/3
Windstream Energy LLC v. Government of Canada [2013] PCA Case No. 2013-22
Yulia Bogdanova v. Republic of Moldova [2012] SCC Case No. 091/2012

Treaties

ASEAN Comprehensive Investment Agreement (ACIA)
Bulgaria - United Kingdom BIT (1995)
Canada Model BIT (2021) (FIPA)
Comprehensive and Progressive Agreement for Trans-Pacific Partnership (2018) (CPTPP)
Canada - EU Comprehensive Economic and Trade Agreement (2016) (CETA)
EU - Vietnam Investment Protection Agreement (2019) (EVIPA)
France - Mexico BIT (1998)
Germany Model BIT (2008)
North America Free Trade Agreement (1992) (NAFTA)
US Model BIT (2012)
Vienna Convention on the Law of Treaty (1969) (VCLT)

Bibliography

Banerjee A, Weber S (2021) The 2019 Morocco Model BIT: moving forwards, backwards or roundabout in circles? ICSID Rev 36(3):536–562

Benedetto SD (2013) International investment law and the environment. Edward Elgar, Cheltenham

Bernasconi-Osterwalder N, Brauch MD, Schacherer S (2018) International investment law and sustainable development: key cases from 2010s. International Institute for Sustainable Development

Berner K (2016) Reconciling investment protection and sustainable development-a plea for an interpretative U-turn. In: Hindelang S, Krajewski M (eds) Shifting paradigms in international investment law: more balanced, less isolated, increasingly diversified. Oxford University Press, Oxford

Bonnitcha J (2014) Substantive protection under investment treaties: a legal and economic analysis. Cambridge University Press

Chi M (2018) Integrating sustainable development in international investment law: normative incompatibility, system integration and governance implications. Routledge

Coleman J, Johnson LJ, Sachs LE, Lobel N (2019) International Investment Agreements 2017 – a review of trends and new approaches. In: Sachs L, Johnson LJ, Coleman J (eds) Yearbook on international investment law and policy 2017. Oxford University Press, Oxford

Dat Bui Tien (2020) Due-process-evading justice: the case of Vietnam. Int J Law Crime Justice 63. https://www.sciencedirect.com/science/article/pii/S1756061620300768

Dolzer R (2007) The impact of international investment treaties on domestic administrative law. NYU J Int Law Polit 37:953–972

Dolzer R, Schreuer C (2012) Principles of international investment law, 2nd edn. Oxford University Press, Oxford

Drukteiniene S, Paleviciene S (2020) Limits of state regulatory power in investment law and under national legislation: search for common denominator. Entrepreneurs Sustain Iss 8(2):1197–1210. https://doi.org/10.9770/jesi.2020.8.2(71)

Dung Tran Chi (2019) Bảo vệ Công lý trong Hoạt động Xét xử của Toà án Nhân dân ở Việt Nam hiện nay [Ensuring Justice in Trials of the Vietnamese People's Court]. Doctoral Dissertation. Ha Noi Law University. https://drive.google.com/file/d/1P-n74aVOgQEMYYQ1p7Uu3AlGyv12z2E-/view

Grierson-Weiler T, Laird IA (2008) Standards of treatment. In: Muchlinski P, Ortino F, Schreuer C (eds) The Oxford handbook of international investment law. Oxford University Press, Oxford

Ha Le Thi Ngoc (2021) Vietnam's international investment agreements: various substantive compatibility thresholds for legislative measures. Doctoral Dissertation. La Trobe University

Hai Nguyen Thi Thanh (2019) Pháp luật Quốc tế về Quyền Tiếp cận Công lý và Thực tiễn ở Việt Nam [International law on the right to access to justice and practice in Vietnam]. Vietnam J Soc Sci 4:73

Henckels C (2016) Protecting regulatory autonomy through greater precision in investment treaties: the TPP, CETA and TTIP. J Int Econ Law 19(1):27–50. https://doi.org/10.1093/jiel/jgw001

Jacob M, Schill SW (2017) Fair and equitable treatment: content, practice, method. Amsterdam Law School Legal Studies Research Paper No. 2017-24. ACIL Research Paper 2017-2020

Keller M (ed) (2023) EU Investment Protection Law – Chapter Eight of CETA, Vietnam and Singapore Free Trade Agreement and EU Regulations 1219/2012, 912/2014 and 2019/452: Article by article commentary. C.H. Beck, Hart Publishing and Nomos Verlagsgesellschaft

Kingsbury B, Schill SW (2010) Public law concepts to balance investors rights with state regulatory actions in the public interest – the concept of proportionality. In: Schill SW (ed) International investment law and comparative public law. Oxford University Press, Oxford, pp 75–104

Kläger R (2011) Fair and equitable treatment. In: International Investment Law. Cambridge University Press, Cambridge

Kläger R (2016) Revising treatment standards – fair and equitable treatment in light of sustainable development. In: Hindelang S, Krajewski M (eds) Shifting paradigms in international investment law: more balanced, less isolated, increasingly diversified. Oxford University Press, Oxford

Kriebaum U (2016) FET and expropriation in the comprehensive economic trade agreement between the European Union and Canada (CETA). Transnatl Dispute Manag 13(1)

Levashova Y (2019) The right of states to regulate in international investment law: the search for balance between public interest and fair and equitable treatment. Wolters Kluwer

Martini C (2017) Balancing investors' rights with environmental protection in international investment arbitration: an assessment of recent trends in investment treaty drafting. Int Lawyer 50(3):529–584

Muchlinski P (2016) Negotiating new generation international investment agreements: new sustainable development oriented initiatives. In: Hindelang S, Krajewski M (eds) Shifting paradigms in international investment law: more balanced, less isolated, increasingly diversified. Oxford University Press, Oxford

Newcombe A, Paradell L (2009) Law and practice of investment treaties: standards of treatment. Kluwer Law International

Nghi Pham Huu (2012) Nguyên tắc bình đẳng, không phân biệt đối xử trong Tuyên ngôn thế giới về quyền con người và trong pháp luật Việt Nam [Principle of Equality and Non-Discrimination in the Universal Declaration of Human Rights]. World Law J 6

Nyer D (2015) The investment chapter of the EU-Canada Comprehensive Economic and Trade Agreement. J Int Arbitration 32(6):697–710

Ortino F (2017) Investment treaties, sustainable development and reasonableness review: a case against strict proportionality balancing. Leiden J Int Law 30(1):77–91

Van QN, Bich TN (2020) Các Quyền Thủ tục Công bằng trong Tố tụng Dân sự ở một số Quốc gia trên Thế giới và ở Việt Nam [Due Process Rights in Civil Procedures: A Comparative Study of Vietnam and Selected Countries]. VNU J Sci Legal Stud 36(1):51–62. https://doi.org/10.25073/2588-1167/vnuls.4282

Reinisch A, Schreuer C (2020) International protection of investments: the substantive standards. Cambridge University Press, Cambridge

Schefer KN (2020) International investment law: text, cases and materials, 3rd edn. Edward Elgar, Cheltenham

Schill SW (2009) The multilateralization of international investment law. Cambridge University Press, Cambridge

Subedi SP (2008) International investment law – reconciling policy and principle. Hart Publishing

Supreme People's Court of the Socialist Republic of Viet Nam (2022) Summary Report and Strategic Directions for Courts in 2023. https://www.toaan.gov.vn/webcentre/portal/tdkt/chitiettthongbao?dDocName=TAND284234

Swedish National Board of Trade (2015) "The Right to Regulate" in the Trade Agreement between the EU and Canada – and its implications for the agreement with the USA
Tudor I (2008) The fair and equitable treatment standard in the international law of foreign investment. Oxford University Press, Oxford
UNCTAD (2012a) Fair and equitable treatment: a sequel. UNTAD Series on Issues in International Investment Agreement II
UNCTAD (2012b) International policy framework for sustainable development, 2012 edn. https://unctad.org/publication/investment-policy-framework-sustainable-development-2012-edition
UNCTAD (2015) Investment policy framework for sustainable development, 2015 edn. https://unctad.org/publication/investment-policy-framework-sustainable-development-2015-edition
UNCTAD (2018) UNCTAD's Reform Package for the International Investment Regime. https://investmentpolicy.unctad.org/uploaded-files/document/UNCTAD_Reform_Package_2018.pdf
VLA and UNDP Vietnam (2016) 2015 Justice Index: towards a justice system for the people. https://www.undp.org/vietnam/publications/2015-justice-index
Valenti M (2014) The protection of general interests of host states in the application of the fair and equitable treatment standard. In: Sacerdoti G, Acconci P, Valenti M, De Luca A (eds) General interests of host states in international investment law. Cambridge University Press, Cambridge
Vandevelde KJ (2010a) Bilateral investment treaties-history, policy, and interpretation. Oxford University Press, Oxford
Vandevelde KJ (2010b) A unified theory of fair & equitable treatment. NYU J Int'l L Pol 43(1):43–106. https://papers.ssrn.com/sol3/papers.cfm?abstract_id=2357642.
Viñuales JE (2012) Foreign investment and the environment in international law. Cambridge University Press
Zhu Y (2018) Fair and equitable treatment of foreign investors in an era of sustainable development. Nat Resour J 58(2):319–364

Documents

EU Council (2012) Meeting document from the European Commission to the Trade Policy Committee on EU - Canada Comprehensive and Economic Trade Agreement - Landing zones. DS 1744/12. https://www.bilaterals.org/IMG/pdf/-29.pdf
EU Council (2016) Joint Interpretative Instrument on the Comprehensive Economic and Trade Agreement (CETA) between Canada and the European Union and its Member States. 13541/16, Brussels. https://data.consilium.europa.eu/doc/document/ST-13541-2016-INIT/en/pdf
European Parliament (2011) Resolution on the Future European International Investment Policy.
Government of Vietnam (2021). Decree 144/2021/NĐ-CP on Administrative penalties for violations against regulations on social safety, security, order; social evils, fire prevention and firefighting; rescue; domestic violence prevention and control (31 December 2021)
NAFTA Free Trade Commission (2001) Notes of Interpretation of Certain Chapter 11 Provisions. http://www.sice.oas.org/tpd/nafta/Commission/CH11understanding_e.asp
National Assembly of Vietnam (2015) Civil Procedure Code No. 92/2015/QH13 (25 November 2015) with amendments in 2019
National Assembly of Vietnam (2015) Criminal Procedure Code No. 101/2015/QH13 (27 November 2015)
National Assembly of Vietnam (2015) Law No. 93/2015/QH13 on Administrative Procedures (25 November 2015)
National Assembly of Vietnam (2017) Law No. 10/2017/QH14 on State Compensation Liability (20 June 2017)

Chapter 8
Preamble and the Right-to-Regulate Clause in the EVIPA

Abstract Chapter 1 briefly introduced the intertwined concepts of sustainable development and the right to regulate. In fact, sustainable development is inherently embedded in the right to regulate, particularly through environmental protection, which constitutes one of the three pillars of sustainable development. Therefore, this chapter examines these two concepts collectively, although each is explored in separate sections.

Historically, in earlier IIAs, the right to regulate was commonly assessed in the context of regulatory measures accused of violating indirect expropriation, FET, or NT. However, it was not typically considered as an independent clause on the right to regulate. Regarding such an independent regulatory clause, it remains to be seen what precedents the ICS tribunal will rely on. Therefore, the evaluation of the EVIPA's provisions is primarily based on existing observations drawn from relevant ISDS practice.

Furthermore, similar to the case of indirect expropriation or FET, the focus on regulatory measures involves evaluating how these measures have been implemented, placing requirements on the host state related to good faith and transparency. This chapter will not reevaluate these aspects concerning Vietnam's domestic regulations. Instead, it examines the experience accumulated from ISDS practice. It anticipates the approaches that ICS tribunals may adopt to balance public and private interests when reviewing the provision on the right to regulate included in the EVIPA.

N. T. Lan Huong, *Investment Protection and Environmental Governance*, European Yearbook of International Economic Law 47,
https://doi.org/10.1007/978-3-032-05332-9_8

8.1 Sustainable Development, Environmental Concerns and the Right to Regulate in International Investment Law and ISDS Practice

- **Sustainable Development**

As mentioned before, early IIAs seldom mentioned sustainable development, environmental protection, or the ongoing regulatory authority of host states[1] because these agreements prioritised stability and favourable conditions for investments and cooperation.[2] Over time, an increasing number of investment treaties are now incorporating environmental concerns, and there is a diverse range of approaches. A survey by the OECD, conducted since 2011 covering 1623 IIAs, reveals this trend.[3] Among the seven types of provisions addressing environmental concerns in IIAs, integrating these concerns into the general language in preambles was the second most frequently observed provision.[4]

Regarding the inclusion of the term "sustainable development," several agreements explicitly incorporate it into the preamble. Examples include NAFTA, COMESA, the Australia–Chile FTA, and several Canadian IIAs. Specifically, NAFTA expresses the Parties' commitment to "Promote sustainable development." In some cases, IIAs indirectly refer to sustainable development through components such as the obligation to achieve economic development "in a manner consistent with the protection of health, safety, and the environment, and the promotion of internationally recognised labour rights" (as seen in the United States–Rwanda BIT) or "without relaxing regulatory standards in fields of environment, health, or safety" (as observed in IIAs signed by Finland, the Netherlands, Japan, and the United States).[5]

As can be seen, incorporating sustainable development and environmental concerns into the preamble is a favoured means for countries to address non-investment concerns in their IIAs. However, merely acknowledging these issues without establishing a hierarchy between objectives[6] and without incorporating them into substantive provisions does not significantly balance the host state's right to regulate with the investment protection objective.

- **The Right to Regulate**

---

[1] However, there is an exception. Some preambles in Bilateral Investment Treaties (BITs) signed between the United States and its partners during the 1990s explicitly state that the parties will not relax health, safety, and environmental measures of general application. See Honduras–US BIT (1995); Nicaragua–US BIT (1995); Croatia–US BIT (1996); Jordan–US BIT (1997); Bolivia–US BIT (1998); El Salvador–US BIT (1999).

[2] Muchlinski (2016), p. 46; Henckels (2016), p. 28.

[3] Gordon, Pohl (2011), p. 12.

[4] Ibid., p. 13.

[5] Gehring, Kent (2013), p. 203.

[6] Ibid., p. 16.

Undoubtedly, over the decades, the states' primary focus when drafting IIAs has been to enhance investment conditions for investors from contracting states to the agreement. Consequently, similar to the concept of "sustainable development," the right to regulate has been given limited attention in trade and investment agreements.[7] However, arbitral practices have highlighted that even reasonable and legitimate actions taken by states can be financially burdensome due to the risk of facing claims from foreign investors.

Divergent opinions have emerged after the rendering of final awards in various cases, questioning whether tribunals have done justice to disputing states by considering the factual backgrounds and objective circumstances of the case. This scrutiny partly arises from the absence of specific provisions regarding the state's right to regulate or the failure to reaffirm this right in earlier IIAs. It should be noted that the lack of a substantive clause on the right to regulate in IIAs does not eliminate its relevance in the context of ISDS.[8] On the contrary, as Trujillo observes, investment tribunals have tended to display a greater respect for the regulatory frameworks established by the parties involved than their counterparts in trade dispute resolution.[9] Nonetheless, despite this tendency, the scope of the right to regulate within traditional IIAs remain somewhat ambiguous. In light of the escalating concerns regarding environmental sustainability and human rights, the conversation about the right to regulate is gaining substantial traction. This dialogue is becoming increasingly important in the negotiation of both trade agreements and BITs.[10]

Indeed, one of the most crucial approaches to address the tension between investment protection standards and broader non-investment considerations, which has gained prominence in recent years, involves acknowledging the regulatory powers of the state.[11] Indeed, scholars believe that establishing an adequate balance in international investment agreements is best achieved by affirming the host state's right to regulate.[12] Within this framework, the term "public interests," expressed in various forms such as "common concerns," "general interest," or "public purpose," particularly within general international law, including IIL,[13] inherently encompasses environmental and human rights protection. Consequently, it substantively aligns and overlaps with the principles of sustainable development. Such a provision is anticipated to serve as a "last" affirmation by contracting states regarding the sovereignty right of host states to adopt and implement measures that address their

[7] Hush (2018), p. 104.

[8] This right can be explored alongside several significant legal doctrines in IIL such as indirect expropriation, fair and equitable treatment, and national treatment. Se further in Trujillo (2018), pp. 2739–2740.

[9] Ibid., pp. 2738–2739.

[10] Ibid.

[11] Viñuales (2012), p. 291.

[12] Bacchus (2018), p. 281.

[13] Chi (2018a), p. 88; Kulick (2012); Sacerdoti G et al. (ed.) (2014).

specific public concerns. This regulation is designed to offer comprehensive coverage for state regulatory actions across all areas related to regulatory objectives.[14]

Regarding preserving the right to regulate, until 2018, states primarily safeguarded their right to regulate through preambular clauses, non-precluded measures clauses, general provisions, and non-lowering of standards clauses.[15] As an illustration, the 2016 Slovakia–Iran BIT included the following language in the preamble: "Acknowledging the rights and responsibilities of the Contracting Parties to regulate investment within their territories to meet their own policy objectives." However, it's important to note that preambles do not establish independent legal rights or obligations within the context of the interpretation of international investment treaties.[16] They have typically been employed by some tribunals to address interpretative gaps in the treaty. Therefore, the preamble functions as a balancing tool for host states, aiding in securing regulatory space and preventing overly broad interpretations of investment protection guarantees by investor-state tribunals.

The significant role of the preamble in supporting the interpretation of substantive provisions in treaties is backed by the VCLT Articles 31.1 and 31.2. Article 31.2(a) of the Vienna Convention explains the term "context" in Article 31.1, explicitly referencing the role of the preamble and annexes in interpreting a treaty: "...The context for the purpose of the interpretation of a treaty shall comprise, in addition to the text, including its preamble and annexes…". Therefore, including the term "sustainable development" imposes an obligation on the investment tribunal to clarify it within the relevant context.

Despite the support of the VCLT on the interpretative role of treaty preambles, the practice in ISDS reveals a lack of serious consideration for the role of the preamble by investment tribunals. For instance, in the *Metalclad v. Mexico* case, despite NAFTA's Preamble explicitly mentioning the protection of the environment and sustainable development,[17] the tribunal did not consider the environmental purpose of the measure when interpreting the notion of a measure tantamount to expropriation under Article 1110.2 of NAFTA.[18]

Notably, many investment tribunals continue to prioritise protecting investments and the creation of favourable conditions for investments.[19] This perspective often stems from the fact that environmental protection is usually mentioned in IIAs as a

[14] VanDuzer et al. (2013), p. 239.

[15] Coleman et al. (2018), p. 74.

[16] Newcombe and Paradell (2009), p. 124.

[17] The NAFTA's Preamble states that the parties are committed to "ensure a predictable commercial framework for business planning and investment... in a manner consistent with environmental protection and conservation;" and to "promote sustainable development… and strengthen the development and enforcement of environmental laws and regulations."

[18] Martini (2017), p. 566.

[19] For instance, *MTD Equity Sdn. Bhd. And MTD Chile S.A. v. Chile* (*MTD v. Chile*) [2001], ICSID Case No. ARB/01/7, Award, 25 May 2004, para. 104; *SGS Société Générale de Surveillance S.A. v. Republic of the Philippines* (*SGS v. Philippines*) [2002] ICSID Case No. ARB/02/6, Award, 29 January 2004, para. 116. See further, Spears (2011), pp. 291–292; See also Martini (2017), p. 565.

concern rather than an "objective." Consequently, the common conception of tribunals regarding the object and purpose of IIAs poses a significant challenge for environmental references inserted in preambles.[20] Due to these factors, the anticipated contributions to the interpretative role of the Preamble are likely to be less effective.

In response to this trend, in addition to mentioning the right to regulate in the preamble, countries seek other ways to acknowledge this right. In the drafting and negotiation of IIAs, references to the right to regulate, or what can be called as safeguard provisions,[21] may be found in the preamble, in separate or independent substantive provisions, in general exception clauses, non-lowering of standards provisions, or clarifications of specific treaty standards that strongly constrain regulatory space, as discussed in Chaps. 6 and 7.[22] Another indirect method to protect the state's policy space is to narrow the scope of certain agreements.[23] Overall, the scope and form of regulatory provisions differ significantly across investor protection provisions, bringing varying impacts to the host state's right to regulate.[24] However, despite earnest attempts to safeguard regulatory space, skepticism from scholars persists.[25] Part of the reason for this skepticism will be discussed in this chapter. To assess the effectiveness of including a substantive provision that reserves the state's right to regulate, this section examines the origin and standing of this right in both international law and ISDS practice.

Broadly recognised as a "basic attribute of sovereignty under international law,"[26] the right to regulate is the bedrock for any regulatory actions undertaken by a host state.[27] These regulatory endeavours aim to safeguard public interests concerning health, the environment, and human rights.[28] Given these characteristics, exercising the right to regulate often raises concerns about potential violations of investment standards designed to ensure the activities of investors within the host state's territory.

The problem arises when this right is examined under the context of relevant IIAs. While regulatory measures are acknowledged in many disputes,[29] as articu-

---

[20] Martini (2017), p. 565.

[21] Korzun (2017), p. 387.

[22] See further in Coleman et al. (2018), p. 72–73; Korzun (2017), pp. 387–388.

[23] Coleman et al. (2018), p. 74.

[24] See further Korzun (2017), p. 388.

[25] Coleman et al. (2018), p. 74.

[26] Titi (2014), p. 32.

[27] Baltag FCIArb et al. (2023), p. 385.

[28] Hindelang and Sassenrath (2015), p. 18.

[29] Some tribunals support the right to act in the public interest of the host state, as shown *Marvin Roy Feldman Karpa v. United Mexican States* (*Marvin Roy v. Mexico*) [1999] ICSID Case No. ARB(AF)/99/1, Award, 16 December 2002, para. 103; and *Methanex Corp. v. United States of America* (*Methanex v. USA*) [1999] UNCITRAL, 44 ILM 1345, Final Award on Jurisdiction and Merits, 3 August 2005, para. 9, 15. Other tribunals, although acknowledging the state's right to regulate, still held that the applied measure constitutes a breach of investment protection standards. See, for instance, *Venezuela Holdings BV, Mobil Cerro Negro Holding LTD et al. v. Venezuela* (*BG*

lated by the tribunal in *SAUR International SA v. Republic of Argentina*, "the exercise of these powers is not absolute and must, on the contrary, be combined with respect for the rights and guarantees guaranteed to the foreign investor" under the IIA.[30] Crucially, safeguarding the state's right to regulate may conflict with the overarching purpose for which IIAs were conceived and ratified, necessitating a narrow interpretation of exceptions designed to protect policy space.[31]

Due to this prevailing approach and the increasing number of policy measures facing claims in international investment arbitration, as highlighted throughout this book, discussions affirming respect for states' regulatory space are gaining recognition in both domestic and international forums. It is evident that, despite its existence beyond treaty law, the right to regulate is not firmly guaranteed in ISDS practice, particularly when this right lacks recognition through a substantive provision.

In the current landscape, recent analyses of international investment treaties highlight the frequent emergence of the term "right to regulate" in various contexts. This term has found its way into states' policy positions and public statements in negotiating IIAs. Following discussions at the domestic level, it has been incorporated into the texts of both new model IIAs and the next generation of agreements. On the global stage, the term has been a focal point in the broader debate on reforming the international investment regime.[32] Consequently, while questions surrounding the position of this right in the context of international investment law continue to grow, it is now uncommon to encounter new investment treaties that lack provisions preserving the state's right to regulate.[33]

The increasing references to the right to regulate in concluded IIAs are often seen as a response to the "regulatory chill" effect in host states where the fear of potential claims submitted to ISDS tribunals influences regulatory actions. Additionally, it addresses the growing imperative to safeguard the state's regulatory space in

---

Group v. Argentina) [2007] ICSID Case No. ARB/07/27, Award, 24 December 2007; *S.D. Myers, Inc. v. Government of Canada* (*SD Myers v. Canada*) [1998], UNCITRAL, NAFTA, partial Award, 13 November 2000; *Joseph Charles Lemire v. Ukraine* (*Lemire v. Ukraine*) [2006] ICSID Case No. ARB/06/18, Award, 28 March 2011.

[30] *SAUR International v. Argentine Republic* [2004], ICSID Case No. ARB/04/4, Award, 6 June 2012.

[31] *Enron Corporation and Ponderosa Assets, L.P. v. Argentine Republic* (*Enron v. Argentina*) [2001] ICSID Case No. ARB/01/3, Award, 22 May 2007, para. 331: "In examining this discussion, the Tribunal must first note that the object and purpose of the Treaty is, as a general proposition, to apply in situations of economic difficulty and hardship that require the protection of the international guaranteed rights of its beneficiaries. To this extent, any interpretation resulting in an escape route from the obligations defined cannot be easily reconciled with that object and purpose. Accordingly, a restrictive interpretation of any such alternative is mandatory." See also *Sempra Energy International v. Argentine Republic* (*Sempra v. Argentina*) [2002] ICSID Case No. ARB/02/16, Award, 28 September 2007.

[32] See the discussion of this trends in Coleman et al. (2018), p. 72.

[33] See further dicussion in Titi (2014), p. 13.

tackling global challenges like climate change.[34] According to the mentioned OECD study, as early as the 2010s, clauses preserving policy space were most commonly associated with environmental texts.[35] However, as illustrated in the following sections of this chapter, regulatory provisions included in new generation IIAs, such as CETA and CPTPP, have expanded the scope of policy objectives much more than environmental protection objectives included in the IIAs in the 2010s.

Another contributing factor to the rising prominence of the right-to-regulate clause in IIA negotiations is the shifting landscape of interests and power distribution at the negotiating table. Recently, IIAs have been more frequently negotiated between developed economies than the historical trend of negotiations primarily involving developing and developed nations.[36] This shift has altered the primary purpose of signing IIAs, moving away from the sole protection of investors from developed capital-exporting states against potential misconduct by developing country governments. This transformation is evident in the early inclusion of regulations preserving policy space in Model BITs drafted by developed countries such as the United States and Canada, which are subsequently reflected in their official treaties.[37]

In IIA negotiations worldwide, the agreements entered into by the EU with its partners unmistakably mirror the prevailing trend of incorporating the right to regulate and sustainable development into various components of the agreements. This chapter will delve into the integration of these values into both the EVFTA and the EVIPA. The assessment in this chapter will commence by scrutinising the pertinent provisions embedded in the EVFTA and EVIPA, exploring the chosen language and structure employed by the drafters. A comparative analysis with analogous provisions in the same generation of IIAs will provide a comprehensive perspective. Subsequently, the discussion will move into the nuanced implications of these regulations, exploring their practical application and the legal consequences they may entail.

8.2 The Role of "Sustainable Development" in the Preamble of EVFTA and EVIPA

As previously emphasised, the global landscape of international investment agreements has undergone a transformation, with an increasing emphasis on sustainable development and the right to regulate. The EVIPA aligns with this evolving trend.

---

[34] See further in Coleman et al. (2018), pp. 72–73.

[35] Gordon, Pohl (2011), p. 10.

[36] See further in Coleman et al. (2018), pp. 72–73.

[37] See the statistic of 1623 IIAs signed by 49 countries conducted by the Gordon and Pohl (2011), pp. 10–12.

Indeed, sustainable development has been identified as a central value that the EU aims to promote through various trade collaborations with its partners.

Given that EVIPA is distinct from the EVFTA, its Preamble essentially mirrors the content of the EVFTA's Preamble. Regarding sustainable development and environmental protection, the agreement explicitly states the following:

> Determining to strengthen their economic, trade, and investment relationship in accordance with the objective of sustainable development, in its economic, social, and environmental dimensions, and to promote investment under this Agreement in a manner of high levels of environmental and labour protection and relevant internationally recognised standards and agreements;
>
> ...
>
> Reaffirming their commitments to the principles of sustainable development in the Free Trade Agreement.

The prominence of sustainable development within the EVIPA is evident. The inclusion of this concept, both directly and through the principles of sustainable development, in the EVFTA underscores the clear intent of both parties to achieve long-term development by striking a balance between investor interests and the stability of states. Although the language remains extensive, akin to that added in traditional IIAs,[38] the objective of "economic, social, and environmental dimensions" in this preamble emphasises the importance of proportionality or balancing among the interests of economics, society, and the environment. When aligned with the principles of sustainable development in the EVFTA, it offers explicit guidance on the parties' perspectives concerning environmental protection, ensuring the right to regulate and pursue economic development and investment attraction goals.

Under Article 31.2 of the VCLT, it is widely accepted that substantive provisions should be interpreted in light of what is stated in the preamble.[39] Consequently, in the case of EVIPA, the evaluation of investment protection obligations outlined in EVIPA must also consider the instructions of its Preamble, along with regulations related to sustainable development and environmental protection included in Chapter 13 on Trade and Environment of EVFTA.

In essence, the EVIPA does not explicitly mention the right to regulate in its Preamble. Instead, its Preamble highlights sustainable principles, a concept initially outlined in the EVFTA. Looking back to the EVFTA, the right to regulate is also not directly addressed in the Preamble, aside from emphasising the overarching goal to "strengthen their economic, trade, and investment relationship in accordance with the objective of sustainable development, in its economic, social, and environmental dimensions, and to promote trade and investment under this Agreement in a mindful manner of high levels of environmental… and relevant internationally recognised

[38] For instance, The Energy Charter Treaty states that: "Recognizing the increasingly urgent need for measures to protect the environment, including the decommissioning of energy installations and waste disposal, and for internationally-agreed objectives and criteria for these purposes." The Australia–Chile FTA Preamble states the following: "Implement this Agreement in a manner consistent with sustainable development and environmental protection and conservation."

[39] Swedish National Board of Trade (2015), p. 11.

standards and agreements…". It should be noted that the EVFTA includes a crucial provision in Chapter 13 on Trade and Sustainable Development, specifically Articles 13.2 , which reserves the right to regulate for the Parties. This provision serves as an important interpretative tool for specific EVFTA provisions.

Regarding the value of the inclusion of sustainable development in EVIPA's Preamble, while some authors argue that "the object and purpose of an investment treaty cannot merely be the protection of foreign investments but entails a variety of aims, interests, and values, including sustainable development," and thus criticise certain tribunal approaches as insufficient,[40] the explicit reference to "sustainable development" in the Preamble appears to provide a more unequivocal guarantee. The wording used in the Preamble of the EVIPA signifies that, in the parties' intention, the position and importance of the sustainable development objective, as well as the environmental protection objective, have been accorded a similar level of significance as the goal of providing investment protection. Consequently, the inclusion of sustainable development and the environmental dimension in EVIPA's Preamble serves not only as a reminder for contracting parties to consider these aspects while fortifying their trading relationship but also serves as an instruction for the ICS tribunals to take heed of these concerns. This proactive stance aims to prevent investor-state tribunals from interpreting investment protection guarantees too broadly, encroaching into the host state's policy space.[41] This extension of the treaty's long-term purpose imparts meaning to the various open-textured provisions of investment treaties.[42]

While some may argue against placing high expectations on the role of the preamble, given that it does not establish substantive obligations or exceptions beyond the explicit treaty text,[43] one should not underestimate its active role, particularly when there is an interpretive gap in the treaty.[44] This becomes particularly relevant in IIL, which involves numerous legal terms that tribunals need to interpret and assess in specific circumstances, following the requirement of a "fact-based inquiry." The significance of the preamble is underscored by Article 31.2 of the 1969 VCLT, which highlights the importance of the context and purpose of a treaty as mentioned in the treaty's preamble. In IIL, where terms such as "legitimate expectation" and "like circumstances" lack uniform interpretation and their effects on sustainable development objectives remain unclear, the Preamble's role becomes even more crucial.[45] It plays a vital role in supporting tribunals in interpreting investment protection standards, addressing uncertainties, and contributing to a more comprehensive understanding of the treaty's objectives.

---

[40] Ortino (2017), p. 76.

[41] See VanDuzer et al. (2013), p. 238–239 (suggesting that the right-to-regulate concept is too open-ended to succeed in IIA negotiations); Julie (2018), pp. 323–324; Prislan and Zandvliet (2014), p. 385.

[42] Ortino (2017), p. 77.

[43] Tudor (2008), p. 20; Ha (2021), p. 150.

[44] Tudor (2008), p. 20; Julie (2018), pp. 325–326.

[45] Gehring and Kent (2013), p. 212.

When comparing the Preamble of the EVFTA with that of the CETA, it becomes evident that the CETA delves deeper into expressing the parties' intentions. While the EVFTA makes a general statement about promoting economic development, trade, and investment relationships "in a mindful manner of high levels of environment," CETA takes a significant step by explicitly acknowledging and preserving the Parties' right to regulate within their territories. Furthermore, CETA outlines five legitimate objectives: public health, safety, environment, public morals, and the promotion and protection of cultural diversity, where the Parties have the authority to legislate and make decisions as needed. This articulation of the right to regulate in the public interest is conspicuously absent from both the EVFTA and the EVIPA.

While scholars presently hold differing opinions on the efficacy of preamble statements affirming the right to regulate in safeguarding the host state's policy space,[46] there is an anticipation that expressing the intent to preserve the right to regulate in the preamble could assist a host state in securing its regulatory space. This becomes particularly crucial when the object and purpose of a treaty are scrutinised in an investor-state dispute, especially in cases where the investment tribunal employs a teleological method of interpretation that overly emphasises the "object and purpose" element of Article 31.1 of the VCLT, as observed in cases like *Siemens v. Argentina* or *SGS v. Philippines*.[47] Indeed, scholars, analysing the case of CETA, suggest that in disputes between the state and investors, arbitration tribunals must consider the underlying principles found in the preamble and the other articles related to the right to regulate.[48] This inference is drawn from the explicit confirmation of the right to regulate in the preamble itself.

Additionally, CETA signatories affirm their commitment to implementing the agreement in a manner consistent with enforcing their respective labour and environmental laws, enhancing levels of labour and environmental protection, and building upon their international commitments on these matters. The statements included in the CETA Preamble provide much more specific guidance for future tribunals in interpreting the agreement's provisions compared to the relatively less detailed Preamble of the EVFTA. The clarity of context, object, and purpose in the CETA Preamble emphasises the signatories' commitment to robustly ensuring their right to regulate in their economic relationship.

Scholars widely applaud the integration of sustainable development in conjunction with international trade, particularly in the Preamble of CETA. They argue that this positioning signifies a departure from the idea that sustainable development is subordinate to trade and investment within the CETA framework. Instead, it suggests that trade and investment should be pursued in a manner that actively

---

[46] Kawharu (2015), pp. 7, 9.

[47] *Siemens A.G. v. Republic of Argentina (Siemens v. Argentina)* [2002] ICSID Case No. ARB/02/8, Award, 3 August 2004; *SGS Société Générale de Surveillance S.A. v. Republic of the Philippines* (*SGS v. Philippines*) [2002] ICSID Case No. ARB/02/6, Award, 29 January 2004. See Julie (2018), pp. 325–326.

[48] Swedish National Board of Trade (2015), p. 06-07.

promotes the overarching goal of sustainable development.[49] While this affirmation may not be exhaustive, given the need for verification conditions, particularly in how arbitral tribunals approach sustainability, it is indisputable that environmental protection has been purposefully incorporated into the preamble of the EU agreements, as well as other sections of the treaties. This intentional choice conveys a clear message and offers enhanced guidance to arbitral tribunals.

Interestingly, similar to CETA, both the trade and investment agreements between the EU and Singapore also reference the right to regulate. It's worth recalling that structurally, the agreements with the EU's two Asian partners, Vietnam and Singapore, share a higher degree of similarity than CETA. This is because the agreements with the Asian partners are divided into two distinct trade and investment agreements, unlike CETA, which combines both aspects into a single agreement. Consequently, one might have expected the EU–Vietnam IPA and EU–Singapore IPA to exhibit similar structures and language. However, while EVIPA's Preamble does not mention the right to regulate, the EU–Singapore IPA includes a confirmation on "each Party's right to adopt and enforce measures necessary to pursue legitimate policy objectives". Given the limited availability of published documents addressing the negotiation process on these specific issues, it remains unclear why the EU allowed such differences to emerge in its agreements, potentially leading to confusion in managing and applying distinct rules across these agreements.

In the context of this study, it is interesting to compare the agreements signed by the EU with a new-generation FTA drafted by the United States, namely the CPTPP. Generally, the environmental protection regulations in the CPTPP are limited, appearing in the Preamble and in Article 20.3 on General Commitments. This indicates minimal changes compared to previous versions of FTAs. However, the CPTPP introduces an important element in its Preamble by emphasising the ongoing powers of host states to regulate and take action to promote public welfare. Specifically, CPTPP's Preamble acknowledges:

> Recognise their inherent right to regulate and resolve to preserve the flexibility of the Parties to set legislative and regulatory priorities, preserve public welfare, and protect legitimate public welfare objectives, such as public health, safety, the environment, the conservation of living or non-living exhaustible natural resources, the integrity and stability of the financial system and public morals;

This expression is believed to clarify the context for interpreting a treaty under Article 31 of the 1969 VCLT, especially Paragraph (2).[50] Accordingly, it emphasises that Parties reserve their right to set legislative and regulatory priorities and protect legitimate public welfare objectives. In addition to this valuable acknowledgement, both the CPTPP Preamble and Article 20.3 are excessively broad, featuring numerous declarative characteristics that establish a foundation only tentatively for future legitimate decisions of CPTPP's Members.

---

[49] Hush (2018), p. 9.

[50] Zamir and Barker (2017), p. 215.

Compared to the CPTPP, EVIPA lacks a value proposition to ensure the position of the pursuit of legitimate public objectives in connection with investment protection goals, a feature evident in the Preamble of agreements such as CPTPP, CETA, and the EU–Singapore IPA. The absence of such affirmation in the Preamble of both trade and investment agreements within the EU–Vietnam relations is regrettable for securing the policy space of the host state. Including such a declaration could guide the tribunal in interpreting the entire agreement. According to Article 31.1 of the VCLT, the overall objectives of the treaty carry significant weight, influencing the interpretation of disputed provisions based on their plain meaning and immediate context.[51]

The inclusion of the right to regulate in the preamble would have a far-reaching impact on all provisions of the agreement, ensuring that the host state's right to regulate is consistently considered by ICS tribunals when evaluating deviations from any substantive standards. Essentially, it would serve as an indication that the right to regulate is reserved for the host state alongside the investment protection outlined in the relevant IIAs.[52] Conversely, a substantive provision on regulatory power may only be applied within a narrower, specifically defined scope.

While both EVFTA and EVIPA incorporate substantive provisions that preserve the right to regulate, expected to provide a legally enforceable right, these provisions lack the overarching impact of clearly articulating the goal of reserving the regulatory rights of the host state in addition to the objective of investment protection. This distinction will be further explained in the following section of this chapter.

8.3 The Role of the Right-to-Regulate Clause in EVFTA and EVIPA

As analysed earlier, EVIPA's Preamble does not explicitly mention the right to regulate. Nevertheless, this agreement includes a significant provision that affirms the right to implement regulatory measures and permits parties to pursue legitimate objectives. This provision is articulated in Article 2.2 of EVIPA on "Investment and Regulatory Measures and Objectives," as quoted below:

> ARTICLE 2.2 Investment and Regulatory Measures and Objectives
>
> 1. The Parties reaffirm their right to regulate within their territories to achieve legitimate policy objectives, such as the protection of public health, safety, environment or public morals, social or consumer protection, or promotion and protection of cultural diversity.
>
> 2. For greater certainty, this Chapter shall not be interpreted as a commitment from a Party that it will not change its legal and regulatory framework, including in a manner that may negatively affect the operation of investments or the investor's expectations of profits.

[51] Hush (2018), p.126.

[52] Korzun (2017), p. 407.

> 3. For greater certainty and subject to paragraph 4, a Party's decision not to issue, renew or maintain a subsidy or a grant shall not constitute a breach of this Chapter in the following circumstances:
>
> (a) in the absence of any specific commitment to an investor of the other Party or to a covered investment under law or contract to issue, renew, or maintain that subsidy or grant; or
>
> (b) in accordance with any terms or conditions attached to the issuance, renewal or maintenance of the subsidy or grant.
>
> 4. For greater certainty, nothing in this Chapter shall be construed as preventing a Party from discontinuing the granting of a subsidy or requesting its reimbursement, or as requiring that Party to compensate the investor therefor, where such action has been ordered by one of its competent authorities listed in Annex 1 (Competent Authorities).

The language employed in Paragraphs 1 and 2 of Article 2.2 in the EVIPA, specifically the terms "reaffirm" or "shall not be interpreted…," resembles expressions commonly found in preambles rather than in substantive clauses. However, these expressions also effectively eliminate doubt by emphasising the intent to exercise the right to regulate by the host state, leaving no room for investors to challenge measures that are made for the listed purposes.

Paragraph 1 of Article 2.2 in the EVIPA broadly preserves the regulatory rights of both parties in the public interest, while Paragraph 2 explicitly underscores that obligations for investment protection do not constrain the host country from altering its legal and regulatory framework. The term "such as" indicates that the cases included in this provision are only an illustrative list. This is perhaps reflected in the "self-judging"[53] nature of measures enacted to protect "public interest" or public purpose, essentially intended to create conditions for countries to exercise sovereignty. In this illustrative list, in addition to public health, safety, and the environment—traditional elements under legitimate objectives—this paragraph is notable for referring to "public morals, social or consumer protection, or promotion and protection of cultural diversity," objectives that are rarely seen in other IIAs.[54]

According to Article 31.2 of the 1969 VCLT, which states that "the context for the purpose of the interpretation of a treaty shall include ... the text, including its preamble and annexes," when reviewing the text of Article 2.2 EVIPA, we can draw the following observations. First, the use of broad terms such as "cultural diversity" and "social protection" that can be flexibly interpreted by host states and tribunals in practice,[55] along with the structure guided by an illustrative list, creates many possibilities for preserving a broad span of states' regulatory power. ISDS practice shows that such an illustrative list does not exclude the possibility of other legitimate policy objectives.[56]

[53] Salacuse (2015), pp. 378–379.

[54] Chi (2018a), p. 107.

[55] Ibid.

[56] As observed by the Swedish National Board of Trade (2015), the dispute between Philip Morris and Australia regarding "plain packaging" would most likely be seen as a legitimate policy objective. However, there is no clarification such as the one in CETA written into Australia's 1993 Agreement, which is the reason for the dispute. See Swedish National Board of Trade (2015), p. 12.

Second, *Paragraph 2 of Article 2.2 EVIPA* clarifies that the introduction of investment protection commitments shall not be interpreted by a Party that it will not change its legal and regulatory framework, even if such changes may negatively affect the operation of investments or the investor's expectations of profits. The mention of the investor's expectations in this context suggests that this provision may be considered in conjunction with Article 2.5 on the FET of EVIPA. Once again, EVIPA shows that the signatories to this agreement pay special attention to limiting the ability of investors' expectations to constrain the state's right to regulate.

Paragraphs 3 and 4 of Article 2.2 in the EVIPA address "specific commitments" related to subsidies provided or granted by the host state. For instance, Paragraph 3(a) specifies that unless the investor obtains a specific commitment from the host state, decisions made by the state regarding subsidies will not be deemed a violation of this chapter. These provisions serve two main purposes. Firstly, they restrict the range of state actions that investors can challenge through investor-state arbitration.[57] Secondly, by clarifying which types of state actions will not constitute a breach of the treaty and be subject to investor recourse, they offer clarity to the tribunals regarding the intentions of the parties, as well as to the investors regarding the jurisdictional scope of the ICS tribunal in interpreting the agreement's language.

Article 2.2 EVIPA emphasises Paragraphs 1 and 2 as these regulations establish generally applicable rules for investment protection obligations. These paragraphs serve as a clear defence against claims alleging the violation of specific investment standards, such as FET or expropriation, particularly those related to exercising the host state's regulatory powers in pursuit of environmental and other public objectives. As Paragraphs 3 and 4 of Article 2.2 EVIPA cover more specific situations related to subsidies, the evaluation in this book primarily focuses on Paragraphs 1 and 2.

Structurally, Article 2.2 EVIPA is similar to Article 8.9 CETA, both comprising four paragraphs, except for the provisions in Paragraph 2. The wording of Paragraph 2 Article 8.9.2 CETA differs slightly. According to Article 8.9.2, CETA specifically excludes modifications of laws that negatively affect an investment or interfere with an investor's expectations, including expectations of profits, amounting to a breach of an obligation under Section D on Investment Protection. The explicit mention of investor expectations, a key element of the FET standard, seems to prevent a broad interpretation of legitimate expectations from the investor.[58] Indeed, as highlighted in Levashova's study on case law, an investor's expectations based on the stability of a general regulatory framework are among the four elements considered to establish the legitimacy of investor expectations capable of limiting the state's right to regulate.[59]

---

[57] Aziz (2017), p. 15.

[58] Levashova (2019), p. 33.

[59] Other three elements that emerged out of her research as important elements in the decision-making process of tribunals with regard to legitimate expectations are: the specific representations made by the host state to an investor; the economic and sociopolitical circumstances in the host state; and the investor's conduct. See further in Levashova (2019), p. 246.

Limiting the possibility that a change in law could become the basis for a breach of a particular investment protection obligation, such as the FET, appears to have been the common intention of the drafters of both EVIPA and CETA regardless of the general consensus from the investment tribunals that a state's legal framework is "by definition subject to change as it adapts to new circumstances day by day and a state has the sovereign right to exercise its powers which include legislative acts."[60] Levashova's study indicates that an investor's claim based on the instability of a general regulatory framework can be successful only in limited situations. These situations include when the altered framework results in a severe negative impact on the investor and its investment or when the transformation of the regulatory framework is conducted in an extraordinary manner.[61] Even in these situations, for a violation of the FET standard, the changes must be drastic and/or discriminatory, having a severe financial impact on the investor.[62] In addition, the manner in which the transformation was conducted should be extreme and unpredictable.[63] This practice demonstrates that the threshold for violating the FET concerning legitimate expectations associated with the stability of a general regulatory framework is set at a high level by tribunals. Hence, the possibility that the disputing measure is considered to disappoint the investor's legitimate expectation is not significantly high. In this context, the inclusion of a regulation emphasising the host state's right to change the legal framework in both EVIPA and CETA once again underscores the state's desire for maximum control over policy space in the context of related IIAs.

While commendable for their efforts to balance economic objectives with environmental considerations,[64] the language employed in the right-to-regulate clauses under CETA and EVIPA remains notably ambiguous. For example, if a change in laws does not amount to a breach, the specific consequences that may arise from this provision are unclear.[65] Moreover, the term "mere fact" implies that this provision does not preclude tribunals from considering the modification of laws in conjunction with other elements that could violate the FET standard, such as bad faith conduct or manifest arbitrariness.[66] In such cases, the contested measure may still be deemed a breach. Therefore, this regulation does not entirely foreclose the possibility that a change in law could be regarded as a violation of the investment protection

---

[60] *AES Summit Generation Limited and AES-Tisza Erömü Kft. v. Republic of Hungary* (*AES Summit v. Hungary*) [2007] ICSID Case No. ARB/07/22, Award, 23 September 2010.

[61] See further Levashova (2019), p. 247.

[62] As shown in *Toto Costruzioni Generali S.p.A. v. Republic of Lebanon* (*Toto v. Lebanon*) [2007] ICSID Case No. ARB/07/12, Award, 7 June 2012, para. 244; *El Paso Energy International Company v. The Argentine Republic* (*El Paso v. Argentina*) [2006] ICSID Case No. ARB/03/15, Award, 31 October 2011, para. 510. See Levashova (2019), p. 248.

[63] Ibid.

[64] Yotova (2019), p. 398.

[65] Coleman et al. (2018), p. 86.

[66] Levashova (2019), p. 265.

commitment.[67] These arguments are indeed valid.[68] However, semantically, the manner in which it is articulated in Article 8.9.2 CETA essentially rules out the notion that altering the law, even if it has a negative impact on an investment, constitutes a breach of the investment protection standards.

In the case of EVIPA, Paragraph 2 Article 2.2 EVIPA explicitly asserts that investment protection commitments do not imply that the parties will refrain from modifying their legal and regulatory framework, even if such modifications may negatively affect the operation of investments or the investor's expectations of profits. This indicates that the state's right to regulate is safeguarded to a certain extent. However, it does not entirely eliminate the possibility that such a change in law could not lead to a breach of the investment protection standard, particularly when the conditions specified in the relevant investment protection obligation are met. This outcome does not seem fundamentally different from the application of Article 8.9.2 CETA. Due to the limited availability of published documents related to EVIPA negotiations from both Vietnam and the EU, the reasons for this difference remain unclear.

Compared to EVIPA, CETA incorporates a mechanism highly appreciated by scholars for enhancing the right to regulate of the Parties, known as the Joint Interpretative Instrument (JII).[69] According to the Parties, this instrument offers "a clear and unambiguous statement of what Canada and the European Union and its Member States agreed in a number of CETA provisions that have been the object of public debate and concerns and provides an agreed interpretation herein." The JII is anticipated to carry legal weight and elucidate the agreed-upon understanding in CETA, aligning with Article 31.2(a) of the VCLT, which underscores the value of supporting treaty interpretation through agreements made by all parties in connection with the treaty's conclusion.[70] This Joint Interpretative Instrument provides crucial guidance to the ICS tribunal on how to interpret the right to regulate, emphasising its content multiple times. Furthermore, it asserts that CETA's provisions on environmental protection are "comprehensive and binding,"[71] serving as an effective tool both legally by offering sufficient guidance for the ICS tribunal and impactfully by directing the tribunal's attention to the parties' concerns.[72]

In addition to the JII, CETA empowers the CETA Joint Committee[73] to provide binding interpretations of the treaty text to ICS tribunals.[74] This practice, akin

[67] Ibid., p. 247.

[68] Coleman et al. (2018), p. 86.

[69] EU Council (2016).

[70] Hush (2018), p. 145.

[71] EU Council (2016), para 7(b).

[72] Hush (2018), p. 147.

[73] It should be noticed that the EU–Singapore FTA has also established a Trade Committee comprising of representatives from both parties under Article 17.1 EUSFTA.

[74] CETA Article 8.31.3: "*Where serious concerns arise as regards matters of interpretation that may affect investment, the Committee on Services and Investment may, pursuant to Article 8.44.3(a), recommend to the CETA Joint Committee the adoption of interpretations of this*

to the submissions by NAFTA's members to tribunals on interpretation issues in NAFTA cases[75] or the Joint Interpretative Statement published by the Indian Government in 2016,[76] has garnered high praise from scholars for actively shaping the substantive content of investment treaties by states under international law.

Within the framework of the EU–Vietnam Trade and Investment relationship, a Trade Committee has also been instituted in accordance with Article 17.1 of the EVFTA. This committee, endowed with significant responsibilities such as overseeing the FTA's implementation and issuing binding decisions,[77] is further empowered to "adopt interpretations of the provisions" outlined in the EVFTA (Para. 4(d) Article 17.1 EVFTA). While the full extent of the Trade Committee's authority remains unexplored,[78] it is anticipated to substantially mitigate the potential uncertainty arising from a broad interpretation by the ICS tribunals.[79] Additionally, EVIPA creates its own Investment Commitee under Article 4.1 that will supervise and facilitate the implementation and application of the agreement. This Committee also has the authority to consider and recommend to the Parties amendments to EVIPA. Considering the prescribed functions of the Investment Committee, it is conceivable that this committee serves as a mechanism to elucidate the agreed-upon terms in the EVIPA.

Notably, in CETA, the autonomy of host states is safeguarded through an alternative provision articulated in Paragraph 7 of Article 8.10. This provision expressly precludes the option of utilising ISDS to challenge state measures under national law.[80] Such a provision significantly confines the jurisdiction of ICS tribunals, restricting them to considering only CETA's provisions and deferring the determination of the legality of a state's measure under domestic law to the competent authorities of that state. The practice of ISDS demonstrates that a "blatant disregard" for domestic rules by state authorities often leads to a violation of the FET standard.[81] The absence of a similar limitation on the jurisdiction of ICS tribunals in

---

Agreement. An interpretation adopted by the CETA Joint Committee shall be binding on a Tribunal established under this Section. The CETA Joint Committee may decide that an interpretation shall have binding effect from a specific date."

[75] Coleman et al. (2018), pp. 48–49.

[76] Government of India, Ministry of Finance (2016).

[77] Daly and Ahmad (2015).

[78] Scholar have commented that the decisions of the Trade Committee become binding on the Parties. Similarly, interpretations adopted by the Trade Committee are binding on the tribunal deciding a claim. However, the usage of the word 'adopted' indicates the Trade Committee's decisions would not have a retroactive element. See further Aziz (2017), p. 16.

[79] Ibid., p. 17.

[80] Paragraph 7 Article 8.10 CETA: *"For greater certainty, the fact that a measure breaches domestic law does not, in and of itself, establish a breach of this Article. In order to ascertain whether the measure breaches this Article, a Tribunal must consider whether a Party has acted inconsistently with the obligations in paragraph 1."*

[81] See further discussion in Levashova (2019), p. 267.

the EVIPA is noteworthy, especially given the EU's expressed concerns on this matter in its agreement with Canada.[82]

Compared with contemporaneous FTAs such as the CPTPP, the efficacy of the EVIPA and the CETA provisions stands out, particularly in articulating the parties' commitment to safeguarding policy autonomy. Indeed, despite the anticipation that the CPTPP would establish elevated benchmarks for labour and environmental protections, along with reinforced safeguards for the majority of its member countries,[83] Article 9.16 within the Investment Chapter of the CPTPP falls short, presenting a statement considerably less robust than those found in EVIPA and CETA. The pertinent excerpt from Article 9.16 CPTPP reads as follows:

> Nothing in this Chapter shall be interpreted to prevent a Party from adopting, maintaining, or enforcing any measure otherwise consistent with this Chapter that it considers appropriate to ensure that investment activity in its territory is undertaken in a manner sensitive to environmental, health, or other regulatory objectives.

Although this provision mirrors Article 1114 of NAFTA, which exclusively addresses measures to protect the environment, Article 9.16 of the CPTPP expands its scope to encompass various regulatory objectives. This self-judging provision that using the structure "nothing in this… shall be construed to prevent…" is acknowledged as a weak expression, as IIAs inherently do not outright proscribe or prohibit specific conduct.[84] Furthermore, Article 9.16 of the CPTPP imposes an additional condition, stipulating that the applied measure must be "otherwise consistent" with the relevant chapter. Regulations formulated with such language are criticised for constraining a state's latitude to regulate in the public interest, potentially compromising the primary objective of IIAs, which is to furnish protection for investments.[85]

Moreover, this regulation proves counterproductive, as even in the absence of such permission granted by this provision, the state retains the ability to enact measures in harmony with investment protection standards.[86] In contrast, the clarity of language employed in Article 2.2 of the EVIPA and Article 8.9 of the CETA is commendable. They avoid such expressions, thereby fortifying the protection of the state's policy space.

Adding to the limitations, the right to regulate provision within the CPTPP introduces a constraint through the term "otherwise consistent," creating the "illusion of retaining regulatory space".[87] In reality, however, this wording fails to offer substantial protection for the right to regulate, as pursuing policy objectives inherently poses a significant risk of violating investment protection standards. Provisions

[82] European Commission (2016).

[83] The statement was given by Obama Administration. See Zients (2015).

[84] Coleman et al. (2018), p. 80.

[85] Ejims (2019), pp. 79–80.

[86] Titi (2022), p. 29; Martini (2017), p. 568.

[87] UNCTAD (2015), p. 131.

incorporating such language merely serve to affirm the state's legitimate rights without providing concrete protection for these rights.

The regulatory rights outlined in Article 2.2 of the EVIPA can be seen as a "safe hall" for contracting parties to exercise their regulatory authority. To some extent, this article reaffirms the rights to regulate and modify the legal framework governing covered investments and investors. This perspective discourages investors from viewing the treaty as an absolute "insurance policy" that guarantees protection for their investments under all circumstances, even when there are changes in the host state's legal framework. While the outcomes of tribunal decisions in EVIPA disputes depend on various facts and factors, the tribunals now have a more substantial basis to consider the state's right to implement specific changes, especially in situations related to police powers or public purpose.

8.4 Experiences from ISDS Practice

As the provision concerning the right to regulate is relatively new, experience derived from the interpretation of ISDS practices is quite limited. In this section, this book discusses some factors pertaining to the application of the right to regulate provision, drawing insights from investor-state arbitration practices.

Within the context of investment arbitration, investment tribunals typically balance the legitimacy of regulatory measures with investors' rights through their interpretation of standards such as FET, NT, and indirect expropriation.[88] When assessing the application of regulatory measures, the tribunals prioritise determining the legitimacy of the state's measure objective. In this context, ISDS practices reveal that tribunals often consider the following criteria:[89] First, they examine whether the measure in dispute aims to serve public interests, concentrating on the intended goal of the measure. Next, they evaluate whether there is sufficient evidence to substantiate the legitimacy of those objectives, focusing on the justification for the presence of the required objective.

Addressing the first criterion, Levashova's study findings indicate that the spectrum of recognised public interests in ISDS practice is extensive, encompassing areas such as modernising the transport sector, protecting ecological interests, safeguarding human rights, ensuring the right to access to clean water, promoting public health, preserving indigenous peoples' rights, protecting cultural heritage, reforming the banking sector, combating corruption, and curbing excessive profits of energy companies.[90] In assessing the legitimacy of these objectives, unacceptable objectives typically involve measures enacted in bad faith or those that are

[88] Trujillo (2018), pp. 2739, 2743; Nadakavukaren and Lazo (2023), pp. 14–18.

[89] Levashova (2019), p. 251.

[90] Ibid., pp. 239, 251–252.

manifestly without reason.[91] For instance, in the case of *Philip Morris v. Uruguay*, the tribunal concluded that "the responsibility for public health measures rests with the government and investment tribunals should pay great deference to governmental judgments of national needs in matters such as the protection of public health. In such cases, respect is due to the discretionary exercise of sovereign power, not made irrationally and not exercised in bad faith [...] involving many complex factors".[92] The overall trend observed is that tribunals generally hold high respect for the right of domestic authorities to regulate matters within their borders,[93] except when measures are one-sided, mainly motivated by a specific state authority's "political agenda," or lack a rational basis.[94]

Regarding the second element, the justification for the state's objective plays a vital role in establishing the legitimacy of the state's measure. ISDS tribunals typically insist that the state's measure objective must be logical and substantiated in the state's records.[95] However, the evaluation of these factors is not straightforward. In practice, tribunals do not uniformly apply a similar rule when assessing the necessity and reasonableness of the applied measure to scrutinise the legitimacy of its objective. Indeed, when adjudicating claims under the traditional FET standard, some tribunals tend to appreciate the state's choices of measures taken to achieve public interest objectives. Notably, in *Philip Morris v. Uruguay*, the tribunal invoked the doctrine of "the margin of appreciation," asserting that higher deference should be accorded to public health objectives pursued by states.[96] The rationale was that states' specialised public health bodies possess superior expertise in making decisions concerning public health compared to arbitrators lacking such specific knowledge.[97]

However, alternative approaches have also been observed. In *AWG Group v. Argentina*, a tribunal, while acknowledging the reasonableness of some of Argentina's arguments, suggested that Argentina could have chosen alternative measures that would not disturb the balance between rights and obligations in the concession.[98] Generally, the criteria set out in these two cases against Argentina closely mirror the test applied in Article XX of the GATT concerning the necessity

[91] Ibid., pp. 251–252.

[92] *Philip Morris Brands Sàrl, Philip Morris Products S.A. and Abal Hermanos S.A. v. Oriental Republic of Uruguay* (*Philip Morris v. Uruguay*) [2010], ICSID Case No. ARB/10/7, Award, 8 July 2016, para. 399.

[93] Other tribunals follow this approach including *S.D. Myers, Inc. v. Government of Canada* (*Myers v. Canada*) [1998] UNCITRAL, NAFTA, Partial Award, 13 November 2000, para. 263; *Mesa Power Group LLC v. Canada* (*Mesa Power v. Canada*) [2011] PCA Case No. 2012-17, Award, 24 March 2016.

[94] Levashova (2019), pp. 251–252.

[95] Ibid., p. 252.

[96] *Philip Morris v. Uruguay* [2010], ICSID Case No. ARB/10/7, Award, 8 July 2016, para. 399.

[97] Levashova (2019), p. 252.

[98] *Impregilo S.p.A. v. Argentine Republic* (*Impregilo v. Argentina*) [2007] ICSID Case No. ARB/07/17, Award, 21 June 2011, para. 330.

test to fulfil policy objectives, which will be discussed further below. The Panel in Thailand–Cigarettes established that a measure is "necessary" within the meaning of Article XX(b) only when there are no alternative measures consistent with the GATT or less inconsistent with it, which the defending Member could reasonably be expected to employ to achieve its objective.[99]

These experiences were garnered in the context of examining the validity of the applied measure's objective under the FET standard. This may not align seamlessly with the application of an independent provision on the right to regulate, specifically concerning the proportionality test, as discussed below. Nevertheless, these experiences can offer insights into the potential approaches that future ICS tribunals may adopt when evaluating the justification for the state's objective under the right-to-regulate clause of the EVIPA.

When considering the provisions on the right to regulate independently in the case of Article 2.2 EVIPA as well as similar provisions in CETA, it is possible that the method of review applied by the ICS tribunals under EVIPA or CETA could involve a proportionality analysis.[100] This analytical approach, often referred to as a "reasonableness test," involves balancing competing interests and is commonly employed in various domestic and supranational contexts. This fundamental principle is applied in ISDS practices to qualify the state's regulatory power in alignment with the standards of protection in IIAs, a deficiency that Calamita has highlighted in investment treaties.[101]

The potential application of proportionality analysis in evaluating Article 2.2 of EVIPA is entirely reasonable, as evident in a growing number of cases, such as *PL Holdings Sàrl v. Republic of Poland*[102] and *Occidental v. Ecuador II*,[103] where Tribunals explicitly adopted this approach. Moreover, proportionality analysis has been employed or relied upon in other disputes, including *Tecmed v. Mexico*,[104] *Saluka v. Czech Republic*,[105] *Electrabel v. Hungary*,[106] *Philip Morris v. Uruguay*.[107]

---

[99] See WTO Panel Report, Thailand—Restrictions on Importation of and Internal taxes on Cigarettes, DS10/R – 37S/200, 7 November 1990, para. 75.

[100] This principle has been especially applied by the Court of Justice of the European Union and the European Court of Human Rights. By the popular of the application of this approach, it is also called as "European-style Proportionality Analysis". See Henckels (2018), para. 12.

[101] Calamita (2013), p. 175.

[102] *PL Holdings S.a.r.l. v. Poland* [2014] SCC Case No. 2014/163, Partial Award, 28 June 2017, paras. 355–357, 375, 389–91.

[103] *Occidental Petroleum Corporation and Occidental Exploration and Production Company v. Republic of Ecuador* (*Occidental v. Ecuador II*) [2006] ICSID Case No. ARB/06/11, Award, 5 October 2012, paras. 428–36, 445–46.

[104] *Técnicas Medioambientales Tecmed, S.A. v. The United Mexican States* (*Tecmed v. Mexico*) [2003] ICSID Case No. ARB(AF)/00/2, Award, 29 May 2003.

[105] *Saluka Investments B.V. v. The Czech Republic* (*Saluka v. Czech Republic*) [2001] PCA Case No. 2001-04, Partial Award, 17 March 2006.

[106] *Electrabel S.A. v. The Republic of Hungary* [2007] ICSID Case No. ARB/07/19, Award, 25 November 2015.

[107] *Philip Morris v. Uruguay* [2010], ICSID Case No. ARB/10/7, Award, 8 July 2016.

In these cases, investment tribunals seem to have invoked the principle of proportionality as a tool to strike a balance between the rights of investors and the rights of states to regulate for public purposes, even though none of the treaties involved explicitly calls for the application of the principle of proportionality.

The proportionality test has traditionally been applied to evaluate the exercise of regulatory power under Article XX of the GATT within the WTO. It plays a crucial role in advancing environmental policy among WTO member parties throughout the functioning of the organisation's dispute resolution mechanisms.[108]

The application of the principle of proportionality or reasonableness involves a comprehensive three-pronged test:[109]

(i) Suitability: Is the applied measure suitable to achieve the pursued aim?
(ii) Necessity: Is the applied measure necessary to achieve the pursued aim?
(iii) Proportionality Stricto Sensu: Even if there are no less restrictive measures, is the burden on the individual excessive relative to the benefits secured by the state objective?

In a context where IIAs provide limited clarification on specific issues such as regulatory rights, tribunals typically do not solely rely on the text of the investment treaty. Recognising the established rules of treaty interpretation, arbitral tribunals may refer to other sources when interpreting guarantees within an investment treaty, such as international law in general.[110] This forms the basis for future ICS tribunals to apply the principle of proportionality, which is not explicitly recognised in the EVIPA when assessing the state's right to regulate under Article 2.2 of this Agreement. This principle is anticipated to guide ICS tribunals in resolving conflicting interests and acknowledging an appropriate balancing level of deference toward states without resorting to judicial borrowing operations.[111]

In this scenario, if applying the proportionality principle demonstrates that the state's measure is indeed proportionate, the host state will not be held responsible for any compensation. This outcome aligns with the approach adopted by many tribunals in assessing regulatory measures applied by host states in cases of indirect expropriation, as seen in cases such as *Tecmed v. Mexico*,[112] *LG&E v. Argentina*,[113] *Azurix v. Argentina*,[114] and *Vattenfall v. Germany*.[115] When applying this approach, scholars have also agreed that adopting a deferential approach is preferable over a

---

[108] Hush (2018), p. 129.

[109] Calamita (2013), p. 175; Ortino (2017), p. 87; Aikaterini TiTi (2018), p. 113.

[110] Calamita (2013) p. 177.

[111] Zarra (2017), p. 115; Henckels (2012), p. 255.

[112] *Tecmed v. Mexico* [2003] ICSID Case No. ARB(AF)/00/2, Award, 29 May 2003.

[113] *LG&E Energy Corp., LG&E Capital Corp., and LG&E International, Inc. v. Argentine Republic (LG&E v. Argentina)* [2002] ICSID Case No. ARB/02/1, Award, 3 October 2006.

[114] *Azurix Corp. v. The Argentine Republic (Azurix v. Argentina)* [2001] ICSID Case No. ARB/01/12, Award, 31 October 2011.

[115] *Vattenfall AB, Vattenfall Europe AG, Vattenfall Europe Generation AG v. Federal Republic of Germany (Vattenfall v. Germany)* [2009] ICSID Case No. ARB/09/6, Award, 06 December 2016.

strict proportionality stance. This approach allows greater flexibility for host states to enact measures in the interest of their populations without incurring liability for compensating foreign investors.[116]

8.5 Sustainable Development and the Right-to-Regulate Clause in EVIPA: Unclear Contribution to State's Regulatory Right

Arbitral practice reveals that in the absence of a specific provision explicitly declaring the right to regulate in a treaty, tribunals can invoke Article 31(3)(c) of the VCLT to maintain the application of these powers, as affirmed in cases like *Marfin v. Cyprus*[117] and *Philip Morris v. Uruguay*.[118] Despite this, the explicit affirmation of such rights through a specific regulation would provide greater assurance, clearly demonstrating the contracting parties' intent to prioritise national policy space.[119]

The right-to-regulate provision in the EVIPA is also mirrored in two other EU agreements frequently referenced in this book: CETA (Article 8.9) and the EU–Singapore IPA (Article 2.2). This demonstrates a strong consistency in actively affirming the state's right to regulate and, more precisely, delineating the extent and nature of their obligations to investors. However, when assessing the effectiveness of the right-to-regulate clause in preserving policy space, it becomes evident that this type of regulation does not necessarily offer a robust guarantee for the protection of the state's policy space.[120] Several reasons for these weaknesses are outlined below.

Firstly, the language of this regulation, similar with the wording of CETA,[121] resembles text typically found in a preamble rather than in the agreement text.[122] Such "affirmation" is akin to mere statements that do not create specific rights or obligations. Moreover, it fails to provide tribunals with specific guidance on assessing the legitimacy of the applied measure or weighing public interest arguments against investors' rights.[123] This contrasts with the widely recognised right to

[116] Henckels (2012), p. 255; Ortino (2017), pp. 90–91.

[117] *Marfin Investment Group Holdings S.A., Alexandros Bakatselos and others v. Republic of Cyprus (Marfin v. Cyprus)* [2013] ARB/13/27, Award, 26 July 2018, para. 827.

[118] *Philip Morris v. Uruguay* [2010], ICSID Case No. ARB/10/7, Award, 8 July 2016, para. 307.

[119] Baltag FCIArb et al. (2023), p. 395.

[120] Many scholars share this view, for instance, see Chi (2018a), p. 107; Julie (2018), p. 289.

[121] Swedish National Board of Trade (2015), p. 12.

[122] Indeed, similar wording such as the objectives of the treaty can be achieved "in a manner consistent with the protection of health, safety and the environment" can be found in the US Model BIT (2012).

[123] Martini (2017), p. 568.

regulate, rooted in the international legal principle of state sovereignty,[124] as shown in ISDS's practice,[125] making such an affirmation essentially unnecessary.

Secondly, in the context of IIL, the scope of the right to regulate remains unclear, and there is uncertainty regarding how an arbitral tribunal would interpret it in relation to investment protection obligations in IIAs.[126] When invoked by the host state to justify the legitimate objective of the disputing measure, this provision acts as an exception to the violation of a specific substantive standard. However, the most pressing concern arises from whether the successful invocation of this provision would absolve the host state from compensation obligations. Can we infer that a successfully proven regulatory measure operates as a carve-out from all investment protection obligations? Unfortunately, the answer is not straightforward. As shown in Chaps. 6 and 7, determining whether a state's measure is legitimate or constitutes a violation of a particular investment protection obligation depends on the outcome of inquiries established in specific standards, relevant customary law, and international treaties. Investment tribunals are obligated to adhere to these rules when evaluating a specific claim. Hence, a mere declaration, as seen in Article 2.2 EVIPA and Article 8.9.2 CETA, is fundamentally insufficient to provide reasonable guidance in this complex matter.

Thirdly, another limitation of this regulation is the lack of detailed articulation of the consequences of the right-to-regulate clause.[127] The criteria needed to legitimise policy objectives are not clarified in this provision, creating ambiguity.[128] While litigation practice may offer some guidance,[129] the diversity of state objectives in the public interest, combined with the absence of specific criteria in Paragraph 1, Article 2.2 EVIPA, renders this regulation less effective in protecting the host state's policy space.

Despite its numerous limitations, particularly in application, the acknowledgement of the right-to-regulate clause as a substantive provision, to some extent, signifies the parties' intent to require ICS tribunals to regard it as an integral component of the treaty. Such substantive provision establishes clear rights and obligations between parties, offering guarantees that a preamble cannot propose. It is essential to note that, according to Articles 31.1 and 31.2 of the VCLT, a preamble can only

---

[124] Levashova (2019), p. 238.

[125] *AWG Group Ltd. v. The Argentine Republic* (*AWG v. Argentina*) [2003] UNCITRAL, Award, 30 July 2010; *Impregilo v. Argentina* [2007] ICSID Case No. ARB/07/17, Award, 21 June 2011; *Urbaser S.A. and Consorcio de Aguas Bilbao Biskaia, Bilbao Biskaia Ur Partzuergoa v. Argentine Republic* (*Urbaser v. Argentina*) [2007], ICSID Case No. ARB/07/26, Award, 8 December 2016; *Chemtura Corporation (formerly Crompton Corporation) v. Government of Canada* (*Chemtura v. Canada*) [2002] PCA Case No. 2008-01, Award, 2 August 2010.

[126] See further VanDuzer et al. (2013), p. 239.

[127] See further in Coleman et al. (2018), p. 86.

[128] Levashova (2019), p. 266.

[129] In such cases, the tribunals usually identify whether the objective can be substantiated by the host state through records and other evidence. In several cases, compliance with national law or international obligations under international treaties other than the applicable IIA has also served as adequate justification. Levashova (2019), p. 267.

offer guidance regarding the context of the treaty for interpretation purposes. The significance of incorporating the right-to-regulate clause lies in compelling the tribunal to approach it with a balanced perspective, avoiding the one-sided approach often seen in traditional IIAs.

Moreover, an independent right-to-regulate clause, when included in an IIA, imposes an additional burden of proof on investors. In addition to demonstrating a violation of a substantive obligation, investors must prove that the disputed measure was "not a legitimate exercise" of the right to regulate. The burden of proof then shifts to the host state to justify the measure within its right to regulate, as provided in Article 2.2 EVIPA. While this doesn't significantly change the responsibility for the host state, it adds complexity for the investor, making the claim more challenging. It's crucial to note that a right to regulate drafted as an exception clause does not create the same consequences. In such cases, only the host state bears the burden of justifying its measure. An independent right-to-regulate clause, therefore, is preferable over an exception clause to ensure it does not unintentionally displace states' rights to regulate under international law.[130] In this perspective, Article 2.2 EVIPA shows a deliberate choice by the parties to acknowledge this provision.

Lastly, although EVIPA does not establish a Joint Interpretative Instrument like CETA, it does create a Committee comprised of representatives from both the EU and Vietnam, co-chaired by the Minister of Planning and Investment of Vietnam and the Member of the European Commission responsible for trade, or their respective delegates (Para. (2) Article 4.1 EVIPA). This Investment Committee, is mandated under EVIPA to "supervise and facilitate the implementation and application of this Agreement" (Para. 3(b) Article 4.1 EVIPA). Moreover, the Committee is empowered to consider and recommend amendments to the Agreement (Para. 4(b) Article 4.1 EVIPA). Significantly, the Committee is also authorised to adopt interpretations of the Agreement's provisions, encompassing all substantive provisions of EVIPA (Para. 4(c) Article 4.1 EVIPA). These interpretations are binding on the Parties and all bodies established under the Agreement, including arbitration panels and tribunals (Para. 4(c) Article 4.1 EVIPA).

With these prerogatives, once operational, the Committee has the potential to further enhance the policy space of the host states if the parties so agree on such matters. While the establishment of relevant committees under EVFTA–EVIPA is still underway, it is indisputable that these agreements provide a mechanism to enable parties to clarify their intentions in drafting international treaties.

---

[130] Henin et al. (2019), p. 64.

8.6 Interim Conclusion

In the context of the EU's trade and investment agreements, it is evident that negotiations between the parties are unfolding within the framework of the IIA reformation process[131] occurring across continents. The inclusion of the principle of sustainable development, which,"as a standard rule of international investment law, has yet to be firmly rooted,"[132] is observed in numerous preambles. These preambles express the shared concern of the parties regarding economic development in connection with sustainable development. Despite scepticism from scholars[133] regarding the efficacy of including sustainable objectives in the preamble of IIAs, this reform has laid the initial groundwork for considering "sustainability" and "environmental protection" on the same platform as investment protection at investor-state tribunals.[134] The objective of "economic, social and environmental dimensions" strongly affirms the importance of proportionality or balancing by considering economic, social, and environmental interests. The purpose of the treaty is to help the future tribunals define reasonableness while examining the regulatory measures applied by the host state. Based on this inclusion of the term sustainable development, future tribunals will have been provided with interpretative arguments in favour of the right to regulate.[135]

The concerning aspect is that EVIPA does not specifically mention the right to regulate in its Preamble. In contrast, both agreements negotiated before or concurrently with EVIPA, namely CETA and the EU–Singapore FTA and IPA, clearly articulate the state's right to regulate in their preamble. These agreements underscore the shared objectives of the agreement, emphasising the importance of ensuring the country's policy space alongside the goal of investment protection. The absence of such a statement in EVIPA represents a missed opportunity to declare the mutual intention of the parties to prioritise and carve out space for the state's regulatory rights.[136]

Examining the right-to-regulate clauses included in EVFTA (Article 13.2 and 13.3) and EVIPA (Article 2.2), the language of these provisions resembles to the preamble rather than substantive provisions. Despite this form, the inclusion of such a regulation marks a significant advancement in the negotiation and signing of IIAs. This shift in approach officially acknowledges the host state's right to regulate, fostering a better balance between the goals of IIAs and moving beyond a singular focus on protecting investments. As highlighted in this chapter, it's important to

---

[131] Chi (2018b), p. 17.

[132] Julie (2018) p. 289.

[133] Ibid.

[134] Infact, many Arbitral tribunals examined the preamble to help support their considerations. See *Siemens A.G. v. Republic of Argentina* [2002] ICSID Case No. ARB/02/8, Award, 3 August 2004; *SGS v. Philippines* [2002] ICSID Case No. ARB/02/6, Award, 29 January 2004.

[135] Titi (2022), p. 38.

[136] Aziz (2017), pp. 14–15.

note that this provision does not imply that environmental measures pursued by a country causing harm to investors cannot be found to violate investor protection commitments. Any such determination must be made after tribunals thoroughly assess the criteria specified in the specific substantive provision. However, this regulation serves as crucial guidance for ICS tribunals, affirming that commitments to protect foreign investors do not entail limiting or excluding the exercise of sovereign rights by the host state. This, to a certain extent, ensures the ability of host states to pursue legitimate public objectives in the future.

Considering the anticipated effects of this provision, as clarified in this chapter, including a right-to-regulate clause imposes a more challenging burden of proof on investors when bringing claims alleging a violation of investment protection standards. Consequently, it is expected to limit potential abuses of the ISDS mechanism, as observed in investor-state arbitration. Furthermore, the superiority of a right-to-regulate clause over an exception clause is emphasised, as a closed list of exceptions in the latter may compel states to demonstrate how their disputing measures align with the cases listed in the exception clause. Article 2.2 EVIPA, therefore, contributes to enhancing states' freedom to determine public objectives within their sovereign power.

While the inclusion of the right-to-regulate clause in international agreements is anticipated to contribute to a balanced framework between investment protection and the sovereign right to regulate, the findings from this chapter underscore that its success hinges largely on the approach adopted by ICS tribunals. The question of whether a successfully proven regulatory measure operates as a carve-out from all investment protection obligations remains a crucial point for clarification. Equally important is the establishment of clear principles for evaluating the application of this regulation.

This book supposes that the principle of proportionality will likely guide the assessment of the right-to-regulate clause, given its inherent need to balance the interests at stake. This aligns with the rationale behind including the right-to-regulate clause in the negotiation and drafting of IIAs. While the principle of proportionality imposes stringent demands on the selection and application of a host state's policy measures, these requirements are deemed necessary to prevent regulatory abuse in the public's interest.

Even with applying the principle of proportionality, the host state's pursuit of public policy-related goals is expected to proceed unimpeded, provided the applied measures adhere to the principles of "good faith" and do not result in a "disguised restriction" on international investment. The lessons drawn from the implementation of Article XX of the GATT under the WTO support this assertion. Host states should note that until the role of the right-to-regulate clause and the applicable principles are clarified, the assessment of a violation of a substantive standard will continue to be based on inquiries specified in that standard. As articulated by Gary Born, an arbitrator in the case of Philip Morris v. Uruguay, in his dissenting opinion: "Deference to sovereign measures is the starting point, but not the ending point, of the evaluation of fair and equitable treatment claims. Instead, a sensitive and nuanced consideration of the nature of the government measure, the character and context of the government judgment, the relationship between the measure and its stated purpose, and the measure's impact on protected investments is necessary."[137] Put differently, acknowledging the sovereignty rights of the host state is a crucial factor when assessing whether a state measure aligns with its objectives, but it is not the sole determinant in this evaluation.[138]

In conclusion, the EVIPA's Preamble does not reveal significant breakthroughs in preserving policy space for the host state when compared to traditional IIAs. Meanwhile, concerns persist regarding the overall effectiveness of the right-to-regulate clause, with answers to these concerns likely emerging only when the ICS tribunal examines the first dispute related to this regulation.

References

ISDS Cases

AES Summit Generation Limited and AES-Tisza Erömü Kft. v. Republic of Hungary [2007] ICSID Case No. ARB/07/22
AWG Group Ltd. v. The Argentine Republic [2003] UNCITRAL
Azurix Corp. v. The Argentine Republic [2001] ICSID Case No. ARB/01/12
Chemtura Corporation (formerly Crompton Corporation) v. Government of Canada [2002] PCA Case No. 2008-01
El Paso Energy International Company v. The Argentine Republic [2006] ICSID Case No. ARB/03/15
Electrabel S.A. v. The Republic of Hungary [2007] ICSID Case No. ARB/07/19
Enron Corporation and Ponderosa Assets, L.P. v. Argentine Republic [2001] ICSID Case No. ARB/01/3
Impregilo S.p.A. v. Argentine Republic [2007] ICSID Case No. ARB/07/17
Joseph Charles Lemire v. Ukraine [2006], ICSID Case No. ARB/06/18
LG&E Energy Corp., LG&E Capital Corp., and LG&E International, Inc. v. Argentine Republic [2002] ICSID Case No. ARB/02/1
Marfin Investment Group Holdings S.A., Alexandros Bakatselos and others v. Republic of Cyprus [2013] ICSID Case No. ARB/13/27
Marvin Roy Feldman Karpa v. United Mexican States [1999] ICSID Case No. ARB(AF)/99/1
Mesa Power Group LLC v. Canada [2011] PCA Case No. 2012-17
Methanex Corp. v. United States of America [1999] UNCITRAL, 44 ILM 1345
MTD Equity Sdn. Bhd. And MTD Chile S.A. v. Chile [2001] ICSID Case No. ARB/01/7

[137] Gary Born (2016) Dissenting Opinion (8 July 2016) appended to the *Philip Morris v. Uruguay* Award, para. 142 <https://www.italaw.com/cases/460>.

[138] Zarra (2017), p. 100.

Occidental Petroleum Corporation and Occidental Exploration and Production Company v. Republic of Ecuador [2006] ICSID Case No. ARB/06/11
Philip Morris Brands Sàrl, Philip Morris Products S.A. and Abal Hermanos S.A. v. Oriental Republic of Uruguay [2010] ICSID Case No. ARB/10/7
PL Holdings S.a.r.l. v. Poland [2014] SCC Case No. 2014/163
SAUR International v. Argentine Republic [2004] ICSID Case No. ARB/04/4
S.D. Myers, Inc. v. Government of Canada [1998] UNCITRAL, NAFTA
Saluka Investments B.V. v. The Czech Republic [2001] PCA Case No. 2001-04
Sempra Energy International v. Argentine Republic [2002] ICSID Case No. ARB/02/16
SGS Société Générale de Surveillance S.A. v. Republic of the Philippines [2002] ICSID Case No. ARB/02/6
Siemens A.G. v. Republic of Argentina [2002] ICSID Case No. ARB/02/8
Técnicas Medioambientales Tecmed, S.A. v. The United Mexican States [2003] ICSID Case No. ARB(AF)/00/2
Toto Costruzioni Generali S.p.A. v. Republic of Lebanon [2007] ICSID Case No. ARB/07/12
Urbaser S.A. and Consorcio de Aguas Bilbao Biskaia, Bilbao Biskaia Ur Partzuergoa v. Argentine Republic [2007] ICSID Case No. ARB/07/26
Vattenfall AB, Vattenfall Europe AG, Vattenfall Europe Generation AG v. Federal Republic of Germany [2009] ICSID Case No. ARB/09/6
Venezuela Holdings BV, Mobil Cerro Negro Holding LTD et al. v. Venezuela [2007] ICSID Case No. ARB/07/27

Other Cases

WTO Panel Report, *Thailand – Restrictions on Importation of and Internal taxes on Cigarettes*, DS10/R – 37S/200, adopted on 7 November 1990.

Treaties

Australia–Chile FTA (2008)
Bolivia–US BIT (1998)
Croatia–US BIT (1996)
El Salvador–US BIT (1999)
Energy Charter Treaty (2017)
EU–Canada Comprehensive Economic and Trade Agreement (2017) (CETA)
EU–Singapore Free Trade Agreement (2019) (EUSFTA)
Honduras–US BIT (1995)
Jordan–US BIT (1997)
Nicaragua–US BIT (1995)

North America Free Trade Agreement (1992) (NAFTA)
Slovakia–Iran BIT (2016)
United States–Rwanda BIT (2008)
US Model BIT (2012)
Vienna Convention on the Law of Treaties (1969) (VCLT)

Bibliography

Aziz SS (2017) The investment protection chapter of the EU-Singapore Free Trade Agreement: a model for the post-Brexit UK IIAs. J East Asia Int Law 10(1):7–26

Bacchus J (2018) The willing world: shaping and sharing a sustainable global prosperity. Cambridge University Press

Baltag FCIArb C, Joshi R, Duggal K (2023) Recent trends in investment arbitration on the right to regulate, environment, health and corporate social responsibility: too much or too little? ICSID Rev 38 (2): 381-421.

Born G (2016) Dissenting opinion appended to the *Philip Morris v. Uruguay* Award, 8 July 2016. https://www.italaw.com/cases/460

Calamita NJ (2013) International human rights and the interpretation of international investment treaties: constitutional considerations. In: Baetens F (ed) Investment law within international law-integrationist perspectives. Cambridge University Press

Chi M (2018a) Integrating sustainable development in international investment law: normative incompatibility, System integration and governance implications. Routledge

Chi M (2018b) Sustainable development provisions in investment treaties', Economic and Social Commission for Asia and the Pacific, United Nations 2018. https://www.unescap.org/sites/default/files/Sustainable%20Development%20Provisions%20in%20Investment%20Treaties.pdf

Coleman J et al (2018) International Investment Agreements 2015–16: a review of trends and new approaches in Lisa E Sachs, Lise Johnson, 2015–2016 Yearbook on International Investment Law and Policy. Oxford University Press

Daly MP, Ahmad J (2015) The EU-Vietnam FTA: what does it all mean? What does it mean for the future? Kluwer Arbitration Blog. 14 December 2015. https://arbitrationblog.kluwerarbitration.com/2015/12/14/the-eu-vietnam-fta-what-does-it-all-mean-what-does-it-mean-for-the-future/

Ejims O (2019) The 2016 Morocco – Nigeria bilateral investment treaty: more practical reality in providing a balanced investment treaty? ICSID Rev 34(1)

Gehring WM, Kent A (2013) International investment agreements and the emerging green economy: rising to the challenge. In: Baetens F (ed) Investment law within international law-integrationist perspectives. Cambridge University Press

Gordon K, Pohl J (2011) Environmental concerns in international investment agreements: a survey. OECD Working Papers on International Investment, 2011/1. www.oecd.org/daf/investment/workingpapers/

Ha Le Thi Ngoc (2021) Vietnam's international investment agreements: various substantive compatibility thresholds for legislative measures. Doctoral Dissertation. La Trobe University

Henckels C (2012) Indirect expropriation and the right to regulate: revisiting proportionality analysis and the standard of review in investor-state arbitration. J Int Econ Law 15(1):255

Henckels C (2016) Protecting regulatory autonomy through greater precision in investment treaties: the TPP, CETA and TTIP. J Int Econ Law 19(1):27

Henckels C, Balancing Test: Investment Arbitration, *Max Planck Encyclopedias of International Law*, https://opil.ouplaw.com/display/10.1093/law-mpeipro/e3420.013.3420/law-mpeipro-e3420?prd=MPIL (2018).

Henin P, Howley J, Keene A, Peart N (2019) Innovating international investment agreements: a proposed green investment protocol for climate change mitigation and adaption. J Int Arbitr 36(1):64

Hindelang S, Sassenrath CP (2015) The investment chapters of the EU's international trade and investment agreements in a comparative perspective. European Parliament Directorate-General for External Policies Policy Department

Hush E (2018) Where no man has gone before: the future of sustainable development in the comprehensive economic and trade agreement and new generation free trade agreements. Columbia J Environ Law 43(1) https://journals.library.columbia.edu/index.php/cjel/article/view/3741

Julie K (2018) Balancing regulatory interests through an exceptions framework under the right to regulate provision in international investment agreements. George Washington Int Law Rev 50(2):289

Kawharu A (2015) TPPA: Chapter 9 on Investment, Expert Paper No.2 WordPress.com: TPP Legal. December 2015. https://tpplegal.files.wordpress.com/2015/12/ep2-amokura-kawharu.pdf

Korzun V (2017) The right to regulate in investor – state arbitration: slicing and dicing regulatory carve-outs. Vanderbilt J Transnl Law 50:355

Kulick A (2012) Global public interest in international investment law. Cambridge University Press

Levashova Y (2019) The right of states to regulate in international investment law: the search for balance between public interest and fair and equitable treatment. Wolters Kluwer

Muchlinski M (2016) Negotiating new generation international investment agreements: new sustainable development oriented initiatives. In: Hindelang S, Krajewski M (eds) Shifting paradigms in international investment law: more balanced, less isolated, increasingly diversified. Oxford University Press

Nadakavukaren K, Lazo R P (2023) Legal opinion on right to regulate on Investment Treaties: Canada, European Union, Japan, Netherlands, and United States of America. Swiss Institute of Comparative Law. www.isdc.ch

Newcombe A, Paradell L (2009) Law and practice of investment treaties: standards of treatment. Kluwer Law International

Martini C (2017) Balancing investors' rights with environmental protection in international investment arbitration: an assessment of recent trends in investment treaty drafting. International Lawyer 50(3):529

Ortino F (2017) Investment treaties, sustainable development and reasonableness review: a case against strict proportionality balancing. Leiden J Int Law 30(1):76

Prislan V, Zandvliet R (2014) Labour provisions in international investment agreements: prospects for sustainable development. In: Bjorklund (ed) Yearbook on International Investment Law & Policy 2012-2013. Oxford University Press, New York

Sacerdoti G, Acconi P, Valenti M, De Luca A (eds) (2014) General interest of host states in international investment law. Cambridge University Press

Salacuse JW (2015) The law of investment treaties, 2nd edn. Oxford University Press

Spears SA (2011) Making way for the Public Interest in International Investment Agreements. In: Brown C, Miles K (eds) Evolution in investment treaty law and arbitration. Cambridge University Press

Swedish National Board of Trade (2015) "The Right to Regulate" in the Trade Agreement between the EU and Canada – and Its Implications for the Agreement with the USA

Titi C (2014) The right to regulate in international investment law. Nomos and Hart

TiTi A (2018) Refining the expropriation clause: what role for proportionality. In: Chaisse J (ed) China – European Union investment relationships: towards a new leadership in global investment governance? Edward Elgar. https://papers.ssrn.com/sol3/papers.cfm?abstract_id=2978530

Titi C (2022) The right to regulate in international investment law. International and Comparative Law Research Centre. https://ssrn.com/abstract=4058447

Trujillo E (2018) Balancing sustainability, the right to regulate, and the need for investor protection: lessons from the trade regime. Boston College Law Rev 59:2735

Tudor I (2008) The fair and equitable treatment standard in the international law of foreign investment. Oxford University Press

UNCTAD (2015) World Investment Report 2015: reforming international investment governance. https://unctad.org/system/files/official-document/wir2015_en.pdf
VanDuzer JA, Simons P, Maeda G (2013) Integrating sustainable development into international investment agreements: a guide for developing country negotiators. Commonwealth Secretaria. https://www.thecommonwealth-ilibrary.org/index.php/comsec/catalog/book/168
Viñuales JE (2012) Foreign investment and the environment in international law. Cambridge University Press
Yotova R (2019) Balancing economic objectives and environmental considerations in new EU investment agreements: a brave new world? In: Miles K (ed) Research Handbook on Environment and Investment Law. Edward Elgar
Zamir N, Barker P (2017) The trans-pacific partnership agreement and states' right to regulate under international investment law. Denver J Int Law Policy 45(2):215
Zarra G (2017) Right to regulate, margin of appreciation and proportionality: current status in investment arbitration in light of *Philip Morris v. Uruguay*. Brazilian J Int Law 14(2):100
Zients J (2015) Investor-State Dispute Settlement (ISDS) questions and answers. The White House: Blog. 26 February 2015. https://obamawhitehouse.archives.gov/blog/2015/02/26/investor-state-dispute-settlement-isds-questions-and-answers

Documents

EU Council (2016) Joint Interpretative Instrument on the Comprehensive Economic and Trade Agreement (CETA) between Canada and the European Union and its Member States. 13541/16 Brussels (27 October 2016). https://data.consilium.europa.eu/doc/document/ST-13541-2016-INIT/en/pdf
European Commission (2016) CETA: EU and Canada Agree on New Approach on Investment in Trade Agreement. 29 February 2016. https://ec.europa.eu/commission/presscorner/detail/en/IP_16_399
Government of India, Ministry of Finance (2016) Office Memorandum: Issuing Joint Interpretative Statements for Indian Bilateral Investment Treaties. 8 February 2016. http://indiainbusiness.nic.in/newdesign/upload/Consolidated_Interpretive-Statement.pdf

Chapter 9
General Exception Clause Under the EVIPA

Abstract This chapter examines the role of the general exception clause (Article 4.6) in safeguarding Vietnam's regulatory autonomy under the EVIPA. This clause can potentially refine the interpretation of core obligations, such as NT and MFN treatment, which in EVIPA closely resemble those found in traditional investment treaties. While the exception clause offers a crucial mechanism for balancing investor rights with Vietnam's regulatory needs, its effectiveness hinges significantly on the approach adopted by the ICS tribunals. To maximise the clause's utility, ongoing dialogue between the EU and Vietnam is essential to clarify its scope and ensure its consistent application in practice.

9.1 Exception Clauses in International Investment Law and Environmental Protection

9.1.1 Exception Clauses as a Tool to Rebalance IIAs

In IIA negotiations, incorporating exception clauses is essential to navigate complex conflicts arising from divergent value systems.[1] As part of efforts to redesign investment treaties with a heightened emphasis on sustainable development and to restore balance to IIAs, nations are advocating for the inclusion of general exception clauses alongside the clarification of traditional substantive standards.[2] These general exceptions serve to address non-commercial concerns primarily centred on public interest, encompassing measures aimed at safeguarding essential security interests, preserving and enhancing life and health standards, protecting the environment, maintaining public order, and implementing various financial and taxation

[1] Benedetto (2013), p.158.

[2] Vandevelde (2013), p. 449; Chi (2018), p. 66.

N. T. Lan Huong, *Investment Protection and Environmental Governance*, European Yearbook of International Economic Law 47,
https://doi.org/10.1007/978-3-032-05332-9_9

measures.[3] By incorporating exception clauses, states seek to preserve their regulatory autonomy in specific policy areas from undue constraints arising from investment treaty obligations.

Amid efforts to embed sustainable development considerations within IIAs and to preserve policy space for host states to pursue their sustainable development objectives, the inclusion of general exception clauses has become increasingly prevalent in IIAs worldwide. Notably, in FTAs with investment provisions, specific instances of general exception clauses can be observed. For instance, NAFTA Chapter 21, particularly Article 2101, explicitly incorporates Article XX of the General Agreement on Tariffs and Trade under the WTO regime. Similarly, the ASEAN Comprehensive Investment Agreement of 2009, Article 17; the Agreement between the Republic of Singapore and Japan for a New Age Economic Partnership of 2002, Article 83; the European Community–Chile FTA (2002), Article 91; the India–Singapore Comprehensive Economic Cooperation Agreement (2005), Article 6.11; the Canada–States of the European Free Trade Association (Iceland, Liechtenstein, Norway, and Switzerland) FTA (2008), Article 22; the COMESA Investment Agreement (2007) includes a provision on "General Exceptions" in Article 22.

Agreements signed by countries in the Asia Pacific region are no exception to this trend. More specifically, the Australia–Korea FTA (2014), Article 22.1; the Japan–Mongolia Economic Partnership Agreement (2015), Article 1.10; the Korea–New Zealand FTA (2015), Chapter 20; Vietnam–South Korea FTA (2015), Article 16.1(2); and the Australia–China FTA (2015), Article 9.8, all include clauses on general exceptions.

While the general exception clause in BITs is not as prevalent as in FTAs, its popularity has steadily increased in recent years within the BIT negotiation context. According to the 2017 World Investment Report, 43% of BITs concluded between 2011 and 2016 included public policy exceptions.[4] Notably, several Model BITs, such as the 2004 Canadian Model BIT, Article 10; India 2015 Model BIT, Article 32; Norway 2015 Draft Model BIT, Article 24; Japan–Uruguay BIT (2015), Article 22(1); Japan–Iran BIT (2016), Article 13(1), and Azerbaijan Model BIT (2016), Article 5, have incorporated general exception clauses. Notably, all Chinese BITs concluded after 2010 include general exceptions.

Canada stands out among countries that follow this trend of including exception clauses in BITs. It is the countries that most frequently include WTO-like exceptions in its IIAs.[5] Diverging from the approach of many other nations, Canada extends these exceptions to the investment protection provisions. Indeed, general exceptions are prevalent in a significant number of Canadian BITs concluded with

[3] Vandevelde (2013), pp. 449–450.

[4] UNCTAD (2017) pp. 119, 122.

[5] Benedetto (2013), p. 197; Todic and Al-Nakid (2020).

various partners.[6] However, this policy has undergone a recent change. Canada has ceased to include the general exception clause in its current model BIT. The subsequent analysis in this chapter will shed light on the reasons behind this shift in strategy.

The trend above underscores a growing consensus among states to incorporate general exceptions, particularly those modelled on WTO general exceptions such as GATT Article XX and GATS Article XIV, into trade and investment agreements. However, the exact wording of these general exception provisions may vary depending on the respective policy priorities of the negotiating parties.[7] Furthermore, the scope of application of general exception clauses in IIAs is subject to diverse regulations. These clauses may be designed to apply to all obligations under an IIA, as seen in certain BITs signed by Canada, or they may be limited to specific investment obligations. General exceptions can have varied impacts depending on the language used in introducing such clauses and the described scope of application.[8]

In essence, general exception clauses are anticipated to be more effective and appropriate than industry carve-outs[9] and exclusions for safeguarding domestic policy space. This is because they offer necessary clarification regarding permissible governmental actions and inform investors of potential risks before deciding to invest.[10] Despite their utility, discussions surrounding these clauses have sparked considerable scepticism, with debates focusing on whether it is necessary to include exception clauses in IIAs and what can be expected from these clauses in terms of preserving regulatory space.

Regarding the first question, there are two points of view. The first perspective suggests that general exceptions can help preserve a state's policy space, but they also present various application challenges.[11] Specifically, Simon has noted that these clauses often lack clarity in scope, leading to difficulties in their implementation.[12] Moreover, broad and ambiguous investment protection obligations, such as the FET standard, differ significantly from the narrower and well-defined obligations under the WTO. Consequently, there is scepticism about the feasibility of applying such exception clauses within the context of investment treaties.[13] Muchlinski further suggests that the general provisions modelled on Article XX of

---

[6] For instance, see Canada–China BIT (2012) Article 33.2; Canada–Philippines BIT (1995) Article XVII.3; Canada–Ecuador BIT (1996), Art. XVII.3; Canada–Thailand BIT (1997) Article XVII; Canada–Czech Republic BIT (2009) Article IX; Canada–Jordan BIT (2009) Article 10. Refer Canada's Trade and Investment Agreement in <https://www.international.gc.ca/trade-commerce/trade-agreements-accords-commerciaux/agr-acc/index.aspx?lang=eng>.

[7] Chi (2018), pp. 70–71; Benedetto (2013), p. 193; Julie (2018), pp. 343–344.

[8] Mitchell et al. (2018), p. 38.

[9] An example of an industry carve-out can be found in CPTPP Article 29.5. This provision provides specific carve-out regarding tobacco control measures.

[10] Lester and Mercurio (2017), pp. 04, 10.

[11] See, for instance, Julie (2018), p. 343; Lester (2014).

[12] Ibid.

[13] Ibid.

the GATT may pose challenges by allowing adjudicators significant discretion in determining the consistency of a public policy measure with the exception.[14]

The second viewpoint posits that the inclusion of general exceptions in IIAs is unnecessary because the substantive obligations themselves, if properly interpreted, are sufficient to safeguard regulatory space,[15] provided that precisely drafted norms are included in the IIAs.[16] Thus, Newcombe has predicted that incorporating general exceptions is likely to hold little practical significance in the jurisprudence of IIAs.[17]

Regarding the second question, scholars diverge on the potential impacts of exception clauses in rebalancing the system of IIAs. Viñuales asserts that the effects of clauses formulated as exceptions to specific investment protection provisions should not be underestimated.[18] He suggests that these clauses could have a significant impact by neutralising conflicts, thereby absolving the host state of liability.[19] However, Simon counters this argument by stating that the language of such clauses does not expand the policy rights of states, as investment obligations typically only require compensation and do not prohibit any measures.[20] Moreover, satisfying a standard based on investor-based discrimination may be more challenging compared to nationality-based discrimination under the GATT framework.[21]

In evaluating the potential effect of exception clauses, some scholars go as far as to argue that exception clauses with a closed list of protected areas could restrict the scope of bona fide public policy objectives.[22] They contend that while the inclusion of general exceptions aims to bolster the regulatory autonomy of host states, it may inadvertently curtail the flexibility and recognition of regulatory purpose within the substantive investment obligations to which those exceptions apply.[23] Others express scepticism that exception clauses might exacerbate the existing uncertainty encountered by investment tribunals when assessing violations of substantive obligations resulting from regulatory measures implemented by the host state.[24] Chauvel, in particular, is concerned that incorporating such exceptions could prompt ISDS tribunals to deviate from what has become a prevailing practice.[25]

In assessing the effectiveness of applying general exceptions in IIAs, practical interpretations and applications of GATT Article XX could provide valuable insights

---

[14] Muchlinski (2016), p. 56.

[15] Newcombe and Paradell (2009), pp. 503–505.

[16] Henckels (2018), pp. 2838–2839.

[17] Newcombe (2008), p. 3.

[18] Viñuales (2012), p. 286.

[19] Ibid.

[20] Lester (2014).

[21] Ibid.

[22] See for instance, Martini (2017), p. 578; See also Gehring and Kent (2013), p. 206; Henckels (2018), p. 2836.

[23] Mitchell et al. (2018), p. 36.

[24] See further Brew (2019), p. 213.

[25] Chauvel (2017), p. 156.

due to the cross-reference between the WTO and ISDS jurisprudence.[26] However, the likelihood of successfully invoking exceptions is low for several reasons. Firstly, in interpreting IIAs, the primary objective of protecting and promoting foreign investments takes precedence. Secondly, as demonstrated in WTO litigation, WTO Panels and Appellate bodies often establish a high threshold for invoking general exceptions.[27] Moreover, due to the challenges associated with invoking exceptions in IIAs, Chi argued that their practical effectiveness should be improved. Consequently, it remains challenging, if not impossible, for states to defend their regulatory measures relying on exception clauses in IIAs.[28]

There is also concern that WTO case law regarding general exceptions is tailored to the trade context and may not readily translate to the investment context.[29] Indeed, the WTO has developed an extensive body of law elucidating the scope, degree of deference, and other facets of general exceptions that should be clarified in examining exception clauses.[30] Meanwhile, significant disparities exist between trade and investment regimes and between the dispute resolution mechanisms of the WTO and ISDS systems, making the application of similar criteria and approaches impractical. Specifically, the WTO Appellate body has endorsed a consistent and coherent interpretation of the general exception clause through a two-tier analysis. In contrast, the landscape of international investment arbitration is fragmented, with each claim being adjudicated in a different forum. Consequently, establishing an appellate mechanism within the IIL framework becomes imperative to furnish a more predictable framework for implementing environmental regulations without encountering excessive challenges from investors.[31]

Moreover, the dispute resolution practices under GATT Article XX of the WTO, which recognise Members' right to determine their desired level of protection for specific objectives, have been respected to some extent by the Panel and Appellate Body. This principle, central to the necessity test under GATT Article XX and GATS Article XIV, affords WTO members a degree of latitude in setting their level of protection.[32] Conversely, the proportionality tests applied by investment tribunals in cases concerning expropriation, fair and equitable treatment, or non-discrimination may produce outcomes less deferential to the host state's policy space.[33] Furthermore, the proportionality *stricto sensu* approach adopted by some investment tribunals may encroach upon domestic democratic processes and unduly constrain states' regulatory autonomy.[34] The asymmetry in the degree of deference accorded to a

[26] Read more in Chi (2018), p. 72.

[27] Ibid., pp. 72–73, 82.

[28] Ibid., p. 82.

[29] Henckels (2016), p. 48.

[30] Korzun (2017), p. 391.

[31] Martini (2017), p. 581.

[32] Mitchell et al. (2018), p. 27.

[33] Ibid., pp. 23, 27; Korzun (2017), p. 391.

[34] Brew (2019), p. 216.

state 's chosen level of protection across these international dispute settlement systems may thus lead to divergent outcomes.

9.1.2 Exception Clauses in ISDS Practice

Research indicates that there is limited direct experience in applying general exceptions, particularly those fashioned after WTO exception clauses, in investor-state litigation practice. Among the disputes where tribunals have examined exceptions included in relevant IIAs, this provision has seldom been successfully invoked.[35] The findings of the review of ISDS tribunals' approaches to interpreting exception clauses underscore the aforementioned challenges. According to a study by Henckels, while tribunals do not explicitly outline the basis for their decisions, their rulings reveal two discernible trends in assessing exception clauses.[36] Some tribunals seem to regard exceptions as an affirmative defence, particularly those in early cases involving the security exception under the *United States–Argentina BIT*,[37] such as *CMS v. Argentina*,[38] *Enron v. Argentina* in 2007,[39] and *Sempra v. Argentina*.[40] A similar approach was observed in two other disputes involving Argentina, *LG&E v. Argentina* and *El Paso Energy International Company v. Argentine Republic*.[41] Specifically, in *LG&E v. Argentina*, the tribunal emphasised on scrutinising the circumstances surrounding Argentina's actions to ascertain their justification under the exception rather than evaluating compliance with fair and equitable treatment. As a result of this analysis, the tribunal found Argentina in breach of FET but ultimately not liable due to the successful invocation of the security exception.[42] Notably, the tribunals in *Bear Creek v. Peru* even commented that the exception clause should serve to legitimise otherwise unfair conduct, akin to Article XX of the GATT.[43] In these cases, violations of treaty obligations are preliminarily deemed to have

---

[35] Chi (2018), p. 82, 157; See also Newcombe (2008), pp. 8–12.

[36] Henckels (2018), pp. 2831–2834.

[37] United States–Argentina BIT (1991) Article XI.

[38] *CMS Gas Transmission Co. v. Republic of Argentina* [2001] ICSID Case No. ARB/01/8, Award, 12 May 2004, paras. 320–324, 329, 355–356, 374.

[39] *Enron Creditors Recovery Corporation and Ponderosa Assets, L.P. v. Argentine Republic* (*Enron v. Argentina*) [2001] ICSID Case No. ARB/01/3, Award, 22 May 2007, paras. 334, 339.

[40] *Sempra Energy International v. Argentine Republic* [2002] ICSID Case No. ARB/02/16, Award, 28 September 2007, paras. 376, 388.

[41] *LG&E Energy Corp., LG&E Capital Corp., and LG&E International, Inc. v. Argentine Republic*, ICSID Case No. ARB/02/1; *El Paso Energy International Company v. The Argentine Republic*, ICSID Case No. ARB/03/15.

[42] *LG&E v. Argentina* [2002] ICSID Case No. ARB/02/1, Award, 3 October 2006, para. 132.

[43] *Bear Creek Mining Corporation v. Republic of Peru* [2014] ICSID Case No. ARB/14/21, Award, 30 November 2017, para. 475.

occurred, and successful reliance on exceptions is seen as a means for the host state to evade the consequences of its actions.

Diverging from the perspective adopted by tribunals in the aforementioned cases, other Tribunals advocate for the interpretation of exception clauses as permissions that delimit the scope of investment protections in the treaty.[44] In two cases concerning the security exception under the United States–Argentina BIT, namely *CMS v. Argentina*[45] (Annulment Committee) and *Continental Casualty Company v. Argentine Republic*, the Annulment Committee and the tribunal asserted that this provision "reserved rights" of state parties under the treaty, implying that when it applied, substantive obligations would be "set aside or suspended."[46] Scholars also underscore the significance of the tribunal's decision in *Copper Mesa v. Ecuador*, which involved a general exception clause akin to Article XX of the GATT. In this case, the tribunal held that an expropriation claim would be established, in part, by the "non-application" of the exception.[47] This interpretation suggests that the tribunal perceives the provision as circumscribing the treaty's scope, requiring the claimant to demonstrate that the impugned measure fell outside the purview of treaty protection.[48] In other words, exceptions function as permissions that exempt specific measures from the scope of treaty obligations.

These divergent trends underscore the inconsistency in ISDS tribunals' approaches to assessing the role of exception clauses and the ambiguity surrounding their relationship with substantive obligations. Henckels posits that interpreting exceptions as defences may constrain rather than enhance states' regulatory flexibility.[49] Moreover, she contends that exceptions may entail a stricter nexus requirement compared to the application of relevant substantive norms by investment tribunals, as exception clauses additionally mandate that the applied measure satisfy the "necessity test".[50] Henckels also critiques the notion of treating an exception as a defence, as it may lead tribunals to adopt a restrictive interpretation, considering exceptions as deviations from general principles and thus warranting narrow construal.[51]

Although general exception clauses, including those modelled after Article XX of the GATT, are commonly included in IIAs, the practice above underscores the importance of carefully drafting exception clauses and adopting a more nuanced approach to interpreting them within the context of investment agreements. To

[44] Henckels (2018), p. 2832.

[45] *CMS Gas Transmission Co. v. Republic of Argentina* [2001] ICSID Case No. ARB/01/8, Award, 12 May 2004, para. 129.

[46] *Continental Casualty Company v. Argentine Republic* [2003] ICSID Case No. ARB/03/9, Award, 5 September 2008, para. 168.

[47] *Copper Mesa Mining Corporation v. Republic of Ecuador* [2011] PCA No. 2012-2, Award, 15 March 2016, para. 6.58.

[48] Henckels (2018), p. 2832.

[49] See further discussion in Henckels, ibid., pp. 2836–2837.

[50] Ibid., p. 2837.

[51] Ibid., pp. 2837–2838.

achieve this goal, scholars have proposed that the drafting of exception clauses should not be confined to an exhaustive list but rather allow non-listed objectives to be permissible as long as they meet the "legitimate" criteria specified.[52] Moreover, employing language tailored to international investment law is crucial to fostering consistent outcomes in investor-state arbitration.[53] Certain state objectives should be articulated precisely to minimise ambiguity and constrain unexpected tribunal interpretations.[54] This approach would provide greater assurance to treaty parties that tribunals will interpret these provisions as intended.[55]

When interpreting this clause, it is crucial to perceive the exception clause as permissions that limit the scope of the investment protections in the relevant treaty rather than as defenses used to justify potentially unlawful conduct.[56] Viewing exceptions as permissions offers several advantages, notably, it ensures that regulatory purpose is taken into account when assessing a government's compliance with the treaty's substantive obligations.[57] This approach sends a clear signal to tribunals and potential claimants that states maintain regulatory authority in the specified areas covered by the provision, with regulatory purpose playing a central role in determining breach.[58] Moreover, this perspective aligns well to foster sustainable economic development, as it positions investment protection as a means to that end.[59] By striking a balance between investment protection and governmental autonomy to pursue policy objectives, this approach promotes a more holistic and equitable framework for international investment agreements.

9.2 Enhancing Regulatory Autonomy: The Role of the General Exceptions Clause in EVIPA

In the current landscape, where exception clauses are increasingly used to safeguard states' regulatory rights, the EVIPA also incorporates numerous exceptions within Chapter 4. Notably, it delineates exceptions on taxation (Article 4.1) and security considerations (Article 4.8). Among those, the general exceptions provided in Article 4.6 of the EVIPA are worth examining as they are expected to justify the state's policy measures.

Article 4.6, on General exceptions under EVIPA, is texted as a special exception stating that this regulation is an escape from NT and MFN treatment obligations.

[52] Brew (2019), pp. 218–219.

[53] Julie (2018), p. 344; Martini (2017), p. 579.

[54] Brew (2019), pp. 219–220.

[55] Henckels (2016), p. 47.

[56] Henckels (2018), p. 2843.

[57] Ibid., p. 2825.

[58] Ibid., p. 2843.

[59] Ibid.

With due regard to sustainability and environmental protection, this article includes, among others, measures that are applied to protect "human, animal or plant life or health" or to conserve "exhaustible natural resources" as below:

> Article 4.6
>
> Subject to the requirement that such measures are not applied in a manner which would constitute a means of arbitrary or unjustifiable discrimination between countries where like conditions prevail, or a disguised restriction on covered investment, nothing in Articles 2.3 (National Treatment) and 2.4 (Most-Favoured-Nation Treatment) shall be construed as preventing the adoption or enforcement by any Party of measures:
>
> (a) necessary to protect public security or public morals or to maintain public order;
>
> (b) necessary to protect human, animal or plant life or health;
>
> (c) relating to the conservation of exhaustible natural resources if such measures are applied in conjunction with restrictions on domestic investors or on the domestic supply or consumption of services;
>
> (d) necessary for the protection of national treasures of artistic, historic or archaeological value;
>
> ....

Among the objectives outlined in Article 4.6 of the EVIPA, those delineated in subparagraphs (b) and (c) hold particular relevance to the research context of this book. These sub-paragraphs will be further explored in the subsequent section of this chapter.

Article 4.6 of the EVIPA, addressing general exceptions, mirrors the language found in Article XX of the GATT and Article XIV of the GATS, particularly in its references to "discrimination between countries where the same conditions prevail." Interestingly, it does not replace this language with a more precise phrase tailored to the context of IIAs, such as "discrimination between investments or between investors," as observed in Canada's 2004 Model IIA (Article 10).[60] However, Article 4.6 of the EVIPA presents a shorter list of policy objectives than GATT Article XX's list.

In the EVIPA, Article 4.6 stands as a distinct provision, granting exemption from non-discriminatory regulations, including NT and MFN treatment obligations. With a focus on sustainability and environmental protection, this clause encompasses measures aimed at protecting "human, animal, or plant life or health" (Para. (b)) and conserving "exhaustible natural resources" (Para. (c)). Consequently, measures aimed at safeguarding all environmental protection-related objectives are covered under this exception.

It is anticipated that determining whether a specific measure falls within the scope of those aimed at pursuing these particular objectives will not pose a challenge for the tribunals, as such considerations are commonplace in both investment arbitration and international trade dispute settlement contexts. Furthermore, WTO Panels and the Appellate Body have broadly interpreted the objectives outlined in general exceptions, typically affording states the benefit of the doubt regarding

[60] It's noteworthy that while Canada 2021 Model FIPA includes General Exceptions in Article 22, the language and scope of this clause differ significantly from the general exception clause included in its earlier 2004 version.

whether a challenged measure aligns with the relevant category.[61] It is also expected that determining whether a specific measure aligns with a policy objective under a general exception in the ISDS context does not necessitate stringent and intricate criteria as in WTO practice. However, ICS tribunals still require a certain grasp of key public policy concepts, such as "relating to," "conservation," or "exhaustible natural resources." Thus, referencing WTO jurisprudence becomes essential to delineate the meaning and scope of these terms accurately.[62]

Notably, Article 4.6 employs distinct expressions when referring to different policy objectives. The use of the terms "necessary" and "relating to" yields varying implications. In the case of protecting human, animal, or plant life or health, the applied measure must be "necessary," establishing a stringent standard for the state to satisfy. Conversely, in the context of conserving exhaustible natural resources, Paragraph (c) merely mentions a measure that is "relating to" conservation.

In addition to Article 4.6 on general exceptions, Annex 2 of the EVIPA includes a noteworthy exemption for Vietnam regarding national treatment in the preservation of natural resources. This exemption aligns with sustainable objectives and encompasses activities such as oil and gas exploration, mineral and natural resources exploration, prospecting, and exploitation, fishery and aquaculture, and forestry and hunting. This provision explicitly excludes certain sectors from national treatment-related commitments under the EVIPA. It reflects the Vietnamese government's prioritisation of sectors associated with the exploitation of natural resources. However, since these exemptions do not present significant application challenges, they will not be assessed in this chapter.

This section will now turn to assess the implementation of Article 4.6 of the EVIPA and highlight potential challenges that could impact the objective of preserving the regulatory rights of the contracting parties under this agreement. Drawing from the precedent set by WTO jurisprudence, an ICS tribunal is anticipated to initially scrutinise whether a measure is deemed "necessary" to achieve a legitimate objective. Subsequently, the tribunal will evaluate whether such measures meet the criteria outlined in the introductory part of this exception. These examinations will be elaborated upon in the following discussion.

---

[61] Henckels (2016), p. 47.

[62] For example, the objective to protect human, animal, or plant life or health pertains to measures intended for health-related policies, as elucidated in the Thailand cigarettes case. Similarly, the objective to conserve exhaustible natural resources is clarified in cases like Canada – Measures Affecting Exports of Unprocessed Herring and Salmon, L/6268 – 35S/98, WTO Panel Report, adopted on 22 March 1988 and *United States – Prohibition of Imports of Tuna and Tuna Products from Canada*, L/5198 – 29S/91, WTO Panel Report, adopted on 22 February 1982.

9.2.1 The "Necessity" Test Under Sub-paragraph (b) and (d) Article 4.6 EVIPA

As highlighted earlier, Article 4.6 of the EVIPA raises the standard for qualifying a state's measure by imposing the requirement of being "necessary" when invoking exceptions for the protection of human, animal, or plant life or health. However, similar to other exception clauses included in IIAs, Article 4.6 of the EVIPA does not clearly define this term.[63] The absence of a clear definition of "necessary" under Article 4.6 of the EVIPA leads scholars to observe that adjudicators will possess broader discretion in assessing compliance with the requirements.[64] However, this book contends that the future ICS—a quasi-judicial system with a two-level trial system comprising the tribunal and the Appeal tribunal (Para. 3 Article 3.27 EVIPA)—will establish a consistent "legal test" adapted to relevant concepts. Such practices have been observed in the WTO dispute settlement system over approximately three decades of operation.

In the context of GATT-WTO dispute settlement practice, establishing the "necessity" requirement proves challenging, as it necessitates an examination of the absence of alternative measures,[65] as discussed in Chap. 8. It has been suggested that tribunals can consider WTO jurisprudence and the customary necessity defence to define "necessary" in IIA exception clauses, as applied by some IIA tribunals.[66] Specifically, the customary necessity defence is widely considered to be codified by Article 25 of the International Law Commission's Draft Articles on Responsibility of States for Internationally Wrongful Acts, which stipulates that the act should be "the only way for the State to secure an essential interest."[67] This "only way" requirement aligns with the WTO's approach to evaluating the "necessity" requirement under WTO law. Specifically, besides weighing and balancing various factors,[68] the WTO necessity test includes a so-called "least-restrictive-means"

[63] In general, IIAs seldom elabourate on what constitutes "necessary". A notable exception is the Indian Model BIT 2016 which includes a footnote in Article 32.1 (footnote no. 6) explaining that "in considering whether a measure is 'necessary', the tribunal shall take into account whether there was no less restrictive alternative measure reasonably available to a Party." See further Brew (2019), p. 221.

[64] Henckels (2016), p. 48.

[65] Regan (2007), p. 348.

[66] Brew (2019), pp. 221–224.

[67] Ibid.

[68] These factor include the "importance of the objective" pursued by the measure, the measure's "contribution... to that objective," and the measure's "trade-restrictiveness," as mentioned in WTO Appellate Body Report, *European Communities – Measures Prohibiting the Importation and Marketing of Seal Products*, WT/DS/400/R; WT/DS401/AB/R, adopted on 22 May 2014, para 5.169. See further Brew (2019), p. 224.

analysis. In this analysis, an alternative measure must be less restrictive while providing an equivalent contribution to achieving the objective pursued.[69]

However, it has been argued that when referencing WTO conceptions, ICS tribunals must exercise caution because not all aspects align with the investment context, particularly the "weighing and balancing" approach.[70] Specifically, IIA exception clauses should only specify that "necessity" is assessed through a least-restrictive-means test, where a measure is deemed not "necessary" if a reasonably available and less investment-restrictive alternative measure would contribute equally or more effectively to the state's chosen level of protection of its objective. Even when the least-restrictive-means test is applied, there's concern that it typically excludes justification for the most severe investment-restrictive methods of achieving a legitimate objective.

In the case of sub-paragraph (c) of Article 4.6 of the EVIPA, the language regarding a measure "relating to" the conservation of exhaustible natural resources doesn't impose as stringent requirements as those for a measure deemed "necessary." Under the WTO regime, the concept of "relating to" entails that a measure is "primarily aimed at" achieving an objective, implying "a close and genuine relationship of ends and means" between the measure and the objective.[71] However, due to limited precedents at investment tribunals, it's challenging to predict whether they will adopt the same interpretation as the WTO's Appellate Body. Nevertheless, the use of "relating to" in Paragraph (c) of Article 4.6 of the EVIPA instead of "necessary" in other sub-paragraphs suggests that this provision may be invoked more easily and could be more applicable than the case requiring measures deemed "necessary."

9.2.2 *Requirements Under the Introduction of Article 4.6 EVIPA*

Similar to Article XX of the GATT and Article XIV of the GATS, Article 4.6 of the EVIPA also contains an introductory clause, or chapeau, which establishes additional requirements alongside those outlined in specific sub-paragraphs. Generally, these chapeau requirements serve as safeguards against the abuse and misuse of exceptions,[72] a stance commonly supported by scholars.[73]

The introductory part of Article 4.6 of the EVIPA mirrors the language found in the chapeau of Article XX of the GATT. The stipulations outlined in this chapeau

[69] WTO Appellate Body Report, *Brazil – Measures Affecting Imports of Retreaded Tyres* (Brazil–Retreaded Tyres), WT/DS332/AB/R, adopted on 3 December 2007, para. 156. See further Brew (2019), p. 225.

[70] Brew (2019), pp. 226–228.

[71] WTO Appellate Body Report, *United States – Standards for Reformulated and Conventional Gasoline*, WT/DS2/AB/R, adopted on 29 April 1996, paras. 18–19.

[72] Ibid., para. 22.

[73] Brew (2019), pp. 232–233.

primarily focus on the requirement of "good faith" in the application of relevant measures, ensuring that such measures are not implemented in a manner that would constitute arbitrary or unjustifiable discrimination between countries with similar conditions or serve as a disguised restriction on covered investment. Consequently, this provision mandates that tribunals assess whether the application of a specific measure could potentially result in (i) arbitrary or unjustifiable discrimination or (ii) a disguised restriction on covered investment or not.

In the context of ISDS, the determination of whether a measure engenders arbitrary or unjustifiable discrimination typically revolves around whether foreign investments are subjected to unfavourable treatment.[74] Regarding the terms "arbitrary" or "unjustifiable", WTO jurisprudence does not draw a clear distinction between these terms.[75] Furthermore, WTO case law underscores the importance of scrutinising the application of exceptions to specific measures, as they have the potential to inadvertently foster arbitrary and unjustifiable discrimination, as evidenced in cases such as *Brazil–Retreated Tyres*,[76] a significant dispute relating to the interplay between the right to regulate and free trade under the WTO regime.

In this case, Brazil implemented an import ban on used and retreated tyres alongside various measures aimed at addressing the issue of waste tyre disposal. However, this ban came with two exemptions: one granted to MERCOSUR members, allowing the importation of retreaded tyres (the MERCOSUR exemption), and another permitting the importation of used tyres in specific cases due to a Brazilian court injunction (the Brazilian court injunction exemption). Notably, the import of recycled tyres from the European Community and other non-MERCOSUR countries remained prohibited. When challenged at the WTO's Dispute Settlement System by the European Community, Brazil argued that its measures were justified under Article XX(b) of the GATT 1994, as they were deemed "necessary to protect human, animal, or plant life or health."

While the WTO's Appellate Body agreed that the import ban was provisionally justified as "necessary" under Article XX(b), it ruled that the exemptions resulted in arbitrary or unjustifiable discrimination, as they were not aligned with the general objective of the measure.[77] This case underscores the importance of ensuring that any exceptions to a measure which treats investors differently must be justified by the overarching purpose of the measure itself.[78] Such exceptions in domestically applied policies aimed at promoting state-directed investment are commonplace and carry a risk of failing to meet the requirements outlined in the chapeau of the

---

[74] Ibid., p. 233.

[75] Ibid.

[76] WTO Appellate Body Report, *Brazil–Retreaded Tyres*, WT/DS332/AB/R, adopted on 17 December 2007.

[77] Ibid., para. 258.

[78] Chauvel (2017), p. 152.

general exception. For example, states frequently implement tax policies with exemptions to incentivise activities aligned with policy objectives.[79]

In the investment context, Brew argues that measures meeting the necessity to contribute to a legitimate objective have already satisfied the requirement of being the "least trade/investment restrictive means" to achieve the desired level of host state protection.[80] Consequently, the stringent standard of review under the necessity test renders the requirements set out in the introductory section unnecessary. Brew commented that it is impossible for an arbitrary restriction to be considered as the least investment restrictive means.[81] While this perspective has merit, this book maintains that the chapeau requirements serve as a vital filter to mitigate measures that pose disguised restrictions to be justified under the exception clause. Moreover, as seen in the *Brazil–Retreated Tyre*s case, while the import ban was deemed "necessary" under Article XX(b) and provisionally justified under that provision,[82] its two exemptions rendered its application discriminatory, highlighting the significance of adhering to the chapeau of Article XX.[83]

Regarding the requirement for "a disguised restriction," it is essential to note that this element aims to uncover whether a measure's true intent is to restrict international investment. Uncovering the underlying motive behind a measure or series of measures can be complex. It may involve examining broader circumstances, including the state's legislative framework, its conduct, and the political context surrounding the measure.[84] Brew suggests that tribunals may need to consider evaluating multiple measures collectively, besides the disputed measure, to achieve stated legitimate objectives, especially in environmental objectives, where a single measure may not suffice.[85]

Assessing whether a measure violates a substantive obligation often relies on specific requirements outlined in relevant substantive obligations. Within the framework of the EVIPA, the assessment of a measure's hidden motives is inherently intertwined with elements present in regulations on indirect expropriation and fair and equitable treatment, while not explicitly stated in the wording of NT and MFN clauses. Therefore, this inquiry may aid in determining whether a particular measure imposes restrictions on protected entities.

Indeed, EVIPA provisions on NT (Article 2.3) and MFN treatment (Article 2.4) do not differ much from the approach taken in the majority of traditional IIAs. The purpose and scope of these provisions remain ambiguous under the current wording, lacking sufficient factors for tribunals to consider when determining whether an

---

[79] Ibid.

[80] Brew (2019), p. 233.

[81] Ibid.

[82] WTO Appellate Body Report, *Brazil–Retreaded Tyres*, WT/DS332/AB/R, adopted on 3 December 2007, para 258.

[83] Ibid.

[84] Brew (2019), pp. 234–235.

[85] Ibid.

investor is treated less favourably than domestic investors (in the case of NT treatment) or investors of third states (in the case of MFN treatment) in similar circumstances. This ambiguity grants arbitrators broad interpretive discretion.[86] This characteristic is consistent with most trade-investment treaties featuring a general exception clause that follows GATT Article XX, regardless of whether they include clarifications to be applied to specific investment obligations or not[87] as these treaties typically do not clarify the meaning of "like circumstances."[88]

A more robust drafting model for the NT clause can be observed in the CPTPP, which incorporates considerations directly into the substantive obligation rather than introducing separate exceptions alongside the NT clause.[89] Notably, the CPTPP lacks a comparable exception clause specifically applied to investment standards. Chapter 29 of the CPTPP outlines various general exceptions applicable to the agreement overall. However, those resembling the general exceptions in the WTO concerning trade in goods and services (Article 29.1) do not extend to the investment chapter.

Given that the NT and MFN obligations under the EVIPA do not offer detailed guidance, an exception clause in the EVIPA, particularly the conditions outlined in its introduction part, holds significant importance in aiding the ICS tribunals in interpreting these nondiscrimination clauses. Specifically, suppose a specific measure targets a policy objective. In that case, the state's measure will still be upheld unless there is evidence of arbitrary or unjustifiable discrimination or a disguised restriction on covered investment.

9.3 Reflections from ISDS Practice

As previously noted, relatively few cases of general exception clauses have been invoked in investment arbitration thus far. The rare cases that have arisen primarily pertain to the Argentina–United States BIT concerning emergency measures implemented by the government during its economic crisis in 2001–2002. These cases underscore the broad discretion afforded to legislatures in this domain and suggest the importance of drafting some of the objectives referenced in these clauses with

---

[86] Mitchell et al. (2018), p. 43. See also the assessments given by investment tribunals in the process of identifying an appropriate comparator for the purpose of non-discrimination obligations in Mitchell et al. (2018), pp. 16–17.

[87] For instance, CETA; Australia–New Zealand Investment Protocol (2011) Article 19; Korea–Australia FTA (2014) Article 22.1.3.

[88] Departing from this trend, the IIA between Nigeria and Singapore signed in 2016 includes a footnote guiding tribunals, ensuring that the application of general exceptions to these provisions does not diminish governments' ability to take measures where investors are not in like circumstances due to legitimate regulatory objectives. Nigeria–Singapore BIT (2016) Article 28.

[89] Henckels (2018), p. 2841. For a deeper exploration of notable innovations regarding the National Treatment clause in the CPTPP, refer Henckels' analysis in Henckels (2016), p. 50. See also Chauvel (2017), p. 155.

greater precision. This would provide greater assurance to treaty parties that tribunals will interpret these provisions as intended. This section examines lessons drawn from the application of exception clauses in ISDS proceedings to identify potential solutions to enhance the effectiveness of including such clauses in IIAs generally and the application of Article 4.6 of the EVIPA in particular.

In practice, some tribunals, such as in the *Pope and Talbot v. Canada*, have expressed concern that a blanket exception for regulatory measures could create a "gaping loophole" in international investment protections.[90] This apprehension may partly explain why investment tribunals have generally approached the application of this clause cautiously, particularly concerning public welfare objectives and its interaction with expropriation clauses. For example, in cases like *Enron v. Argentina* and *Sempra v. Argentina*, tribunals have advocated for a "restrictive" interpretation of exception clauses in IIAs.[91] Obviously, this narrow approach by investment tribunals cannot contribute to preserving the state's right to regulate.

One notable dispute stemming from measures prohibiting mining activities in an environmental conservation zone, covered by a general exceptions clause regarding environmental measures in the Canada–Colombia FTA (2008) Article 2201(3), is the *Eco Oro v. Colombia* case.[92] The approach taken by the tribunal in Eco Oro regarding the exception clause under the Canada–Colombia FTA has sparked significant controversy. Initially, the tribunal referred to Article 31(1) of the VCLT 1969, emphasising interpretation "in good faith in accordance with the ordinary meaning of the terms of the treaty in their context and in the light of its object and purpose" (Para. 827). However, instead of focusing on the ordinary meaning of the exception clause, the tribunal analysed the Preamble to elucidate the FTA's object and purpose. From this perspective, the tribunal concluded that "neither environmental protection nor investment protection is subservient to the other; they must co-exist in a mutually beneficial manner" (Para. 828). Within this framework, the tribunal interpreted Article 2201(3) as "permissive, ensuring a Party is not prohibited from adopting or enforcing a measure to protect human, animal, or plant life and health, provided that such measures are not arbitrary or unjustifiably discriminatory between investment or between investors or a disguised restriction on international trade or investment" (Para. 829). However, the tribunal arrived at the surprising conclusion that "there is no provision in Article 2201(3) permitting such action to be taken without the payment of compensation" (Para. 829). It further explained that "a State may adopt or enforce a measure regarding the stated objectives in Article 2201(3) without finding itself in breach of the FTA; however, this

---

[90] *Pope and Talbot v. The Government of Canada* [1999] UNCITRAL, Award on the Merits of Phase 2, 10 April 2001, para. 99.

[91] *Enron Creditors Recovery Corporation and Ponderosa Assets, L.P. v. Argentine Republic* [2001] ICSID Case No. ARB/01/3, Award, 22 May 2007, para. 373; *Sempra Energy International v. Argentine Republic* [2002] ICSID Case No. ARB/02/16, Award, 28 September 2007, para. 373. These cases relating to claims based on Article XI of the United States–Argentina BIT (1991).

[92] *Eco Oro Minerals Corp. v. Republic of Colombia* [2016] ICSID Case No. ARB/16/41, Award, 15 July 2024.

does not prevent an investor from claiming compensation under Chapter 8 [the relevant investment chapter], even if the measure is lawful under the treaty's exception clause." (Para. 830) This interpretation essentially undermines the role and purpose of exceptions in IIAs.

Regrettably, these assessments were seemingly made without considering a non-disputing party submission (NDPS) from Canada,[93] submitted on February 27, 2020. In this NDPS, Canada clarified the order of operation for two types of norms: exceptions operating after a prima facie breach of an investment standard.[94] According to Canada, "whether a measure is justified under an exception is a distinct inquiry that must be viewed through a different lens" from the evaluation of substantive standards. Importantly, Canada highlighted that an exception clause can only be activated following a finding of breach. Specifically, the order of operation for the two types of norms should be as follows: exceptions operate after a prima facie breach of an investment standard has been established. This exception is only triggered after a finding of a breach and operates to inquire if there are grounds for not finding a state liable despite that breach.[95] Therefore, while this proposal approaches the exception clause as a defence rather than permission, it still merits precedence over the approach taken by the tribunal in the Eco Oro case.

Regarding the tribunal's approach to the role of the exception clause in the Canada Colombia FTA, Canada underscored in its NDPS that "if the general exception applies, then there is no violation of the Agreement and no State liability. Payment of compensation would therefore not be required."[96] Regrettably, the Eco Oro tribunal does not align with Canada's perspective on this matter.

Scholars generally endorse the view that the insertion of a general exception clause aims to "enhance regulatory flexibility by permitting host states to regulate foreign investment without incurring international liability for their actions."[97] Given this understanding of the exception clause's role, the Eco Oro tribunal's proposition of an approach that disregards the explicit intent of the treaty parties is truly confounding. Essentially, such an exception clause in an IIA affirms the right to implement policy measures as long as they adhere to the stipulated requirements in its text. In such cases, the state is free from the obligation to provide compensation. Ultimately, the purpose of the public order carve-out is to allow exceptions in IIAs for measures deemed necessary for maintaining public order.[98]

In addition to the dispute above, the *Bear Creek v. Peru* case also drew significant criticism from scholars regarding the tribunal's interpretations.[99] In this instance,

---

[93] A non-disputing party submission may function as a form of 'subsequent practice' under Article 31(3) of the VCLT.

[94] Todic and Al-Nakib (2020).

[95] Ibid.

[96] *Eco Oro v. Colombia* [2016] ICSID Case No. ARB/16/41, Non-disputing Party Submission of Canada, 27 February 2020, para. 16.

[97] Sabanogullari (2015); Levashova (2019), p. 27.

[98] Julie (2018), p. 340.

[99] Titi (2022), p. 55.

when assessing the general exception clause in the Canada–Peru FTA, the tribunal remarked that "the exception clause must lead to the conclusion that no other exceptions from general international law or otherwise can be considered applicable in this case."[100] This comment is contentious because it suggests that by incorporating general exceptions for public welfare interests, states nullify all defences under international law. This conclusion disregards the lex specialis–lex generalis conflict rule under international law.[101] Notably, echoing the stance of the tribunals in *Eco Oro v. Colombia*, which asserted that "the exception in Article 2201 of the FTA does not offer any waiver from the obligation... to compensate for the expropriation,"[102] the tribunal in Bear Creek concluded that "irrespective of a possible applicability of the Exception in Article 2201 of the FTA", two of the breaches of Article 812 of the FTA (on expropriation)…remain and thus Supreme Decree 032 must be considered a breach of the FTA.[103]

The reasoning and conclusions drawn in the aforementioned cases have essentially nullified the significance of the general exception clause, prompting considerable concerns about its future application. Titi proposes two possibilities leading to this situation.[104] Firstly, these clauses introduce broad exceptions, posing challenges for tribunals in giving them full effect. Secondly, it underscores the necessity for arbitrators with a robust background in public international law, or at the very least, competence in interpreting IIAs. It remains unclear whether Canada's decision not to retain a similar language for the exception clause in its Canada 2021 Model FIPA was directly influenced by these experiences. Nonetheless, these concerns offer valuable insights for ICS tribunals when faced with situations involving invocating exception clauses.

The interpretive challenges surrounding the general exception clause, modelled after GATT Article XX and GATS Article XIV in ISDS, underscore the complexities of applying trade principles in the investment context due to inherent differences between the two domains. To ensure effective application, investment arbitrators must navigate novel and intricate questions, including the extent to which they should draw from WTO jurisprudence and how to appropriately apply such clauses in the international investment regime.[105] Moreover, Vietnam and the EU should collaborate to provide guidance to the ICS tribunals, outlining the extent to which they expect tribunals to consider WTO jurisprudence in applying exceptions. In fact, Article 3.21 EVIPA has mentioned that the arbitration panel needs to take into account relevant interpretation in reports of panel and Appellate Body adopted

[100] *Bear Creek Mining Corporation v. Republic of Peru*, ICSID Case No. ARB/14/2, Award, 30 November 2017, para. 473.

[101] Titi (2014), p. 55.

[102] *Bear Creek v. Peru*, ICSID Case No. ARB/14/2, Award, 30 November 2017, para. 476.

[103] Ibid., para 478.

[104] Titi (2022), p. 58.

[105] Julie (2018), p. 343; See also Roberts (2013), p. 46.

by the WTO's Dispute Settlement Body.[106] However, any reference to the WTO's experience should be tailored and applied in accordance with the unique context of investment treaties. Resolving these issues necessitates extensive knowledge of international law and a keen understanding of the parties' intentions to safeguard policy space. Consequently, members of ICS tribunals must possess these qualifications. Contracting parties of the EVIPA should, therefore, carefully consider these factors to facilitate the application of the general exception clause under EVIPA.

9.4 Exception Clause Under EVIPA: The Need for Clarification

This section examines the application of Article 4.6 EVIPA on general exceptions in investment arbitration proceedings. When Article 4.6 EVIPA is invoked during the litigation process, the focus shifts away from proving violations of NT or MFN obligations. Instead, the inquiry centres on whether the measure meets the requirement of "necessity" or is "related to" specific legitimate objectives outlined in the relevant sub-paragraph of Article 4.6 EVIPA. If these conditions are met, factors such as arbitrary or unjustifiable discrimination or disguised restrictions will be further examined.

During the determination of these factors, the burden of proof is shifted between the disputing parties, commencing with the host state tasked with proving that the disputing measure is necessary to achieve the relevant legitimate policy objective as stated in sub-paragraphs (b) or (c) of Article 4.6 EVIPA. This burden is not easily discharged for the host state, as any chosen measure leading to differential treatment between national and foreign investors (in the case of NT) or among foreign investors (in the case of MFN) must be no more restrictive than necessary to achieve its legitimate objective at the expected level of protection. Nonetheless, the host state possesses significant advantages, with ample resources within its administrative mechanism and sufficient information (from both international organisations and domestic authorities) to provide proof of the necessity to apply the measure. If successful, the host state's demonstration of the measure's necessity positively excludes the existence of "like circumstances" between national and foreign investors or among foreign investors.[107]

Subsequently, the burden shifts to the investor, who must prove that the applied measure is not "necessary." To meet this requirement, the investor must identify a reasonable alternative that is less restrictive than the contested measure while making an equivalent contribution to the objective. This task poses a significant

[106] The contracting parties of CPTPP have adopted a similar proactive approach to support their Panel under Paragraph 3 Article 28.12 Chapter 28 CPTPP on dispute settlement.

[107] Refer to the analysis applied by the Tribunal in *Pope and Talbot v. Canada* [1999] UNCITRAL, Award on the Merits of Phase 2, 10 April 2001, ICSID Reports, Vol. 7, p. 102, para. 78–79. See further discussion on this process in Chauvel (2017), p. 142.

challenge for the investor, lacking the advantages of human resources, knowledge, and information the host states enjoy. Even if the investor invests substantial resources in hiring lawyers, experts, and support mechanisms for this analysis, gathering all necessary information to propose a less restrictive, reasonable alternative measure that achieves the same objective remains complex.

In case such a reasonable available alternative is indicated by the investor, the burden shifts to the host state, which must prove that the alternative measure would not suffice to achieve its desired level of protection concerning the pursued objective.[108] Should the host state successfully demonstrate this element, the burden remains with the investor, who must prove that the measure resulted in arbitrary or unjustifiable discrimination, or led to a disguised restriction on covered investment. This allocation of the burden of proof to the claimant aligns with established positions in international law.[109] By placing the burden of proof on both the host state and the investor, the ISDS system becomes more balanced, promoting fairness and transparency in the authoritative decision-making process.[110]

However, it is essential to recognise the challenges in proving these factors for both the investor and the host state, particularly given the stringent standard of review required by the necessity test. Therefore, the evaluation of the ICS tribunal regarding the necessity test and the characteristics of the applied measure is crucial. If the investor successfully proves these elements, the exception clause is deemed unsuccessfully invoked, and the host state is held liable for violating relevant substantive IIA obligations. Conversely, the measure the host state applied is considered not to violate NT or MFN standards. This scenario is drawn on the basis of considering the role of the exception clause as permission for the treaty's obligation because this approach is more consistent with the intentions of the EVIPA's contracting parties, which means it will contribute more to promoting sustainable development.

In ISDS litigation practice, when assessing the NT obligation in light of regulatory concerns, ISDS tribunals typically employ simpler tests compared to those under Article 4.6 EVIPA. Specifically, after determining whether a foreign investor received less favourable treatment than national investors in similar circumstances, tribunals often consider whether any differential treatment was justified by a legitimate public policy objective.[111] This latter analysis is relatively lenient, as it does not entail the stringent "necessary" requirements or the conditions outlined in the chapeau. However, the introduction of Article 4.6 EVIPA complicates matters, potentially making it challenging for a host state's measure to comply with NT or MFN obligations and thus possibly leading to regulatory chill.[112] This concern is not

[108] As observed in *United States – Measures affecting the Cross-border supply of Gambling and Betting Services,* WT/DS285/AB/R, Appellate Body Report, adopted on 7 April 2005, para. 308.

[109] Julie (2018), p. 340.

[110] Ibid, p. 341.

[111] Chauvel (2017), p. 142.

[112] Ibid, p. 152.

unfounded, given the difficulty for both investors and host states in meeting the "necessity" or "least trade/investment restrictive" requirements. Therefore, the approach adopted by the ICS tribunal becomes crucial. It is advisable for the tribunal to utilise causation or impossibility analyses to interpret NT in a manner that safeguards the right to regulate.[113]

When comparing the exception clauses across various agreements signed by the EU, notable differences emerge, highlighting the complexities involved. For instance, Paragraph 2 of Article 28.3 in CETA on general exceptions is limited to non-discriminatory treatment (Section C CETA) and obligations related to the establishment of investments (Section B CETA). Conversely, in the EU–Singapore IPA, although Chapter 4 mirrors EVIPA's structure, no equivalent general exceptions clause exists. The only similarity among the general exceptions clauses in the EU's trade-investment agreements appears to be their exclusion from applying to other core investment protection standards such as expropriation and FET. This omission sidesteps the question of how general exceptions influence the policy scope already embedded in those obligations. While these differences may stem from varying concerns among the EU's partners, their presence across agreements is likely to complicate the EU's management and application,[114] as highlighted in Chap. 8.

As outlined in Chapter 8, EVIPA establishes a mechanism—the Investment Committee—to supervise and facilitate its implementation and application (under Para. 3(b) Article 4.1 EVIPA). To ensure the exception clause effectively balances the parties' objectives of investment protection and state regulatory autonomy, EVIPA's contracting parties must address the uncertainties raised in this chapter, including:

- Clarifying the exception clause's role in limiting the scope of investment obligations (permissive role) or providing a defence for the host state against what might otherwise be deemed unfair conduct. As has been repeatedly emphasised, the permissive role is preferable to promote sustainable development.
- Correspondingly, it is also imperative to determine how the burden of proof is shared between parties to the dispute or whether it rests with the claimant to establish non-compliance with the exception.[115]

Overall, the approach adopted by the ICS tribunals in interpreting nondiscrimination obligations and the general exception under EVIPA remains unclear. Therefore, Vietnam must pay close attention to the requirements outlined by NT and MFN

[113] The causation analysis, as proposed by Chauvel, suggests that a case of less favorable treatment should be established if the disputed measure itself is found to be responsible for a significant disparate impact, thereby excluding less favorable treatment attributed solely to the circumstances of the case. See Chauvel (2017), pp. 152–153.

[114] As argued by Martini, while safeguarding investors' legitimate rights and addressing the host country's regulatory requirements are primary objectives, it is also essential to maintain the overall coherence of the investment framework. Martini (2017), p. 583.

[115] Henckels (2018), p. 2842.

obligations, as well as those included in the general exception clause. Ensuring equal treatment for all domestic and foreign investors within the same economic sector is paramount. Any differential treatment must be justified by specific legitimate public objectives outlined in the sub-paragraphs of Article 4.6 EVIPA. This means that Vietnam has to make sure that an alternative, less restrictive measure for the foreign investor is unavailable. Additionally, any exceptions to measure application must align with the relevant public objectives as well as with the conditions included in the introduction of the Exception clause.

9.5 Interim Conclusion

The review in this chapter shows that exceptions have been invoked in a limited number of IIA cases today, and they were rarely successful. In the rare cases where the general exception clause is considered, tribunals may adopt different approaches, such as the "permission" and "defence" frameworks. The tribunal's choice of approach has significant implications for safeguarding the regulatory space of the host state.

The inclusion of exceptions in EVIPA aligns with the prevailing trend in international trade and investment. Assessing the efficacy of this clause in preserving the host state's policy space necessitates an evaluation alongside other substantive provisions of EVIPA, particularly the NT and MFN clauses. Therefore, the interplay between this exception clause and the NT and MFN clauses requires clarification by the contracting parties.

Regarding concerns that the incorporation of the general exception may bolster the state's right to regulate at the expense of investors' rights, the stringent requirements related to the necessity test and the conditions outlined in the introduction part suggest a contrary outcome. These requirements ensure that legitimate policy objectives are not easily endorsed, potentially making the clause overly burdensome for a state's right to regulate.[116] Consequently, commentators have proposed alternative drafting approaches to mitigate this weakness.[117]

This book contends that the divergence in ISDS tribunals' approaches to the role of the general exception clause observed thus far may not necessarily translate to the context of the EVIPA. This is due to the fact that EVIPA's provisions will be evaluated by the ICS tribunals, comprising members selected for their expertise in international law and proficiency in applying established techniques of interpretation and conflict resolution.[118] If the ICS tribunals meet these criteria, it is conceivable to

[116] Chauvel (2017), p. 153.

[117] Brew (2019), p. 242; Chauvel (2017), pp. 155–156.

[118] Titi has suggested that interpretation techniques encompass principles such as the general rule of interpretation in the VCLT (Article 31), effective treaty interpretation (Article 32 VCLT), and the lex specialis conflict rule. See further Titi (2022), pp. 61–62.

apply EVIPA's general exceptions clause in a manner consistent with international law and the parties' intentions.

Despite scholars' reservations regarding the contribution of the exception clause in preserving the right to regulate,[119] this book maintains that the value of including the general exception clause in EVIPA for balancing the rights of host states and investors should not be underestimated. By necessitating the consideration of a legitimate objective that may justify the disputed measure, such a clause reduces the likelihood that the tribunal will solely base a breach of NT obligation on differential treatment between a foreign investor and a national or among foreign investors "in like circumstances."[120] Provided that the parties adequately address the issues identified in this chapter, the general exceptions clause can be regarded as making a substantive contribution to the protection of states' policy space and the promotion of sustainable development objectives in IIAs, notably within the framework of the EVIPA. Additionally, including this provision in EVIPA helps rebalance the burden of proof between the parties when invoking this clause, thereby partially ensuring the pursuit of the state's policy objectives.

References

ISDS Cases

Bear Creek Mining Corporation v. Republic of Peru [2014] ICSID Case No. ARB/14/21

CMS Gas Transmission Co. v. Republic of Argentina [2001] ICSID Case No. ARB/01/8

Continental Casualty Company v. Argentine Republic [2003] ICSID Case No. ARB/03/9

Copper Mesa Mining Corporation v. Republic of Ecuador [2011] PCA No. 2012-2

Eco Oro Minerals Corp. v. Republic of Colombia [2016a] ICSID Case No. ARB/16/41

Enron Creditors Recovery Corporation and Ponderosa Assets, L.P. v. Argentine Republic [2001] ICSID Case No. ARB/01/3

LG&E v. Argentine Republic [2002] ICSID Case No. ARB/02/1

Minerals Corp. v. Republic of Colombia [2016b] ICSID Case No. ARB/16/41

Pope and Talbot v. The Government of Canada [1999] UNCITRAL

Sempra Energy International v. Argentine Republic [2002] ICSID Case No. ARB/02/16

[119] See, for instance, Gehring and Kent (2013), p. 205.

[120] Chauvel (2017), p. 153.

Other Cases

WTO (1982) *United States - Prohibition of Imports of Tuna and Tuna Products from Canada*, L/5198 - 29S/91, 22 February 1982
WTO (1996) *United States - Standards for Reformulated and Conventional Gasoline*, WT/DS2/AB/R, 29 April 1996
WTO (1998) *Canada - Measures Affecting Exports of Unprocessed Herring and Salmon*, L/6268 - 35S/98, 22 March 1998
WTO (2005) *United States – Measures affecting the Cross-border supply of Gambling and Betting Services,* WT/DS285/AB/R, 7 April 2005
WTO (2007) *Brazil - Measures Affecting Imports of Retreaded Tyres (Brazil - Retreaded Tyres)*, WT/DS332/AB/R, 3 December 2007
WTO (2014) *European Communities - Measures Prohibiting the Importation and Marketing of Seal Products*, WT/DS/400/R, WT/DS401/AB/R, 22 May 2014

Treaties

ASEAN Comprehensive Investment Agreement (2009)
Australia–China FTA (2015)
Australia–Korea FTA (2014)
Australia–New Zealand The Protocol on Investment to the Australia New Zealand Closer Economic Relations Trade Agreement (2011)
Azerbaijan Model BIT (2016)
Canada Model BIT (2004)
Canada Model BIT (2021) (FIPA)
Canada–China BIT (2012)
Canada–Colombia FTA (2008)
Canada–Czech Republic BIT (2009)
Canada–Ecuador BIT (1996)
Canada–Jordan BIT (2009)
Canada–Philippines BIT (1995)
Canada–Thailand BIT (1997)
Canada–States of the European Free Trade Association (Iceland, Liechtenstein, Norway, and Switzerland) FTA (2008)
COMESA Investment Agreement (2007)
Comprehensive and Progressive Agreement for Trans – Pacific Partnership (CPTPP)
EU–Canada Comprehensive Economic and Trade Agreement (2017) (CETA)
EU–Vietnam Investment Protection Agreement (EVIPA) (2019)
European Community–Chile FTA (2002)
India Model BIT (2015)
India–Singapore Comprehensive Economic Cooperation Agreement (2005)
Japan–Iran BIT (2016)

Japan–Mongolia Economic Partnership Agreement (2015)
Japan–Uruguay BIT (2015)
Korea–New Zealand FTA (2015)
Nigeria–Singapore BIT (2016)
North America Free Trade Agreement (1992) (NAFTA)
Norway Draft Model BIT (2015)
Singapore–Japan Agreement for a New Age Economic Partnership (2002)
United States–Argentina BIT (1991)
Vienna Convention on the Law of Treaties (VCLT) (1969)
Vietnam–South Korea FTA (2015)
WTO General Agreement on Tariffs and Trade (GATT) (1994)
WTO General Agreement on Trade in Services (GATS) (1994)

Bibliography

Benedetto SD (2013) International investment law and the environment. Edward Elgar

Brew R (2019) Exception clauses in international investment agreements as a tool for appropriately balancing the right to regulate with investment protection. Canterbury Law Rev 25:205

Chauvel LM (2017) The influence of general exceptions on the interpretation of national treatment in international investment law. Brazilian J Int Law 14

Chi M (2018) Integrating sustainable development in international investment law: normative incompatibility, system integration and governance implications. Routledge

Gehring MW, Kent A (2013) International investment agreements and the emerging green economy: rising to the challenge. In: Baetens F (ed) Investment law within international law – integrationist perspectives. Cambridge University Press

Henckels C (2016) Protecting regulatory autonomy through greater precision in investment treaties: the TPP, CETA and TTIP. J Int Econ Law 19(1):27

Henckels C (2018) Should investment treaties contain public policy exceptions? Boston College Law Rev 59(8):2825

Julie K (2018) Balancing regulatory interests through an exceptions framework under the right to regulate provision in international investment agreements. George Washington Int Law Rev 50(2)

Korzun V (2017) The right to regulate in investor - state arbitration: slicing and dicing regulatory carve-outs. Vanderbilt J Transnl Law 50(2)

Lester S (2014) Improving investment treaties through general exceptions provisions: the Australian example. Investment Treaty News. 14 May 2014. https://www.iisd.org/itn/en/2014/05/14/improving-investment-treaties-through-general-exceptions-provisions-the-australian-example/

Lester S, Mercurio B (2017) Safeguarding policy space in investment agreements. Institute of International Economic Law, Issue Brief

Levashova Y (2019) The right of states to regulate in international investment law: the search for balance between public interest and fair and equitable treatment. Wolters Kluwer

Martini C (2017) Balancing investors' rights with environmental protection in international investment arbitration: an assessment of recent trends in investment treaty drafting. Int Lawyer 50(3)

Mitchell AD, Munro J, Voon T (2018) Importing WTO general exceptions into international investment agreements: proportionality, myths and risks. Yearbook on International Investment Law & Policy 2016–2017. Oxford University Press. https://papers.ssrn.com/sol3/papers.cfm?abstract_id=3084663

Muchlinski P (2016) Negotiating new generation international investment agreements: new sustainable development oriented initiatives. In: Hindelang S, Krajewski M (eds) Shifting paradigms in international investment law: more balanced, less isolated, increasingly diversified. Oxford University Press

Newcombe A (2008) General exceptions in international investment agreements. Draft Discussion Paper, BIICL Eighth Annual WTO Conference. 13, 14 May 2008. London. https://www.biicl.org/files/3866_andrew_newcombe.pdf

Newcombe A, Paradell L (2009) Law and practice of investment treaties: standards of treatment. Kluwer Law International

Roberts A (2013) Clash of paradigms: actors and analogies shaping the investment treaty system. Am J Int Law 107(1):45–94

Regan DH (2007) The meaning of "necessary" in GATT Article XX and GATS Article XIV: the myth of cost-benefit balancing. World Trade Rev 6

Sabanogullari L (2015) The merits and limitations of general exception clauses in contemporary investment treaty practice. Investment Treaty News. https://www.iisd.org/itn/en/2015/05/21/the-merits-and-limitations-of-general-exception-clauses-in-contemporary-investment-treaty-practice/

Titi A (2014) The Right to Regulate in International Investment Law, *Nomos and Hart*, https://catharinetiti.com/the-right-to-regulate-in-international-investment-law/

Titi C (2022) The right to regulate in international investment law (revisited). International and Comparative Law Research Center. https://papers.ssrn.com/sol3/papers.cfm?abstract_id=4058447

Todic J, Al-Nakid HA (2020) What Next for interpreting general exceptions in international investment agreements? Canada's Non-disputing party submission in *Eco Oro Minerals v. Colombia*. Kluwer Arbitration Blog. https://arbitrationblog.kluwerarbitration.com/2020/07/18/what-next-for-interpreting-general-exceptions-in-international-investment-agreements-canadas-non-disputing-party-submission-in-eco-oro-minerals-v-colombia/

UNCTAD (2017) World Investment Report 2017: investment and the digital economy. https://unctad.org/system/files/official-document/wir2017_en.pdf

Vandevelde KJ (2013) Rebalancing through exceptions. Lewis Clark Law Rev 17(2)

Viñuales JE (2012) Foreign investment and the environment in international law. Cambridge University Press

Part IV
Environmental Protection in Vietnam's FDI Policy: Toward Better Integration

Chapter 10
EVIPA and Vietnam's Right to Regulate: Implications for Policy and Governance

Abstract This chapter initiates a detailed exploration of the initiatives outlined in the EVIPA, focusing on how they safeguard state policy autonomy. By doing so, it delivers a comprehensive evaluation of the overall effectiveness of these initiatives. This chapter also examines the Vietnamese government's capacity to pursue its policy objectives, particularly environmental protection, within the constraints of the EVIPA. This analysis is crucial for developing countries like Vietnam, where attracting FDI is vital for economic growth but often necessitates navigating complex trade-offs with environmental sustainability. Based on this analysis, the chapter offers recommendations for the Vietnamese government to align FDI with sustainable development goals. The insights from this research may provide valuable lessons for other developing countries facing similar challenges, particularly those in Asia.

10.1 Exercising Regulatory Rights Under EVIPA: It Is Far from Achieving the Goals?

10.1.1 Anticipated Progress in Safeguarding States' Regulatory Rights Within the EVIPA

Part III of this book focuses on clarifying what can be expected from the design of EVIPA regulations, aiming to strike a balance between the policy space of the signatories and the traditional goals associated with investment protection in IIAs. Additionally, this section assesses the compatibility of relevant Vietnamese domestic laws with EVIPA provisions. It is crucial to recognise that achieving effective rebalancing of IIAs requires a comprehensive approach rather than relying solely on individual improvements. Furthermore, the analysis conducted in this book highlights the significance of the approach adopted by ICS tribunal members in influencing the assurance of policy space under EVIPA.

N. T. Lan Huong, *Investment Protection and Environmental Governance*, European Yearbook of International Economic Law 47,
https://doi.org/10.1007/978-3-032-05332-9_10

As discussed, the variability in the interpretation of substantive obligations across different ISDS tribunals poses an issue that could restrict states' regulatory autonomy. This variability partly arises from the broad discretion granted to tribunals by the expansive wording of IIA provisions.[1] Such uncertainties complicate the determination of which public policy regulations may trigger liability and/or compensation obligations, leading to a regulatory chill. Additionally, these uncertainties leave investors unsure about their position when challenging a public policy measure.[2]

The accurate integration of regulatory rights into substantive provisions and other mechanisms within EVIPA hinges on the considerations and methodologies adopted by the first ICS tribunals. However, until these tribunals commence their deliberations and apply their review methods, accurately predicting the extent of integration remains challenging. Furthermore, crucial details concerning these factors remain unclear since the ICS established under the EVIPA has not been set up. Meanwhile, a similar mechanism established under CETA has yet to become operational. As a result, the assessments presented in this book regarding the EVIPA primarily rely on existing knowledge documented in international investment law and ISDS practice. The key findings of this book relating to the host states' regulatory autonomy are summarised as follows:

Firstly, the inclusion of regulatory rights of the host state within EVIPA does not represent groundbreaking innovations but rather aligns with established trends observed in the evolution of IIAs to safeguard the legitimate rights of parties within the international investment relationship. This practice underscores EVIPA's adherence to the prevailing trend of supporting states' right to regulate. The retention of substantive obligations resembling those found in traditional IIAs and the mechanism of investment dispute resolution indicate the EU and Vietnam's preference to uphold the fundamental legitimacy of international investment law and the core features of the investment treaty regime rather than seeking a top-down overhaul. This perspective contrasts with approaches from certain countries, which posit that "ISDS is intrinsically flawed," suggesting that no reform efforts could salvage the system.[3]

Secondly, substantive obligations frequently invoked to challenge measures in ISDS practice, including indirect expropriation provisions and FET treatment, have been clarified to a greater extent, elucidating situations where government actions may constitute a violation. This clarification is believed to better balance regulatory freedom and investment protection.[4]

In particular, EVIPA's FET clause offers clear guidance, ensuring that interpretations by ICS tribunals closely align with the intentions of the parties. This FET clause establishes a more defined framework for states to implement environmental

[1] Aaken (2009), pp. 520, 527–528.

[2] Brew (2019), pp. 212–213.

[3] This viewpoint is expressed by Brazil's position on ISDS in the UNCITRAL Working Group III.

[4] Newcombe (2012), p. 269; Henckels (2018a), p. 2839.

measures within their sovereignty. This clarification in the interpretation of the FET clause demonstrates a proactive stance by signatories in controlling the interpretation of investment agreement terms, thereby safeguarding the policy space of the host state. Additionally, parties retain the right to actively negotiate, even after the conclusion of EVIPA.

The regulations on indirect expropriation under EVIPA have undergone significant changes, aiming to narrow down the concept compared to IIAs signed in the 1990s. However, this model of indirect expropriation clause has received mixed reviews from scholars due to several unclear factors, as analysed in this book. These uncertainties raise concerns about the limited predictability of these provisions. Indeed, the analysis presented in Part III of this book suggests that these regulations merely echo practices in resolving investment disputes over the past 50 years rather than introducing an apparent breakthrough. Even the exception outlined in Paragraph 3 of Annex 4 fails to provide adequate guarantees for the state's regulatory authority, as much of the assessment and decision-making power remains with the ICS tribunals. Therefore, while it's anticipated that these provisions may prompt tribunals to exercise more caution when evaluating measures under the host state's regulatory authority, this ultimately relies on the parties' efforts to address the issues highlighted in this book.

Thirdly, regarding other substantive obligations such as NT and MFN, EVIPA includes a general exceptions clause (Article 4.6) allowing environmental protection measures to meet specific conditions to avoid being deemed a violation of non-discrimination obligations. However, as discussed in Chap. 9, based on WTO jurisprudence and ISDS practice, the language of Article 4.6 in EVIPA might lead ICS tribunals to apply a stricter standard of review than traditional ISDS tribunals, potentially resulting in regulatory chill. Therefore, to safeguard the policy space of the EU and Vietnam, both parties may need to negotiate and provide guidance to ICS tribunals, clarifying that the role of the exception clause is to grant permissions that limit the scope of substantive treaty obligations rather than serving as defences to justify prima facie unlawful actions. Under this approach, both parties may also need to specify that the burden of proof lies with the claimant to demonstrate non-compliance with the exception.[5]

Furthermore, given that Article 4.6 of EVIPA is formulated based on the general exceptions clause of the WTO, it might be helpful to reference WTO jurisprudence. However, it is worth noting that WTO Panels and the Appellate Body have historically treated the exception clause as a defence. This perspective may not entirely align with international investment law. Therefore, parties may need to reach a mutual understanding and provide guidance to ICS tribunals regarding the extent to which they should consider WTO jurisprudence when applying exceptions. It's essential to recognise that while there are valuable lessons to be gleaned from WTO jurisprudence, the differences between trade and investment sectors necessitate a

[5] Ibid., p. 2842.

careful selection and application of these experiences within the context of investment treaties.

Fourthly, in addition to clarifying the aforementioned substantive obligations, other mechanisms within EVIPA also contribute to bolstering states' regulatory rights. The preamble and the right-to-regulate provision hold particular significance in addressing the parties' concerns. These advancements lay down a legal foundation for ICS Tribunals to structure their rulings' reasoning, a crucial element in enhancing the legitimacy of the ISDS system.[6]

Moreover, the emphasis placed on the right to regulate within EVIPA and in IIAs contemporaneously signed underscores a clear commitment to preserving this right alongside the obligation to provide investment protection. This declaration holds valuable implications for both ICS tribunals and investors. Firstly, these provisions serve as guiding principles for tribunals, emphasising the overarching goal of investment protection that states aim to achieve through their treaties. By adopting this approach, policy measures adopted by host states will be evaluated within the broader treaty context,[7] rather than solely through the lens of traditional investment treaty objectives. This shift fosters a more balanced consideration of public interest within the IIL framework. Secondly, IIAs containing such provisions send a clear message to investors regarding the evolving goals of investment treaties, prompting them to realign their expectations regarding the investment environment.[8]

The regrettable aspect of this set of regulations lies in EVIPA's Preamble, which fails to explicitly mention the objective of safeguarding the states' right to regulate. While the Preamble's value may be limited compared to substantive provisions, its simultaneous alignment with substantive standards referencing the right to regulate within the treaty text, supported by exceptions, could foster a mutually reinforcing interpretation of treaty terms.[9] Additionally, a weakness is apparent in the provision concerning the right to regulate itself. As noted, this provision lacks specificity, resembling more of a statement in the Preamble rather than a substantive clause. Implementing such a new and unclear regulation within an ISDS context with limited experience in interpreting such provisions hampers its effectiveness in enhancing the regulatory powers of the host state.

Fifthly, the redrafting of investment protection standards, as seen in EVIPA, purportedly grants broad discretion to arbitrators by employing evaluative language such as "rare circumstances," "excessive," and "necessary." However, as suggested by Henckels,[10] greater precision in language may promote norm compliance and limit tribunals from straying too far from the parties' intentions. Yet, overly precise regulations can lack flexibility, especially in unforeseen situations. Calculated ambiguity in treaty text may be necessary to secure political agreement, particularly

[6] Ranjan (2019), p. 102. See also Federico Ortino (2012), p. 34.

[7] Coleman et al. (2018), p. 87.

[8] Baltag FCIArb et al. (2023), p. 387.

[9] Martini (2017), p. 567.

[10] Henckels (2016), pp. 30–31.

in multilateral negotiations.[11] These considerations likely influence the norm choices in EVIPA. Moreover, as discussed in Chaps. 6 and 7, most of these norms are familiar to ISDS practice, and ICS tribunals are expected to interpret them without difficulty. Finally, surrounding EVIPA are numerous tools signalling parties' attention to sustainable development concerns, aiding tribunals in aligning with the parties' intentions.

Overall, the enhancements incorporated into EVIPA may not introduce entirely novel and robust measures. Still, they arguably bolster the legal foundation for states' right to regulate in the name of public welfare without incurring liability under IIL. Furthermore, they offer tribunals more guidance in assessing future challenges to specific policy measures. These clauses are anticipated to lend greater coherence and legitimacy to IIL by rectifying the asymmetric structure of IIAs and directly incorporating public concerns into the text of agreements.[12]

To shed light on this possibility, the forthcoming section will explore how developments under EVIPA might be evaluated collectively by the ICS tribunals, guided by Articles 31.1 and 31.2 of the VCLT. As stipulated in Article 3.21 EVIPA on Rules of Interpretation, the ICS tribunal shall interpret the provisions outlined in Article 3.2 (Scope) in accordance with the customary rules of interpretation of public international law, including those codified in the VCLT 1969. Article 31.1 VCLT emphasises interpreting a treaty in good faith, considering the ordinary meaning of its terms in context and in light of its object and purpose. Additionally, Article 31.2 underscores that the relevant context encompasses the entire text, including the preamble, annex and related agreements or instruments accepted by the parties at the time of its conclusion. Furthermore, Article 31.3 highlights the significance of "any subsequent agreement between the parties regarding the interpretation of the treaty" and "any subsequent practice in the application of the treaty" in interpreting the treaty.

Examining the tools provided for interpreting international treaties by the VCLT, it becomes evident that EVIPA currently incorporates most of these tools, ensuring support for interpreting the parties' agreements under this treaty. Specifically, if the ICS tribunal needs to adjudicate claims related to indirect expropriation, FET, or if NT or MFN obligations are examined alongside the general exceptions clause, several sources will be considered, in addition to the ordinary meaning of the relevant provisions, including:

(i) The disputed clause's direct context, object, and purpose.
(ii) The broader object and purpose of the treaty.
(iii) Documents connected with the conclusion of the treaty.
(iv) The instrument in connection with the conclusion of EVIPA.
(v) Subsequent agreements between the parties regarding the interpretation of EVIPA

[11] Ibid., p. 31.

[12] Martini (2017), p. 534.

In examining these sources, EVIPA offers certain safeguards to regulatory rights when specific investment standards, such as indirect expropriation or FET, are discussed. For example, provisions on expropriation and indirect expropriation necessitate a case-by-case, fact-based inquiry considering the object, context, and intent of the applied measure and its economic impact and duration. Moreover, EVIPA significantly diminishes the likelihood of non-discriminatory measures designed to protect legitimate public policy objectives being deemed indirect expropriation. Regarding the FET standard, EVIPA provides an exhaustive list to guide ICS tribunals in evaluating FET claims. Article 2.5 sets a high threshold for proving a breach of the FET standard. Additionally, relevant provisions curtail the role of investors' legitimate expectations in constituting a violation of the FET standard.

When Article 2.2 of EVIPA is considered alongside these substantive obligations, it underscores the parties' commitment to preserving their policy space, reminding the ICS tribunal not to prioritise investment protection standards over the parties' rights to regulate. Furthermore, regardless of the investment protection commitments made, the parties retain the right to alter the legal and regulatory framework. Legitimate objectives in this context encompass a broad range, including environmental protection. Additionally, decisions regarding subsidies shall not breach investment protection obligations under Chap. 2. on Investment Protection of the EVIPA.

However, when evaluating these substantive provisions in a broader context, particularly in the context of the treaty's object and purpose, the preamble of EVIPA falls short by not explicitly mentioning the right to regulate. Despite its emphasis on promoting economic development in line with sustainable development objectives, the absence of the right to regulate in the preamble fails to provide an overarching impact on EVIPA's regulations. While it is anticipated that protection provisions in EVIPA should align with sustainable development objectives shared by the signatories,[13] relying solely on the ICS tribunal to interpret the various values encompassed in the concept of sustainable development outlined in the preamble of EVIPA may not yield definitive results.

In examining the last two sources for treaty interpretation, EVIPA and its Investment Committee promise to actively contribute to guiding ICS tribunals in aligning with the shared concerns between the contracting parties. As discussed in Chap. 8, this instrument is granted full authority to adopt interpretations of EVIPA provisions (Article 4.1 EVIPA), thereby carrying legal weight with the parties and relevant stakeholders. However, the challenge remains that concerted efforts are needed from the parties to establish and refine this mechanism post-EVIPA ratification and implementation to ensure its effective operation.

In addition to the five sources supporting the interpretation of international treaties mentioned above, the VCLT also underscores an equally significant source in Paragraph 3(c) of Article 31: "any relevant rules of international law applicable in the relations between the parties." Consequently, it is recommended that

[13] Sacerdoti (2016), pp. 38–39.

the obligations under IIAs should not be construed or interpreted in isolation, but rather in context with other instruments -such as treaties on human rights, the environment, health, and labour standards -that are binding upon the signatories or to which they are subscribed .[14] This holistic approach ensures a comprehensive understanding of the legal framework within which IIAs operate, fostering coherence and consistency across various areas of international law.

10.1.2 Sustainable IIAs: The Critical Role of the Investment Court System and Supporting Mechanisms

The scenario presented above illustrates that while EVIPA may not be exhaustive in its approach,[15] it does provide an effective framework for addressing situations where policy measures are challenged by investors. In such cases, the ICS tribunals have sufficient groundwork to evaluate these measures, both through substantive clauses and relevant exceptions. Thus, the legal framework established by EVIPA initially acts as a shield to safeguard the parties' right to regulate. However, to fully ensure this potential protection and uphold the goal of preserving the state's right to regulate under EVIPA, it is imperative to address drafting uncertainties, such as the applicable standard of review, and ensure overall consistency in implementation.[16] Although EVIPA may not encompass all the tools found in CETA to enhance the parties' initiative in shaping desired policy spaces,[17] it offers valuable mechanisms akin to those in CETA, especially the ICS and the Investment Committee.

Clarifying ambiguities not clearly stipulated in EVIPA can be achieved through the activities of the Investment Committee. This committee can deliberate, reach agreements, and offer additional guidance to assist ICS tribunals in aligning with the parties' intentions. Specifically, it can help determine that the goals of investment protection and safeguarding states' policy space are balanced objectives. Utilising this tool ensures maximum oversight by signatories in EVIPA's implementation, fostering its continuous improvement over time to accurately reflect the desires of contracting parties. While the full extent of the Trade-Investment Committee's powers under all EU's IIAs remains to be explored, such mechanisms transform EVIPA into a dynamic and evolving agreement rather than a treaty with fixed obligations observed in traditional IIAs.

---

[14] Ibid.

[15] Such a lackadaisical approach has been criticized in the case of Comprehensive and Progressive Agreement for Trans-Pacific Partnership (CPTPP). See Zamir and Barker (2017), p. 224.

[16] Paparinskis (2015), p. 669.

[17] CETA's signatories have used 'pro-active' tools, which give the CETA Parties the possibility to re-interpret the CETA provisions. More specific: (1) Joint Binding Interpretations, (2) Joint Committees, (3) Interfering in Disputes as Non-Disputing State Party, (4) Determining the Correct Respondent (5) The European Commission's Proposal for an Investment Court System (ICS) (6) The A Priori Exclusion of Any Direct Effect of the CETA. Refer Lavranos (2016), p. 312.

As previously mentioned, the ISDS mechanism plays a crucial role in accommodating regulatory measures and achieving the objective of rebalancing IIAs. Despite recognising the state's right to regulate, traditional investment tribunals may not be best suited for evaluating the policy preferences of states.[18] Therefore, implementing a dispute settlement mechanism more aligned with the state's regulatory rights, rather than eliminating the ISDS mechanism from investment treaties, is imperative.

The functioning of the ICS under EVIPA is anticipated to play a vital role in supporting the objective of rebalancing the agreement. Serving as the primary body responsible for reviewing and assessing substantive obligations, as discussed throughout this book, the ICS operates as a quasi-judicial mechanism sharing similarities with the dispute settlement mechanism of the WTO. It comprises two levels: a first instance level and an appellate level, with members appointed by the EVIPA Committee in accordance with the provisions outlined in Paragraphs 2 and 3 of Article 3.39, as well as Paragraph 5(a) of Article 4.1 of EVIPA.

Insights drawn from the operation of the WTO's dispute settlement body suggest that the ICS, with its two-tiered court system, is likely to align closely with the priorities outlined by the parties in the agreement text. This structured approach is expected to promote greater consistency in rulings, thereby increasing predictability in the interpretation and application of relevant regulations—a characteristic that traditional IIAs, along with ad-hoc tribunals established by these agreements, often fail to provide.

The appointment of ICS Members, who will serve as the future interpreters of EVIPA, necessitates meticulous consideration, ensuring they possess the requisite expertise in international law and the nuances of international arbitration. These qualifications are inherently complex, as Paparinskis highlighted in his paper.[19] Assessing international investment law demands a multitude of qualifications, including the ability to identify the meaning of treaty rules by reference to their textual expression in accordance with the principles of treaty interpretation outlined in the VCLT. Furthermore, navigating the myriad rules governing jurisdiction, admissibility, the scope and content of obligations, as well as exceptions in primary rules and applicable secondary rules, requires careful handling to determine the existence of responsibility or the success of a particular claim. Given that the international investment treaty system is a mixed-up system with characteristics from various legal regimes,[20] clarifying regulations within investment treaties often necessitates reference and comparison with other legal fields to address gaps,

---

[18] Brew argues that these tribunals' detachment from domestic constitutional regimes suggests their inadequacy in undertaking the delicate balancing required, as domestic institutions would. Therefore, insisting that tribunals weigh investment protection against states' policy interests, despite their unsuitability for this task, unjustly impinges on states' regulatory autonomy. See Brew (2019), pp. 212–216.

[19] Paparinskis (2015), pp. 664–666.

[20] The investment treaty system in considered as a part of public international law while grafting private international law dispute resolution mechanisms onto public international law treaties.

resolve ambiguities, or understand the system's nature.[21] Consequently, the interpretation of investment treaties may entail consideration of customary law and rules from other regimes of international law, such as international human rights law or international health law.[22] Moreover, arbitrators within the ICS must comprehend domestic prioritisation decisions, particularly understanding the preservation of policy space goals outlined by the EVIPA signatories. While individuals possessing such multifaceted qualities may be scarce, establishing and nurturing such a body is imperative to ensure a balanced approach between investment protection and regulatory autonomy under EVIPA.

For the above reasons, establishing the ICS and refining its appropriate operations is paramount in balancing investors' rights and states' regulatory powers. Such a centralised dispute settlement mechanism addresses the shortcomings observed in the ISDS system, where investment tribunals have employed varied methods of review to balance state and investor interests.[23] Selecting and applying appropriate review methods in evaluating substantive investment standards are crucial for determining liability or the success of a claim. With the consistent application of review methods by ICS tribunals, the ability to uphold the expected regulatory rights of the parties will be further ensured.

Following the ratification of the EVFTA, the Vietnamese government issued Decision 1201/QD-TTg (August 6, 2020), endorsing the Plan for EVFTA Implementation. Under this decision, the Vietnam Prime Minister has tasked relevant ministries with appointing individuals to compile a list of arbitrators in accordance with the provisions outlined in EVFTA–EVIPA to handle arising disputes.

However, establishing the ICS with each treaty partner poses challenges for the EU due to the limited availability of individuals with the necessary qualifications. Under EVIPA, the EU must designate five individuals, and together with Vietnam, designate five others, none of whom are nationals or permanent residents of either party, to serve as chairperson of the arbitration panel (Paras. 1 and 2, Article 3.23 EVIPA). Similar requirements exist in CETA and the EU–Singapore IPA.[24] Naturally, the EU may appoint the same five individuals to serve in the ICS established under its various IPAs. However, finalizing the composition of the remaining five members with different partners poses a considerable challenge, a difficulty further compounded by the nationality requirements. Consequently, the operation of the ICS is likely to require additional time.

In essence, the text of EVIPA aligns with contemporary practices in global IIA negotiations, wherein substantive obligations are delineated with greater precision alongside a clearer recognition of the right to regulate. This enhances control over the interpretation of investment treaties by investment tribunals, particularly in

[21] Roberts (2013), pp. 45–47.

[22] See further Paparinskis (2015), p. 665.

[23] As highlighted by Henckels, arbitrators' application of methodologies has often lacked clarity; references to balancing, proportionality, and similar tests, as well as comparisons with other legal systems, do not consistently indicate a specific analytical process. Henckels (2018b), para. 3.

[24] See Paragraph 3, Article 13.20 CETA and Article 3.44 EU–Singapore IPA.

ensuring the appropriate consideration of regulatory rights within the international investment context. Models of investment treaties similar to EVIPA, such as CETA or TTIP, represent initial steps towards achieving this objective.[25]

Nevertheless, countries have yet to devise a definitive solution to fully preserve their regulatory powers, indicating that there is still much work to be done to realise the potential of these developments in advancing sustainable development through international investment treaties. One proposed approach for EVIPA's Parties involves directing the ICS tribunal's attention toward various elements showcasing the growing global significance of sustainable development. For instance, the Paris Agreement and declarations from the UN Climate Change Conferences illustrate that a majority of nations worldwide are increasingly prioritising sustainable development as a global imperative and striving to reduce carbon emissions to sustainable levels. It is suggested that as sustainable development evolves into a customary principle of international law, it gains greater persuasive power.[26] Furthermore, the domestic laws of both parties or existing environmental agreements between them can indicate the Parties' intentions.[27] These options offer avenues for parties to more effectively integrate sustainable development into their agreements and ensure that sustainable development receives appropriate attention, balancing it with investor protection under EVIPA. Referencing environmental obligations under international treaties is believed to strengthen the host state's right to regulate in the public interest and enables states to assert successful counterclaims in this area.[28] In this context, Hush provides practical suggestions, including transforming statements and regulations related to sustainable development from soft to hard verbs, thus imbuing them with stronger legal force.[29] Additionally, incorporating sustainable development into each enumeration of the right to regulate and clearly linking sustainable development to both the right to regulate and investment protection standards could significantly enhance the influence of sustainable development.

Moreover, assigning actionable responsibilities to investors could alter the incentive structure of FTAs and position investors as partners with the states in advancing these objectives.[30] In this regard, Muchlinski suggests that investor obligations could be voluntary, mandatory, or a combination of both.[31] Models for increasing investor responsibility in IIAs can be found in the frameworks introduced by the UNCTAD and the Commonwealth Secretariat, as discussed in Chap. 1 of this book. All these obligations contribute to reshaping investors' perspectives and positioning them as partners with the states in advancing these objectives.[32]

---

[25] Henckels (2016), pp. 49–50.

[26] Hush (2018), p. 148.

[27] Ibid.

[28] Gore (2024).

[29] Hush (2018), pp. 154–155.

[30] Ibid., p.156.

[31] Muchlinski (2016), pp. 57–58.

[32] Hush (2018), p. 156.

As highlighted in this book, the ICS and the Investment Committee hold significant potential to advance the parties' objective of safeguarding regulatory space by facilitating ongoing monitoring of their treaty. However, the success of these tools hinges on the parties' initiative and efforts in collaborative endeavours. Fortunately, this cooperation is likely facilitated by the strong, longstanding relationship between the two parties, particularly given the EU's economic and political strength and extensive legislative experience. In addition to the matters previously identified as requiring clarification by the parties, it should be recalled that the scope of regulatory autonomy under the EVIPA and comparable EU agreements is largely dependent on the practical functioning of the ICS. Therefore, ongoing research is essential to devising strategies for organising and operating the ICS to support the realisation of this framework effectively.

Furthermore, it is acknowledged that achieving a meaningful rebalancing of the international investment regime will necessitate far-reaching measures beyond the incremental developments discussed in this book.[33] It is imperative to recognise that reconciling competing interests within the international investment regime is inherently complex. While the inclusion of language about environmental protection, sustainable development, and the right to regulate in IIAs, in general, and EVIPA, in specific, represents a step forward, it's a fundamental prerequisite to address the legitimacy crisis of international investment law and advancing toward a more inclusive approach to economic development.[34]

As clarified in Part III of this book, although substantive investment protection standards have been improved, the discretion afforded to the ICS tribunals in determining whether a particular measure violates these standards remains notable. Issues such as assessing the severity of measures in indirect expropriation claims or identifying manifestly wrong grounds for targeted discrimination under the FET standard underscore the complexity of adjudicating state policy measures. While the flexibility may be warranted given the diverse and intricate nature of state policies, it underscores the critical role of a well-designed ISDS system in ensuring accurate interpretation of substantive regulations in BIT language that aligns with the contracting parties' intentions. Consequently, a comprehensive examination of the new EU proposals for a two-tiered ICS system is imperative to optimise discussions and outcomes in this study area.

[33] Coleman et al. (2018), p. 64.

[34] Martini (2017), p. 582.

10.2 Chasing Sustainable Development Goals: What Direction for Vietnam?

This book has examined Vietnam's current environmental and international investment policies and legal framework, analysing the compatibility of domestic regulations with the EVIPA provisions. It has assessed Vietnam's utilisation of the right to regulate in the context of foreign investment management and environmental protection, as safeguarded by EVIPA. The findings have highlighted that, while the EVIPA introduces various tools to bolster the host state's regulatory rights, the extent of this empowerment depends on the continuing efforts of the signatories.

This underscores the need for Vietnam to evaluate whether it can leverage its IIAs to address existing challenges, particularly in achieving environmental and sustainable development objectives . Pursuing these goals requires substantial financial resources. Given that FDI constitutes a significant source of external financing for Vietnam's development,[35] this book has explores potential strategies for integrating sustainability requirements into its IIA-making process.

10.2.1 Addressing Urgent Environmental Challenges: Imperatives for Vietnam

A notable trend is the divergence in priorities between developing and developed countries regarding investment promotion and environmental considerations. Developing nations, including Vietnam, prioritise measures to attract across various sectors, while developed countries emphasise incentivising investments with positive environmental impacts.[36] Chapter 3shed light on Vietnam's efforts to attract FDI, revealing scattered and directionless initiatives thus far.

During the opening phase of Vietnam's economy and into the 2000s, the country exhibited a degree of passivity in shaping the content of its international investment agreements. Like most BITs signed globally during the same period, these agreements primarily focused on ensuring investment protection. Key provisions included MFN treatment, NT, FET, full protection and security, and commitments to non-expropriation. This emphasis on investor protection was understandable, as BITs served as diplomatic tools to integrate Vietnam into the global economy and attract foreign capital. Even in more recent treaties such as the Vietnam–UK BIT (2002), Vietnam–Japan BIT (2003), and Vietnam–Korea BIT (2003), substantive obligations remained largely unchanged. These agreements continued to prioritise investor protection over the right to regulate, offering broad substantive protections to foreign investors.

[35] UNCTAD (2018a), p. 88.

[36] UNCTAD (2023), p. 92–93.

This situation was not unique to Vietnam but was characteristic of many developing countries worldwide during the 1990s–2000s.[37] During this period, developing nations faced significant resource constraints, particularly in understanding international investment negotiations and their unequal bargaining power vis-à-vis developed countries in IIAs negotiations.[38] Moreover, the primary focus of these countries during this period was on economic development goals, often prioritising them over other concerns.

Vietnam's passive stance in IIAs negotiations persisted until around 2007, when Vietnamese enterprises increasingly invested abroad. However, even as Vietnam became more active in negotiating IIAs, environmental protection requirements were seldom mentioned alongside the primary goal of attracting foreign investment. Among the 67 BITs signed by Vietnam, the Vietnam–Japan BIT (2003) and the Vietnam–Morocco BIT (2012) are exceptional cases as they explicitly address environmental issues or establish connections between investment promotion and environmentally related measures.[39]

Until recently, amidst the global trend of reforming IIAs and ISDS systems and the emergence of new-generation FTAs that encompass commitments to investment protection while addressing concerns about states' regulatory autonomy, Vietnam's FTAs-IIAs have seen a gradual integration of environmental and sustainable development concerns. However, these developments are not necessarily proactive proposals from Vietnam, rather, they primarily stem from the influence and vision of more developed partners. This observation is based on insights gained from observing the negotiation process of agreements between Vietnam and the EU, as well as discussions within Vietnam's legislature regarding the ratification of these agreements.

The focus of trade-investment negotiations can vary depending on the partner involved, with each side prioritising concerns that align with their respective aims in the relationship. For instance, a partner that frequently faces investment disputes may be more inclined to limit investment protection obligations, while partners with

[37] For instance, see the case of India in Baltag FCIArb et al. (2023), p. 415 or see the case of Mexico in Gallagher and Zarsky (2005), p. 13.

[38] VanDuzer (2019), p. 42. See also, Puig (2019), p. 259.

[39] Vietnam–Japan BIT includes in the Preamble the declaration to "not relaxing health, safety and environmental measures of general application." Article 21 of this BIT also emphasises that: "The Contracting Parties recognise that it is inappropriate to encourage investment by investors of the other Contracting Party by relaxing environmental measures. To this effect each Contracting Party should not waive or otherwise derogate from such environmental measures as an encouragement for the establishment, acquisition or expansion in its Area of investments by investors of the other Contracting Party." Moreover, Article 2 Vietnam–Morocco BIT on promotion and protection of investments also exclude investment protections if the measures that have to be taken by the Contracting Party for reasons public security, order or public health or protection of environment provided that such measures are not applied in a manner which would constitute a means of arbitrary or unjustified discrimination. While the broad or narrow interpretation of these regulations remains uncertain, their inclusion and correlation of investment with the environment in these agreements represent a progressive step that aligns well with the current international investment landscape.

a strong emphasis on sustainable issues, like the EU and Canada,[40] may seek ambitious commitments in agreements such as CETA. However, in the case of negotiations between the EU and Vietnam, although environmental protection is a shared concern, the EU's emphasis on enhancing labour standards and workers' rights in Vietnam has raised more implementation concerns for the Vietnamese government. Consequently, prioritising discussions on ratifying the three remaining core conventions of the International Labour Organisation has taken precedence over other issues in Vietnam's National Assembly sessions, while sustainable development, environmental protection, and the preservation of policy space under the EVFTA – EVIPA have not received much attention.[41]

In Vietnam, information regarding Vietnam's negotiating position on specific treaty issues is only limitedly disclosed to the public if those matters are deliberated in the National Assembly. While some basic trade negotiation documents on the EU side may be published, documents within the framework of EVIPA negotiations are kept private due to political reasons. Along with this lack of transparency in the international treaty negotiation process, in practical legislative activities within Vietnam, sustainable development, environmental protection, and the preservation of policy space under the EVFTA – EVIPA have received little attention and discussion from the Vietnamese side. Specifically, issues related to investment protection agreements often do not spark much debate in the National Assembly and are generally supported with a high rate of consensus, as evidenced by the approval of the Resolution on the recognition and enforcement of judgments of the ISDS under the EVIPA by 93% of National Assembly delegates.[42]

This practice highlights a concern articulated by VanDuzer, indicating that despite the availability of resources to bolster efforts by developing countries, "systemic barriers continue to hinder developing country capacity to adopt new and improved approaches to IIAs."[43] Another reason for this imbalance in trade-investment negotiations might be that, as discussed in Chap. 5, the EVFTA does not mandate specific obligations on Vietnam regarding climate change.[44] Another indicator is that the Vietnamese government shares this perspective with the EU, as it aligns with the country's development strategies and broader interests. However, these indications reveal capacity challenges in trade-investment negotiations for developing countries in the current context, where developed countries are again successful in imposing their model on developing countries.[45]

Generally, the lack of initiative from developing countries in negotiating trade-investment agreements is not entirely negative, as it enables developed countries to

---

[40] European Comission (2017).

[41] See VietnamPlus (2020a, b, c).

[42] VietnamPlus (2020d).

[43] VanDuzer (2019), p. 43.

[44] See also a study of legal gap assessment for Vietnam's implementaltion of the EVFTA in a publication of World Bank (2020), pp. 39–51.

[45] VanDuzer (2019), p. 45.

strengthen their standards in specific relations, indirectly elevating the standards of developing countries, particularly in non-trade concerns such as sustainable development and the environment. However, relying solely on IIAs drafted by developed countries can only partially address the economic circumstances and development objectives of developing countries.[46] Moreover, such a passive approach does not effectively address Vietnam's increasingly urgent environmental pollution, especially given the current context, where the adverse effects of climate change, such as droughts, water shortages, and saline intrusion, pose significant threats to Vietnam.

It is evident that the current challenging context, coupled with the imperative to address urgent environmental and climate change issues, requires Vietnam to abandon its passive stance in IIAs negotiations. Chapter 4 underscored that Vietnam's environmental situation is increasingly alarming due to the pursuit of rapid economic development policies while lacking the necessary attention to environmental protection for nearly four decades. Specifically, the GDP data provided in Chap. 3 illustrates Vietnam's success in economic development policies. However, akin to most of its Southeast Asian neighbours, the government has faced criticism for adopting a "develop first, clean up later" approach.[47]

The rapid economic growth accompanying Vietnam's drive towards industrialisation and modernisation has exerted a significant toll on the environment, evident in numerous recent environmental incidents across the country. The pursuit of economic development through industrialisation has escalated demands for energy and raw materials. Concurrently, urban areas are expanding unchecked in many regions, often neglecting sustainable development requirements and overlooking environmental considerations in socio-economic planning. Consequently, this neglect has resulted in a decline in the quality of the living environment.

Vietnam's geographical location and natural conditions are compounding these challenges, rendering it one of the countries most vulnerable to climate change. The impacts of climate change are increasingly disrupting Vietnam's economy, with costs already eroding growth. Initial assessments from the recent Country Environmental Analysis indicate that Vietnam incurred a loss of 10 billion USD in 2020, equivalent to 3.2% of its GDP, due to climate change impacts. The magnitude of these damages, which are foreseen to increase rapidly, intensifies the need for Vietnam to adapt to the risks posed by climate change.[48]

The presented scenario underscores the escalating domestic environmental challenges and climate change risks in Vietnam, coupled with the mounting international commitments made by government representatives. This convergence of factors exerts immense pressure on the government to act swiftly and decisively in response to climate change. Consequently, Vietnam is compelled to explore and devise more effective strategies to address the evolving climate crisis.

[46] Ibid., p. 50.

[47] Lee (2024).

[48] World Bank (2022), p. 6.

The intertwined nature of trade, investment, and environmental challenges highlights the necessity of concurrently integrating policies for economic development, investment attraction, and environmental protection. Failure to reconcile these interrelated systems could exacerbate environmental risks and incidents such as soil, water, and air pollution, as well as resource depletion. To navigate this complex landscape, it is imperative to bolster political will and enhance the capacity of mainstream institutions to integrate environmental considerations into development strategies, plans, and state's budgets. This concerted effort will foster a "demand-pull" for environment-development information and options, ensuring a more harmonious and sustainable approach.[49]

Moreover, it is essential to acknowledge that Vietnam has encountered challenges in accessing international support since attaining middle-income country status in 2010.[50] Consequently, accessing international credit lines with favourable conditions has become increasingly challenging.[51] In this context, FDI assumes heightened importance as a crucial avenue for Vietnam to pursue sustainable development in the current and forthcoming periods.

10.2.2 *Navigating Vietnam's Course: Leveraging Available Tools*

In the current context, the Vietnamese government must earnestly consider IIAs as a viable solution to address present and potential future environmental challenges. While still evolving, IIAs hold promise as a mechanism to harmonise the advantages of foreign investment while safeguarding environmental interests.[52] However, leveraging IIAs to advance sustainable development goals presents its own set of challenges.

Research on the impact of FDI in developing countries reveals various outcomes on economic growth, efficiency spillovers, and environmental performance, ranging from positive to neutral to even negative.[53] Crucial determining factors include domestic policies, institutional capacities, and regulatory frameworks.[54] Experts underscore that not all investment pathways lead to sustainability and equity.[55] The efficacy of FDI in promoting clean technology transfer and fostering better environmental management hinges significantly on the governance framework in place.[56]

[49] Bass et al. (2010), p. 56.

[50] World Bank (2024).

[51] Schirmbeck (2017), p. 5.

[52] Baltag FCIArb et al. (2023), pp. 419–421.

[53] Gallagher and Zarsky (2004), p. 13.

[54] Ibid.

[55] Lyuba Zarsky (2004), p. 1.

[56] Ibid.

Without robust governance mechanisms, FDI inflows risk overwhelming domestic capacities for environmental and social oversight, potentially resulting in net costs rather than benefits for local communities and national revenue streams.[57] International bodies such as UNCTAD highlight that IIAs extend beyond mere investment facilitation, holding broader implications for policy coherence and capacity-building at a systemic level.[58]

To date, akin to numerous other nations globally,[59] despite the acknowledgement of sustainable development as a vital objective in national development agendas, FDI in Vietnam often fails to align with the locations, sectors, or activities essential for fostering sustainable outcomes. Many investments even contribute to or exacerbate social and environmental detriments. This underscores the inadequacy of the domestic policy and legal frameworks governing foreign investment, which are yet to be effectively integrated with sustainable development objectives.

There is no need for a comprehensive analysis of FDI flows' impact on Vietnam's sustainable development as the practice shown in Chaps. 3 and 4 of this book demonstrates that while a large volume of FDI flowed in Vietnam recently, particularly before the onset of the COVID-19 pandemic, the realisation of technology and knowledge spillovers has been limited.[60] Conversely, rapid economic expansion lacking meticulous environmental policies has led to severe environmental degradation in Vietnam.

The multifaceted nature of sustainable development necessitates diverse approaches to address its various dimensions. Striking a balance between domestic rgulatory frameworks and international investment laws is pivotal in charting this new direction. The following recommendations serve as a starting point for cultivating more intricate innovations.

Vietnamese policymakers must recognise the paramount importance of sustainable development in formulating economic development strategies. This necessitates the seamless integration of sustainable development imperatives into every facet of economic development goals, making investment attraction an indispensable component. Scholars agree that the relationship between FDI and the green economy[61] exhibits a dual nature.[62] While private sector investments are crucial to addressing climate change, fostering job creation, advancing biodiversity, and pro-

[57] Ibid., pp. 03–04.

[58] According to the UNCTAD, IIAs can help improve countries' regulatory and institutional frameworks, including by adding an international dimension to them and by promoting the rule of law and enhancing good governance. UNCTAD (2018b), p. 16.

[59] Coleman et al.'s (2021), pp. 118, 160.

[60] This situation is similar with Mexico's experience in the 1990s. Gallagher and Zarsky (2005), p. 13.

[61] The term defined by the UNEP as an economy that "should contribute to eradicating poverty as well as sustained economic growth, enhancing social inclusion, imroving human welfare and creating opportunities for employment and decent work for all, while maintaining the healthy functioning of the earth's ecosystems". See United Nations (2012), para. 56.

[62] UNCTAD (2010), p. 136.

moting the development of environmentally friendly technologies and sustainable agriculture, they also pose challenges to achieving sustainable development objectives.

The concept of a green economy or green growth has gained traction recently and has been enshrined in policy through the Vietnam National Green Growth Strategy for the 2021–2030 period, with a vision to 2050.[63] This strategy outlines critical objectives and delineates key targets, serving as a roadmap for restructuring Vietnam's prevailing growth model to achieve economically prosperous and environmentally sustainable development, while also promoting social equity. This policy framework is regarded as instrumental in advancing sustainable development objectives and curbing greenhouse gas emissions, ultimately steering Vietnam towards a carbon-neutral economy in the long term.

Furthermore, to operationalise the National Green Growth Strategy, a specific action plan has been formulated—the National Action Plan on Green Growth covering the period from 2021 to 2030.[64] This plan, endorsed by the Prime Minister through Decision 882/QĐ-TTg in July 2022, delineates the targets essential for realising the objectives outlined in the strategy. Additionally, the Ministry of Planning and Investment recently issued Circular 10/2023/TT-BKHDT, which outlines the statistical indicators to measure the impacts of the National Green Growth Strategy.[65]

Regrettably, despite these initiatives, there appears to be a need for more attention to IIAs as a mechanism for advancing green growth in Vietnam. When situated within the context of economic development and the imperatives posed by climate change, IIAs transcend mere investment policies, extending their implications to various policy domains across different levels of governance. Given their wide-ranging applicability and the diverse operations of foreign investment, IIA provisions intersect with policies related to trade, labour standards, social issues, taxation, intellectual property rights, land tenure, sector-specific regulations, national security concerns, cultural policies, as well as health and environmental protection.[66] Due to the intricate linkages and potential impacts on various socio-economic sectors, IIA negotiation policies must align cohesively with Vietnam's economic and social development objectives.

This book delineates a number of directions aimed at promoting sustainable development and addressing climate change through the governance of foreign investment as below:

(i) **Shaping FDI Capital Flows Toward Sustainable Development Goals**

[63] Prime Minister of Vietnam (2021) Decision No. 1658/QĐ-TTg.

[64] This plan was approved by the Prime Minister of Vietnam, Decision 882/QĐ-TTg.

[65] This Circular disaggregates the National Green Growth Strategy into four primary objectives: Reduction of greenhouse gas emissions; Implementation of green economic reforms by sector; Promotion of sustainable urban development and consumption practices; Enhancement of equality, inclusion, and resilience.

[66] See further UNCTAD (2018b), p. 17.

Existing studies suggest that IIAs play a supportive role at best, with economic factors wielding more significant influence over investment decisions.[67] Consequently, the conventional approach of offering extensive investment protection to attract capital is losing favour. Conversely, recognising the dual nature of the relationship between FDI and sustainable development,[68] IIAs can serve as strategic tools in advancing sustainable development goals through foreign investment.[69]

It is widely recognised that IIAs play a crucial role in the governance framework, offering a distinct opportunity for collaboration with treaty partners to shape investment flows between parties actively. This collaboration catalyses international investment aligned with sustainable development goals and prevents support for investments that counteract these goals.[70] In fact, IIAs have demonstrated their capacity to influence FDI capital flows by establishing criteria for qualifying investments eligible for treaty benefits. These criteria typically require investments to contribute to the economic development of the host state or operate in compliance with its laws.[71] Additionally, provisions within IIAs, such as denial of benefits clauses and measures promoting responsible investor conduct, including adherence to anti-corruption regulations and corporate social responsibility standards, further guide FDI inflows towards countries aligning with their developmental concerns and objectives.

Given the potential of IIAs to advance sustainable development objectives, Vietnam should explore how these treaties can best support its overarching development strategy, taking into account its unique circumstances. By leveraging IIAs effectively, Vietnam can steer FDI capital flows in directions that promote sustainable development, aligning with its national priorities and goals.[72] This book recommends that the Vietnamese government refrain from signing additional BITs or engaging in negotiations to amend expiring agreements until a Model BIT is drafted. This model should prioritise sustainable development issues and incorporate environmental concerns into its content. Alternatively, when entering into IIA negotiations, it is essential for Vietnamese negotiators to explicitly state that their purpose is to promote and safeguard investments contributing to sustainable development. However, as this requirement is challenging to quantify, governments may consider incorporating the most pertinent principles of international environmental law into investment agreements.

Drawing inspiration from the balanced approach of agreements like the EVFTA and the EVIPA, which integrate measures to advance the transition to a green economy, governments can adjust substantive obligations and include fundamental notions emphasising sustainable development and the right to regulate. For instance,

---

[67] Coleman et al. (2018), p. 62.

[68] UNCTAD (2010), p. 136.

[69] VanDuzer (2019), p. 43.

[70] Coleman et al. (2021), p. 118.

[71] See India–Kyrgyzstan BIT (2019) Article 1.4.

[72] VanDuzer (2019), p. 43.

EVFTA includes a commitment to remove or reduce non-tariff barriers to trade and investment in renewable energy generation.

These actions reflect a shared commitment among all parties to promote the transition to a green economy actively.[73] These efforts highlight the significant role these agreements play in supporting climate change responses within the territories of the signatory parties. The EVFTA – EVIPA is a valuable example for Vietnam, offering insights into effectively integrating sustainable development objectives into future trade and investment agreements. The innovations introduced in those agreements establish a legal foundation that supports the pursuit of the host country's legitimate goals while mitigating the risk of investor claims in cases involving implementing environmental management measures that may adversely affect investors. While the inclusion of such provisions in specific BITs largely depends on the stance of the host country, adept integration of the host country's environmental protection policies is crucial and feasible, especially given that the prevailing trend and awareness among countries worldwide also support this approach.

Notably, major capitalist nations across the northern and southern globe, such as the EU, Canada, Australia, and New Zealand, are keen on aligning their trade and investment agreements with sustainable development objectives. Interestingly, China, Vietnam's neighbouring country, also moved in this direction early on. Since the late 1970s, when China embarked on its opening-up journey after a prolonged period of international isolation,[74] its initial agreements focused solely on encouraging, promoting, and protecting investments to stimulate business initiatives and foster prosperity.[75] However, beginning around 2010, China's approach to IIAs has shown a discernible shift towards environmental friendliness, with a notable emphasis on sustainable development, as evidenced by agreements such as the BIT between China and Canada. Agreements like those signed between China, Japan, and Korea, while not explicitly mentioning sustainability, include vital elements indicative of such orientation. This sustainable development orientation has become a consistent feature of China's modern IIA framework, reflecting a mainstream practice in the country's approach to IIAs.[76]

With its involvement in numerous BITs with various partners, Vietnam has garnered sufficient experience to formulate a Model BIT that aligns with its current conditions and aspirations more proactively. This Model BIT should delineate the concessions in each investment protection standard and adopt a comprehensive approach to steering FDI flows towards its sustainable development objectives. Vietnam's participation in negotiating and signing new-generation trade and investment agreements, such as the CPTPP and the EVFTA – EVIPA, reflects a modern

[73] Scholars have proposed several levels of integrating green economy goals into IIAs, including incorporating such objectives into the pre-conclusion phase of IIAs, embedding sustainable development within the procedural aspects of dispute settlement mechanisms, and integrating green economy objectives into substantive provisions. See further UNCTAD (2010), p. 190.

[74] Chi (2018), p. 19.

[75] Preamble China–Africa BIT (1997); See Chi (2018), Ibid.

[76] Ibid.

and progressive approach. Leveraging these agreements can elevate Vietnam's investment protection standards to match the evolving landscape of IIAs in the contemporary context.

This book does not aim to draft a comprehensive Model BIT encompassing all provisions that reserve the host state's rights to regulate. Therefore, several emerging trends in IIA negotiation practices have not been extensively explored within this book's scope. Notable innovative approaches include the inclusion of obligations imposed on investor,[77] clauses mandating investor assessment of environmental and social impacts[78] or non-relaxation clause[79] and consistency with the IIA obligations clause.[80] Further studies are encouraged to analyse and develop sufficient provisions that comprehensively safeguard the host country's right to regulate, addressing issues identified under agreements like the EVIPA or referring to IIA negotiation practice while respecting investors' rights.[81]

Moreover, adopting a "two-way street" approach in designing IIAs, as seen in the Morocco 2019 Model BIT and other "new generation" model BITs published in recent years, could prove beneficial for Vietnam. These model BITs, including the SADC 2012 Model BIT, the Brazil 2015 Model BIT, the Colombia 2017 Model BIT, and the Netherlands 2019 Model BIT, incorporate provisions on investor obligations alongside standard investor protection mechanisms. This two-way street framework imposes obligations on both the host state and the foreign investor, nudging corporations and stakeholders towards environmentally conscious practices through the instrument of IIAs.[82]

Developed countries often formulate a model BIT that effectively encapsulates their own goals and intentions, such as the US 2012 Model BIT.[83] They then utilise this model to negotiate with various partners. Another approach involves developing a unified negotiation policy or framework that clarifies general and specific goals and other targets, ensuring negotiations adhere to this direction—a strategy adopted by the EU.[84] For Vietnam, before embarking on the research and construction of a Model BIT as proposed above, the government must first assess the current conditions and characteristics of the domestic economy. This will allow the customisation of the Model BIT to closely align with current needs and conditions. In essence, it is essential to delineate the expected regulatory scope to determine if additional

[77] For instance, Morocco Model BIT 2019 Section III, which is most noticeable is Article 20 on social and environmental responsibility. Other Agreement applied similar approach can be named as Netherlands Model BIT (2019) Article 7; Draft Pan-African Investment Code (2016); SADC Model BIT (2012) Article 15.2; Colombian Model BIT (2017) 'Investors Social Responsibility.

[78] As proposed by the SADC Model BIT (2012) Article 2.

[79] Singapore–Myanmar BIT (2019) (not yet entered into force) Preamble.

[80] As seen in Australia–Hong Kong, China SAR BIT (2019) Article 15.

[81] Baltag FCIArb et al. (2023), pp. 420–421.

[82] Ibid.

[83] Office of the US Trade Representative.

[84] European Commission (2015), p. 35.

policy space, particularly in specific areas, is warranted.[85] For instance, an economy like Vietnam may require greater discretion on policy matters to transition towards cleaner forms of energy. This is crucial due to the dynamic nature of energy policy, where evolving regulatory schemes incentivise projects that contribute to both economic development and cleaner energy forms.[86] As observed in ISDS practice, failure to provide a stable legal environment may lead to disputes and result in foreign investors experiencing unexpected losses. In fact, the members of the ECT have faced a significant number of ISDS cases due to their new regulations in the fossil fuel industry aimed at transitioning away from a carbon-intensive economy.[87] To address this situation, the ECT Members reached an "Agreement in Principle" amending the ECT in 2022.[88] Along with other changes, this amendment introduced a "flexibility mechanism" that allows Parties, based on a conference decision, to exclude investment protection for fossil fuels in their territories. Such specific concerns can also be clarified in Vietnam's Model BIT.

Moreover, Vietnam's Model BIT should address specific factors and concerns, including investment provisions that address climate change challenges through investment-facilitation measures. These measures aim to increase investments in environmentally friendly goods and services, as seen in agreements such as those between the EU–Japan and EU–Singapore.[89] Prioritising policies for renewable energy development is also essential and should be integrated into Vietnam's Model BIT. Developing renewable energy as a substitute for fossil fuels is recognised as an effective strategy for combating climate change, especially for reaching climate neutrality,[90] a direction Vietnam has been pursuing for many years. However, traditional IIL often fails to reflect such investment incentive policies, resulting in countries facing claims from investors, as seen in cases like *Foresight Luxembourg Solar v. Spain* or *Antaris GMBH v. the Czech Republic*.[91] Therefore, it is imperative to incorporate these considerations into Vietnam's Model BIT to safeguard the country's interests and promote sustainable development.

[85] OECD (2015), para. 36.

[86] Trujillo (2018), pp. 2744–2745.

[87] For instance, Netherlands faced with an indirect expropriation and FET claim concerning its Coal Ban Act in *RWE AG and RWE Eemshaven Holding II BV v. Kingdom of the Netherlands* [2021] ICSID Case, ARB/21/4 and in *Uniper SE, Uniper Benelux Holding B.V. and Uniper Benelux N.V. v. Kingdom of the Netherlands* [2021], ARB/21/22. Canada has faced with similar claim in *Westmoreland Coal Company v. Canada* [2022] UNCT/23/2 (Pending). See Zhu (2024), p. 184; Medici-Colombo (2024), pp. 138–141.

[88] It should be noticed that after failing to secure a majority, the EU Commission opted to remove the adoption of the Agreement in Principle from the agenda of the annual summit and postpone it. See Mauro (2024), p. 63; Medici-Colombo (2024), p. 144.

[89] Thrasher (2021), p. 2.

[90] UNEP (2022), p. 41–42.

[91] *Foresight Luxembourg Solar 1 S. Á.R1. and others v. Kingdom of Spain*, SCC Case No. 2015/150, Award, 14 November 2018; *Antaris GMBH v. the Czech Republic, 2014-01*, PCA Case No. 2014-01, Award, 2 May 2018.

As discussed in Chap. 6 on Expropriation and Chap. 7 on FET, even the phase-out of projects detrimental to the environment or reliant on fossil fuels, such as oil, gas, and coal, poses the risk of potential claims against the host state for alleged violations of investment treaty obligations. Indeed, a 2021 report by the IISD notes that the fossil fuel industry is by far the most litigious under IIL, with most cases decided in favour of investors.[92] UNCTAD experts have similarly observed that ISDS could complicate or increase the cost of the energy transition.[93] Therefore, Vietnam must heed this warning with great caution.

In recent times, demonstrating a commitment to sharing the burden of climate change with the global community, Vietnam has signed numerous environmental and climate change agreements, most notably the Paris Agreement. However, there is scant evidence that Vietnam has aligned investment treaty incentives with the Paris Agreement and other environmental agreements. Meanwhile, coal thermal power projects, like other energy ventures, require substantial capital investment. In Vietnam, these projects heavily depend on FDI and state funding.[94] For instance, the Van Phong 1 BOT Thermal Power Plant, with an investment of 2.58 billion USD by the Sumitomo Group, is Vietnam's largest coal power plant.[95]

Given that withdrawing from ISDS and investment treaties may not be viable for Vietnam, it is imperative to explore BIT models that facilitate the implementation of climate adaptation policies, promote green industrial growth, and discourage environmentally harmful fuels. Hippolyte argues that improving the country's position by adopting strategies to enhance its participation in the regime and increase the level of FDI it currently attracts should be the preferred approach, rather than dismissing the importance of FDI.[96] This study supports this viewpoint. At a minimum, BITs should include provisions that support the host state's policy measures rather than relying solely on the right to regulate clause.

While it remains unclear whether there is a horizontal conflict between investment and climate treaties, primarily due to the flexible nature of climate treaty obligations, the inclusion of a climate treaty conflict clause in investment treaties, as suggested by Ying Zhu, might help resolve conflicts between state climate measures and their investment treaty obligations.[97] Another option proposed by the OECD is

---

[92] According to this report, disputes involving the fossil fuel industry account for nearly 20% of all known ISDS cases across various sectors. See Salvatore (2021), pp. iii, iv. Another statistics from UNCTAD in 2023 indicate that fossil fuel investors were involved in over 15% of all treaty-based cases—specifically 219 out of 1257 cases in 2022. See UNCTAD (2023), p. 92. This data suggests that claims related to policies on the energy transition will continue to pose a significant threat to both developing and developed countries in the near future.

[93] UNCTAD (2023), p. 91.

[94] Refer to the list of coal projects in Vietnam as of October 2020 in: Open Development Vietnam (2020).

[95] Ngọc Điệp (2024).

[96] Hippolyte (2019), p. 75.

[97] The author proposes two models for resolving conflicts between climate and investment treaties: (1) A subordination clause that stipulates that the climate treaty should have priority over the investment treaty in case of a conflict between the two; (2) A coordination clause that requires

to negotiate an ISDS carve-out for climate change measures.[98] This climate carve-out could be drafted in a format applicable to existing IIAs via a plurilateral opt-in agreement that modifies the applicable IIAs or as an amendment to existing IIAs or incorporated into new IIAs. These options, which exclude treaty coverage for measures aimed at reducing greenhouse gas emissions and thereby preserve policy space for states to enact fossil fuel-related policies, should be carefully considered in Vietnam's IIA negotiation policy.

Moreover, abrupt shifts in energy development policies away from fossil fuels towards renewables and new technologies,[99] as observed in the transition from Vietnam's Seventh Power Development Plan VII (PDP VII)[100] to Vietnam's Eight Power Development Plan (PDP VIII),[101] are anticipated to present substantial challenges for the Vietnamese government in effectively implementing these policies. Such transitions entail domestic management complexities and carry the risk of unsettling foreign investors whose interests may be impacted by policy changes. As Vietnam navigates its energy transition, careful consideration of domestic management activities is essential to ensure a smooth transition while mitigating risks to investor interests.

In the realm of IIA negotiation policy, it is crucial for developing countries to maintain flexibility and responsiveness to the evolving needs of their constituents. New IIAs should reflect this reality, adopting an approach that allows countries to assess both the short- and long-term impacts of FDI on their economies.[102] This approach enables governments to navigate the complexities of FDI inflows while safeguarding their national interests and promoting sustainable development objectives.

Reaching specific agreements in IIAs is contingent upon various factors, including the negotiating partner, alignment on specific goals, and the role of capital importation/exportation between the countries. Nonetheless, a Model BIT serves as a valuable blueprint for Vietnamese negotiators in crafting individual IIAs and establishing boundaries for concessions. By drafting a Model BIT, Vietnam can ensure that its IIAs align with the country's sustainable development orientation, striking a balance between investment protection and sustainable development goals. This approach safeguards Vietnam's sovereign rights in pursuing environmental protection and sustainable development objectives while protecting the legitimate rights of Vietnamese investors abroad.

Implementing a consistent IIA negotiation policy enhances the effectiveness of IIA management and implementation, reducing resource strain. Furthermore,

contracting parties to engage in consultation to reach a mutually satisfactory solution to the conflict. See Zhu (2024), pp. 191–193.

[98] Paine and Sheargold (2024).

[99] PwC (2023).

[100] Prime Minister of Vietnam (2016) Decision No. 428/QĐ-TTg.

[101] Prime Minister of Vietnam (2023) Decision No. 500/QĐ-TTg.

[102] Thrasher (2021).

leveraging the Model BIT facilitates decision-making regarding whether to enter into IIAs and what provisions they should entail as part of a comprehensive strategy concerning foreign investment and sustainable development.[103]

However, it's crucial to acknowledge that the effectiveness of Model BITs hinges on negotiators' awareness, understanding of their benefits, and ability to negotiate treaties incorporating them.[104] This presents a significant challenge for negotiators from developing economies like Vietnam. Therefore, continued capacity-building efforts for negotiators are imperative if the Vietnamese government intends to harness the potential of IIAs effectively.

(ii) **Sustainability Impact Assessments—An Available Tool to Evaluate Sustainable Development Characteristics of IIA Negotiations**

The extensive array of agreements inked by the EU with its partners across continents underscoring the emphasis on environmental concerns and climate change might be supported by the adept utilisation of impact assessment mechanisms or sustainable impact assessments. They are valuable tools for evaluating such an agreement's economic, environmental, and social implications. By comprehensively assessing these impacts, decision-makers gain insights into the advantages and disadvantages of each proposal, enabling them to understand the synergies between different policy fields and how they can mutually support each other.[105]

Canada has been employing impact assessments since around 1994, conducting ex-post environmental reviews of agreements in the Uruguay Round to understand the synergies between the different fields and how one policy can support another.[106] Subsequently, it adopted a set of tools—Environmental Assessments for trade negotiations in 2001 and has applied them since then.[107] Similarly, the United States developed its environmental review mechanism, known as Environmental Reviews, in 1992, which became an obligatory assessment for trade negotiations by 1999.[108]

The European Commission has also utilised impact assessment mechanisms since 1999, significantly shaping its trade and investment agreement negotiation practices.[109] Recent agreements signed by the EU demonstrate a notable emphasis on addressing climate change and promoting sustainable development, including treaties signed with Vietnam. Leveraging these practices, the Vietnamese government can adopt and apply impact assessment mechanisms in future trade and investment negotiations, drawing upon the EU's experiences as a useful reference point. Furthermore, as Gehring and Kent suggest, impact assessment mechanisms are not limited to the international level but are also prevalent at the national level. They are

---

[103] VanDuzer (2019), p. 60.

[104] Ibid., p. 49.

[105] UNCTAD (2010), p. 192.

[106] Ibid, p. 194.

[107] Ibid.

[108] Ibid, p. 195.

[109] EU Commission (2016).

commonly utilised for assessing domestic environmental and planning laws concerning significant projects and can even be employed to evaluate the direct impacts of individual FDI projects.

Sauvant and Gabor propose that investment projects should be designed to prioritise commercial viability and efforts to contribute to the economic, social, and environmental development of host countries within the framework of fair governance mechanisms. Such investment endeavours, termed "sustainable FDI," involve direct corporate actions to enhance the developmental impact of FDI.[110] While this concept is not novel, it remains imperative as the focal point for attracting FDI capital. The Vietnamese government must earnestly pursue this direction, establishing characteristics of FDI sustainability alongside an indicative list of such traits.

However, analogous conditions should also be applied to domestic enterprises when integrating FDI sustainability characteristics into foreign investment, as stipulated in the 2023 updated ILO Tripartite Declaration of Principles Concerning Multinational Enterprises and Social Policies.[111] The intention here is not to create a distinction between multinational and domestic enterprises. Adhering to such a requirement may pose a significant burden for domestic businesses, particularly during the post-pandemic recovery period when resources are limited. Nevertheless, this orientation remains imperative in the long run if Vietnam is earnest about achieving its sustainable development goals.

Given its asymmetric negotiating position, there may be concerns regarding Vietnam's ability to proactively persuade future negotiating partners in IIAs to integrate sustainable development concerns. However, this concern may hold less weight for several reasons. Firstly, despite fluctuations due to various factors, including the COVID-19 pandemic, Vietnam's overseas investment reached 2.67 billion USD in 2022.[112] This increased investment potential abroad has bolstered Vietnam's negotiating position, making it easier to advocate for shared views in IIA negotiations compared to the past, particularly the 1990s.

Secondly, the parties' negotiating positions in IIA negotiations are influenced by numerous factors, with economic potential being just one aspect. Expectations set by each party within the specific BIT relationship also play a crucial role.[113] As highlighted in Chap. 2, even developing partners prioritise environmental protection and regulatory rights due to shifts in the international investment landscape and growing environmental concerns. Environmental issues have become increasingly urgent globally, making sustainable development a shared concern in IIA negotiations, transcending Vietnam's individual interests.

Moreover, if Vietnam finds its negotiating position unbalanced and its partner unwilling to integrate sustainable development into IIAs, it can explore multilateral negotiations as an alternative. In multilateral settings, proposals regarding

[110] Sauvant and Gabor (2021), p. 267.

[111] ILO (2023), p. 3.

[112] World Bank data.

[113] Mills (2014), p. 449.

sustainable development in trade and investment negotiations are more likely to garner support. Multilateral negotiations operate based on generalised principles of conduct, focusing on appropriate conduct for a class of actions rather than the specific interests of individual parties or strategic considerations.[114]

Another concern frequently expressed in the literature is that developing countries like Vietnam should refrain from negotiating for additional protection for sustainable development policies due to fierce competition for investment with other nations. The fear is that commitments related to sustainable development in BITs may deter prospective investors.[115] However, research indicates that the belief that providing more investment guarantees through IIAs leads to increased FDI capital is flawed.[116] The influx of FDI capital depends on multifaceted factors. Moreover, sacrificing regulatory rights to attract investment is no longer a viable objective for Vietnam, particularly considering the country's escalating environmental pollution and the impacts of climate change.

(iii) **Aligning Domestic Legal and Policy Frameworks to Advance Sustainable Development Goals**

As suggested by UNCTAD, the extensive scope and obligations of IIAs necessitate comprehensive internal policy coordination at national and subnational levels during the development of a country's IIA negotiation strategy and throughout the negotiation process.[117] Moreover, it is crucial to ensure coherence between IIA obligations and domestic policies and achieve consistency between IIAs and other international commitments of the contracting parties involved.[118] These recommendations underscore that the potential benefits of IIAs can only be fully realised with an appropriate domestic policy and implementation framework in place.

It is essential to recognise that IIAs are tools to advance sustainable development objectives. Still, they cannot be transformed into instruments of development cooperation due to their inherent focus on investment protection.[119] Therefore, while efforts to enhance policy space within IIAs are valuable, Vietnam must continue to prioritise integrating sustainable development policies across different economic and social governance areas. This includes enhancing the capacity and efficiency of state management, particularly in environmental management and foreign investment activities. Such efforts are necessary because the impacts of investments are significantly influenced by domestic laws, policies, and institutions that govern investments, monitor compliance, and enforce regulations. The role and

[114] Schill (2014), p. 111.

[115] VanDuzer (2016), p.175.

[116] See, for instance, Hallward-Driemeier (2003), pp. 22–23; Ryan Suda (2006).

[117] UNCTAD (2018b), p. 17.

[118] Ibid.

[119] Sacerdoti (2016), p. 32. See also VanDuzer (2016), p. 144.

effectiveness of domestic policymaking and institutions are crucial for shaping investment and its impacts and serve as foundational elements of sustainable development.[120]

Currently, the Vietnamese government recognises sustainable development as a global imperative, with the digital economy, circular economy, and green growth emerging as preferred development models worldwide.[121] Aligning with this trend, the 2021–2030 strategy, similar to its predecessor, underscores sustainable development as a paramount requirement, emphasising the vital role of science, technology, innovation, and digital transformation.[122] Moreover, Vietnam acknowledges the significance of leveraging FDI capital to advance its green growth agenda, particularly in technology transfer, as the country transitions its economy toward cleaner production methods. The latest Vietnam Social-Economic Development Strategy 2021–2030 advocates for a shift in foreign investment attraction and cooperation policy from quantity to quality. It emphasises high-value projects, efficiency, and technology utilisation, environmental protection, and sustainable development goals. The strategy emphasises the importance of prioritising projects with advanced technology, innovation capacity, and integration into global supply chains.[123]

While these strategic directions are commendable, their implementation remains unclear. Hence, there is a need to reassess the role of FDI capital flows in the national strategy for achieving sustainable development goals, aiming to promote better and channel investments toward sustainable development objectives. Additionally, efforts should focus on enhancing responsible investment practices.[124] Policies aimed at supporting priority FDI capital flows must be developed and implemented with transparency, clarity, and strict adherence.

Besides, in managing foreign investment, attention should be directed towards the following requirements:

- It is imperative to ensure consistency in pursuing sustainable development goals, particularly in investment management activities. All decisions related to investment licensing and foreign investors' investments must integrate sustainable development considerations.[125]
- The balanced policy space under the EVIPA does not automatically guarantee that general regulatory measures will positively impact sustainable development. It remains the regulatory task of the host state to ensure that its measures serve the goal of sustainable development.[126]

---

[120] Coleman et al. (2021), p. 125.

[121] Communist Party of Vietnam (2021).

[122] Central Committee of Communist Party (2020).

[123] Communist Party of Vietnam (2021).

[124] UNCTAD (2018b), p. 17.

[125] Hush (2018), p, 151.

[126] Stifter and Reinisch (2016), p. 96.

- The FET obligation is closely linked to the concept of integrity, which requires that applied measures be open and principled.[127] Vietnam must exercise extreme caution in its decisions or applied measures, even when pursuing sustainable development. Such measures should be enacted transparently, in good faith, without discrimination, and meeting specific conditions in each relevant substantive obligation.
- Environmental conditions are dynamic, necessitating flexible and adaptive policies. This flexibility should extend to the management of investment activities related to the environment. For instance, policy measures should be implemented flexibly, drawing from experiences in trade relations within the WTO regime, such as the Shrimp-Turtle case.[128] Fostering flexibility toward investor rights demonstrates good faith and maximises the State's regulatory space.[129] Therefore, the state should provide opportunities for discussion between investors and the state to clarify unclear issues in guidelines, policies, and instructions on compliance with newly issued regulations. Offering deadline extensions in extraordinary circumstances and providing investors with various tools or options to comply with measures demonstrates flexibility.[130]
- While the role of legitimate expectations in threatening policy space has been limited under EVIPA, the indemnification of losses suffered by foreign investors when significantly affected in their operations must be anticipated when planning significant policy changes. This aligns with good governance principles and the duty of states to observe their obligations under BITs while furthering the general interest.[131]

To ensure sustainable development with the support of the IIA negotiation policy, the government must review, build, and align investment attraction and management policies with environmental policies. This involves reconciling investors' rights to protection with the country's right to pursue sustainable environmental policies within the existing relationship framework.

(iv) **Strengthening Institutional Capacity for Sustainable Development**

The research findings presented in Parts II and III of this book indicate that Vietnam's domestic regulations concerning environmental protection and investment management generally align with the requirements set forth in the EVIPA, particularly regarding indirect expropriation and FET. This suggests that adherence to domestic legal regulations can help mitigate the risk of investor-state disputes. This implication is supported by a 2014 study examining 163 disputes in ICSID case records, Lexis-Nexis news archives, and other sources, which found a low

[127] Vandevelde (2010), p. 105.

[128] Hush (2018), p. 141.

[129] Ibid.

[130] Ibid, pp. 142, 151.

[131] Sacerdoti (2016), pp. 38–39.

incidence of disputes involving legislative activities.[132] Empirical evidence from that study also highlights that most government decisions leading to investor arbitration are associated with actions taken by the executive branch. Therefore, the effective management of investor-state disputes requires attention to the capacity for problem assessment and decision-making within the administrative apparatus. This holds significance not only for dispute management but also for administrative and judicial reform in Vietnam.

Vietnam's administrative and judicial systems have significantly improved, particularly since the comprehensive reform period following WTO accession. In the years following 2005–2007, Vietnam actively engaged in numerous regional and inter-regional trade agreements to become an attractive destination for foreign investment. Consequently, there is a continuous need for institutional reform and enhancement of the efficiency of national administrative and judicial operations. This proposition is advocated in several policy studies within Vietnam, notably highlighted in the Vietnam 2015 Justice Index.[133]

In the past 10 years, amidst heightened scrutiny of the legitimacy of ISDS mechanisms in various international forums, the Vietnamese government has increasingly recognised the risks associated with investor-state disputes. This awareness can also be attributed to Vietnam's involvement as the defendant in 13 ISDS cases. As a response, the government has established an investment dispute prevention mechanism and organised numerous training workshops to enhance the understanding of investment protection obligations among government officials at both central and local levels. However, these efforts, though commendable, are insufficient in addressing the systemic weaknesses prevalent in state management. These weaknesses, which extend from policy formulation to implementation, monitoring, and performance measurement, pose significant challenges.

As highlighted in Chaps. 3 and 4, Vietnam's environmental policies lack specificity and are characterised by a declarative and directive nature. There needs to be more research into specific mechanisms for policy implementation. Moreover, the organisational structure of state management agencies in Vietnam is mainly fragmented and lacks coordination. The absence of effective liaison among relevant political actors results in disjointed environmental management and investment activities, leading to inefficiencies.

Furthermore, the capacity for management and oversight within environmental agencies needs to be improved. The sprawling nature of the environmental management system, spanning multiple sectors, hampers its ability to effectively address macro and interdisciplinary issues. Environmental agencies typically have limited involvement in foreign investment management beyond the appraisal of environmental impact assessment reports. Conversely, investment management agencies

132 Caddel and Jensen (2014).

133 This document recommends a shift in focus from creating new legislation to the implementation of existing laws at all levels. VLA and UNDP (2016), p. 56.

often view environmental requirements as procedural formalities during licensing activities.

Crucially, government officials within these agencies often lack awareness of investment obligations, including Vietnam's commitments under its IIAs. This deficiency undermines their ability to manage conflicts and address disputes with investors effectively.[134] At the local level, provincial government officials responsible for managing FDI issues exhibit limited understanding of investment protection standards, leading to inconsistencies in their approach.

Sustainable development is intrinsically linked to effective governance.[135] Hence, the weaknesses identified in environment and investment management systems, as outlined above, are prevalent in many emerging economies, including Vietnam, and pose significant barriers to realising the benefits of signed IIAs. Deficiencies in management may lead to potential claims that restrict Vietnam's ability to exercise its right to regulate effectively.

Therefore, while clarifying and elaborating on the provisions of IIAs can help ensure a strict interpretation more aligned with the parties' intentions, enhancing the domestic implementation system is equally imperative. Throughout Vietnam's economic integration and development period, FTAs and IIAs have played a significant role in strengthening the capacity and legitimacy of domestic systems and institutions. Therefore, the obligations outlined in EVIPA and other IIAs in which Vietnam participates have the potential to further bolster good governance at the domestic level of this country.

(v) **Harnessing Social Resources for the Development of Sustainable Investment and Environmental Policies**

Negotiating and ratifying international trade and investment treaties often faces numerous hurdles due to public opposition stemming from various concerns. For example, the Trans-Pacific Partnership faced obstacles in the United States Congress due to its contentious nature during President Obama's election season, which was eventually cancelled by President Trump. Similarly, the CETA faced challenges when a subnational region in Belgium threatened to block the necessary approval under Belgian law, jeopardising the entire treaty.[136] These instances underscore the significant impact that the monitoring role of various societal stakeholders can have on the formulation and fate of trade and investment treaties.[137]

In contrast, in Vietnam, public engagement in discussions on the participation and ratification of international treaties is limited. While individuals may contribute opinions to the government through seminars and conferences organised by major legal research institutions, there is no guarantee that relevant government agencies will acknowledge these opinions. Government bodies have primarily led

---

[134] VanDuzer (2019), p. 50.

[135] Walde (2004); UNDP (2014).

[136] See further in Coleman et al. (2018), p. 54.

[137] Ibid.

discussions on such matters and are not open to the public. Commentary on, for example, managing investor-state disputes, if any, typically originates from a decision of the Ministry of Justice, often funded by foreign countries and international organisations.[138] Besides these "solicited" opinions, it is uncommon for researchers' viewpoints to receive widespread attention. Gathering feedback on draft laws through state agencies' websites is mainly ineffective and fails to reach a broad segment of society.

In the case of the EVFTA and EVIPA, publicly available information mainly focuses on the economic benefits of the trade cooperation agreement, with little discussion on the specific commitments regarding investment protection standards and related issues. While it may be argued that such topics are complex and require specialised knowledge, this complexity poses a challenge for the National Assembly's members and citizens alike. This absence of proper oversight from citizens leaves government activities unchecked.

Therefore, this study suggests that, in the long term, the government should broaden its efforts to gather feedback from society regarding the content of international treaties in general, especially the IIAs that Vietnam is considering negotiating. This approach would involve engaging external professional resources separate from state management activities, including external experts. Leveraging resources outside the government can also help address capacity challenges within the state apparatus. As previously noted, not all government officials or members of the National Assembly possess expertise in trade and investment treaties or understand international commitments under IIAs. In contrast, scholars and experts may offer valuable insights relevant to ensuring that foreign investment contributes to sustainable development. Importantly, they can provide impartial perspectives as outsiders, offering beneficial opinions for developing specific policies or laws.

Fostering such practices can provide policymakers with essential information to make policy decisions and promote greater democratic participation. This approach aligns with trends observed in advanced democracies such as the European Union, where the influence of stakeholders outside government agencies has gained prominence, notably during discussions on agreements like the CETA and the TTIP. Discussions within UNCTAD on reforming the IIA regime also underscore the importance of engaging regulators, arbitrators, the private sector, and independent experts alongside policymakers to reconcile differing legal frameworks.[139]

One of the core principles outlined in the UNCTAD Policy Framework (revised version, 2015) is that "investment policies should be developed involving all stakeholders." Encouraging public participation in shaping policy-making legislation can ensure that public policies and investment decisions are guided by a bottom-up, strategic vision of sustainable development based on local and national

[138] For instance, in 2020, a report aimed at enhancing the effectiveness of investor-state dispute resolution in Vietnam was conducted by Ms. Dinh Anh Tuyet of IDVN Law Firm by the sponsor of UNDP–UK 2019–2020 Prjoject. See Tuyết Đinh Ánh (2020).

[139] Trujillo (2018), p. 2759–2760.

aspirations.[140] Incorporating input from diverse sectors of society can better reflect society's capacity to pursue and implement specific policy goals, making policies and laws more relevant to people's lives and enhancing their enforceability.

In general, in Vietnam, sustainable development remains an overarching goal characterised by fragmented and disparate objectives, existing more as an orientation rather than a cohesive, action-oriented strategy. Notably, recent government strategies for sustainable development spanning the periods of 2011–2020 and 2021–2030 do not explicitly integrate foreign investment and signing IIAs as integral components of the national strategy to achieve sustainable development goals. This study advocates for a different approach, suggesting that the government should evaluate how various societal resources, including foreign direct investment, can best contribute to the country's overall development strategy. Sustainable development objectives should be integrated into a comprehensive vision that links all sectors of the economy, fostering cohesive cooperation among them.

Pursuing a green economic development policy requires stringent and consistent management across multiple levels and scopes. While some proposed solutions may pose immediate challenges given Vietnam's current conditions and resource constraints, as is the case for many developing countries, the strength of a single-party government lies in its ability to pursue predetermined objectives consistently. Once a target is established, the entire system, including resources, mechanisms, and people, aligns toward achieving it. Vietnam's accession to the WTO over 15 years ago is a testament to this phenomenon. In the lead-up to 2007, Vietnam underwent substantial legal reforms to meet transparency requirements and adhere to WTO agreements. This period witnessed the enactment of numerous new or revised laws and decrees, resulting in Vietnam developing a comprehensive legal system in compliance with WTO standards. The country's WTO accession showcased its unwavering determination and diligent efforts, earning recognition from the global community. Given the parallels between the WTO accession process and the negotiation of trade–investment agreements with the EU, a similar approach can be expected.

While there is strong political commitment to achieving the ambitious objectives presented to the international community, a persistent challenge lies in addressing the existing shortcomings within Vietnam's governance and administrative frameworks. The country's current stage of development may also constrain the availability of societal resources necessary for the effective realisation of these objective.

Addressing these issues effectively as a non-discretionary imperative, rather than an optional requirement, is crucial for streaming FDI to drive sustainable development outcomes, as these positive effects are not inherent or automatic.[141] Indeed, Vietnam's approximately four decades of experience with FDI flows have demonstrated instances of suboptimal efficacy. In the prevailing landscape of global trade volatility, FDI continues to represent a critical channel for the transnational transfer

[140] Lorenzo Cotula (2016), p. viii.

[141] Johnson (2019), p. 128.

of capital, technology, specialised skills, information, and other essential resources. Consequently, the nation is compelled to optimise its utilisation of these inflows. Furthermore, as underscored by Johnson,[142] policy frameworks, including those at the international level, are indispensable for maximising the potential of FDI to contribute meaningfully to sustainable development objectives. Therefore, it's time for the Vietnamese government to systematically improve the prevailing IIAs regime and to concurrently establish a comprehensive policy for IIA negotiations in the near future. This holds particular significance for Vietnam within the current globalised and digitalised context, where FDI decisions are no longer solely predicated on geographical advantages or preferential policies, but increasingly demand transparency, shared responsibility, and contributions to sustainable development.

References

Jurisprudence

Antaris Solar GmbH and Dr. Michael Göde v. The Czech Republic [2013] PCA Case No. 2014-01

Foresight Luxembourg Solar 1 S. Á.R1. and others v. Kingdom of Spain [2015] SCC Case No. 2015/150

RWE AG and RWE Eemshaven Holding II BV v. Kingdom of the Netherlands [2021] ICSID Case No. ARB/21/4

Uniper SE, Uniper Benelux Holding B.V. and Uniper Benelux N.V. v. Kingdom of the Netherlands [2021] ICSID Case No. ARB/21/22

Westmoreland Coal Company v. Canada [2022] ICSID Case, UNCT/23/2 (Pending)

Treaties

Australia–Hong Kong, China SAR BIT (2019)

Brazil Model BIT (2015)

China–South Africa BIT (1997)

Comprehensive and Progressive Agreement for Trans-Pacific Partnership (CPTPP)

Canada–EU Comprehensive Economic and Trade Agreement (2016a) (CETA)

Colombian Model BIT (2017)

Draft Pan-African Investment Code (2016)

Energy Charter Treaty (1991) (ECT)

EU–Canada Comprehensive Economic and Trade Agreement (2016b) (CETA)

EU–Singapore BIT (2018) (EUSIPA)

[142] Ibid., p. 142.

EU–Vietnam Investment Protection Agreement (EVIPA) (2019)
ILO Tripartite Declaration of Principles Concerning Multinational Enterprises and Social Policies (2023)
India–Kyrgyzstan BIT (2019)
Morocco Model BIT (2019)
Myanmar–Singapore BIT (2019)
Netherlands Model BIT (2019)
Singapore–Myanmar BIT (2019)
South African Development Community (SADC) Model BIT (2012)
Transatlantic Trade and Investment Partnership (TTIP)
US Model BIT (2012)
Vietnam–Japan BIT (2003)
Vietnam–Korea BIT (2003)
Vietnam–Morocco BIT (2012)
Vietnam–UK BIT (2002)
Vienna Convention on the Law of Treaties (VCLT) (1969)

Bibliography

Aaken AV (2009) International investment law between commitment and flexibility: a contract theory analysis. J Int Econ Law 12(2)
Baltag C, Joshi R, Duggal K (2023) Recent trends in investment arbitration on the right to regulate, environment, health and corporate social responsibility: too much or too little? ICSID Rev 38(2):381–421
Bass S et al. (2010) Integrating environment and development in Vietnam: achievements, challenges and next step. Paper resulting from the Viet Nam Environmental Mainstreaming 'Lessons Learned Review', International Institute for Environment and Development. https://www.iied.org/17505iied
Brew R (2019) Exception clauses in international investment agreements as a tool for appropriately balancing the right to regulate with investment protection. Canterbury Law Rev 25
Caddel J, Jensen NM (2014) Which host country government actors are most involved in disputes with foreign investors? Columbia FDI Perspectives No.120. Columbia University. Vale Columbia Centre on Sustainable International Investment. https://academiccommons.columbia.edu/doi/10.7916/D8M32SWK
Chi M (2018) Integrating sustainable development in international investment law: normative incompatibility, system integration and governance implications. Routledge
Chu XD (2020) Laws of environmental protection in Vietnam – situation and solutions. J Phys Conf Ser 1515:052082. https://iopscience.iop.org/article/10.1088/1742-6596/1515/5/052082
Coleman J, Johnson L et al (2018) International investment agreements, 2015–16: a review of trends and new approaches. In: Sachs LE, Johnson L (eds) Yearbook on International Investment Law and Policy 2015–2016. Oxford University Press
Coleman J, Johnson LJ, Merrill E, Sachs LE (2021) Investment treaties and models in 2019 (mis) aligned with the SDGs? In: Sachs LE, Johnson LJ, Coleman J (eds) Yearbook on International Investment Law & Policy 2019. Oxford University Press
Cotula L (2016) Foreign investment, law and sustainable development: a handbook on agriculture and extractive industries. Natural Resource Issues No 3, 2nd edn. International Institute for Environment and Development, London

Gallagher KP, Zarky L (2004) No Miracle Drug: Foreign Direct Investment and Sustainable Development, *Zarsky L (ed) International Investment for Sustainable Development - Balancing Rights and Rewards, Routledge*, https://www.routledge.com/International-Investment-for-Sustainable-Development-Balancing-Rights-and-Rewards/Zarsky/p/book/9781844070398

Gallagher KP, Zarsky L (2005) No miracle drug: foreign direct investment and sustainable development. In: Zarsky L (ed) International investment for sustainable development – balancing rights and rewards. Earthscan

Gore KN (2024) Opportunity for ESG-related counterclaims in international investment arbitrations: a trip down the rabbit hole. Kluwer Arbitration Blog. 17 April 2024. https://arbitrationblog.kluwerarbitration.com/2024/04/17/opportunities-for-esg-related-counterclaims-in-international-investment-arbitrations-a-trip-down-the-rabbit-hole/

Hallward-Driemeier M (2003) Do bilateral investment treaties attract FDI? World Bank – Research Department; World Bank – Development Research Group. https://ssrn.com/abstract=636541

Henckels C (2016) Protecting regulatory autonomy through greater precision in investment treaties: the TPP, CETA and TTIP. J Int Econ Law 19(1):27

Henckels C (2018a) Should investment treaties contain public policy exceptions? Boston College Law Rev 59(8):2839

Henckels C (2018b) Balancing test: investment arbitration. Max Planck Encyclopedias of International Law. https://opil.ouplaw.com/display/10.1093/law-mpeipro/e3420.013.3420/law-mpeipro-e3420?prd=MPIL

Hippolyte AR (2019) Foreign investment law and developing countries. In: Krajewski M, Hoffmann RT (eds) Research handbook on foreign direct investment. Edward Elgar

Hush E (2018) Where no man has gone before: the future of sustainable development in the comprehensive economic and trade agreement and new generation free trade agreements. Columbia J Environ Law 43(1):93. https://doi.org/10.7916/cjel.v43i1.3741

Johnson L (2019) FDI, international investment agreements and the sustainable development goals. In: Krajewski M, Hoffmann RT (eds) Research handbook on foreign direct investment. Edward Elgar

Lavranos N (2016) How the European Commission and the EU member states are reasserting their control over their investment treaties and ISDS rules. In: Kulick A (ed) States' reassertion of control over international investment agreements and international investment treaty dispute settlement. Cambridge University Press

Lee S (2024) Vietnam's renewables surge, but serious pollution concerns persist. Asia Pacific Foundation of Canada. https://www.asiapacific.ca/publication/vietnams-renewables-surge-serious-pollution-concerns-persist

Martini C (2017) Balancing investors' rights with environmental protection in international investment arbitration: an assessment of recent trends in investment treaty drafting. Int Lawyer 50(3):567

Mauro MR (2024) Energy security, energy transition, and foreign investments: an evolving complex relationship. Laws 13(4):48. https://doi.org/10.3390/laws13040048

Medici-Colombo G (2024) The European Green Deal and the Energy Charter Treaty – Chronicle of a breakup foretold. In: Eritja MC, Fernández-Pons X (eds) Deploying the European Green Deal protecting the environment beyond the EU borders. Routledge Studies in Environmental Policy Series

Mills A (2014) The balancing and unbalancing of interests in international investment law and arbitration. In: Douglas Z, Pauwelyn J, Viñuales JE (eds) The foundation of international investment law: bringing theory into practice. Oxford University Press

Muchlinski P (2016) Negotiating new generation international investment agreements: new sustainable development oriented initiatives. In: Hindelang S, Krajewski M (eds) Shifting paradigms in international investment law: more balanced, less isolated, increasingly diversified. Oxford University Press

Newcombe A (2012) The use of general exceptions in IIAs: increasing legitimacy or uncertainty? In: Mestral AD, Lévesque C (eds) Improving international investment agreements. Routledge
Ngọc Điệp (2024) Tập đoàn Nhật sở hữu nhà máy điện than 2,58 tỷ USD lớn nhất Việt Nam vừa khánh thành: Bắt tay BRG làm dự án 4,2 tỷ USD, đầu tư vào loạt doanh nghiệp hàng đầu ở nhiều lĩnh vực [The Japanese corporation owns the largest 2.58 billion USD coal power plant in Vietnam has just inaugurated: Joining hands with BRG to build a 4.2 billion USD project, investing in a series of leading enterprises in many fields]. Cafef. 15 March 2024. https://cafef.vn/tap-doan-dang-sau-nha-may-nhiet-dien-258-ty-usd-tai-khu-kinh-te-van-phong-cung-cap-85-ty-kwh-dien-hang-nam-188240313160258725.chn
OECD (2015) Summary of discussions of Freedom of Investment Roundtable 23. DAF/INV/WD(2015)15/FINAL. 13–14 October 2015. https://one.oecd.org/document/DAF/INV/WD(2015)15/FINAL/en/pdf
Open Development Vietnam (2020) The list of Coal projects in Vietnam as of October 2020. https://data.vietnam.opendevelopmentmekong.net/vi/dataset/thermal-coal-plants-in-vietnam-by-october-2020/resource/34b33a9f-d513-4c42-bbc3-ac65d9813d0a?view_id=2614bc2c-5c23-45c4-a74c-b39dee5351d4
Ortino F (2012) Legal reasoning of international investment tribunals: a typology of egregious failures. J Int Dispute Settlement 3(1):31
Paine J, Sheargold E (2024) Carving-out climate action from Investor–State Dispute Settlement (ISDS): suggested treaty language and commentary. OECD 9th Annual Conference on Investment Treatie. 11 March 2024. https://one.oecd.org/document/DAF/INV/TR1/RD(2024)1/en/pdf
Paparinskis M (2015) International investment law and the European Union: a reply to Catharine Titi. Eur J Int Law 26(3)
Puig S (2019) In search of a more balanced international economic order - lessons from international investment law. In: Pauwelyn J, Wang M (eds) Building legal capacity for a more inclusive globalization. The Graduate Institute, Geneva
PwC (2023) Vietnam's Eight Power Development Plan – insights and key considerations for investor. August 2023. https://www.pwc.com/vn/en/publications/vietnam-publications/pdp8-insights.html
Ranjan P (2019) Police power, indirect expropriation in international investment law, and Article 31(3)(c) of the VCLT: a critique of *Phipip Morris v. Uruguay*. Asian J Int Law 98:9
Roberts A (2013) Clash of paradigms: actors and analogies shaping the investment treaty system. Am J Int Law 107(1):45–94
Sacerdoti G (2016) Investment protection and sustainable development – key issues. In: Hindelang S, Krajewski M (eds) Shifting paradigms in international investment law: more balanced, less isolated, increasingly diversified. Oxford University Press
Salvatore LD (2021) Investor–state disputes in the fossil fuel industry. International Institute for Sustainable Development Report. https://www.iisd.org/system/files/2022-01/investor–state-disputes-fossil-fuel-industry.pdf
Sauvant KP, Gabor E (2021) Facilitating sustainable FDI for sustainable development in a WTO investment facilitation framework: four concrete proposals. J World Trade 55(2)
Schirmbeck S (2017) Vietnam's environmental policies at a crossroads – salinated rice fields, hunted-out national parks, and eroding beaches – and what we can do about it. Friedrich Ebert Stiftung. https://asia.fes.de/news/vietnams-environmental-policies-at-a-crossroads
Schill SW (2014) Ordering paradigms in international investment law: bilateralism – multilateralism – multilateralization. In: Douglass Z, Pauwelyn J, Viñuales JE (eds) The foundations of international investment law: bringing theory into practice. Oxford University Press
Stifter L, Reinisch A (2016) Expropriation in the light of the UNCTAD investment policy framework for sustainable development. In: Hindelang S, Krajewski M (eds) Shifting paradigms in international investment law: more balanced, less isolated, increasingly diversified. Oxford University Press

Suda R (2006) The effect of bilateral investment treaties on human rights enforcement and realization. In: Schutter OD (ed) Transnational corporations and human rights. Studies in International Law. Bloomsbury Collections. Hart Publishing, London

Tin Vo Trung (2019) Assessing Vietnam's environmental laws and direction for improvement. Vietnamese J Legal Sci 1(1)

Thrasher R (2021). Room to Move: building flexibility into investment treaties to meet climate-change commitments. Columbia FDI Perspective No. 296. Columbia Centre on Sustainable Development. 25 January 2021. https://www.econstor.eu/handle/10419/254130

Tuyết Đinh Ánh (2020) Báo cáo nghiên cứu: Nâng cao hiệu quả giải quyết tranh chấp tại Việt Nam [Research Report: Improving Dispute Resolution Efficiency in Vietnam]. Ministry of Justice of Vietnam, UK Government and UNDP Vietnam. https://moj.gov.vn/tttp/tintuc/Lists/NghienCuuTraoDoi/Attachments/62/Consultation%20report%20_%20final_%20upload.pdf

Trujillo E (2018) Theoretical perspectives and cross-cutting issues: balancing sustainability, the right to regulate, and the need for investor protection: lessons from the trade regime. Boston College Law Rev 59(8):2735

UNCTAD (2010) World Investment Report 2010: investing in a low Carbon. https://unctad.org/system/files/official-document/wir2010_en.pdf

UNCTAD (2018a) World Investment Report 2018: investment and new industrial policies. UNCDAT/WIR/2018. https://unctad.org/system/files/official-document/wir2018_en.pdf

UNCTAD (2018b) UNCTAD's reform package for the international investment regime. https://investmentpolicy.unctad.org/uploaded-files/document/UNCTAD_Reform_Package_2018.pdf

UNCTAD (2023) World Investment Report 2023: investing in sustainable energy for all. https://unctad.org/system/files/official-document/wir2023_en.pdf

UNDP (2014) Governance for sustainable development- integrating governance in the post-2015 development framework. Discussion Paper. https://www.undp.org/sites/g/files/zskgke326/files/publications/Discussion-Paper%2D%2DGovernance-for-Sustainable-Development.pdf

UNEP (2022) Emissions Gap Report 2022: The closing window – climate crisis calls for rapid transformation of societies. https://www.unep.org/resources/emissions-gap-report-2022

United Nations (2012) The future we want. A/RES/66/288. Sustainable Development Knowledge Platform. https://sustainabledevelopment.un.org/futurewewant.html

VLA and UNDP (2016) 2015 Justice Index: towards a justice system for the people (Vietnam). https://www.undp.org/vietnam/publications/2015-justice-index

Vandevelde KJ (2010) A unified theory of fair & equitable treatment. N Y Univ J Int Law Politics 43(1). https://papers.ssrn.com/sol3/papers.cfm?abstract_id=2357642

VanDuzer JA (2016) Sustainable development provisions in international trade treaties. In: Hindelang S, Krajewski M (eds) Shifting paradigms in international investment law: more balanced, less isolated, increasingly diversified. Oxford University Press

VanDuzer JA (2019) Can international investments be instruments of sustainable development? Systemic capacity challenges for developing countries. In: Pauwelyn J, Wang M (eds) Building legal capacity for a more inclusive globalization. The Graduate Institute, Geneva

VietnamPlus (2020a) Ratification of EU-Vietnam deals, ILO convention makes NA's highlight. 8 June 2020. https://en.vietnamplus.vn/ratification-of-euvietnam-deals-ilo-convention-makes-nas-highlight/174580.vnp

VietnamPlus (2020b) NA ratifies Vietnam's membership of ILO convention against forced labour. 8 June 2020. https://en.vietnamplus.vn/na-ratifies-vietnams-membership-of-ilo-convention-against-forced-labour/174539.vnp

VietnamPlus (2020c) Quốc hội thảo luận Công ước số 98 của Tổ chức Lao động quốc tế' [National Assembly discusses Convention No. 98 of the International Labour Organisation]. 7 June 2020. https://www.vietnamplus.vn/quoc-hoi-thao-luan-cong-uoc-so-98-cua-to-chuc-lao-dong-quoc-te/573504.vnp

VietnamPlus (2020d) Công nhận phán quyết của cơ quan giải quyết tranh chấp theo EVIPA [Recognition of the Decision of the Dispute Resolution Body under EVIPA]. 18 June 2020.

https://www.vietnamplus.vn/cong-nhan-phan-quyet-cua-co-quan-giai-quyet-tranh-chap-theo-evipa/646248.vnp
Walde TW (2004) Natural resources and sustainable development: from “good intentions” to “good consequences”. In: Schrijver N, Weiss F (eds) International law and sustainable development – principle and practice. Koninklijke Brill NV
World Bank data. Foreign Direct Investment, net outflow – Vietnam. https://data.worldbank.org/indicator/BM.KLT.DINV.CD.WD?locations=VN
World Bank (2020) Vietnam: deepening international integration and implementing the EVFTA. https://documents1.worldbank.org/curated/en/866871589557725251/pdf/Vietnam-Deepening-International-Integration-and-Implementing-the-EVFTA.pdf
World Bank (2022) Vietnam – country climate and development report. http://vepg.vn/wp-content/uploads/2022/07/CCDR-Full-report_01.07_FINAL-1.pdf
World Bank (2024) Vietnam: overview. 19 April 2024. https://www.worldbank.org/en/country/vietnam/overview
Zamir N, Barker P (2017) The trans-pacific partnership agreement and states right to regulate under international investment law. Denver J Int Law Policy 45(2):205
Zarsky L (2004) Introduction: balancing rights and rewards in investment rules. In: Zarsky L (ed) International investment for sustainable development – balancing rights and rewards. Routledge
Zhu Y (2024) A quasi-normative conflict: resolving the tension between investment treaties and climate action. Rev Eur Compar Int Environ Law. Wiley Periodicals LLC 183

Documents

Central Committee of Communist Party (2020) Dự thảo Báo cáo Tổng kết Thực hiện Chiến lược Phát triển Kinh tế - Xã hội 10 năm 2011 - 2020, Xây dựng Chiến lược Phát triển Kinh tế - Xã hội 10 năm 2021 – 2030 [Draft Report Summarizing the Implementation of the 10-year Socio-economic Development Strategy for 2011 - 2020, Preparing the 10-year Socio-economic Development Strategy for 2021 – 2030]. https://vuit.org.vn/Document/Detail/981
Communist Party of Vietnam (2021) Chiến lược phát triển kinh tế - xã hội 10 năm 2021-2030 [Vietnam Social-Economic Development Strategy 2021-2030]. https://tulieu-vankien.dangcongsan.vn/ban-chap-hanh-trung-uong-dang/dai-hoi-dang/lan-thu-xiii/chien-luoc-phat-trien-kinh-te-xa-hoi-10-nam-2021-2030-3735
European Commission (2015) Trade for all: towards a more responsible trade and investment policy. COM/2015/0497 final. https://www.europarl.europa.eu/cmsdata/92121/Commission%20Communication.pdf
EU Commission (2016) Handbook for sustainability impact assessment, 2nd edn https://op.europa.eu/en/publication-detail/-/publication/8b3a2b37-1028-11e6-ba9a-01aa75ed71a1
European Parliament (2008) Resolution on trade and economic relations with the Association of South East Asian Nations (ASEAN). 2007/2265(INI). 8 May 2008. https://www.europarl.europa.eu/doceo/document/TA-6-2008-0195_EN.html
European Comission (2017) EU-Canada Comprehensive Economic and Trade Agreement (CETA). https://policy.trade.ec.europa.eu/eu-trade-relationships-country-and-region/countries-and-regions/canada/eu-canada-agreement_en
Gallagher KP, & Zarky L, No Miracle Drug: Foreign Direct Investment and Sustainable Development, *Zarsky L (ed) International Investment for Sustainable Development - Balancing Rights and Rewards, Routledge*, https://www.routledge.com/International-Investment-for-Sustainable-Development-Balancing-Rights-and-Rewards/Zarsky/p/book/9781844070398 (2004).
Office of the US Trade Representative. Fact Sheet: Model Bilateral Investment Treaty. https://ustr.gov/about-us/policy-offices/press-office/fact-sheets/2012/april/model-bilateral-investment-treaty

Prime Minister of Vietnam (2016) Decision No. 428/QĐ-TTg (18 March 2016) on approving the revised National Power Development Master Plan for the 2011-2020 period, Vision to 2030

Prime Minister of Vietnam (2021) Decision No. 1658/QĐ-TTg (1 October 2021) on approving National Green Growth Strategy 2021–2030, vision to 2050

Prime Minister of Vietnam (2022) Decision No. 882/QĐ-TTg (22 July 2022) on approving the National Action Plan on Green Growth for the 2021–2030 period

Prime Minister of Vietnam (2023) Decision No. 500/QĐ-TTg (15 May 2023) on approving National Electricity Development Plan for the period 2021–2030, vision to 2050

Chapter 11
Outlook

This book offers a thorough exploration of environmental protection and the pursuit of sustainable development goals within the framework of IIL. Additionally, it examines the regulatory power of EVIPA signatories based on relevant initiatives of this agreement. Moreover, it evaluates the status of environmental protection and foreign investment management in Vietnam, aiming to establish connections between these two interrelated fields within the context of sustainable development.

Balancing economic development objectives with non-commercial goals like environmental protection poses inherent complexities and challenges. The impacts of current trade and investment agreement negotiation policies in reshaping international investment law and ISDS mechanisms to prioritise sustainable development goals necessitate time to evaluate. Likewise, stakeholders must adapt to these changes and assess their implications. Therefore, a cautious approach and comprehensive assessment tools remain imperative in pursuing specific policies or directions.

An individual nation is less likely to diverge from the prevailing global trends. Nevertheless, it is equally rational to acknowledge that specific conditions may necessitate a tailored approach that aligns with its unique requirements. In the domestic context, the linkage between sustainable development and environmental protection has yet to be explored in the context of investment treaty negotiations. Until recently, Vietnam, as a developing country partner, has often assumed a passive role in investment treaty negotiations, with sustainable development remaining an isolated policy rather than an integral aspect, notwithstanding the consensus that sustainable development encompasses the integration of both environmental preservation and economic growth.[1]

Vietnam stands at a crucial juncture in its economic development, actively engaging in trade and investment agreements with developed nations, particularly those that emphasize sustainable development, such as the EU. This participation not only accelerates access to global standards in drafting and negotiating IIAs but also equips Vietnam with the tools necessary to adapt to the dynamic landscape of IIA negotiations.

[1] Fuentes (2002), p. 109.

N. T. Lan Huong, *Investment Protection and Environmental Governance*, European Yearbook of International Economic Law 47,
https://doi.org/10.1007/978-3-032-05332-9_11

To truly capitalise on this cooperation, Vietnam must invest in strengthening its state officials' capacities. Moreover, EVIPA presents significant advantages, offering mechanisms that protect the host state's regulatory autonomy—an improvement over earlier IIAs and the CPTPP. However, to maximise these benefits, Vietnam needs to take a proactive stance by working collaboratively with the EU to enhance the frameworks provided by the EVIPA, particularly focusing on the ICS system and the Investment Committee. This collaboration is not just beneficial; it is essential for safeguarding Vietnam's policy space in the face of escalating environmental challenges. By embracing this partnership with urgency and intent, Vietnam can pave the way for sustainable growth while protecting its regulatory authority.

The outcomes of this study hold significant potential to assist Vietnamese management agencies in formulating comprehensive mechanisms and policies for sustainable economic development within the framework of their IIA-making strategy. This is imperative to attract sustainable investments in Vietnam and similar emerging economies. Achieving this goal may necessitate a series of organisational reforms and the establishment of a more defined division of responsibilities among relevant state management entities. The enhancement of institutional capacity remains an indispensable prerequisite. Moreover, appointing a central agency to oversee consultations and provide technical support to both central and local state management bodies in making specific decisions related to investors, especially in cases involving the potential breach of investment protection commitments under EVIPA and other IIAs, is equally essential.

While there have been recent training initiatives in Vietnam to enhance knowledge of international investment agreements, the grasp of these concepts among local state management bodies remains insufficient. Therefore, it is crucial to prioritise training on the provisions of the EVIPA. This training should specifically address regulations that directly impact licensing decisions and the investment management activities of local officials. Although this responsibility lies with the Vietnamese government, the EU's support through resources and experts can significantly enhance these efforts. Ultimately, preventing and minimising the potential for disputes constitutes a more sustainable approach than engaging in litigation, regardless of the effectiveness of the dispute resolution mechanisms in place.

For the long-term success of Vietnam, it is crucial to further research and develop the Model BIT in line with the country's specific priorities. The country does not require economic development that leads to higher income at the expense of the environment, as this can result in declining agricultural activities and increasingly serious health issues for the population. This Model BIT holds significant importance because it will ensure that the management of FDI flows is effectively aligned with sustainable development goals. Additionally, this Model BIT will help protect Vietnam from the risks associated with ISDS claims. Prioritising this goal in future studies and research is essential for Vietnam's sustainable development.

The findings presented in this book underscore the necessity of addressing the adverse effects of climate change and mitigating the repercussions of previous policies that prioritised rapid economic development followed by Vietnam. These challenges present the Vietnamese government with a more intricate dilemma than simply achieving economic growth during the early stages of globalisation. Economic activities and public interest considerations, including environmental preservation and natural resource protection, are inherently intertwined.[2] Hence, a systematic and holistic policy approach must supersede the fragmented approach. In this process, central government institutions play a vital role in determining the feasibility and effectiveness of integrating environmental and developmental objectives.[3] Consequently, fostering government awareness of the pressing challenges, coupled with an open and inquisitive approach, is crucial in advancing the country's sustainable development strategy.

Furthermore, mobilising the entire system to fulfil these commitments and safeguard the planet's ecosystem demands a scientific approach. Developing evidence-based and strategic laws and policies is vital to implementing sustainability measures and protecting the earth's environment effectively. Through such concerted efforts, Vietnam can navigate the complexities of sustainable development and pave the way for a more harmonious balance between economic prosperity and environmental preservation.

References

Bass S et al (2010) Integrating environment and development in vietnam: achievements, challenges and next step. Paper resulting from the Viet Nam Environmental Mainstreaming 'Lessons Learned Review'. IIED. The Viet Nam/UNDP Poverty Environment Programme 2010

Fuentes X (2002) International law-making in the field of sustainable development: the unequal competition between development and the environment. International Environmental Agreements: Politics, Law and Economics 2

Martini C (2017) Balancing investors' rights with environmental protection in international investment arbitration: an assessment of recent trends in investment treaty drafting. International Lawyer 50(3):562

[2] Martini (2017), p. 562.

[3] Bass et al. (2010), p. 15.

MIX
Papier aus verantwortungsvollen Quellen
Paper from responsible sources
FSC® C105338

If you have any concerns about our products,
you can contact us on
ProductSafety@springernature.com

In case Publisher is established outside the EU,
the EU authorized representative is:
Springer Nature Customer Service Center GmbH
Europaplatz 3, 69115 Heidelberg, Germany

Printed by Libri Plureos GmbH
in Hamburg, Germany